IMPOR

HERE IS YOUR REGISTRATION C
PREMIUM CONTENT AND MCGRA

For key premium online resources you need THIS CODE to gain access. Once the code is entered, you will be able to use the web resources for the length of your course.

Access is provided only if you have purchased a new book.

If the registration code is missing from this book, the registration screen on our website, and within your WebCT or Blackboard course will tell you how to obtain your new code. Your registration code can be used only once to establish access. It is not transferable

To gain access to these online resources

1. USE your web browser to go to: **http://www.mhhe.com/kinickiob2e**
2. CLICK on "First Time User"
3. ENTER the Registration Code printed on the tear-off bookmark on the right
4. After you have entered your registration code, click on "Register"
5. FOLLOW the instructions to setup your personal UserID and Password
6. WRITE your UserID and Password down for future reference. Keep it in a safe place.

If your course is using WebCT or Blackboard, you'll be able to use this code to access the McGraw-Hill content within your instructor's online course.

To gain access to the McGraw-Hill content in your instructor's WebCT or Blackboard course simply log into the course with the user ID and Password provided by your instructor. Enter the registration code exactly as it appears to the right when prompted by the system. You will only need to use this code the first time you click on McGraw-Hill content.

These instructions are specifically for student access. Instructors are not required to register via the above instructions.

The McGraw-Hill Companies

Thank you, and welcome to your McGraw-Hill/Irwin Online Resources.

Kinicki/Kreitner
Organizational Behavior:
Key Concepts, Skills & Best Practices, 2/E
0-07-313603-4

AT34-T3KK-EAM9-B3QM-T7HM

REGISTRATION CODE
REGISTRATION CODE

The McGraw-Hill Companies
McGraw-Hill Irwin

organizational behavior

key concepts, skills & best practices

second edition

organizational behavior

key concepts, skills & best practices

Angelo Kinicki

Robert Kreitner

Both of
Arizona State University

Boston Burr Ridge, IL Dubuque, IA Madison, WI New York San Francisco St. Louis
Bangkok Bogotá Caracas Kuala Lumpur Lisbon London Madrid Mexico City
Milan Montreal New Delhi Santiago Seoul Singapore Sydney Taipei Toronto

ORGANIZATIONAL BEHAVIOR: KEY CONCEPTS, SKILLS & BEST PRACTICES

Published by McGraw-Hill/Irwin, a business unit of The McGraw-Hill Companies, Inc., 1221 Avenue of the Americas, New York, NY, 10020.

This book is printed on acid-free paper.

3 4 5 6 7 8 9 0 QWV/QWV 0 9 8 7 6 5

ISBN 0-07-282932-X

Editorial director: *John E. Biernat*
Executive editor: *John Weimeister*
Senior developmental editor: *Christine Scheid*
Senior marketing manager: *Lisa Nicks*
Producer, Media technology: *Mark Molsky*
Senior project manager: *Lori Koetters*
Senior production supervisor: *Rose Hepburn*
Lead designer: *Matthew Baldwin*
Senior photo research coordinator: *Jeremy Cheshareck*
Photo researcher: *Jennifer Blankenship*
Senior media project manager: *Rose M. Range*
Developer, Media technology: *Brian Nacik*
Cover images: © Corbis
Typeface: *10.5/12 Times Roman*
Compositor: *GTS–Los Angeles, CA Campus*
Printer: *Von Hoffmann Corporation*

Library of Congress Cataloging-in-Publication Data

Kinicki, Angelo.
Organizational behavior : key concepts, skills & best practices / Angelo Kinicki, Robert Kreitner.—2nd ed.
p. cm.
Includes bibliographical references and index.
ISBN 0-07-282932-X (alk. paper)
1. Organizational behavior. I. Kreitner, Robert. II. Title.
HD58.7.K5265 2006
658.3—dc22

2004056941

www.mhhe.com

DEDICATION

To Ken and Mary Lou Polak, in-laws by chance, friends by choice. Thanks for spoiling me on every occasion we see each other. Your commitment to family, friends, and work is admirable.

—A.K.

In loving memory of our parents: Leo and Jean Sova and Robert and Caroline Kreitner

—B.K.

ABOUT THE AUTHORS

Angelo Kinicki (pictured on the right) is a Professor and Dean's Council of 100 Distinguished Scholar at Arizona State University. He joined the faculty in 1982, the year he received his doctorate in business administration from Kent State University. His specialty is Organizational Behavior.

Angelo is recognized for both his research and teaching. He has published over 75 articles in a variety of leading academic and professional journals, and has coauthored three textbooks. Angelo's success as a researcher also resulted in his selection to serve on the editorial review boards for the *Academy of Management Journal, Journal of Vocational Behavior,* and the *Journal of Management*. He received the All Time Best Reviewer Award from the *Academy of Management Journal* for the period of 1996–1999. Angelo's outstanding teaching performance resulted in his selection as the Graduate Teacher of the Year and the Undergraduate Teacher of the Year in the W. P. Carey School of Business at Arizona State University. He also was acknowledged as the Instructor of the Year for Executive Education from the Center for Executive Development at Arizona State University.

One of Angelo's strengths is his ability to teach students at all levels within a university. He uses an interactive environment to enhance undergraduates' understanding about management and organizational behavior. He focuses MBAs on applying management concepts to solve complex problems; PhD students learn the art and science of conducting scholarly research.

Angelo also is a busy consultant and speaker with companies around the world. His clients are many of the *Fortune* 500 companies as well as a variety of entrepreneurial firms. Much of his consulting work focuses on creating organizational change aimed at increasing organizational effectiveness and profitability. One of Angelo's most important and enjoyable pursuits is the practical application of his knowledge about management and organizational behavior.

Angelo and his wife Joyce have enjoyed living in the beautiful Arizona desert for 22 years, but are natives of Cleveland, Ohio. They enjoy traveling, golfing, and hiking.

Robert Kreitner, PhD, is a Professor Emeritus of Management at Arizona State University. Prior to joining ASU in 1975, Bob taught at Western Illinois University. He also has taught organizational behavior at the American Graduate School of International Management (Thunderbird). Bob is a popular speaker who has addressed a diverse array of audiences worldwide on management topics. He is a member of ASU's W. P. Carey School of Business Faculty Hall of Fame. Bob has authored articles for journals such as *Organizational Dynamics, Business Horizons,* and *Journal of Business Ethics.* He also is the co-author (with Fred Luthans) of the award-winning book *Organizational Behavior Modification and Beyond: An Operant and Social Learning Approach,* and the author of *Management,* 9th edition, a best-selling introductory management text.

Among his consulting and executive development clients have been American Express, SABRE Computer Services, Honeywell, Motorola, Amdahl, the Hopi Indian Tribe, State Farm Insurance, Goodyear Aerospace, Doubletree Hotels, Bank One-Arizona, Nazarene School of Large Church Management, US Steel, Ford, Caterpillar, and Allied-Signal. In 1981–82 he served as Chairman of the Academy of Management's Management Education and Development Division.

On the personal side, Bob was born in Buffalo, New York. After a four-year enlistment in the US Coast Guard, including service on the icebreaker EASTWIND in Antarctica, Bob attended the University of Nebraska–Omaha on a football scholarship. Bob also holds an MBA from the University of Nebraska–Omaha and a PhD from the University of Nebraska–Lincoln. While working on his PhD in Business at Nebraska, he spent six months teaching management courses for the University in Micronesia. In 1996, Bob taught two courses in Albania's first-ever MBA program (funded by the US Agency for International Development and administered by the University of Nebraska–Lincoln). He taught a summer leadership program in Switzerland from 1995 to 1998. Bob and his wife, Margaret, live in Phoenix with their two cats and a pet Starling, and they enjoy travel, hiking, woodcarving, and fishing.

preface

In our many years of teaching organizational behavior and management to undergraduate and graduate students in various countries, we *never* had a student say, "I want a longer, more expensive textbook with more chapters." We got the message! Indeed, there is a desire for shorter and less expensive textbooks in today's fast-paced world where overload and tight budgets are a way of life. Within the field of organizational behavior, so-called "essentials" texts have attempted to satisfy this need. Too often, however, brevity has been achieved at the expense of up-to-date examples, artful layout, and learning enhancements. We believe "brief" does not have to mean outdated and boring.

A New Standard

Kinicki and Kreitner's *Organizational Behavior: Key Concepts, Skills & Best Practices,* 2nd edition, represents a new standard in OB essentials textbooks. The following guiding philosophy inspired our quest for this new standard: "Create a short, up-to-date, practical, user-friendly, interesting, and engaging introduction to the field of organizational behavior." Thus, in this book, you will find lean and efficient coverage of topics recommended by AACSB International conveyed with pedagogical features found in full-length OB textbooks. Among those pedagogical enhancements are current, real-life chapter-opening vignettes, a rich array of contemporary in-text examples, a strong skills emphasis including Skills & Best Practices boxes in every chapter, at least one interactive exercise integrated into each chapter, an appealing four-color presentation, interesting captioned photos, poignant cartoons, instructive chapter summaries, and chapter-closing Ethical Dilemma exercises.

Efficient and Flexible Structure

The 16 chapters in this text (including the ethics module following Chapter 1) are readily adaptable to traditional 15-week semesters, 10-week terms, summer and intersessions, management development seminars, and distance learning programs via the Internet. Following up-front coverage of important topics—including ethics, international OB, and managing diversity—the topical flow of this text goes from micro (individuals) to macro (groups, teams, and organizations). Mixing and matching chapters (and topics within each chapter) in various combinations is not only possible but strongly encouraged to create optimum teaching/learning experiences.

A Rich Array of OB Research Insights

To enhance the instructional value of our coverage of major topics, we systematically cite "hard" evidence from five different categories. Worthwhile evidence was obtained by drawing upon the following *priority* of research methodologies:

- *Meta-analyses.* A **meta-analysis** is a statistical pooling technique that permits behavioral scientists to draw general conclusions about certain variables from many different studies. It typically encompasses a vast number of subjects, often reaching the thousands. Meta-analyses are instructive because they focus on general patterns of research evidence, not fragmented bits and pieces or isolated studies.
- *Field studies.* In OB, a **field study** probes individual or group processes in an organizational setting. Because field studies involve real-life situations, their results often have immediate and practical relevance for managers.
- *Laboratory studies.* In a **laboratory study,** variables are manipulated and measured in contrived situations. College students are commonly used as subjects. The highly controlled nature of laboratory studies enhances research precision. But generalizing the results to organizational management requires caution.
- *Sample surveys.* In a **sample survey,** samples of people from specified populations respond to questionnaires. The researchers then draw conclusions about the relevant population. Generalizability of the results depends on the quality of the sampling and questioning techniques.
- *Case Studies.* A **case study** is an in-depth analysis of a single individual, group, or organization. Because of their limited scope, case studies yield realistic but not very generalizable results.

meta-analysis
Pools the results of many studies through statistical procedure.

field study
Examination of variables in real-life settings.

laboratory study
Manipulation and measurement of variables in contrived situations.

sample survey
Questionnaire responses from a sample of people.

case study
In-depth study of a single person, group, or organization.

Emphasis on Ethics in the Second Edition

Two new features in the second edition—a comprehensive module on Ethics and Organizational Behavior following Chapter 1 and an Ethical Dilemma exercise at the end of every chapter—set a proper moral tone for managing people at work. The 16 Ethical Dilemma exercises raise contemporary ethical issues, ask tough questions, and have corresponding interpretations on our Web site at www.mhhe.com/kinickiob2e. An instructive Group Exercise, "Investigating the Difference in Moral Reasoning between Men and Women," follows the Ethics in OB module.

ethics learning module

IBM Cuts Retirees' Health Benefits to Boost Profits

FOR DISCUSSION

Do you think it is ethical for a company like IBM to raise retirees' contributions to health benefits while its own decrease? Explain. For an interpretation of this case and additional comments, visit our Online Learning Center:

www.mhhe.com/kinickiob2e

The loud message comes from one company after another: Surging health-care costs for retired workers are creating a giant burden. So companies have been cutting health benefits for their retirees or requiring them to contribute more of the cost.

Time for a reality check: In fact, no matter how high health-care costs go, well over half of large American corporations face only limited impact from the increases when it comes to their retirees. They have established ceilings on how much they will ever spend per retiree for health care. If health costs go above the caps, it's the retiree, not the company, who's responsible.

Yet numerous companies are cutting retirees' health benefits anyway. One possible factor: When companies cut these benefits, they create instant income. This isn't just the savings that come from not spending as much. Rather, thanks to complex accounting rules, the very act of cutting retirees' future health-care benefits lets companies reduce a liability and generate an immediate accounting gain.

In some cases it flows straight to the bottom line. More often it sits on the books like a cookie jar, from which a company takes a piece each year that helps it meet earnings estimates. . . .

The fate of retirees can be very different. When Robert Eggleston retired from International Business Machines Corp. 12 years ago, he was paying $40 a month toward health-care premiums for himself and his wife, LaRue, with IBM paying the rest. In 1993, IBM set ceilings on its own health-care spending for retirees. For those on Medicare, which provides basic hospital and doctor-visit coverage, the cap was $3,000 or $3,500, depending on when they retired. For those younger than 65, the cap was $7,000 or $7,500. Spending hit the caps for the older retirees in 2001, the company says, pushing future health-cost increases onto retirees' shoulders.

Mr. Eggleston, 66 years old, has seen his premiums jump to $365 a month for the couple. Deductibles and copayments for drugs and doctor visits added $663 a month last year. "It just eats up all the pension," which is $850 a month, Mrs. Eggleston says. Her husband has brain cancer. Though he gets free supplies of a tumor-fighting drug through a program for low-income families, he has cashed in his 401(k) account, and he and LaRue have taken out a second mortgage on their Lake Dallas, Texas, home.

IBM retirees as a group saw their health-care premiums rise nearly 29% in 2003, on the heels of a 67%-plus increase in 2002. For IBM, with its caps in place, spending on retiree health care declined nearly 5%, after a drop of 18% the year before.

IBM confirms that retirees' spending has risen as its own has fallen.[1]

26

ethical dilemma

You Mean Cheating Is Wrong?

College students are disturbed by recent corporate scandals: Some 84% believe the U.S. is having a business crisis, and 77% think CEOs should be held personally responsible for it.

But when the same students are asked about their own ethics, it's another story. Some 59% admit cheating on a test (66% of men, 54% of women). And only 19% say they would report a classmate who cheated (23% of men, but 15% of women—even though recent whistle-blowers have been women).

The survey of 1,100 students on 27 U.S. campuses was conducted by Students in Free Enterprise (SIFE), a nonprofit that teams up with corporations to teach students

How Should We Interpret This Hypocritical Double Standard?

1. Don't worry, most students know the difference between school and real life. They'll do the right thing when it really counts. Explain your rationale.
2. Whether in the classroom or on the job, pressure for results is the problem. People tend to take shortcuts and bend the rules when they're pressured. Explain.
3. A cheater today is a cheater tomorrow. Explain.
4. College professors need to do a better job with ethics education. How?

New Features and Material in the Second Edition

All 17 of the opening vignettes for the 16 chapters and the Ethics and OB module are new. Twenty-four of the 42 Skills & Best Practices boxes are new. Five of the 19 Hands-On Exercises are new and two have been updated. More than 270 of our source material references are dated 2004.

New topics include:

- Building human and social capital
- Positive psychology/OB
- E-leadership
- Model of ethical behavior
- Decision tree for ethical decisions
- Framework for understanding organizational culture
- Socialization tactics
- Nine basic cultural dimensions and leadership lessons from the GLOBE Project
- Impact of perception on interpersonal influence
- Techniques to improve the selling of ideas
- Attributional realignment
- Building self-esteem in self and others
- The proactive personality
- How to make your own luck
- Emotional contagion
- Emotional labor
- How to develop your emotional intelligence
- Employee engagement
- Intrinsic motivation
- Organizational citizenship behavior
- Work–family relationships
- Organizational justice
- Managerial implications of expectancy theory
- Goalsharing programs
- Improving goal commitment
- Combining 360-degree feedback and coaching
- Pay for performance
- Modern incentive plans
- Knowledge management
- Minority dissent in group decision making
- Rules for brainstorming
- Developing teamwork competence
- Indirect influence tactics in self-managed teams
- Why people avoid conflict
- Programming functional conflict with devil's advocacy and the dialectic method
- How to negotiate your pay and benefits
- Perceptual model of communication
- Communication competence
- Listening styles
- Wi-Fi communication
- Credibility and influence
- New tips for keeping organizational politics within bounds
- Followership
- Leader trait research findings
- House's revised path–goal theory of leadership
- Full-range theory of leadership
- Transformational leadership
- Shared leadership
- Level 5 leadership
- Organizations as military/mechanical bureaucracies
- Expanded discussion of virtual organizations
- How to manage geographically dispersed employees
- Customers as a force for change
- OD interventions for implementing change
- Commitment to change

Active Learning

Engaging Pedagogy

We have a love and a passion for teaching organizational behavior in the classroom and via textbooks because it deals with the intriguing realities of working in modern organizations. Puzzling questions, insights, and surprises hide around every corner. Seeking useful insights about how and why people behave as they do in the workplace is a provocative, interesting, and oftentimes fun activity. After all, to know more about organizational behavior is to know more about both ourselves and life in general. We have designed this text to facilitate *active* learning by relying on the following learning enhancements:

HANDS-ON EXERCISE

How Strong Is Your Potential for Ethnocentrism?

INSTRUCTIONS: If you were born and raised or have spent most of your life in the United States, select one number from the following scale for each item. If you are from a different country or culture, substitute the country/language you most closely identify with for the terms "American" and "English," and then rate each item.

	Strongly Disagree	Disagree	Neutral	Agree	Strongly Agree
1. I was raised in a way that was [truly] American.	1	2	3	4	5
2. Compared to how much I criticize other cultures, I criticize American culture less.	1	2	3	4	5
3. I am proud of American culture.	1	2	3	4	5
4. American culture has had a positive effect on my life.	1	2	3	4	5
5. I believe that my children should read, write, and speak [only] English.	1	2	3	4	5
6. I go to places where people are American.	1	2	3	4	5
7. I admire people who are American.	1	2	3	4	5
8. I would prefer to live in an American community.	1	2	3	4	5
9. At home, I eat [only] American food.	1	2	3	4	5
10. Overall, I am American.	1	2	3	4	5

SCORING 10–23 = Low potential for ethnocentrism
24–36 = Moderate potential for ethnocentrism
37–50 = High potential for ethnocentrism

SOURCE: Adapted from and survey items excerpted from J L Tsai, Y-W Ying, and P A Lee, "The Meaning of 'Being Chinese' and 'Being American': Variation among Chinese American Young Adults," *Journal of Cross-Cultural Psychology*, May 2000, pp 302–32.

Hands-On Exercises—

These exercises (one per chapter) are included to help readers personalize and expand upon key concepts as they are presented in the text. These exercises encourage active and thoughtful interaction rather than passive reading.

Chapter-Opening Vignettes—

For some real-world context, these brief cases use topics that are timely and relevant to actual life situations. The text's Web site also features interpretations for each case.

COSTCO'S CULTURE PRODUCES SATISFIED CUSTOMERS

James D. Sinegal, the president and CEO of Costco, has no palace guard and no profile to speak of, particularly compared to a retail legend like Sam Walton. Yet he's the guy who in 20 years has taken Costco from a startup to the FORTUNE 50 using, as surely as Mr. Sam, highly distinctive practices. He caps Costco's markups at 14% (department store markups can reach 40%). He offers the best wages and benefits in retail (full-time hourly workers make $40,000 after four years). He gives customers blanket permission for returns: no receipts; no questions; no time limits, except for computers—and even then the grace period is six months. . . .

Analysts have pounded on Sinegal to trim the company's generous health benefits and to otherwise reduce labor costs. But he's taken only limited steps in that direction, like modestly increasing employees' share of health-insurance premiums. That doesn't satisfy critics like Deutsche Bank analyst Bill Dreher, who recently wrote, "Costco continues to be a company that is better at serving the club member and employee than the shareholder."

Sinegal just shrugs. . . . "We think when you take care of your customer and your employees, your shareholders are going to be rewarded in the long run. And I'm one of them [the shareholders]; I care about the stock price. But we're not going to do something for the sake of one quarter that's going to destroy the fabric of our company and what we stand for." . . . The axioms Costco lives by . . .

AXIOM NO. 1: Obey the law.

AXIOM NO. 2: Take care of your customers.

AXIOM NO. 3: Take care of your employees.

AXIOM NO. 4: Practice the intelligent loss of sales. Many retailers' shelves are crowded with a plethora of products: different brands, different sizes, many choices. Costco offers relatively few choices. That means some customers may pass up purchases, because the gallon jar of mayonnaise is too big or the brand isn't their favorite. But the benefits far exceed the lost sales. Stocking fewer items streamlines distribution and hastens inventory turns—and nine out of ten customers are perfectly happy with the mayonnaise. . . .

Sinegal manages to be demanding without being intimidating. His bare-bones office helps set the tone for that style. So does his open-collared shirt and the nametag he wears, like everyone else. Not that he needs one. To walk with Sinegal from his headquarters building to the Costco next door is to hear a nonstop chorus of "Hi, Jim. . . . Hi, Jim. . . . Hi, Jim." He returns the greetings by using first names, without appearing to consult nametags. Sinegal has also

Active Learning features

SKILLS & BEST PRACTICES

Building an Effective Mentoring Network

1. Become the perfect protégé. It is important to invest ample time and energy to develop and maintain a network of developmental relationships. Trust and respect are needed among network members.
2. Engage in 360-degree networking. Share information and maintain good relationships with those above, below, and at the same status/responsibility level as yourself.
3. Commit to assessing, building, and adjusting the mentor network. Begin by assessing the competencies you want to build. Next, find mentors that can assist in building your desired competencies. Finally, change network members commensurate with changes in your experience and knowledge.
4. Develop diverse, synergistic connections. Find and develop relationships with multiple, diverse mentors. Pursue both formal and informal mentoring opportunities.
5. Realize that change is inevitable and that all good things come to an end. Most mentoring relationships last an average of five years. When a relationship ceases to be beneficial, end the mentoring relationship.

Skills & Best Practices Boxes— These additional readings and practical application items (one to four per chapter) are designed to sharpen users' skills by either recommending how to apply a concept, theory, or model, or by giving an exemplary corporate application. Students will benefit from real-world experiences and direct skill-building opportunities.

For example, J. M. Smucker, the number one company to work for in America in 2003 according to *Fortune,* is a 107-year-old family-run business that is headed by co-CEOs Tim and Richard Smucker. The brothers encourage all Smucker employees to adhere to a set of values created by their father, Paul Smucker. No. 3: "Listen with your full attention, look for the good in others, have a sense of humor, and say thank you for a job well done."[7] Because espoused values constitute aspirations that are explicitly communicated to employees, managers such as Tim and Richard Smucker hope that espoused values will directly influence. . . .

Up-to-Date Real-World Examples— Nothing brings material to life better than in-text examples featuring real companies, people, and situations. These examples permeate the text.

Active Learning features

chapter summary

- *Discuss the layers and functions of organizational culture.* The three layers of organizational culture are observable artifacts, espoused values, and basic underlying assumptions. Each layer varies in terms of outward visibility and resistance to change. Four functions of organization culture are organizational identity, collective commitment, social system stability, and sense-making device.

  Discuss the three general types of organizational culture and their associated normative beliefs. The three general types of organizational culture are constructive, passive–defensive, and aggressive–defensive. Each type is grounded in different normative beliefs. Normative beliefs represent an individual's thoughts and beliefs about how members of a particular group or organization are expected to approach their work and interact with others. A constructive culture is associated with the beliefs of achievement, self-actualizing, humanistic-encouraging, and affiliative. Passive–defensive organizations tend to endorse the beliefs of approval, conventional, dependent, and avoidance. Aggressive–defensive cultures tend to endorse the beliefs of oppositional, power, competitive, and perfectionistic.
- *Summarize the methods used by organizations to embed their cultures.* Embedding a culture amounts to teaching employees about the organization's preferred values, beliefs, expectations, and behaviors. This is accomplished by using one or more of the following 11 mechanisms: (a) formal statements of organizational philosophy, mission, vision, values, and materials used for recruiting, selection, and socialization; (b) the design of physical space, work environments, and buildings; (c) slogans, language, acronyms, and sayings; (d) deliberate role modeling, training programs; teaching, and coaching by managers and supervisors; (e) explicit rewards, status symbols, and promotion criteria; (f) stories, legends, and myths about key people and events; (g) the organizational activities, processes, or outcomes that leaders pay attention to, measure, and control; (h) leader reactions to critical incidents and organizational crises; (i) the workflow and organizational structure; (j) organizational systems and procedures; and (k) organizational goals and associated criteria used for recruitment, selection, development, promotion, layoffs, and retirement of people.
- *Describe the three phases in Feldman's model of organizational socialization.* The three phases of Feldman's model are anticipatory socialization, encounter, and change and acquisition. Anticipatory socialization begins before an individual actually joins the organization. The encounter phase begins when the employment contract has been signed. Phase 3 involves the period in which employees master important tasks and resolve any role conflicts.
- *Discuss the various socialization tactics used to socialize employees.* There are six key socialization tactics. They are collective versus individual, formal versus informal, sequential versus random, fixed versus variable, serial versus disjunctive, and investiture versus divestiture (see Table 2–2). Each tactic provides organizations with two opposing options for socializing employees.
- *Explain the four types of development networks derived from a developmental network model of mentoring.* The four development networks are receptive, traditional, entrepreneurial, and opportunistic. A receptive network is composed of a few weak ties from one social system. A traditional network contains a few strong ties between an employee and developers that all come from one social system. An entrepreneurial network is made up of strong ties among developers from several social systems, and an opportunistic network is associated with having weak ties with multiple developers from different social systems.

Chapter Summaries—
This section includes responses to the learning objectives in each chapter, making it a handy review tool for all users.

discussion questions

1. In the context of the chapter-opening vignette, how much does family history affect one's self-esteem and emotional intelligence? Explain.
2. How is someone you know with low self-efficacy, relative to a specified task, "programming themselves for failure"? What could be done to help that individual develop high self-efficacy?
3. What importance do you attach to self-talk in self-management? Explain.
4. On scales of low = 1 to high = 10, how would you rate yourself on the Big Five personality dimensions? Is your personality profile suitable for your present (or chosen) line of work? Explain.
5. Which of the four key components of emotional intelligence is (or are) your strong suit? Which is (or are) your weakest? What are the everyday implications of your EI profile?

Discussion Questions—
Focused and challenging, these questions help facilitate classroom discussion or review material. Answers and interpretations can be found at our Web site www.mhhe.com/kinickiob2e.

Active Learning

features

New! Ethical Dilemmas—

These 16 new exercises raise contemporary ethical issues, ask tough questions, and have corresponding interpretations on the Online Learning Center at www.mhhe.com/kinickiob2e.

ethical dilemma

You Mean Cheating Is Wrong?

College students are disturbed by recent corporate scandals: Some 84% believe the U.S. is having a business crisis, and 77% think CEOs should be held personally responsible for it.

But when the same students are asked about their own ethics, it's another story. Some 59% admit cheating on a test (66% of men, 54% of women). And only 19% say they would report a classmate who cheated (23% of men, but 15% of women—even though recent whistle-blowers have been women).

The survey of 1,100 students on 27 U.S. campuses was conducted by Students in Free Enterprise (SIFE), a non-profit that teams up with corporations to teach students ethical business practices. "There's a lack of understanding about ethics and how ethics are applied in real life," says Alvin Rohrs, SIFE'S CEO. "We have to get young people to stop and think about ethics and the decisions

How Should We Interpret This Hypocritical Double Standard?

1. Don't worry, most students know the difference between school and real life. They'll do the right thing when it really counts. Explain your rationale.
2. Whether in the classroom or on the job, pressure for results is the problem. People tend to take shortcuts and bend the rules when they're pressured. Explain.
3. A cheater today is a cheater tomorrow. Explain.
4. College professors need to do a better job with ethics education. How?
5. Both students and managers need to be held personally accountable for their unethical behavior. How?
6. Invent other interpretations or options. Discuss.

Instructor supplements

Organizational Behavior 2e gives you all the support material you need for an enriched classroom experience.

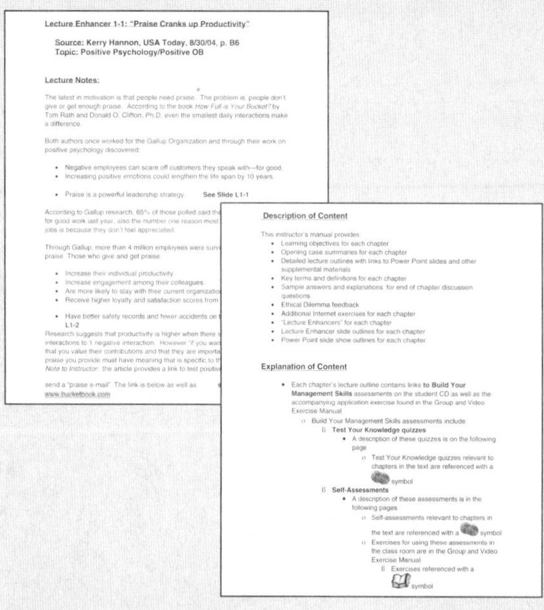

Lecture Enhancer 1-1: "Praise Cranks up Productivity"

Source: Kerry Hannon, USA Today, 8/30/04, p. B6
Topic: Positive Psychology/Positive OB

Lecture Notes:

The latest in motivation is that people need praise. The problem is, people don't give or get enough praise. According to the book *How Full is Your Bucket?* by Tom Rath and Donald O. Clifton, Ph.D. even the smallest daily interactions make a difference.

Both authors once worked for the Gallup Organization and through their work on positive psychology discovered:

- Negative employees can scare off customers they speak with—for good.
- Increasing positive emotions could lengthen the life span by 10 years.
- Praise is a powerful leadership strategy. **See Slide L1-1**

According to Gallup research, 65% of those polled said the … for good work last year, also the number one reason most … jobs is because they don't feel appreciated.

Through Gallup, more than 4 million employees were surv… praise. Those who give and get praise:

- Increase their individual productivity
- Increase engagement among their colleagues.
- Are more likely to stay with their current organizatio…
- Receive higher loyalty and satisfaction scores from …
- Have better safety records and fewer accidents on t… L1-2

Research suggests that productivity is higher when there … interactions to 1 negative interaction. However "if you war… that you value their contributions and that they are importa… praise you provide must have meaning that is specific to th… *Note to Instructor:* the article provides a link to test positiv…

send a "praise e-mail". The link is below as well as … www.bucketbook.com

Description of Content

This instructor's manual provides:

- Learning objectives for each chapter
- Opening case summaries for each chapter
- Detailed lecture outlines with links to Power Point slides and other supplemental materials
- Key terms and definitions for each chapter
- Sample answers and explanations for end of chapter discussion questions
- Ethical Dilemma feedback
- Additional Internet exercises for each chapter
- "Lecture Enhancers" for each chapter
- Lecture Enhancer slide outlines for each chapter
- Power Point slide show outlines for each chapter

Explanation of Content

- Each chapter's lecture outline contains links **to Build Your Management Skills** assessments on the student CD as well as the accompanying application exercise found in the Group and Video Exercise Manual
  - Build Your Management Skills assessments include:
    - **Test Your Knowledge quizzes**
      - A description of these quizzes is on the following page
        - Test Your Knowledge quizzes relevant to chapters in the text are referenced with a symbol
    - **Self-Assessments**
      - A description of these assessments is in the following pages
        - Self-assessments relevant to chapters in the text are referenced with a symbol
        - Exercises for using these assessments in the class room are in the Group and Video Exercise Manual
          - Exercises referenced with a symbol

Instructor's Resource Guide

The Instructor's Manual is a creative guide to understanding organizational behavior. It combines traditional elements of Instructor's Manuals with newer features such as teaching tips throughout the lecture outline, additional discussion ideas for the Opening Vignettes, note pages for the PPT slides, a matrix on how to incorporate Hot Seat DVD material or the Build Your Management Skills exercises, answers to Discussion Questions and End of Chapter material, and much more. Each element will assist the instructor and students in maximizing the ideas, issues, concepts, and important organizational behavior approaches included in each chapter.

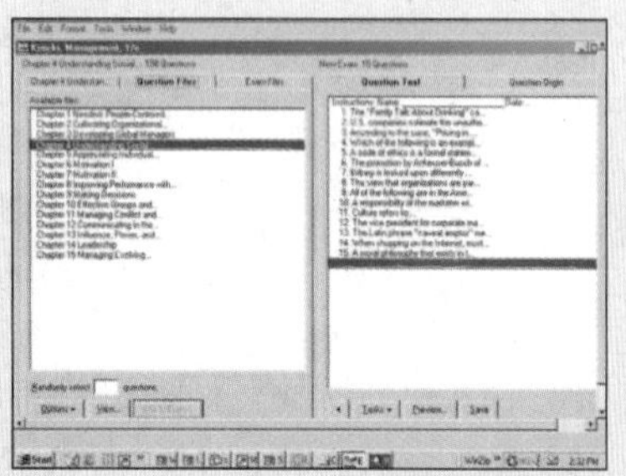

Computerized Test Bank

The Test Bank contains approximately 1,200 questions, with a mix of true/false, multiple-choice, and essay questions. Multiple-choice questions are ranked (easy, medium, or hard) to help the instructor provide the proper mix of questions.

Instructor's CD-ROM

ISBN: 007-304659-0

All of the above-mentioned materials, including PowerPoint slides, can be located on the Instructor's CD-ROM. This CD-ROM allows professors to easily create their own custom presentation. They can pull from resources on the CD, like the Instructor's Manual, the Test Bank, and PowerPoint, or from their own files. Additional downloads of figures and tables from the text are available for use.

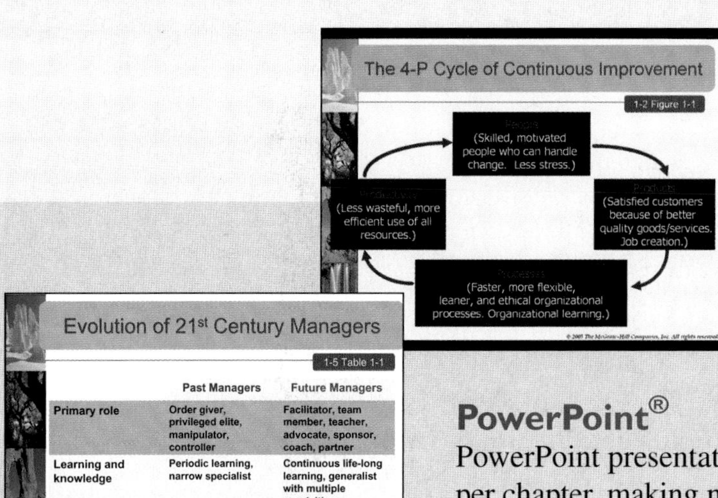

PowerPoint®

PowerPoint presentations feature approximately 20 slides per chapter, making notetaking easier for all your students.

VHS Videos

ISBN: 007-304657-4

An almost entirely new video collection is available for you to enhance your classroom presentation, and for students to see real companies applying organizational behavior topics. With a mixture of footage from PBS, NBC, and uniquely produced and newly created videos for the text, the collection offers the opportunity for you to go beyond the text material into such companies as The Container Store and Wal-Mart, and such hot topics as Money and Ethics, and Executive Perks.

Online Learning Center for Instructors

www.mhhe.com/kinickiob2e

More and more students are studying online. That's why we offer an Online Learning Center (OLC) that follows *Organizational Behavior* chapter by chapter. It doesn't require any building or maintenance on your part. It's ready to go the moment you and your students type in the URL.

Instructor supplements

As your students study, they can refer to the OLC Web site for such benefits as:

- Internet-based activities
- Self-grading quizzes
- Learning objectives
- Chapter summaries
- Additional video

A secured Instructor Resource Center stores your essential course materials to save you prep time before class. The Instructor's Manual, PowerPoint, and sample syllabi are now just a couple of clicks away. You will also find useful packaging information and Video notes.

PowerWeb provides high-quality, peer-reviewed content including up-to-date articles from leading periodicals and journals, current news, weekly updates with assessment, interactive exercises, Web research guide, study tips, and much more. PowerWeb is free with your *Organizational Behavior* adoption.

The OLC Web site also serves as a doorway to other technology solutions like PageOut, which is free to *Organizational Behavior* adopters.

Primis Online

You can customize this text by using McGraw-Hill's Primis Online digital database. This feature offers you the flexibility to customize your course to include material from the largest online collection of textbooks, readings, and cases. Primis leads the way in customized eBooks with hundreds of titles available at prices that save your students over 20% off bookstore prices. Additional information is available at 800-228-0634.

Student supplements

Student CD-ROM

All NEW copies of this text are packaged with a special Student CD-ROM. This added-value feature includes:

- Interactive modules that encourage hands-on learning about such topics as Motivation, Leadership, and Organizational Communication
- Interactive chapter quizzes
- Videos of real-world companies
- Exercises and quizzes to enhance videos
- A special link to Kinicki/Kreitner's Online Learning Center

To package the free Student CD-ROM with the text for your students, ask your McGraw-Hill/Irwin Sales Representative, or order ISBN: 007-313833-9.

Online Learning Center for Students

The Student Resources area of the Online Learning Center is loaded with beneficial exercises and study material that follow *Organizational Behavior* chapter-by-chapter to help your students understand and absorb key concepts and topics. Some of the features include:

- Internet-based activities
- Self-grading quizzes
- Learning objectives
- Additional videos

Grateful Appreciation

Our sincere thanks and gratitude go to our Editor, John Weimeister, and his first-rate team at McGraw-Hill/Irwin who encouraged and facilitated our pursuit of "something better." Key contributors include Christine Scheid, Senior Developmental Editor; Lisa Nicks, Marketing Manager; and Lori Koetters, Project Manager. We would also like to thank Amanda Johnson for her wonderful work on the PowerPoint presentation, the Instructor's Resource Guide, and the Student CD quizzes, and Amit Shah of Frostburg State University for his work on the Test Bank.

We'd also like to give a special thank you to those colleagues who gave their comments and suggestions to help us create an even better second edition. They are:

Abe Bakhshesy
University of Utah

Joy Benson
University of Illinois–Springfield

Linda Boozer
Suny AG & Tech College–Morrisville

Emilio Bruna
University of Texas at El Paso

Mark Butler
San Diego State University

Holly Buttner
University of North Carolina–Greensboro

John Byrne
St. Ambrose University

Diane Caggiano
Fitchburg State College

Dave Carmichel
Oklahoma City University

Xiao-Ping Chen
University of Washington

Bongsoon Cho
SUNY–Buffalo

Savannah Clay
Central Piedmont Community College

Ray Coye
DePaul University

Denise Daniels
Seattle Pacific University

W. Gibb Dyer, Jr.
Brigham Young University

Mark Fichman
Carnegie Mellon University

David A. Foote
Middle Tennessee State University

Lucy Ford
Rutgers University

Thomas Gainey
State University of West Georgia

Jacqueline Gilbert
Middle Tennessee State University

Leonard Glick
Northeastern University

Barbara Hassell
IUPUI–Indianapolis

Hoyt Hayes
Columbia College–Columbia

Kim Hester
Arkansas State University

Chad Higgins
University of Washington

David Jalajas
Long Island University

Andrew Johnson
Bellevue Community College

Dong Jung
San Diego State University

Jordan Kaplan
Long Island University

John Keeling
Old Dominion University

Karen Markel
Oakland University

Tom McDermott
Pittsburgh Technical Institute

Edward Miles
Georgia State University

Linda Morable
Richland College

Jay Nathan
St. John's University

Regina Oneil
Suffolk University

Amy Randel
Wake Forest University

Clint Relyea
Arkansas State University

Patricia Rice
Finger Lakes Community College

Janet Romaine
St. Anselm College

Paula Silva
University of New Mexico

Randi Sims
Nova University

Peggy Takahashi
University of San Francisco

Jennie Carter Thomas
Belmont University

Matthew Valle
Elon University

Andrew Ward
Emory University

John Washbush
University of Wisconsin

John Watt
University of Central Arkansas

Ken Weidner
St. Josephs University

Scott Williams
Wright State University

Lynn Wilson
Saint Leo University

We'd also like to acknowledge and thank those who helped us with their feedback for the first edition:

Jodi Barnes-Nelson
NC State–Raleigh

Linda Boozer
SUNY AG & Tech College–Morrisville

Jack Chirch
Hampton University

Jacqueline Gilbert
Middle Tennessee State University

Kristine Hoover
Bowling Green State University

Claire Killian
University of Wisconsin–River Falls

Linda Morable
Richland College

Joseph Petrick
Wright State University

Dave Phillips
Purdue University–Westville

Brian Usilaner
University of Maryland–University College

Finally, we would like to thank our wives, Joyce and Margaret. Their love and support are instrumental to *everything* we do. They lift our tired spirits when needed and encourage us at every turn.

This project has been a fun challenge from start to finish. Not only did we enjoy reading and learning more about the latest developments within the field of organizational behavior, but completion of this edition has deepened a friendship between us that has spanned more than 20 years. We hope you enjoy this textbook. Best wishes for success and happiness!

Angelo & Bob

brief contents

contents

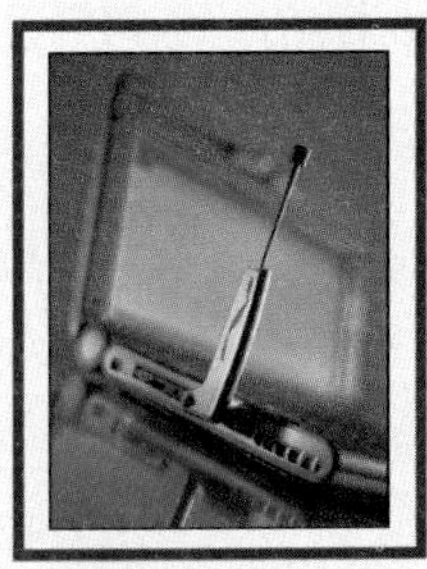

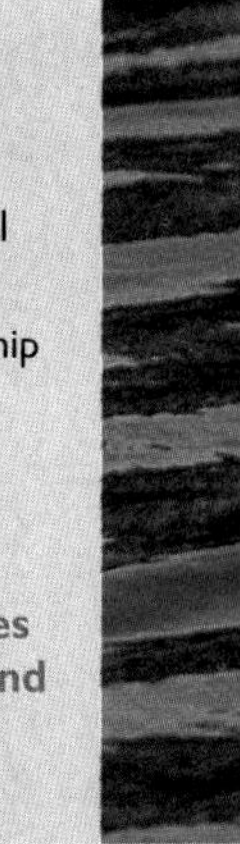

part One

Managing People in a Global Economy

chapter One

Needed: People-Centered Managers and Workplaces

LEARNING OBJECTIVES

After reading the material in this chapter, you should be able to:

- Identify at least four of Pfeffer's people-centered practices, and define the term *management.*
- Contrast McGregor's Theory X and Theory Y assumptions about employees.
- Explain the managerial significance of Deming's 85–15 rule, and identify the four principles of total quality management (TQM).
- Contrast human and social capital, and explain why we need to build both.
- Explain the impact of the positive psychology movement on the field of organizational behavior (OB).
- Define the term *E-business,* and specify five ways the Internet is affecting the management of people at work.

HEWLETT-PACKARD'S FOUNDERS PUT PEOPLE FIRST

The plaque outside the ramshackle two-family house at 367 Addison St. in Palo Alto, Calif., identifies the dusty one-car garage out back as the "birthplace of Silicon Valley." But the site, where Dave Packard and Bill Hewlett first set up shop, in 1938, is more than that. It's the birthplace of a new approach to management, a West Coast alternative to the traditional, hierarchical corporation. Sixty-five years later, the methods of Hewlett and Packard remain the dominant DNA for tech companies—and a major reason for U.S. preeminence in the Information Age.

The partnership began when the pair met as students at Stanford University. Packard, an opinionated star athlete from the hardscrabble town of Pueblo, Colo., had a commanding presence to match his 6-ft.-5-in. frame. Hewlett, whose technical genius was obscured from teachers by undiagnosed dyslexia, favored dorm-room pranks and bad puns. While different in temperament, the two soon discovered a shared passion for camping and fishing—and for turning engineering theory into breakthrough products.

The result was one of the most influential companies of the 20th century. Hewlett-Packard Co. (they flipped a coin to decide whose name went first) cranked out a blizzard of geeky electronic tools that were crucial to the development of radar, computers, and other digital wonders. Still, the pair's greatest innovation was managerial, not technical. From the first days in the garage, they set out to create a company that would attract like-minded techies. They shunned the rigid hierarchy of companies back East in favor of an egalitarian, decentralized system that came to be known as "the HP Way." The essence of the idea, radical at the time, was that employees' brainpower was the company's most important resource.

To make the idea a reality, the young entrepreneurs instituted a slew of pioneering practices. Starting in 1941, they granted big bonuses to all employees when the company improved its productivity. That evolved into one of the first all-company profit-sharing plans. When HP went public in 1957, the founders gave shares to all employees. Later, they were among the first to offer tuition assistance, flex time, and job sharing.

Even HP's offices were unusual. To encourage the free flow of ideas, employees worked in open cubicles. Even supply closets were to be kept open. Once, Hewlett sawed a lock off a closet and left a note: "HP trusts its employees."

If HP's policies were progressive, there was nothing coddling about either man. Until his death in 1996, Packard was a fearsome paragon of corporate integrity. He was famous for flying to distant branches to make a show of firing managers who skirted ethical lines. Neither man would hesitate to kill a business if it wasn't hitting its profits goals. The result: HP grew nearly 20% a year for 50 years without a loss.

Today, the behavior of the two founders remains a benchmark for business. Hewlett, who died in 2001, and Packard expected employees to donate their time to civic causes. And they gave more than 95% of their fortunes to charity. "My father and Mr. Packard felt they'd made this money almost as a fluke," says Hewlett's son Walter. "If anything, the employees deserved it more than they did." It's an insight that changed Corporate America—and the lives of workers everywhere.[1]

FOR DISCUSSION

Which of HP's employee-friendly practices do you think had the greatest motivational impact? Explain. For an interpretation of this case and additional comments, visit our Online Learning Center (OLC):

www.mhhe.com/kinickiob2e

HOW IMPORTANT ARE PEOPLE to organizational success? For a quick answer, we go to Bill Ford, CEO of the Ford Motor Company. When asked, "What keeps you up at night?," Ford replied, "People issues. Motivating and focusing people."[2] With 327,531 employees, Ford must lose some sleep.[3]

A longer research-based answer comes from Stanford's Jeffrey Pfeffer: "There is a substantial and rapidly expanding body of evidence, some of it quite methodologically sophisticated, that speaks to the strong connection between how firms manage their people and the economic results achieved."[4] His review of research from the United States and Germany showed *people-centered practices* strongly associated with higher profits and lower employee turnover. Seven people-centered practices in successful companies are:

1. Job security (to eliminate fear of layoffs).
2. Careful hiring (emphasizing a good fit with the company culture).
3. Power to the people (via decentralization and self-managed teams).
4. Generous pay for performance.
5. Lots of training.
6. Less emphasis on status (to build a "we" feeling).
7. Trust building (through the sharing of critical information).[5]

Importantly, these factors are a *package* deal, meaning they need to be installed in a coordinated and systematic manner—not in bits and pieces.

Sadly, too many managers act counter to their declarations that people are their most important asset. Pfeffer blames a number of modern management trends and practices. For example, undue emphasis on short-term profit precludes long-term efforts to nurture human resources. Also, excessive layoffs, when managers view people as a cost rather than an asset, erode trust, commitment, and loyalty.[6] *Only 12% of today's organizations, according to Pfeffer, have the systematic approaches and persistence to qualify as true people-centered organizations, thus giving them a competitive advantage.*[7] No surprise, then, that "a recent Gallup Poll shows 71% of U.S. workers consider themselves 'disengaged' clock-watchers who can't wait to go home."[8]

To us, an 88% shortfall in the quest for people-centered organizations represents a tragic loss, both to society and to the global economy. We all need to accept the challenge to do better.[9] *Fortune* magazine's annual list of "The 100 Best Companies to Work For" shows what is being done at progressive organizations that put people first. For example, Northwestern Mutual, the Milwaukee life insurance firm with 4,382 employees, "hasn't laid off a single person in 145 years."[10] Importantly, as documented in a recent study, companies making *Fortune*'s "100 Best" list tend to outperform the competition.[11]

The mission of this book is to help increase the number of people-centered managers and organizations around the world. Our jumping-off point is the 4-P model of strategic results in Figure 1–1. The 4-P model emphasizes the larger strategic context for managing people. Of course, other factors such as planning, technology, and finances also require good management. Further, the 4-P model stresses the importance of day-to-day *continuous improvement* in all aspects of organizational endeavor to cope with more demanding customers and stiffer competition.

In this chapter, we discuss the manager's job, define and examine organizational behavior and its evolution, and explore new directions.

FIGURE 1–1 Strategic Results: The 4-P Cycle of Continuous Improvement

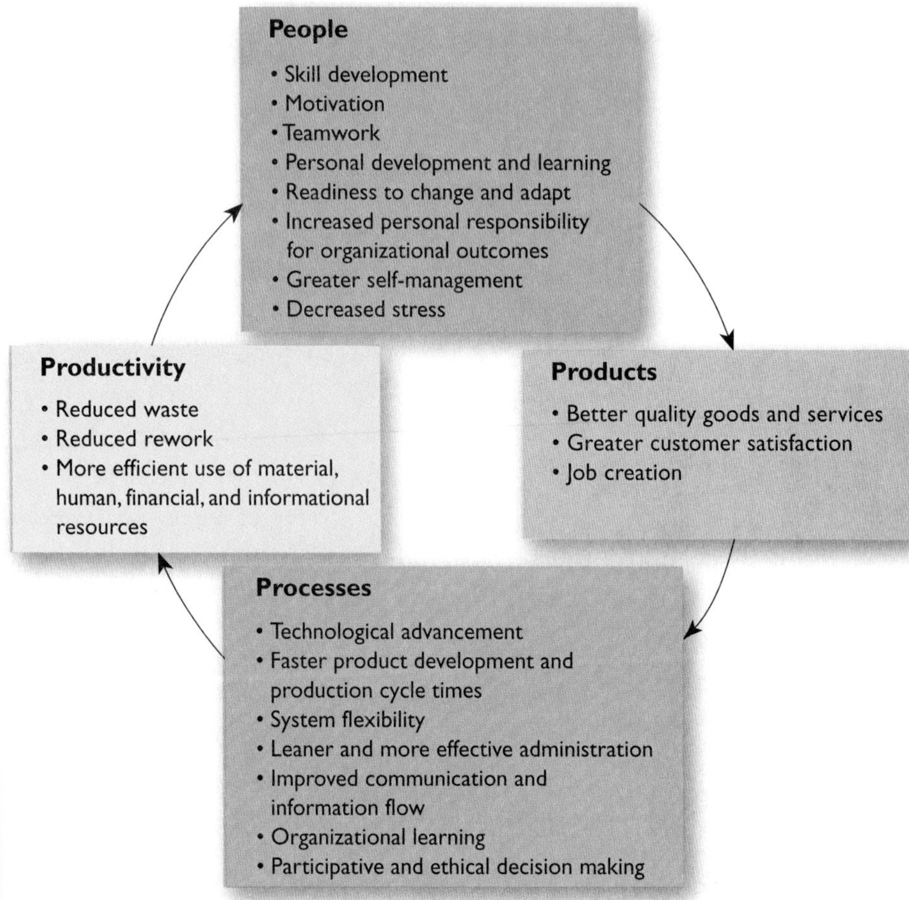

People
• Skill development
• Motivation
• Teamwork
• Personal development and learning
• Readiness to change and adapt
• Increased personal responsibility for organizational outcomes
• Greater self-management
• Decreased stress
Products
• Better quality goods and services
• Greater customer satisfaction
• Job creation
Processes
• Technological advancement
• Faster product development and production cycle times
• System flexibility
• Leaner and more effective administration
• Improved communication and information flow
• Organizational learning
• Participative and ethical decision making
Productivity
• Reduced waste
• Reduced rework
• More efficient use of material, human, financial, and informational resources

Managers Get Results with and through Others

> **management**
> Process of working with and through others to achieve organizational objectives efficiently and ethically.

For better or for worse, managers touch our lives in many ways. Schools, hospitals, government agencies, and large and small businesses all require systematic management. Formally defined, **management** is the process of working with and through others to achieve organizational objectives in an efficient and ethical manner. From the standpoint of organizational behavior, the central feature of this definition is "working with and through others." Managers play a constantly evolving role. Today's successful managers are no longer the I've-got-everything-under-control order givers of yesteryear. Rather, they need to creatively envision and actively sell bold new directions in an ethical and sensitive manner. Effective managers are team players empowered by the willing and active support of others who are driven by conflicting self-interests. Each of us has a huge stake in how well managers carry out their evolving role. Henry Mintzberg, a respected management scholar, observed: "No job is more vital to our society than that of the manager. It is the manager who determines whether our social institutions serve us well or whether they squander our talents and resources."[12]

Extending our managerial thrust, let us take a closer look at the skills managers need to perform and the future direction of management.

A Skills Profile for Managers

Observational studies by Mintzberg and others have found the typical manager's day to be a fragmented collection of brief episodes.[13] Interruptions are commonplace, while large blocks of time for planning and reflective thinking are not. In one particular study, four top-level managers spent 63% of their time on activities lasting less than nine minutes each. Only 5% of the managers' time was devoted to activities lasting more than an hour.[14] But what specific skills do effective managers perform during their hectic and fragmented workdays?

Many attempts have been made over the years to paint a realistic picture of what managers do.[15] Diverse and confusing lists of managerial functions and roles have been suggested. Fortunately, a stream of research over the past 25 years by Clark Wilson and others has given us a practical and statistically validated profile of managerial *skills*[16] (see Skills & Best Practices). Wilson's managerial skills profile focuses on 11 observable categories of managerial behavior. This is very much in tune with today's emphasis on managerial competency.[17] Wilson's unique skills-assessment technique goes beyond the usual self-report approach with its natural bias. In addition to surveying a given manager about his or her 11 skills, the Wilson approach also asks those who report directly to the manager to answer questions about their boss's skills. According to Wilson and his colleagues, the result is an assessment of skill *mastery,* not simply skill awareness.[18] The logic behind Wilson's approach is both simple and compelling. Who better to assess a manager's skills than the people who experience those behaviors on a day-to-day basis—those who report directly to the manager?

The Wilson managerial skills research yields three useful lessons:

1. Dealing effectively with *people* is what management is all about. The 11 skills constitute a goal creation/commitment/feedback/reward/accomplishment cycle with human interaction at every turn.
2. Managers with high skills mastery tend to have better subunit performance and employee morale than managers with low skills mastery.[19]
3. *Effective* female and male managers *do not* have significantly different skill profiles,[20] contrary to claims in the popular business press in recent years.[21]

SKILLS & BEST PRACTICES

The Effective Manager's Skill Profile

1. *Clarifies goals and objectives* for everyone involved.
2. *Encourages participation,* upward communication, and suggestions.
3. *Plans and organizes* for an orderly work flow.
4. Has *technical and administrative expertise* to answer organization-related questions.
5. *Facilitates work* through team building, training, coaching, and support.
6. *Provides feedback* honestly and constructively.
7. *Keeps things moving* by relying on schedules, deadlines, and helpful reminders.
8. *Controls details* without being overbearing.
9. Applies reasonable *pressure for goal accomplishment.*
10. *Empowers and delegates* key duties to others while maintaining goal clarity and commitment.
11. *Recognizes good performance* with rewards and positive reinforcement.

SOURCE: Adapted from material in F Shipper, "A Study of the Psychometric Properties of the Managerial Skill Scales of the Survey of Management Practices," *Educational and Psychological Measurement,* June 1995, pp 468–79; and C L Wilson, *How and Why Effective Managers Balance Their Skills: Technical, Teambuilding, Drive* (Columbia, Maryland: Rockatech Multimedia Publishing, 2003).

TABLE 1–1 Evolution of the 21st-Century Manager

	Past Managers	Future Managers
Primary role	Order giver, privileged elite, manipulator, controller	Facilitator, team member, teacher, advocate, sponsor, coach, partner
Learning and knowledge	Periodic learning, narrow specialist	Continuous life-long learning, generalist with multiple specialties
Compensation criteria	Time, effort, rank	Skills, results
Cultural orientation	Monocultural, monolingual	Multicultural, multilingual
Primary source of influence	Formal authority	Knowledge (technical and interpersonal)
View of people	Potential problem	Primary resource
Primary communication pattern	Vertical	Multidirectional
Decision-making style	Limited input for individual decisions	Broad-based input for joint decisions
Ethical considerations	Afterthought	Forethought
Nature of interpersonal relationships	Competitive (win–lose)	Cooperative (win–win)
Handling of power and key information	Hoard and restrict access	Share and broaden access
Approach to change	Resist	Facilitate

21st-Century Managers

Today's workplace is indeed undergoing immense and permanent changes.[22] Organizations have been "reengineered" for greater speed, efficiency, and flexibility.[23] Teams are pushing aside the individual as the primary building block of organizations.[24] Command-and-control management is giving way to participative management and empowerment.[25] Ego-centered leaders are being replaced by customer-centered leaders. Employees increasingly are being viewed as internal customers. All this creates a mandate for a new kind of manager in the 21st century.[26] Table 1–1 contrasts the characteristics of past and future managers. As the balance of this book will demonstrate, the managerial shift in Table 1–1 is not just a good idea, it is an absolute necessity in the new workplace.

The Field of Organizational Behavior: Past and Present

organizational behavior
Interdisciplinary field dedicated to better understanding and managing people at work.

Organizational behavior, commonly referred to as OB, is an interdisciplinary field dedicated to better understanding and managing people at work. By definition, organizational behavior is both research and application oriented. Three basic levels of analysis in OB are individual, group, and organizational. OB draws upon a diverse array of disciplines, including psychology, management, sociology, organization theory, social psychology, statistics, anthropology, general systems theory, economics, information technology, political science, vocational counseling, human stress management, psychometrics, ergonomics, decision theory, and ethics. This rich heritage has spawned many competing perspectives and theories about human work behavior. In fact, one researcher has identified 73 established OB theories.[27]

Organizational behavior is an academic designation. With the exception of teaching/research positions, OB is not an everyday job category such as accounting, marketing, or finance. Students of OB typically do not get jobs in organizational behavior, per se. This reality in no way demeans OB or lessens its importance in effective organizational management. OB is a *horizontal* discipline that cuts across virtually every job category, business function, and professional specialty. Anyone who plans to make a living in a large or small, public or private, organization needs to study organizational behavior. Both managers and nonmanagers alike need a solid grounding in OB.

A historical perspective of the study of people at work helps in studying organizational behavior. According to a management history expert, this is important because

> Historical perspective is the study of a subject in light of its earliest phases and subsequent evolution. Historical perspective differs from history in that the object of historical perspective is to sharpen one's vision of the present, not the past.[28]

In other words, we can better understand where the field of OB is today and where it appears to be headed by appreciating where it has been. Let us examine three significant landmarks in the evolution of understanding and managing people:

1. The human relations movement.
2. The total quality management movement.
3. The contingency approach to management.

The Human Relations Movement

A unique combination of factors during the 1930s fostered the human relations movement. First, following legalization of union–management collective bargaining in the United States in 1935, management began looking for new ways of handling employees. Second, behavioral scientists conducting on-the-job research started calling for more attention to the "human" factor. Managers who had lost the battle to keep unions out of their factories heeded the call for better human relations and improved working conditions. One such study, conducted at Western Electric's Chicago-area Hawthorne plant, was a prime stimulus for the human relations movement. Ironically, many of the Hawthorne findings have turned out to be more myth than fact.

The Hawthorne Legacy Interviews conducted decades later with three subjects of the Hawthorne studies and reanalysis of the original data with modern statistical techniques do not support initial conclusions about the positive effect of supportive supervision. Specifically, money, fear of unemployment during the Great Depression, managerial discipline, and high-quality raw materials—not supportive supervision—turned out to be responsible for high output in the relay assembly test room experiments.[29] Nonetheless, the human relations movement gathered momentum through the 1950s, as academics and managers alike made stirring claims about the powerful effect that individual needs, supportive supervision, and group dynamics apparently had on job performance.

TABLE 1–2 McGregor's Theory X and Theory Y

Outdated (Theory X) Assumptions about People at Work	Modern (Theory Y) Assumptions about People at Work
1. Most people dislike work; they avoid it when they can.	1. Work is a natural activity, like play or rest.
2. Most people must be coerced and threatened with punishment before they will work. People require close direction when they are working.	2. People are capable of self-direction and self-control if they are committed to objectives.
3. Most people actually prefer to be directed. They tend to avoid responsibility and exhibit little ambition. They are interested only in security.	3. People generally become committed to organizational objectives if they are rewarded for doing so.
	4. The typical employee can learn to accept and seek responsibility.
	5. The typical member of the general population has imagination, ingenuity, and creativity.

SOURCE: Adapted from D McGregor, *The Human Side of Enterprise* (New York: McGraw-Hill, 1960), Ch 4.

The Writings of Mayo and Follett Essential to the human relations movement were the writings of Elton Mayo and Mary Parker Follett. Australian-born Mayo, who headed the Harvard researchers at Hawthorne, advised managers to attend to employees' emotional needs in his 1933 classic, *The Human Problems of an Industrial Civilization.* Follett was a true pioneer, not only as a female management consultant in the male-dominated industrial world of the 1920s, but also as a writer who saw employees as complex bundles of attitudes, beliefs, and needs. Mary Parker Follett was way ahead of her time in telling managers to motivate job performance instead of merely demanding it, a "pull" rather than "push" strategy. She also built a logical bridge between political democracy and a cooperative spirit in the workplace.[30]

McGregor's Theory Y In 1960, Douglas McGregor wrote a book entitled *The Human Side of Enterprise,* which has become an important philosophical base for the modern view of people at work.[31] Drawing upon his experience as a management consultant, McGregor formulated two sharply contrasting sets of assumptions about human nature (see Table 1–2). His Theory X assumptions were pessimistic and negative and, according to McGregor's interpretation, typical of how managers traditionally perceived employees. To help managers break with this negative tradition, McGregor formulated his **Theory Y,** a modern and positive set of assumptions about people. McGregor believed managers could accomplish more through others by viewing them as self-energized, committed, responsible, and creative beings.

Theory Y

McGregor's modern and positive assumptions about employees being responsible and creative.

A survey of 10,227 employees from many industries across the United States challenges managers to do a better job of acting on McGregor's Theory Y assumptions. From the employees' perspective, Theory X management practices are the major barrier to productivity improvement and employee well-being. The researcher concluded:

> The most noteworthy finding from our survey is that an overwhelming number of American workers—some 97%—desire work conditions known to facilitate high productivity. Workers uniformly reported—regardless of the type of organization, age, gender, pay schedule, or level in the organizational hierarchy—that they needed and wanted in their own workplaces the conditions for collaboration, commitment, and creativity research has demonstrated as necessary for both productivity and health. Just as noteworthy, however, is the finding that the actual conditions of work supplied by management are those conditions that research has identified as *competence suppressors*—procedures, policies, and practices that prevent or punish expressions of competence and most characterize unproductive organizations.[32]

New Assumptions about Human Nature Unfortunately, unsophisticated behavioral research methods caused the human relationists to embrace some naive and misleading conclusions. For example, human relationists believed in the axiom, "A satisfied employee is a hardworking employee." Subsequent research, as discussed later in this book, shows the satisfaction–performance linkage to be more complex than originally thought.

Despite its shortcomings, the human relations movement opened the door to more progressive thinking about human nature. Rather than continuing to view employees as passive economic beings, managers began to see them as active social beings and took steps to create more humane work environments.

The Total Quality Management Movement

In 1980, NBC aired a television documentary titled "If Japan Can . . . Why Can't We?" It was a wake up call for North American companies to dramatically improve product quality or continue losing market share to Japanese electronics and automobile companies. A full-fledged movement ensued during the 1980s and 1990s. Much was written, said, and done about improving the quality of both goods and services.[33] Thanks to the concept of *total quality management* (TQM), the quality of much of what we buy today is significantly better than in the past. The underlying principles of TQM are more important than ever given the growth of both E-business on the Internet and the overall service economy. According to one business writer:

> A company stuck in the industrial-age mentality is very likely to get squashed because "zero-defect" quality has become an ante to compete, not a differentiator. Even "zero-time" operations that address customers' expectations for immediate response and gratification are becoming common in today's digital age.[34]

In a survey of 1,797 managers from 36 countries by the American Management Association, "customer service" and "quality" ranked as the corporate world's top two concerns.[35] TQM principles have profound practical implications for managing people today.[36]

What Is TQM? Experts on the subject offered this definition of **total quality management:**

> TQM means that the organization's culture is defined by and supports the constant attainment of customer satisfaction through an integrated system of tools, techniques, and training. This involves the continuous improvement of organizational processes, resulting in high-quality products and services.[37]

total quality management

An organizational culture dedicated to training, continuous improvement, and customer satisfaction.

Quality consultant Richard J Schonberger sums up TQM as "continuous, customer-centered, employee-driven improvement."[38] TQM is necessarily employee driven because product/service quality cannot be continuously improved without the

SKILLS & BEST PRACTICES

Quality Improvement Was the Right Rx for This Ailing Florida Hospital

Despite its idyllic setting amid palm trees and sea breezes on Florida's West Coast, Sarasota Memorial Hospital was not a tranquil place back in 1998. The 828-bed facility was far below par in numbers of patients served and levels of worker retention. In a survey of 800 hospitals by Press Ganey Associates, a health care research firm in South Bend, Ind., Sarasota Memorial's customer satisfaction ratings were down in the 17th percentile that year. Staff turnover was running at an annual rate of 25.2%, and the not-for-profit organization posted a $2.2 million shortfall.

In 2002, three years into a targeted effort to refocus the organization, Sarasota Memorial had $27 million in excess revenues after expenses, turnover for the system's 3,500 employees had dropped to 16.6%, and customer satisfaction had risen to the 90th percentile.

The turnabout, achieved against a backdrop of cost-cutting pressures and industry workforce shortages, was accomplished without layoffs, restructuring or major capital investments. . . .

What finally cemented the efforts at Sarasota Memorial, [Service Excellence Director Pam] Beitlich says, was an approach adapted from the "pillars of excellence" concept in place at another Florida hospital, Pensacola Baptist. During benchmarking that involved hospitals throughout the country, including two others in Florida and one each in Illinois and Connecticut, Pensacola Baptist kept coming up as one of the best, she says. Quint Studer, then president at Pensacola, shared his pillar concept. Later his consulting firm, the Studer Group, contracted with Sarasota to help with the customer service initiative.

Sarasota's pillars of excellence are service, people, quality, finance and growth. "We do all our meetings, all our strategic planning around these five," [CEO Dr. Duncan] Findlay says. Beitlich adds: "Everybody sets goals based on the pillars. It's simple. Five things, that's it. If what you are doing as a leader doesn't contribute in some way to those five pillars, then you need to [reexamine] what you're doing." The evaluation process for leaders was changed to support those pillars, Studer says. Now a leader is responsible for how much his or her customer satisfaction improves.

SOURCE: Excerpted from L H Heuring, "Patients First," *HR Magazine*, July 2003, pp 64–69. Copyright 2003 by Society for Human Resource Management. Reproduced with permission of Society for Human Resource Management via Copyright Clearance Center.

active learning and participation of *every* employee. Thus, in successful quality improvement programs, TQM principles are embedded in the organization's culture (see Skills & Best Practices).

The Deming Legacy TQM is firmly established today thanks in large part to the pioneering work of W Edwards Deming.[39] Ironically, the mathematician credited with Japan's post–World War II quality revolution rarely talked in terms of quality. He instead preferred to discuss "good management" during the hard-hitting seminars he delivered right up until his death at age 93 in 1993.[40] Although Deming's passion was the statistical measurement and reduction of variations in industrial processes, he had much to say about how employees should be treated. Regarding the human side of quality improvement, Deming called for the following:

- Formal training in statistical process control techniques and teamwork.
- Helpful leadership, rather than order giving and punishment.
- Elimination of fear so employees will feel free to ask questions.
- Emphasis on continuous process improvements rather than on numerical quotas.
- Teamwork.
- Elimination of barriers to good workmanship.[41]

One of Deming's most enduring lessons for managers is his 85–15 rule.[42] Specifically, when things go wrong, there is roughly an 85% chance the *system* (including management, machinery, and rules) is at fault. Only about 15% of the time is the individual employee at fault. Unfortunately, as Deming observed, the typical manager spends most of his or her time wrongly blaming and punishing individuals for system failures. Statistical analysis is required to uncover system failures.

Principles of TQM Despite variations in the language and scope of TQM programs, it is possible to identify four common TQM principles:

1. Do it right the first time to eliminate costly rework.
2. Listen to and learn from customers and employees (see Hands-On Exercise).
3. Make continuous improvement an everyday matter.
4. Build teamwork, trust, and mutual respect.[43]

Deming's influence is clearly evident in this list. Once again, as with the human relations movement, we see people as the key factor in organizational success.

HANDS-ON EXERCISE

Who Comes First? Customers, Employees, or Stockholders?

INSTRUCTIONS

1. Drawing from your own value system and business philosophy, rank the three groups in the title of this exercise first, second, and third in terms of managerial priority. What is the rationale for your ranking?
2. Read the two brief quotes below.
3. Based on the opinions of these two respected business leaders, would you change your initial priority ranking? Why? With whom do you agree more, Iacocca or Schultz? Why?

Consult our Web site for an interpretation of this exercise: www.mhhe.com/kinickiob2e.

Lee Iacocca, Former President of Ford and Retired CEO of Chrysler:

*Just be sure to take care of your customers. You have to go eyeball to eyeball with them and say, "Do I have a deal for you!" And then stand behind your product or service. Don't worry about stockholders or employees. If you take care of your customers, everything else will fall into place.**

Howard Schultz, Chairman and Founder of Starbucks (as recalled by business partner Dan Levitan):

*He made it very clear that his hierarchy of importance was employees first, customers second, and shareholders third.***

SOURCES: *As quoted in L McCauley and C Canabou, eds., "Unit of One: The Voice of Experience," *Fast Company,* May 2001, p 82. **Excerpted from J B Dann, "Find a Hit as Big as Starbucks," *Business 2.0,* May 2004, pp 66, 68.

In summary, TQM advocates have made a valuable contribution to the field of OB by providing a *practical* context for managing people. When people are managed according to TQM principles, everyone is more likely to get the employment opportunities and high-quality goods and services they demand. As you will see many times in later chapters, this book is anchored to Deming's philosophy and TQM principles.

The Contingency Approach to Management

Scholars have wrestled for many years with the problem of how best to apply the diverse and growing collection of management tools and techniques. Their answer is the contingency approach. The **contingency approach** calls for using management concepts and techniques in a situationally appropriate manner, instead of trying to rely on "one best way."

contingency approach

Using management tools and techniques in a situationally appropriate manner; avoiding the one-best-way mentality.

The contingency approach encourages managers to view organizational behavior within a situational context. According to this modern perspective, evolving situations, not hard-and-fast rules, determine when and where various management techniques are appropriate. Harvard's Clayton Christensen recently put it this way: "Many of the widely accepted principles of good management are only situationally appropriate."[44] For example, as will be discussed in Chapter 14, contingency researchers have determined that there is no single best style of leadership. Organizational behavior specialists embrace the contingency approach because it helps them realistically interrelate individuals, groups, and organizations. Moreover, the contingency approach sends a clear message to managers in today's global economy: Carefully read the situation and then apply lessons learned from published research studies, observing role models, self-study and training, and personal experience in situationally appropriate ways.

New Directions in OB

AFLAC offers a broad line of insurance products to more than 40 million people worldwide. Its customer service stands second to none, with most claims paid within four days. Chairman and CEO Dan Ramos believes in a strong commitment to employee development and has confidence that investment in human capital will produce a successful business outcome.

The field of OB is a dynamic work in progress—not static and in final form. As such, OB is being redirected and reshaped by various forces both inside and outside the discipline, including new concepts, models, and technology. In this section, we explore three general new directions for OB: human and social capital, *positive* organizational behavior, and impacts of the Internet revolution.

The Age of Human and Social Capital

Management is a lot like juggling. Everything is constantly in motion, with several things up in the air at any given time. Strategically speaking, managers juggle human, financial, material, informational, and technological resources. Each is vital to success in its own way. But jugglers remind us that some objects are rubber and some are glass. Dropped rubber objects bounce; dropped glass objects break. As more and more managers have come to realize, we cannot afford to drop the people factor (referred to in Figure 1–2 as human and social capital).

What Is Human Capital? (Hint: Think BIG) A team of human resource management authors recently offered this perspective:

> We're living in a time when a new economic paradigm—characterized by speed, innovation, short cycle times, quality, and customer satisfaction—is highlighting the importance of intangible assets, such as brand recognition, knowledge, innovation, and particularly human capital.[45]

human capital
The productive potential of one's knowledge and actions.

Human capital is the productive potential of an individual's knowledge and actions.[46] *Potential* is the operative word in this intentionally broad definition. When you are hungry, money in your pocket is good because it has the potential to buy a meal. Likewise, a present or future employee with the right combination of knowledge, skills, and motivation to excel represents human capital with the potential to give the organization a competitive advantage. Computer chip maker Intel, for example, is a high-tech company whose future depends on innovative engineering. It takes years of math and science studies to make world-class engineers. Not wanting to leave the future supply of engineers to chance, Intel annually spends millions of dollars funding education at all levels. The company encourages youngsters to study math and science and sponsors science competitions with generous scholarships for the winners.[47] Additionally, Intel encourages its employees to volunteer at local schools by giving the schools $200 for every 20 hours contributed.[48] Will all of the students end up working for Intel? No. That's not the point. The point is much bigger—namely, to build the *world's* human capital.

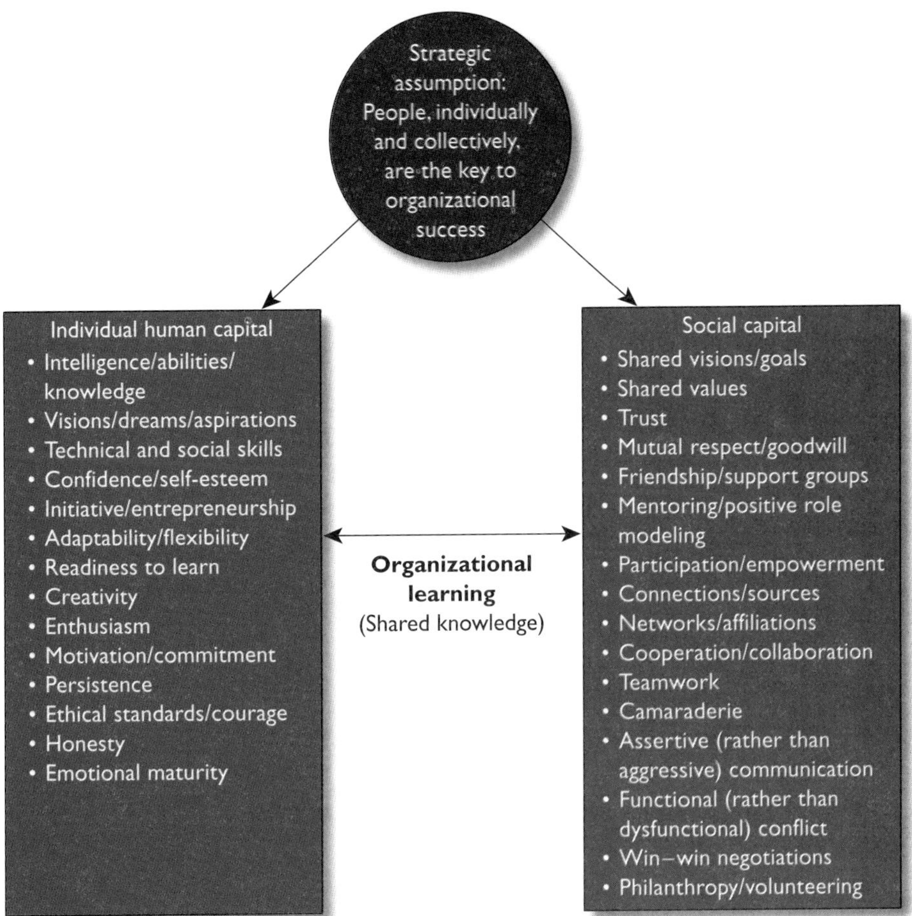

FIGURE 1–2 The Strategic Importance and Dimensions of Human and Social Capital

SOURCES: Based on discussions in P S Adler and S Kwon, "Social Capital: Prospects for a New Concept," *Academy of Management Review,* January 2002, pp 17–40; and C A Bartlett and S Ghoshal, "Building Competitive Advantage through People," *MIT Sloan Management Review,* Winter 2002, pp 34–41.

What Is Social Capital? Our focus now shifts from the individual to social units (e.g., friends, family, company, group or club, nation). Think *relationships.* **Social capital** is productive potential resulting from strong relationships, goodwill, trust, and cooperative effort.[49] Again, the word *potential* is key. According to experts on the subject: "It's true: the social capital that used to be a given in organizations is now rare and endangered. But the social capital we can build will allow us to capitalize on the volatile, virtual possibilities of today's business environment."[50] Relationships do matter. In a recent general survey, 77% of the women and 63% of the men rated "Good relationship with boss" extremely important. Other factors—including good equipment, resources, easy commute, and flexible hours—received lower ratings.[51]

social capital

The productive potential of strong, trusting, and cooperative relationships.

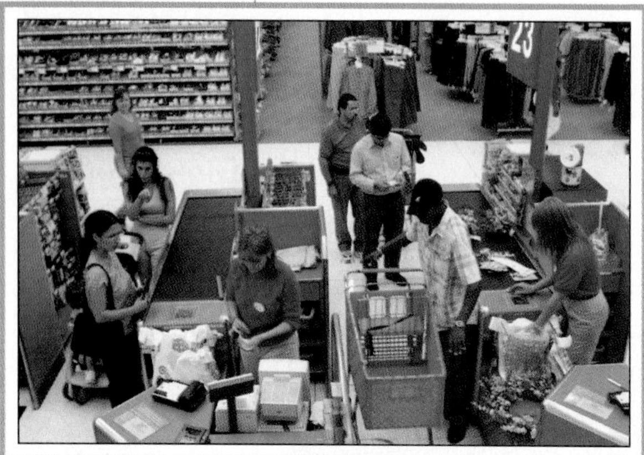

Target has been recognized for its financial performance and strength. It has been honored as one of America's most admired companies, one of the best companies for both working mothers and Latinos, one of the best corporate citizens, and a leader in its commitment to the education and training of its people. To what extent do you think its positive work environment affects its financial success?

How to Build Human and Social Capital Making the leap from concept to practice within this broad domain appears to be a daunting task. But we have a handy shortcut to jump-start your imagination. *Fortune* magazine, as mentioned earlier, publishes its annual list of "The 100 Best Companies to Work For" every January. Reading the brief side comments about the 100 selected companies is time well spent because they are both interesting and inspiring (as well as being a great resource for job hunters). These model companies are good at building human and/or social capital (for example, see Skills & Best Practices). Another area to watch is the *social entrepreneurship* movement that challenges students and businesspeople to create businesses with a dual bottom line. Laura D'Andrea Tyson, Dean of London Business School, explains:

> At the broadest level, a social entrepreneur is one driven by a social mission, a desire to find innovative ways to solve problems that are not being or cannot be addressed by either the market or the public sector. . . . Well-documented cases of grassroots entrepreneurial activities to tackle such diverse social problems as child abuse, disability, illiteracy, and environmental degradation give life to it. . . . Such businesses have a dual or "blended" bottom line that encompasses both a financial rate of return and a social rate of return.[52]

This promising initiative meshes nicely with the areas of corporate social responsibility and business ethics. Meanwhile, relative to the field of OB, many of the ideas discussed in this book relate directly or indirectly to building human and social capital (e.g., managing diversity, self-efficacy, self-management, emotional intelligence, goal setting, positive reinforcement, group problem-solving, group development, building trust, teamwork, managing conflict, communicating, empowerment, leadership, and organizational learning).

The Emerging Area of Positive Organizational Behavior (POB)

OB draws heavily on the field of psychology. So major shifts and trends in psychology eventually ripple through to OB. One such shift being felt in OB is the positive psychology movement. This exciting new direction promises to broaden the scope and practical relevance of OB.

The Positive Psychology Movement Something curious happened to the field of psychology during the last half of the 20th century. It took a distinctly negative turn. Theory and research became preoccupied with mental and behavioral pathologies; in other words, what was *wrong* with people! Following the traditional medical model, most researchers and practicing psychologists devoted their attention to diagnosing what was wrong with people and trying to make them better. At the turn of the 21st century, bits and pieces of an alternative perspective advocated by pioneering psychologists such as Abraham Maslow and Carl Rogers were pulled together under the label of positive psychology. This approach recommended focusing on human strengths and potential as a way to possibly *prevent* mental and behavioral problems and improve the general quality of life. A pair of positive psychologists described their new multilevel approach as follows:

> The field of positive psychology at the subjective level is about valued subjective experiences: well-being, contentment, and satisfaction (in the past); hope and optimism (for the future); and flow and happiness (in the present). At the individual level, it is about positive individual traits: the capacity for love and vocation, courage, interpersonal skill, aesthetic sensibility, perseverance, forgiveness, originality, future mindedness, spirituality, high talent, and wisdom. At the group level, it is about the civic virtues and the institutions that move individuals toward better citizenship: responsibility, nurturance, altruism, civility, moderation, tolerance, and work ethic.[53]

This is an extremely broad agenda for understanding and improving the human condition. However, we foresee a productive marriage between the concepts of human and social capital and the positive psychology movement, as it evolves into POB.[54]

SKILLS & BEST PRACTICES

Building Human Capital

Company	Program or activity
TDIndustries Dallas 1,393 employees	"Education is foremost at this construction company, where all employees—called 'partners'—are allowed 100% reimbursement of tuition, fees, and books at any state-supported college."
A.G. Edwards St. Louis 16,482 employees	"The brokerage . . . spends $75,000 per worker on training, and just built AGEU, a 200,000-square-foot education center for new financial consultants."

Building Social Capital

Company	Program or activity
Microsoft Redmond, Washington 36,665 employees	"The software giant . . . matches charity donations up to $12,000."
American Express New York 43,477 employees	"The 153-year-old travel and financial services firm . . . recently reinstated 12-week sabbaticals, [so] staff can take time off to work at nonprofits."
Timberland Stratham, New Hampshire 2,116 employees	"The maker of rugged footwear gives employees up to 40 hours a year of paid time off for community service."

SOURCE: Adapted and excerpted from R Levering and M Moskowitz, "2004 Special Report: The 100 Best Companies to Work For," *Fortune*, January 12, 2004, pp 56–80.

Positive Organizational Behavior: Definition and Key Dimensions

University of Nebraska OB scholar Fred Luthans defines **positive organizational behavior (POB)** as "the study and application of positively oriented human resource strengths and psychological capacities that can be measured, developed, and effectively managed for performance improvement in today's workplace."[55] His emphasis on study and measurement (meaning a coherent body of theory and research evidence) clearly sets POB apart from the quick-and-easy self-improvement books

positive organizational behavior (POB)
The study and improvement of employees' positive attributes and capabilities.

"So what's the problem with morale now?"

commonly found on best-seller lists. Also, POB focuses positive psychology more narrowly on the workplace. Luthans created the CHOSE acronym to identify five key dimensions of POB (see Table 1–3). Progressive managers already know the value of a positive workplace atmosphere, as evidenced by the following situations: At Perkins Coie, in Seattle, "'Happiness committees' roam the law firm's halls leaving baskets of candies and other thank-you treats on employees' desks."[56] Meanwhile, in Atlanta, at Barton Protective Services, "'Love' appears nine times in this security-guard agency's outline of company values."[57]

The Internet Revolution and OB

We can be forgiven if the Internet revolution has left us a bit dizzy.[58] In just a few short years, dot-coms exploded onto the scene, with promises of *everything* for sale *cheap* on the Internet. Then, just as suddenly, many dot-coms truly did explode, leaving their overworked employees jobless and their founders telling bizarre riches-to-rags stories.[59] Strange and unforeseen things happened. For example, Pets.com, with a popular and expensive advertising campaign, went broke trying to underprice pet supply stores. But, by 2004, Google had become a household name as the Internet

TABLE 1–3 Luthans' CHOSE Model of Key POB Dimensions (with cross-references to related topics in this textbook)

Confidence/self-efficacy: One's belief (confidence) in being able to successfully execute a specific task in a given context. (See Chapter 5.)
Hope: One who sets goals, figures out how to achieve them (identify pathways) and is self-motivated to accomplish them, that is, willpower and "waypower." (See Chapters 5 and 7.)
Optimism: Positive outcome expectancy and/or a positive causal attribution, but is still emotional and linked with happiness, perseverance, and success. (See Chapters 4, 5, 7, and 16.)
Subjective well-being: Beyond happiness emotion, how people cognitively process and evaluate their lives, the satisfaction with their lives. (See Chapters 4, 5, and 6.)
Emotional intelligence: Capacity for recognizing and managing one's own and others' emotions—self-awareness, self-motivation, being empathetic, and having social skills. (See Chapters 5, 10, 11, 12, 13, and 14.)

SOURCE: From *The Academy of Management Executive: The Thinking Manager's Source* by F. Luthans. Copyright © 2002 by Academy of Management. Reproduced with permission of Academy of Management via Copyright Clearance Center.

search company processed "more than 3,000 searches every second of the day"[60] and the value of annual transactions on eBay was expected to pass $20 billion.[61]

As we continue to sift through the wreckage of the 2000–2001 dot-com crash looking for winning formulas, one thing is very clear. The **Internet**—the global network of computers, software, cables, servers, switches, and routers—is here to stay as a business tool. John Chambers, CEO of Cisco Systems, the giant Internet equipment firm that was badly whiplashed during the dot-com crash, recently offered this perspective: "During boom times, people get overly excited, and during busts, they get overly pessimistic. . . . We believe the Internet is going to change the way people live, learn and play."[62] Meanwhile, *Business Week* offered an OB-related Internet challenge: "The real imperative for the next few years, though, will be adapting new technology to people and their work, rather than forcing people to adapt to it."[63]

Who doesn't remember the goofy, but endearing "mascot" of the now defunct Web site Pets.com? Pets.com spent huge advertising dollars on the concept and the ads, only to fall victim of the dot-com crash. Don't get too teary-eyed, though, because our pseudo-canine friend has landed another gig to hawk auto loans to people with bad credit for 1-800-Bar-None.

The purpose of this section is to define *E-business* and identify significant OB implications in the ongoing Internet revolution (as signs of what lies ahead).

E-business Is Much More than E-Commerce Experts on the subject draw an important distinction between *E-commerce* (buying and selling goods and services over the Internet) and **E-business,** using the Internet to facilitate *every* aspect of running a business.[64] Says one industry observer: "Strip away the highfalutin talk, and at bottom, the Internet is a tool that dramatically lowers the cost of communication. That means it can radically alter any industry or activity that depends heavily on the flow of information."[65] Relevant information includes everything from customer needs and product design specifications to prices, schedules, finances, employee performance data, and corporate strategy. Intel, discussed earlier as a champion of human capital, has taken this broad view of the Internet to heart. The computer-chip giant is striving to become what it calls an E-corporation, one that relies primarily on the Internet to not only buy and sell things, but also to facilitate all business functions, exchange knowledge among its employees, and build partnerships with outsiders. Intel is on the right track according to this recent observation by *Business Week:*

Internet

The global system of networked computers.

E-business

Running the *entire* business via the Internet.

> . . . take a look around, and you'll see that e-business has become a pillar of the economy. Consumers are more avid than ever to go places where only the Web can take them, and the corporations making the smartest use of the Internet outclass their brethren when it comes to operating nimbly and efficiently.[66]

E-business has significant implications for managing people at work because it eventually will seep into every corner of life both on and off the job.

E-business Implications for OB The following list is intended to open doors and explore possibilities, not serve as a final analysis. It also is a preview of later discussions in this book.

- *E-management*—21st-century managers, profiled earlier in Table 1–1, are needed in the fast-paced Internet age. They are able to create, motivate, and lead teams of far-flung specialists linked by Internet E-mail and project-management software and by fax and phone. Networking skills, applied both inside and outside the organization, are essential today.

- *E-leadership*—Because it involves electronically mediated interactions, in combination with the traditional face-to-face variety, experts say E-leadership raises these major issues for modern management:

  1. Leaders and followers have more access to information and each other, and this is changing the nature and content of their interactions.
  2. Leadership is migrating to lower and lower organizational levels and out through the boundaries of the organization to both customers and suppliers.
  3. Leadership creates and exists in networks that go across traditional organizational and community boundaries.
  4. Followers know more at earlier points in the decision-making process, and this is potentially affecting the credibility and influence of leaders.
  5. Unethical leaders with limited resources can now impact negatively a much broader audience of potential followers.
  6. The amount of time and contact that even the most senior leaders can have with their followers has increased, although the contact is not in the traditional face-to-face mode.[67]

  Making wise hiring and job assignment decisions, nurturing productive relationships, and building trust are more important than ever in the age of E-leadership.

- *E-communication*—E-mail has become one of the most used and abused forms of organizational communication. Today's managers need to be masters of concise, powerful e-mail and voice mail messages. Communicating via the

Telecommuters need to strike a productive balance between independence and feelings of isolation.

Internet's World Wide Web is fast and efficient for those who know how to fully exploit it. Consider the experience of Pietro Senna, a buyer for Nestlé in Switzerland:

> The time savings are immense. Each country's hazelnut buyer, for example, used to visit processing plants in Italy and Turkey. Hazelnuts, a key ingredient in chocolate bars, are prone to wild price swings and uneven quality. But after Senna stopped by some Turkish plants, he posted his report on the Web—and within a week, 73 other Nestlé buyers from around the globe had read it, saving them the trouble of a trip to Turkey. "For the first time, I get to take advantage of Nestlé's size," he says.[68]

Additionally, employees who "telecommute" from home or report in from remote locations via the Internet present their managers with unique motivational and performance measurement problems. For their part, telecommuters must strike a productive balance between independence and feelings of isolation.

- *Goal setting and feedback*—Abundant research evidence supports the coupling of clear and challenging goals and timely and constructive feedback for keeping employees headed in the right direction. Thanks to Web-based software programs such as *eWorkbench,* managers can efficiently create, align, and track their employees' goals.[69]
- *Organizational structure*—The Internet and modern telecommunications technology have given rise to "virtual teams" and "virtual organizations."[70] Time zones, facilities, and location no longer are hard constraints on getting things accomplished. Got a great product idea but don't have the time to build a factory? No problem. Just connect with someone via the Internet who can get the job done. This virtual workplace, with less face-to-face interaction, requires managers and employees who are flexible and adaptable and not bound by slow and rigid bureaucratic structures and methods.
- *Job design*—The *work itself* is a powerful motivator for many employees today, especially those in information technology. A New Economy study by Harvard's Rosabeth Moss Kanter led to this conclusion:

> [They] are attracted by the chance to take on big responsibility and stretch their skills even further. The "stickiest" work settings (the ones people leave less frequently and more reluctantly) involve opportunity and empowerment. Cutting-edge work with the best tools for the best customers is important in the present because it promises even greater responsibility and rewards in the future.[71]

Boring and unchallenging and/or dead-end jobs will repel rather than attract top talent in the Internet age.

- *Decision making*—Things indeed are moving faster and faster in the Internet age. Just ask the typical overloaded manager. A survey asking 479 managers about their last three years uncovered these findings: 77% reported making more decisions while 43% said they had less time to make decisions.[72] Adding to the pressure, databases linked to the Internet give today's decision makers unprecedented amounts of both relevant and irrelevant data. The trick is to be energized and selective, not overwhelmed. A clear sense of purpose is

SKILLS & BEST PRACTICES

E-Learning Saves Time and Money at Hewlett-Packard

Daisy Ng, Hewlett-Packard's vice president of workforce development, also is devoted to making the workforce more productive while keeping costs down.

To be able to offer "a total customer experience to an internal learner at low cost," Ng said, "I have to use technology." That means a portal—"Learn@HP"—that acts as a single gateway for employees in nearly 60 countries.

Hewlett-Packard continually reduces the amount of time employees spend in the classroom. "Last year 25 percent of learning was using e-learning; now it's 38 to 40 percent. We are leading the way" in training, Ng said.

And in saving money. When Hewlett-Packard's merger with Compaq Computer Corp. was completed in May 2002, e-learning training was used to help define the new corporate structure. "It speeded up the merger, and we saved the company $50 million," she said.

A recent arrangement with Microsoft means retraining 3,000 workers, according to Ng. "If we do not use e-learning, it will take us three months to re-skill those individuals. By using e-learning and virtual classrooms, we have been able to improve the certification rate and do it in eight weeks. We save $10 million."

SOURCE: Excerpted from S Overman, "Dow, Hewlett-Packard Put E-Learning to Work to Save Time and Money," *HR Magazine*, February 2004, p 32. Copyright 2004 by Society for Human Resource Management. Reproduced with permission of Society for Human Resource Management via Copyright Clearance Center.

necessary when sifting for useful information. Moreover, decision makers cannot ignore the trend away from command-and-control tactics and toward employee empowerment and participation. In short, there is more "we" than "me" for Internet-age decision makers.

- *Knowledge management*—Of growing importance today are E-training, E-learning, and distance learning via the Internet.[73] In fact, a recent "survey of some 296 organizations shows that organizations today are becoming more inclusive when it comes to e-learning, with 56 percent of respondents offering e-learning to the majority of their employees."[74] (See Skills & Best Practices.) Brandon Hall, a Sunnyvale, California, training specialist, recommends a contingency approach in this evolving area:

  > The old arguments about e-learning vs. classroom learning have been replaced by the common sense of a blended learning approach. When you can draw from a multitude of online and face-to-face components for a given learning program, blended learning offers the most options for best addressing the underlying performance need.[75]

- *Speed, conflict, and stress*—The name of the popular Internet-age magazine, *Fast Company,* says it all. Unfortunately, conflict and stress are unavoidable by-products of strategic and operational speed. The good news, as you will learn in later chapters, is that conflict and stress can be managed.
- *Change and resistance to change*—As Old Economy companies race to become E-corporations, employees are being asked to digest huge doses of change in every aspect of their worklives. Inevitable conflict and resistance to change will need to be skillfully managed.
- *Ethics*—Internet-centered organizations are littered with ethical landmines needing to be addressed humanely and responsibly. Among them are around-the-clock work binges, offshoring of jobs to India and elsewhere, exaggerated promises about rewards, electronic monitoring, questionable antiunion tactics, repetitive-motion injuries from excessive keyboarding, unfair treatment of part-timers, and privacy issues.[76]

Overall, the problems, challenges, and opportunities embodied in the Internet revolution are immense. Skillful management is needed.

key terms

contingency approach 13
E-business 19
human capital 14
Internet 19
management 6
organizational behavior (OB) 8
positive organizational behavior (POB) 17
social capital 15
Theory Y 10
total quality management 11

chapter summary

- *Identify at least four of Pfeffer's people-centered practices, and define the term* management. Pfeffer's seven people-centered practices are job security, careful hiring, power to the people, generous pay for performance, lots of training, less emphasis on status, and trust building. *Management* is the process of working with and through others to achieve organizational objectives in an efficient and ethical manner.
- *Contrast McGregor's Theory X and Theory Y assumptions about employees.* Theory X employees, according to traditional thinking, dislike work, require close supervision, and are primarily interested in security. According to the modern Theory Y view, employees are capable of self-direction, of seeking responsibility, and of being creative.
- *Explain the managerial significance of Deming's 85–15 rule, and identify the four principles of total quality management (TQM).* Deming claimed that about 85% of organizational failures are due to system breakdowns involving factors such as management, machinery, or work rules. He believed the workers themselves are responsible for failures only about 15% of the time. Consequently, Deming criticized the standard practice of blaming and punishing individuals for what are typically *system* failures beyond their immediate control. The four principles of TQM are (a) do it right the first time to eliminate costly rework; (b) listen to and learn from customers and employees; (c) make continuous improvement an everyday matter; and (d) build teamwork, trust, and mutual respect.
- *Contrast human and social capital and explain why we need to build both.* The first involves *individual* characteristics, the second involves *social* relationships. Human capital is the productive potential of an individual's knowledge and actions. Dimensions include such things as intelligence, visions, skills, self-esteem, creativity, motivation, ethics, and emotional maturity. Social capital is productive potential resulting from strong relationships, goodwill, trust, and cooperative effort. Dimensions include such things as shared visions and goals, trust, mutual respect, friendships, empowerment, teamwork, win–win negotiations, and volunteering. Social capital is necessary to tap individual human capital for the good of the organization through knowledge sharing and networking.
- *Explain the impact of the positive psychology movement on the field of OB.* Reversing psychology's long-standing preoccupation with what is wrong with people, positive psychology instead focuses on identifying and building human strengths and potential. Accordingly, Luthans recommends positive organizational behavior (POB) and identifies its basic elements with the CHOSE model. This acronym stands for Confidence/self-efficacy, Hope, Optimism, Subjective well-being, and Emotional intelligence.
- *Define the term* E-business, *and specify five ways the Internet is affecting the management of people at work. E-business* involves using the Internet to more effectively and efficiently manage *every* aspect of a business. The Internet is reshaping the management of people in the following areas: E-management (networking), E-leadership, E-communication (E-mail and telecommuting), goal setting and feedback, organizational structure (virtual teams and organizations), job design (desire for more challenge), decision making (greater speed and employee empowerment), knowledge management (E-learning), conflict and stress triggered by increased speed, rapid change and inevitable conflict and resistance, and ethical problems such as overwork and privacy issues.

discussion questions

1. Which of Pfeffer's seven people-centered practices are evident in the chapter-opening vignette on Hewlett-Packard? Explain.
2. In your opinion, what are the three or four most important strategic results in Figure 1–1? Why?
3. What is your personal experience with Theory X and Theory Y managers (see Table 1–2)? Which did you prefer? Why?
4. What are you doing to build human and social capital?
5. As the field of positive organizational behavior (POB) evolves, what potential impacts on the practice of management do you foresee?

ethical dilemma

You Mean Cheating Is Wrong?

College students are disturbed by recent corporate scandals: Some 84% believe the U.S. is having a business crisis, and 77% think CEOs should be held personally responsible for it.

But when the same students are asked about their own ethics, it's another story. Some 59% admit cheating on a test (66% of men, 54% of women). And only 19% say they would report a classmate who cheated (23% of men, but 15% of women—even though recent whistle-blowers have been women).

The survey of 1,100 students on 27 U.S. campuses was conducted by Students in Free Enterprise (SIFE), a non-profit that teams up with corporations to teach students ethical business practices. "There's a lack of understanding about ethics and how ethics are applied in real life," says Alvin Rohrs, SIFE'S CEO. "We have to get young people to stop and think about ethics and the decisions they're making." Otherwise, today's students may be tomorrow's criminals.[77]

How Should We Interpret This Hypocritical Double Standard?

1. Don't worry, most students know the difference between school and real life. They'll do the right thing when it really counts. Explain your rationale.
2. Whether in the classroom or on the job, pressure for results is the problem. People tend to take shortcuts and bend the rules when they're pressured. Explain.
3. A cheater today is a cheater tomorrow. Explain.
4. College professors need to do a better job with ethics education. How?
5. Both students and managers need to be held personally accountable for their unethical behavior. How?
6. Invent other interpretations or options. Discuss.

For an interpretation of this situation, visit our Web site, www.mhhe.com/kinickiob2e.

If you're looking for additional study materials, be sure to check out the Online Learning Center at

www.mhhe.com/kinickiob2e

for more information and interactivities that correspond to this chapter.

ethics learning module

IBM Cuts Retirees' Health Benefits to Boost Profits

> **FOR DISCUSSION**
>
> **Do you think it is ethical for a company like IBM to raise retirees' contributions to health benefits while its own decrease? Explain. For an interpretation of this case and additional comments, visit our Online Learning Center:**
>
> **www.mhhe.com/kinickiob2e**

The loud message comes from one company after another: Surging health-care costs for retired workers are creating a giant burden. So companies have been cutting health benefits for their retirees or requiring them to contribute more of the cost.

Time for a reality check: In fact, no matter how high health-care costs go, well over half of large American corporations face only limited impact from the increases when it comes to their retirees. They have established ceilings on how much they will ever spend per retiree for health care. If health costs go above the caps, it's the retiree, not the company, who's responsible.

Yet numerous companies are cutting retirees' health benefits anyway. One possible factor: When companies cut these benefits, they create instant income. This isn't just the savings that come from not spending as much. Rather, thanks to complex accounting rules, the very act of cutting retirees' future health-care benefits lets companies reduce a liability and generate an immediate accounting gain.

In some cases it flows straight to the bottom line. More often it sits on the books like a cookie jar, from which a company takes a piece each year that helps it meet earnings estimates. . . .

The fate of retirees can be very different. When Robert Eggleston retired from International Business Machines Corp. 12 years ago, he was paying $40 a month toward health-care premiums for himself and his wife, LaRue, with IBM paying the rest. In 1993, IBM set ceilings on its own health-care spending for retirees. For those on Medicare, which provides basic hospital and doctor-visit coverage, the cap was $3,000 or $3,500, depending on when they retired. For those younger than 65, the cap was $7,000 or $7,500. Spending hit the caps for the older retirees in 2001, the company says, pushing future health-cost increases onto retirees' shoulders.

Mr. Eggleston, 66 years old, has seen his premiums jump to $365 a month for the couple. Deductibles and copayments for drugs and doctor visits added $663 a month last year. "It just eats up all the pension," which is $850 a month, Mrs. Eggleston says. Her husband has brain cancer. Though he gets free supplies of a tumor-fighting drug through a program for low-income families, he has cashed in his 401(k) account, and he and LaRue have taken out a second mortgage on their Lake Dallas, Texas, home.

IBM retirees as a group saw their health-care premiums rise nearly 29% in 2003, on the heels of a 67%-plus increase in 2002. For IBM, with its caps in place, spending on retiree health care declined nearly 5%, after a drop of 18% the year before.

IBM confirms that retirees' spending has risen as its own has fallen.[1]

IBM's situation highlights the "grayness" that accompanies discussions about organizational ethics. The problem is that there is no universal standard of ethical behavior. For example, companies like IBM that raise employees' contributions to health care while simultaneously lowering their own contributions are not violating the law, but they may be acting unethically. The IBM vignette also underscores the fact that top management's ethical or unethical behavior can significantly affect the lives of present and past employees such as Robert Eggleston. Ethics and ethical behavior are receiving greater attention today. This interest is partly due to reported cases of questionable or potential unethical behavior involving companies such as Enron, Tyco, WorldCom (now MCI), and Arthur Andersen, and the associated costs of unethical behavior. In fact, the U.S. government filed 600 indictments and convicted 200 executives from March 2002 to March 2004.[2]

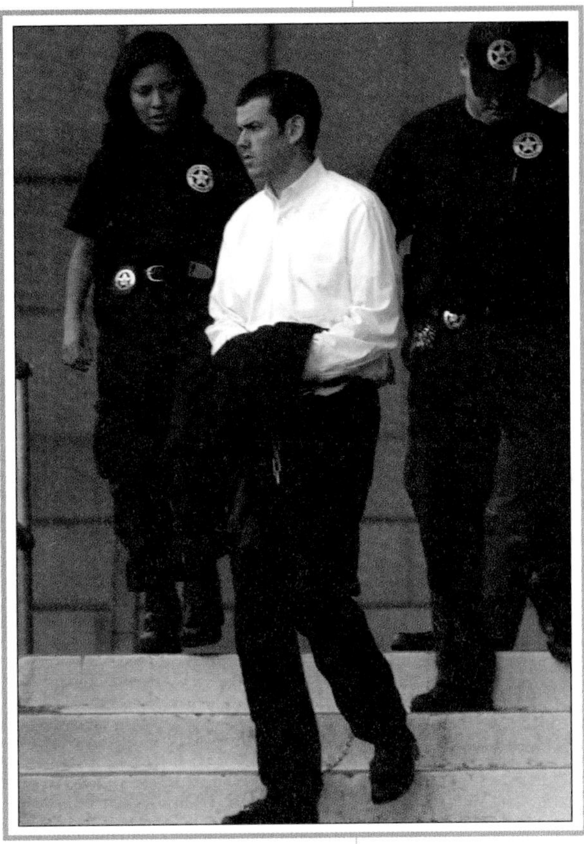

Former Enron treasurer Ben Glisan is led in chains from the federal courthouse in Houston.

U.S. industries lose about $400 billion a year from unethical and criminal behavior. Another nationwide survey revealed that over 50% of the respondents felt some pressure to compromise their organization's ethical standards.[3] Unethical behavior is a relevant issue for all employees. It occurs from the bottom to the top of the organization. For example, a recent survey of job applicants for executive positions indicated that 64% had been misinformed about the financial condition of potential employers, and 58% of these individuals were negatively impacted by this misinformation.[4] It is very likely that some of these affected individuals moved their families and left their friends only to find out that the promise of a great job in a financially stable organization was a lie. As you will learn, there are a variety of individual and organizational characteristics that contribute to unethical behavior. OB is an excellent vantage point for better understanding and improving workplace ethics. If OB can provide insights about managing human work behavior, then it can teach us something about avoiding *misbehavior*.

ethics Study of moral issues and choices.

Ethics involves the study of moral issues and choices. It is concerned with right versus wrong, good versus bad, and the many shades of gray in supposedly black-and-white issues. Moral implications spring from virtually every decision, both on and off the job. Managers are challenged to have more imagination and the courage to do the right thing. For example, do you think credit card companies should actively inform consumers that they are charging additional fees on any international transactions? Visa and MasterCard regularly tack on a 1% fee to cover the cost of international purchases.

> Now, many of the banks that issue the cards have been quietly adding separate fees of their own. Earlier this month, First USA added a 2% surcharge to all overseas transactions for cards that didn't already have one. That means users of its popular Visa cards will pay an additional 3% on all foreign charges. . . .

> In many instances, the credit card fees don't show up separately on travelers' monthly credit card statements. Instead, the surcharges are folded into the cost of each item charged. The fees are disclosed only in the fine print when you first sign up for your card, or sometimes your card issuer will send you an official notice that it's raising the fee. One notable exception is Chase, which discloses the fee on the bill.[5]

Are Visa and MasterCard engaging in sound business practices or unethical behavior? The answer will ultimately be resolved in the courts. *The Wall Street Journal* reports that these hidden charges have instigated a number of lawsuits against both Visa and MasterCard.

To enhance your understanding about ethics and organizational behavior, we discuss (1) a conceptual framework of ethical behavior, (2) a decision tree for diagnosing ethical decisions, (3) whether moral orientations vary by gender, (4) general moral principles for managers, and (5) how to improve an organization's ethical climate.

A Model of Ethical Behavior

Ethical and unethical conduct is the product of a complex combination of influences (see Figure A–1). At the center of the model in Figure A–1 is the individual decision maker. He or she has a unique combination of personality characteristics, values, and moral principles, leaning toward or away from ethical behavior. Personal experience with being rewarded or reinforced for certain behaviors and punished for others also shapes the individual's tendency to act ethically or unethically. Finally, gender plays an important role in explaining ethical behavior. Men and women have different moral orientations toward organizational behavior.[6] This issue is discussed later in this section.

Next, Figure A–1 illustrates two major sources of influence on one's role expectations. People assume many roles in life, including those of employee or manager.

FIGURE A–1 A Model of Ethical Behavior in the Workplace

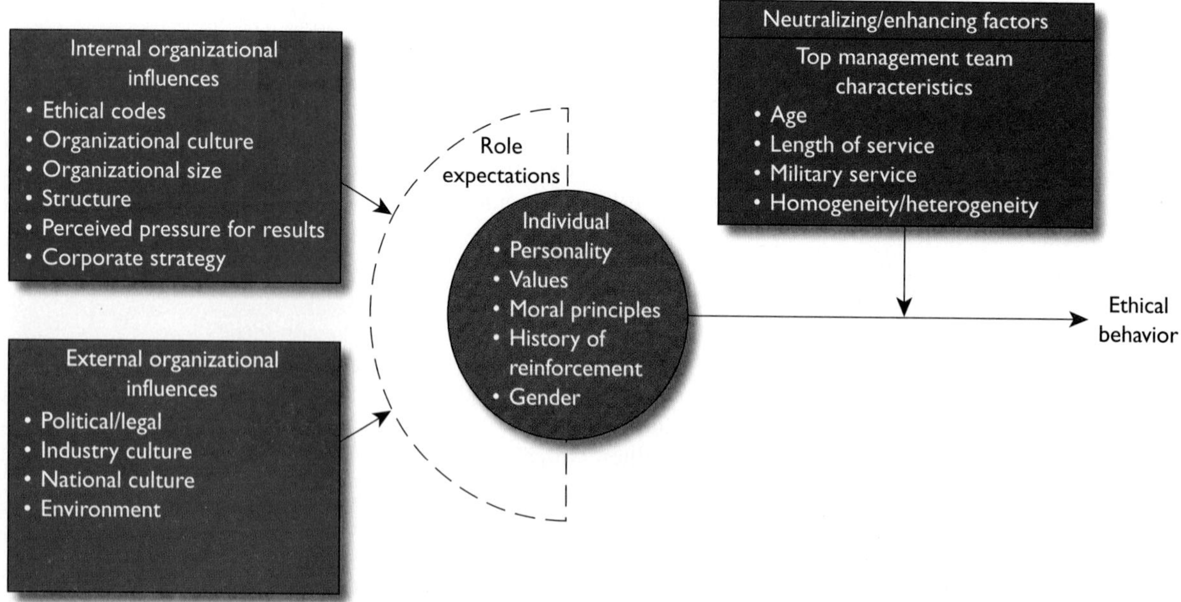

SOURCE: Based in part on A J Daboub, A M A Rasheed, R L Priem, and D A Gray, "Top Management Team Characteristics and Corporate Illegal Activity," *Academy of Management Review*, January 1995, pp 138–70.

One's expectations for how those roles should be played are shaped by a combination of internal and external organizational factors. Let us now examine how various internal and external organizational influences impact ethical behavior and how these effects are neutralized or enhanced by characteristics possessed by an organization's top management team.

Internal Organizational Influences

Figure A–1 shows six key internal organizational influences on ethical behavior.[7] Corporate ethical codes of conduct and organizational culture, discussed in Chapter 2, clearly contribute to reducing the frequency of unethical behavior. Consider the example of Rudder Finn, the world's largest privately owned public relations agency.

> Rudder Finn established an ethics committee early on in its history because the founders maintain that public relations professionals have a special obligation to believe in what they are doing. David Finn, co-founder and CEO, chairs every ethics committee meeting to demonstrate how seriously he takes this issue. In part, these meetings perform the function of a training program in that all members of staff are invited to participate in an open forum, during which actual ethical problems are freely discussed and an outside adviser provides objectivity. "Employees have to trust that if they go to a line manager to discuss a delicate situation or seek advice, they can do so without fear of repercussions," says Finn.[8]

This example also illustrates the importance of top management support in creating an ethical work environment.

A number of studies have uncovered a positive relationship between organizational size and unethical behavior: Larger firms are more likely to behave illegally. Interestingly, research also reveals that managers are more likely to behave unethically in decentralized organizations. Unethical behavior is suspected to occur in this context because lower-level managers want to "look good" for the corporate office. In support of this conclusion, many studies have found a tendency among middle- and lower-level managers to act unethically in the face of perceived pressure for results. By fostering a pressure-cooker atmosphere for results, managers can unwittingly set the stage for unethical shortcuts by employees who seek to please and be loyal to the company. Consider what happened at Qwest under the leadership of the company's former CEO Joe Nacchio.

> "The market was collapsing," recounts Nik Nesbitt, a former Qwest senior vice president. "[There were] unreachable demands: 'We need to sell this many millions of dollars in hosting services in the next 90 days,' when the lead time to sell hosting services was 180 days. You'd ask questions, and it was just, 'Don't ask questions. Just go and do it, and if you don't do it, you're not part of the team.'"
>
> Managers were terrified they wouldn't match Nacchio's expectations. . . . Down through the hierarchy, Qwest managers believed they had to make their numbers in any way possible. "[Managers would say] 'What can I do? My arm is being twisted. I just gotta do what the boss says,'" recalls Nesbitt.[9]

Nacchio ultimately lost his job, being forced out by Qwest's board of directors while in the midst of a multibillion-dollar accounting scandal. This example also reinforces that individuals are more likely to behave ethically/unethically when they have incentives to do so. Managers are encouraged to examine their reward systems to ensure that the preferred types of behaviors are being reinforced.

HANDS-ON EXERCISE

How Ethical Are These Behaviors?

INSTRUCTIONS Evaluate the extent to which you believe the following behaviors are ethical. Circle your responses on the rating scales provided. Compute your average score and compare it to the norms.

	Very Unethical	Unethical	Neither Ethical nor Unethical	Ethical	Very Ethical
Accepting gifts/favors in exchange for preferential treatment	1	2	3	4	5
Giving gifts/favors in exchange for preferential treatment	1	2	3	4	5
Divulging confidential information	1	2	3	4	5
Calling in sick to take a day off	1	2	3	4	5
Using the organization's materials and supplies for personal use	1	2	3	4	5
Doing personal business on work time	1	2	3	4	5
Taking extra personal time (breaks, etc.)	1	2	3	4	5
Using organizational services for personal use	1	2	3	4	5
Passing blame for errors to an innocent co-worker	1	2	3	4	5
Claiming credit for someone else's work	1	2	3	4	5
Not reporting others' violations of organizational policies	1	2	3	4	5
Concealing one's errors	1	2	3	4	5
Average score = ____________					

Norms (average scores by country)

United States = 1.49

Great Britain = 1.70

Australia = 1.44

France = 1.66

China = 1.46

Average of all 10 countries = 1.67

SOURCE: The survey behaviors were taken from T Jackson, "Cultural Values and Management Ethics: A 10-Nation Study," Human Relations, October 2001, pp 1287–88.

External Organizational Influences

Figure A–1 identifies four key external influences on role expectations and ethical behavior. The political/legal system clearly impacts ethical behavior. As previously mentioned, the United States is currently experiencing an increase in the extent to which its political/legal system is demanding and monitoring corporate ethical behavior. As a case in point, Computer Associates International, a $3 billion software company, is facing criminal indictments from the U.S. government based on charges of securities fraud and obstruction of justice. At the request of the federal government, an internal probe resulted in the dismissal of 15 employees, a demotion for the CEO, and a restatement of corporate earnings. Legal experts believe that the company is going to have to pay a large fine for its misdeeds.[10] Past research also uncovered a tendency for firms in certain industries to commit more illegal acts. Researchers partially explained this finding by speculating that an industry's culture, defined as shared norms, values, and beliefs among firms, predisposes managers to act unethically.

Moreover, Figure A–1 shows that national culture affects ethical behavior (national cultures are discussed in Chapter 3). This conclusion was supported in a multi-nation study (including the United States, Great Britain, France, Germany, Spain, Switzerland, India, China, and Australia) of management ethics. Managers from each country were asked to judge the ethicality of the 12 behaviors used in the Hands-On Exercise. Results revealed significant differences across the 10 nations.[11] That is, managers did not agree about the ethicality of the 12 behaviors. What is your attitude toward these behaviors? (You can find out by completing the Hands-On Exercise.) Finally, the external environment influences ethical behavior. For example, unethical behavior is more likely to occur in environments that are characterized by less generosity and when industry profitability is declining.

Neutralizing/Enhancing Factors

In their search for understanding the causes of ethical behavior, OB researchers uncovered several factors that may weaken or strengthen the relationship between the internal and external influencers shown in Figure A–1 and ethical behavior. These factors all revolve around characteristics possessed by an organization's top management team (TMT): A TMT consists of the CEO and his or her direct reports.[12] The relationship between ethical influencers and ethical behavior is weaker with increasing average age and increasing tenure among the TMT. This result suggests that an older and more experienced group of leaders is less likely to allow unethical behavior to occur. Further, the ethical influencers are less likely to lead to unethical behavior as the number of TMT members with military experience increases and when the TMT possesses heterogenous characteristics (e.g., diverse in terms of gender, age, race, religion, etc.). This conclusion has two important implications.

First, it appears that prior military experience favorably influences the ethical behavior of executives. While OB researchers are uncertain about the cause of this relationship, it may be due to the military's practice of indoctrinating recruits to endorse the values of duty, discipline, and honor. Regardless of the cause, military experience within a TMT is positively related to ethical behavior. Organizations thus should consider the merits of including military experience as one of its selection criteria when hiring or promoting managers. Second, organizations are encouraged to increase the diversity of its TMT if they want to reduce the chances of unethical decision making. Chapter 4 thoroughly discusses how employee diversity can increase creativity, innovation, group problem solving, and productivity.

A Decision Tree for Ethical Decisions

Ethical decision making frequently involves tradeoffs. The opening vignette to this learning module is a good example. IBM's decision to raise their retirees' health benefit contributions saved the company money and thereby created a positive impact on shareholder value. On the other hand, individuals like Robert Eggleston were hurt by this decision. He ultimately had to take out a second mortgage on his home to pay for health-related expenses. This section presents a decision tree that managers can use to help navigate through ethical questions such as the one faced by IBM in the opening vignette.

The decision tree is shown in Figure A–2 and it can be applied to any type of decision or action that an individual manager or corporation is contemplating.[13] Looking at the tree, the first question to ask is whether or not the proposed action is legal. If the action is illegal, do not do it. If the action is legal, then consider the impact of the action on shareholder value. A decision maximizes shareholder value when it results in a more favorable financial position (e.g., increased profits) for an organization. Whether or not an action maximizes shareholder value, the decision tree shows that managers still need to consider the ethical implications of the decision or action. For example, if an action maximizes shareholder value, the next question to consider is whether or not the action is ethical. The answer to this question is based on considering the positive effect of the action on

FIGURE A–2
An Ethical Decision Tree

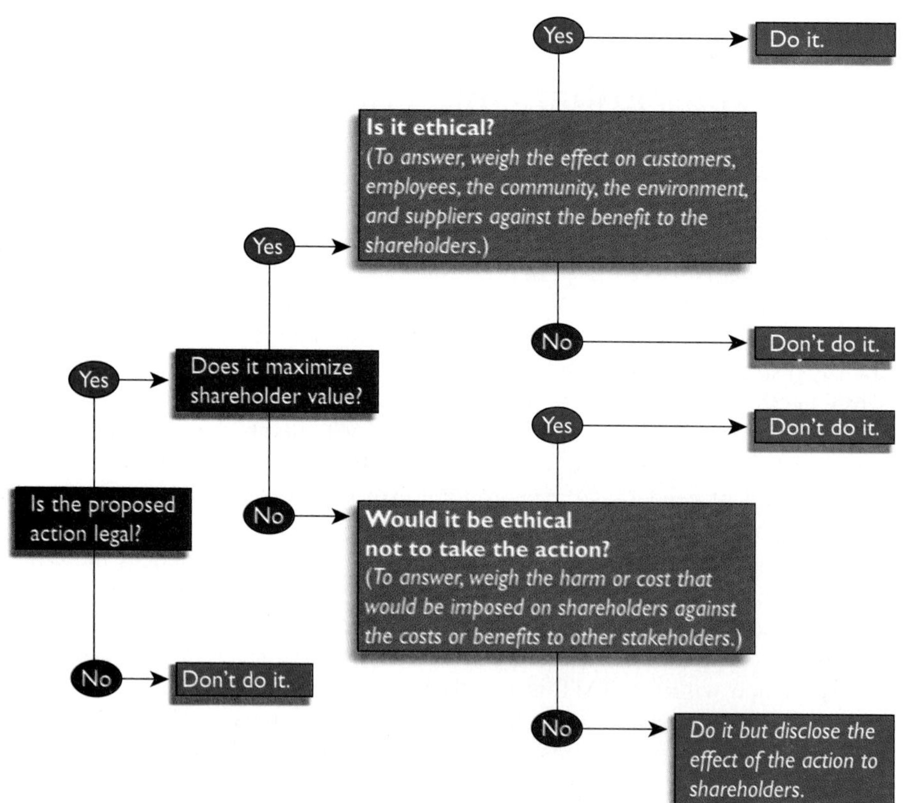

SOURCE: Reprinted by permission of *Harvard Business Review.* From Constance E. Bagley, "The Ethical Leader's Decision Tree," *Harvard Business Review,* February 2003, p 19. Copyright © 2003 by Harvard Business School Publishing Corporation; all rights reserved.

an organization's other key constituents (i.e., customers, employees, the community, the environment, and suppliers) against the benefit to the shareholders. According to the decision tree framework, managers should make the decision to engage in an action if the benefits to the shareholders exceed the benefits to the other key constituents. Managers should not engage in the action if the other key constituents benefit more from the action than shareholders.

Figure A–2 illustrates that managers use a slightly different perspective when their initial conclusion is that an action does not maximize shareholder value. In this case, the question becomes "Would it be ethical not to take action?" This question necessitates that a manager consider the *harm or cost* of an action to shareholders against the *costs or benefits* to other key constituents. If the costs to shareholders from a managerial decision exceed the costs or benefits to other constituents, the manager or company should not engage in the action. Conversely, the manager or company should take action when the perceived costs or benefits to the other constituents are greater than the costs to shareholders. Let us apply this decision tree to the example in the opening vignette on IBM.

Is it legal for a company to decrease its contribution to retiree health-care benefits while simultaneously raising retirees' contributions? The answer is yes.[14] Does an organization maximize shareholder value by decreasing its retiree health-care expenses? Again, the answer is yes. We now have to consider the overall benefits to shareholders against the overall benefits to other key constituents. The answer to this question is more complex than it appears and is contingent on an organization's corporate values. Consider the following two examples. In company one, the organization is losing money and it needs cash in order to invest in new product development. Management believes that new products will fuel the company's economic growth and ultimate survival. This company's statement of corporate values also reveals that the organization values profits and shareholder return more than employee loyalty. In this case, the company should make the decision to increase retirees' health-care contributions. Company two, in contrast, is profitable and has been experiencing increased market share with its products. This company's statement of corporate values also indicates that employees are the most important constituent it has, even more than shareholders: Southwest Airlines is a good example of a company with these corporate values. In this case, the company should not make the decision to decrease its contribution to retirees' benefits.

It is important to keep in mind that the decision tree cannot provide a quick formula that managers and organizations can use to assess every ethical question. It does, however, provide a framework for considering the trade-offs between managerial and corporate actions and managerial and corporate ethics. Try using this decision tree the next time you are faced with an ethical question or problem.

Do Moral Orientations Vary by Gender?

It is interesting to note that two women, Sherron Watkins and Maureen Castaneda, played key roles as whistle-blowers (i.e., when an employee informs others about corporate wrongdoing) in the Enron fiasco. "Watkins, Enron's vice president of corporate development, wrote the prescient memo to Enron's chief executive that warned him the company was in deep financial trouble. Castaneda, Enron's director of foreign exchange, is the one who told authorities that Enron was still shredding documents after its officials were ordered to preserve every piece of paper."[15] Does this suggest that women are more likely to be whistle-blowers because they have different moral principles than men?

At great risk to her career, Enron executive Sherron Watkins reported financial misconduct as a whistle-blower. Would you have the courage to do so?

A study of 300 self-described whistle-blowers revealed that gender was not related to employees' reporting wrongdoing.[16] Still, other research suggests that men and women view moral problems and situations differently. Carol Gilligan, a well-known psychologist, proposed one underlying cause of these gender differences. Her research revealed that men and women differed in terms of how they perceived moral problems. Males perceived moral problems in terms of a **justice perspective,** whereas women relied on a **care perspective.** The two perspectives are described as follows:

> A justice perspective draws attention to problems of inequality and oppression and holds up an ideal of reciprocal rights and equal respect for individuals. A care perspective draws attention to problems of detachment or abandonment and holds up an ideal of attention and response to need. Two moral injunctions, not to treat others unfairly and not to turn away from someone in need, capture these different concerns.[17]

This description underscores the point that men are expected to view moral problems in terms of rights, whereas women are predicted to conceptualize moral problems as an issue of care involving empathy and compassion.

A meta-analysis of 113 studies tested these ideas by examining whether or not the justice and care orientations varied by gender. Results did not support the expectation that the care perspective was used predominantly by females and the justice orientation predominantly by males.[18] The authors concluded that "although distinct moral orientations may exist, these orientations are not strongly associated with gender."[19] This conclusion suggests that future research is needed to identify the source of moral reasoning differences between men and women. Which moral perspective do you prefer: justice or care?

General Moral Principles

Management consultant and writer Kent Hodgson has helpfully taken managers a step closer to ethical decisions by identifying seven general moral principles (see Table A–1). Hodgson calls them "the magnificent seven" to emphasize their timeless and worldwide relevance. Both the justice and care perspectives are clearly evident in the magnificent seven, which are more detailed and, hence, more practical. Importantly, according to Hodgson, there are no absolute ethical answers for decision makers. The goal for managers should be to rely on moral principles so their decisions are *principled, appropriate,* and *defensible.*[20]

The Magnificent Seven: General Moral Principles for Managers TABLE A–1

1. *Dignity of human life: The lives of people are to be respected.* Human beings, by the fact of their existence, have value and dignity. We may not act in ways that directly intend to harm or kill an innocent person. Human beings have a right to live; we have an obligation to respect that right to life. Human life is to be preserved and treated as sacred.
2. *Autonomy: All persons are intrinsically valuable and have the right to self-determination.* We should act in ways that demonstrate each person's worth, dignity, and right to free choice. We have a right to act in ways that assert our own worth and legitimate needs. We should not use others as mere "things" or only as means to an end. Each person has an equal right to basic human liberty, compatible with a similar liberty for others.
3. *Honesty: The truth should be told to those who have a right to know it.* Honesty is also known as integrity, truth telling, and honor. One should speak and act so as to reflect the reality of the situation. Speaking and acting should mirror the way things really are. There are times when others have the right to hear the truth from us; there are times when they do not.
4. *Loyalty: Promises, contracts, and commitments should be honored.* Loyalty includes fidelity, promise keeping, keeping the public trust, good citizenship, excellence in quality of work, reliability, commitment, and honoring just laws, rules, and policies.
5. *Fairness: People should be treated justly.* One has the right to be treated fairly, impartially, and equitably. One has the obligation to treat others fairly and justly. All have the right to the necessities of life—especially those in deep need and the helpless. Justice includes equal, impartial, unbiased treatment. Fairness tolerates diversity and accepts differences in people and their ideas.
6. *Humaneness.* There are two parts: (1) *Our actions ought to accomplish good,* and (2) *we should avoid doing evil.* We should do good to others and to ourselves. We should have concern for the well-being of others; usually, we show this concern in the form of compassion, giving, kindness, serving, and caring.
7. *The common good: Actions should accomplish the "greatest good for the greatest number" of people.* One should act and speak in ways that benefit the welfare of the largest number of people, while trying to protect the rights of individuals.

SOURCE: From *A Rock and a Hard Place: How to Make Ethical Business Decisions When the Choices Are Tough,* by Kent Hodgson, 1992, American Management Association. Reprinted with permission of the author.

Fannie Mae is a good example of a company trying to follow this recommendation. The company was ranked as the Best Corporate Citizen in the United States for 2004 by *Business Ethics* magazine. The following profile of Fannie Mae was offered.

> This firm is dedicated to "the American Dream business, helping Americans become home owners—the company buys mortgages from local lenders and repackages them for sale as securities. Fannie Mae's dominant presence in the mortgage market enables it to play a critical role in keeping mortgage rates down. Yet its most visible impact is on helping those who traditionally have been underserved obtain home loans.

justice perspective

Based on the ideal of reciprocal rights and driven by rules and regulations.

care perspective

Involves compassion and an ideal of attention and response to need.

In 2003, more than $240 billion in home mortgages were financed for 1.6 million minority first-time homebuyers, an increase of 60 percent over the year prior. Most uniquely, a $10 million Fannie Mae partnership was established with an Islamic financial institution to open up southern California's real estate market to Muslims. It accommodates Islamic Law's ban on paying or collecting interest on debt, by negotiating monthly payments based on a property's sale price and fair rental value instead of interest rate.[21]

How to Improve the Organization's Ethical Climate

A team of management researchers recommended the following actions for improving on-the-job ethics:[22]

- *Behave ethically yourself.* Managers are potent role models whose habits and actual behavior send clear signals about the importance of ethical conduct. Ethical behavior is a top-to-bottom proposition.
- *Screen potential employees.* Surprisingly, employers are generally lax when it comes to checking references, credentials, transcripts, and other information on applicant résumés. More diligent action in this area can screen out those given to fraud and misrepresentation. Integrity testing is fairly valid but is no panacea.[23]
- *Develop a meaningful code of ethics.* Codes of ethics can have a positive impact if they satisfy these four criteria:
  1. They are *distributed* to every employee.
  2. They are firmly *supported* by top management.
  3. They refer to *specific* practices and ethical dilemmas likely to be encountered by target employees (e.g., salespersons paying kickbacks, purchasing agents receiving payoffs, laboratory scientists doctoring data, or accountants "cooking the books").
  4. They are evenly *enforced* with rewards for compliance and strict penalties for noncompliance.
- *Provide ethics training.* Employees can be trained to identify and deal with ethical issues during orientation and through seminar, video, and Internet training sessions.[24]
- *Reinforce ethical behavior.* Behavior that is reinforced tends to be repeated, whereas behavior that is not reinforced tends to disappear. Ethical conduct too often is punished while unethical behavior is rewarded.
- *Create positions, units, and other structural mechanisms to deal with ethics.* Ethics needs to be an everyday affair, not a one-time announcement of a new ethical code that gets filed away and forgotten. Boeing, for example, has hired an outside ethics watchdog in response to several breaches of ethics. Ethics transgressions have cost the company billions of dollars in government contracts and resulted in the firing of several top-level executives. The new external ethics compliance officer will oversee Boeing's new ethics-compliance programs and will report directly to the U.S. Air Force.[25]

group exercise

Investigating the Difference in Moral Reasoning between Men and Women

Objectives

1. To determine if men and women resolve moral/ethical problems differently.
2. To determine if males and females use justice and care perspectives, respectively, to solve moral/ethical problems.
3. To improve your understanding about the moral reasoning used by men and women.

Introduction

Men and women view moral problems and situations dissimilarly. This is one reason men and women solve identical moral or ethical problems differently. Some researchers believe that men rely on a justice perspective to solve moral problems whereas women are expected to use a care perspective. This exercise presents two scenarios that possess a moral/ethical issue. You will be asked to solve each problem and to discuss the logic behind your decision. The exercise provides you with the opportunity to hear the thought processes used by men and women to solve moral/ethical problems.

Instructions

Your instructor will divide the class into groups of four to six. (An interesting option is to use gender-based groups.) Each group member should first read the scenario alone and then make a decision about what to do. Once this is done, use the space provided to outline the rationale for your decision for this scenario. Next, read the second scenario and follow the same procedure: Make a decision and explain your rationale. Once all group members have completed their analyses for both scenarios, meet as a group to discuss the results. One at a time, each group member should present his or her final decision and the associated reasoning for the first scenario. Someone should keep a running tally of the decisions so that a summary can be turned in to the professor at the end of your discussion. Follow the same procedure for the second scenario.[26]

Scenario 1

You are the manager of a local toy store. The hottest Christmas toy of the year is the new "Peter Panda" stuffed animal. The toy is in great demand and almost impossible to find. You have received your one and only shipment of 12, and they are all promised to people who previously stopped in to place a deposit and reserve one. A woman comes by the store and pleads with you, saying that her six-year-old daughter is in the hospital very ill, and that "Peter Panda" is the one toy she has her heart set on. Would you sell her one, knowing that you will have to break your promise and refund the deposit to one of the other customers? (There is no way you will be able to get an extra toy in time.)

Your Decision: ______

	Would Sell	**Would Not Sell**	**Unsure**
Men			
Women			

Rationale for your decision:

Scenario 2

You sell corporate financial products, such as pension plans and group health insurance. You are currently negotiating with Paul Scott, treasurer of a *Fortune* 500 firm, for a sale that could be in the millions of dollars. You feel you are in a strong position to make the sale, but two competitors are also negotiating with Scott, and it could go either way. You have become friendly with Scott, and over lunch one day he confided in you that he has recently been under treatment for manic depression. It so happens that in your office there is a staff psychologist who does employee counseling. The thought has occurred to you that such a trained professional might be able to coach you on how to act with and relate to a personality such as Scott's, so as to persuade and influence him most effectively. Would you consult the psychologist?

Your Decision: ______

	Would Consult	**Would Not Consult**	**Unsure**
Men			
Women			

Rationale for your decision:

Questions for Discussion

1. Did males and females make different decisions in response to both scenarios? (Comparative norms can be found in Note 27.)
2. What was the moral reasoning used by women and men to solve the two scenarios?[28]
3. To what extent did males and females use justice and care perspectives, respectively?
4. What useful lessons did you learn from this exercise?

discussion questions

1. Use Figure A–1 to identify the most important influences on IBM's decision to increase retirees' contributions to health benefits while decreasing its contributions.
2. Why do you think there is an increase in the number of indictments against executives in the United States?
3. If you were a professor at a university, what would you do to discourage students from cheating on assignments and exams? Explain your recommendations.

chapter Two

Organizational Culture, Socialization, and Mentoring

LEARNING OBJECTIVES

After reading the material in this chapter, you should be able to:

- Discuss the layers and functions of organizational culture.
- Describe the three general types of organizational culture and their associated normative beliefs.
- Summarize the methods used by organizations to embed their cultures.
- Describe the three phases in Feldman's model of organizational socialization.
- Discuss the various socialization tactics used to socialize employees.
- Explain the four types of developmental networks derived from a developmental network model of mentoring.

COSTCO'S CULTURE PRODUCES SATISFIED CUSTOMERS AND EMPLOYEES

James D. Sinegal, the president and CEO of Costco, has no palace guard and no profile to speak of, particularly compared to a retail legend like Sam Walton. Yet he's the guy who in 20 years has taken Costco from a startup to the FORTUNE 50 using, as surely as Mr. Sam, highly distinctive practices. He caps Costco's markups at 14% (department store markups can reach 40%). He offers the best wages and benefits in retail (full-time hourly workers make $40,000 after four years). He gives customers blanket permission for returns: no receipts; no questions; no time limits, except for computers—and even then the grace period is six months. . . .

Analysts have pounded on Sinegal to trim the company's generous health benefits and to otherwise reduce labor costs. But he's taken only limited steps in that direction, like modestly increasing employees' share of health-insurance premiums. That doesn't satisfy critics like Deutsche Bank analyst Bill Dreher, who recently wrote, "Costco continues to be a company that is better at serving the club member and employee than the shareholder."

Sinegal just shrugs. . . . "We think when you take care of your customer and your employees, your shareholders are going to be rewarded in the long run. And I'm one of them [the shareholders]; I care about the stock price. But we're not going to do something for the sake of one quarter that's going to destroy the fabric of our company and what we stand for." . . . The axioms Costco lives by . . .

AXIOM NO. 1: Obey the law.

AXIOM NO. 2: Take care of your customers.

AXIOM NO. 3: Take care of your employees.

AXIOM NO. 4: Practice the intelligent loss of sales. Many retailers' shelves are crowded with a plethora of products: different brands, different sizes, many choices. Costco offers relatively few choices. That means some customers may pass up purchases, because the gallon jar of mayonnaise is too big or the brand isn't their favorite. But the benefits far exceed the lost sales. Stocking fewer items streamlines distribution and hastens inventory turns—and nine out of ten customers are perfectly happy with the mayonnaise. . . .

Sinegal manages to be demanding without being intimidating. His bare-bones office helps set the tone for that style. So does his open-collared shirt and the nametag he wears, like everyone else. Not that he needs one. To walk with Sinegal from his headquarters building to the Costco next door is to hear a nonstop chorus of "Hi, Jim. . . . Hi, Jim. . . . Hi, Jim." He returns the greetings by using first names, without appearing to consult nametags. Sinegal has also kept himself in the good graces of subordinates by limiting his pay. His $350,000 salary last year was practically cause for drumming him out of the FORTUNE 500 CEO club; and at his own request, he took no bonus for the third consecutive year. He does have $16.5 million worth of options, but he's intent on capping his salary and bonus at about twice the level of a Costco store manager.

Sinegal is careful not to lop off managers' heads for taking chances, because, he says, "The art form of our business is intuition." Costco buyers have to take big chances. A warehouse stocks less than 10% of the items of a typical Wal-Mart, so buyers can't spread their bets around. If a high-end product doesn't move fast, it leaves a lot of money tied up in inventory. Bill Prescott, the chief buyer for consumer electronics, makes some of the toughest judgments about when new products are affordable enough and hot enough to be put on the Costco floor. He sensed the time had come for plasma TVs earlier this year, when the price fell below $5,000. He placed his order and held his breath. "You take an educated gamble," he says. "If you don't occasionally make a mistake, you're not doing your job." The TVs turned out to be a hit.[1]

FOR DISCUSSION

Do you think Sinegal should reduce the amount Costco pays its employees? Explain. For an interpretation of this case and additional comments, visit our Online Learning Center:

www.mhhe.com/kinickiob2e

THE OPENING CASE HIGHLIGHTS the role of organizational culture in contributing to organizational effectiveness. Costco's culture, which highly values employees and customers, significantly contributes to the organization's success. For example, Costco's labor costs are lower than Wal-Mart's as a percentage of sales, and its 68,000 hourly employees in the United States generate more operating profit per hourly employee than Sam's club, the Wal-Mart division that directly competes with Costco. Costco also has one of the lowest employee turnover rates in the industry.[2] The case also highlights that an organization's culture originates from a core set of values, or axioms in Costco's case.

This chapter will help you better understand how managers can use organizational culture as a competitive advantage. After defining and discussing the context of organizational culture, we examine (1) the dynamics of organizational culture, (2) the organization socialization process, and (3) the embedding of organizational culture through mentoring.

Organizational Culture: Definition and Context

organizational culture
Shared values and beliefs that underlie a company's identity.

Organizational culture is "the set of shared, taken-for-granted implicit assumptions that a group holds and that determines how it perceives, thinks about, and reacts to its various environments."[3] This definition highlights three important characteristics of organizational culture. First, organizational culture is passed on to new employees through the process of socialization, a topic discussed later in this chapter. Second, organizational culture influences our behavior at work. Finally, organizational culture operates at different levels.

Figure 2–1 provides a conceptual framework for reviewing the widespread impact organizational culture has on organizational behavior.[4] It also shows the linkage between this chapter—culture, socialization, and mentoring—and other key

FIGURE 2–1 A Conceptual Framework for Understanding Organizational Culture

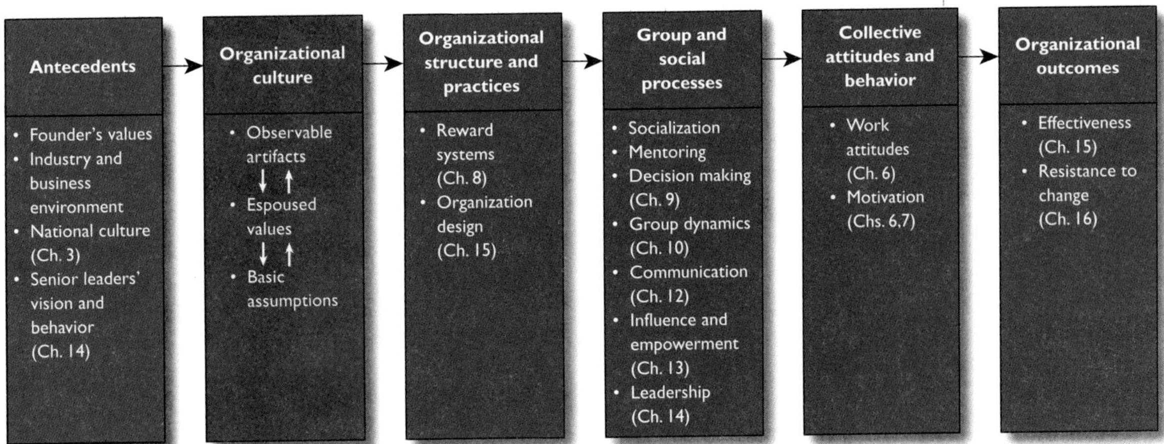

SOURCE: Adapted in part from C Ostroff, A Kinicki, and M Tamkins, "Organizational Culture and Climate," in *Handbook of Psychology*, vol 12, eds W C Burman, D R Ilgen, and R J Klimoski (New York: Wiley and Sons, 2003), pp 565–93.

topics in this book. Figure 2–1 reveals organizational culture is shaped by four key components: the founders' values, the industry and business environment, the national culture, and the senior leaders' vision and behavior. In turn, organizational culture influences the type of organizational structure adopted by a company and a host of practices, policies, and procedures implemented in pursuit of organizational goals. These organizational characteristics then affect a variety of group and social processes. This sequence ultimately affects employees' attitudes and behavior and a variety of organizational outcomes. All told, Figure 2–1 reveals that organizational culture is a contextual variable influencing individual, group, and organizational behavior.

Dynamics of Organizational Culture

To provide a better understanding of how organizational culture is formed and used by employees, this section begins by discussing the layers of organizational culture. It then reviews the four functions of organizational culture, types of organizational culture, outcomes associated with organizational culture, and how cultures are embedded within organizations.

Layers of Organizational Culture

Figure 2–1 shows the three fundamental layers of organizational culture. Each level varies in terms of outward visibility and resistance to change, and each level influences another level.[5]

Observable Artifacts At the more visible level, culture represents observable artifacts. Artifacts consist of the physical manifestation of an organization's culture. Organizational examples include acronyms, manner of dress, awards, myths and stories told about the organization, published lists of values, observable rituals and ceremonies, special parking spaces, decorations, and so on. This level also includes visible behaviors exhibited by people and groups. Artifacts are easier to change than the less visible aspects of organizational culture.

values

Enduring belief in a mode of conduct or end-state.

espoused values

The stated values and norms that are preferred by an organization.

Espoused Values Values possess five key components. "**Values** (1) are concepts or beliefs, (2) pertain to desirable end-states or behaviors, (3) transcend situations, (4) guide selection or evaluation of behavior and events, and (5) are ordered by relative importance."[6] It is important to distinguish between values that are espoused versus those that are enacted.

Espoused values represent the explicitly stated values and norms that are preferred by an organization. They are generally established by the founder of a new or small company and by the top management team in a larger organization. For example, J. M. Smucker, the number one company to work for in America in 2003 according to *Fortune,* is a 107-year-old family-run business that is headed by co-CEOs Tim and Richard Smucker. The brothers encourage all Smucker employees to adhere to a set of values created by their father, Paul Smucker. No. 3: "Listen with your full attention, look for the good in others, have a sense of humor, and say thank you for a job well done."[7] Because espoused values constitute aspirations that are explicitly communicated to employees, managers such as Tim and Richard Smucker hope that espoused values will directly influence employee behavior. Unfortunately, aspirations do not automatically produce the desired behaviors because people do not always "walk the talk."

Enacted values, on the other hand, represent the values and norms that actually are exhibited or converted into employee behavior. Let us consider the difference between these two types of values. Home Depot, for instance, has espoused that it values customer service and safety. If the organization displays customer service and safety through its store layouts and behavior of employees, then the espoused value is enacted and individual behavior is being influenced by the values of customer service and safety. Unfortunately, Home Depot appears to have a discrepancy between its espoused and enacted values:

enacted values
The values and norms that are exhibited by employees.

> "Home Depot advertises having the best customer service, but it seems like everybody is so busy," says Priscilla High, a customer shopping in Atlanta recently for a rug and kitchen sink. "Lowe's [a Home Depot rival] has more customer service." . . . as sales volumes soared and product lines expanded in recent years, that busy warehouse action became a liability. Shoppers complained that pallets of merchandise cluttered the aisles. Injuries from falling merchandise grabbed headlines. And the company says many employees became more concerned with stocking socket wrenches than helping customers. . . . On a recent morning at a Home Depot near Stone Mountain, [Georgia], assistant manager Jill Roberts found three pallets of space heaters clogging an aisle of kitchen sinks and plumbing supplies. . . . Another priority for Home Depot is improved store safety in the wake of three deaths last year [2000] and other injuries caused by falling merchandise.[8]

It is important to reduce gaps between espoused and enacted values because they can significantly influence employee attitudes and organizational performance. For example, a study of 312 British rail drivers revealed that employees were more cynical about safety when they believed that senior managers' behaviors were inconsistent with the stated values regarding safety.[9] Home Depot is aware of this important

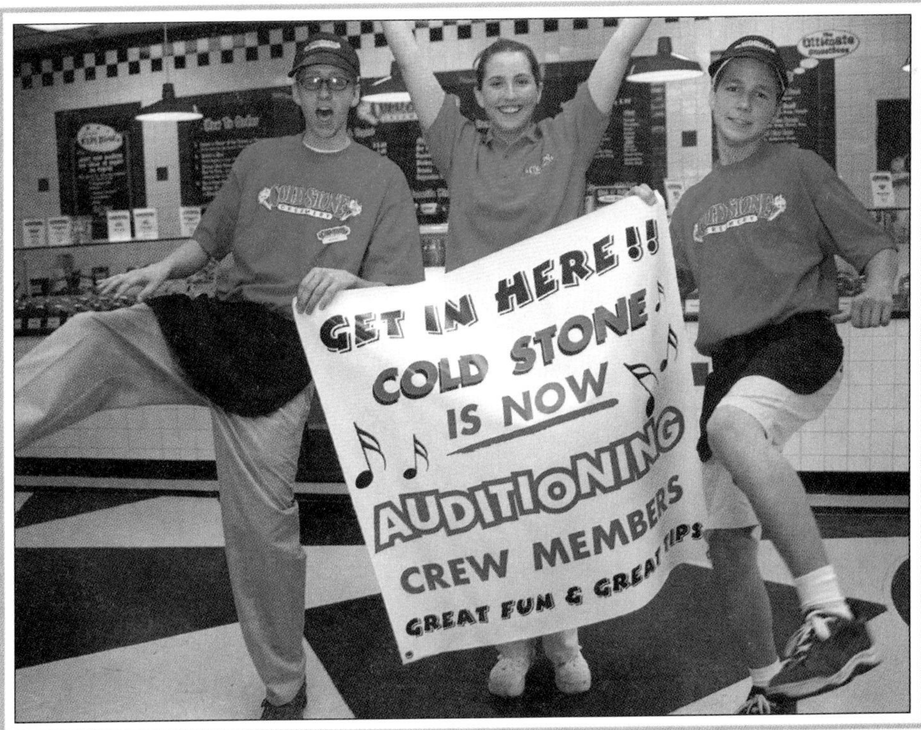

Some organizations display their **enacted values** when recruiting employees. Scottsdale, Arizona–based Cold Stone Creamery conveys their culture of fun and performing for customers by holding "auditions" for new workers. Would you like to work there?

issue and has instituted a program labeled Service Performance Improvement, or SPI, to reduce the gap between espoused and enacted values regarding customer service and safety. Preliminary results from six test stores indicated increases in store sales and the amount of time store employees spent helping customers.[10]

Basic Assumptions Basic underlying assumptions are unobservable and represent the core of organizational culture. They constitute organizational values that have become so taken for granted over time that they become assumptions that guide organizational behavior. They thus are highly resistant to change. When basic assumptions are widely held among employees, people will find behavior based on an inconsistent value inconceivable. Southwest Airlines, for example, is noted for operating according to basic assumptions that value employees' welfare and providing high-quality service. Employees at Southwest Airlines would be shocked to see management act in ways that did not value employees' and customers' needs.

Four Functions of Organizational Culture

As illustrated in Figure 2–2, an organization's culture fulfills four functions.[11] To help bring these four functions to life, let us consider how each of them has taken shape at Southwest Airlines. Southwest is a particularly instructive example because it has grown to become the fourth-largest US airline since its inception in 1971 and has achieved 32 consecutive years of profitability. *Fortune* has ranked Southwest in the top five of the Best Companies to Work For in America from 1997–2000: Southwest has chosen not to participate in this ranking process since 2000. Southwest also was ranked as the second most admired company in the

FIGURE 2–2
Four Functions of Organizational Culture

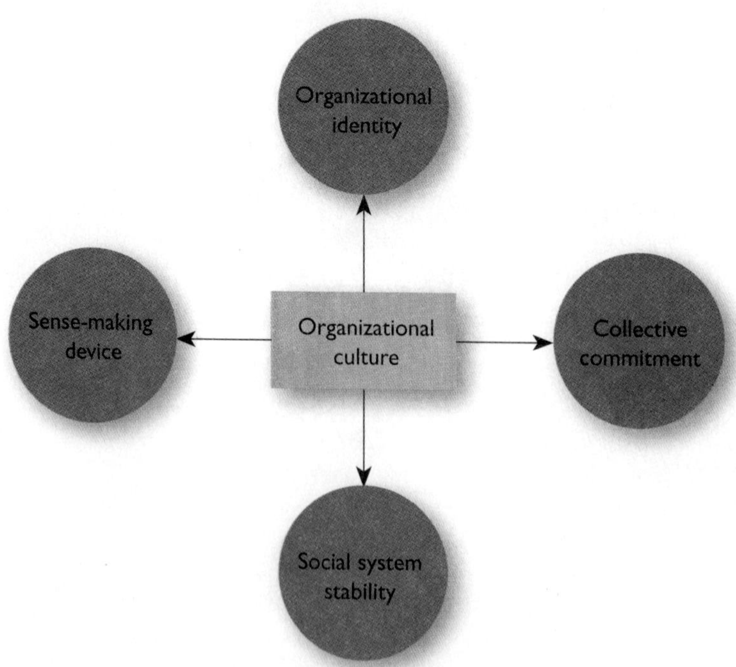

SOURCE: Adapted from discussion in L Smircich, "Concepts of Culture and Organizational Analysis," *Administrative Science Quarterly*, September 1983, pp 339–58. Reprinted with permission.

United States by *Fortune* in 2003, partly due to its strong and distinctive culture.[12]

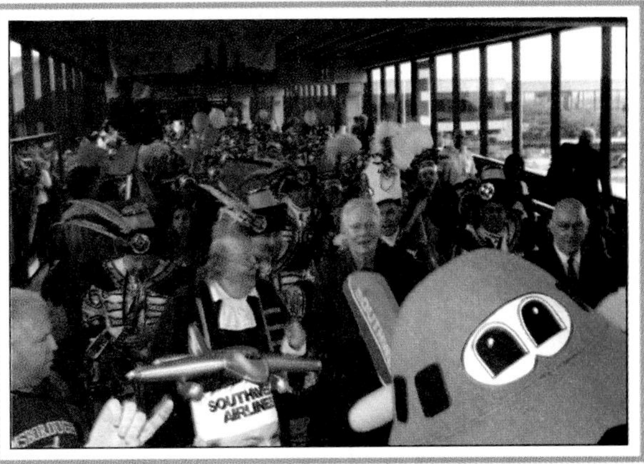

Fun is the norm at Southwest Airlines. Executive Chairman Herb Kelleher noted, "The employees come first. If they're happy, satisfied, dedicated, and energetic, they'll take real good care of the customers." Do you agree with Herb's philosophy?

1. *Give members an organizational identity.* Southwest Airlines is known as a fun place to work that values employee satisfaction and customer loyalty over corporate profits. Herb Kelleher, executive chairman, commented on this issue.

   > Who comes first? The employees, customers, or shareholders? That's never been an issue to me. The employees come first. If they're happy, satisfied, dedicated, and energetic, they'll take real good care of the customers. When the customers are happy, they come back. And that makes the shareholders happy.[13]

   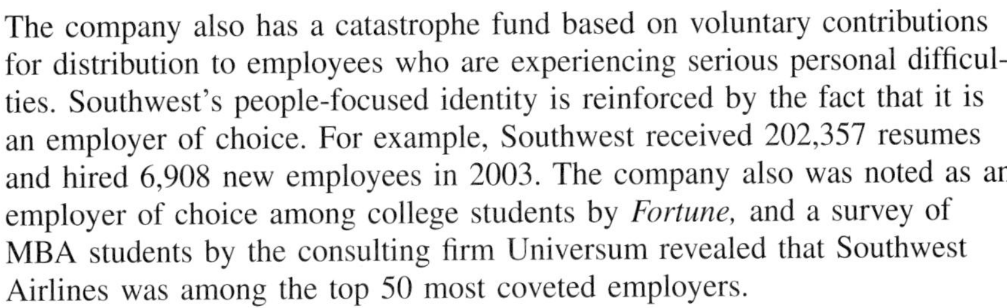

   The company also has a catastrophe fund based on voluntary contributions for distribution to employees who are experiencing serious personal difficulties. Southwest's people-focused identity is reinforced by the fact that it is an employer of choice. For example, Southwest received 202,357 resumes and hired 6,908 new employees in 2003. The company also was noted as an employer of choice among college students by *Fortune,* and a survey of MBA students by the consulting firm Universum revealed that Southwest Airlines was among the top 50 most coveted employers.

2. *Facilitate collective commitment.* The mission of Southwest Airlines "is dedication to the highest quality of Customer Service delivered with a sense of warmth, friendliness, individual pride, and Company Spirit."[14] Southwest's more than 35,000 employees are committed to this mission. The Department of Transportation's Air Travel Consumer Report reported Southwest was ranked number one in fewest customer complaints for the last 13 consecutive years.

3. *Promote social system stability.* Social system stability reflects the extent to which the work environment is perceived as positive and reinforcing, and the extent to which conflict and change are effectively managed. Southwest is noted for its philosophy of having fun, having parties, and celebrating. For example, each city in which the firm operates is given a budget for parties. Southwest also uses a variety of performance-based awards and service awards to reinforce employees. The company's positive and enriching environment is supported by the lowest turnover rates in the airline industry and the employment of 1,000 married couples.

4. *Shape behavior by helping members make sense of their surroundings.* This function of culture helps employees understand why the organization does what it does and how it intends to accomplish its long-term goals. Keeping in mind that Southwest's leadership originally viewed ground transportation as their main competitor in 1971, employees come to understand why the airline's primary vision is to be the best primarily short-haul, low-fare, high-frequency, point-to-point carrier in the United States. Employees understand they must achieve exceptional performance, such as turning a plane in 20 minutes, because they must keep costs down in order to compete against Greyhound and the use of automobiles. In turn, the company reinforces the

importance of outstanding customer service and high performance expectations by using performance-based awards and profit sharing. Employees own at least 10% of the company stock.

Types of Organizational Culture

Researchers have attempted to identify and measure various types of organizational culture in order to study the relationship between types of culture and organizational effectiveness. This pursuit was motivated by the possibility that certain cultures were more effective than others. Unfortunately, research has not uncovered a universal typology of cultural styles that everyone accepts.[15] Just the same, there is value in providing an example of various types of organizational culture. Table 2–1 is thus presented as an illustration rather than a definitive conclusion about the types of organizational culture that exist. Awareness of these types provides you with greater understanding about the manifestations of culture.

Table 2–1 shows that there are three general types of organizational culture—constructive, passive–defensive, and aggressive–defensive—and that each type is associated with a different set of normative beliefs.[16] **Normative beliefs** represent an individual's thoughts and beliefs about how members of a particular group or organization are expected to approach their work and interact with others. A *constructive culture* is one in which employees are encouraged to interact with others and to work on tasks and projects in ways that will assist them in satisfying their need to grow and develop. This type of culture endorses normative beliefs associated with achievement, self-actualizing, humanistic-encouraging, and affiliative. In contrast, a *passive–defensive culture* is characterized by an overriding belief that employees must interact with others in ways that do not threaten their own job security. This culture reinforces the normative beliefs associated with approval, conventional, dependent, and avoidance (see Table 2–1). Mitsubishi is a good example of a company with a passive–defensive culture. According to *Business Week* reporters:

normative beliefs

Thoughts and beliefs about expected behavior and modes of conduct.

> This was a company whose managers were so reluctant to relay bad news to higher-ups that they squelched complaints about quality defects for decades to avoid costly product recalls. Many Daimler [DaimlerChrysler spent $2.4 billion to obtain a 37% stake in Mitsubishi] critics also say its culture contributed to the failed turnaround: The push was always on for results, and few wanted to alert Stuttgart to major problems. Later, to help U.S. sales, Mitsubishi resorted to an ultragenerous financing campaign—no money down and no payments for a year. The result was almost half a billion in bad loans.[17]

Finally, companies with an *aggressive–defensive culture* encourage employees to approach tasks in forceful ways in order to protect their status and job security. This type of culture is more characteristic of normative beliefs reflecting oppositional, power, competitive, and perfectionistic. Joe Nacchio, former CEO of Qwest, had a leadership style that reinforced an aggressive–defensive culture. "Managers were terrified they wouldn't match Nacchio's expectations. In meetings, he would pretend not to listen when he was unhappy, then suddenly zero in on what he thought was the weakest point of an executive's presentation, subjecting him to what even a friend describes as a terrifying experience."[18]

Although an organization may predominately represent one cultural type, it can manifest normative beliefs and characteristics from the others. Research demonstrates that organizations can have functional subcultures, hierarchical subcultures based on one's level in the organization, geographical subcultures, occupational subcultures

General Types of Culture	Normative Beliefs	Organizational Characteristics
Constructive	Achievement	Organizations that do things well and value members who set and accomplish their own goals. Members are expected to set challenging but realistic goals, establish plans to reach these goals, and pursue them with enthusiasm. (Pursuing a standard of excellence)
Constructive	Self-actualizing	Organizations that value creativity, quality over quantity, and both task accomplishment and individual growth. Members are encouraged to gain enjoyment from their work, develop themselves, and take on new and interesting activities. (Thinking in unique and independent ways)
Constructive	Humanistic-encouraging	Organizations that are managed in a participative and person-centered way. Members are expected to be supportive, constructive, and open to influence in their dealings with one another. (Helping others to grow and develop)
Constructive	Affiliative	Organizations that place a high priority on constructive interpersonal relationships. Members are expected to be friendly, open, and sensitive to the satisfaction of their work group. (Dealing with others in a friendly way)
Passive–defensive	Approval	Organizations in which conflicts are avoided and interpersonal relationships are pleasant—at least superficially. Members feel that they should agree with, gain the approval of, and be liked by others. ("Going along" with others)
Passive–defensive	Conventional	Organizations that are conservative, traditional, and bureaucratically controlled. Members are expected to conform, follow the rules, and make a good impression. (Always following policies and practices)
Passive–defensive	Dependent	Organizations that are hierarchically controlled and nonparticipative. Centralized decision making in such organizations leads members to do only what they are told and to clear all decisions with superiors. (Pleasing those in positions of authority)
Passive–defensive	Avoidance	Organizations that fail to reward success but nevertheless punish mistakes. This negative reward system leads members to shift responsibilities to others and avoid any possibility of being blamed for a mistake. (Waiting for others to act first)
Aggressive–defensive	Oppositional	Organizations in which confrontation and negativism are rewarded. Members gain status and influence by being critical and thus are reinforced to oppose the ideas of others. (Pointing out flaws)
Aggressive–defensive	Power	Nonparticipative organizations structured on the basis of the authority inherent in members' positions. Members believe they will be rewarded for taking charge, controlling subordinates and, at the same time, being responsive to the demands of superiors. (Building up one's power base)
Aggressive–defensive	Competitive	Winning is valued and members are rewarded for outperforming one another. Members operate in a "win–lose" framework and believe they must work against (rather than with) their peers to be noticed. (Turning the job into a contest)
Aggressive–defensive	Perfectionistic	Organizations in which perfectionism, persistence, and hard work are valued. Members feel they must avoid any mistake, keep track of everything, and work long hours to attain narrowly defined objectives. (Doing things perfectly)

SOURCE: Adapted from R A Cooke and J L Szumal, "Measuring Normative Beliefs and Shared Behavioral Expectations in Organizations: The Reliability and Validity of the Organizational Culture Inventory," *Psychological Reports*, 1993, Vol. 72, pp 1299–1330.

based on one's title or position, social subcultures derived from social activities such as a bowling or golf league and a reading club, and counter-cultures.[19] It is important for managers to be aware of the possibility that conflict between subgroups that form subcultures can undermine an organization's overall performance.

Outcomes Associated with Organizational Culture

Both managers and academic researchers believe that organizational culture can be a driver of employee attitudes and organizational effectiveness and performance. To test this possibility, various measures of organizational culture have been correlated with a variety of individual and organizational outcomes. So what have we learned? First, several studies demonstrated that organizational culture was significantly correlated with employee behavior and attitudes. For example, a constructive culture was positively related with job satisfaction, intentions to stay at the company, and innovation and was negatively associated with work avoidance. In contrast, passive–defensive and aggressive–defensive cultures were negatively correlated with job satisfaction and intentions to stay at the company.[20] These results suggest that employees seem to prefer organizations that encourage people to interact and work with others in ways that assist them in satisfying their needs to grow and develop. Second, results from several studies revealed that the congruence between an individual's values and the organization's values was significantly associated with organizational commitment, job satisfaction, intention to quit, and turnover.[21]

Third, a summary of 10 quantitative studies showed that organizational culture did not predict an organization's financial performance.[22] This means that there is not one type of organizational culture that fuels financial performance. That said, however, a study of 207 companies from 22 industries for an 11-year period demonstrated that financial performance was higher among companies that had adaptive and flexible cultures.[23] Finally, studies of mergers indicated that they frequently failed due to incompatible cultures. Due to the increasing number of corporate mergers around the world, and the conclusion that 7 out of 10 mergers and acquisitions failed to meet their financial promise, managers within merged companies would be well advised to consider the role of organizational culture in creating a new organization.[24]

These research results underscore the significance of organizational culture. They also reinforce the need to learn more about the process of cultivating and changing an organization's culture. An organization's culture is not determined by fate. It is formed and shaped by the combination and integration of everyone who works in the organization.

How Cultures Are Embedded in Organizations

An organization's initial culture is an outgrowth of the founder's philosophy. For example, an achievement culture is likely to develop if the founder is an achievement-oriented individual driven by success. Over time, the original culture is either embedded as is or modified to fit the current environmental situation. Edgar Schein, an OB scholar, notes that embedding a culture involves a teaching process. That is, organizational members teach each other about the organization's preferred values, beliefs, expectations, and behaviors. This is accomplished by using one or more of the following mechanisms:[25]

1. *Formal statements of organizational philosophy, mission, vision, values, and materials used for recruiting, selection, and socialization.* Sam Walton, the

founder of Wal-Mart, established three basic beliefs or values that represent the core of the organization's culture. They are (1) respect for the individual, (2) service to our customer, and (3) striving for excellence.[26]

2. *The design of physical space, work environments, and buildings.*
3. *Slogans, language, acronyms, and sayings.* For example, Bank One promoted its desire to provide excellent client service through the slogan "whatever it takes." Employees were encouraged to do whatever it takes to exceed customer expectations.
4. *Deliberate role modeling, training programs, teaching, and coaching by managers and supervisors.* General Semiconductor implemented the "People Plus" program. It is an in-house leadership development and problem-solving training program that uses the company's mission and values as the springboard for creating individual development plans.
5. *Explicit rewards, status symbols (e.g., titles), and promotion criteria.* Charles Haldeman, the CEO of Putnam Investments, is trying to change the company's culture by creating a new set of performance criteria and incentives for employees.

> Now, instead of swinging for the fences as Putnam's leadership did in the go-go days of the 1990s, Haldeman has ordered managers to aim for reliable returns over the long haul. Haldeman wants each of Putnam's 54 funds to rank in the top half of its category every year. . . . In the future, managers will earn bonuses by achieving just that—and not get a penny more for edging their funds into the top 10%, as they once did.[27]

Haldeman is implementing this new approach because the old performance criteria and incentives were partly responsible for serious trading scandals that resulted in investors pulling out $70 billion of their money from Putnam's funds.

6. *Stories, legends, and myths about key people and events.* Southwest Airlines, for example, does an excellent job at telling stories to reinforce the company's commitment to customer service. One example involves a mechanic in Buffalo who used a snowmobile during a blizzard to drive seven miles in 20 feet of snow in order to get to the airport to free up a plane for takeoff.[28] The Skills & Best Practices contains recommendations for how managers can find stories with impact.
7. *The organizational activities, processes, or outcomes that leaders pay attention to, measure, and control.* Consider the behavior of Chung Mong Koo, chairman of Hyundai Motor Co.

> Hyundai's focus on quality comes straight from the top. Since 1999, Chairman Chung has boosted the quality team to 865 workers from 100, and virtually all employees have had to attend special seminars on improving Hyundai's cars. Chung

SKILLS & BEST PRACTICES

How Do Managers Develop Stories That Have Impact?

The task involves (1) observing day-to-day activities with an eye toward looking for stories and (2) being a good listener. Observe the following people and note how they achieve outstanding results.

- Successful individuals
- Risk takers
- Informal leaders
- Organizational heroes
- People who go beyond the call of duty
- People who truly live the organization's values
- People who help others to succeed

Managers can also derive stories by talking with satisfied customers and suppliers.

SOURCE: Derived from Barbara Kaufman, "Stories that Sell, Stories that Tell," *Journal of Business Strategy,* March/April 2003, pp 11–15.

"We're in awe of your ability to fit in here, Ms. Stoughton."

presides over twice-monthly quality meetings in a special conference room and an adjacent workshop, with vehicle lifts and high-intensity spotlights for comparing Hyundais head-to-head with rivals. And this team has teeth: In the past year, the introduction of three new models was delayed by months as engineers scrambled to boost quality in response to problems found by the team.[29]

8. *Leader reactions to critical incidents and organizational crises.*
9. *The workflow and organizational structure.* Hierarchical structures are more likely to embed an orientation toward control and authority than a flatter organization.
10. *Organizational systems and procedures.* An organization can promote achievement and competition through the use of sales contests.
11. *Organizational goals and the associated criteria used for recruitment, selection, development, promotion, layoffs, and retirement of people.* PepsiCo reinforces a high-performance culture by setting challenging goals.

The Organizational Socialization Process

organizational socialization
Process by which employees learn an oraganization's values, norms, and required behaviors.

Organizational socialization is defined as "the process by which a person learns the values, norms, and required behaviors which permit him to participate as a member of the organization."[30] As previously discussed, organizational socialization is a key mechanism used by organizations to embed their organizational cultures. In short, organizational socialization turns outsiders into fully functioning insiders by promoting and reinforcing the organization's core values and beliefs. This section introduces a three-phase model of organizational socialization and examines the practical application of socialization research.

A Three-Phase Model of Organizational Socialization

One's first year in a complex organization can be confusing. There is a constant swirl of new faces, strange jargon, conflicting expectations, and apparently unrelated events. Some organizations treat new members in a rather haphazard, sink-or-swim manner. More typically, though, the socialization process is characterized by a sequence of identifiable steps.[31]

Organizational behavior researcher Daniel Feldman has proposed a three-phase model of organizational socialization that promotes deeper understanding of this important process. As illustrated in Figure 2–3, the three phases are (1) anticipatory socialization, (2) encounter, and (3) change and acquisition. Each phase has its associated

FIGURE 2–3 A Model of Organizational Socialization

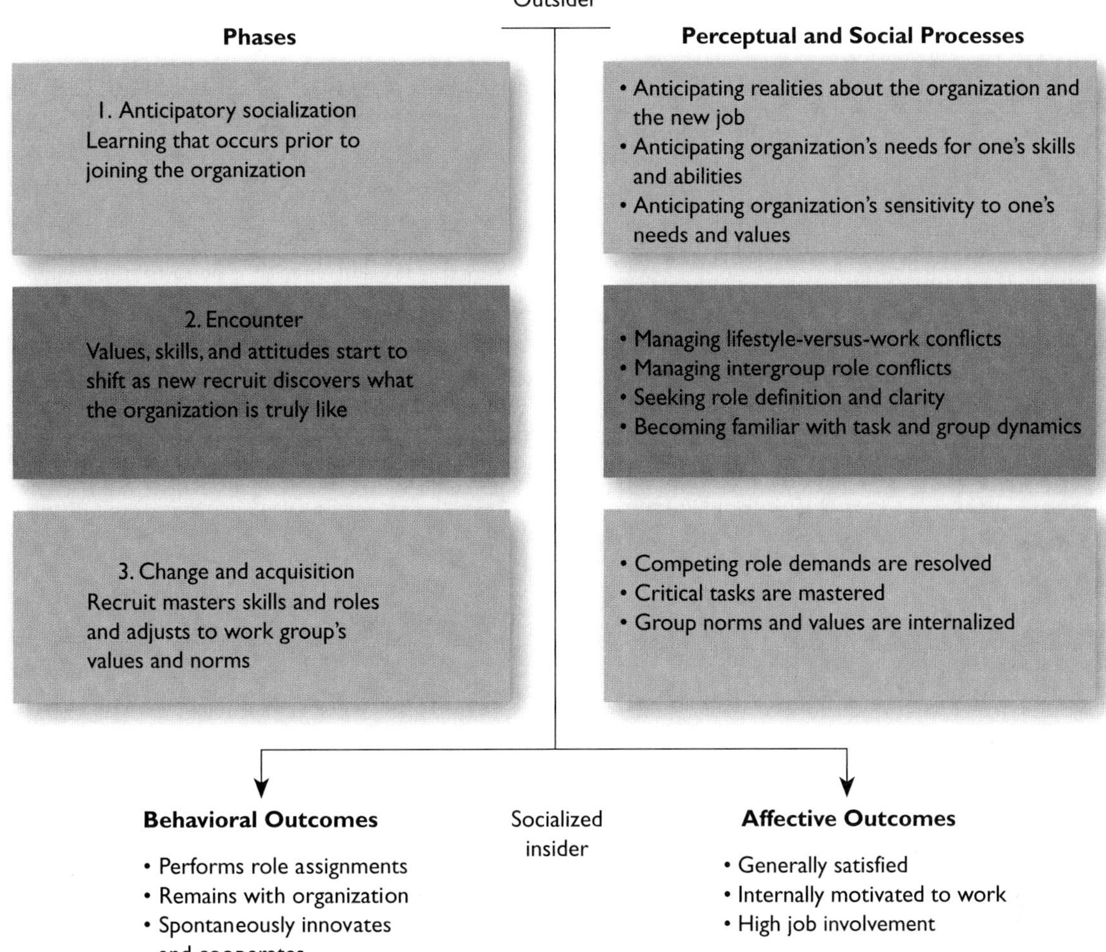
Outsider
Phases
Perceptual and Social Processes
1. Anticipatory socialization
Learning that occurs prior to joining the organization
• Anticipating realities about the organization and the new job
• Anticipating organization's needs for one's skills and abilities
• Anticipating organization's sensitivity to one's needs and values
2. Encounter
Values, skills, and attitudes start to shift as new recruit discovers what the organization is truly like
• Managing lifestyle-versus-work conflicts
• Managing intergroup role conflicts
• Seeking role definition and clarity
• Becoming familiar with task and group dynamics
3. Change and acquisition
Recruit masters skills and roles and adjusts to work group's values and norms
• Competing role demands are resolved
• Critical tasks are mastered
• Group norms and values are internalized
Behavioral Outcomes
• Performs role assignments
• Remains with organization
• Spontaneously innovates and cooperates
Socialized insider
Affective Outcomes
• Generally satisfied
• Internally motivated to work
• High job involvement

SOURCE: Adapted from material in D C Feldman, "The Multiple Socialization of Organization Members," *Academy of Management Review,* April 1981, pp 309–18.

perceptual and social processes. Feldman's model also specifies behavioral and affective outcomes that can be used to judge how well an individual has been socialized. The entire three-phase sequence may take from a few weeks to a year to complete, depending on individual differences and the complexity of the situation.

Phase 1: Anticipatory Socialization **Anticipatory socialization** occurs before an individual actually joins an organization. It is represented by the information people have learned about different careers, occupations, professions, and organizations. For example, anticipatory socialization partially explains the different perceptions you might have about working for the US government versus a high-technology company like Intel or Microsoft.

anticipatory socialization
Occurs before an individual joins an organization, and involves the information people learn about different careers, occupations, professions, and organizations.

All of this information—whether formal or informal, accurate or inaccurate—helps the individual anticipate organizational realities. Unrealistic expectations about the nature of the work, pay, and promotions are often formulated during phase I.

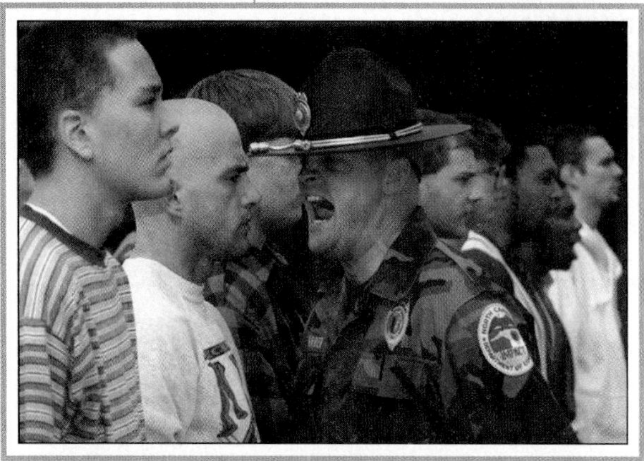

Boot camp, which is part of the encounter phase, is used by the military to quickly and firmly instill values endorsed by the military.

Phase 2: Encounter This second phase begins when the employment contract has been signed. During the **encounter phase** employees come to learn what the organization is really like. It is a time for reconciling unmet expectations and making sense of a new work environment. Many companies use a combination of orientation and training programs to socialize employees during the encounter phase. Consider the combination used at Capital One.

> On their first day as a Capital One associate, new hires can literally hit the ground running thanks to a recruiting process that identifies the required competencies for each position and incorporates job simulation into the pre-hire evaluation process. Candidates for a customer contact position, for example, can experience the job before a position is offered or accepted. Once on board, orientation includes a departmental new hire training program, which, depending on the job, can range anywhere from two to six weeks. After training but before phone associates join permanent teams, they spend time "nesting," taking customer calls in a controlled environment with many experienced associates to coach them.[32]

encounter phase

Employees learn what the organization is really like and reconcile unmet expectations.

change and acquisition

Requires employees to master tasks and roles and to adjust to work group values and norms.

Phase 3: Change and Acquisition The **change and acquisition** phase requires employees to master important tasks and roles and to adjust to their work group's values and norms. Table 2–2 presents a list of socialization processes or tactics used by organizations to help employees through this adjustment process. Trilogy, for example, uses a variety of these tactics in its renowned socialization program. The three-month program takes place at the organization's corporate university, called Trilogy University.

> **Month One.** When you arrive at Trilogy University, you are assigned to a section and to an instruction track. Your section, a group of about 20, is your social group for the duration of TU. . . . Tracks are designed to be microcosms of future work life at Trilogy. . . . The technical challenges in such exercises closely mimic real customer engagements, but the time frames are dramatically compressed. The assignments pile up week after week for the first month, each one successively more challenging than the last. During that time, you're being constantly measured and evaluated, as assignment grades and comments are entered into a database monitoring your progress. . . .
>
> **Month Two.** Month two is TU project month. . . . In teams of three to five people, they have to come up with an idea, create a business model for it, build the product, and develop the marketing plan. In trying to launch bold new ideas in a hyperaccelerated time frame, they gain a deep appreciation of the need to set priorities, evaluate probabilities, and measure results. Mind you, these projects are not hypothetical—they're the real thing. . . .
>
> **Month Three.** Month three at Trilogy University is all about finding your place and having a broader impact in the larger organization. A few students continue with their TU projects, but most move on to "graduation projects," which generally are assignments within various Trilogy business units. People leave TU on a rolling basis as they find sponsors out in the company who are willing to take them on.[33]

The change and acquisition phase at Trilogy is stressful, exhilarating, and critical for finding one's place within the organization. How would you like to work there? Returning to Table 2–2, can you identify the socialization tactics used by Trilogy?

Socialization Tactics TABLE 2–2

Tactic	Description
Collective vs. individual	Collective socialization consists of grouping newcomers and exposing them to a common set of experiences rather than treating each newcomer individually and exposing him or her to more or less unique experiences.
Formal vs. informal	Formal socialization is the practice of segregating a newcomer from regular organization members during a defined socialization period versus not clearly distinguishing a newcomer from more experienced members. Army recruits must attend boot camp before they are allowed to work alongside established soldiers.
Sequential vs. random	Sequential socialization refers to a fixed progression of steps that culminate in the new role, compared to an ambiguous or dynamic progression. The socialization of doctors involves a lock-step sequence from medical school, to internship, to residency before they are allowed to practice on their own.
Fixed vs. variable	Fixed socialization provides a timetable for the assumption of the role, whereas a variable process does not. American university students typically spend one year apiece as freshmen, sophomores, juniors, and seniors.
Serial vs. disjunctive	A serial process is one in which the newcomer is socialized by an experienced member, whereas a disjunctive process does not use a role model.
Investiture vs. divestiture	Investiture refers to the affirmation of a newcomer's incoming global and specific role identities and attributes. Divestiture is the denial and stripping away of the newcomer's existing sense of self and the reconstruction of self in the organization's image. During police training, cadets are required to wear uniforms and maintain an immaculate appearance, they are addressed as "officer," and told they are no longer ordinary citizens but are representatives of the police force.

SOURCE: Descriptions were taken from B E Ashforth, *Role Transitions in Organizational Life: An Identity-Based Perspective* (Mahwah, NJ: Lawrence Erlbaum Associates, 2001), pp 149–83.

Practical Application of Socialization Research

Past research suggests four practical guidelines for managing organizational socialization.

1. Managers should avoid a haphazard, sink-or-swim approach to organizational socialization because formalized socialization tactics positively affect new hires. A formalized orientation program positively influenced 116 new employees in a variety of occupations.[34]
2. Managers play a key role during the encounter phase. Studies of newly hired accountants demonstrated that the frequency and type of information

obtained during their first six months of employment significantly affected their job performance, their role clarity, and the extent to which they were socially integrated.[35] Managers need to help new hires integrate within the organizational culture. National City Corporation followed this advice and experienced significant cost savings and revenue growth.

> Hiring managers were taught how to prepare for the arrival of new employees and make their transition to a new job smoother. New employees were paired with experienced bank "sponsors" who had attended a half-day workshop on employee development.
>
> The program paid off. New hires are now 50% less likely to quit within their first three months, which saves the company at least $1.35 million annually. Absenteeism among new employees is down 25%, for an annual savings of $306,000. And as new hires complete workshops, the improvement in sales and product referrals has led to a revenue jump of $3.7 million.[36]

Take a moment now to complete the Hands-On Exercise. It measures the extent to which you have been socialized into your current work organization. Have you been adequately socialized? If not, you may need to find a mentor. Mentoring is discussed in the next section.

3. The organization can benefit by training new employees to use proactive socialization behaviors. A study of 154 entry-level professionals showed that effectively using proactive socialization behaviors influenced the newcomers' general anxiety and stress during the first month of employment and their motivation and anxiety six months later.[37]

4. Managers should pay attention to the socialization of diverse employees. Research demonstrated that diverse employees, particularly those with disabilities, experienced different socialization activities than other newcomers. In turn, these different experiences affected their long-term success and job satisfaction.[38]

Embedding Organizational Culture through Mentoring

mentoring

Process of forming and maintaining developmental relationships between a mentor and a junior person.

The modern word *mentor* derives from Mentor, the name of a wise and trusted counselor in Greek mythology. Terms typically used in connection with mentoring are *teacher, coach, sponsor,* and *peer*. **Mentoring** is defined as the process of forming and maintaining intensive and lasting developmental relationships between a variety of developers (i.e., people who provide career and psychosocial support) and a junior person (the protégé, if male; or protégée, if female).[39] Mentoring can serve to embed an organization's culture when developers and the protégé/protégée work in the same organization for two reasons. First, mentoring contributes to creating a sense of oneness by promoting the acceptance of the organization's core values throughout the organization. Second, the socialization aspect of mentoring also promotes a sense of membership.

Not only is mentoring important as a tactic for embedding organizational culture, but research suggests it can significantly influence the protégé/protégée's future career. For example, mentored employees performed better on the job and experienced more rapid career advancement than nonmentored employees. Mentored employees also

HANDS-ON EXERCISE

Have You Been Adequately Socialized?

INSTRUCTIONS: Complete the following survey items by considering either your current job or one you held in the past. If you have never worked, identify a friend who is working and ask that individual to complete the questionnaire for his or her organization. Read each item and circle your response by using the rating scale shown below. Compute your total score by adding up your responses and compare it to the scoring norms.

	Strongly Disagree	Disagree	Neutral	Agree	Strongly Agree
1. I have been through a set of training experiences that are specifically designed to give newcomers a thorough knowledge of job-related skills.	1	2	3	4	5
2. This organization puts all newcomers through the same set of learning experiences.	1	2	3	4	5
3. I did not perform any of my normal job responsibilities until I was thoroughly familiar with departmental procedures and work methods.	1	2	3	4	5
4. There is a clear pattern in the way one role leads to another, or one job assignment leads to another, in this organization.	1	2	3	4	5
5. I can predict my future career path in this organization by observing other people's experiences.	1	2	3	4	5
6. Almost all of my colleagues have been supportive of me personally.	1	2	3	4	5
7. My colleagues have gone out of their way to help me adjust to this organization.	1	2	3	4	5
8. I received much guidance from experienced organizational members as to how I should perform my job.	1	2	3	4	5
Total Score	_____	_____	_____	_____	_____

SCORING NORMS

8–18 = Low socialization 19–29 = Moderate socialization 30–40 = High socialization

SOURCE: Adapted from survey items excerpted from D Cable and C Parsons, "Socialization Tactics and Person-Organization Fit," *Personnel Psychology*, Spring 2001, pp 1–23.

Bill Wear, a program manager for security at Hewlett-Packard, started out hacking into phone lines at the age of 10. At 14, he hacked into his school computer using a password he'd stolen from his guidance counselor. The counselor knew Wear had stolen the password, so he left this message for him: "I know that you're using my account. I also know about your father. I know he abuses you. I also know that we can do something. Call me. Let me help." The counselor helped get him into a private school, and through two engineering degrees. Wear today is a mentor. He even wrote a handbook for the company's e-mail-mentoring program.

reported higher job and career satisfaction and working on more challenging job assignments.[40] With this information in mind, this section focuses on how people can use mentoring to their advantage. We discuss the functions of mentoring, the developmental networks underlying mentoring, and the personal and organizational implications of mentoring.

Functions of Mentoring

Kathy Kram, a Boston University researcher, conducted in-depth interviews with both members of 18 pairs of senior and junior managers. As a byproduct of this study, Kram identified two general functions—career and psychosocial—of the mentoring process. Five *career functions* that enhanced career development were sponsorship, exposure-and-visibility, coaching, protection, and challenging assignments. Four *psychosocial functions* were role modeling, acceptance-and-confirmation, counseling, and friendship. The psychosocial functions clarified the participants' identities and enhanced their feelings of competence.[41]

Developmental Networks Underlying Mentoring

Historically, it was thought that mentoring was primarily provided by one person who was called a mentor. Today, however, the changing nature of technology, organizational structures, and marketplace dynamics requires that people seek career information and support from many sources. Mentoring is currently viewed as a process in which protégés and protégées seek developmental guidance from a network of people, who are referred to as developers. Lori McKee, a project manager with Chubb Group of Insurance Cos., is a good example of someone who used a network of people to advance her career. She started a book club at the company, and 19 Chubb Group women across the country meet via teleconference once a month to discuss career issues associated with books they have read. "As a result of her increased visibility at the company, the 31-year-old Ms. McKee says she has been offered bigger assignments, including one to help upgrade the company's financial systems world-wide. 'The way I got it was through these discussions and getting mentoring from other women in the group,' she says."[42] This example implies that the diversity and strength of a person's network of relationships is instrumental in obtaining the type of career assistance needed to manage his or her career. Figure 2–4 presents a developmental network typology based on integrating the diversity and strength of developmental relationships.[43]

diversity of developmental relationships

The variety of people in a network used for developmental assistance.

The **diversity of developmental relationships** reflects the variety of people within the network an individual uses for developmental assistance. There are two subcomponents associated with network diversity: (1) the number of different people the person is networked with and (2) the various social systems from which the networked relationships stem (e.g., employer, school, family, community, professional associations, and religious affiliations). As shown in Figure 2–4, developmental relationship diversity ranges from low (few people or social systems) to high (multiple people or social systems).

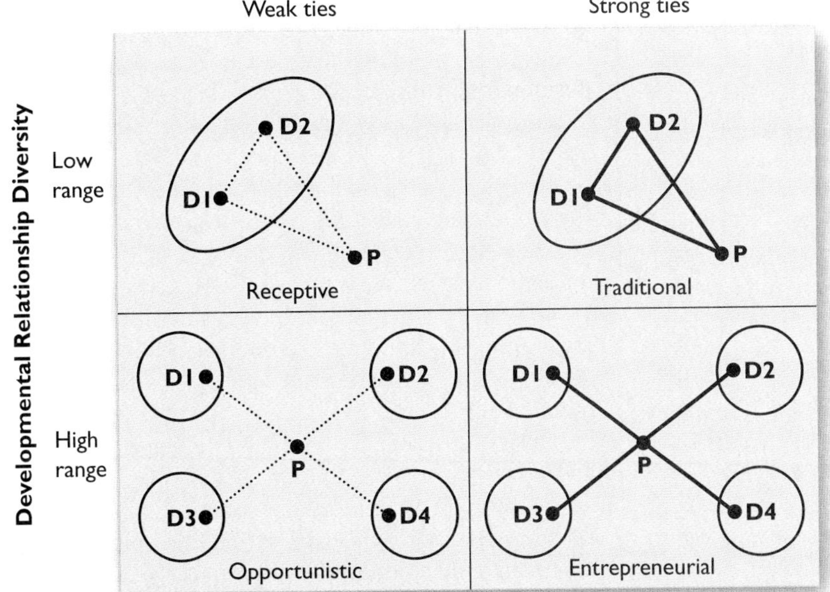

FIGURE 2–4 Developmental Networks Associated with Mentoring

SOURCE: From *Academy of Management Review* by M Higgins and K Kram, "Reconceptualizing Mentoring at Work: A Developmental Network Perspective," April 2001, p 270. Copyright 2001 by Academy of Management. Reproduced with permission of Academy of Management via Copyright Clearance Center.

developmental relationship strength The quality of relationships among people in a network.

Developmental relationship strength reflects the quality of relationships among the individual and those involved in his or her developmental network. For example, strong ties are reflective of relationships based on frequent interactions, reciprocity, and positive affect. Weak ties, in contrast, are based more on superficial relationships. Together, the diversity and strength of developmental relationships results in four types of developmental networks (see Figure 2–4): receptive, traditional, entrepreneurial, and opportunistic.

A *receptive* developmental network is composed of a few weak ties from one social system such as an employer or a professional association. The single oval around D1 and D2 in Figure 2–4 is indicative of two developers who come from one social system. In contrast, a *traditional* network contains a few strong ties between an employee and developers that all come from one social system. An entrepreneurial network, which is the strongest type of developmental network, is made up of strong ties among several developers (D1–D4) who come from four different social systems. Finally, an opportunistic network is associated with having weak ties with multiple developers from different social systems.

Personal and Organizational Implications

There are two key personal implications to consider. First, job and career satisfaction are likely to be influenced by the consistency between an individual's career goals and the type of developmental network at his or her disposal. For example, people with an entrepreneurial developmental network are more likely to experience change in their careers and to benefit from personal learning than people with receptive, traditional, and opportunistic networks. If this sounds attractive to you, you should try to increase the diversity and strength of your developmental relationships. In contrast, lower levels of job satisfaction are expected when employees have receptive developmental networks

SKILLS & BEST PRACTICES

Building an Effective Mentoring Network

1. Become the perfect protégé. It is important to invest ample time and energy to develop and maintain a network of developmental relationships. Trust and respect are needed among network members.
2. Engage in 360-degree networking. Share information and maintain good relationships with those above, below, and at the same status/responsibility level as yourself.
3. Commit to assessing, building, and adjusting the mentor network. Begin by assessing the competencies you want to build. Next, find mentors that can assist in building your desired competencies. Finally, change network members commensurate with changes in your experience and knowledge.
4. Develop diverse, synergistic connections. Find and develop relationships with multiple, diverse mentors. Pursue both formal and informal mentoring opportunities.
5. Realize that change is inevitable and that all good things come to an end. Most mentoring relationships last an average of five years. When a relationship ceases to be beneficial, end the mentoring relationship.

SOURCE: Derived from Suzanne C de Janasz, Sherry E Sullivan, and Vicki Whiting, "Mentor Networks and Career Success: Lessons for Turbulent Times," *Academy of Management Executive,* November 2003, pp 78–91.

and they desire to experience career advancement in multiple organizations. Receptive developmental networks, however, can be satisfying to someone who does not desire to be promoted up the career ladder.[44] Second, a developer's willingness to provide career and psychosocial assistance is a function of the protégé/protégée's ability, potential, and the quality of the interpersonal relationship.[45] This implies that you must take ownership for enhancing your skills, abilities, and developmental networks if you desire to experience career advancement throughout your life (see Skills & Best Practices).

Research also supports the organizational benefits of mentoring. In addition to the obvious benefit of employee development, mentoring enhances the effectiveness of organizational communication. Specifically, mentoring increases the amount of vertical communication both up and down an organization, and it provides a mechanism for modifying or reinforcing organizational culture. As found at Blue Cross and Blue Shield of North Carolina, an effective mentoring program can also reduce employee turnover and increase productivity. Their program pairs employees with company leaders for one year.

> Designed to identify high-potential employees, develop talent, enhance cross-functional relationships and create networking opportunities, the program consists of nine-month commitments on the part of the mentor and mentee. Employees who are accepted into the program (anyone can apply) are paired with a mentor who has completed rigorous training and is typically from a different department and/or division than the mentee. . . . Since the program's inauguration in 2000, turnover among mentees has averaged 46 percent lower than BCBSNC's general employee population. What's more, the BCBSNC's Corporate Leadership Council's formula for calculating the cost of turnover showed that this program, which costs less than $4,500 per year in out-of-pocket expense, generated a cost avoidance of more than $1.4 million. Additionally, 18 percent of mentees in 2001 and 25 percent in 2002 received outstanding performance ratings, compared to 10 percent for the general population for the same periods.[46]

key terms

chapter summary

- *Discuss the layers and functions of organizational culture.* The three layers of organizational culture are observable artifacts, espoused values, and basic underlying assumptions. Each layer varies in terms of outward visibility and resistance to change. Four functions of organizational culture are organizational identity, collective commitment, social system stability, and sense-making device.

  Discuss the three general types of organizational culture and their associated normative beliefs. The three general types of organizational culture are constructive, passive–defensive, and aggressive–defensive. Each type is grounded in different normative beliefs. Normative beliefs represent an individual's thoughts and beliefs about how members of a particular group or organization are expected to approach their work and interact with others. A constructive culture is associated with the beliefs of achievement, self-actualizing, humanistic-encouraging, and affiliative. Passive–defensive organizations tend to endorse the beliefs of approval, conventional, dependent, and avoidance. Aggressive–defensive cultures tend to endorse the beliefs of oppositional, power, competitive, and perfectionistic.
- *Summarize the methods used by organizations to embed their cultures.* Embedding a culture amounts to teaching employees about the organization's preferred values, beliefs, expectations, and behaviors. This is accomplished by using one or more of the following 11 mechanisms: (a) formal statements of organizational philosophy, mission, vision, values, and materials used for recruiting, selection, and socialization; (b) the design of physical space, work environments, and buildings; (c) slogans, language, acronyms, and sayings; (d) deliberate role modeling, training programs, teaching, and coaching by managers and supervisors; (e) explicit rewards, status symbols, and promotion criteria; (f) stories, legends, and myths about key people and events; (g) the organizational activities, processes, or outcomes that leaders pay attention to, measure, and control; (h) leader reactions to critical incidents and organizational crises; (i) the workflow and organizational structure; (j) organizational systems and procedures; and (k) organizational goals and associated criteria used for recruitment, selection, development, promotion, layoffs, and retirement of people.
- *Describe the three phases in Feldman's model of organizational socialization.* The three phases of Feldman's model are anticipatory socialization, encounter, and change and acquisition. Anticipatory socialization begins before an individual actually joins the organization. The encounter phase begins when the employment contract has been signed. Phase 3 involves the period in which employees master important tasks and resolve any role conflicts.
- *Discuss the various socialization tactics used to socialize employees.* There are six key socialization tactics. They are collective versus individual, formal versus informal, sequential versus random, fixed versus variable, serial versus disjunctive, and investiture versus divestiture (see Table 2–2). Each tactic provides organizations with two opposing options for socializing employees.
- *Explain the four types of development networks derived from a developmental network model of mentoring.* The four development networks are receptive, traditional, entrepreneurial, and opportunistic. A receptive network is composed of a few weak ties from one social system. A traditional network contains a few strong ties between an employee and developers that all come from one social system. An entrepreneurial network is made up of strong ties among developers from several social systems, and an opportunistic network is associated with having weak ties with multiple developers from different social systems.

discussion questions

1. How would you describe the type of organizational culture that exists at Costco? Be sure to provide examples about the extent to which Costco displayed the 12 types of normative beliefs shown in Table 2–1.
2. How would you respond to someone who made the following statement? "Organizational cultures are not important as far as managers are concerned."
3. Can you think of any organizational heroes who have influenced your work behavior? Describe them, and explain how they affected your behavior.
4. Why is socialization essential to organizational success?
5. Have you ever had a mentor? Explain how things turned out.

ethical dilemma

Arthur Andersen's Pursuit of Consulting Income Created Ethical Challenges in Its Auditing Operations[47]

Andersen realized long ago that no one was going to get rich doing just audits. So for partners to share in hundreds of thousands of dollars of firm profits each year, Andersen would have to boost its lucrative consulting business. That quest for revenue is how the firm lost sight of its obligation to cast a critical eye on its clients' accounting practices, some critics say. . . .

The problems with focusing on consulting are evident in Andersen's biggest accounting blowups. Consider Waste Management Inc., which generated millions of dollars in consulting fees for Andersen. Last year, securities regulators alleged that Andersen bent the accounting rules so far the firm committed fraud. Time and again, starting in 1988 up through 1997, when Waste Management announced what at the time was the biggest financial restatement in US history, Andersen auditors knew the company was violating generally accepted accounting principles, the Securities and Exchange Commission said in a settled complaint filed in a Washington, DC, federal court.

Throughout the late 1990s, Andersen proposed hundreds of millions of dollars of accounting adjustments to rectify the situation, the SEC said in its suit. But when Waste Management refused to follow their recommendations, to the auditors' disappointment, they caved in. Those decisions were backed at the highest levels of Andersen's Chicago office, the SEC suit says.

Before taking over Waste Management's audit in 1991, Andersen partner Robert Allgyer had been in charge of coordinating the Chicago office's efforts to cross-sell nonaudit services to Andersen's audit clients. Indeed, for Andersen, nonaudit services were the only potential source of revenue growth from the trash hauler. That year, Waste Management had capped the amount of audit fees it would pay Andersen. The company, however, allowed Andersen to earn additional fees for "special work."

What Would You Have Done If You Were Auditing Waste Management's Financial Statements?

1. Vigorously challenge Waste Management employees to correct their accounting practices.
2. Go to your manager when you first realize Waste Management was not following generally accepted accounting principles and tell him or her that you will not work on this account until Waste Management changes its ways.
3. Complete the work as best you can because your efforts contribute to Andersen's financial goals.
4. Invent other options. Discuss.

For an interpretation of this situation, visit our Web site, www.mhhe.com/kinickiob2e.

If you're looking for additional study materials, be sure to check out the Online Learning Center at

www.mhhe.com/kinickiob2e

for more information and interactivities that correspond to this chapter.

chapter Three

Developing Global Managers

LEARNING OBJECTIVES

After reading the material in this chapter, you should be able to:

- Define *ethnocentrism,* and explain what Hofstede concluded about applying American management theories in other countries.
- Identify and describe the nine cultural dimensions from the GLOBE project.
- Draw a distinction between individualistic cultures and collectivist cultures.
- Demonstrate your knowledge of these two distinctions: high-context versus low-context cultures and monochronic versus polychronic cultures.
- Explain what the GLOBE project has taught us about leadership.
- Explain why US managers have a comparatively high failure rate in foreign assignments, and identify an OB trouble spot for each stage of the foreign assignment cycle.

GE'S DAY BEGINS IN INDIA

Pulling into General Electric's John F. Welch Technology Center, a uniformed guard waves you through an iron gate. Once inside, you leave the dusty, traffic-clogged streets of Bangalore and enter a leafy campus of low buildings that gleam in the sun. Bright hallways lined with plants and abstract art—"it encourages creativity," explains a manager—lead through laboratories where physicists, chemists, metallurgists, and computer engineers huddle over gurgling beakers, electron microscopes, and spectrophotometers. Except for the female engineers wearing saris and the soothing Hindi pop music wafting through the open-air dining pavilion, this could be GE's giant research-and-development facility in the upstate New York town of Niskayuna.

It's more like Niskayuna than you might think. The center's 1,800 engineers—a quarter of them have PhDs—are engaged in fundamental research for most of GE's 13 divisions. In one lab, they tweak the aerodynamic designs of turbine-engine blades. In another, they're scrutinizing the molecular structure of materials to be used in DVDs for short-term use in which the movie is automatically erased after a few days. In another, technicians have rigged up a working model of a GE plastics plant in Spain and devised a way to boost output there by 20%. Patents? Engineers here have filed for 95 in the U.S. since the center opened in 2000.

Pretty impressive for a place that just four years ago was a fallow plot of land. Even more impressive, the Bangalore operation has become vital to the future of one of America's biggest, most profitable companies. "The game here really isn't about saving costs but to speed innovation and generate growth for the company," explains Bolivian-born Managing Director Guillermo Wille, one of the center's few non-Indians.

The Welch center is at the vanguard of one of the biggest mind-melds in history. Plenty of Americans know of India's inexpensive software writers and have figured out that the nice clerk who booked their air ticket is in Delhi. But these are just superficial signs of India's capabilities. Quietly but with breathtaking speed, India and its millions of world-class engineering, business, and medical graduates are becoming enmeshed in America's New Economy in ways most of us barely imagine. "India has always had brilliant, educated people," says tech-trend forecaster Paul Saffo of the Institute for the Future in Menlo Park, Calif. "Now Indians are taking the lead in colonizing cyberspace."

This techno take-off is wonderful for India—but

terrifying for many Americans. In fact, India's emergence is fast turning into the latest Rorschach test on globalization. Many see India's digital workers as bearers of new prosperity to a deserving nation and vital partners of Corporate America. Others see them as shock troops in the final assault on good-paying jobs.[1]

FOR DISCUSSION

What is your opinion about this sort of "offshoring" of jobs in today's global economy? For an interpretation of this case and additional comments, visit our Online Learning Center:

www.mhhe.com/kinickiob2e

WE HEAR A LOT about the global economy these days. On one level, it all seems so grand, so vague, and so distant. But, on another level, it is here, it is now, and it is *very* personal. For example, consider this scenario:

> Liz awakens to a new workday in her San Diego home as her made-in-China alarm clock buzzes. She flips on a Japanese lamp with a bulb made by Philips, a Dutch company. After showering and applying French makeup, she puts on an outfit sewn in Singapore and slips into her favorite hand-crafted Italian shoes. A quick check of the weather on her assembled-in-Mexico television accompanies a hurried breakfast of juice from Brazilian oranges, an apple from New Zealand, a chunk of Danish cheese, and toast smeared with British marmalade. As she stops her German Mercedes SUV (made in Alabama) to fill up on gasoline refined from Venezuelan crude oil, her cell phone made by Finland's Nokia rings and she chats with her best friend thanks to equipment from Canada's Nortel Networks. Down the road, Liz parks outside the offices of her employer, Qualcomm, the wireless technology firm that "has employees originating from more than 100 countries who altogether speak over 50 languages."[2]

Yes, welcome to the global economy! And *you* are a big part of it—just check the labels on the products you buy and the clothes on your back. As *USA Today* pointed out during a recent year-end shopping season: "More than 80% of the toys, bikes and Christmas ornaments sold in the USA come from China. About 90% of all sporting goods and 95% of shoes are foreign-made."[3] Goods, money, and talent are crossing international borders at an accelerating pace. For better or for worse, even more economic globalization lies ahead. For example, when the European Union grew by 10 countries (for a total of 25) in May 2004, the world suddenly had another giant trading block encompassing 455 million people (versus a US population of 291 million at the time).[4] Those worried about having their jobs "offshored" to lower-cost foreign countries can take some comfort in this recent perspective from *Business Week:* "there's still plenty of demand in the U.S. for people who combine technical skills with industry-specific knowledge and people skills."[5] From an OB standpoint, continued globalization means an exponential increase in both cross-cultural interactions and the demand for managers who are comfortable and effective working with people from other countries and cultures.

How ready are you to manage in the burgeoning global economy? Michelangelo (Mike) Volpi, chief strategist at Cisco Systems, the Internet equipment giant, is an inspiring measuring stick. *Business Week* recently offered this profile:

> With workers from all its acquisitions roaming the halls, Cisco sometimes resembles a mini United Nations. It's the perfect environment for Volpi's multicultural upbringing. Born in Milan to Italian parents, he still holds his Italian citizenship. He spent 12 years in Japan—from age 5 to 17—and speaks three languages: English, Italian, and Japanese. His father, Vittorio Volpi, the head of the Japanese subsidiary of Swiss UBS Bank, says his son has learned flexibility from the Italians, subtlety from the Japanese, and pragmatism and fairness from American business culture. "He is an interesting cocktail of cultures," the elder Volpi says.[6]

Indeed, competition for both business and top jobs in the global economy promises to be very tough. The purpose of this chapter is to help you move toward meeting the challenge.

Developing a Global Mind-Set

Managing in a global economy is as much about patterns of thinking and behavior as it is about trade agreements, goods and services, and currency exchange rates. Extended periods in a single dominant culture ingrain assumptions about how things are and should be. Today's managers, whether they work at home for a foreign-owned company or actually work in a foreign country, need to develop a global mind-set (involving open-mindedness, adaptability, and a strong desire to learn).[7]

This section encourages a global mind-set by defining societal culture and contrasting it with organizational culture, discussing ethnocentrism, exploring ways to become a global manager, and examining the applicability of American management theories in other cultures.

A Model of Societal and Organizational Cultures

societal culture

Socially derived, taken-for-granted assumptions about how to think and act.

Societal culture involves "shared meanings" that generally remain below the threshold of conscious awareness because they involve *taken-for-granted assumptions* about how one should perceive, think, act, and feel.[8] Cultural anthropologist Edward T Hall put it this way:

> Since much of culture operates outside our awareness, frequently we don't even know what we know. We pick . . . [expectations and assumptions] up in the cradle. We unconsciously learn what to notice and what not to notice, how to divide time and space, how to walk and talk and use our bodies, how to behave as men or women, how to relate to other people, how to handle responsibility, whether experience is seen as whole or fragmented. This applies to all people. The Chinese or the Japanese or the Arabs are as unaware of their assumptions as we are of our own. We each assume that they're part of human nature. What we think of as "mind" is really internalized culture.[9]

Peeling the Cultural Onion Culture is difficult to grasp because it is multilayered. International management experts Fons Trompenaars (from the Netherlands) and Charles Hampden-Turner (from Britain) offer this instructive analogy in their landmark book, *Riding the Waves of Culture:*

> Culture comes in layers, like an onion. To understand it you have to unpeel it layer by layer.
>
> On the outer layer are the products of culture, like the soaring skyscrapers of Manhattan, pillars of private power, with congested public streets between them. These are expressions of deeper values and norms in a society that are not directly visible (values such as upward mobility, "the more-the-better," status, material success). The layers of values and norms are deeper within the "onion," and are more difficult to identify.[10]

Thus, the September 11, 2001, destruction of the New York World Trade Center towers by terrorists was as much an attack on American cultural values as it was on lives and property. That deepened the hurt and made the anger more profound for Americans and their friends around the world. In both life and business, culture is a serious matter.

Merging Societal and Organizational Cultures As illustrated in Figure 3–1, culture influences organizational behavior in two ways. Employees bring their

Cultural Influences on Organizational Behavior **FIGURE 3–1**

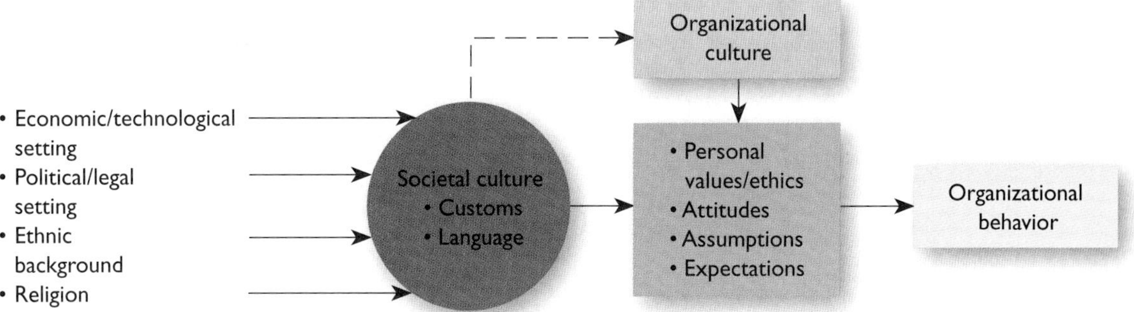

societal culture to work with them in the form of customs and language. Organizational culture, a by-product of societal culture, in turn affects the individual's values, ethics, attitudes, assumptions, and expectations.[11] The term *societal* culture is used here instead of national culture because the boundaries of many modern nation-states were not drawn along cultural lines. The former Soviet Union, for example, included 15 republics and more than 100 ethnic nationalities, many with their own distinct language.[12] Meanwhile, English-speaking Canadians in Vancouver are culturally closer to Americans in Seattle than to their French-speaking compatriots in Quebec. Societal culture is shaped by the various environmental factors listed in the left-hand side of Figure 3–1.

Once inside the organization's sphere of influence, the individual is further affected by the *organization's* culture. Mixing of societal and organizational cultures can produce interesting dynamics in multinational companies. For example, with French and American employees working side by side at General Electric's medical imaging production facility in Waukesha, Wisconsin, unit head Claude Benchimol witnessed some culture shock:

> The French are surprised the American parking lots empty out as early as 5 PM; the Americans are surprised the French don't start work at 8 AM. Benchimol feels the French are more talkative and candid. Americans have more of a sense of hierarchy and are less likely to criticize. But they may be growing closer to the French. Says Benchimol: "It's taken a year to get across the idea that we are all entitled to say what we don't like to become more productive and work better."[13]

Same company, same company culture, yet GE's French and American co-workers have different attitudes about time, hierarchy, and communication. They are the products of different societal cultures.[14]

When managing people at work, the individual's societal culture, the organizational culture, and any interaction between the two need to be taken into consideration.[15] For example, American workers' cultural orientation toward quality improvement differs significantly from the Japanese cultural pattern:

> Unlike Japanese workers, Americans aren't interested in making small step-by-step improvements to increase quality. They want to achieve the breakthrough, the impossible dream. The way to motivate them: Ask for the big leap, rather than for tiny steps.[16]

Ethnocentrism: Removing a Cultural Roadblock in the Global Economy

ethnocentrism

Belief that one's native country, culture, language, and behavior are superior.

Ethnocentrism, the belief that one's native country, culture, language, and modes of behavior are superior to all others, has its roots in the dawn of civilization. First identified as a behavioral science concept in 1906, involving the tendency of groups to reject outsiders,[17] the term *ethnocentrism* generally has a more encompassing (national or societal) meaning today.

Worldwide evidence of ethnocentrism is plentiful. For example, consider these awkward cross-cultural circumstances reported from the war in Iraq in 2003:

> . . . for [Lt. Col. Hector] Mirabile's troopers, the culture gap still yawns in ways that feel not only alien but threatening. In their wraparound shades and body armor, the soldiers look like creatures from outer space to the Iraqis (who generally do not wear sunglasses and suspect that the Americans' Ray-Bans have been engineered to look through women's clothes). After the mortar attack, "the police chief came over to talk," says Sgt. William Sanchez, 33. "He was gonna give me that Arab kiss thing. I said, 'I don't kiss, buddy. How ya doin'?'"[18]

Ethnocentrism led to deadly "ethnic cleansing" in Bosnia and Kosovo and genocide in the African nations of Rwanda, Burundi, and Sudan.

Less dramatic, but still troublesome, is ethnocentrism within managerial and organizational contexts. Experts on the subject framed the problem this way:

> [Ethnocentric managers have] a preference for putting home-country people in key positions everywhere in the world and rewarding them more handsomely for work, along with a tendency to feel that this group is more intelligent, more capable, or more reliable. . . . Ethnocentrism is often not attributable to prejudice as much as to inexperience or lack of knowledge about foreign persons and situations. This is not too surprising, since most executives know far more about employees in their home environments. As one executive put it, "At least I understand why our own managers make mistakes. With our foreigners, I never know. The foreign managers may be better. But if I can't trust a person, should I hire him or her just to prove we're multinational?"[19]

Hundreds of ethnic Albanians were persecuted and killed by ethnocentric Serbs in Kosovo. Here Albanians mourn over relatives and friends reportedly killed by Serbian police.

HANDS-ON EXERCISE

How Strong Is Your Potential for Ethnocentrism?

INSTRUCTIONS: If you were born and raised or have spent most of your life in the United States, select one number from the following scale for each item. If you are from a different country or culture, substitute the country/language you most closely identify with for the terms "American" and "English," and then rate each item.

	Strongly Disagree	Disagree	Neutral	Agree	Strongly Agree
1. I was raised in a way that was [truly] American.	1	2	3	4	5
2. Compared to how much I criticize other cultures, I criticize American culture less.	1	2	3	4	5
3. I am proud of American culture.	1	2	3	4	5
4. American culture has had a positive effect on my life.	1	2	3	4	5
5. I believe that my children should read, write, and speak [only] English.	1	2	3	4	5
6. I go to places where people are American.	1	2	3	4	5
7. I admire people who are American.	1	2	3	4	5
8. I would prefer to live in an American community.	1	2	3	4	5
9. At home, I eat [only] American food.	1	2	3	4	5
10. Overall, I am American.	1	2	3	4	5

SCORING 10–23 = Low potential for ethnocentrism
24–36 = Moderate potential for ethnocentrism
37–50 = High potential for ethnocentrism

SOURCE: Adapted from and survey items excerpted from J L Tsai, Y-W Ying, and P A Lee, "The Meaning of 'Being Chinese' and 'Being American': Variation among Chinese American Young Adults," *Journal of Cross-Cultural Psychology,* May 2000, pp 302–32.

Research Insight Research suggests ethnocentrism is bad for business. A survey of 918 companies with home offices in the United States (272 companies), Japan (309), and Europe (337) found ethnocentric staffing and human resource policies to be associated with increased personnel problems. Those problems included recruiting difficulties, high turnover rates, and lawsuits over personnel policies. Among the three regional samples, Japanese companies had the most ethnocentric human resource practices and the most international human resource problems.[20]

Dealing with Ethnocentrism in Ourselves and Others Current and future managers can effectively deal with ethnocentrism through education, greater cross-cultural awareness, international experience, and a conscious effort to value cultural diversity.[21] (Take a moment to complete the Hands-On Exercise.) Results of the Hands-On Exercise need to be interpreted cautiously because this version has not been scientifically validated; thus, it is for instructional and discussion purposes only.

SKILLS & BEST PRACTICES

Steps You Can Take *Now* to Become Global Manager Material

Skills	Action Steps
Global perspective	Broaden focus from one or two countries to a global business perspective.
Cultural responsiveness	Become familiar with many cultures.
Appreciate cultural synergies	Learn the dynamics of multicultural situations.
Cultural adaptability	Be able to live and work effectively in many different cultures.
Cross-cultural communication	Engage in cross-cultural interaction every day, whether at home or in a foreign country.
Cross-cultural collaboration	Work effectively in multicultural teams where everyone is equal.
Acquire broad foreign experience	Move up the career ladder by going from one foreign country to another, instead of taking frequent home-country assignments.

SOURCE: Adapted from N J Adler and S Bartholomew, "Managing Globally Competent People," *Academy of Management Executive,* August 1992, Table 1, pp 52–65.

Becoming a Global Manager

On any given day in today's global economy, a manager can interact with colleagues from several different countries or cultures. For instance, at PolyGram, the British music company, the top 33 managers are from 15 different countries.[22] If they are to be effective, managers in such multicultural situations need to develop *global* skills (see Skills & Best Practices). Developing skilled managers who move comfortably from culture to culture takes time. Consider, for example, this comment by the head of Gillette, who wants twice as many global managers on the payroll. "We could try to hire the best and the brightest, but it's the experience with Gillette that we need. About half of our [expatriates] are now on their fourth country—that kind of experience. It takes 10 years to make the kind of Gillette manager I'm talking about."[23]

Importantly, these global skills will help managers in culturally diverse countries such as the United States and Canada do a more effective job on a day-to-day basis.

The Hofstede Study: How Well Do US Management Theories Apply in Other Countries?

The short answer to this important question: *not very well.* This answer derives from a landmark study conducted nearly 30 years ago by Dutch researcher Geert Hofstede. His unique cross-cultural comparison of 116,000 IBM employees from 53 countries worldwide focused on four cultural dimensions:

- *Power distance.* How much inequality does someone expect in social situations?
- *Individualism-collectivism.* How loosely or closely is the person socially bonded?
- *Masculinity-femininity.* Does the person embrace stereotypically competitive, performance-oriented masculine traits or nurturing, relationship-oriented feminine traits?
- *Uncertainty avoidance.* How strongly does the person desire highly structured situations?

The US sample ranked relatively low on power distance, very high on individualism, moderately high on masculinity, and low on uncertainty avoidance.[24]

The high degree of variation among cultures led Hofstede to two major conclusions: (1) Management theories and practices need to be adapted to local cultures. This is particularly true for made-in-America management theories (e.g., Maslow's need hierarchy) and Japanese team management practices. *There is no one best way to manage across cultures.*[25] (2) Cultural arrogance is a luxury individuals, companies, and nations can no longer afford in a global economy.

Becoming Cross-Culturally Competent

Cultural anthropologists believe interesting and valuable lessons can be learned by comparing one culture with another. Many dimensions have been suggested over the years to help contrast and compare the world's rich variety of cultures. Five cultural perspectives, especially relevant to present and aspiring global managers, discussed in this section are basic cultural dimensions, individualism versus collectivism, high-context and low-context cultures, monochronic and polychronic time orientation, and cross-cultural leadership. Separately or together these cultural distinctions can become huge stumbling blocks when doing business across cultures.

A qualification needs to be offered at this juncture. It is important to view all of the cultural differences in this chapter and elsewhere as *tendencies and patterns,* rather than as absolutes. As soon as one falls into the trap of assuming *all* Germans are this, *all* British are that, and so on, potentially instructive generalizations become mindless stereotypes. Well-founded cultural generalizations are fundamental to successfully doing business in other cultures. But one needs to be constantly alert to *individuals* who are exceptions to the local cultural tendency. For instance, it is possible to encounter talkative and aggressive Japanese and quiet and deferential Americans who simply do not fit their respective cultural molds. Also, tipping the scale against clear cultural differences are space age transportation; global telecommunications, television, and computer networks; tourism; global marketing; and music and entertainment. These areas are homogenizing the peoples of the world. The result, according to experts on the subject, is an emerging "world culture" in which, someday, people may be more alike than different.[26]

Nine Basic Cultural Dimensions from the GLOBE Project

Project GLOBE (Global Leadership and Organizational Behavior Effectiveness) is the brainchild of University of Pennsylvania professor Robert J House.[27] It is a massive and ongoing attempt to "develop an empirically based theory to describe, understand, and predict the impact of specific cultural variables on leadership and organizational processes and the effectiveness of these processes."[28] GLOBE has evolved into a network of more than 160 scholars from 62 societies since the project was launched in Calgary, Canada, in 1994. Most of the researchers are native to the particular cultures they study, thus greatly enhancing the credibility of the project. During the first two phases of the GLOBE project, a list of nine basic cultural dimensions was developed and statistically validated. Translated questionnaires based on the nine dimensions were administered to thousands of managers in the banking, food, and telecommunications industries around the world to build a database. Results are being published on a regular basis.[29] Much work and many years are needed if the project's goal, as stated above, is to be achieved. In the meantime, we have been given a comprehensive, valid, and up-to-date tool for better understanding cross-cultural similarities and differences.

Genevieve Bell, an anthropologist employed by Intel Research, has been researching how people use technology in Asia and the Pacific to learn more about values and habits in emerging markets. Much of what Bell has learned challenges Western assumptions regarding technology and its use across the globe. Countries like Japan have little "private" space in homes and therefore younger occupants are attracted to text-messaging. The South Korean electronics company LG Electronics has introduced a mobile phone with an embedded compass to allow Muslim users to locate the direction of Mecca using Global Positioning System technology. All of these considerations can make it difficult for one company like Intel to market one product globally. Pictured here is one of the many mobile phone chargers that can be found across China.

The nine cultural dimensions from the GLOBE project are:

- *Power distance:* How much unequal distribution of power should there be in organizations and society?
- *Uncertainty avoidance:* How much should people rely on social norms and rules to avoid uncertainty and limit unpredictability?
- *Societal collectivism:* How much should leaders encourage and reward loyalty to the social unit, as opposed to the pursuit of individual goals?
- *In-group collectivism:* How much pride and loyalty should individuals have for their family or organization?
- *Gender egalitarianism:* How much effort should be put into minimizing gender discrimination and role inequalities?
- *Assertiveness:* How confrontational and dominant should individuals be in social relationships?
- *Future orientation:* How much should people delay gratification by planning and saving for the future?
- *Performance orientation:* How much should individuals be rewarded for improvement and excellence?
- *Humane orientation:* How much should society encourage and reward people for being kind, fair, friendly, and generous?[30]

Notice how the two forms of collectivism, along with the dimensions of power distance and uncertainty avoidance, correspond to the similarly labeled variables in Hofstede's classic study, discussed earlier.

Bringing the GLOBE Cultural Dimensions to Life A fun and worthwhile exercise is to reflect on your own cultural roots, family traditions, and belief system and develop a personal cultural profile, using as many of the GLOBE dimensions as possible. As a case in point, which of the GLOBE cultural dimensions relates to the following biographical sketch?

> Christopher Jones, 24, [is] a UCLA grad who's a musician, playing with his rock band at clubs in Los Angeles.
>
> Like many his age, he has no money for rainy-day savings, let alone the long term.
>
> "At this point, my attitude of life is 'carpe diem.' If I have some money, take a trip, something like that," Jones said.
>
> "I understand that being a young person and saving money is the right thing to do. But finding happiness is more important to me than having a little money down the line."[31]

If you said "future orientation," you're right! Indeed, like too many Americans (of all ages), Christopher Jones scores low on future orientation and thus has inadequate savings for the future.

Country Profiles and Practical Implications How do different countries score on the GLOBE cultural dimensions? Data from 18,000 managers yielded the profiles in Table 3–1. A quick overview shows a great deal of cultural diversity

TABLE 3–1 Countries Ranking Highest and Lowest on the GLOBE Cultural Dimensions

Dimension	Highest	Lowest
Power distance	Morocco, Argentina, Thailand, Spain, Russia	Denmark, Netherlands, South Africa—black sample, Israel, Costa Rica
Uncertainty avoidance	Switzerland, Sweden, German—former West, Denmark, Austria	Russia, Hungary, Bolivia, Greece, Venezuela
Societal collectivism	Sweden, South Korea, Japan, Singapore, Denmark	Greece, Hungary, Germany—former East, Argentina, Italy
In-group collectivism	Iran, India, Morocco, China, Egypt	Denmark, Sweden, New Zealand, Netherlands, Finland
Gender egalitarianism	Hungary, Poland, Slovenia, Denmark, Sweden	South Korea, Egypt, Morocco, India, China
Assertiveness	Germany—former East, Austria, Greece, US, Spain	Sweden, New Zealand, Switzerland, Japan, Kuwait
Future orientation	Singapore, Switzerland, Netherlands, Canada—English speaking, Denmark	Russia, Argentina, Poland, Italy, Kuwait
Performance orientation	Singapore, Hong Kong, New Zealand, Taiwan, US	Russia, Argentina, Greece, Venezuela, Italy
Humane orientation	Philippines, Ireland, Malaysia, Egypt, Indonesia	Germany—former West, Spain, France, Singapore, Brazil

SOURCE: Adapted from M Javidan and R J House, "Cultural Acumen for the Global Manager: Lessons from Project GLOBE," *Organizational Dynamics,* Spring 2001, pp 289–305.

around the world. But thanks to the nine GLOBE dimensions, we have more precise understanding of *how* cultures vary. Closer study reveals telling cultural *patterns,* or cultural fingerprints for nations. The US managerial sample, for instance, scored high on assertiveness and performance orientation. Accordingly, Americans are widely perceived as pushy and hardworking. Switzerland's high scores on uncertainty avoidance and future orientation help explain its centuries of political neutrality and world-renowned banking industry. Singapore is known as a great place to do business because it is clean and safe and its people are well educated and hardworking. This is no surprise, considering Singapore's high scores on social collectivism, future orientation, and performance orientation. In contrast, Russia's low scores on future orientation and performance orientation could foreshadow a slower than hoped for transition from a centrally planned economy to free enterprise capitalism. These illustrations bring us to an important practical lesson: *Knowing the cultural tendencies of foreign business partners and competitors can give you a strategic competitive advantage.*

Individualism versus Collectivism: A Closer Look

Have you ever been torn between what you personally wanted and what the group, organization, or society expected of you? If so, you have firsthand experience with a fundamental and important cultural distinction in both the Hofstede and GLOBE studies: individualism versus collectivism. Awareness of this distinction, as we will soon see, can spell the difference between success and failure in cross-cultural business dealings.

individualistic culture

Primary emphasis on personal freedom and choice.

collectivist culture

Personal goals less important than community goals and interests.

Individualistic cultures, characterized as "I" and "me" cultures, give priority to individual freedom and choice. **Collectivist cultures,** oppositely called "we" and "us" cultures, rank shared goals higher than individual desires and goals. People in collectivist cultures are expected to subordinate their own wishes and goals to those of the relevant social unit. A worldwide survey of 30,000 managers by Trompenaars and Hampden-Turner, who prefer the term *communitarianism* to collectivism, found the highest degree of individualism in Israel, Romania, Nigeria, Canada, and the United States. Countries ranking lowest in individualism—thus qualifying as collectivist cultures—were Egypt, Nepal, Mexico, India, and Japan. Brazil, China, and France also ended up toward the collectivist end of the scale.[32]

A Business Success Factor

Of course, one can expect to encounter both individualists and collectivists in culturally diverse countries such as the United States.[33] For example, imagine the frustration of Dave Murphy, a Boston-based mutual fund salesperson, when he recently tried to get Navajo Indians in Arizona interested in saving money for their retirement. After several fruitless meetings with groups of Navajo employees, he was given this cultural insight by a local official: "If you come to this environment, you have to understand that money is different. It's there to be spent. If you have some, you help your family."[34] To traditional Navajos, enculturated as collectivists, saving money is an unworthy act of selfishness. Subsequently, the sales pitch was tailored to emphasize the *family* benefits of individual retirement savings plans.

Allegiance to Whom?

The Navajo example brings up an important point about collectivist cultures. Specifically, which unit of society predominates? For the Navajos, family is the key reference group. But, as Trompenaars and Hampden-Turner observe, important differences exist among collectivist (or communitarian) cultures:

> For each single society, it is necessary to determine the group with which individuals have the closest identification. They could be keen to identify with their trade union, their family, their corporation, their religion, their profession, their nation, or the state apparatus. The French tend to identify with *la France, la famille, le cadre;* the Japanese with the corporation; the former eastern bloc with the Communist Party; and Ireland with the Roman Catholic Church. Communitarian goals may be good or bad for industry depending on the community concerned, its attitude and relevance to business development.[35]

High-Context and Low-Context Cultures

high-context cultures Primary meaning derived from nonverbal situational cues.

People from **high-context cultures**—including China, Korea, Japan, Vietnam, Mexico, and Arab cultures—rely heavily on situational cues for meaning when perceiving and communicating with others.[36] Nonverbal cues such as one's official position, status, or family connections convey messages more powerfully than do spoken words. Thus, we come to better understand the ritual of exchanging *and reading* business cards in Japan. Japanese culture is relatively high context. One's business card, listing employer and official position, conveys vital silent messages about one's status to members of Japan's homogeneous society. Also, people from high-context cultures who are not especially talkative during a first encounter with a stranger are not necessarily being unfriendly; they are simply taking time to collect "contextual" information.

low-context cultures Primary meaning derived from written and spoken words.

Reading the Fine Print in Low-Context Cultures In **low-context cultures,** written and spoken words carry the burden of shared meanings. Low-context cultures include those found in Germany, Switzerland, Scandinavia, North America, and Great Britain. True to form, Germany has precise written rules for even the smallest details of daily life. In *high*-context cultures, agreements tend to be made on the basis of someone's word or a handshake, after a rather prolonged get-acquainted and trust-building period. Low-context Americans and Canadians, who have cultural roots in Northern Europe, see the handshake as a signal to get a signature on a detailed, lawyer-approved, ironclad contract.

Avoiding Cultural Collisions Misunderstanding and miscommunication often are problems in international business dealings when the parties are from high- versus low-context cultures. A Mexican business professor recently made this instructive observation:

> Over the years, I have noticed that across cultures there are different opinions on what is expected from a business report. US managers, for instance, take a pragmatic, get-to-the-point approach, and expect reports to be concise and action-oriented. They don't have time to read long explanations: "Just the facts, ma'am."
>
> Latin American managers will usually provide long explanations that go beyond the simple facts. . . .
>
> I have a friend who is the Latin America representative for a United States firm and has been asked by his boss to provide regular reports on sales activities. His reports are long, including detailed explanations on the context in which the events he is reporting on occur and the possible interpretations that they might have. His boss regularly answers these reports with very brief messages, telling him to "cut the crap and get to the point!"[37]

SKILLS & BEST PRACTICES

Breaking through the Context Barrier in Culturally Diverse US Workplaces

- People on both sides of the context barrier must be trained to make adjustments.
- A new employee should be greeted by a group consisting of his or her boss, the secretary, several colleagues who have similar duties, and an individual located near the newcomer.
- Background information is essential when explaining anything. Include the history and personalities involved.
- Do not assume the newcomer is self-reliant. Give explicit instructions not only about objectives, but also about the process involved.
- High-context workers from abroad need to learn to ask questions outside their department and function.
- Foreign workers must make an effort to become more self-reliant.

SOURCE: Excerpted from R Drew, "Working with Foreigners," *Management Review,* September 1999, p 6.

Awkward situations such as this can be avoided when those on both sides of the context divide make good-faith attempts to understand and accommodate their counterparts (see Skills & Best Practices).

Cultural Perceptions of Time

In North American and Northern European cultures, time seems to be a simple matter. It is linear, relentlessly marching forward, never backward, in standardized chunks. To the American who received a watch for his or her third birthday, time is like money. It is spent, saved, or wasted.[38] Americans are taught to show up 10 minutes early for appointments. When working across cultures, however, time becomes a very complex matter.[39] Imagine a New Yorker's chagrin when left in a waiting room for 45 minutes, only to find a Latin American government official dealing with three other people at once. The North American resents the lack of prompt and undivided attention. The Latin American official resents the North American's impatience and apparent self-centeredness.[40] This vicious cycle of resentment can be explained by the distinction between **monochronic time** and **polychronic time:**

> The former is revealed in the ordered, precise, schedule-driven use of public time that typifies and even caricatures efficient Northern Europeans and North Americans. The latter is seen in the multiple and cyclical activities and concurrent involvement with different people in Mediterranean, Latin American, and especially Arab cultures.[41]

monochronic time
Preference for doing one thing at a time because time is limited, precisely segmented, and schedule driven.

polychronic time
Preference for doing more than one thing at a time because time is flexible and multidimensional.

A Matter of Degree Monochronic and polychronic are relative rather than absolute concepts. Generally, the more things a person tends to do at once, the more polychronic that person is.[42] Thanks to computers and advanced telecommunications systems, highly polychronic managers can engage in "multitasking."[43] For instance, it is possible to talk on the telephone, read and respond to E-mail messages, print a report, check a cell phone message, *and* eat a stale sandwich all at the same time. Unfortunately, this extreme polychronic behavior too often is not as efficient as hoped and can be very stressful. Monochronic people prefer to do one thing at a time. What is your attitude toward time?

Practical Implications Low-context cultures, such as that of the United States, tend to run on monochronic time while high-context cultures, such as that of Mexico, tend to run on polychronic time. People in polychronic cultures view time as flexible, fluid, and multidimensional. The Germans and Swiss have made an exact science of monochronic time. In fact, a radio-controlled watch made by a German company, Junghans, is "guaranteed to lose no more than one second in 1 million years."[44] Many a visitor has been a minute late for a Swiss train, only to see its taillights leaving the station. Time is more elastic in polychronic cultures. During the Islamic holy month of Ramadan in Middle Eastern nations, for example, the faithful fast during daylight hours, and the general pace of things markedly slows. Managers need to reset their mental clocks when doing business across cultures.

Leadership Lessons from the GLOBE Project

In direct contrast to the Hofstede tradition of searching for cultural differences, researchers from the GLOBE project set out to discover which, if any, attributes of leadership were universally liked or disliked. They surveyed 15,022 middle managers from 60 societies/cultures.[45] The responding managers worked for a total of 779 different organizations. Twenty-two leader attributes were found to be universally liked, 8 were universally disliked, and 35 received mixed reviews. Table 3–2 highlights the findings by listing the most liked, most disliked, and most disputed leader attributes.

This study represents a refreshing redirection in cross-cultural management research. Specifically, it stakes out some *common* cultural ground in the important area of leadership. Among the practical implications:

- According to the researchers, leader attributes associated with the charismatic/transformational leadership style, discussed in Chapter 14, are globally applicable.
- Certain leader attributes, listed in the middle column of Table 3–2, should be avoided in all cultures.

TABLE 3–2 Leader Attributes Universally Liked, Universally Disliked, and Most Strongly Disputed across 60 Cultures Worldwide

Leader Attributes Universally Liked*	Leader Attributes Universally Disliked**	Most Disputed Leader Attributes***
• Trustworthy	• Noncooperative	• Subdued
• Dynamic	• Irritable	• Intragroup conflict avoider
• Motive arouser	• Egocentric	• Cunning
• Decisive	• Ruthless	• Sensitive
• Intelligent	• Dictatorial	• Provocateur
• Dependable	• Loner/self-centered	• Self-effacing
• Plans ahead		• Willful
• Excellence oriented		
• Team builder		
• Encouraging		

Selection criteria for this table:

*Mean score of 6.14 or higher on 1–7 scale.

**Mean score of 2.06 or lower on 1–7 scale.

***Standard deviation of .84 or higher.

SOURCE: Adapted from Den Hartog et al., "Emics and Etics of Culturally-Endorsed Implicit Leadership Theories: Are Attributes of Charismatic/Transformational Leadership Universally Endorsed?" *Leadership Quarterly,* in press. This paper is available on the Web at: www.ucalgary.ca/mg/GLOBE/public/publications_2001.html

- Leader attributes that are widely disputed across cultures need to be used (or avoided) on a culture-by-culture basis. In other words, the contingency approach applies.[46]

Preparing for a Foreign Assignment

As the reach of global companies continues to grow, many opportunities for living and working in foreign countries will arise. Imagine, for example, the opportunities for foreign duty and cross-cultural experiences at Siemens, the German electronics giant. "While Siemens' corporate headquarters is near Munich, nearly 80% of the firm's business is international. Worldwide the company has 470,000 employees, including 75,000 in the United States and 25,000 in China."[47] Siemens and other global players need a vibrant and growing cadre of employees who are willing and able to do business across cultures. Thus, the purpose of this final section is to help you prepare yourself and others to work successfully in foreign countries.

Reprinted by permission of Dave Carpenter from *Harvard Business Review,* October 2003.

A Poor Track Record for American Expatriates

As we use the term here, **expatriate** refers to anyone living and/or working outside their home country. Hence, they are said to be *expatriated* when transferred to another country and *repatriated* when transferred back home. US expatriate managers usually are characterized as culturally inept and prone to failure on international assignments. Sadly, research supports this view. A pair of international management experts offered this assessment:

expatriate
Anyone living or working in a foreign country.

> Over the past decade, we have studied the management of expatriates at about 750 US, European, and Japanese companies. We asked both the expatriates themselves and the executives who sent them abroad to evaluate their experiences. In addition, we looked at what happened after expatriates returned home. . . .
>
> Overall, the results of our research were alarming. We found that between 10% and 20% of all US managers sent abroad returned early because of job dissatisfaction or difficulties in adjusting to a foreign country. Of those who stayed for the duration, nearly one-third did not perform up to the expectations of their superiors. And perhaps most problematic, one-fourth of those who completed an assignment left their company, often to join a competitor, within one year after repatriation. That's a turnover rate double that of managers who did not go abroad.[48]

Because of the high cost of sending employees and their families to foreign countries for extended periods, significant improvement is needed.

Research has uncovered specific reasons for the failure of US expatriate managers. Listed in decreasing order of frequency, the seven most common reasons are as follows:

1. The manager's spouse cannot adjust to new physical or cultural surroundings.
2. The manager cannot adapt to new physical or cultural surroundings.
3. Family problems.
4. The manager is emotionally immature.
5. The manager cannot cope with foreign duties.
6. The manager is not technically competent.
7. The manager lacks the proper motivation for a foreign assignment.[49]

Collectively, *family and personal adjustment problems,* not technical competence, are the main stumbling block for American managers working in foreign countries.

This conclusion is reinforced by the results of a survey that asked 72 human resource managers at multinational corporations to identify the most important success factor in a foreign assignment. "Nearly 35% said cultural adaptability: patience, flexibility, and tolerance for others' beliefs. Only 22% of them listed technical and management skills."[50] A recent Australian study documented how preparing the *entire family* for a foreign assignment was a key success factor.[51] Clearly, US multinational companies need to do a better job of managing the foreign assignment cycle.

Some Good News: North American Women on Foreign Assignments

Historically, a woman from the United States or Canada on a foreign assignment was a rarity. Things are changing, albeit slowly. A review of research evidence and anecdotal accounts uncovered these insights:

- The proportion of corporate women from North America on foreign assignments grew from about 3% in the early 1980s to between 11% and 15% in the late 1990s.
- Self-disqualification and management's assumption that women would not be welcome in foreign cultures—not foreign prejudice, itself—are the primary barriers for potential female expatriates.
- Expatriate North American women are viewed first and foremost by their hosts as being foreigners, and only secondarily as being female.
- North American women have a very high success rate on foreign assignments.[52]

Research shows that being an expatriate is a bigger hurdle to "fitting in" or socializing in a foreign business culture than being a woman.

Considering the rapidly growing demand for global managers, self-disqualification and management's prejudicial policies are counterproductive. Our advice to women who have their heart set on a foreign assignment: "Go for it!" (See Skills & Best Practices.)

SKILLS & BEST PRACTICES

Tips for Women (and Men) for Landing a Foreign Assignment

- While still in school, pursue foreign study opportunities and become fluent in one or more foreign languages.
- Starting with the very first job interview, clearly state your desire for a foreign assignment.
- Become very knowledgeable about foreign countries where you would like to work (take vacations there).
- Network with expatriates (both men and women) in your company to uncover foreign assignment opportunities.
- Make sure your family fully supports a foreign assignment.
- Get your boss's support by building trust and a strong working relationship.
- Be visible: make sure upper management knows about your relevant accomplishments and unique strengths.
- Stay informed about your company's international strategies and programs.
- Polish your cross-cultural communication skills daily with foreign-born co-workers.

SOURCE: Based on discussions in A Varma, L K Stroh, and L B Schmitt, "Women and International Assignments: The Impact of Supervisor-Subordinate Relationships," *Journal of World Business*, Winter 2001, pp 380-88; and T Wilen, "Women Working Overseas," *Training and Development*, May 2001, pp 120–22.

Avoiding OB Trouble Spots in the Foreign Assignment Cycle

Finding the right person (often along with a supportive and adventurous family) for a foreign position is a complex, time-consuming, and costly process.[53] For our purposes, it is sufficient to narrow the focus to common OB trouble spots in the foreign assignment cycle. As illustrated in Figure 3–2, the first and last stages of the cycle occur at home. The middle two stages occur in the foreign or host country. Each stage hides an OB-related trouble spot that needs to be anticipated and neutralized. Otherwise, the bill for another failed foreign assignment will grow.

Avoiding Unrealistic Expectations with Cross-Cultural Training Realistic job previews (RJPs) have proven effective at bringing people's unrealistic expectations about a pending job assignment down to earth by providing a realistic balance of good and bad news. People with realistic expectations tend to quit less often and be more satisfied than those with unrealistic expectations. RJPs are a must for future expatriates. In addition, cross-cultural training is required.

Cross-cultural training is any type of structured experience designed to help departing employees adjust to a foreign culture. The trend is toward more such training. Although costly, companies believe cross-cultural training is less expensive than failed foreign assignments. Programs vary widely in type and also in rigor.[54] Of course, the greater the difficulty, the greater the time and expense:

cross-cultural training
Structured experiences to help people adjust to a new culture/country.

- *Easiest.* Predeparture training is limited to informational materials, including books, lectures, films, videos, and Internet searches.
- *Moderately difficult.* Experiential training is conducted through case studies, role playing, assimilators (simulated intercultural incidents), and introductory language instruction.
- *Most difficult.* Departing employees are given some combination of the preceding methods plus comprehensive language instruction and field experience in the target culture. As an example of the latter, PepsiCo Inc. transfers "about 25 young foreign managers a year to the US for one-year assignments in bottling plants."[55]

Which approach is the best? Research to date does not offer a final answer. One study involving US employees in South Korea led the researcher to recommend a

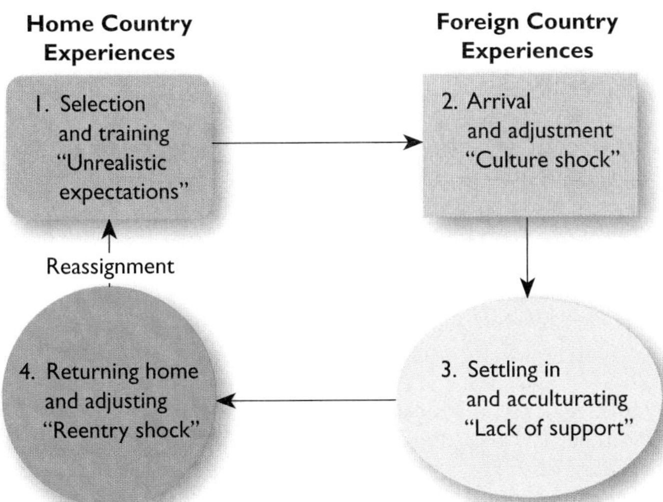

FIGURE 3–2 The Foreign Assignment Cycle (with OB Trouble Spots)

combination of informational and experiential predeparture training.[56] As a general rule of thumb, the more rigorous the cross-cultural training, the better. Our personal experience with teaching OB to foreign students both in the United States and abroad reminds us that there really is no substitute for an intimate knowledge of the local language and culture.[57]

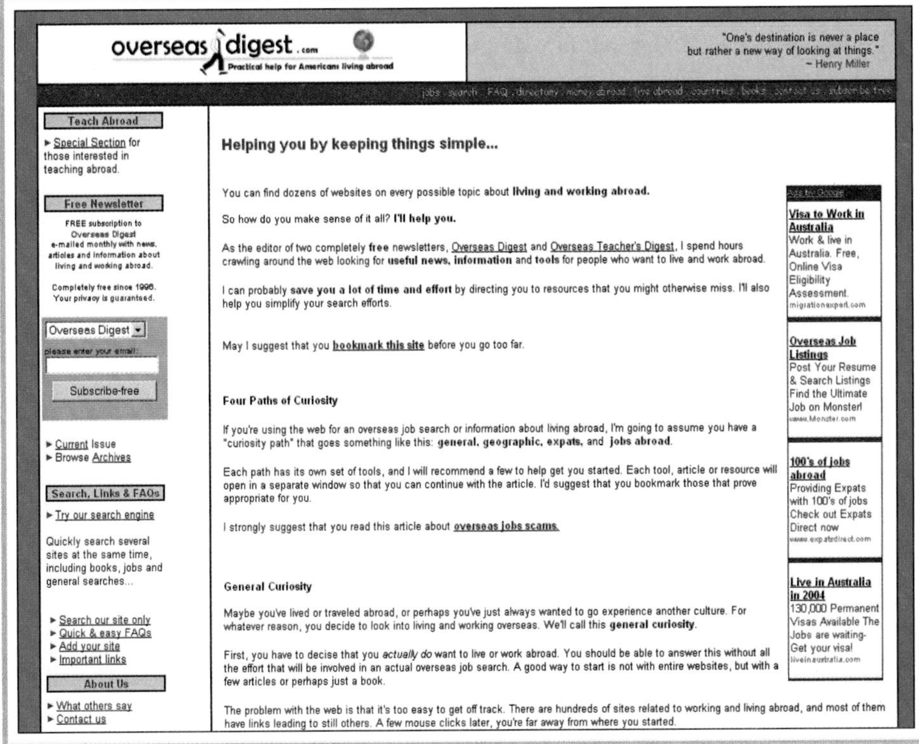

Web sites like overseasdigest.com offer tips for living and working abroad.

Avoiding Culture Shock Have you ever been in a totally unfamiliar situation and felt disoriented and perhaps a bit frightened? If so, you already know something about culture shock. According to anthropologists, **culture shock** involves anxiety and doubt caused by an overload of unfamiliar expectations and social cues.[58] For example, consider the experience of US Secretary of Labor Elaine Chao as a young immigrant unable to speak English:

culture shock

Anxiety and doubt caused by an overload of new expectations and cues.

> Chao sailed with her mother, Ruth, and two siblings in 1961 to the USA to join her father, Chinese student James Chao, when she was 8. He had come to New York three years earlier while the rest of the family waited in Taiwan until he had saved enough money to send for them. Her parents had three children in the USA; Chao is the oldest of six girls.
>
> It was a culture shock. One afternoon in October, Chao and her sisters opened the door to find other children dressed in ghost and goblin costumes, holding out bags. Believing they were being robbed, they gave the trick-or-treaters their meager weekly provisions of food, including cereal and bread.[59]

College freshmen often experience a variation of culture shock. An expatriate manager, or family member, may be thrown off balance by an avalanche of strange sights, sounds, and behaviors. Among them may be unreadable road signs, strange-tasting food, inability to use your left hand for social activities (in Islamic countries, the left hand is the toilet hand), or failure to get a laugh with your sure-fire joke. For the expatriate manager trying to concentrate on the fine details of a business negotiation, culture shock is more than an embarrassing inconvenience. It is a disaster! Like the confused college freshman who quits and goes home, culture-shocked employees often panic and go home early.

The best defense against culture shock is comprehensive cross-cultural training, including intensive language study. Once again, the only way to pick up subtle—yet important—social cues is via the local language. Quantum, the Milpitas, California, maker of computer hard-disk drives has close ties to its manufacturing partner in Japan, Matsushita-Kotobuki Electronics (MKE):

> MKE is constantly proposing changes in design that make new disk drives easier to manufacture. When the product is ready for production, 8 to 10 Quantum engineers descend on MKE's plant in western Japan for at least a month. To smooth teamwork, Quantum is offering courses in Japanese language and culture, down to mastering etiquette at a tea ceremony.[60]

This type of program reduces culture shock by taking the anxiety-producing mystery out of an unfamiliar culture.

Support During the Foreign Assignment Especially during the first six months, when everything is so new to the expatriate, a support system needs to be in place.[61] *Host-country sponsors,* assigned to individual managers or families, are recommended because they serve as "cultural seeing-eye dogs." In a foreign country, where even the smallest errand can turn into an utterly exhausting production, sponsors can get things done quickly because they know the cultural and geographical territory. Honda's Ohio employees, for example, enjoyed the help of family sponsors when training in Japan:

> Honda smoothed the way with Japanese wives who once lived in the US. They handled emergencies such as when Diana Jett's daughter Ashley needed stitches in her chin. When Task Force Senior Manager Kim Smalley's daughter, desperate to

fit in at elementary school, had to have a precisely shaped bag for her harmonica, a Japanese volunteer stayed up late to make it.[62]

Another way to support expatriates during the transition phase of a new foreign assignment is to maintain an active dialog with established *mentors* from back home. This can be accomplished via E-mail, telephone, and, when possible, an occasional face-to-face meeting.[63]

Avoiding Reentry Shock Strange as it may seem, many otherwise successful expatriate managers encounter their first major difficulty only after their foreign assignment is over. Why? Returning to one's native culture is taken for granted because it seems so routine and ordinary. But having adjusted to another country's way of doing things for an extended period of time can put one's own culture and surroundings in a strange new light. Three areas for potential reentry shock are work, social activities, and general environment (e.g., politics, climate, transportation, food). Ira Caplan's return to New York City exemplifies reentry shock:

> During the past 12 years, living mostly in Japan, he and his wife had spent their vacations cruising the Nile or trekking in Nepal. They hadn't seen much of the US. They are getting an eyeful now. . . .
>
> Prices astonish him. The obsession with crime unnerves him. What unsettles Mr Caplan more, though, is how much of himself he has left behind.
>
> In a syndrome of return no less stressful than that of departure, he feels displaced, disregarded, and diminished. . . .
>
> In an Italian restaurant, crowded at lunchtime, the waiter sets a bowl of linguine in front of him. Mr Caplan stares at it. "In Asia, we have smaller portions and smaller people," he says.
>
> Asia is on his mind. He has spent years cultivating an expertise in a region of huge importance. So what? This is New York.[64]

Work-related adjustments were found to be a major problem for samples of repatriated Finnish, Japanese, and American employees.[65] Upon being repatriated, a 12-year veteran of one US company said: "Our organizational culture was turned upside down. We now have a different strategic focus, different 'tools' to get the job done, and different buzzwords to make it happen. I had to learn a whole new corporate 'language.'"[66] Reentry shock can be reduced through employee career counseling and home-country mentors and sponsors. Simply being aware of the problem of reentry shock is a big step toward effectively dealing with it.[67]

Overall, the key to a successful foreign assignment is making it a well-integrated link in a career chain rather than treating it as an isolated adventure.

key terms

chapter summary

- *Define* ethnocentrism, *and explain what Hofstede concluded about applying American management theories in other countries.* Ethnocentrism is a prejudicial belief that one's native country, culture, language, behavior, and traditions are better than all others. Due to the wide variations in key dimensions Hofstede found among cultures, he warned against directly applying American-made management theories to other cultures without adapting them first. He said there is no one best way to manage across cultures.
- *Identify and describe the nine cultural dimensions from the GLOBE project.* (1) *Power distance*—How equally should power be distributed? (2) *Uncertainty avoidance*—How much should social norms and rules reduce uncertainty and unpredictability? (3) *Societal collectivism*—How much should loyalty to the social unit override individual interests? (4) *In-group collectivism*—How strong should one's loyalty be to family or organization? (5) *Gender egalitarianism*—How much should gender discrimination and role inequalities be minimized? (6) *Assertiveness*—How confrontational and dominant should one be in social relationships? (7) *Future orientation*—How much should one delay gratification by planning and saving for the future? (8) *Performance orientation*—How much should individuals be rewarded for improvement and excellence? (9) *Humane orientation*—How much should individuals be rewarded for being kind, fair, friendly, and generous?
- *Draw a distinction between individualistic cultures and collectivist cultures.* People in individualistic cultures think primarily in terms of "I" and "me" and place a high value on freedom and personal choice. Collectivist cultures teach people to be "we" and "us" oriented and to subordinate personal wishes and goals to the interests of the relevant social unit (such as family, group, organization, or society).
- *Demonstrate your knowledge of these two distinctions: high-context versus low-context cultures and monochronic versus polychronic cultures.* People in high-context cultures (such as China, Japan, and Mexico) derive great meaning from situational cues, above and beyond written and spoken words. Low-context cultures (including Germany, the United States, and Canada) derive key information from precise and brief written and spoken messages. In monochronic cultures (e.g., the United States), time is precise and rigidly measured. Polychronic cultures, such as those found in Latin America and the Middle East, view time as multidimensional, fluid, and flexible. Monochronic people prefer to do one thing at a time, while polychronic people like to tackle multiple tasks at the same time.
- *Explain what the GLOBE project has taught us about leadership.* Across 60 cultures, they identified three categories of leader attributes: universally liked, universally disliked, and disputed. The universally liked leader attributes—including trustworthy, dynamic, motive arouser, decisive, and intelligent—are associated with the charismatic/transformational leadership style that is widely applicable. Universally disliked leader attributes—such as noncooperative, irritable, egocentric, and dictatorial—should be avoided in all cultures. Disputed leader attributes need to be used or avoided on a culture-by-culture contingency basis.
- *Explain why US managers have a comparatively high failure rate in foreign assignments, and identify an OB trouble spot for each stage of the foreign assignment cycle.* American expatriates are troubled by family and personal adjustment problems; in other words, cultural problems, *not* technical competence problems. The four stages of the foreign assignment cycle (and OB trouble spots) are (a) selection and training (unrealistic expectations), (b) arrival and adjustment (culture shock), (c) settling in and acculturating (lack of support), and (d) returning home and adjusting (reentry shock).

discussion questions

1. Relative to the chapter-opening vignette, how should today's managers reconcile these two competing demands: (1) North American companies are being forced to off-shore work to low-wage countries because competitors are doing so and because customers demand low-cost goods and services. (2) Offshoring has become a major political issue, with companies that outsource jobs to foreign countries being called "Benedict Arnold" companies.
2. How would you describe the prevailing culture in your country to a stranger from another land, in terms of the nine GLOBE project dimensions?
3. Why are people from high-context cultures such as China and Japan likely to be misunderstood by low-context Westerners?
4. How strong is your desire for a foreign assignment? Why? If it is strong, where would you like to work?

Why? How prepared are you for a foreign assignment? What do you need to do to be better prepared?

5. What is your personal experience with culture shock? Which of the OB trouble spots in Figure 3–2 do you believe is the greatest threat to expatriate employee success? Explain.

ethical dilemma

3M Tries to Make a Difference in Russia

Russian managers aren't inclined . . . to reward people for improved performance. They spurn making investments for the future in favor of realizing immediate gains. They avoid establishing consistent business practices that can reduce uncertainty. Add in the country's high political risk and level of corruption, and it's no wonder that many multinationals have all but given up on Russia. . . .

The Russian business environment can be corrupt and dangerous; bribes and protection money are facts of life. But unlike many international companies, which try to distance themselves from such practices by simply banning them, 3M Russia actively promotes not only ethical behavior but also the personal security of its employees. . . .

3M Russia also strives to differentiate itself from competitors by being an ethical leader. For example, it holds training courses in business ethics for its customers.[68]

Should 3M Export Its American Ethical Standards to Russia?

1. If 3M doesn't like the way things are done in Russia, it shouldn't do business there. Explain your rationale.
2. 3M should do business in Russia but not meddle in Russian culture. "When in Russia, do things the Russian way." Explain your rationale.
3. 3M has a basic moral responsibility to improve the ethical climate in foreign countries where it does business. Explain your rationale.
4. 3M should find a practical middle ground between the American and Russian ways of doing business. How should that happen?
5. Invent other options. Discuss.

For an interpretation of this situation, visit our Web site, www.mhhe.kinickiob2e.

If you're looking for additional study materials, be sure to check out the Online Learning Center at

www.mhhe.com/kinickiob2e

for more information and interactivities that correspond to this chapter.

part Two

Managing Individuals

chapter Four

Understanding Social Perception and Managing Diversity

LEARNING OBJECTIVES

After reading the material in this chapter, you should be able to:

- Describe *perception* in terms of the social information processing model.
- Identify and briefly explain four managerial implications of social perception.
- Explain, according to Kelley's model, how external and internal causal attributions are formulated.
- Demonstrate your familiarity with the demographic trends that are creating an increasingly diverse workforce.
- Identify the barriers and challenges to managing diversity.
- Discuss the organizational practices used to manage diversity identified by Ann Morrison.

EMPLOYEES USE COSMETIC SURGERY TO IMPROVE THEIR IMAGE

When the executive in the adjacent office returns from a two-week vacation minus any bags under his eyes or deep lines around his mouth, forget what he tells you about a certain Caribbean resort. Chances are, he has been under the knife.

Cosmetic surgery, botox and other de-aging skin treatments are becoming de rigueur for baby-boomer executives of both sexes who fear being judged as over the hill. For many, including some top CEOs who haven't yet gone public, plastic surgery is the next step in their rigorous fitness and beauty regimens that include several hours a week at the gym, expensive personal trainers and diet consultants, and hair treatments. "I can't tell you the number of men I know who no longer are gray or who have covered bald spots with hair transplants," says Pat Cook, president of Cook & Co., a Bronxville, N.Y., executive-search firm.

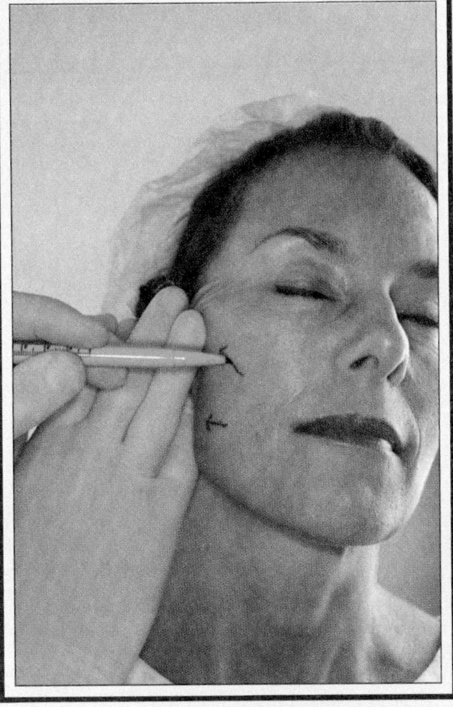

In addition to vanity, these executives are driven by job insecurity. They believe that looking older in business now means looking vulnerable, not wise and experienced, as might have been the case in the past. So many 50-something managers have suffered layoffs and early retirement that survivors in this age bracket feel pressured to look and act as young as possible to hang onto their posts. And even 45-year-olds who are unemployed in today's tight market worry that wrinkles will cut them out of the running.

They ignore the financial expense (work on eyelids costs $3,000 to $6,000 and facelifts, $15,000 to $25,000) and the medical risks (Novelist Olivia Goldsmith died last month at the age of 54 during a chin-tuck operation).

A recent survey of senior executives by ExecuNet, a networking and job-search service, found that 82% consider age bias a "serious problem," up from 78% three years ago. And 94% of these respondents, who were mostly in their 40s and 50s, said they thought age had cost them a shot at a particular job.

"Ageism is unfortunate but it exists, and if you aren't looking good, you aren't a player, especially now when so many companies are run by younger executives," says Rick Miners, president of FlexCorp Systems, a New York business-process outsourcing company. "It isn't only women waiting for appointments with cosmetic surgeons, it's a lot of men, too, and not just senior executives but middle managers who want to stay competitive." . . .

It isn't something most executives want to discuss publicly, however. A 56-year-old public-relations manager at a New Jersey technology company, who had his lower eyelids done last April, says he was delighted when colleagues told him he looked more rested than they had ever seen him. But he didn't counter their belief that he had just returned from a cruise. "I didn't want to call attention to my age by saying I needed this to look younger," he says. But his new look has given him more confidence at work, prompting him to volunteer for new projects, he adds.

Even more executives are choosing less expensive and less invasive treatments, such as botox injections, which average several hundred dollars per session. Dr. Diana Bihova, a New York dermatologist, *says 40% of her patients seeking botox and other cosmetic treatments, including chemical peels and collagen, are now men. . . .*

A major focus for both sexes is removing frown lines between the brows or on the forehead. One woman claimed that losing her worried look helped her land a new job.

Looking younger, however, isn't the most crucial way to counter ageism on the job. Managers who don't repeatedly rejuvenate their thinking—failing to stay informed about current events and popular culture—inevitably date themselves and limit their chances to advance.[1]

FOR DISCUSSION

Would you go under the knife in order to enhance your career opportunities? Why or why not? For an interpretation of this case and additional comments, visit our Online Learning Center:

www.mhhe.com/kinickiob2e

HOW IMPORTANT IS THE perception process? As highlighted in the chapter opening vignette, perception is important enough that people are using cosmetic surgery to change the way they are perceived by others. Our perceptions and feelings are influenced by information we receive from newspapers, magazines, television, radio, family, and friends. You see, we all use information stored in our memories to interpret the world around us, and our interpretations, in turn, influence how we respond and interact with others. As human beings, we constantly strive to make sense of our surroundings. The resulting knowledge influences our behavior and helps us navigate our way through life. Think of the perceptual process that occurs when meeting someone for the first time. Your attention is drawn to the individual's physical appearance, mannerisms, actions, and reactions to what you say and do. You ultimately arrive at conclusions based on your perceptions of this social interaction. The brown-haired, green-eyed individual turns out to be friendly and fond of outdoor activities. You further conclude that you like this person and then ask him or her to go to a concert, calling the person by the name you stored in memory.

This reciprocal process of perception, interpretation, and behavioral response also applies at work. Consider the situation faced by Stephanie Odle and other women employed at Wal-Mart. Stephanie's job perceptions changed after she found a W-2 lying around in the Riverside, Calif., Sam's Club where she worked as an assistant manager.

> The W-2 belonged to a male assistant manager who turned out to be making $10,000 more a year than she was. She says she was told that her co-worker was paid more because he had "a wife and kids to support." When the single mother protested, she was asked to submit a personal household budget. She did and was granted a $40 a week raise. "It was humiliating," says Odle. And she was still making less than the male manager. Odle claims that she was eventually fired for speaking up. . . .
>
> Other women tell stories of management trips to strip clubs and business meetings at Hooters. One was allegedly advised that if she wanted a better job she needed to "doll up" more and "blow the cobwebs from her makeup."[2]

Stephanie Odle and a host of other women are suing Wal-Mart because they perceive the company is discriminating. In contrast, the company perceives that it fairly compensates women and men and that the organization treats its employees with dignity: a fundamental component of Wal-Mart's organizational culture. This example illustrates the interplay between perceptual processes and managing diverse employees.

Managing diversity is a sensitive, potentially volatile, and sometimes uncomfortable issue. Yet managers are required to deal with it in the name of organizational survival. Accordingly, the purpose of this chapter is to enhance your understanding of the perceptual process and how it influences the manner in which managers manage diversity. We begin by focusing on a social information processing model of perception and then discuss the perceptual outcome of causal attributions. Next, we define diversity and describe the organizational practices used to manage diversity effectively.

FIGURE 4–1 Social Perception: A Social Information Processing Model

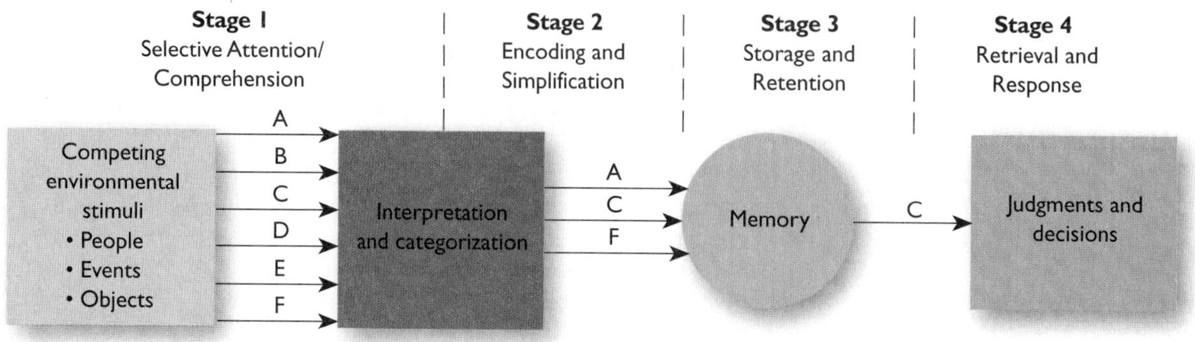

SOURCE: R Kreitner and A Kinicki, *Organizational Behavior* (6th ed) (McGraw-Hill), p 225.

A Social Information Processing Model of Perception

perception

Process of interpreting one's environment.

Perception is a cognitive process that enables us to interpret and understand our surroundings. Recognition of objects is one of this process's major functions. For example, both people and animals recognize familiar objects in their environments. You would recognize a picture of your best friend; dogs and cats can recognize their food dishes or a favorite toy. Reading involves recognition of visual patterns representing letters in the alphabet. People must recognize objects to meaningfully interact with their environment. But since OB's principal focus is on people, the following discussion emphasizes *social* perception rather than object perception.

Social perception involves a four-stage information processing sequence (hence, the label "social information processing"). Figure 4–1 illustrates a basic social information processing model. Three of the stages in this model—selective attention/comprehension, encoding and simplification, and storage and retention—describe how specific social information is observed and stored in memory. The fourth and final stage, retrieval and response, involves turning mental representations into real-world judgments and decisions.

Keep the following everyday example in mind as we look at the four stages of social perception. Suppose you were thinking of taking a course in, say, personal finance. Three professors teach the same course, using different types of instruction and testing procedures. Through personal experience, you have come to prefer good professors who rely on the case method of instruction and essay tests. According to social perception theory, you would likely arrive at a decision regarding which professor to take following the steps outlined in the following sections.

Stage 1: Selective Attention/Comprehension

People are constantly bombarded by physical and social stimuli in the environment. Because they do not have the mental capacity to fully comprehend all this information, they selectively perceive subsets of environmental stimuli. This is where attention plays a role. **Attention** is the process of becoming consciously aware of something or someone. Attention can be focused on information either from the environment or from memory. Regarding the latter situation, if you sometimes find yourself thinking about totally unrelated events or people while reading a textbook, your memory is the focus of your attention. Research has shown that people tend to pay attention to salient stimuli.

attention

Being consciously aware of something or someone.

Salient Stimuli Somethings is *salient* when it stands out from its context. For example, a 250-pound man would certainly be salient in a women's aerobics class but not at a meeting of the National Football League Players' Association. One's needs and goals often dictate which stimuli are salient. For a driver whose gas gauge is on empty, an Exxon or Shell sign is more salient than a McDonald's or Burger King sign. The reverse would be true for a hungry driver with a full gas tank. Moreover, research shows that people have a tendency to pay more attention to negative than positive information. This leads to a negativity bias.[3] This bias helps explain the gawking factor that slows traffic to a crawl following a car accident.

If you're reading this textbook late at night and having a munchie attack, this photo might have caught your attention before anything else on the page. It's an example of *salient* stimuli, or something that stands out from its context. The context for this example is the text on this page. One's needs or goals often affect what stimuli are salient. If you're having a munchie attack, a Whopper would be *very* salient right now.

Back to Our Example You begin your search for the "right" personal finance professor by asking friends who have taken classes from the three professors. You also may interview the various professors who teach the class to gather still more relevant information. Returning to Figure 4–1, all the information you obtain represents competing environmental stimuli labeled A through F. Because you are concerned about the method of instruction (e.g., line A in Figure 4–1), testing procedures (e.g., line C), and past grade distributions (e.g., line F), information in those areas is particularly salient to you. Figure 4–1 shows that these three salient pieces of information thus are perceived, and you then progress to the second stage of information processing. Meanwhile, competing stimuli represented by lines B, D, and E in Figure 4–1 fail to get your attention and are discarded from further consideration.

Stage 2: Encoding and Simplification

Observed information is not stored in memory in its original form. Encoding is required; raw information is interpreted or translated into mental representations. To accomplish this, perceivers assign pieces of information to **cognitive categories.** "By *category* we mean a number of objects that are considered equivalent. Categories are generally designated by names, e.g., *dog, animal.*"[4] People, events, and objects are interpreted and evaluated by comparing their characteristics with information contained in schemata (or schema in singular form).

cognitive categories

Mental depositories for storing information.

Schema According to social information processing theory, a **schema** represents a person's mental picture or summary of a particular event or type of stimulus.[5] For example, picture your image of a sports

schema

Mental picture of an event or object.

car. Does it contain a smaller vehicle with two doors? Is it red? If you answered yes, you would tend to classify all small, two-door, fire-engine-red vehicles as sports cars because this type of car possesses characteristics that are consistent with your "sports car schema."

stereotype

Beliefs about the characteristics of a group.

Stereotypes Are Used During Encoding People use stereotypes during encoding in order to organize and simplify social information.[6] "A **stereotype** is an individual's set of beliefs about the characteristics or attributes of a group."[7] Stereotypes are not always negative. For example, the belief that engineers are good at math is certainly part of a stereotype. Stereotypes may or may not be accurate. Engineers may in fact be better at math than the general population. In general, stereotypic characteristics are used to differentiate a particular group of people from other groups.

Unfortunately, stereotypes can lead to poor decisions; can create barriers for women, older individuals, people of color, and people with disabilities; and can undermine loyalty and job satisfaction. For example, a study of 44 African-American managers and 80 white managers revealed that African-American managers experienced slower rates of promotion and less psychological support than white managers.[8] It thus is not surprising that the turnover rate for African-American executives is 40% higher than for their white counterparts.[9] Another sample of 69 female executives and 69 male executives indicated women reported greater promotional barriers and fewer overseas assignments, and had more assignments with nonauthority relationships than men.[10]

Stereotyping is a four-step process. It begins by categorizing people into groups according to various criteria, such as gender, age, race, and occupation. Next, we infer that all people within a particular category possess the same traits or characteristics (e.g., all women are nurturing, older people have more job-related accidents, all African-Americans are good athletes, all professors are absentminded). Then, we form expectations of others and interpret their behavior according to our stereotypes. Finally, stereotypes are maintained by (1) overestimating the frequency of stereotypic behaviors exhibited by others, (2) incorrectly explaining expected and unexpected behaviors, and (3) differentiating minority individuals from oneself.[11] Although these steps are self-reinforcing, there are ways to break the chain of stereotyping.

Research shows that the use of stereotypes is influenced by the amount and type of information available to an individual and his or her motivation to accurately process information.[12] People are less apt to use stereotypes to judge others when they encounter salient information that is highly inconsistent with a stereotype. For instance, you are unlikely to assign stereotypic "professor" traits to a new professor you have this semester if he or she rides a Harley-Davidson, wears leather pants to class, and has a pierced nose. People also are less likely to rely on stereotypes when they are motivated to avoid using them. That is, accurate information processing requires mental effort. Stereotyping is generally viewed as a less effortful strategy of information processing.

Encoding Outcomes We use the encoding process to interpret and evaluate our environment. Interestingly, this process can result in differing interpretations and evaluations of the same person or event. Table 4–1 describes five common perceptual errors that influence our judgments about others. Because these perceptual errors often distort the evaluation of job applicants and of employee performance, managers need to guard against them.

Commonly Found Perceptual Errors **TABLE 4–1**

Perceptual Error	Description	Example
Halo	A rater forms an overall impression about an object and then uses that impression to bias ratings about the object.	Rating a professor high on the teaching dimensions of ability to motivate students, knowledge, and communication because we like him or her.
Leniency	A personal characteristic that leads an individual to consistently evaluate other people or objects in an extremely positive fashion.	Rating a professor high on all dimensions of performance regardless of his or her actual performance. The rater who hates to say negative things about others.
Central tendency	The tendency to avoid all extreme judgments and rate people and objects as average or neutral.	Rating a professor average on all dimensions of performance regardless of his or her actual performance.
Recency effects	The tendency to remember recent information. If the recent information is negative, the person or object is evaluated negatively.	Although a professor has given good lectures for 12 to 15 weeks, he or she is evaluated negatively because lectures over the last 3 weeks were done poorly.
Contrast effects	The tendency to evaluate people or objects by comparing them with characteristics of recently observed people or objects.	Rating a good professor as average because you compared his or her performance with three of the best professors you have ever had in college. You are currently taking courses from the three excellent professors.

Back to Our Example Having collected relevant information about the three personal finance professors and their approaches, you compare this information with other details contained in schemata. This leads you to form an impression and evaluation of what it would be like to take a course from each professor. In turn, the relevant information contained on paths A, C, and F in Figure 4–1 are passed along to the third stage of information processing.

Stage 3: Storage and Retention

This phase involves storage of information in long-term memory. Long-term memory is like an apartment complex consisting of separate units connected to one another. Although different people live in each apartment, they sometimes interact. In addition, large apartment complexes have different wings (such as A, B, and C). Long-term memory similarly consists of separate but related categories. Like the individual apartments inhabited by unique residents, the connected categories contain different types of information. Information also passes among these categories. Finally, long-term memory is made up of three compartments (or wings) containing categories of information about events, semantic materials, and people.[13]

Event Memory This compartment is composed of categories containing information about both specific and general events. These memories describe appropriate sequences of events in well-known situations, such as going to a restaurant, going on a job interview, going to a food store, or going to a movie.[14]

Semantic Memory Semantic memory refers to general knowledge about the world. In so doing, it functions as a mental dictionary of concepts. Each concept contains a definition (e.g., a good leader) and associated traits (outgoing), emotional states (happy), physical characteristics (tall), and behaviors (works hard). Just as there are schemata for general events, concepts in semantic memory are stored as schemata. Given our previous discussion of international OB in Chapter 3, it should come as no surprise that there are cultural differences in the type of information stored in semantic memory.

Person Memory Categories within this compartment contain information about a single individual (your supervisor) or groups of people (managers).

Back to Our Example As the time draws near for you to decide which personal finance professor to take, your schemata of them are stored in the three categories of long-term memory. These schemata are available for immediate comparison and/or retrieval.

Stage 4: Retrieval and Response

People retrieve information from memory when they make judgments and decisions. Our ultimate judgments and decisions are either based on the process of drawing on, interpreting, and integrating categorical information stored in long-term memory or on retrieving a summary judgment that was already made.[15]

Concluding our example, it is registration day and you have to choose which professor to take for personal finance. After retrieving from memory your schemata-based impressions of the three professors, you select a good one who uses the case method and gives essay tests (line C in Figure 4–1). In contrast, you may choose your preferred professor by simply recalling the decision you made two weeks ago.

Managerial Implications

Social cognition is the window through which we all observe, interpret, and prepare our responses to people and events. A wide variety of managerial activities, organizational processes, and quality-of-life issues are thus affected by perception. Consider, for example, the following implications.

"Actually, I'm the CEO of a very successful company. I just don't like being hassled about my salary."

Hiring Interviewers make hiring decisions based on their impression of how an applicant fits the perceived requirements of a job. Inaccurate impressions in either direction produce poor hiring decisions. Moreover, interviewers with racist or sexist schemata can undermine the accuracy and legality of hiring decisions. Those invalid schemata need to be confronted and improved through coaching and training. Failure to do so can lead to poor hiring decisions. For example, a study of 46 male and 66 female financial institution managers revealed that their hiring decisions were biased by the physical attractiveness of applicants. More attractive men and women were hired over less attractive applicants with equal qualifications.[16] On the positive side, however, a study demonstrated that interviewer training can reduce the use of invalid schema. Training improved interviewers' ability to obtain high-quality, job-related information and to stay focused on the interview task. Trained interviewers provided more balanced judgments about applicants than did nontrained interviewers.[17]

Performance Appraisal Faulty schemata about what constitutes good versus poor performance can lead to inaccurate performance appraisals, which erode work motivation, commitment, and loyalty. For example, a study of 166 production employees indicated that they had greater trust in management when they perceived that the performance appraisal process provided accurate evaluations of their performance.[18] Therefore, it is important for managers to accurately identify the behavioral characteristics and results indicative of good performance at the beginning of a performance review cycle. These characteristics then can serve as the benchmarks for evaluating employee performance. The importance of using objective rather than subjective measures of employee performance was highlighted in a meta-analysis involving 50 studies and 8,341 individuals. Results revealed that objective and subjective measures of employee performance were only moderately related. The researchers concluded that objective and subjective measures of performance are not interchangeable.[19] Managers are thus advised to use more objectively based measures of performance as much as possible because subjective indicators are prone to bias and inaccuracy. In those cases where the job does not possess objective measures of performance, however, managers should still use subjective evaluations. Furthermore, because memory for specific instances of employee performance deteriorates over time, managers need a mechanism for accurately recalling employee behavior. Research reveals that individuals can be trained to be more accurate raters of performance.[20]

Carolyn Kepcher, Trump's right-hand woman on *The Apprentice,* told the women in one episode that she "wanted to see less sexuality and more 'smarts.'" Not long after the show was over, some of these same women posed rather scantily clad for a magazine. Do you think it was in their best interest to do this? Do you still "take them seriously" as effective and successful businesswomen?

Leadership Research demonstrates that employees' evaluations of leader effectiveness are influenced strongly by their schemata of good and poor leaders. A leader will have a difficult time influencing employees when he or she exhibits behaviors contained in employees' schemata of poor leaders. A team of researchers investigated the behaviors contained in our schemata of good and poor leaders. Good leaders were perceived as exhibiting the following behaviors: (1) assigning specific tasks to group members, (2) telling others that they had done well, (3) setting specific goals for the group, (4) letting other group members make decisions, (5) trying to get the group to work as a team, and (6) maintaining definite standards of performance. In contrast, poor leaders

SKILLS & BEST PRACTICES

Avoid Four Behavioral Tendencies That Are Negatively Perceived When Trying to Sell or Pitch an Idea

1. **Being a pushover.** This tendency involves giving up on an idea rather than defending it. Be prepared to defend your ideas with facts, figures, and passion. Do not simply drop an idea because someone questions it.
2. **Being a robot.** This tendency involves a communication style and approach that is too formulaic. When answering questions about your ideas, do not use canned answers. Rather, first try to understand the other individual's point of view or source of confusion/resistance. You then can provide an answer that specifically responds to the person's concerns.
3. **Being a used-car salesman.** This tendency involves being pushy, close-minded, and argumentative. Remember, you can catch more bees with honey than with vinegar.
4. **Being a charity case.** This tendency is characterized by desperation and pleading.

SOURCE: Reprinted by permission of *Harvard Business Review.* This information was derived from K D Elsbach, "How to Pitch a Brilliant Idea," *Harvard Business Review,* September 2003, p 119.

were perceived to exhibit these behaviors: (1) telling others that they had performed poorly, (2) insisting on having their own way, (3) doing things without explaining themselves, (4) expressing worry over the group members' suggestions, (5) frequently changing plans, and (6) letting the details of the task become overwhelming.[21]

Communication and Interpersonal Influence

Managers must remember that social perception is a screening process that can distort communication, both coming and going. Because people interpret oral and written communications by using schemata developed through past experiences, your ability to influence others is affected by information contained in others' schemata regarding age, gender, ethnicity, appearance, speech, mannerisms, personality, and other personal characteristics. It is important to keep this in mind when trying to influence others or when trying to sell your ideas. For example, consider the advice that Carolyn Kepcher, chief operating officer for Trump Industries and advisor to the reality show *The Apprentice,* gave to the women on one episode who were trying to win a job working for Donald Trump. "Kepcher told the women she wanted to see less sexuality and more 'smarts.'"[22] She perceived that the women were using risqué clothing rather than intelligence in order to gain an advantage over their male competitors, and she viewed this behavior as unprofessional. The Skills & Best Practices identifies four behavioral tendencies that are negatively perceived by others when trying to pitch or sell them an idea. Avoiding these tendencies can help you to achieve greater acceptance of your ideas or opinions.

Causal Attributions

Attribution theory is based on the premise that people attempt to infer causes for observed behavior. Rightly or wrongly, we constantly formulate cause-and-effect explanations for our own and others' behavior. Attributional statements such as the following are common: "Joe drinks too much because he has no willpower; but I need a couple of drinks after work because I'm under a lot of pressure." Formally defined, **causal attributions** are suspected or inferred causes of behavior. Even though our causal attributions tend to be self-serving and are often invalid, it is important to understand how people formulate attributions because they profoundly affect organizational behavior. For example, a supervisor who attributes an employee's poor performance to a lack of effort might reprimand that individual. However, training might be deemed necessary if the supervisor attributes the poor performance to a lack of ability.

causal attributions
Suspected or inferred causes of behavior.

Generally speaking, people formulate causal attributions by considering the events preceding an observed behavior. This section introduces Harold Kelley's model of attribution and two important attributional tendencies.

FIGURE 4–2 Performance Charts Showing Low and High Consensus, Distinctiveness, and Consistency Information

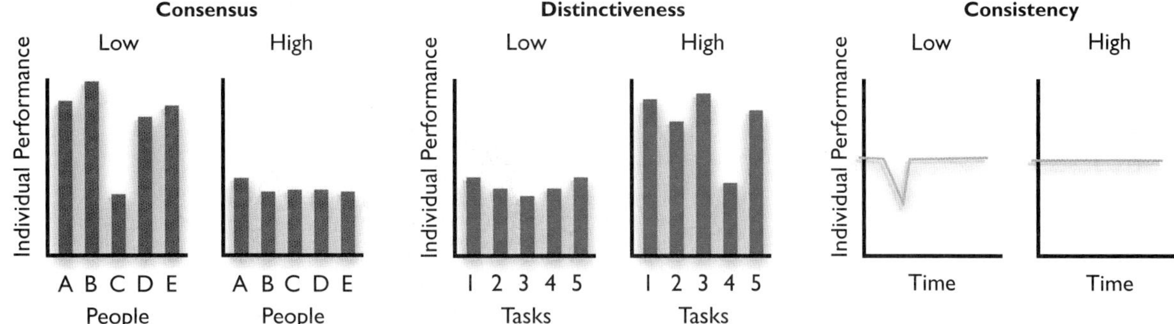

SOURCE: K A Brown, "Explaining Group Poor Performance: An Attributional Analysis," *Academy of Management Review,* January 1984, p 56. Copyright 2001 by Academy of Management. Reproduced with permission of Academy of Management via Copyright Clearance Center.

Kelley's Model of Attribution

Current models of attribution, such as Kelley's, are based on the pioneering work of the late Fritz Heider. Heider, the founder of attribution theory, proposed that behavior can be attributed either to **internal factors** within a person (such as ability) or to **external factors** within the environment (such as a difficult task). Building on Heider's work, Kelley attempted to pinpoint major antecedents of internal and external attributions. Kelley hypothesized that people make causal attributions after gathering information about three dimensions of behavior: consensus, distinctiveness, and consistency.[23] These dimensions vary independently, thus forming various combinations and leading to differing attributions.

internal factors
Personal characteristics that cause behavior.

external factors
Environmental characteristics that cause behavior.

Figure 4–2 presents performance charts showing low versus high consensus, distinctiveness, and consistency. These charts are now used to help develop a working knowledge of all three dimensions in Kelley's model.

- *Consensus* involves a comparison of an individual's behavior with that of his or her peers. There is high consensus when one acts like the rest of the group and low consensus when one acts differently. As shown in Figure 4–2, high consensus is indicated when persons A, B, C, D, and E obtain similar levels of individual performance. In contrast, person C's performance is low in consensus because it significantly varies from the performance of persons A, B, D, and E.
- *Distinctiveness* is determined by comparing a person's behavior on one task with his or her behavior on other tasks. High distinctiveness means the individual has performed the task in question in a significantly different manner than he or she has performed other tasks. Low distinctiveness means stable performance or quality from one task to another. Figure 4–2 reveals that the employee's performance on task 4 is highly distinctive because it significantly varies from his or her performance on tasks 1, 2, 3, and 5.
- *Consistency* is determined by judging if the individual's performance on a given task is consistent over time. High consistency implies that a person performs a certain task the same, time after time. Unstable performance of a given task

over time would mean low consistency. The downward spike in performance depicted in the consistency graph of Figure 4–2 represents low consistency. In this case, the employee's performance on a given task varied over time.

It is important to remember that consensus relates to other *people,* distinctiveness relates to other *tasks,* and consistency relates to *time.* The question now is: How does information about these three dimensions of behavior lead to internal or external attributions?

Kelley hypothesized that people attribute behavior to *external* causes (environmental factors) when they perceive high consensus, high distinctiveness, and low consistency. *Internal* attributions (personal factors) tend to be made when observed behavior is characterized by low consensus, low distinctiveness, and high consistency. So, for example, when all employees are performing poorly (high consensus), when the poor performance occurs on only one of several tasks (high distinctiveness), and the poor performance occurs during only one time period (low consistency), a supervisor will probably attribute an employee's poor performance to an external source such as peer pressure or an overly difficult task. In contrast, performance will be attributed to an employee's personal characteristics (an internal attribution) when only the individual in question is performing poorly (low consensus), when the inferior performance is found across several tasks (low distinctiveness), and when the low performance has persisted over time (high consistency). Many studies supported this predicted pattern of attributions.[24]

Attributional Tendencies

Researchers have uncovered two attributional tendencies that distort one's interpretation of observed behavior—*fundamental attribution bias* and *self-serving bias.*

fundamental attribution bias

Ignoring environmental factors that affect behavior.

Fundamental Attribution Bias The **fundamental attribution bias** reflects one's tendency to attribute another person's behavior to his or her personal characteristics, as opposed to situational factors. This bias causes perceivers to ignore important environmental forces that often significantly affect behavior. For example, a study of 1,420 employees of a large utility company demonstrated that supervisors tended to make more internal attributions about worker accidents than did the workers. Interestingly, research also shows that people from Westernized cultures tend to exhibit the fundamental attribution bias more than individuals from East Asia.[25]

self-serving bias

Taking more personal responsibility for success than failure.

Self-Serving Bias The **self-serving bias** represents one's tendency to take more personal responsibility for success than for failure. The self-serving bias suggests employees will attribute their success to internal factors (high ability or hard work) and their failures to uncontrollable external factors (tough job, bad luck, unproductive co-workers, or an unsympathetic boss). For example, after losing to the US hockey team in the 2002 winter Olympics, Russian hockey coach Slava Fetisov blamed the referees and the disparity in penalties for his team's loss. He also "leveled charges of conspiracy, saying the tournament was 'designed to have a final with Canada and the US, and you have this final.'"[26]

Managerial Application and Implications Attribution models can be used to explain how managers handle poorly performing employees. One study revealed that managers gave employees more immediate, frequent, and negative feedback when they attributed their performance to low effort. This reaction was even more pronounced when the manager's success was dependent on an employee's performance. A second study indicated that managers tended to transfer employees whose poor performance was attributed to a lack of ability. These same managers also decided to take no immediate action when poor performance was attributed to external factors beyond an individual's control.[27]

The preceding situations have several important implications for managers. First, managers tend to disproportionately attribute behavior to *internal* causes.[28] This can result in inaccurate evaluations of performance, leading to reduced employee motivation. No one likes to be blamed because of factors they perceive to be beyond their control. Further, because managers' responses to employee performance vary according to their attributions, attributional biases may lead to inappropriate managerial actions, including promotions, transfers, layoffs, and so forth. This can dampen motivation and performance. Attributional training sessions for managers are in order. Basic attributional processes can be explained, and managers can be taught to detect and avoid attributional biases. Finally, an employee's attributions for his or her own performance have dramatic effects on subsequent motivation, performance, and personal attitudes such as self-esteem. For instance, people tend to give up, develop lower expectations for future success, and experience decreased self-esteem when they attribute failure to a lack of ability. In contrast, employees are more likely to display high performance and job satisfaction when they attribute success to internal factors such as ability and effort.[29] Fortunately, attributional realignment can improve both motivation and performance.

The goal of attributional realignment is to shift failure attributions away from ability and towards attributions of low effort or some other external cause (e.g., lack of resources). Dennis Green, the new head coach of the Arizona Cardinals NFL football team, is trying to use attributional realignment to motivate his players. After taking over leadership of a team that won 4 and lost 12 in 2003, Green concluded, "I think you want to convince them [the players] that they are good, that they're (just) not playing good."[30] Dennis Green clearly is attempting to shift the players' attributions for their losses from a lack of ability to a lack of effort. Based on past research, this attributional shift should pave the way for improved motivation and performance among the team's players. Time will tell.

Defining and Managing Diversity

diversity

The host of individual differences that make people different from and similar to each other.

Diversity represents the multitude of individual differences and similarities that exist among people.[31] This definition underscores a key issue about managing diversity. There are many different dimensions or components of diversity. This implies that diversity pertains to everybody. It is not an issue of age, race, or gender. It is not an issue of being heterosexual, gay, or lesbian or of being Catholic, Jewish, Protestant, or Muslim. Diversity also does not pit white males against all other groups of people. Diversity pertains to the host of individual differences that make all of us unique and different from others.

This section begins our journey into managing diversity by first reviewing the key dimensions of diversity. Because many people associate diversity with affirmative action, we then compare affirmative action with managing diversity. Next, we review the demographic trends that are creating an increasingly diverse workforce.

FIGURE 4–3 The Four Layers of Diversity

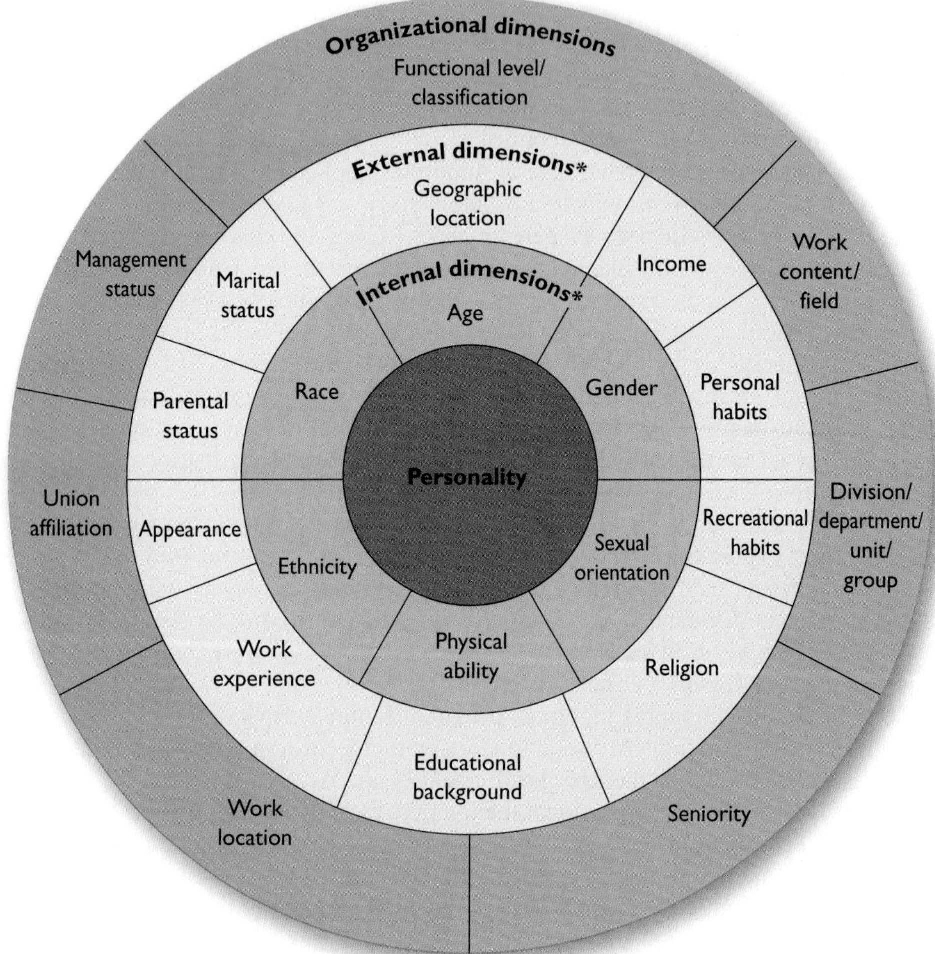

*Internal Dimensions and External Dimensions are adapted from Loden and Rosener, *Workforce America!* (Homewood, IL: Business One Irwin, 1991).

SOURCE: From L Gardenswartz and A Rowe, *Diverse Teams at Work: Capitalizing on the Power of Diversity,* 1994, 2003, p 33. Published by the Society for Human Resource Management. Reprinted with permission.

This section concludes by describing the organizational practices used to effectively manage diversity.

Layers of Diversity

Like seashells on a beach, people come in a variety of shapes, sizes, and colors. This variety represents the essence of diversity. Lee Gardenswartz and Anita Rowe, a team of diversity experts, identified four layers of diversity to help distinguish the important ways in which people differ (see Figure 4–3). Taken together, these layers define your personal identity and influence how each of us sees the world.[32]

Figure 4–3 shows that personality is at the center of the diversity wheel. Personality is at the center because it represents a stable set of characteristics that is responsible for a person's identity: The dimensions of personality are discussed later in

Chapter 5. The next layer of diversity consists of a set of internal dimensions that are referred to as the primary dimensions of diversity.[33] These dimensions, for the most part, are not within our control, but strongly influence our attitudes and expectations and assumptions about others, which, in turn, influence our behavior. Take the encounter experienced by an African-American woman in middle management while vacationing at a resort:

> While she was sitting by the pool, "a large 50-ish white male approached me and demanded that I get him extra towels. I said, 'Excuse me?' He then said, 'Oh, you don't work here,' with no shred of embarrassment or apology in his voice."[34]

Stereotypes regarding one or more of the primary dimensions of diversity most likely influenced this man's behavior toward the woman.

Figure 4–3 reveals that the next layer of diversity is composed of external influences, which are referred to as secondary dimensions of diversity. They represent individual differences that we have a greater ability to influence or control. Examples include where you grew up and live today, your religious affiliation, whether you are married and have children, and your work experiences. These dimensions also exert a significant influence on our perceptions, behavior, and attitudes.

Consider religion as an illustration. Given that Islam is expected to surpass Judaism as the second-most commonly practiced religion in the United States (Christianity is first), organizations need to consider Muslim employees when implementing their policies, procedures, and programs. Argenbright Security Inc. in Atlanta created problems for itself when management sent home seven Muslim women for wearing Islamic headscarves at their security jobs at Dulles International Airport. Because wearing headscarves in no way affected their job performance, the company had to reimburse the women for back pay and other relief in a settlement negotiated with the Equal Employment Opportunity Commission.[35] In contrast, Ford Motor Co. proactively conducted a series of Islam 101 training sessions in Dearborn, Michigan, after the September 11 terrorist attacks. They did this because the Dearborn area is home to one of the largest Arab-American and Middle Eastern communities in the United States and the company wanted to raise awareness about the Islamic faith.[36]

As you can see from these examples, an organization's level of awareness about the external layer of diversity can cause either negative or positive feelings among employees. The final layer of diversity includes organizational dimensions such as seniority, job title and function, and work location.

Affirmative Action and Managing Diversity

Effectively managing diversity requires organizations to adopt a new way of thinking about differences among people. Rather than pitting one group against another, managing diversity entails recognition of the unique contribution every employee can make. As found at Designer Blinds, a 170-employee company located in Omaha, Nebraska, with a turnover rate of 167%, effectively managing diversity can lower turnover and increase productivity and quality.

> Top managers began by viewing recruiting and retention strategically and quantitatively. An entirely new approach to hiring was launched. One aspect was networking with representatives of various cultures, including the local Sudanese community, which had not been well represented in the workforce. Company supervisors and coworkers studied the culture and embraced it. The firm also

> identified Hispanics as the fastest-growing group in the area and made a sincere effort to welcome members of the community and to provide English-as-a-second-language classes.
>
> The diversification of the workplace has produced good results for several years, especially the last two. Employee efficiency and productivity is skyrocketing, quality is a benchmark for the industry, and turnover has plunged from stratospheric highs to 8 percent a year.[37]

The management philosophies used at Designer Blinds earned the company the 2003 Optimas Award for excellence in people management and are much different from the management philosophies associated with affirmative action. This section highlights the differences between affirmative action and managing diversity.

affirmative action

Voluntary and involuntary efforts to achieve equality of opportunity for everyone.

Affirmative Action **Affirmative action** represents "voluntary and mandatory efforts undertaken by federal, state, and local governments; private employers; and schools to combat discrimination and to promote equal opportunity in education and employment for all."[38] Affirmative action is proactive. That is, the goal of affirmative action is to eliminate discrimination and to create equal opportunity for everyone. According to a variety of Equal Employment Opportunity laws, it is illegal to discriminate on the basis of race, color, religion, gender, national origin, age, religious affiliation, and physical abilities. Affirmative action, however, does not legitimize quotas. Quotas are illegal. They can only be imposed by judges who conclude that a company has engaged in discriminatory practices. It also is important to note that under no circumstances does affirmative action require companies to hire unqualified people.

Managing diversity helps people perform to their maximum potential.

Although affirmative action created tremendous opportunities for women and minorities, it does not foster the type of thinking that is needed to effectively manage diversity.[39] For example, affirmative action is resisted more by white males than women and minorities because it is perceived as involving preferential hiring and treatment based on group membership. Affirmative action plans are more successful when employees view them as fair and equitable.[40]

Affirmative action programs also were found to negatively affect the women and minorities expected to benefit from them. Research demonstrated that women and minorities, supposedly hired on the basis of affirmative action, felt negatively stigmatized as unqualified or incompetent. They also experienced lower job satisfaction and more stress than employees supposedly selected on the basis of merit.[41]

managing diversity

Creating organizational changes that enable all people to perform up to their maximum potential.

Managing Diversity **Managing diversity** enables people to perform up to their maximum potential. It focuses on changing an organization's culture and infrastructure such that people provide the highest productivity possible. Ann Morrison, a diversity expert, conducted a study of 16 organizations that successfully managed diversity. Her results uncovered three key strategies for success: education, enforcement, and exposure. She describes them as follows:

> The education component of the strategy has two thrusts: one is to prepare nontraditional managers for increasingly responsible posts, and the other is to help traditional managers overcome their prejudice in thinking about and interacting with people who are of a different sex or ethnicity. The second component of the strategy, enforcement, puts teeth in diversity goals and encourages behavior change. The third component, exposure to people with different backgrounds and characteristics, adds a more personal approach to diversity by helping managers get to know and respect others who are different.[42]

In summary, both consultants and academics believe that organizations should strive to manage diversity rather than only valuing it or simply using affirmative action.

"After three decades during which increasing numbers of women have moved into the tech sector, the drive appears to have stalled at the corner office. A 2003 survey . . . by Catalyst, a national women's business advocacy organization, found that women occupied only 9.3% of board seats at technology companies, vs 12.4% at other outfits. In the executive ranks, the differential is worse. Women represent only 11% of corporate-officer positions in tech companies. Outside tech, they hold 15.7%." (Business Week Online, May 12, 2004) Pictured is Karen Richardson, CEO of E. piphany, a customer-relationship-management software company.

Increasing Diversity in the Workforce

This section explores four demographic trends that are creating an increasingly diverse workforce: (1) women continue to enter the workforce in increasing numbers, (2) people of color (non-Caucasian) represent a growing share of the labor force, (3) there is a critical mismatch between workers' educational attainment and occupational requirements, and (4) the workforce is aging.

Women Entering the Workforce Table 4–2 shows that approximately 50.4% of the new entrants into the workforce between 2000 and 2010 are expected to be women. It also shows that women will account for 44.6% of the departures from the workforce. Men account for the largest share of retirement-bound employees.

In spite of the fact that women constituted 46% of the labor force in 1996 and are expected to represent 48% by 2010, they continue to encounter the **glass ceiling.** The glass ceiling represents an invisible barrier that separates women and minorities from advancing into top management positions. It can be particularly demotivating because employees can look up and see coveted top management positions through the transparent ceiling but are unable to obtain them. A variety of statistics support the existence of a glass ceiling.

As of March 2004, women were still underpaid relative to men: Women received 76% of men's earnings.[43] Even when women are paid the same as men, they may suffer in other areas of job opportunities. For example, a study of 69 male and female executives from a large multinational financial services corporation revealed no differences in base salary or bonus. However, the women in this sample received fewer stock options than the male executives, even after controlling for level of education, performance, and job function, and reported less satisfaction with future

glass ceiling
Invisible barrier blocking women and minorities from top management positions.

TABLE 4–2 Projected Entrants and Departures in the US Workforce from 2000 to 2010

	Entrants*		Departures*	
	2000–2010	Percent	2000–2010	Percent
Total**	41,048	100.0%	24,191	100.0%
Men	20,379	49.6	13,406	55.4
Women	20,669	50.4	10,785	44.6
White non-Hispanic	24,873	60.6	18,717	77.4
Men	12,583	30.7	10,404	43.0
Women	12,290	29.9	8,314	34.4
African-American	5,627	13.7	2,843	11.8
Men	2,463	6.0	1,525	6.3
Women	3,164	7.7	1,318	5.4
Hispanic	7,331	17.9	1,752	7.2
Men	3,820	9.3	1,016	4.2
Women	3,511	8.6	736	3.0
Asian and other races	3,218	7.8	879	3.6
Men	1,513	3.7	461	1.9
Women	1,705	4.2	417	1.7

*Labor force entrants and departures, in thousands, 2000–2010.

**All groups add to total.

Note: Numbers may not add up due to rounding.

SOURCE: Data were taken from Table 9 in H Fullerton Jr and M Toossi, "Labor Force Projections to 2010: Steady Growth and Changing Composition," *Monthly Labor Review,* November 2001, p 35. (www.bls.gov/opub/mlr/2001/11/art2abs.htm)

career opportunities.[44] A follow-up study of 13,503 female managers and 17,493 male managers from the same organization demonstrated that women at higher levels in the managerial hierarchy received fewer promotions than males at comparable positions.[45] Would you be motivated if you were a woman working in this organization?

Women still have not broken into the highest echelon of corporate America to a significant extent. For example, there were only 8 and 16 female CEOs in the *Fortune* 500 and *Fortune* 1000 as of May 2004, respectively.[46] Women also accounted for only 15.7% of corporate-officer positions and 5.2% of top earners at *Fortune* 500 companies in 2002. Further, the majority of women in top jobs are working in staff rather than line positions.[47] In general, roles associated with line jobs contain more power and influence than staff positions.

How can women overcome the glass ceiling? A team of researchers attempted to answer this question by surveying 461 executive women who held titles of vice president or higher in *Fortune* 1000 companies. Respondents were asked to evaluate the extent to which they used 13 different career strategies to break through the glass ceiling. The 13 strategies are shown in the Hands-On Exercise. Before discussing the results from this study, we would like you to complete the Hands-On Exercise.

HANDS-ON EXERCISE

What Are the Strategies for Breaking the Glass Ceiling?

INSTRUCTIONS: Read the 13 career strategies shown below that may be used to break the glass ceiling. Next, rank order each strategy in terms of its importance for contributing to the advancement of a woman to a senior management position. Rank the strategies from 1 (most important) to 13 (least important). Once this is completed, compute the gap between your rankings and those provided by the women executives who participated in this research. Their rankings are presented in Endnote 48 at the back of the book. In computing the gaps, use the absolute value of the gap. (Absolute values are always positive, so just ignore the sign of your gap.) Finally, compute your total gap score. The larger the gap, the greater the difference in opinion between you and the women executives. What does your total gap score indicate about your recommended strategies?

Strategy	My Rating	Survey Rating	Gap $\lvert$Your Rating − Survey Rating$\rvert$
1. Develop leadership outside office	_____	_____	_____
2. Gain line management experience	_____	_____	_____
3. Network with influential colleagues	_____	_____	_____
4. Change companies	_____	_____	_____
5. Be able to relocate	_____	_____	_____
6. Seek difficult or high-visibility assignments	_____	_____	_____
7. Upgrade educational credentials	_____	_____	_____
8. Consistently exceed performance expectations	_____	_____	_____
9. Move from one functional area to another	_____	_____	_____
10. Initiate discussion regarding career aspirations	_____	_____	_____
11. Have an influential mentor	_____	_____	_____
12. Develop style that men are comfortable with	_____	_____	_____
13. Gain international experience	_____	_____	_____

SOURCE: Strategies and data were taken from B R Ragins, B Townsend, and M Mattis, "Gender Gap in the Executive Suite: CEOs and Female Executives Report on Breaking the Glass Ceiling," *The Academy of Management Executive,* February 1998, pp 28–42.

Findings indicated that the top nine strategies were central to the advancement of these female executives. Within this set, however, four strategies were identified as critical toward breaking the glass ceiling: consistently exceeding performance expectations, developing a style with which male managers are comfortable, seeking out difficult or challenging assignments, and having influential mentors.[49]

People of Color in the US Workforce People of color in the United States are projected to add 39.4% of the new entrants in the workforce from 2000 to 2010 (see Table 4–2). Hispanics are predicted to account for the largest share of this increase (17.9%). The Hispanic population also continues to grow at a faster rate than other racial groups, and it will surpass the African-American population by 2010. Projecting forward, the Census Bureau estimates that people of color will represent 49.9% of the population by 2050.[50]

Unfortunately, four additional trends suggest that people of color are experiencing their own glass ceiling. First, people of color are advancing even less in the managerial and professional ranks than women. For example, African-Americans and Hispanics held 11.3% and 10.9%, respectively, of all managerial and professional jobs in 2001; women held 46.6% of these positions. Second, the number of race-based charges of discrimination that were deemed to show reasonable cause by the US Equal Employment Opportunity Commission increased from 294 in 1995 to 1,422 in 2003. Companies paid a total of $69.6 million to resolve these claims outside of litigation in 2003.[51] Third, people of color also tend to earn less than whites. Median household income in 2002 was $30,032, $33,946, and $47,194 for African-Americans, Hispanics, and whites, respectively. Interestingly, Asians and Pacific Islanders had the highest median income—$54,910.[52] Finally, a number of studies show that people of color experience more perceived discrimination than whites.[53]

Mismatch between Educational Attainment and Occupational Requirements Approximately 27% of the labor force has a college degree.[54] Unfortunately, many of these people are working in jobs for which they are overqualified. This creates underemployment. **Underemployment** exists when a job requires less than a person's full potential as determined by his or her formal education, training, or skills. Underemployment is associated with higher arrest rates and the likelihood of becoming an unmarried parent for young adults. It also is negatively correlated with job satisfaction, work commitment, job involvement, internal work motivation, life satisfaction, and psychological well-being. Underemployment also is related to higher absenteeism and turnover.[55] On a positive note, however, underemployment is one of the reasons more new college graduates are starting businesses of their own. Moreover, research reveals that over time a college graduate's income ranges from 50% to 100% higher than that obtained by a high-school graduate. For example, the median income in the United States was $29,200 and $47,000 for employees with a high-school diploma and a bachelor's degree, respectively, in 2001.[56] It pays to graduate from college!

underemployment

The result of taking a job that requires less education, training, or skills than possessed by a worker.

There is another important educational mismatch. The national high-school dropout rate is approximately 16%, and more than 20% of the adult US population read at or below a fifth-grade level, a level which is below that needed to earn a living wage. More than 40 million Americans age 16 and older also are illiterate.[57] Literacy is defined as "an individual's ability to read, write, and speak in English, compute and solve problems at levels of proficiency necessary to function on the job and in society, to achieve one's goals, and develop one's knowledge and potential."[58] These statistics are worrisome because 70% of on-the-job reading materials are written for ninth-grade to college levels.

The Aging Workforce America's population and workforce are getting older. Between 1995 and 2020, the number of individuals in the United States over age 65 will increase by 60%, the 45- to 64-year-old population by 34%, and those between ages 18 and 44 by 4%.[59] Life expectancy is increasing as well. The number of people living into their 80s is increasing rapidly, and this group disproportionately suffers from chronic illness. The United States is not the only country with an aging population. Japan, Eastern Europe, and former Soviet republics, for example, are expected to encounter significant economic and political problems due to an aging population.

Managerial Implications of Increasing Diversity Highly skilled women and people of color will be in high demand. To attract and retain the best workers, companies need to adopt policies and programs that meet the needs of women and people of color. Programs such as day care, elder care, flexible work schedules, and benefits such as paternal leaves, less rigid relocation policies, and mentoring programs are likely to become more popular. Before implementing such initiatives, however, companies should consider the recommendations derived from Deloitte & Touche's successful Women's Initiative program (see Skills & Best Practices). The company initiated this program after determining that it was having a problem retaining high-quality women in the firm.

Given the projected increase in the number of Hispanics entering the workforce over the next 20 years, managers should consider progressive methods to recruit, retain, and integrate this segment of the population into their organizations. Consider the examples set by Kmart, the University of North Carolina Health Care System at Chapel Hill, Pricewaterhouse-Coopers, Chevron, and PepsiCo:

> K-mart recruits at colleges and universities that have large numbers of Hispanic students. The company also advertises in Hispanic publications and uses online Hispanic job boards. It also has translated employment and benefit information into Spanish. The University of North Carolina Health Care System at Chapel Hill, NC, has brought in Spanish interpreters at its new-employee orientations and printed part of its job application information in Spanish. . . . PricewaterhouseCoopers . . . set up employee support and socialization groups where Hispanic managers act as leaders to Hispanic employees, and the company provides scholarships for Hispanic accounting students. Chevron sponsors a Hispanic employee network . . . Pepsi works with national Hispanic organizations to help with recruiting and is planning a leadership forum for some Hispanic executives. The program will give the executives access to the CEO and other company leaders.[60]

Mismatches between the amount of education needed to perform current jobs and the amount of education possessed by members of the workforce are growing.

SKILLS & BEST PRACTICES

Recommendations from Deloitte & Touche's Women's Initiative

Recommendations	Supportive Tactics
1. Make sure senior management is front and center.	The CEO actively led the Women's Initiative.
2. Make an airtight business case for cultural change.	The company documented the business imperative for change before it could justify the investment and effort required by the initiative.
3. Let the world watch you.	The company appointed an external advisory council and informed the press about its plans. The company did not the let the initiative become another "program of the year" that led nowhere.
4. Begin with dialogue as the platform for change.	Employees were required to attend intensive workshops to reveal and examine gender-based assumptions in mentoring and client assignments.
5. Use a flexible system of accountability.	Local offices measured their efforts with women professionals. Management worked with office heads to select their focus areas of change under the initiative.
6. Promote work-life balance for men and women.	The company implemented policies for flexible work arrangements and lighter travel schedules.

SOURCE: Excerpted and adapted from D M McCracken, "Winning the Talent War for Women: Sometimes It Takes a Revolution," *Harvard Business Review,* November–December 2000, p 166.

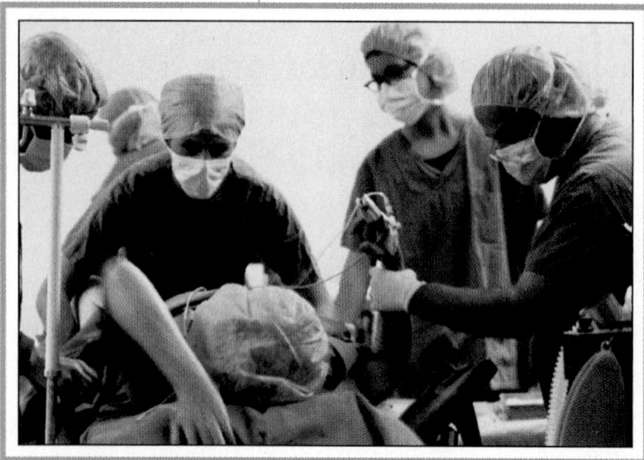

Good communication is essential during surgical procedures. Imagine what would happen if a doctor's instructions were unclear and misunderstood by a surgical team. Miscommunication could be deadly! Given the multinational nature of medical professionals, the health-care industry has been offering foreign language classes to health-care professionals.

Underemployment among college graduates threatens to erode job satisfaction and work motivation. As well-educated workers begin to look for jobs commensurate with their qualifications and expectations, absenteeism and turnover likely will increase. This problem underscores the need for job redesign (see the discussion in Chapter 6). On-the-job remedial skills and literacy training will be necessary to help the growing number of dropouts and illiterates cope with job demands. The influx of workers whose first language is something other than English is likely to require more companies to offer foreign language training. Consider the need for foreign language training within the health-care industry.

> "For health care, it is almost unthinkable that an organization would not offer these classes," says Deborah Lance, director of professional development for Erlanger Health System in the Southeast, in Chattanooga, Tenn. "We deal with life and death situations every day, and patient safety and education is vital. We need to be able to communicate with all our patients and families, and foreign language education is one way to help us meet that need."[61]

There are two general recommendations for helping organizations effectively adapt to an aging workforce. The first involves the need to help employees deal with personal issues associated with elder care. Elder care is a critical issue for employees that have aging parents, and failing to deal with it can drive up an employer's costs. For example, MetLife estimates that a lack of elder care costs organizations at least $11 billion a year in lost productivity and increased absenteeism, workday interruptions, and turnover.[62] Second, employers need to make a concerted effort to keep older workers engaged and committed and their skills current. The following seven initiatives can help accomplish this objective.[63]

1. Provide challenging work assignments that make a difference to the firm.
2. Give the employee considerable autonomy and latitude in completing a task.
3. Provide equal access to training and learning opportunities when it comes to new technology.
4. Provide frequent recognition for skills, experience, and wisdom gained over the years.
5. Provide mentoring opportunities whereby older workers can pass on accumulated knowledge to younger employees.
6. Ensure that older workers receive sensitive, high-quality supervision.
7. Design a work environment that is both stimulating and fun.

Organizational Practices Used to Effectively Manage Diversity

Many organizations throughout the United States are unsure of what it takes to effectively manage diversity. In addition, the sensitive and potentially volatile nature of managing diversity has led to significant barriers when trying to move forward with diversity initiatives. This section reviews the barriers to managing diversity and discusses a framework for categorizing organizational diversity initiatives developed by Ann Morrison.

Barriers and Challenges to Managing Diversity

Organizations encounter a variety of barriers when attempting to implement diversity initiatives. It thus is important for present and future managers to consider these barriers before rolling out a diversity program. The following is a list of the most common barriers to implementing successful diversity programs.[64]

1. *Inaccurate stereotypes and prejudice.* This barrier manifests itself in the belief that differences are viewed as weaknesses. In turn, this promotes the view that diversity hiring will mean sacrificing competence and quality.
2. *Ethnocentrism.* The ethnocentrism barrier represents the feeling that one's cultural rules and norms are superior or more appropriate than the rules and norms of another culture.
3. *Poor career planning.* This barrier is associated with the lack of opportunities for diverse employees to get the type of work assignments that qualify them for senior management positions.
4. *An unsupportive and hostile working environment for diverse employees.* Diverse employees are frequently excluded from social events and the friendly camaraderie that takes place in most offices.
5. *Lack of political savvy on the part of diverse employees.* Diverse employees may not get promoted because they do not know how to "play the game" of getting along and getting ahead in an organization. Research reveals that women and people of color are excluded from organizational networks.[65]
6. *Difficulty in balancing career and family issues.* Women still assume the majority of the responsibilities associated with raising children. This makes it harder for women to work evenings and weekends or to frequently travel once they have children. Even without children in the picture, household chores take more of a woman's time than a man's time.
7. *Fears of reverse discrimination.* Some employees believe that managing diversity is a smoke screen for reverse discrimination. This belief leads to very strong resistance because people feel that one person's gain is another's loss.
8. *Diversity is not seen as an organizational priority.* This leads to subtle resistance that shows up in the form of complaints and negative attitudes. Employees may complain about the time, energy, and resources devoted to diversity that could have been spent doing "real work."
9. *The need to revamp the organization's performance appraisal and reward system.* Performance appraisals and reward systems must reinforce the need to effectively manage diversity. This means that success will be based on a new set of criteria. Employees are likely to resist changes that adversely affect their promotions and financial rewards.
10. *Resistance to change.* Effectively managing diversity entails significant organizational and personal change. As discussed in Chapter 16, people resist change for many different reasons.

Ann Morrison Identifies Specific Diversity Initiatives

Ann Morrison conducted a landmark study of the diversity practices used by 16 organizations that successfully managed diversity. Her results uncovered 52 different practices, 20 of which were used by the majority of the companies sampled. She classified the 52 practices into three main types: accountability, development, and recruitment.[66] The top 10 practices associated with each type are shown in Table 4–3. They are discussed next in order of relative importance.

accountability practices

Focus on treating diverse employees fairly.

Accountability Practices **Accountability practices** relate to managers' responsibility to treat diverse employees fairly. Table 4–3 reveals that companies predominantly accomplish this objective by creating administrative procedures aimed at integrating diverse employees into the management ranks (practice numbers 3, 4, 5, 6, 8, 9, and 10). In contrast, work and family policies, practice 7, focuses on creating an environment that fosters employee commitment and productivity. Progress Energy, an energy company that serves the Carolinas and Florida, uses a variety of accountability practices in its attempt to manage diversity.

> The chairman of the diversity council is also the chairman and CEO of the company, William Cavanaugh III. The council meets once a quarter and subcouncils

TABLE 4–3 Common Diversity Practices

Accountability Practices	Development Practices	Recruitment Practices
1. Top management's personal intervention	1. Diversity training programs	1. Targeted recruitment of nonmanagers
2. Internal advocacy groups	2. Networks and support groups	2. Key outside hires
3. Emphasis on EEO statistics, profiles	3. Development programs for all high-potential managers	3. Extensive public exposure on diversity (AA)
4. Inclusion of diversity in performance evaluation goals, ratings	4. Informal networking activities	4. Corporate image as liberal, progressive, or benevolent
5. Inclusion of diversity in promotion decisions, criteria	5. Job rotation	5. Partnerships with educational institutions
6. Inclusion of diversity in management succession planning	6. Formal mentoring program	6. Recruitment incentives such as cash supplements
7. Work and family policies	7. Informal mentoring program	7. Internships (such as INROADS)
8. Policies against racism, sexism	8. Entry development programs for all high-potential new hires	8. Publications or PR products that highlight diversity
9. Internal audit or attitude survey	9. Internal training (such as personal safety or language)	9. Targeted recruitment of managers
10. Active AA/EEO committee, office	10. Recognition events, awards	10. Partnership with nontraditional groups

SOURCE: Abstracted from Tables A.10, A.11, and A.12 in A M Morrison, *The New Leaders: Guidelines on Leadership Diversity in America* (San Francisco: Jossey-Bass, 1992).

throughout the company meet monthly. In addition, every manager in the company is accountable for the way diversity is both perceived and practiced within his or her organization. Every year employees fill out a written questionnaire that evaluates employee satisfaction with the work environment. If a particular group provides negative feedback regarding issues (including diversity), the company follows up and addresses the issues.[67]

Development Practices The use of development practices to manage diversity is relatively new compared with the historical use of accountability and recruitment practices. **Development practices** focus on preparing diverse employees for greater responsibility and advancement. These activities are needed because most nontraditional employees have not been exposed to the type of activities and job assignments that develop effective leadership and social networks. Table 4–3 indicates that diversity training programs, networks and support groups, and mentoring programs are among the most frequently used developmental practices. Consider the networking practices used by Xerox and Fannie Mae.

development practices

Focus on preparing diverse employees for greater responsibility and advancement.

Many years ago when Xerox was trying to ensure more participation from blacks in its workforce, a caucus established among black employees had the blessing of then-CEO David Kearns, who encouraged black employees to get together periodically to talk about their challenges in moving through the organization and to get help from other managers. After that, there arose a women's caucus, an Hispanic caucus, and so on. Fannie Mae has taken the idea of employee caucus groups a step further. It has 14 Employee Networking Groups for African-Americans, Hispanics, Native Americans, Catholics, Christians, Muslims, older workers, gays, lesbians, veterans, and so forth. The groups serve as social and networking hubs, and they foster workplace communication about diversity issues among all employees, including senior managers.[68]

Recruitment Practices **Recruitment practices** focus on attracting job applicants at all levels who are willing to accept challenging work assignments. This focus is critical because people learn the leadership skills needed for advancement by successfully accomplishing increasingly challenging and responsible work assignments. As shown in Table 4–3, targeted recruitment of nonmanagers (practice 1) and managers (practice 9) are commonly used to identify and recruit women and people of color.

recruitment practices

Attempts to attract qualified, diverse employees at all levels.

key terms

chapter summary

- *Describe perception in terms of the social information processing model.* Perception is a mental and cognitive process that enables us to interpret and understand our surroundings. Social perception, also known as social cognition and social information processing, is a four-stage process. The four stages are selective attention/comprehension, encoding and simplification, storage and retention, and retrieval and response. During social cognition, salient stimuli are matched with schemata, assigned to cognitive categories, and stored in long-term memory for events, semantic materials, or people.
- *Identify and briefly explain four managerial implications of social perception.* Social perception affects hiring decisions, performance appraisals, leadership perceptions, communication, and interpersonal influence. Inaccurate schemata or racist and sexist schemata may be used to evaluate job applicants. Similarly, faulty schemata about what constitutes good versus poor performance can lead to inaccurate performance appraisals. Invalid schemata need to be identified and replaced with appropriate schemata through coaching and training. Further, managers are advised to use objective rather than subjective measures of performance. With respect to leadership, a leader will have a difficult time influencing employees when he or she exhibits behaviors contained in employees' schemata of poor leaders. Finally, because people interpret oral and written communications by using schemata developed through past experiences, an individual's ability to influence others is affected by information contained in others' schemata regarding age, gender, ethnicity, appearance, speech, mannerisms, personality, and other personal characteristics.
- *Explain, according to Kelley's model, how external and internal causal attributions are formulated.* Attribution theory attempts to describe how people infer causes for observed behavior. According to Kelley's model of causal attribution, external attributions tend to be made when consensus and distinctiveness are high and consistency is low. Internal (personal responsibility) attributions tend to be made when consensus and distinctiveness are low and consistency is high.
- *Demonstrate your familiarity with the demographic trends that are creating an increasingly diverse workforce.* There are four key demographic trends: (a) half of the new entrants into the workforce between 2000 and 2010 will be women, (b) people of color will account for more than a third of the new entrants into the workforce between 2000 and 2010, (c) a mismatch exists between workers' educational attainment and occupational requirements, and (d) the workforce is aging.
- *Identify the barriers and challenges to managing diversity.* There are 10 barriers to successfully implementing diversity initiatives: (a) inaccurate stereotypes and prejudice, (b) ethnocentrism, (c) poor career planning, (d) an unsupportive and hostile working environment for diverse employees, (e) lack of political savvy on the part of diverse employees, (f) difficulty in balancing career and family issues, (g) fears of reverse discrimination, (h) diversity is not seen as an organizational priority, (i) the need to revamp the organization's performance appraisal and reward system, and (j) resistance to change.
- *Discuss the organizational practices used to manage diversity identified by Ann Morrison.* Ann Morrison's study of diversity practices identified three main types or categories of activities. Accountability practices relate to a manager's responsibility to treat diverse employees fairly. Development practices focus on preparing diverse employees for greater responsibility and advancement. Recruitment practices emphasize attracting job applicants at all levels who are willing to accept challenging work assignments. Table 4–3 presents a list of activities that are used to accomplish each main type.

discussion questions

1. In the context of the chapter-opening vignette, to what extent does an age bias exist in today's organizations? Explain.
2. Why is it important for managers to have a working knowledge of perception and attribution?
3. How would you formulate an attribution, according to Kelley's model, for the behavior of a classmate who starts arguing in class with your professor?
4. Does diversity suggest that managers should follow the rule, "Do unto others as you would have them do unto you"?
5. How can Ann Morrison's diversity initiatives be helpful in overcoming the barriers and challenges to managing diversity?

ethical dilemma

Enron Employees Try to Alter the Perceptions of Wall Street Analysts[69]

Some current and former employees of Enron's retail-energy unit say the company asked them to pose as busy electricity and natural-gas sales representatives one day in 1998 so the unit could impress Wall Street analysts visiting its Houston headquarters.

Enron rushed 75 employees of Enron Energy Services—including secretaries and actual sales representatives—to an empty trading floor and told them to act as if they were trying to sell energy contracts to businesses over the phone, the current and former employees say.

"When we went down to the sixth floor, I remember we had to take the stairs so the analysts wouldn't see us," said Kim Garcia, who at the time was an administrative assistant for Enron Energy Services and was laid off in December.

"We brought some of our personal stuff, like pictures, to make it look like the area was lived in," Ms Garcia said in an interview. "There were a bunch of trading desks on the sixth floor, but the desks were totally empty. Some of the computers didn't even work, so we worked off of our laptops. When the analysts arrived, we had to make believe we were on the phone buying and selling electricity and natural gas. The whole thing took like 10 minutes."

Penny Marksberry—who also worked as an Enron Energy Services administrative assistant in 1998 and was laid off in December—and two employees who still work at the unit also say they were told to act as if they were trying to sell contracts.

"They actually brought in computers and phones and they told us to act like we were typing or talking on the phone when the analysts were walking through," Ms Marksberry said. "They told us it was very important for us to make a good impression and if the analysts saw that the operation was disorganized, they wouldn't give the company a good rating."

What Would You Do If You Were Asked to Act Busy in Front of the Analysts?

1. Follow the company's instructions by going to the sixth floor and acting busy in front of the analysts.
2. Explain to your manager that this behavior is inconsistent with your personal values and that you will not participate.
3. Go to the sixth floor in support of the company's request, but do not act busy or bring personal artifacts to create a false impression.
4. Invent other options. Discuss.

For an interpretation of this situation, visit our Web site, www.mhhe.com/kinickiob2e.

If you're looking for additional study materials, be sure to check out the Online Learning Center at

www.mhhe.com/kinickiob2e

for more information and interactivities that correspond to this chapter.

chapter Five

Appreciating Individual Differences: Self-Concept, Personality, Emotions

LEARNING OBJECTIVES

After reading the material in this chapter, you should be able to:

- Distinguish between self-esteem and self-efficacy.
- Contrast high and low self-monitoring individuals, and describe resulting problems each may have.
- Explain the social learning model of self-management.
- Identify and describe the Big Five personality dimensions, specify which one is correlated most strongly with job performance, and describe the proactive personality.
- Explain the difference between an internal and external locus of control.
- Explain the concepts of emotional contagion and emotional labor, and identify the four key components of emotional intelligence.

ARE DYSFUNCTIONAL FAMILIES PARTLY TO BLAME FOR BAD MANAGERS?

For Peter Tilton, the office revelation came last February. He was sitting in a conference room at company headquarters, meeting with the group he managed, when an "incompetent" colleague began needling him about his own progress on a project. Tilton felt the trip wire go off, the raw rush that made him feel as if he were slipping into a state of adolescent siege.

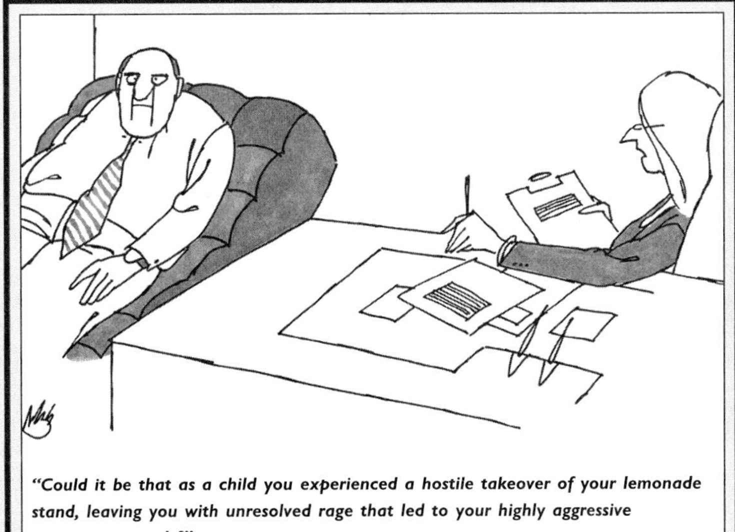

"Could it be that as a child you experienced a hostile takeover of your lemonade stand, leaving you with unresolved rage that led to your highly aggressive management style?"

Within seconds, he was banging his fist on the whiteboard and "yelling his face off." Even at a place like Microsoft Corp., where Tilton says co-workers routinely blast each others' ideas as "stupid," this wasn't exactly behavior becoming a director-level executive. The emotional outburst, Tilton now realizes, was eerily similar to one he had back in seventh grade, when his parents—"chronic misunderstanders"—forbade him to wear his jeans with the holey knees to school. It was 1967, and he was heavy into his hippie protest phase. "And they wanted me to wear slacks," Tilton says. . . .

That . . . highly rational, utterly left-brained executives are delving into their pasts illustrates a new strain of organizational therapy coursing through the inner sanctums of corporate power. The basic concept: that people tend to recreate their family dynamics at the office. The idea is being fanned by organizational experts, who say that corporate strivers can at times behave a bit like thumb-suckers in knee pants, yearning for pats on the back from boss "daddies and mommies" and wishing those scene-stealing co-worker "siblings" would, well, die. Boardroom arguments can parallel spats at the family dinner table. . . .

Buttressed by new research in workplace dynamics, more high-profile coaches and consultants are applying family-systems therapy to business organizations, to grapple with what has come to be seen as a new frontier in productivity: emotional inefficiency, which includes all that bickering, back-stabbing, and ridiculous playing for approval that are a mark of the modern workplace. A two-year study by Seattle psychologist Brian DesRoches found that such dramas routinely waste 20% to 50% of workers' time. The theory is also gaining more resonance as corporations become ever more cognizant that talented employees quit bosses, not companies, and that CEOs often get hired for their skills—and fired for their personalities.

Looking backward to move forward makes sense, say group dynamic researchers, considering that the first organization people ever belong to is their families, with parents the first bosses and siblings the first colleagues. "Our original notions of an institution, of an authority structure, of power and influence are all forged in the family," says Warren Bennis, management guru and professor of business at the University of Southern California.

. . . by performing psychological X-rays on clients' pasts, coaches have helped executives at companies as diverse as the *Los Angeles Times,* State Farm Insurance, and American Express understand their own and others' dysfunctional behavior. They learn how to recognize the shadowy emotional subtext that drives many encounters, deconstructing how they may be subconsciously sabotaging themselves, shying from authority figures, or engaging in hypercritical judgments of subordinates. Or why they may unwittingly play the role of the hero, scapegoat, or martyr. "I'm not suggesting that our employees are our kids," says Kenneth Sole, a consulting social psychologist who has worked with Apple Computer Inc. and the U.N. "But the psychology is parallel." . . .

Personalities, emotions, behavioral tics—all have started to take on a bigger dimension in an era in which businesses increasingly sell the ideas that come from employees' heads, not just the products from their machines. . . .

Of course, plenty of leaders and their consultants object to therapy invading the office. "The workplace is not the place to explore psychological foibles," says Richard A. Chaifetz, CEO of ComPsych Corp., a Chicago employee-assistance firm. "It can open up a can of worms." Chaifetz approves of this kind of inquiry only if it's done off-site, one-on-one, and with a trained professional. And many work dynamics can't be analyzed solely through a family filter. More likely, say critics, work teams carry traits that are characteristic of all group dynamics. Pairing off, for example, usually happens any time people gather. So does complaining. . . .

In Tilton's case, the Microsoft exec had disdained therapy "ever since my parents tried to send me to a pipe-smoking guy in seventh grade." But in the months he has been working with an executive coach, he only wishes he could have cracked through his denial sooner. Like many, he realizes that being analytically savvy isn't enough. Being emotionally competent is now part of the job, too.[1]

FOR DISCUSSION

Do you think one's family history affects workplace behavior? Explain. For an interpretation of this case and additional comments, visit our Online Learning Center:

www.mhhe.com/kinickiob2e

THANKS TO A VAST array of individual differences, modern organizations have a rich and interesting human texture. On the other hand, individual differences make the manager's job endlessly challenging. In fact, according to research, "variability among workers is substantial at all levels but increases dramatically with job complexity. In life insurance sales, for example, variability in performance is around six times as great as in routine clerical jobs."[2]

Growing workforce diversity compels managers to view individual differences in a fresh new way. Rather than limiting diversity, as in the past, today's managers need to better understand and accommodate employee diversity and individual differences.[3]

This chapter explores the following important dimensions of individual differences: (1) self-concept and self-management, (2) personality traits, (3) attitudes, (4) mental abilities, and (5) emotions. Figure 5–1 is a conceptual model showing the relationship between self-concept (how you view yourself), personality (how you appear to others), and key forms of self-expression. Considered as an integrated package, these factors provide a foundation for better understanding yourself and others as unique and special individuals.

From Self-Concept to Self-Management

Self is the core of one's conscious existence. Awareness of self is referred to as one's self-concept. Individualistic North American cultures have been called self-centered. Not surprisingly, when people ages 16 to 70 were asked in a recent survey what they would do differently if they could live life over again, 48% chose the response category "Get in touch with self."[4] To know more about self-concept is to understand more about life in general. Sociologist Viktor Gecas defines **self-concept** as "the concept the individual has of himself as a physical, social, and spiritual or moral being."[5] In other words, because you have a self-concept, you recognize yourself as a distinct human being. A self-concept would be impossible without the capacity to think. This brings us to the role of cognitions. **Cognitions** represent "any knowledge, opinion, or belief about the environment, about oneself, or about one's behavior."[6] Among many different types of cognitions, those involving anticipation, planning,

self-concept
Person's self-perception as a physical, social, spiritual being.

cognitions
A person's knowledge, opinions, or beliefs.

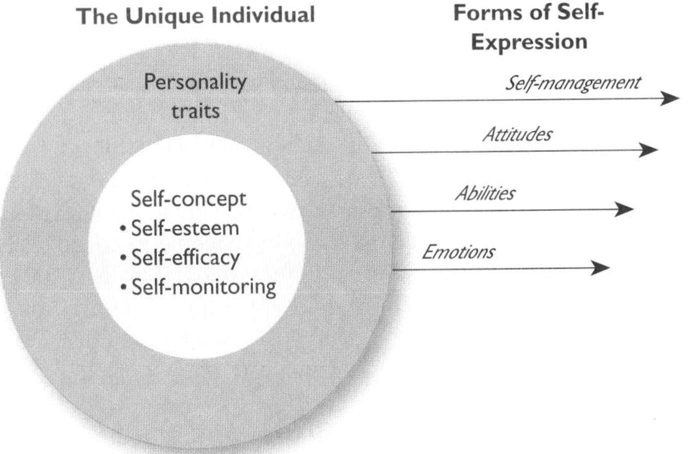

FIGURE 5–1 An OB Model for Studying Individual Differences

goal setting, evaluating, and setting personal standards are particularly relevant to OB. Cognitively based topics covered in this book include social perception, behavioral self-management, modern motivation theories, and decision-making styles.

Importantly, ideas of self and self-concept vary from one historical era to another, from one socioeconomic group to another, and from culture to culture.[7] How well one detects and adjusts to different cultural notions of self can spell the difference between success and failure in international dealings. For example, Japanese–US communication and understanding often are hindered by significantly different degrees of self-disclosure. With a comparatively large public self, Americans pride themselves in being open, honest, candid, and to the point. Meanwhile, Japanese, who culturally discourage self-disclosure, typically view Americans as blunt, prying, and insensitive to formalities. For their part, Americans tend to see Japanese as distant, cold, and evasive.[8] One culture is not right and the other wrong. They are just different, and a key difference involves culturally rooted conceptions of self and self-disclosure.

Keeping this cultural qualification in mind, let us explore three topics invariably mentioned when behavioral scientists discuss self-concept. They are self-esteem, self-efficacy, and self-monitoring. A social learning model of self-management is presented as a practical capstone for this section. Each of these areas deserves a closer look by those who want to better understand and effectively manage people at work. James Champy, the well-known management author and consultant, knows the importance of self-awareness and self-management: "Great leaders are quietly introspective, always asking whether they are a cause of the organization's problems or whether they are doing what needs to be done."[9]

Self-Esteem

self-esteem
One's overall self-evaluation.

Self-esteem is a belief about one's own self-worth based on an overall self-evaluation.[10] Self-esteem is measured by having survey respondents indicate their agreement or disagreement with both positive and negative statements. A positive statement on one general self-esteem survey is: "I feel I am a person of worth, the equal of other people."[11] Among the negative items is: "I feel I do not have much to be proud of."[12] Those who agree with the positive statements and disagree with the negative statements have high self-esteem. They see themselves as worthwhile, capable, and acceptable. People with low self-esteem view themselves in negative terms. They do not feel good about themselves and are hampered by self-doubts.[13]

A Cross-Cultural Perspective What are the cross-cultural implications for self-esteem, a concept that has been called uniquely Western? In a survey of 13,118 students from 31 countries worldwide, a moderate positive correlation was found between self-esteem and life satisfaction. But the relationship was stronger in individualistic cultures (e.g., United States, Canada, New Zealand, Netherlands) than in collectivist cultures (e.g., Korea, Kenya, Japan). The researchers concluded that individualistic cultures socialize people to focus more on themselves, while people in collectivist cultures "are socialized to fit into the community and to do their duty. Thus, how a collectivist feels about him- or herself is less relevant to . . . life satisfaction."[14] Global managers need to remember to deemphasize self-esteem when doing business in collectivist ("we") cultures, as opposed to emphasizing it in individualistic ("me") cultures.[15]

Can General Self-Esteem Be Improved? The short answer is *yes* (see Skills & Best Practices). More detailed answers come from research. In one study, youth-league baseball coaches who were trained in supportive teaching techniques had a positive effect on the self-esteem of young boys. A control group of untrained coaches had no such positive effect.[16] Another study led to this conclusion: "Low self-esteem can be raised more by having the person think of *desirable* characteristics *possessed* rather than of undesirable characteristics from which he or she is free."[17] Yet another comprehensive study threw cold water on the popular view that high self-esteem is the key to better performance. The conclusion:

> . . . self-esteem and school or job performance are correlated. But long overdue scientific scrutiny points out the foolishness of supposing that people's opinion of themselves can be the *cause* of achievement. Rather, high-esteem is the *result* of good performance.[18]

This is where self-efficacy comes to the forefront.

How to Build Self-Esteem in Yourself and Others

SKILLS & BEST PRACTICES

What nurtures and sustains self-esteem in grown-ups is not how others deal with us but how we ourselves operate in the face of life's challenges—the choices we make and the actions we take.

This leads us to the six pillars of self-esteem.

1. *Live consciously:* Be actively and fully engaged in what you do and with whom you interact.
2. *Be self-accepting:* Don't be overly judgmental or critical of your thoughts and actions.
3. *Take personal responsibility:* Take full responsibility for your decisions and actions in life's journey.
4. *Be self-assertive:* Be authentic and willing to defend your beliefs when interacting with others, rather than bending to their will to be accepted or liked.
5. *Live purposefully:* Have clear near-term and long-term goals and realistic plans for achieving them to create a sense of control over your life.
6. *Have personal integrity:* Be true to your word and your values.

Between self-esteem and the practices that support it, there is reciprocal causation. This means that the behaviors that generate good self-esteem are also expressions of good self-esteem.

SOURCE: Excerpted and adapted from Nathaniel Branden, *Self-Esteem at Work: How Confident People Make Powerful Companies* (San Francisco: Jossey-Bass, 1998), pp 33–36.

Self-Efficacy ("I can do that.")

Have you noticed how those who are confident about their ability tend to succeed, while those who are preoccupied with failing tend to fail? Perhaps that explains the comparative golfing performance of your authors! One consistently stays in the fairways and hits the greens. The other spends the day thrashing through the underbrush, wading in water hazards, and blasting out of sand traps. At the heart of this performance mismatch is a specific dimension of self-esteem called self-efficacy. **Self-efficacy** is a person's belief about his or her chances of successfully accomplishing a specific task. According to one OB writer, "Self-efficacy arises from the gradual acquisition of complex cognitive, social, linguistic, and/or physical skills through experience."[19]

Helpful nudges in the right direction from parents, role models, and mentors are central to the development of high self-efficacy. Consider, for example, this interview exchange with Nathan Lane, the successful Broadway and Hollywood actor:

self-efficacy

Belief in one's ability to do a task.

> I asked Lane if he ever considered giving up during his early years of trying to succeed as an actor, when times were tough.
>
> He seemed startled by the question. "What else would I do?" he replied. "I have no other skills. I didn't for a moment think I *wasn't* going to make it. I just thought it may take a while. Certainly, at times you lose confidence, but I always believed there was a place for me. People believing in you is what gives you the confidence to go on. After that, it's a matter of perseverance, luck, and being ready when the opportunity does arrive."[20]

The relationship between self-efficacy and performance is a cyclical one. Efficacy → performance cycles can spiral upward toward success or downward toward failure.[21] Researchers have documented a strong linkage between high self-efficacy expectations and success in widely varied physical and mental tasks, anxiety reduction, addiction control, pain tolerance, illness recovery, and avoidance of seasickness in

learned helplessness

Debilitating lack of faith in one's ability to control the situation.

naval cadets.[22] Oppositely, those with low self-efficacy expectations tend to have low success rates. Chronically low self-efficacy is associated with a condition called **learned helplessness,** the severely debilitating belief that one has no control over one's environment.[23] Although self-efficacy sounds like some sort of mental magic, it operates in a very straightforward manner, as a model will show.

Mechanisms of Self-Efficacy A basic model of self-efficacy is displayed in Figure 5–2. It draws upon the work of Stanford psychologist Albert Bandura.[24] Let us explore this model with a simple illustrative task. Imagine you have been told to

FIGURE 5–2 Self-Efficacy Beliefs Pave the Way for Success or Failure

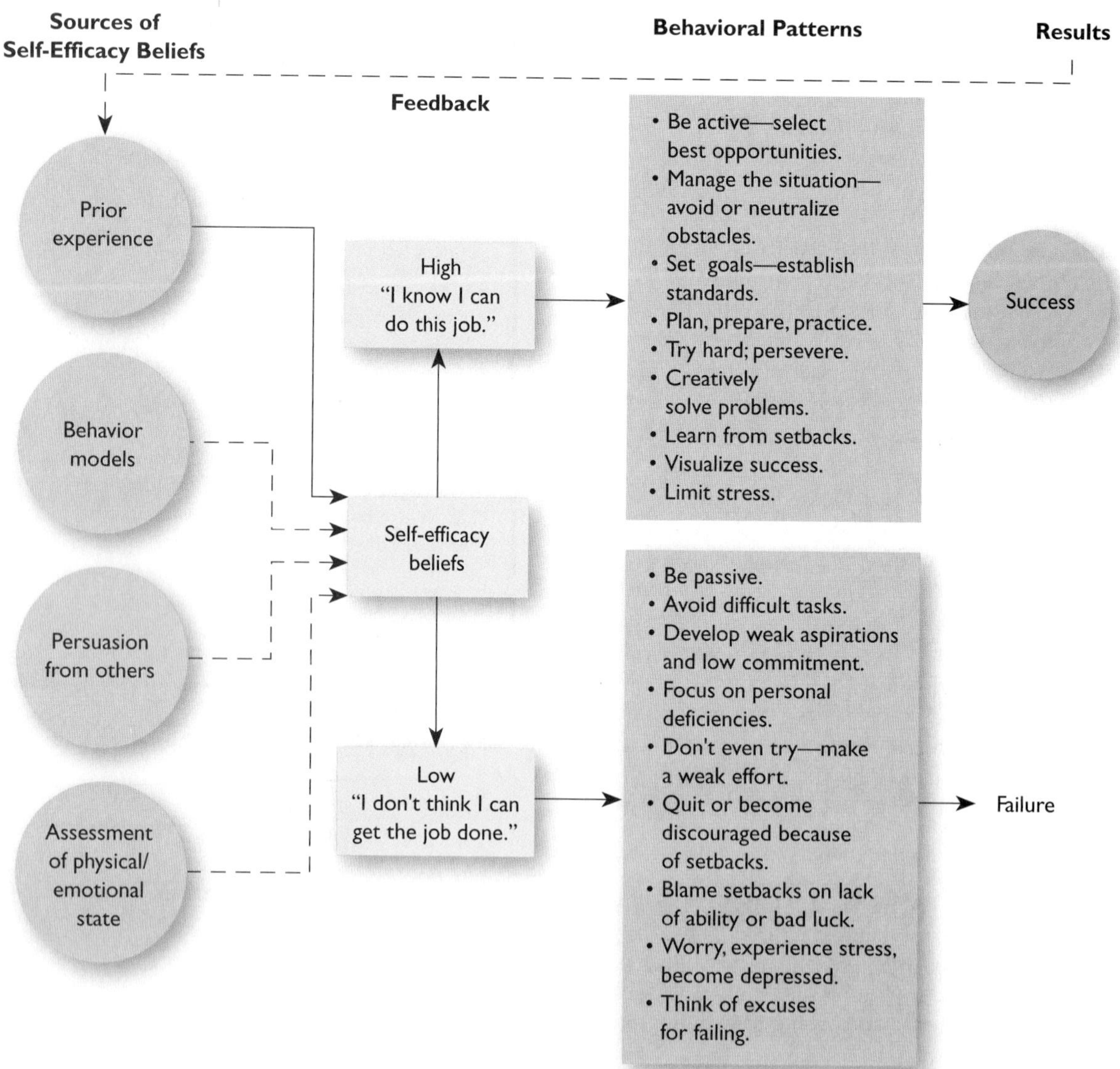

SOURCES: Adapted from discussion in A Bandura, "Regulation of Cognitive Processes through Perceived Self-Efficacy," *Developmental Psychology,* September 1989, pp 729–35; and R Wood and A Bandura, "Social Cognitive Theory of Organizational Management," *Academy of Management Review,* July 1989, pp 361–84.

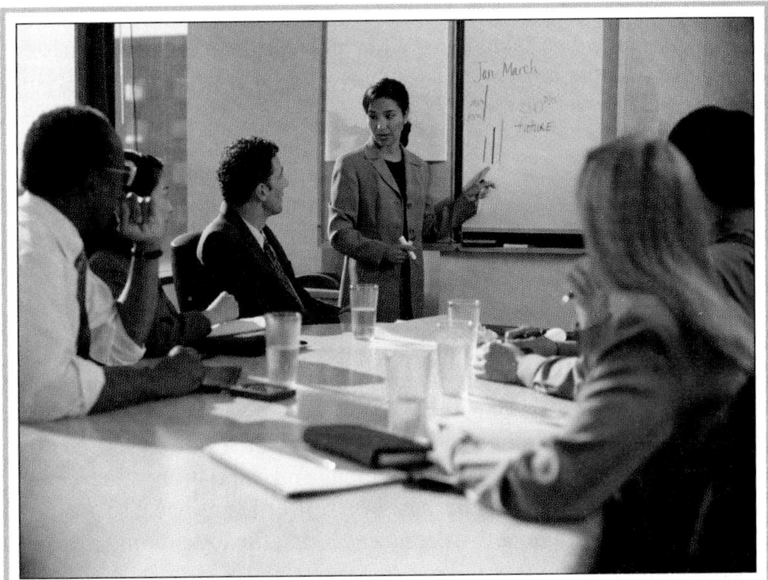

***Self-efficacy* expectations can come into play during public speaking sessions. Prior experience is the most potent source of these beliefs.**

prepare and deliver a 10-minute talk to an OB class of 50 students on the workings of the self-efficacy model in Figure 5–2. Your self-efficacy calculation would involve cognitive appraisal of the interaction between your perceived capability and situational opportunities and obstacles.

As you begin to prepare for your presentation, the four sources of self-efficacy beliefs would come into play. Because prior experience is the most potent source, according to Bandura, it is listed first and connected to self-efficacy beliefs with a solid line.[25] Past success in public speaking would boost your self-efficacy. But bad experiences with delivering speeches would foster low self-efficacy. Regarding behavior models as a source of self-efficacy beliefs, you would be influenced by the success or failure of your classmates in delivering similar talks. Their successes would tend to bolster you (or perhaps their failure would if you were very competitive and had high self-esteem). Likewise, any supportive persuasion from your classmates that you will do a good job would enhance your self-efficacy. Physical and emotional factors also might affect your self-confidence. A sudden case of laryngitis or a bout of stage fright could cause your self-efficacy expectations to plunge. Your cognitive evaluation of the situation then would yield a self-efficacy belief—ranging from high to low expectations for success. Importantly, self-efficacy beliefs are not merely boastful statements based on bravado; they are deep convictions supported by experience.

Moving to the *behavioral patterns* portion of Figure 5–2, we see how self-efficacy beliefs are acted out. In short, if you have high self-efficacy about giving your 10-minute speech you will work harder, more creatively, and longer when preparing for your talk than will your low-self-efficacy classmates. The results would then take shape accordingly. People program themselves for success or failure by enacting their self-efficacy expectations. Positive or negative results subsequently become feedback for one's base of personal experience. Bob Schmonsees, a software entrepreneur, is an inspiring example of the success pathway through Figure 5–2:

> A contender in mixed-doubles tennis and a former football star, Mr Schmonsees was standing near a ski lift when an out-of-control skier rammed him. His legs were paralyzed. He would spend the rest of his life in a wheelchair.

Fortunately, he discovered a formula for his different world: Figure out the new rules for any activity, then take as many small steps as necessary to master those rules. After learning the physics of a tennis swing on wheels and the geometry of playing a second bounce (standard rules), he became the world's top wheelchair player over age 40.[26]

Managerial Implications On-the-job research evidence encourages managers to nurture self-efficacy, both in themselves and in others. In fact, a meta-analysis encompassing 21,616 subjects found a significant positive correlation between self-efficacy and job performance.[27] Self-efficacy requires constructive action in each of the following managerial areas:

1. *Recruiting/selection/job assignments.* Interview questions can be designed to probe job applicants' general self-efficacy as a basis for determining orientation and training needs. Pencil-and-paper tests for self-efficacy are not in an advanced stage of development and validation. Care needs to be taken not to hire solely on the basis of self-efficacy because studies have detected below-average self-esteem and self-efficacy among women and protected minorities.[28]
2. *Job design.* Complex, challenging, and autonomous jobs tend to enhance perceived self-efficacy.[29] Boring, tedious jobs generally do the opposite.
3. *Training and development.* Employees' self-efficacy expectations for key tasks can be improved through guided experiences, mentoring, and role modeling.[30]
4. *Self-management.* Systematic self-management training involves enhancement of self-efficacy expectations.[31]
5. *Goal setting and quality improvement.* Goal difficulty needs to match the individual's perceived self-efficacy.[32] As self-efficacy and performance improve, goals and quality standards can be made more challenging.
6. *Creativity.* Supportive managerial actions can enhance the strong linkage between self-efficacy beliefs and workplace creativity.[33]
7. *Coaching.* Those with low self-efficacy and employees victimized by learned helplessness need lots of constructive pointers and positive feedback.[34]
8. *Leadership.* Needed leadership talent surfaces when top management gives high self-efficacy managers a chance to prove themselves under pressure.
9. *Rewards.* Small successes need to be rewarded as stepping-stones to a stronger self-image and greater achievements.

Self-Monitoring

Consider these contrasting scenarios:

1. You are rushing to an important meeting when a co-worker pulls you aside and starts to discuss a personal problem. You want to break off the conversation, so you glance at your watch. He keeps talking. You say, "I'm late for a big meeting." He continues. You turn and start to walk away. The person keeps talking as if he never received any of your verbal and nonverbal signals that the conversation was over.
2. Same situation. Only this time, when you glance at your watch, the person immediately says, "I know, you've got to go. Sorry. We'll talk later."

In the first all-too-familiar scenario, you are talking to a "low self-monitor." The second scenario involves a "high self-monitor." But more is involved here than an irritating situation. A significant and measurable individual difference in self-expression behavior, called self-monitoring, is highlighted. **Self-monitoring** is the extent to which a person observes their own self-expressive behavior and adapts it to the demands of the situation.[35] Experts on the subject offer this explanation:

self-monitoring

Observing one's own behavior and adapting it to the situation.

> Individuals high in self-monitoring are thought to regulate their expressive self-presentation for the sake of desired public appearances, and thus be highly responsive to social and interpersonal cues of situationally appropriate performances. Individuals low in self-monitoring are thought to lack either the ability or the motivation to so regulate their expressive self-presentations. Their expressive behaviors, instead, are thought to functionally reflect their own enduring and momentary inner states, including their attitudes, traits, and feelings.[36]

In organizational life, both high and low self-monitors are subject to criticism. High self-monitors are sometimes called *chameleons,* who readily adapt their self-presentation to their surroundings. Low self-monitors, on the other hand, often are criticized for being on their own planet and insensitive to others. Importantly, within an OB context, self-monitoring is like any other individual difference—not a matter of right or wrong or good versus bad, but rather a source of diversity that needs to be adequately understood by present and future managers.

A Matter of Degree Self-monitoring is not an either-or proposition. It is a matter of degree; a matter of being relatively high or low in terms of related patterns of self-expression. The Hands-On Exercise is a self-assessment of your self-monitoring tendencies. It can help you better understand your*self.* Take a short break from your reading to complete the 10-item survey. Does your score surprise you in any way? Are you unhappy with the way you present yourself to others? What are the ethical implications of your score (particularly with regard to items 9 and 10)?

Research Insights and Practical Recommendations According to field research, there is a positive relationship between high self-monitoring and career success. Among 139 MBA graduates who were tracked for five years, high self-monitors enjoyed more internal and external promotions than did their low self-monitoring classmates.[37] Another study of 147 managers and professionals found that high self-monitors had a better record of acquiring a mentor (someone to act as a personal career coach and professional sponsor).[38] These results mesh well with an earlier study that found managerial success (in terms of speed of promotions) tied to political savvy (knowing how to socialize, network, and engage in organizational politics).[39]

The foregoing evidence and practical experience lead us to make these practical recommendations:

> *For high, moderate, and low self-monitors:* Become more consciously aware of your self-image and how it affects others (the Hands-On Exercise is a good start).
>
> *For high self-monitors:* Don't overdo it by turning from a successful chameleon into someone who is widely perceived as insincere, dishonest, phoney, and untrustworthy. You cannot be everything to everyone.

HANDS-ON EXERCISE

How Good Are You at Self-Monitoring?

INSTRUCTIONS: In an honest self-appraisal, mark each of the following statements as true (T) or false (F), and then consult the scoring key.

_______ **1.** I guess I put on a show to impress or entertain others.
_______ **2.** In a group of people I am rarely the center of attention.
_______ **3.** In different situations and with different people, I often act like very different persons.
_______ **4.** I would not change my opinions (or the way I do things) in order to please someone or win their favor.
_______ **5.** I have considered being an entertainer.
_______ **6.** I have trouble changing my behavior to suit different people and different situations.
_______ **7.** At a party I let others keep the jokes and stories going.
_______ **8.** I feel a bit awkward in public and do not show up quite as well as I should.
_______ **9.** I can look anyone in the eye and tell a lie with a straight face (if for a right end).
_______ **10.** I may deceive people by being friendly when I really dislike them.

SCORING KEY Score one point for each of the following answers:

I.T; 2. F; 3. T; 4. F; 5. T; 6. F; 7. F; 8. F; 9. T; 10. T

Score: _______

1–3 = Low self-monitoring
4–5 = Moderately low self-monitoring
6–7 = Moderately high self-monitoring
8–10 = High self-monitoring

SOURCE: Excerpted and adapted from M Snyder and S Gangestad, "On the Nature of Self-Monitoring: Matters of Assessment, Matters of Validity," *Journal of Personality and Social Psychology*, July 1986, p 137.

For low self-monitors: You can bend without breaking, so try to be a bit more accommodating while being true to your basic beliefs. Don't wear out your welcome when communicating. Practice reading and adjusting to nonverbal cues in various public situations. If your conversation partner is bored or distracted, stop—because he or she is not really listening.

Self-Management: A Social Learning Model

Albert Bandura, the Stanford psychologist introduced earlier, extended his self-efficacy concept into a comprehensive model of human learning. According to Bandura's *social learning theory,* an individual acquires new behavior through the interplay of environmental cues and consequences and cognitive processes.[40] When you consciously control this learning process yourself, you are engaging in self-management. Bandura explains:

> [A] distinguishing feature of social learning theory is the prominent role it assigns to self-regulatory capacities. By arranging environmental inducements, generating cognitive supports, and producing consequences for their own actions people are able to exercise some measure of control over their own behavior.[41]

A Social Learning Model of Self-Management **FIGURE 5–3**

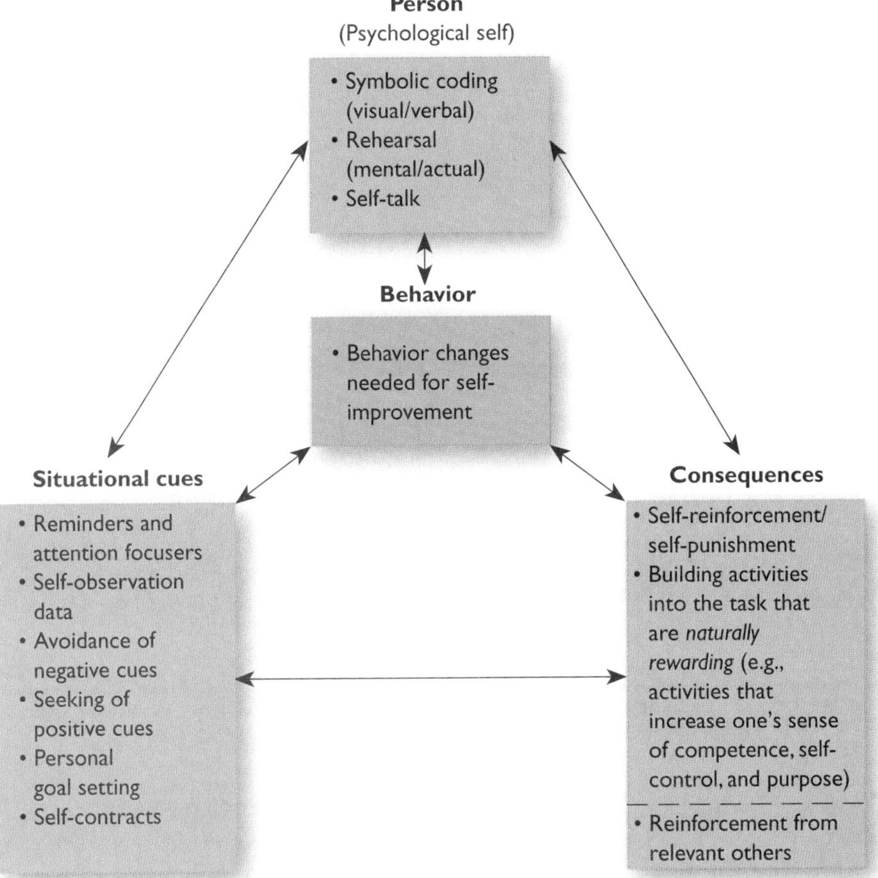

In other words, to the extent that you can control your environment and your cognitive representations of your environment, you are the master of your own behavior. The practical model displayed in Figure 5–3 is derived from social learning theory. The two-headed arrows reflect dynamic interaction among all factors in the model. Each of the four major components of this self-management model requires a closer look. Since the focal point of this model is *behavior change,* let us begin by discussing the behavior component in the center of the triangle.[42]

An Agenda for Self-Improvement In today's fast-paced Internet age, corporate hand-holding is pretty much a thing of the past when it comes to career management. Employees are told such things as "You own your own employability." They must make the best of themselves and any opportunities that may come along. A brochure at one large US company tells employees: "No one is more interested or qualified when it comes to evaluating your individual interests, values, skills, and goals than you are."[43] The new age of *career self-management* challenges you to do a better job of setting personal goals, having clear priorities, being well organized, skillfully managing your time, and developing a self-learning program.[44]

TABLE 5–1 Covey's Seven Habits: An Agenda for Managerial Self-Improvement

1. *Be proactive.* Choose the right means and ends in life, and take personal responsibility for your actions. Make timely decisions and make positive progress.
2. *Begin with the end in mind.* When all is said and done, how do you want to be remembered? Be goal oriented.
3. *Put first things first.* Establish firm priorities that will help you accomplish your mission in life. Strike a balance between your daily work and your potential for future accomplishments.
4. *Think win/win.* Cooperatively seek creative and mutually beneficial solutions to problems and conflicts.
5. *Seek first to understand, then to be understood.* Strive hard to become a better listener.
6. *Synergize.* Because the whole is greater than the sum of its parts, you need to generate teamwork among individuals with unique abilities and potential. Value interpersonal differences.
7. *Sharpen the saw.* "This is the habit of self-renewal, which has four elements. The first is mental, which includes reading, visualizing, planning, and writing. The second is spiritual, which means value clarification and commitment, study, and meditation. Third is social/emotional, which involves service, empathy, synergy, and intrinsic security. Finally, the physical element includes exercise, nutrition, and stress management."

SOURCES: Adapted from discussion in S R Covey, *The 7 Habits of Highly Effective People* (New York: Simon & Schuster, 1989). Excerpt from "Q & A with Stephen Covey," *Training,* December 1992, p 38.

Fortunately, Stephen R Covey, in his best-selling book *The 7 Habits of Highly Effective People,* has given managers a helpful agenda for improving themselves (see Table 5–1). Covey refers to the seven habits, practiced by truly successful people, as "principle-centered, character-based."[45] The first step for putting the model in Figure 5–3 to work is to pick one or more of the seven habits that are personal trouble spots and translate them to specific behaviors. For example, "think win/win" might remind a conflict-prone manager to practice cooperative teamwork behaviors with co-workers. Habit number five might prompt another manager to stop interrupting others during conversations. Next, a supportive environment is needed for the target behavior.

Managing Situational Cues When people try to give up a nagging habit such as smoking, the cards are stacked against them. Many people (friends who smoke) and situations (after dinner, when under stress at work, or when relaxing) serve as subtle yet powerful cues telling the individual to light up. If the behavior is to be changed, the cues need to be rearranged so as to trigger the alternative behavior. Six techniques for managing situational cues are listed in the left column of Figure 5–3.

Reminders and attention focusers do just that. For example, many students and managers cue themselves about deadlines and appointments with Post-it™ notes stuck all over their work areas, refrigerators, and dashboards. Self-observation data, when compared against a goal or standard, can be a potent cue for improvement. Those who keep a weight chart near their bathroom scale will attest to the value of this tactic. Successful self-management calls for avoiding negative cues while seeking positive cues. Managers in Northwestern Mutual Life Insurance Company's new business department appreciate the value of avoiding negative cues: "On Wednesdays, the department shuts off all incoming calls, allowing workers to speed processing of new policies. On those days, the unit averages 23% more policies than on other days."[46]

Goals, as repeatedly mentioned in this text, are the touchstone of good management. So it is with challenging yet attainable personal goals and effective self-management. Personal finance expert Jean Chatzky offers this perspective:

> For setting goals, you get a substantial payoff. For working toward them, you get a greater one. Nearly half—48%—of Americans who are steadily working toward their goals or have already achieved them say they are very happy with their lives overall. A little over 30% of those who have just started to achieve their goals say they are very happy—and only 18% of those who haven't identified goals or taken the first step toward them say they're very happy. People who have at least started to achieve their goals are much more likely to feel useful, content and confident.[47]

Goals simultaneously provide a target and a measuring stick of progress. Finally, a self-contract is an "if-then" agreement with oneself. For example, if you can define all the key terms in this chapter, treat yourself to something special.

Arranging Cognitive Supports Referring to the *person* portion of the self-management model in Figure 5–3, three cognitive supports for behavior change are symbolic coding, rehearsal, and self-talk. These amount to psychological, as opposed to environmental, cues. Yet, according to Bandura, they prompt appropriate behavior in the same manner. Each requires brief explanation:

- *Symbolic coding.* From a social learning theory perspective, the human brain stores information in visual and verbal codes. For example, a sales manager could use the visual picture of a man chopping down a huge tree to remember Woodman, the name of a promising new client. In contrast, people commonly rely on acronyms to recall names, rules for behavior, and other information. An acronym (or verbal code) that is often heard in managerial circles is the KISS principle, standing for "Keep It Simple, Stupid."
- *Rehearsal.* While it is true that practice often makes perfect, mental rehearsal of challenging tasks also can increase one's chances of success. Importantly, experts draw a clear distinction between systematic visualization of how one should proceed and daydreaming about success:

  > The big difference between daydreaming and visualizing is that "visualizing is much more specific and detailed," says Philadelphia consultant Judith Schuster. "A daydream typically has gaps in it—we jump immediately to where we want to wind up. In visualization, we use building blocks and, step-by-step, construct the result we want."[48]

  This sort of visualization has been recommended for use in managerial planning.[49]

  Managers stand to learn a great deal about mental rehearsal and visualization from successful athletes. Kim Woodring, Wittenberg University's two-time All-American volleyball player, is a good example. She effectively combines visualization and self-talk:

  > "I'm always positive," she says. "Even if I'm losing. I talk positively to myself. I go on with the next play and don't worry about the last one. When I visualize, I always see the perfect pass, perfect hit, perfect set, perfect kill, perfect result."[50]

  Job-finding seminars are very popular on college campuses today because they typically involve mental and actual rehearsal of tough job interviews. This sort of manufactured experience can build the confidence and self-efficacy necessary for real-world success.[51]

self-talk

Evaluating thoughts about oneself.

- *Self-talk.* According to an expert on the subject, "**self-talk** is the set of evaluating thoughts that you give yourself about facts and events that happen to you."[52] Personal experience tells us that self-talk tends to be a self-fulfilling prophecy. Negative self-talk tends to pave the way for failure, whereas positive self-talk often facilitates success. Replacing negative self-talk ("I'll never get a raise") with positive self-talk ("I deserve a raise and I'm going to get it") is fundamental to better self-management. One business writer, while urging salespeople to be their own cheerleaders, offered this advice for handling difficult situations:

> Tell yourself there's a positive side to everything and train yourself to focus on it. At first your new self-talk will seem forced and unnatural, but stick with it. Use mental imagery to help you concentrate on the benefits of what you think is a bad situation. If you don't like cold calling, for example, think of how good you'll feel when you're finished, knowing you have a whole list of new selling opportunities. Forming a new habit isn't easy, but the effort will pay off.[53]

Self-Reinforcement The completion of self-contracts and other personal achievements calls for self-reinforcement. According to Bandura, three criteria must be satisfied before self-reinforcement can occur:

1. The individual must have *control over desired reinforcers.*
2. Reinforcers must be *self-administered on a conditional basis.* Failure to meet the performance requirement must lead to self-denial.
3. *Performance standards must be adopted* to establish the quantity and quality of target behavior required for self-reinforcement.[54]

In view of the following realities, self-reinforcement strategies need to be resourceful and creative:

> Self-granted rewards can lead to self-improvement. But as failed dieters and smokers can attest, there are short-run as well as long-run influences on self-reinforcement. For the overeater, the immediate gratification of eating has more influence than the promise of a new wardrobe. The same sort of dilemma plagues procrastinators. Consequently, one needs to weave a powerful web of cues, cognitive supports, and internal and external consequences to win the tug-of-war with status-quo payoffs. Primarily because it is so easy to avoid, self-punishment tends to be ineffectual. As with managing the behavior of others, positive instead of negative consequences are recommended for effective self-management.[55]

In addition, it helps to solicit positive reinforcement for self-improvement from supportive friends, co-workers, and relatives.

Personality Dynamics

personality

Stable physical and mental characteristics responsible for a person's identity.

Individuals have their own way of thinking and acting, their own unique style or *personality.* **Personality** is defined as the combination of stable physical and mental characteristics that give the individual his or her identity. These characteristics or traits—including how one looks, thinks, acts, and feels—are the product of interacting genetic and environmental influences.[56] In this section, we introduce the Big

TABLE 5–2 The Big Five Personality Dimensions

Personality Dimension	Characteristics of a Person Scoring Positively on the Dimension
1. Extraversion	Outgoing, talkative, sociable, assertive
2. Agreeableness	Trusting, good-natured, cooperative, softhearted
3. Conscientiousness	Dependable, responsible, achievement oriented, persistent
4. Emotional stability	Relaxed, secure, unworried
5. Openness to experience	Intellectual, imaginative, curious, broad-minded

SOURCE: Adapted from M R Barrick and M K Mount, "Autonomy as a Moderator of the Relationships between the Big Five Personality Dimensions and Job Performance," *Journal of Applied Psychology,* February 1993, pp 111–18.

Five personality dimensions and discuss key personality dynamics including locus of control, attitudes, intelligence, and mental abilities.

The Big Five Personality Dimensions

Long and confusing lists of personality dimensions have been distilled in recent years to the Big Five.[57] They are extraversion, agreeableness, conscientiousness, emotional stability, and openness to experience (see Table 5–2 for descriptions). Standardized personality tests determine how positively or negatively a person scores on each of the Big Five. For example, someone scoring negatively on extraversion would be an introverted person prone to shy and withdrawn behavior.[58] Someone scoring negatively on emotional stability would be nervous, tense, angry, and worried. A person's scores on the Big Five reveal a personality profile as unique as his or her fingerprints.

But one important question lingers: Are personality models ethnocentric and unique to the culture in which they were developed? At least as far as the Big Five model goes, cross-cultural research evidence points in the direction of "no." Specifically, the Big Five personality structure held up very well in a study of women and men from Russia, Canada, Hong Kong, Poland, Germany, and Finland.[59] However, as emphasized by a recent study of 27,965 adults from 36 different cultures, this does *not* mean there is a global personality profile. Some geographic clustering of the Big Five dimensions was observed. For example, the results "showed a clear contrast of European and American cultures with Asian and African cultures. The former were higher in extraversion and openness to experience and lower in agreeableness."[60] This is useful diversity information for expatriate employees and tourists.

Personality and Job Performance Those interested in OB want to know the connection between the Big Five and job performance. Ideally, Big Five personality dimensions that correlate positively and strongly with job performance would be helpful in the selection, training, and appraisal of employees. A meta-analysis of 117 studies involving 23,994 subjects from many professions offers guidance.[61] Among the Big Five, *conscientiousness* had the strongest positive correlation with job performance and training performance. According to the

Successful movie and rock stars are often considered extraverts due to the fact that they have chosen a profession that places them "in the spotlight." But contrast the two performers pictured here. Jim Carrey would most probably be considered an extravert considering the way he acts both on screen and off. However, what about "stars" who tend to shy away from media attention, such as Prince? Can one be introverted and still be a "star manager"?

researchers, "those individuals who exhibit traits associated with a strong sense of purpose, obligation, and persistence generally perform better than those who do not."[62]

Another expected finding: Extraversion (an outgoing personality) was associated with success for managers and salespeople. Also, extraversion was a stronger predictor of job performance than agreeableness, across all professions. The researchers concluded, "It appears that being courteous, trusting, straightforward, and softhearted has a smaller impact on job performance than being talkative, active, and assertive."[63] Not surprisingly, in a recent study, a strong linkage between conscientiousness and performance was found among those with polished social skills.[64] As an added bonus for extraverts, a recent positive psychology study led to this conclusion: "All you have to do is act extraverted and you can get a happiness boost."[65] So the next time you are on the job go initiate a conversation with someone and be more productive *and* happier!

The Proactive Personality As suggested by the above discussion, someone who scores high on the Big Five dimension of conscientiousness is probably a good worker. Thomas S Bateman and J Michael Crant took this important linkage an additional step by formulating the concept of the proactive personality. They define and characterize the **proactive personality** in these terms: "someone who is relatively unconstrained by situational forces and who effects environmental change. Proactive people identify opportunities and act on them, show initiative, take action, and persevere until meaningful change occurs."[66] In short, people with proactive personalities are "hardwired" to change the status quo. In a review of relevant studies, Crant found the proactive personality to be positively associated with individual, team, and organizational success.[67]

proactive personality
Action-oriented person who shows initiative and perseveres to change things.

internal locus of control
Attributing outcomes to one's own actions.

Successful entrepreneurs exemplify the proactive personality. Take this dynamic duo, for example:

A few years ago, sisters Alka and Mona Srivastava planned to follow in their family's highly educated footsteps—Alka, 30, planned to get a PhD in economics and Mona, 31, a law degree.

But instead, they gave it all up, and in 1995, quit their jobs and moved from the power suit world of New York to the beaches of Los Angeles to start Florentyna Intima, a lingerie firm. Now, their bras, underwear and camisoles are sold in more than 200 specialty shops and catalogs, and sales have grown about 30% each year since the first item was shipped in 1999. . . .

"You are talking about two girls who had no idea about anything to do with manufacturing, except for the fact that we knew that we liked to shop," Mona says. "We had to learn everything as we went along."[68]

People with proactive personalities truly are valuable *human capital,* as defined in Chapter 1. Those wanting to get ahead would do well to cultivate the initiative, drive, and perseverence of someone with a proactive personality.

There Is No "Ideal Employee" Personality A word of caution is in order here. The Big Five personality dimensions of conscientiousness and extraversion and the proactive personality are generally desirable in the workplace, but they are not panaceas. Given the complexity of today's work environments, the diversity of today's workforce, and recent research evidence,[69] the quest for an ideal employee personality profile is sheer folly. Just as one shoe does not fit all people, one personality profile does not fit all job situations. Good management involves taking the time to get to know *each* employee's *unique combination* of personality traits, abilities, and potential and then creating a productive and satisfying person-job fit.

Flexible Flyers Rafting co-owner Stephen Saltsman's business is frequently affected by environmental factors—wildfire, drought, even the price of gas. "Every year, there's something," Saltsman said. "There's hantavirus, rain, no water, recession, gas prices. We're certainly a fragile economy here. It depends on everything all going right." His proactive personality and internal locus of control help keep his business afloat.

Locus of Control: Self or Environment?

Individuals vary in terms of how much personal responsibility they take for their behavior and its consequences. Julian Rotter, a personality researcher, identified a dimension of personality he labeled *locus of control* to explain these differences. He proposed that people tend to attribute the causes of their behavior primarily to either themselves or environmental factors.[70] This personality trait produces distinctly different behavior patterns.

People who believe they control the events and consequences that affect their lives are said to possess an **internal locus of control.** For example, such a person tends to attribute positive outcomes, such as getting a passing grade on an exam, to her or his own abilities. Similarly, an "internal" tends to blame negative events, such as failing an exam, on personal shortcomings—not studying hard enough, perhaps. Many entrepreneurs eventually succeed

SKILLS & BEST PRACTICES

How Lucky People Make Their Own Luck

In an environment marked by rising tensions and diminished expectations, most of us could use a little luck—at our companies, in our careers, with our investments. Richard Wiseman thinks that he can help you find some.

Wiseman, 37, is head of a psychology research department at the University of Hertfordshire in England. For the past eight years, he and his colleagues at the university's Perrott-Warrick Research Unit have studied what makes some people lucky and others not. After conducting thousands of interviews and hundreds of experiments, Wiseman now claims that he's cracked the code. Luck isn't due to kismet, karma, or coincidence, he says. Instead, lucky folks—without even knowing it—think and behave in ways that create good fortune in their lives. In his new book, *The Luck Factor: Changing Your Luck, Changing Your Life: The Four Essential Principles* (Miramax, 2003), Wiseman reveals four approaches to life that turn certain people into luck magnets. . . .

1. **Maximize Chance Opportunities** Lucky people are skilled at creating, noticing, and acting upon chance opportunities. They do this in various ways, which include building and maintaining a strong network, adopting a relaxed attitude to life, and being open to new experiences.
2. **Listen to Your Lucky Hunches** Lucky people make effective decisions by listening to their intuition and gut feelings. They also take steps to actively boost their intuitive abilities—for example, by meditating and clearing their mind of other thoughts.
3. **Expect Good Fortune** Lucky people are certain that the future will be bright. Over time, that expectation becomes a self-fulfilling prophecy because it helps lucky people persist in the face of failure and positively shapes their interactions with other people.
4. **Turn Bad Luck Into Good** Lucky people employ various psychological techniques to cope with, and even thrive upon, the ill fortune that comes their way. For example, they spontaneously imagine how things could have been worse, they don't dwell on the ill fortune, and they take control of the situation.

SOURCE: Excerpted from D H Pink, "How To Make Your Own Luck," *Fast Company*, July 2003, pp 78–82. Reprinted with permission.

because their *internal* locus of control helps them overcome setbacks and disappointments. They see themselves as masters of their own fate and not simply lucky (see Skills & Best Practices).

On the other side of this personality dimension are those who believe their performance is the product of circumstances beyond their immediate control. These individuals are said to possess an **external locus of control** and tend to attribute outcomes to environmental causes, such as luck or fate. Unlike someone with an internal locus of control, an "external" would attribute a passing grade on an exam to something external (an easy test or a good day) and attribute a failing grade to an unfair test or problems at home.

Research Lessons Researchers have found important behavioral differences between internals and externals:

- Internals display greater work motivation.
- Internals have stronger expectations that effort leads to performance.
- Internals exhibit higher performance on tasks involving learning or problem solving, when performance leads to valued rewards.
- There is a stronger relationship between job satisfaction and performance for internals than for externals.
- Internals obtain higher salaries and greater salary increases than externals.
- Externals tend to be more anxious than internals.[71]

Managerial Implications The preceding summary of research findings on locus of control has important implications for managing people at work. Let us examine two of them.

First, since internals have a tendency to believe they control the work environment through their behavior, they will attempt to exert control over the work setting. This can be done by trying to influence work procedures, working conditions, task assignments, or relationships with peers and supervisors. As these possibilities imply, internals may resist a manager's attempts to closely supervise their work. Therefore, management may want to place internals in jobs requiring high initiative and low compliance. Externals, on the other hand, might be more amenable to highly structured jobs requiring greater compliance. Direct participation also can bolster the attitudes and performance of externals. This conclusion comes from a field study of 85 computer system users in a wide variety of business and government organizations. Externals who had been significantly involved in designing their organization's computer information system had more favorable attitudes toward the system than their external-locus co-workers who had not participated.[72]

external locus of control

Attributing outcomes to circumstances beyond one's control.

Second, locus of control has implications for reward systems. Given that internals have a greater belief that their effort leads to performance, internals likely would prefer and respond more productively to incentives such as merit pay or sales commissions.[73]

Attitudes

Hardly a day goes by without the popular media reporting the results of another attitude survey. The idea is to take the pulse of public opinion. What do we think about candidate X, the war on drugs, gun control, or abortion? In the workplace, meanwhile, managers conduct attitude surveys to monitor such things as job and pay satisfaction. All this attention to attitudes is based on the assumption that attitudes somehow influence behavior such as voting for someone, working hard, or quitting one's job.

Attitudes versus Values An **attitude** is defined as "a learned predisposition to respond in a consistently favorable or unfavorable manner with respect to a given object."[74] Attitudes affect behavior at a different level than do values. While values represent global beliefs that influence behavior across *all* situations, attitudes relate only to behavior directed toward *specific* objects, persons, or situations. Values and attitudes generally, but not always, are in harmony. A manager who strongly values helpful behavior may have a negative attitude toward helping an unethical co-worker.

attitude

Learned predisposition toward a given object.

How Stable Are Attitudes? In one landmark study, researchers found the *job* attitudes of 5,000 middle-aged male employees to be very stable over a five-year period. Positive job attitudes remained positive; negative ones remained negative. Even those who changed jobs or occupations tended to maintain their prior job attitudes.[75] More recent research suggests the foregoing study may have overstated the stability of attitudes because it was restricted to a middle-aged sample. This time, researchers asked: What happens to attitudes over the entire span of adulthood? *General* attitudes were found to be more susceptible to change during early and late adulthood than during middle adulthood. Three factors accounted for middle-age attitude stability: (1) greater personal certainty, (2) perceived abundance of knowledge, and (3) a need for strong attitudes. Thus, the conventional notion that general attitudes become less likely to change as the person ages was rejected. Elderly people, along with young adults, can and do change their general attitudes because they are more open and less self-assured.[76]

Intelligence and Cognitive Abilities

intelligence

Capacity for constructive thinking, reasoning, problem solving.

Although experts do not agree on a specific definition, **intelligence** represents an individual's capacity for constructive thinking, reasoning,

TABLE 5–3 Mental Abilities

Ability	Description
1. Verbal comprehension	The ability to understand what words mean and to readily comprehend what is read.
2. Word fluency	The ability to produce isolated words that fulfill specific symbolic or structural requirements (such as all words that begin with the letter b and have two vowels).
3. Numerical	The ability to make quick and accurate arithmetic computations such as adding and subtracting.
4. Spatial	Being able to perceive spatial patterns and to visualize how geometric shapes would look if transformed in shape or position.
5. Memory	Having good rote memory for paired words, symbols, lists of numbers, or other associated items.
6. Perceptual speed	The ability to perceive figures, identify similarities and differences, and carry out tasks involving visual perception.
7. Inductive reasoning	The ability to reason from specifics to general conclusions.

SOURCE: Adapted from M D Dunnette, "Aptitudes, Abilities, and Skills," in *Handbook of Industrial and Organizational Psychology*, ed M D Dunnette (Skokie, IL: Rand McNally, 1976), pp 478–83.

and problem solving.[77] Historically, intelligence was believed to be an innate capacity, passed genetically from one generation to the next. Research since has shown, however, that intelligence (like personality) also is a function of environmental influences.[78] Organic factors have more recently been added to the formula as a result of mounting evidence of the connection between alcohol and drug abuse by pregnant women and intellectual development problems in their children.[79]

Researchers have produced some interesting findings about abilities and intelligence in recent years. A unique five-year study documented the tendency of people to "gravitate into jobs commensurate with their abilities."[80] This prompts the vision of the labor market acting as a giant sorting or sifting machine, with employees tumbling into various ability bins. Meanwhile, a steady and significant rise in average intelligence among those in developed countries has been observed over the last 70 years. Why? Experts at an American Psychological Association conference concluded, "Some combination of better schooling, improved socioeconomic status, healthier nutrition, and a more technologically complex society might account for the gains in IQ scores."[81] So if you think you're smarter than your parents and your teachers, you're probably right!

Two Types of Abilities Human intelligence has been studied predominantly through the empirical approach. By examining the relationships between measures of mental abilities and behavior, researchers have statistically isolated major components of intelligence. Using this empirical procedure, pioneering psychologist Charles Spearman proposed in 1927 that all cognitive performance is determined by two types of abilities. The first can be characterized as a general mental ability needed for *all* cognitive tasks. The second is unique to the task at hand. For example, an individual's ability to complete crossword puzzles is a function of his or her broad mental abilities as well as the specific ability to perceive patterns in partially completed words.

Seven Major Mental Abilities Through the years, much research has been devoted to developing and expanding Spearman's ideas on the relationship between cognitive abilities and intelligence.[82] One research psychologist listed 120 distinct mental abilities. Table 5–3 contains definitions of the seven most frequently cited mental abilities. Of the seven abilities, personnel selection researchers have found verbal ability, numerical ability, spatial ability, and inductive reasoning to be valid predictors of job performance for both minority and majority applicants. Also, according to a recent comprehensive research review, standard intelligence (IQ) tests do a good job of predicting both academic achievement and job performance.[83] This contradicts the popular notion that different cognitive abilities are needed for school and work. Plainly stated: "smarts" are "smarts."

OB Gets Emotional

In the ideal world of management theory, employees pursue organizational goals in a logical and rational manner. Emotional behavior seldom is factored into the equation. Yet day-to-day organizational life shows us how prevalent and powerful emotions can be. Anger and jealousy, both potent emotions, often push aside logic and rationality in the workplace. Managers use fear and other emotions to both motivate and intimidate. For example, consider Selina Y Lo, the head of marketing at Alteon WebSystems in San Jose, California:

> A 15-year veteran of the networking business, she has honed her in-your-face style at three startups, earning a reputation as one of the smartest, toughest managers in the industry. Lo's temper and intensity are legendary: During a product meeting last fall, recalls Alteon software engineer John Taylor, she sprang up yelling from her chair, banged her fist on the table, and shoved a finger in his face after Taylor said he couldn't add a feature she had asked for. Taylor quickly relented. "I've left a few dead bodies behind me," Lo crows.[84]

Less noisy, but still emotion laden, is Intel Chairman Andy Grove's use of Grove's Law to keep a competitive edge in the global computer chip market. According to Grove's Law, "Only the paranoid survive."[85] A combination of curiosity and fear is said to drive Barry Diller, one of the media world's legendary dealmakers. Says Diller: "I and my friends succeeded because we were scared to death of failing."[86] These admired corporate leaders would not have achieved what they have without the ability to be logical and rational decision makers *and* be emotionally charged. Too much emotion, however, could have spelled career and organizational disaster for any one of them.

In this final section, our examination of individual differences turns to defining emotions, reviewing a typology of 10 positive and negative emotions, and

Talk about baptism by fire. Just 10 months after being named CEO of American Express, Kenneth I. Chenault addressed 5,000 of his co-workers in an emotional meeting to begin the healing process following the September 11, 2001, terrorist attacks. The tragedy claimed the lives of 11 AmEx employees and closed the firm's New York headquarters for eight months of repairs. Chenault, seen here presiding over AmEx's May 13, 2002, headquarters homecoming celebration, reportedly handled the post-9/11 meeting with great skill and compassion.

discussing the topics of emotional contagion, emotional labor, and emotional intelligence.

Positive and Negative Emotions

Richard S Lazarus, a leading authority on the subject, defines **emotions** as "complex, patterned, organismic reactions to how we think we are doing in our lifelong efforts to survive and flourish and to achieve what we wish for ourselves."[87] The word *organismic* is appropriate because emotions involve the *whole* person—biological, psychological, and social. Importantly, psychologists draw a distinction between *felt* and *displayed* emotions.[88] For example, you might feel angry (felt emotion) at a rude co-worker but not make a nasty remark in return (displayed emotion). Emotions play roles in both causing and adapting to stress and its associated biological and psychological problems. The destructive effect of emotional behavior on social relationships is all too obvious in daily life.

Lazarus's definition of emotions centers on a person's goals. Accordingly, his distinction between positive and negative emotions is goal oriented. Some emotions are triggered by frustration and failure when pursuing one's goals. Lazarus calls these *negative* emotions. They are said to be goal incongruent. For example, which of the six negative emotions in Figure 5–4 are you likely to experience if you fail the final exam in a required course? Failing the exam would be incongruent with your goal of graduating on time. On the other hand, which of the four *positive* emotions in Figure 5–4 would you probably experience if you graduated on time and with honors? The emotions you would experience in this situation are positive because they are congruent (or consistent) with an important lifetime goal. The individual's goals, it is important to note, may or may not be socially acceptable. Thus, a positive emotion, such as love/affection, may be undesirable if associated with sexual harassment. Oppositely, slight pangs of guilt, anxiety, and envy can motivate extra effort. On balance, the constructive or destructive nature of a particular emotion must be judged in terms of both its intensity and the person's relevant goal.

Good (and Bad) Moods Are Contagious

emotions

Complex human reactions to personal achievements and setbacks that may be felt and displayed.

Have you ever had someone's bad mood sour your mood? That person could have been a parent, supervisor, co-worker, friend, or someone serving you in a store or restaurant. Appropriately, researchers call this *emotional contagion.* We, quite literally, can catch another person's good or bad mood or displayed emotions. This effect was documented in a recent study of 131 bank tellers (92% female) and 220 exit interviews with their customers. Tellers who expressed positive emotions tended to have more satisfied customers.[89] Two field studies with nurses and accountants as subjects found a strong linkage between the work group's collective mood and the individual's mood.[90] Both foul moods and good moods turned out to be contagious.

FIGURE 5–4 Positive and Negative Emotions

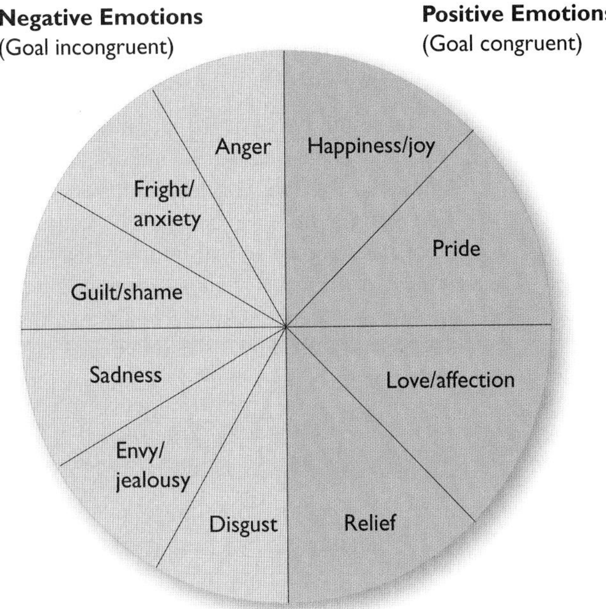

SOURCE: Adapted from discussion in R S Lazarus, *Emotion and Adaptation* (New York: Oxford University Press, 1991), Chs 6, 7.

Perhaps more managers should follow the lead of Lorin Maazel, director of the New York Philharmonic Orchestra:

> I have noticed in my long career that if I am really tired or I have a flu coming on that it's felt. Everybody gets into that mode, and pretty soon, they're playing as sluggishly as I'm conducting. I have learned to come to rehearsal fresh, energetic, projecting enthusiasm and go-go-go. It's got to be irresistible. If I don't think I'm up to it, I take a cold shower. That's my job—to energize people. If they grind it out and couldn't care less, then they wind up hating you and themselves because it's not why they practiced all of their lives. Emotion is what it's all about. Music making without emotion and passion is nothing.[91]

Emotional Labor (It has *not* been a pleasure serving you!)

Although they did not have the benefit of a catchy label or a body of sophisticated research, generations of managers have known about the power of emotional contagion in the marketplace. "Smile, look happy for the customers," employees are told over and over. But what if the employee is having a rotten day? What if they have to mask their true feelings and emotions? What if they have to fake it? Researchers have begun studying the dynamics of what they call *emotional labor.* A pair of authors, one from Australia, the other from the United States, recently summarized the research lessons to date:

> Emotional labor can be particularly detrimental to the employee performing the labor and can take its toll both psychologically and physically. Employees . . . may bottle up feelings of frustration, resentment, and anger, which are not appropriate

SKILLS & BEST PRACTICES

Developing Emotional Intelligence

Personal Competence: These capabilities determine how we manage ourselves.

Self-Awareness

- *Emotional self-awareness:* Reading one's own emotions and recognizing their impact; using "gut sense" to guide decisions.
- *Accurate self-assessment:* Knowing one's strengths and limits.
- *Self-confidence:* A sound sense of one's self-worth and capabilities.

Self-Management

- *Emotional self-control:* Keeping disruptive emotions and impulses under control.
- *Transparency:* Displaying honesty and integrity; trustworthiness.
- *Adaptability:* Flexibility in adapting to changing situations or overcoming obstacles.
- *Achievement:* The drive to improve performance to meet inner standards of excellence.
- *Initiative:* Readiness to act and seize opportunities.
- *Optimism:* Seeing the upside in events.

Social Competence: These capabilities determine how we manage relationships.

Social Awareness

- *Empathy:* Sensing others' emotions, understanding their perspective, and taking active interest in their concerns.
- *Organizational awareness:* Reading the currents, decision networks, and politics at the organizational level.
- *Service:* Recognizing and meeting follower, client, or customer needs.

Relationship Management

- *Inspirational leadership:* Guiding and motivating with a compelling vision.
- *Influence:* Wielding a range of tactics for persuasion.
- *Developing others:* Bolstering others' abilities through feedback and guidance.
- *Change catalyst:* Initiating, managing, and leading in a new direction.
- *Conflict management:* Resolving disagreements.
- *Building bonds:* Cultivating and maintaining a web of relationships.
- *Teamwork and collaboration:* Cooperation and team building.

SOURCE: Reprinted by permission of Harvard Business School Press. D Goleman, R Boyatzis, and A McKee, *Primal Leadership: Realizing the Power of Emotional Intelligence* (Boston: Harvard Business School Press, 2002), p 39.

to express. These feelings result, in part, from the constant requirement to monitor one's negative emotions and express positive ones. If not given a healthy expressive outlet, this emotional repression can lead to a syndrome of emotional exhaustion and burnout.[92]

Interestingly, a pair of laboratory studies with US college students as subjects found no gender difference in *felt* emotions. But the women were more emotionally *expressive* than the men.[93] This stream of research on emotional labor has major practical implications for productivity and job satisfaction, as well as for workplace anger, aggression, and violence. Clearly, managers need to be attuned to (and responsive to) the emotional states and needs of their people. This requires emotional intelligence.

Emotional Intelligence

In 1995, Daniel Goleman, a psychologist turned journalist, created a stir in education and management circles with the publication of his book *Emotional Intelligence.* Hence, an obscure topic among positive psychologists became mainstream. According to Goleman, traditional models of intelligence (IQ) are too narrow, failing to consider interpersonal competence. Goleman's broader agenda includes "abilities such as being able to motivate oneself and persist in the face of frustrations; to control impulse and delay gratification; to regulate one's moods and keep distress from swamping the ability to think; to empathize and to hope."[94] Thus, **emotional intelligence** is the ability to manage oneself and one's relationships in mature and constructive ways. Referred to by some as EI and others as EQ, emotional intelligence is said to have four key components: self-awareness, self-management, social awareness, and relationship management.[95] The first two constitute *personal competence;* the second two feed into *social competence* (see Skills & Best Practices). These emotional intelligence skills need to be well polished in today's pressure-packed workplaces:

> Unanticipated hot spots often flare up during important meetings. Show patience, career experts say. Take deep breaths, compose your thoughts, restate the question—and use humor to defuse tension. If you avoid blurting out the first thing that comes to mind, "people will see your demeanor as cool and professional," observes [executive and author] David F D'Alessandro. . . .
>
> Most people don't do well with the unexpected because they lack a script, notes Dr. [Dory] Hollander. The workplace psychologist recommends acting classes for her clients.

A year of lessons helped one female client advance into the executive ranks at a big technology company. The woman used to perform poorly when colleagues tossed out unforseen questions after presentations. "She looked like she was in pain," Dr. Hollander recalls.

Today, the former middle manager acts confident and appears to enjoy herself even when she lands on the hot seat. "It really is theater," her coach concludes.[96]

emotional intelligence

Ability to manage oneself and interact with others in mature and constructive ways.

Self-assessment instruments supposedly measuring emotional intelligence have appeared in the popular management literature. Sample questions include: "I believe I can stay on top of tough situations,"[97] and "I am able to admit my own mistakes."[98] Recent research, however, casts serious doubt on the reliability and validity of such instruments.[99] Even Goleman concedes, "It's very tough to measure our own emotional intelligence, because most of us don't have a very clear sense of how we come across to other people. . . ."[100] Honest feedback from others is necessary. Still, the area of emotional intelligence is useful for teachers and organizational trainers because, unlike IQ, social problem solving and the ability to control one's emotions can be taught and learned. Scores on emotional intelligence tests definitely should *not* be used for making hiring and promotion decisions until valid measuring tools are developed.

key terms

attitude 137
cognitions 121
emotional intelligence 143
emotions 140
external locus of control 137
intelligence 137
internal locus of control 134
learned helplessness 124
personality 132
proactive personality 134
self-concept 121
self-efficacy 123
self-esteem 122
self-monitoring 127
self-talk 132

chapter summary

- *Distinguish between self-esteem and self-efficacy.* Self-esteem is an overall evaluation of oneself, one's perceived self-worth. Self-efficacy is the belief in one's ability to successfully perform a task.
- *Contrast high and low self-monitoring individuals, and describe resulting problems each may have.* A high self-monitor strives to make a good public impression by closely monitoring his or her behavior and adapting it to the situation. Very high self-monitoring can create a "chameleon" who is seen as insincere and dishonest. Low self-monitors do the opposite by acting out their momentary feelings, regardless of their surroundings. Very low self-monitoring can lead to a one-way communicator who seems to ignore verbal and nonverbal cues from others.
- *Explain the social learning model of self-management.* Behavior results from interaction among four components: (a) situational cues, (b) the person's psychological self, (c) the person's behavior, and (d) consequences. Behavior, such as Covey's seven habits of highly effective people, can be developed by relying on supportive cognitive processes such as mental rehearsal and self-talk. Carefully arranged cues and consequences also help in the self-improvement process.
- *Identify and describe the Big Five personality dimensions, specify which one is correlated most strongly with job performance, and describe the proactive personality.* The Big Five personality dimensions are extraversion (social and talkative), agreeableness (trusting and cooperative),

conscientiousness (responsible and persistent), emotional stability (relaxed and unworried), and openness to experience (intellectual and curious). Conscientiousness is the best predictor of job performance. A person with a proactive personality shows initiative, takes action, and perseveres until a desired change occurs.

- *Explain the difference between an internal and external locus of control.* People with an *internal* locus of control, such as entrepreneurs, believe they are masters of their own fate. Those with an *external* locus of control attribute their behavior and its results to situational forces.
- *Explain the concepts of emotional contagion and emotional labor, and identify the four key components of emotional intelligence.* Emotions are indeed contagious, with good and bad moods "infecting" others. Emotional labor occurs when people need to repress their emotional reactions when serving others. Resentment, frustration, and even anger can result when "putting on a happy face" for customers and others. Four key components of emotional intelligence are self-awareness and self-management (for personal competence) and social awareness and relationship management (for social competence).

discussion questions

1. In the context of the chapter-opening vignette, how much does family history affect one's self-esteem and emotional intelligence? Explain.
2. How is someone you know with low self-efficacy, relative to a specified task, "programming themselves for failure"? What could be done to help that individual develop high self-efficacy?
3. What importance do you attach to self-talk in self-management? Explain.
4. On scales of low = 1 to high = 10, how would you rate yourself on the Big Five personality dimensions? Is your personality profile suitable for your present (or chosen) line of work? Explain.
5. Which of the four key components of emotional intelligence is (or are) your strong suit? Which is (or are) your weakest? What are the everyday implications of your EI profile?

ethical dilemma

Hot Heads!

Situation

You are the human resources vice president at a leading overnight express company. After lunch today, one of your top trainers excitedly plopped down in your office and said "Read this short section I marked in a *Business 2.0* article." You took it and read the following:

> Thrown any good lamps lately? Of course, you're probably too professional and well-bred to show anger at work. Just be aware: Being restrained may not be doing your career any good.
>
> For some years, Larissa Tiedens, an assistant professor of organizational behavior at Stanford Business School, has been studying the effects of anger in the workplace. Her research has revealed that employers have a bias toward promoting employees who get mad now and again. "I don't think we're cognizant of this," Tiedens says. "We make inferences about people all the time, and we don't always know where the information has come from."
>
> Tiedens began testing her hypothesis at a software firm in Palo Alto. She gave 24 of the employees a list of 10 or so emotions and asked them to rate how often their colleagues expressed each one. At the same time, the group managers filled out a questionnaire about how likely they would be to promote each of the employees. Those who were rated high on the anger scale were more likely to be on the promotion list. In a separate experiment, Tiedens had MBA students watch video clips of mock job interviews. In one tape the applicant shows visible signs of anger when discussing a presentation that went wrong, and in the other the candidate is fairly restrained. Most of the MBAs said they would have slotted the angry candidate for the higher-paying position.[101]

As you handed the reading back, you remarked "Let me see if I get this. You want to teach our managers *how* to get angry, or get angry *more often?*" An ethical flag went up in your mind.

What Would You Do?

1. Kill the idea on the spot. Explain how.
2. Take an immediate cue from what you just read and angrily tell the trainer that some research shouldn't be taken so literally. How would you do that?
3. Make an appointment with the trainer to discuss and refine the concept to make it an acceptable part of your management training program. Explain how.
4. Without hurting the trainer's feelings or discouraging creativity, take a few minutes to review the ethical implications of what you just read.
5. Invent other options. Discuss.

For an interpretation of this situation, visit our Web site, www.mhhe.com/kinickiob2e.

If you're looking for additional study materials, be sure to check out the Online Learning Center at

www.mhhe.com/kinickiob2e

for more information and interactivities that correspond to this chapter.

chapter Six

Motivation I: Needs, Job Design, Intrinsic Motivation, and Satisfaction

LEARNING OBJECTIVES

After reading the material in this chapter, you should be able to:

- Discuss the job performance model of motivation.
- Contrast Maslow's and McClelland's need theories.
- Describe the mechanistic, motivational, biological, and perceptual-motor approaches to job design.
- Review the four intrinsic rewards underlying intrinsic motivation, and discuss how managers can cultivate intrinsic motivation in others.
- Discuss the causes and consequences of job satisfaction.
- Critique the four hypotheses that explain the nature of work–family relationships.

SAKS FIFTH AVENUE AND ROCHE DIAGNOSTICS USE EMPLOYEE SURVEYS TO BOOST EMPLOYEE ENGAGEMENT

At Saks Fifth Avenue, the luxury retailer based in New York, executives were looking for ways to boost service to customers in their highly competitive market. Saks officials decided to measure employee engagement and customer engagement at stores, with customer engagement including willingness to make repeat purchases and recommend the store to friends.

"We used both to pinpoint problem spots," says Vice President Jay Redman. Saks found that "there absolutely is a correlation between employee engagement and customer engagement" and that customer engagement creates loyal, repeat customers and increased sales.

"We've seen 20 to 25 percent improvement in stores with great engagement," he says. But it's not just about higher sales figures. "How you get there is important."

There's been a major change in the nature of the dialog between management and the sales force, says Redman. Saks makes a point about asking employees what they need to do their jobs. Every time there is an initiative resulting from such dialog—for example, a flextime program was implemented recently, and many computers were upgraded—managers make sure to remind workers that this resulted from their suggestions.

"We've probably done 100 things over three years" in response to survey results, says Redman. "Some are as simple as opening a stairwell. People said they used to wait five to 10 minutes to go by elevator between floors" in a store.

A key message from Saks management to employees is that the dialog is intended to be a permanent feature. "The first year everyone thinks that it's a program. It's not a program anymore." . . .

At Roche Diagnostics Corp., a diagnostic systems manufacturer based in Indianapolis, high turnover was a troublesome problem. Company officials did some research and concluded that they needed to define and treat the root cause of the too-frequent departures of key workers.

They had what Patty Ayers, vice president for HR, called "a gut feeling" why turnover was high, but employee engagement surveys pinpointed the reasons. The company discovered, for example, that employees had concerns about career development. They needed better computer resources in the field. They wanted to understand the company's business strategy and where they fit in.

"When you get back hard data, it's no longer HR coming in and saying that we've got some problems over here or there. You now have statistical data to support your observations, and you've got a safe way to open direct conversations with employees. You then really get to the heart of the issues."

Many of the improvements that were implemented probably would have occurred without the engagement surveys, but the company made it clear to workers that certain changes were directly related to the feedback and the company's intent that they succeed. With such a dialog, "people walk away feeling that they are being listened to," says Ayers.

Today, "we are dramatically outperforming our competition," she says. "Having this kind of employee commitment is the reason."

She warns that it takes "a huge commitment in time and energy. But relative to some of the other investments you make, it has a pretty good return." And she notes that anyone doing a survey to gauge employee engagement should "expect to hear bad things. If you're only looking for positive feedback, you're going to be disappointed."[1]

FOR DISCUSSION

What are the pros and cons of using surveys to assess employee engagement? Explain. For an interpretation of this case and additional comments, visit our Online Learning Center:

www.mhhe.com/kinickiob2e

EFFECTIVE EMPLOYEE MOTIVATION has long been one of management's most difficult and important duties. Success in this endeavor is becoming more challenging in light of organizational trends to downsize and reengineer and the demands associated with managing a diverse workforce. As revealed in the opening case, companies such as Saks Fifth Avenue and Roche Diagnostics consider employee motivation and satisfaction as critical for organizational success. The purpose of this chapter, as well as the next, is to provide you with a foundation for understanding the complexities of employee motivation.

After discussing the fundamentals of employee motivation, this chapter focuses on (1) an overview of job design methods used to motivate employees, (2) the process of enhancing intrinsic motivation, and (3) job satisfaction and work–family relationships. Coverage of employee motivation extends to Chapter 7.

The Fundamentals of Employee Motivation

The term *motivation* derives from the Latin word *movere,* meaning "to move." In the present context, **motivation** represents "those psychological processes that cause the arousal, direction, and persistence of voluntary actions that are goal directed."[2] Managers need to understand these psychological processes if they are to successfully guide employees toward accomplishing organizational objectives. This section thus provides a conceptual framework for understanding motivation and examines need theories of motivation.

motivation

Psychological processes that arouse and direct goal-directed behavior.

A Job Performance Model of Motivation

Terence Mitchell, a well-known OB researcher, proposed a broad conceptual model that explains how motivation influences job behaviors and performance. This model, which is shown in Figure 6–1, integrates elements from several of the theories we discuss in this book. It identifies the causes and consequences of motivation.[3]

Figure 6–1 shows that individual inputs and job context are the two key categories of factors that influence motivation. As discussed in Chapter 5, employees bring ability, job knowledge, dispositions and traits, emotions, moods, beliefs, and values to the work setting. The job context includes the physical environment, the tasks one completes, the organization's approach to recognition and rewards, the adequacy of supervisory support and coaching, and the organization's culture (recall our discussion in Chapter 2). These two categories of factors influence each other as well as the motivational processes of arousal, direction, and persistence. Consider the motivational implications associated with the job context at Boston Beer Company, the maker of Samuel Adams beer:

> The 370-employee firm offers flexible scheduling and quarterly parties at the brewery, company-subsidized meals and home-brewing contests, paid adoption aid and a week of parental leave for workers with newborns. Employees get between 17 and 22 personal days a year, which they can use for any purpose—vacations, sick days or an opportunity to watch their child's piano recital. "By eliminating questions about why a person isn't coming in on a given day, we get rid of excuses and game-playing," says Jim Koch, chairman and founder. "We create an environment where employees act more responsibility and are treated with greater respect."[4]

FIGURE 6–1 | A Job Performance Model of Motivation

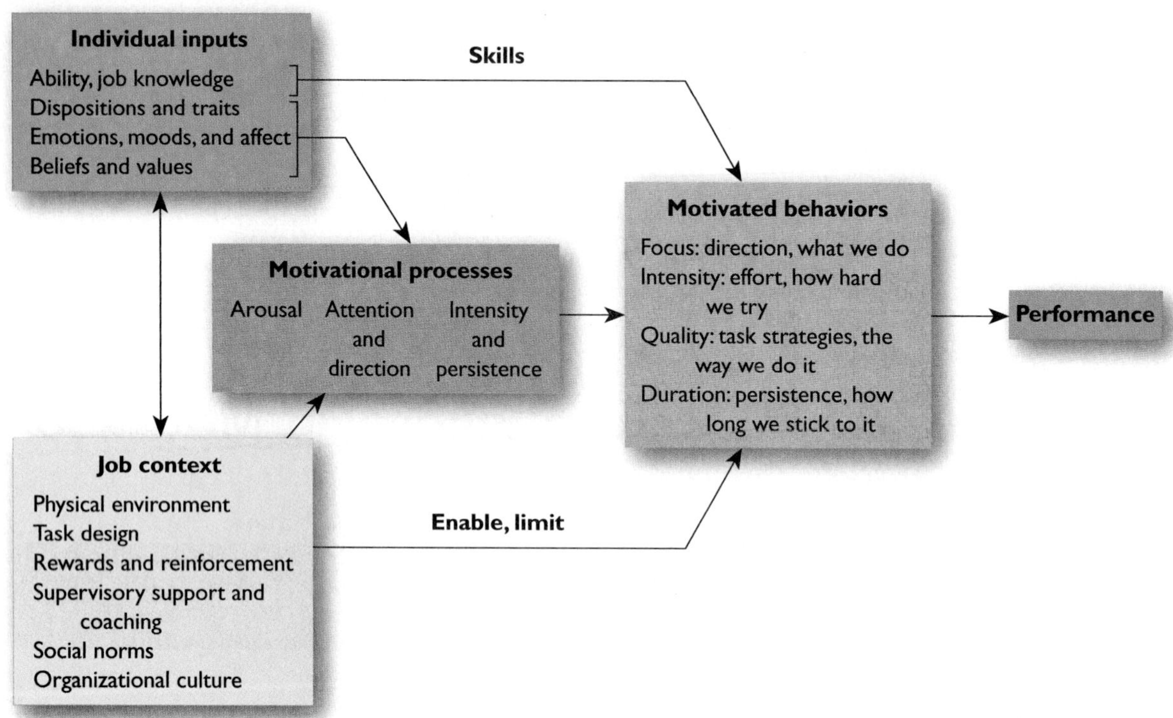

SOURCE: Adapted from T R Mitchell and D Daniels, "Motivation," in *Handbook of Psychology* (Vol 12), eds W C Borman, D R Ilgen, and R J Klimoski (Hoboken, NJ: John Wiley & Sons, Inc., 2003), p 226.

In support of the idea that job context influences employee motivation and performance, economics professors Sandra Black and Lisa Lynch estimated that 89% of the growth in multifactor productivity in the 1990s (i.e., the growth in productivity that goes beyond investments in new technology) was due to innovative workplace practices.[5] Examples include job rotation, which is discussed later in this chapter, tying compensation to performance (see Chapter 8), and employee empowerment (see Chapter 13).

Figure 6–1 further reveals that *motivated behaviors* are directly affected by an individual's ability and job knowledge (skills), motivation, and a combination of enabling and limiting job context factors. For instance, it would be difficult to persist on a project if you were working with defective raw materials or broken equipment. In contrast, motivated behaviors are likely to be enhanced when managers supply employees with adequate resources to get the job done and provide effective coaching. This coaching might entail furnishing employees with successful role models, showing employees how to complete complex tasks, and helping them maintain high self-efficacy and self-esteem (recall the discussion in Chapter 5). Performance is, in turn, influenced by motivated behavior.

needs

Physiological or psychological deficiencies that arouse behavior.

Need Theories of Motivation

Need theories attempt to pinpoint internal factors that energize behavior. **Needs** are physiological or psychological deficiencies that arouse behavior. They can be strong or weak and are influenced by environmental factors.

Human needs thus vary over time and place. Two popular need theories are discussed in this section: Maslow's need hierarchy theory and McClelland's need theory.

Maslow's Need Hierarchy Theory In 1943, psychologist Abraham Maslow published his now-famous need hierarchy theory of motivation. Although the theory was based on his clinical observation of a few neurotic individuals, it has subsequently been used to explain the entire spectrum of human behavior. Maslow proposed that motivation is a function of five basic needs—physiological, safety, love, esteem, and self-actualization.

Maslow said these five need categories are arranged in a prepotent hierarchy. In other words, he believed human needs generally emerge in a predictable stair-step fashion. Accordingly, when one's physiological needs are relatively satisfied, one's safety needs emerge, and so on up the need hierarchy, one step at a time. Once a need is satisfied it activates the next higher need in the hierarchy. This process continues until the need for self-actualization is activated.[6]

Although research does not clearly support this theory of motivation, there is one key managerial implication of Maslow's theory worth noting. That is, a satisfied need may lose its motivational potential. Therefore, managers are advised to motivate employees by devising programs or practices aimed at satisfying emerging or unmet needs. Many companies have responded to this recommendation by offering employees targeted benefits that meet their specific needs. Consider Marriott International, for example:

> The company found that employee participation in some benefits programs significantly reduced turnover and improved profitability in certain parts of the company. It was then able to estimate the impact of changes in base and incentive pay and benefits on the behavior of certain groups of employees—and ultimately on the profitability of different hotel properties. Those estimates were used to help devise strategies to reshape the company's rewards policies.[7]

Other companies are beginning to offer "specialized" benefits aimed at satisfying the needs of unique employees. Consider the case of Tom Tyler:

> With two job offers in hand, mechanical engineer Tom Tyler knew he'd be moving from suburban Detroit to the San Francisco area. The only question was, which employer would get his services? "The only difference between what [his eventual employer] offered me and the other company was the housing assistance," Tyler says. "The other company even offered $5,000 more per year in salary. But, when all was said and done, the house buying and selling assistance was worth somewhere in the neighborhood of $30,000. . . ." The benefit that swayed Tyler's job decision was mortgage help through an employer-assisted housing (EAH) program.[8]

In conclusion, managers are more likely to fuel employee motivation by offering benefits and rewards that meet individual needs.

McClelland's Need Theory David McClelland, a well-known psychologist, has been studying the relationship between needs and behavior since the late 1940s. Although he is most recognized for his research on the need for achievement, he also investigated the needs for affiliation and power. Let us consider each of these needs:

- The **need for achievement** is defined by the following desires:

  To accomplish something difficult. To master, manipulate, or organize physical objects, human beings, or ideas. To do this as rapidly and as independently as possible. To overcome obstacles and attain a high

need for achievement
Desire to accomplish something difficult.

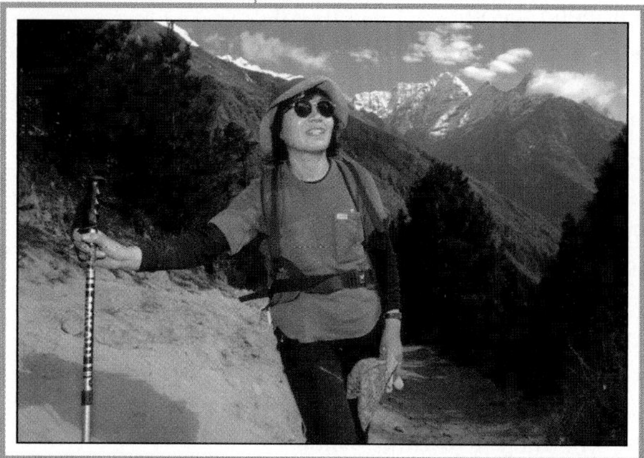

As a child growing up in Japan, Junko Tabei was called weak and frail by other children. In 1975, Tabei led an all-woman expedition to the summit of Mount Everest. Twelve days after living through an avalanche, she became the first woman to ever reach the top.

> standard. To excel one's self. To rival and surpass others. To increase self-regard by the successful exercise of talent.[9]

Achievement-motivated people share three common characteristics: (1) a preference for working on tasks of moderate difficulty; (2) a preference for situations in which performance is due to their efforts rather than other factors, such as luck; and (3) they desire more feedback on their successes and failures than do low achievers. A review of research on the "entrepreneurial" personality showed that entrepreneurs were found to have a higher need for achievement than nonentrepreneurs.[10]

- People with a high **need for affiliation** prefer to spend more time maintaining social relationships, joining groups, and wanting to be loved. Individuals high in this need are not the most effective managers or leaders because they have a hard time making difficult decisions without worrying about being disliked.
- The **need for power** reflects an individual's desire to influence, coach, teach, or encourage others to achieve. People with a high need for power like to work and are concerned with discipline and self-respect. There is a positive and negative side to this need. The negative face of power is characterized by an "if I win, you lose" mentality. In contrast, people with a positive orientation to power focus on accomplishing group goals and helping employees obtain the feeling of competence. More is said about the two faces of power in Chapter 13. Because effective managers must positively influence others, McClelland proposes that top managers should have a high need for power coupled with a low need for affiliation. He also believes that individuals with high achievement motivation are *not* best suited for top management positions. Several studies support these propositions.[11]

need for affiliation
Desire to spend time in social relationships and activities.

need for power
Desire to influence, coach, teach, or encourage others to achieve.

There are three managerial implications associated with McClelland's need theory. First, given that adults can be trained to increase their achievement motivation, and achievement motivation is correlated with performance, organizations should consider the benefits of providing achievement training for employees.[12] Second, achievement, affiliation, and power needs can be considered during the selection process, for better placement. For example, a study revealed that people with a high need for achievement were more attracted to companies that had a pay-for-performance environment than were those with a low achievement motivation.[13] Finally, managers should create challenging task assignments or goals because the need for achievement is positively correlated with goal commitment, which, in turn, influences performance.[14]

Motivating Employees through Job Design

Job design, also referred to as job redesign, "refers to any set of activities that involve the alteration of specific jobs or interdependent systems of jobs with the intent of improving the quality of employee job experience and their on-the-job productivity."[15] A team of researchers examined the various methods for conducting job design and integrated them into an interdisciplinary framework that contains four major approaches: mechanistic, motivational, biological, and perceptual-motor.[16] As you will learn, each approach to job design emphasizes different outcomes.[17] This section discusses these four approaches to job design and focuses most heavily on the motivational methods.

job design
Changing the content and/or process of a specific job to increase job satisfaction and performance.

The Mechanistic Approach

The mechanistic approach draws from research in industrial engineering and scientific management and is most heavily influenced by the work of Frederick Taylor. Taylor, a mechanical engineer, developed the principles of scientific management based on research and experimentation to determine the most efficient way to perform jobs. Because jobs are highly specialized and standardized when they are designed according to the principles of scientific management, this approach to job design targets efficiency, flexibility, and employee productivity.

Designing jobs according to the principles of scientific management has both positive and negative consequences. Positively, employee efficiency and productivity are increased. On the other hand, research reveals that simplified, repetitive jobs also lead to job dissatisfaction, poor mental health, higher levels of stress, and low sense of accomplishment and personal growth.[18] These negative consequences paved the way for the motivational approach to job design.

Motivational Approaches

The motivational approaches to job design attempt to improve employees' affective and attitudinal reactions such as job satisfaction and intrinsic motivation as well as a host of behavioral outcomes such as absenteeism, turnover, and performance.[19] We discuss three key motivational techniques: job enlargement, job enrichment, and a contingency approach called the job characteristics model.

Job Enlargement This technique was first used in the late 1940s in response to complaints about tedious and overspecialized jobs. **Job enlargement** involves putting more variety into a worker's job by combining specialized tasks of comparable difficulty. Some call this *horizontally loading* the job. Researchers recommend using job enlargement as part of a broader approach that uses multiple motivational methods because it does not have a significant and lasting positive effect on job performance by itself.[20]

job enlargement
Putting more variety into a job.

Job Rotation As with job enlargement, job rotation's purpose is to give employees greater variety in their work. **Job rotation** calls for moving employees from one specialized job to another. Rather than performing only one job, workers are trained and given the opportunity to perform two or more separate jobs on a rotating basis. By rotating employees from job to job, managers believe they can stimulate interest and motivation while providing employees with a broader perspective of the organization. Other proposed advantages of job rotation include increased worker flexibility and easier scheduling because employees are cross trained to perform different jobs. General Electric, for example, experienced many of these benefits from its rotation program for human resource (HR) entry-level employees.

job rotation
Moving employees from one specialized job to another.

> The goal of the program is to hire talented people who can become senior HR leaders in the company. . . . The program offers tremendous opportunities to

participants, says Peters [Susan Peters is vice president for executive development]. "The big attraction is the variety they get in the first few years," she says. "They see different businesses and different functions. You might start in labor relations, and then go to compensation, then to staffing, then benefits."

About a decade ago, GE added a cross-functional rotation to the mix, and it has become a key component of the program's success. "You have to go on the audit staff or become a marketing person for one rotation," Peters says. "We've learned that the HR function has to have good connectivity with the business operations and it improves the credibility of the individual later on."[21]

Despite positive experiences from companies like GE, it is not possible to draw firm conclusions about the value of job rotation programs because they have not been adequately researched.

Job Enrichment Job enrichment is the practical application of Frederick Herzberg's motivator–hygiene theory of job satisfaction. Herzberg's theory is based on a landmark study in which he interviewed 203 accountants and engineers.[22] These interviews sought to determine the factors responsible for job satisfaction and dissatisfaction. Herzberg found separate and distinct clusters of factors associated with job satisfaction and dissatisfaction. Job satisfaction was more frequently associated with achievement, recognition, characteristics of the work, responsibility, and advancement. These factors were all related to outcomes associated with the *content* of the task being performed. Herzberg labeled these factors **motivators** because each was associated with strong effort and good performance. He hypothesized that motivators cause a person to move from a state of no satisfaction to satisfaction (see Figure 6–2). Therefore,

motivators
Job characteristics associated with job satisfaction.

FIGURE 6–2 Herzberg's Motivator–Hygiene Model

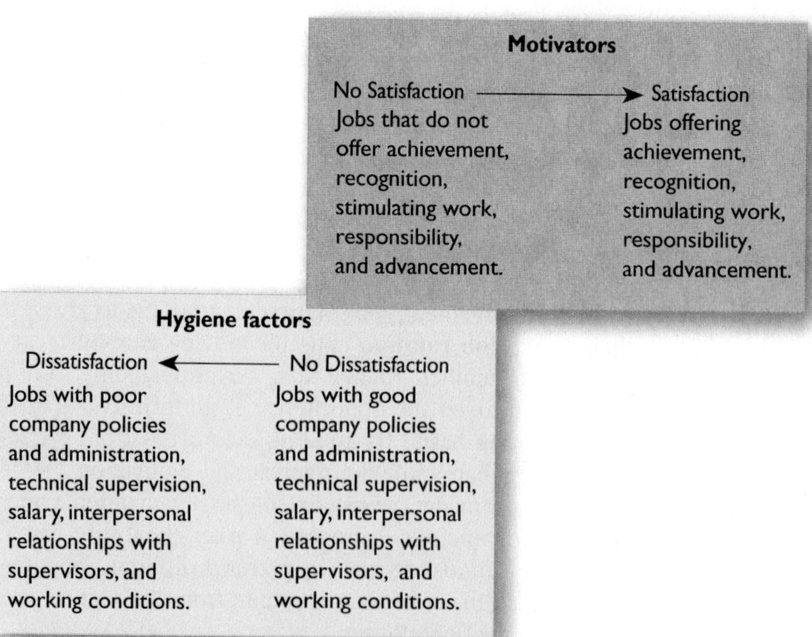

SOURCE: Adapted in part from D A Whitsett and E K Winslow, "An Analysis of Studies Critical of the Motivator–Hygiene Theory," *Personnel Psychology*, Winter 1967, pp 391–415.

Herzberg's theory predicts managers can motivate individuals by incorporating "motivators" into an individual's job.

hygiene factors
Job characteristics associated with job dissatisfaction.

Herzberg found job *dissatisfaction* to be associated primarily with factors in the work *context* or environment. Specifically, company policy and administration, technical supervision, salary, interpersonal relations with one's supervisor, and working conditions were most frequently mentioned by employees expressing job dissatisfaction. Herzberg labeled this second cluster of factors **hygiene factors.** He further proposed that they were not motivational. At best, according to Herzberg's interpretation, an individual will experience no job dissatisfaction when he or she has no grievances about hygiene factors (refer to Figure 6–2). In contrast, employees like Katrina Gill are likely to quit when poor hygiene factors lead to job dissatisfaction.

> Katrina Gill, a 36-year-old certified nursing aide, worked in one of the premiere long-term care facilities near Portland, Ore. From 10:30 p.m. to 7 a.m., she was on duty alone, performing three rounds on the dementia ward, where she took care of up to 28 patients a night for $9.32 an hour. She monitored vitals, turned for bedsores, and changed adult diapers. There were the constant vigils over patients like the one who would sneak into other rooms, mistaking female patients for his deceased wife. Worse was the resident she called "the hitter" who once lunged at her, ripping a muscle in her back and laying her flat for four days. Last month, Gill quit and took another job for 68¢ an hour more, bringing her salary to $14,400 a year.[23]

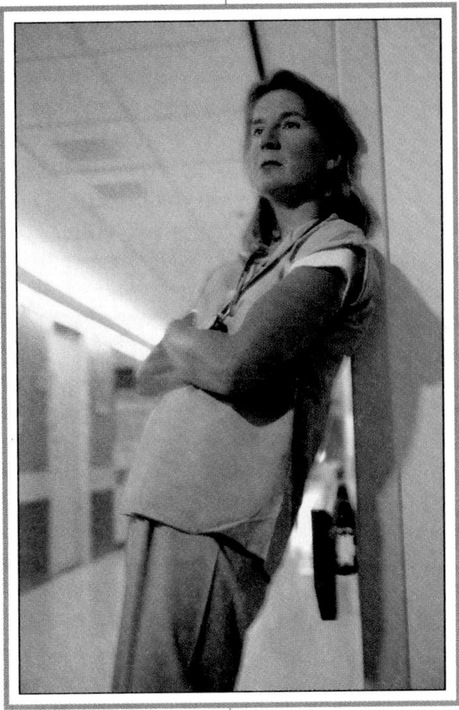

A 36-year-old certified nursing aide in a premiere long-term care facility endured 8 1/2 hours in the dementia ward where she took care of up to 28 patients a night for $9.32 an hour. She then quit and took a job for 68 cents more an hour, with no health benefits. Where would you say she fits on Herzberg's continuum?

The key to adequately understanding Herzberg's motivator–hygiene theory is recognizing that he believes that satisfaction is not the opposite of dissatisfaction. Herzberg concludes that "the opposite of job satisfaction is not job dissatisfaction, but rather no job satisfaction; and similarly, the opposite of job dissatisfaction is not job satisfaction, but no dissatisfaction."[24] Herzberg thus asserts that the dissatisfaction–satisfaction continuum contains a zero midpoint at which dissatisfaction and satisfaction are absent. Conceivably, an organization member who has good supervision, pay, and working conditions but a tedious and unchallenging task with little chance of advancement would be at the zero midpoint. That person would have no dissatisfaction (because of good hygiene factors) and no satisfaction (because of a lack of motivators).

Herzberg's theory generated a great deal of research and controversy. Although research does not support the two-factor aspect of his theory, it does support many of the theory's implications for job design.[25] Job enrichment is based on the application of Herzberg's ideas. Specifically, **job enrichment** entails modifying a job such that an employee has the opportunity to experience achievement, recognition, stimulating work, responsibility, and advancement. These characteristics are incorporated into a job through vertical loading. Rather than giving employees additional tasks of similar difficulty (horizontal loading), *vertical loading* consists of giving workers more responsibility. In other words, employees take on chores normally performed by their supervisors.

job enrichment
Building achievement, recognition, stimulating work, responsibility, and advancement into a job.

The Job Characteristics Model Two OB researchers, J Richard Hackman and Greg Oldham, played a central role in developing the job characteristics approach. These researchers tried to determine how work can be structured so that employees are internally or intrinsically motivated. **Intrinsic motivation** occurs when an individual is "turned on to one's work because of the positive internal feelings that are generated by doing well, rather than being dependent on external factors (such as incentive pay or compliments from the boss) for the motivation to work effectively."[26] These positive feelings power a self-perpetuating cycle of motivation. As shown in Figure 6–3, internal work motivation is determined by three psychological states. In turn, these psychological states are fostered by the presence of five core job dimensions. As you can see in Figure 6–3, the object of this approach is to promote high intrinsic motivation by designing jobs that possess the five core job characteristics shown in Figure 6–3. Let us examine the core job dimensions.

intrinsic motivation
Motivation caused by positive internal feelings.

In general terms, **core job dimensions** are common characteristics found to a varying degree in all jobs. Three of the job characteristics shown in Figure 6–3 combine to determine experienced meaningfulness of work:

core job dimensions
Job characteristics found to various degrees in all jobs.

- *Skill variety.* The extent to which the job requires an individual to perform a variety of tasks that require him or her to use different skills and abilities.
- *Task identity.* The extent to which the job requires an individual to perform a whole or completely identifiable piece of work. In other words, task identity is high when a person works on a product or project from beginning to end and sees a tangible result.

FIGURE 6–3 The Job Characteristics Model

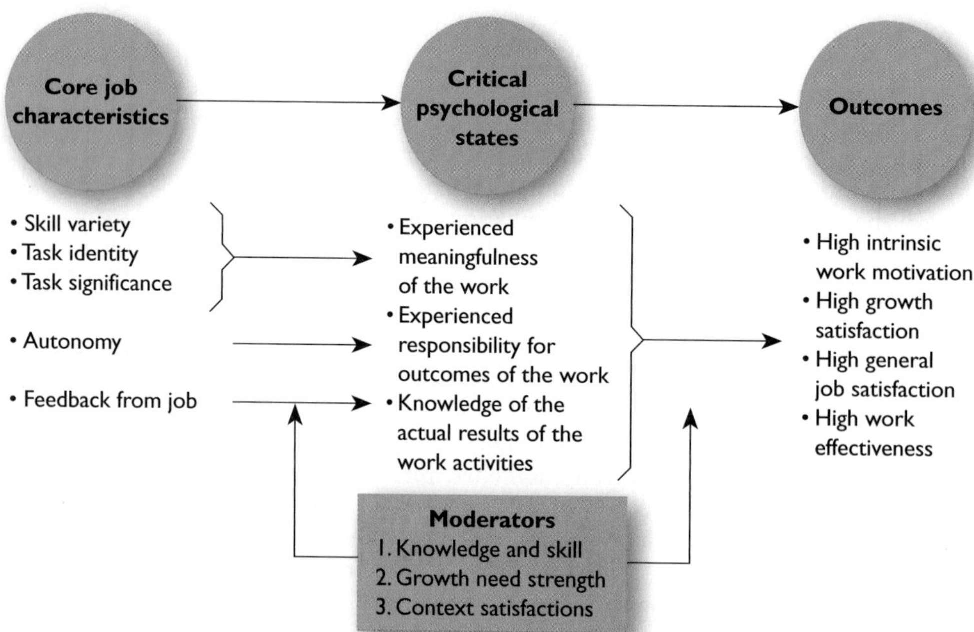

SOURCE: From J R Hackman and G R Oldham, *Work Redesign*, Copyright © 1980. Reprinted by permission of Pearson Education, Inc., Upper Saddle River, New Jersey.

- *Task significance.* The extent to which the job affects the lives of other people within or outside the organization.

Experienced responsibility is elicited by the job characteristic of autonomy, defined as follows:

- *Autonomy.* The extent to which the job enables an individual to experience freedom, independence, and discretion in both scheduling and determining the procedures used in completing the job.

Finally, knowledge of results is fostered by the job characteristic of feedback, defined as follows:

- *Feedback.* The extent to which an individual receives direct and clear information about how effectively he or she is performing the job.[27]

Hackman and Oldham recognized that everyone does not want a job containing high amounts of the five core job characteristics. They incorporated this conclusion into their model by identifying three attributes that affect how individuals respond to job enrichment. These attributes are concerned with the individual's knowledge and skill, growth need strength (representing the desire to grow and develop as an individual), and context satisfactions (see the box labeled Moderators in Figure 6–3). Context satisfactions represent the extent to which employees are satisfied with various aspects of their job, such as satisfaction with pay, co-workers, and supervision.

There are several practical implications associated with using the job characteristics model to enhance intrinsic motivation: Steps for applying this model are shown in Skills & Best Practices. Managers may want to use this model to increase employee job satisfaction. Research overwhelmingly demonstrates a moderately strong relationship between job characteristics and satisfaction.[28] Consistent with this finding, both ARUP Laboratories in Salt Lake City, Utah, and W.L. Gore in Newark, Delaware, attempted to enhance employee satisfaction by designing more autonomy into employees' jobs. ARUP laboratories allows employees to develop their own schedules—30% work seven 10-hour days and then take seven days off—while workers at Gore can choose specific projects they want to work on.[29]

Unfortunately, job redesign appears to reduce the quantity of output just as often as it has a positive effect. Caution and situational appropriateness are advised. For example, one study demonstrated that job redesign works better in less complex organizations (small plants or companies).[30] Nonetheless, managers are likely to find noticeable increases in the quality of performance after a job redesign program. Results from 21 experimental studies revealed that job redesign resulted in a median increase of 28% in the quality of performance.[31] Moreover, two separate meta-analyses support the practice of using the job characteristics model to help managers reduce absenteeism and turnover.[32] Athleta Corp., a sports apparel company in Petaluma, California, for instance, helped reduce employee turnover to less than 1% by using the job characteristic of autonomy to allow employees to set their own schedules and handle personal matters during the workday.[33]

SKILLS & BEST PRACTICES

Steps for Applying the Job Characteristics Model

1. Diagnose the work environment to determine the level of employee motivation and job satisfaction. Job design should be used when employee motivation ranges from low to moderately high. The diagnosis can be made using employee surveys.
2. Determine whether job redesign is appropriate for a given group of employees. Job redesign is most likely to work in a participative environment in which employees have the necessary knowledge and skills to perform the enriched tasks and their job satisfaction is average to high.
3. Determine how to best redesign the job. The focus of this effort is to increase those core job characteristics that are low. Employee input is essential during this step to determine the details of a redesign initiative.

The Freedom Task Chair is designed to conform to a user's shape, and each purchaser gets a custom fitting before he/she receives a chair. Its creator and designer, Niels Diffrient, states, "When design springs from an understanding of the people who are going to use a product, you begin to see forms that you would never have imagined." (from the Humanscale Web site at: www.humanscale.com)

Job characteristics research also underscores an additional implication for companies undergoing reengineering. Reengineering potentially leads to negative work outcomes because it increases job characteristics beyond reasonable levels. This occurs for two reasons: (1) reengineering requires employees to use a wider variety of skills to perform their jobs, and (2) reengineering typically results in downsizing and short-term periods of understaffing.[34] The unfortunate catch is that understaffing was found to produce lower levels of group performance, and jobs with either overly low or high levels of job characteristics were associated with higher stress.[35] Managers are advised to carefully consider the level of perceived job characteristics when implementing reengineering initiatives.

Biological and Perceptual-Motor Approaches

The biological approach to job design is based on research from biomechanics, work physiology, and ergonomics and focuses on designing the work environment to reduce employees' physical strain, fatigue, and health complaints.[36] An attempt is made to redesign jobs so that they eliminate or reduce the amount of repetitive motions from a worker's job. Intel, for example, has implemented the biological approach to job design.

> At Intel, the most common types of workplace injuries are musculoskeletal disorders. That's one reason the company has stepped up efforts to prevent and treat repetitive-motion injuries. When employees change offices, Intel will tear down and rebuild their workstations if needed so that they are ergonomically customized. They've created an ergonomics-profile database for their Santa Clara, CA, facility which includes information on workers' heights, preferred chairs, mouse arrangement, ideal desk heights, and whether employees are left- or right-handed. A companywide database is under development.[37]

The perceptual-motor approach is derived from research that examines human factors engineering, perceptual and cognitive skills, and information processing. This approach to job design emphasizes the reliability of work outcomes by examining error rates, accidents, and workers' feedback about facilities and equipment.[38] IBM and Steelcase are jointly developing a new interactive office system, labeled BlueSpace, that is based on this method of job design. Its features include[39]

- *BlueScreen:* A touch screen that sits next to a user's computer monitor and puts users in control of their heat or cooling, ventilation, and light.
- *Everywhere Display:* A video projector that displays information on walls, floors, desktops, and other surfaces.
- *Monitor rail:* A moving rail that consists of a work surface that travels the length of a work space and a dual monitor arm that rotates to nearly a complete circle, letting users be positioned almost anywhere.
- *Threshold:* An L-shaped partial ceiling and wall on wheels that provides on-demand visual and territorial privacy to a user.

The frequency of using both the biological and perceptual-motor approaches to job redesign is increasing in light of the number of workers who experience injuries related to overexertion or repetitive motion. A study conducted by the National Research Council and the Institute of Medicine revealed "Musculoskeletal disorders cause about 1 million employees to miss work each year and cost the nation $45 billion to $54 billion in compensation costs, lost wages and decreased productivity."[40] Moreover, the Occupational Safety and Health Administration (OSHA) implemented a new set of guidelines regarding ergonomic standards in the workplace due to this trend. The standards went into effect on October 14, 2001.[41]

Cultivating Intrinsic Motivation

The Gallup Organization has been studying employee engagement around the world for many years. It recently completed a study of employee engagement in the United States and 10 other countries. Sadly, results reveal that 27%, 56%, and 17% of the US workforce is actively engaged at work (i.e., loyal, productive, and satisfied), not engaged (i.e., not psychologically committed to their work role), and actively disengaged (i.e., disenchanted with their workplace) at work, respectively.[42] Results further reveal that the pattern of employee engagement is lower among the other 10 countries. These countries include Canada, Germany, Japan, Great Britain, Chile, France, Israel, Australia, New Zealand, and Singapore. Singapore, for instance, ranks among the lowest in the world in employee engagement, costing between $4.9 and $6.7 billion annually in lost productivity.[43]

Managers play a major role in the extent to which employees are engaged at work. Quite simply, employees tend to engage at work when they are intrinsically motivated. It thus is important to have an understanding of how managers can influence employees' intrinsic motivation.

We begin our exploration of intrinsic motivation by discussing the difference between intrinsic and extrinsic motivation and then presenting a model of intrinsic motivation. We conclude by reviewing the research and managerial implications pertaining to the model of intrinsic motivation.

The Foundation of Intrinsic Motivation

Intrinsic motivation was defined earlier as being driven by positive feelings associated with doing well on a task or job. Intrinsically motivated people are driven to act for the fun or challenge associated with a task rather than because of external rewards, pressures, or requests. Motivation comes from the psychological rewards associated with doing well on a task that one enjoys. It is important to note that individual differences exist when it comes to intrinsic motivation. People are intrinsically motivated for some activities and not others, and everyone is not intrinsically motivated by the same tasks.[44] For example, while the authors of this book are intrinsically motivated to write, we do not jump for joy when asked to proofread hundreds of pages. In contrast, someone else may hate to write but love the task of finding typos in a document.

extrinsic motivation

Motivation caused by the desire to attain specific outcomes.

In contrast to completing tasks for the joy of doing them, **extrinsic motivation** drives people's behavior when they do things in order to attain a specific outcome. In other words, extrinsic motivation is fueled by a person's desire to avoid or achieve some type of consequence for his or her behavior.[45] For example, a student who completes homework because he or she wants to avoid the embarrassment of being called on in class without knowing the answer is extrinsically motivated because he or she is doing it to avoid the negative outcome of being embarrassed. Similarly, a student who does homework because he or she believes it will help him or her obtain a job also is extrinsically motivated because he or she is studying for its instrumental value rather than because of pure interest. As you can see, extrinsic motivation is related to the receipt of extrinsic rewards. *Extrinsic rewards* do not come from the work itself; they are given by others (e.g., teachers, managers, parents, friends, or customers). At work, they include things like salaries, bonuses, promotions, benefits, awards, and titles.

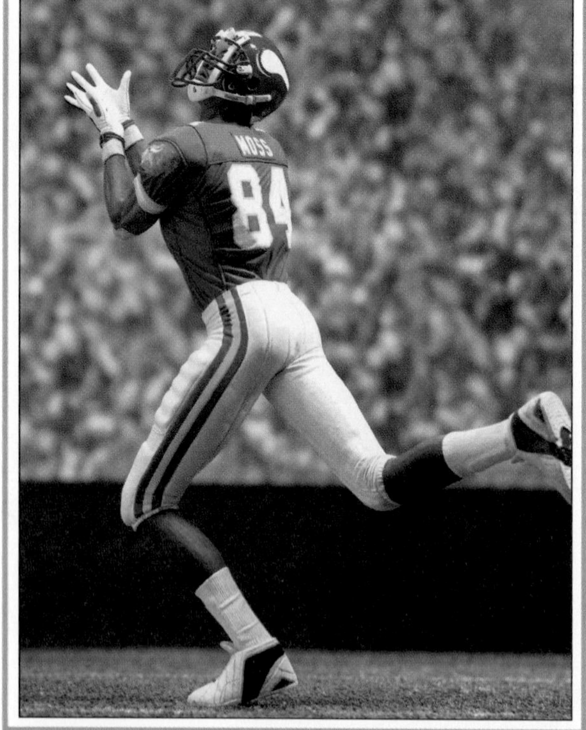

Are professional athletes like Randy Moss intrinsically or extrinsically motivated?

There has been an extensive amount of research on the topic of intrinsic motivation. The majority of this research relied on students performing tasks in laboratory experiments to determine whether or not the use of extrinsic rewards dampened their intrinsic motivation. Unfortunately, the overall pattern of results has created controversy and debate among researchers. Nonetheless, this conclusion does not detract from the value of focusing on the positive application of intrinsic motivation at work.

A Model of Intrinsic Motivation

Kenneth Thomas proposed the most recent model of intrinsic motivation. He developed his model by integrating research on empowerment, which is discussed in Chapter 13, with two previous models of intrinsic motivation.[46] Thomas specifically

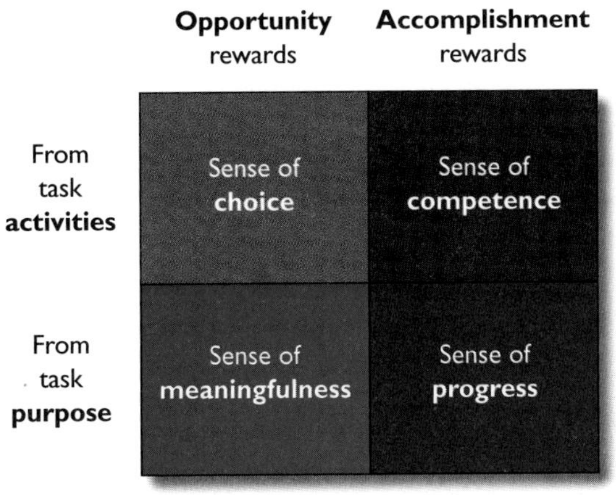

	Opportunity rewards	**Accomplishment** rewards
From task **activities**	Sense of **choice**	Sense of **competence**
From task **purpose**	Sense of **meaningfulness**	Sense of **progress**

FIGURE 6–4
A Model of Intrinsic Motivation

SOURCE: Reprinted with permission of the publisher. From *Intrinsic Motivation at Work: Building Energy and Commitment.* www.bkconnection.com.

linked components of the job characteristics model of job design discussed in the last section with Edward Deci and Richard Ryan's cognitive evaluation theory. Deci and Ryan proposed people must satisfy their needs for autonomy and competence when completing a task for it to be intrinsically motivating.[47] Thomas's model is shown in Figure 6–4.

Figure 6–4 illustrates the four key intrinsic rewards underlying an individual's level of intrinsic motivation. Looking across the rows, rewards of meaningfulness and progress are derived from the purpose for completing various tasks, while the sense of choice and sense of competence come from the specific tasks one completes. Looking down the columns, the sense of choice and meaningfulness are related to the opportunity to use one's own judgment and to pursue a worthwhile purpose. In contrast, accomplishment rewards—a sense of competence and progress—are derived from the extent to which individuals feel competent in completing tasks and successful in attaining their original task purpose, respectively. Thomas believes intrinsic motivation is a direct result of the extent to which an individual experiences these four intrinsic rewards while working. Let us examine these intrinsic rewards in more detail.

Sense of Meaningfulness "A **sense of meaningfulness** is the opportunity you feel to pursue a worthy task purpose. The feeling of meaningfulness is the feeling that you are on a path that is worth your time and energy—that you are on a valuable mission, that your purpose matters in the larger scheme of things."[48] This description reveals that it is not the task itself that drives intrinsic motivation, but rather the overall purpose for completing tasks. People have a desire to do meaningful work, work that makes a difference. This conclusion was supported by results from a national survey of employees. Results revealed that the primary contributor to workplace pride was that employees were doing work that mattered.[49]

sense of meaningfulness
The task purpose is important and meaningful.

Sense of Choice "A **sense of choice** is the opportunity you feel to select task activities that make sense to you and to perform them in ways that seem appropriate. The feeling of choice is the feeling of being free

sense of choice
The ability to use judgment and freedom when completing tasks.

to choose—of being able to use your own judgment and act out of your own understanding of the task."[50] Nordstrom's, for example, grants employees much latitude in determining how best to provide customer service. The company tells employees to use good judgment and to treat their job as if they were running their own business.[51]

sense of competence

Feelings of accomplishment associated with doing high-quality work.

Sense of Competence "A **sense of competence** is the accomplishment you feel in skillfully performing task activities you have chosen. The feeling of competence involves the sense that you are doing good, high-quality work on a task."[52] A sense of competence also is related to the level of challenge associated with completing tasks. In general, people feel a greater sense of competence by completing challenging tasks.

sense of progress

Feeling that one is accomplishing something important.

Sense of Progress "A **sense of progress** is the accomplishment you feel in achieving the task purpose. The feeling of progress involves the sense that the task is moving forward, that your activities are really accomplishing something."[53] A sense of progress promotes intrinsic motivation because it reinforces the feeling that one is wisely spending his or her time. A low sense of progress leads to discouragement. Over time, a low sense of progress can lower enthusiasm and lead to feelings of being stuck or helpless.

Research and Managerial Implications

Before discussing research and managerial implications, we would like you to complete the Hands-On Exercise on page 163. It assesses the level of intrinsic motivation in your current or past job. How did you stack up? Does your job need a dose of intrinsic rewards? If it does, the following discussion outlines how you or your manager might attempt to increase your intrinsic motivation.

Thomas's model of intrinsic motivation has not been subjected to much research at this point in time. This is partly due to its newness in the field of organizational behavior and the fact that the model is based on integrating theories—the job characteristics model and cognitive evaluation theory—that have been supported by past research. This leads us to conclude that the basic formulation of the model appears to be on solid ground, and future research is needed to study the specific recommendations for leading others toward intrinsic motivation.[54] In the meantime, managers are encouraged to use a different set of managerial behaviors to increase each of the four intrinsic rewards. Let us consider these managerial behaviors.

Managers can foster a sense of *meaningfulness* by inspiring their employees and modeling desired behaviors. This can be done by helping employees to identify their passions at work and creating an exciting organizational vision that employees are motivated to pursue. Managers can lead for *choice* by empowering employees and delegating meaningful assignments and tasks. Managers can enhance a sense of *competence* by supporting and coaching their employees. Providing positive feedback and sincere recognition can also be coupled with the assignment of a challenging task to fuel the intrinsic reward of competence.[55] Finally, managers can increase employees' sense of *progress* by monitoring and rewarding them. On-the-spot incentives are a useful way to reward a broader-based group of employees. "If an employee's performance has been exceptional—such as filling in for a sick colleague, perhaps, or working nights or weekends or cutting costs for the company—

HANDS-ON EXERCISE

Are You Intrinsically Motivated at Work?

INSTRUCTIONS: The following survey was designed to assess the extent to which you are deriving intrinsic rewards from your current job: If you are not working, use a past job or your role as a student to complete the survey. There are no right or wrong answers to the statements. Circle your answer by using the rating scale provided. After evaluating each of the survey statements, complete the scoring guide.

	Strongly Disagree	Disagree	Neither Agree or Disagree	Agree	Strongly Agree
1. I am passionate about my work.	1	2	3	4	5
2. I can see how my work tasks contribute to my organization's corporate vision.	1	2	3	4	5
3. I have significant autonomy in determining how I do my job.	1	2	3	4	5
4. My supervisor/manager delegates important projects/tasks to me that significantly impact my department's overall success.	1	2	3	4	5
5. I have mastered the skills necessary for my job.	1	2	3	4	5
6. My supervisor/manager recognizes when I competently perform my job.	1	2	3	4	5
7. Throughout the year, my department celebrates its progress toward achieving its goals.	1	2	3	4	5
8. I regularly receive evidence/information about my progress toward achieving my overall performance goals.	1	2	3	4	5

SCORING KEY

Sense of meaningfulness (add items 1–2) ______

Sense of choice (add items 3–4) ______

Sense of competence (add items 5–6) ______

Sense of progress (add items 7–8) ______

Overall score (add all items) ______

ARBITRARY NORMS

For each intrinsic reward, a score of 2–4 indicates low intrinsic motivation, 5–7 represents moderate intrinsic motivation, and 8–10 indicates high intrinsic motivation. For the overall score, 8–19 is low, 20–30 is moderate, and 31–40 is high.

the employer may reward the worker with a one-time bonus of $50, $100 or $500 shortly after the noteworthy actions."[56]

Job Satisfaction and Work–Family Relationships

An individual's work motivation is related to his or her job satisfaction and work–family relationships. Motivation is not independent of an employee's work environment or personal life. For example, your desire to study for your next OB test is jointly affected by how much you like the course and the state of your health at the time you are studying. It is very hard to study when you have a bad cold or the flu. Consider Warren Buffett's feelings about this issue. Buffett is the founder and chairman and CEO of Berkshire Hathaway, an investment firm located in Omaha, Nebraska, and is one of the wealthiest individuals in the United States. This is what he said to a group of students at the University of Washington:

> I can certainly define happiness, because happy is what I am . . . I get to do what I like to do every single day of the year. I get to do it with people I like, and I don't have to associate with anybody who causes my stomach to churn. I tap-dance to work . . . I'd advise you that when you go to work, work for an organization of people you admire, because it will turn you on. I always worry about people who say, "I'm going to do this for 10 years; I really don't like it very well. And then I'll do this. . . ." That's a little like saving up sex for your old age. Not a very good idea. I have turned down business deals that were otherwise decent deals because I didn't like the people I would have to work with. I didn't see any sense in pretending.[57]

Buffett is clearly motivated by his job and work environment. Because of the dynamic relationships between motivation, job satisfaction, and work–family relationships, we conclude this chapter by discussing the causes and consequences of job satisfaction and work–family relationships. This information will increase your understanding about how to motivate others as well as yourself.

The Causes of Job Satisfaction

job satisfaction

An affective or emotional response to one's job.

Job satisfaction is an affective or emotional response toward various facets of one's job. This definition means job satisfaction is not a unitary concept. Rather, a person can be relatively satisfied with one aspect of his or her job and dissatisfied with one or more other aspects. The Hands-On Exercise, for instance, assesses your satisfaction with recognition, compensation, and supervision. Please take a moment now to determine how satisfied you are with three aspects of your present or most recent job, and then use the norms to compare your score.[58] How do you feel about your job?

Research revealed that job satisfaction varied across countries. A study of 9,300 adults in 39 countries identified the percentage of workers who said they were "very satisfied with their jobs." The top five countries were Denmark (61%), India (urban middle- and upper-class only; 55%), Norway (54%), United States (50%), and Ireland (49%). Experts suggest that job satisfaction is highest in Denmark because labor and management have a great working relationship. The bottom five countries were Estonia (11%), China (11%), Czech Republic (10%), Ukraine (10%), and Hungary (9%). Why do Hungarian employees indicate the lowest job satisfaction? An average monthly salary of $302 and poor labor management relations are two possible

HANDS-ON EXERCISE

How Satisfied Are You with Your Present Job?

	Very Dissatisfied				Very Satisfied
1. The way I am noticed when I do a good job	1	2	3	4	5
2. The recognition I get for the work I do	1	2	3	4	5
3. The praise I get for doing a good job	1	2	3	4	5
4. How my pay compares with that for similar jobs in other companies	1	2	3	4	5
5. My pay and the amount of work I do	1	2	3	4	5
6. How my pay compares with that of other workers	1	2	3	4	5
7. The way my boss handles employees	1	2	3	4	5
8. The way my boss takes care of complaints brought to him/her by employees	1	2	3	4	5
9. The personal relationship between my boss and his/her employees	1	2	3	4	5

Total score for satisfaction with recognition (add questions 1–3), compensation (add questions 4–6), and supervision (add questions 7–9).

Comparative norms for each dimension of job satisfaction are: Total score of 3–6 = Low job satisfaction; 7–11 = Moderate satisfaction; 12 and above = High satisfaction.

SOURCE: Adapted from D J Weiss, R V Dawis, G W England, and L H Lofquist, Manual for the *Minnesota Satisfaction Questionnaire* (Minneapolis: Industrial Relations Center, University of Minnesota, 1967). Used with permission of Vocational Psychology Research, University of Minnesota.

causes.[59] OB researchers have identified other causes of job satisfaction and dissatisfaction.

Five predominant models of job satisfaction specify its causes. They are need fulfillment, discrepancy, value attainment, equity, and dispositional/genetic components. A brief review of these models will provide insight into the complexity of this seemingly simple concept.[60]

Need Fulfillment These models propose that satisfaction is determined by the extent to which the characteristics of a job allow an individual to fulfill his or her needs. For example, a survey of 30 Massachusetts law firms revealed that 35% to 50% of law-firm associates left their employers within three years of starting because the firms did not accommodate family needs. This example illustrates that unmet needs can affect both satisfaction and turnover.[61] Although these models generated a great degree of controversy, it is generally accepted that need fulfillment is correlated with job satisfaction.[62]

Discrepancies These models propose that satisfaction is a result of met expectations. **Met expectations** represent the difference between what an individual expects to receive from a job, such as good pay and promotional opportunities, and what he or she actually receives. When expectations are greater than what is received, a person will be dissatisfied. In contrast, this model predicts the individual will be satisfied when he or she attains outcomes above and beyond expectations. A meta-analysis of 31 studies that included 17,241 people demonstrated that met expectations were significantly

met expectations

The extent to which one receives what he or she expects from a job.

related to job satisfaction.[63] Many companies use employee attitude or opinion surveys to assess employees' expectations and concerns (see Skills & Best Practices).

Value Attainment The idea underlying **value attainment** is that satisfaction results from the perception that a job allows for fulfillment of an individual's important work values.[64] In general, research consistently supports the prediction that value fulfillment is positively related to job satisfaction.[65] Managers can thus enhance employee satisfaction by structuring the work environment and its associated rewards and recognition to reinforce employees' values.

value attainment

The extent to which a job allows fulfillment of one's work values.

Equity In this model, satisfaction is a function of how "fairly" an individual is treated at work. Satisfaction results from one's perception that work outcomes, relative to inputs, compare favorably with a significant other's outcomes/inputs. A meta-analysis involving 190 studies and 64,757 people supported this model. Employees' perceptions of being treated fairly at work were highly related to overall job satisfaction.[66] Managers thus are encouraged to monitor employees' fairness perceptions and to interact with employees in such a way that they feel equitably treated. Chapter 7 explores this promising model in more detail.

SKILLS & BEST PRACTICES

Lockheed Martin Uses Surveys to Assess Employees' Job Satisfaction and Improve Employee Engagement

Bethesda, Md.-based Lockheed Martin (ranked 9 [in *Fortune*'s 100 Best Companies to Work For]) also uses surveys to help measure job retention efforts. The company conducts an all-employee survey biannually to assess satisfaction across 26 job attributes considered critical to recruitment, retention and performance. Survey results in 2001 showed a need for improvement in articulating the corporate mission for objectives and performance management. Lockheed's training organization played a key role in developing programs to meet those needs, including a new performance recognition system, performance management training, a formal mentoring program and training for coaching and mentoring. These carefully targeted programs worked. The results of the 2003 survey showed an 11 to 17 percent gain on all of Lockheed's targeted indices, including intention to remain and job engagement.

SOURCE: Excerpted from G Johnson, "And the Survey Says . . . ," *Training*, March 2004, p 28.

Dispositional/Genetic Components Have you ever noticed that some of your co-workers or friends appear to be satisfied across a variety of job circumstances, whereas others always seem dissatisfied? This model of satisfaction attempts to explain this pattern.[67] Specifically, the dispositional/genetic model is based on the belief that job satisfaction is partly a function of both personal traits and genetic factors. As such, this model implies that stable individual differences are just as important in explaining job satisfaction as are characteristics of the work environment. Although only a few studies have tested these propositions, results support a positive, significant relationship between personal traits and job satisfaction over time periods ranging from 2 to 50 years.[68] Genetic factors also were found to significantly predict life satisfaction, well-being, and general job satisfaction.[69] Overall, researchers estimate that 30% of an individual's job satisfaction is associated with dispositional and genetic components.[70]

The Consequences of Job Satisfaction

This area has significant managerial implications because thousands of studies have examined the relationship between job satisfaction and other organizational variables. Because it is impossible to examine them all, we will consider a subset of the more important variables from the standpoint of managerial relevance.

TABLE 6–1 Correlates of Job Satisfaction

Variables Related with Satisfaction	Direction of Relationship	Strength of Relationship
Motivation	Positive	Moderate
Job involvement	Positive	Moderate
Organizational citizenship behavior	Positive	Moderate
Organizational commitment	Positive	Strong
Absenteeism	Negative	Weak
Tardiness	Negative	Weak
Turnover	Negative	Moderate
Heart disease	Negative	Moderate
Perceived stress	Negative	Strong
Pro-union voting	Negative	Moderate
Job performance	Positive	Moderate
Life satisfaction	Positive	Moderate
Mental health	Positive	Moderate

Table 6–1 summarizes the pattern of results. The relationship between job satisfaction and these other variables is either positive or negative. The strength of the relationship ranges from weak (very little relationship) to strong. Strong relationships imply that managers can significantly influence the variable of interest by increasing job satisfaction. Let us now consider several of the key correlates of job satisfaction.

Motivation A recent meta-analysis of nine studies and 1,739 workers revealed a significant positive relationship between motivation and job satisfaction. Because satisfaction with supervision also was significantly correlated with motivation, managers are advised to consider how their behavior affects employee satisfaction.[71] Managers can potentially enhance employees' motivation through various attempts to increase job satisfaction.

Job Involvement Job involvement represents the extent to which an individual is personally involved with his or her work role. A meta-analysis involving 27,925 individuals from 87 different studies demonstrated that job involvement was moderately related with job satisfaction.[72] Managers are thus encouraged to foster satisfying work environments in order to fuel employees' job involvement.

Organizational Citizenship Behavior **Organizational citizenship behaviors (OCBs)** consist of employee behaviors that are beyond the call of duty. Examples include "such gestures as constructive statements about the department, expression of personal interest in the work of others, suggestions for improvement, training new people, respect for the spirit as well as the letter of housekeeping rules, care for organizational property, and punctuality and attendance well beyond standard or

organizational citizenship behaviors (OCBs)
Employee behaviors that exceed work-role requirements.

"It's good for morale."

FARCUS® is reprinted with permission from LaughingStock Licensing Inc., Ottawa, Canada.

enforceable levels."[73] Managers certainly would like employees to exhibit these behaviors. A meta-analysis covering 7,100 people and 22 separate studies revealed a significant and moderately positive correlation between organizational citizenship behaviors and job satisfaction.[74] Moreover, additional research demonstrated that employees' citizenship behaviors were determined more by leadership and characteristics of the work environment than by an employee's personality.[75] It thus appears that managerial behavior significantly influences an employee's willingness to exhibit citizenship behaviors. This relationship is important to recognize because employees' OCBs were positively correlated with their conscientiousness at work, organizational commitment, and performance ratings.[76] Another recent study demonstrated a broader impact of OCBs on organizational effectiveness. Results revealed that the amount of OCBs exhibited by employees working in 28 regional restaurants was significantly associated with each restaurant's corporate profits one year later.[77]

Organizational Commitment Organizational commitment reflects the extent to which an individual identifies with an organization and is committed to its goals. A meta-analysis of 68 studies and 35,282 individuals uncovered a significant and strong relationship between organizational commitment and satisfaction.[78] Managers are advised to increase job satisfaction in order to elicit higher levels of commitment. In turn, higher commitment can facilitate higher productivity.

Absenteeism Absenteeism is costly, and managers are constantly on the lookout for ways to reduce it. One recommendation has been to increase job satisfaction. If this is a valid recommendation, there should be a strong negative relationship (or negative correlation) between satisfaction and absenteeism. In other words, as satisfaction increases, absenteeism should decrease. A researcher tracked this prediction by synthesizing three separate meta-analyses containing a total of 74 studies. Results revealed a weak negative relationship between satisfaction and absenteeism.[79] It is unlikely, therefore, that managers will realize any significant decrease in absenteeism by increasing job satisfaction.

Turnover Turnover is important to managers because it both disrupts organizational continuity and is very costly. A meta-analysis of 67 studies covering 24,566 people demonstrated a moderate negative relationship between satisfaction and turnover[80] (see Table 6–1). Given the strength of this relationship, managers would be well advised to try to reduce turnover by increasing employee job satisfaction.

Have you ever debated whether or not to quit a job? Based on the above discussion, your job satisfaction probably figured into your deliberations. That said, there are other factors to consider when determining whether or not to leave an organization. The Skills & Best Practices summarizes some telltale signs when it may make sense to quit a job.

Perceived Stress Stress can have very negative effects on organizational behavior and an individual's health. Stress is positively related to absenteeism, turnover, coronary heart disease, and viral infections.[81] Based on a meta-analysis of seven studies covering 2,659 individuals, Table 6–1 reveals that perceived stress has a strong, negative relationship with job satisfaction.[82] It is hoped that managers would attempt to reduce the negative effects of stress by improving job satisfaction.

Job Performance One of the biggest controversies within OB research centers on the relationship between job satisfaction and job performance. Although researchers have identified seven different ways in which these variables are related, the dominant beliefs are either that satisfaction causes performance or performance causes satisfaction.[83] A team of researchers recently attempted to resolve this controversy through a meta-analysis of data from 312 samples involving 54,417 individuals.[84] There were two key findings from this study. First, job satisfaction and performance are moderately related. This is an important finding because it supports the belief that employee job satisfaction is a key work attitude managers should consider when attempting to increase employees' job performance. Second, the relationship between job satisfaction and performance is much more complex than originally thought. It is not as simple as satisfaction causing performance or performance causing satisfaction. Rather, researchers now believe both variables indirectly influence each other through a host of individual differences and work-environment characteristics.[85] There is one additional consideration to keep in mind regarding the relationship between job satisfaction and job performance.

Researchers believe the relationship between satisfaction and performance is understated due to incomplete measures of individual-level performance. For example, if performance ratings used in past research did not reflect the actual interactions and interdependencies at work, inaccurate measures of performance served to lower the reported correlations between satisfaction and performance. Examining the relationship between *aggregate* measures of job satisfaction and organizational performance is one solution to correct this problem.[86] In support of these ideas, a team of researchers conducted a recent meta-analysis of 7,939 business units in 36 companies. Results uncovered significant positive relationships between business-unit-level employee satisfaction and business-unit outcomes of customer satisfaction, productivity, profit, employee turnover, and accidents.[87] It thus appears managers can positively affect a variety of important organizational outcomes, including performance, by increasing employee job satisfaction.

SKILLS & BEST PRACTICES

Telltale Signs That You Should Look for Another Job

- Current job's requirements aren't a good match with your best skills.
- Job doesn't adequately meet your needs in areas you value, such as work-family balance, work location and compensation.
- Requests for advancement or new opportunities are consistently ignored or only half met.
- Is work making you miserable? Family and friends tell you that your job has changed you for the worse.
- Your job ranks low on a "joy and meaning" scale.
- Your standing in the office has been diminished—for example, key clients or vendors no longer deal with you.

SOURCE: G F Ceron, "When Leaving Is the Best Move," *The Wall Street Journal*, Eastern Edition, March 29, 2004, p R4.

Work–Family Relationships

Have you ever been stressed at home because of something that happened at work? Conversely, have you found it hard to focus at work because of problems occurring

Single working-parent families face a tough challenge in balancing work and home life. Single moms—divorced, widowed, or never married—account for over 9 million of single-parent households. For single parents, business travel and other routine demands of a corporate career—including overtime and interoffice transfers—can turn life upside down. Sometimes single parents decline promotions or high-profile assignments to preserve time with their children. In some organizations, experts say, it may be assumed single-mom staffers can't handle new duties because of the responsibilities they're shouldering at home.

at home? If you answered yes, then you have experienced the dynamic interplay between work and family relationships. This relationship is becoming increasingly important in light of the increased number of women in the workforce (particularly those with children), the growth in dual-career couples, an aging population, and organizational pressures to accomplish more with constrained resources.

This section helps you to understand and manage your work–family relationships by examining four alternative hypotheses that explain the interaction between work and family and by discussing organizational responses to this issue.

Hypotheses Regarding Work–Family Relationships OB researchers have proposed a variety of mechanisms linking work and family[88] We discuss four hypotheses that pertain to a subset of these mechanisms. The first hypothesis, called the *compensation effect,* suggests that job and life satisfaction are negatively related. That is, we compensate for low job or life satisfaction by seeking satisfying activities in the other domains. A meta-analysis of 34 studies covering 19,811 people failed to support this prediction. Results revealed a significant and positive correlation between job and life satisfaction.[89] The *segmentation hypothesis* proposes that job satisfaction and life satisfaction are independent—one supposedly does not influence the other. Research also did not confirm this model. Recent research supports the third hypothesis, which is called the *spillover model.*

The **spillover model** hypothesizes that job satisfaction or dissatisfaction spills over into one's personal life and vice versa. In other words, each affects the other both positively and negatively on an ongoing basis. Consider the case of Anne Crum Ross:

> In the months leading up to her wedding last July, Anne Crum Ross says the line between her work and her personal life dissolved. "For every five work calls I made at the office, I made one wedding-planning call," she says. With just three months to go before the ceremony, she changed jobs in real estate and became director of corporate training at Sussex & Reilly in Chicago. She took the wedding-guest and catering files she had stored on her Palm to her new office. "As long as I was doing my work, my bosses didn't have a problem with me doing wedding planning," she says. "It's all about knowing how to multitask."[90]

Anne resolved the spillover of her personal and work lives by being more organized. This example also illustrates the essence of the fourth hypothesis regarding work–family relationships. This hypothesis, labeled *work–family conflict,* is based on the idea that the roles we assume in our work and family domains are mutually incompatible. This means that the roles and associated expectations in one domain of our life (e.g., work) make it difficult to meet the demands in the other (e.g., family). In turn, these competing roles create a fundamental source of work–family conflict that influences our well-being and happiness. Research clearly supports the existence of work–family conflict and its effect on important personal and organizational outcomes.[91]

spillover model

Describes the reciprocal relationship between job and life satisfaction.

Organizational Response to Work–Family Issues Organizations have implemented a variety of "family-friendly" programs and services aimed at helping employees to balance the interplay between their work and personal lives. These programs included providing child-care services, flexible work schedules, cafeteria benefit plans, telecommuting, dry-cleaning services, concierge services, ATM at work, and stress reduction programs.[92] Although these programs are positively received by employees, experts now believe that such efforts are partially misguided because they focus on balancing work–family issues rather than integrating them. Balance is needed for opposites, and work and family are not opposites. Rather, our work and personal lives should be a well-integrated whole. A team of researchers arrived at the following conclusion regarding the need to integrate versus balance work–life issues.

> Gendered assumptions and stereotypes based in the separation of [occupational and family] spheres constrain the choices of both women and men. Our vision of gender equity is to relax these social norms about separation so that men and women are free to experience these two parts of their lives as integrated rather than as separate domains that need to be "balanced." Integration would make it possible for both women and men to perform up to their capabilities and find satisfaction in both work and personal life, no matter how they allocate their time commitment between the two. To convey this goal, we speak of integrating work and personal life rather than balancing. This terminology expresses our belief in the need to diminish the separation between these two spheres of life in ways that will *change both,* rather than merely reallocating—or "balancing"—time between them as they currently exist.[93]

key terms

core job dimensions 156
extrinsic motivation 160
hygiene factors 155
intrinsic motivation 156
job design 153
job enlargement 153
job enrichment 155
job rotation 153
job satisfaction 164
met expectations 165
motivation 149
motivators 154
need for achievement 151
need for affiliation 152
need for power 152
needs 150
organizational citizenship behaviors (OCBs) 167
sense of choice 161
sense of competence 162
sense of meaningfulness 161
sense of progress 162
spillover model 170
value attainment 166

chapter summary

- *Discuss the job performance model of motivation.* Individual inputs and job context variables are the two key categories of factors that influence motivation. In turn, motivation leads to motivated behaviors, which then affect performance.
- *Contrast Maslow's and McClelland's need theories.* Two well-known need theories of motivation are Maslow's need hierarchy and McClelland's need theory. Maslow's notion of a prepotent or stair-step hierarchy of five levels of needs has not stood up well under research. McClelland believes that motivation and performance vary according to the strength of an individual's need for achievement. High achievers prefer moderate risks and situations where

they can control their own destiny. Top managers should have a high need for power coupled with a low need for affiliation.

- *Describe the mechanistic, motivational, biological, and perceptual-motor approaches to job design.* The mechanistic approach is based on industrial engineering and scientific management and focuses on increasing efficiency, flexibility, and employee productivity. Motivational approaches aim to improve employees' affective and attitudinal reactions and behavioral outcomes. Job enlargement, job enrichment, and a contingency approach called the job characteristics model are motivational approaches to job design. The biological approach focuses on designing the work environment to reduce employees' physical strain, effort, fatigue, and health complaints. The perceptual-motor approach emphasizes the reliability of work outcomes.
- *Review the four intrinsic rewards underlying intrinsic motivation, and discuss how managers can cultivate intrinsic motivation in others.* Intrinsic motivation is driven by the opportunity rewards of a sense of meaningfulness and a sense of choice, and the accomplishment rewards of a sense of competence and a sense of progress. Senses of meaningfulness and progress are driven by the purpose underlying task completion, whereas senses of choice and competence revolve around the tasks one performs at work. Managers specifically lead for meaningfulness, choice, competence, and progress by inspiring and modeling, empowering and delegating, supporting and coaching, and monitoring and rewarding, respectively.
- *Discuss the causes and consequences of job satisfaction.* Job satisfaction is an affective or emotional response toward various facets of one's job. Five models of job satisfaction specify its causes. They are need fulfillment, discrepancy, value attainment, equity, and trait/genetic components. Job satisfaction has been correlated with hundreds of consequences. Table 6–1 summarizes the pattern of results found for a subset of the more important variables.
- *Critique the four hypotheses that explain the nature of work–family relationships.* The compensation effect predicts that job and life satisfaction are negatively related, and the segmentation hypothesis proposes that job satisfaction and life satisfaction are independent. Neither of these hypotheses are supported by research. The spillover hypothesis, which is confirmed by research, predicts that job satisfaction and life satisfaction affect each other both positively and negatively on an ongoing basis. The work–family conflict hypothesis is based on the idea that the roles we assume in our work and family life domains are mutually incompatible. This creates an inherent conflict between our work and family relationships.

discussion questions

1. How did the use of employee surveys at Saks Fifth Avenue and Roche Diagnostics help managers apply need theories of motivation and various job design techniques? Explain.
2. Why should the average manager be well versed in the various motivation theories?
3. Which of the four types of job design is most likely to be used in the future? Explain your rationale.
4. To what extent is your behavior and performance as a student a function of intrinsic and extrinsic motivation? Explain.
5. What are the three most valuable lessons about employee motivation that you have learned from this chapter?

ethical dilemma

Should I Ignore the Cheating?

You are taking a college course. The tests and quizzes are online through the class Web site. The professor gives you a three-day window and you take the tests in your personal time. The professor has strict guidelines about cheating. At the beginning of the semester, he told all of you that the tests and quizzes will be timed so you will not have enough time to look the answers up in the book. You are in the computing commons taking one of the quizzes and notice a group of your classmates huddled around a computer. They are taking the quiz as well. One student is looking up the answers in the book, one is taking the quiz, and the other is recording the answers.

As a student, what would you do?

1. Immediately contact your professor about what is going on. It is unfair to the rest of your classmates if these three get away with cheating.
2. Form a similar test group of your own. The professor never specifically said you couldn't take the tests in groups.
3. Ignore the group's behavior and continue taking the test. You are sure these three will be caught eventually and at least you will know you *earned* your grade.
4. Invent other options. Discuss.

If you're looking for additional study materials, be sure to check out the Online Learning Center at

www.mhhe.com/kinickiob2e

for more information and interactivities that correspond to this chapter.

chapter Seven

Motivation II: Equity, Expectancy, and Goal Setting

LEARNING OBJECTIVES

After reading the material in this chapter, you should be able to:

- Discuss the role of perceived inequity in employee motivation.
- Describe the practical lessons derived from equity theory.
- Explain Vroom's expectancy theory.
- Describe the practical implications of expectancy theory.
- Identify five practical lessons to be learned from goal-setting research.
- Specify issues that should be addressed before implementing a motivational program.

CUTTING COSTS CAN DE-MOTIVATE EMPLOYEES

When executives start talking about cutting costs, there are those things—layoffs, tightened travel, revoked benefits and perks—that employees might expect to suffer. And then there are those efforts you can hardly believe.

For Ken Marcus, it was having his former company force employees to pay for the pizza slices their spouses ate on a business trip, and the company's $5 Christmas-party budget (yes, that's $5 total). But the measure that most stood out was when the former chief financial officer ordered employees not to skip lines on interoffice envelopes because, he complained, "we were using too many envelopes."

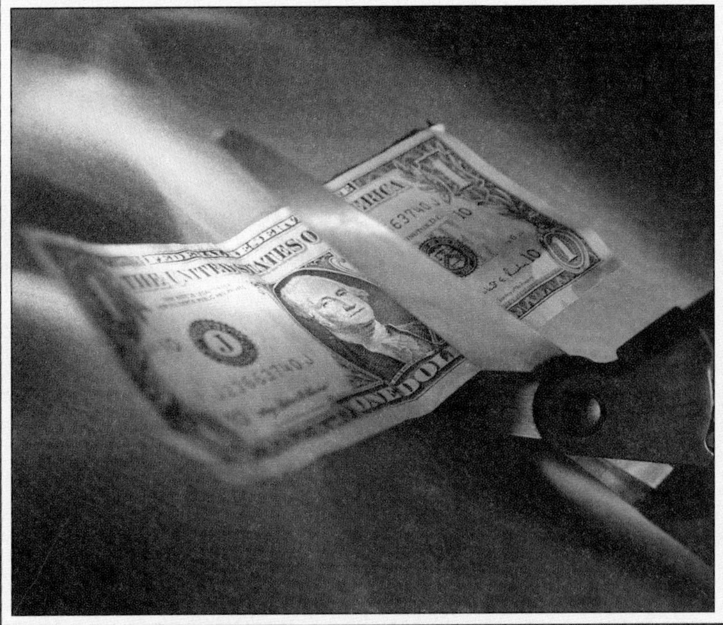

In fairness, the finance chief's thinking might have been something like this: A letter-size interoffice envelope, purchased for nine cents each without volume discounting, can be readdressed 14 times. That means with every line skipped on the envelope, the company gets 0.64 cent closer to the brink of disaster. Let's pull together, people.

But the less-than-inspirational move only reminded employees of a double standard. They recalled that the chief executive stayed at butler-serviced hotels, the name of which was on a need-to-know basis. He was driven daily by a limousine and, Mr. Marcus says, he was widely rumored to have expensed an athletic supporter during a gym visit. Assuming it was a low-grade model for $7.99, that is the equivalent of about 1,248 address lines on an interoffice envelope. "It was so stupid," lamented Mr. Marcus. "You can't make this stuff up."

In one of the more notable cost cuts in recent memory—not counting when Xerox once told its employees to ease up on Xeroxing—Lucent, its name evoking "shining lights," shut them off in the hallways of its esteemed research labs as part of a massive budget-trimming campaign a few years ago.

Rarely have there been so many dumbstruck geniuses under one dimly lighted roof. But being scientists, recalls Jon Bentley, a former Lucent researcher, they started doing back-of-the-envelope calculations and found that the savings in electricity didn't even add up to what it cost in labor for them to do the back-of-the-envelope calculations.

The low point for Mr. Bentley came when he took a visitor to what he called We Love Us museum in the front of the Lucent

building. There, replicas of Nobel prizes won by the lab's scientists were on display—so long as you had night vision goggles to see them.

Mr. Bentley had to pull out the flashlight on his key ring to illuminate the medals. He took the retirement offer a few months later. "I don't know if it was the straw that broke the camel's back," he says. "But it was a pretty hefty two-by-four before the straw."[1]

FOR DISCUSSION

Can companies cut costs and still maintain employee motivation? If yes, discuss how this might be done. For an interpretation of this case and additional comments, visit our Online Learning Center:

www.mhhe.com/kinickiob2e

THE OPENING CASE ILLUSTRATES how an organization's approach to cost cutting can affect employee motivation. Ken Marcus was de-motivated by a perceived double standard between employees and the company's chief executive. This double standard created feelings of inequity. The next section discusses the impact of perceived inequities on employee motivation. In contrast, Jon Bentley was de-motivated because he felt that Lucent's cost cutting devalued the accomplishments of the company's lab's scientists. This chapter completes our discussion of motivation by exploring three cognitive theories of work motivation: equity, expectancy, and goal setting. Each theory is based on the premise that employees' cognitions are the key to understanding their motivation. To help you apply what you have learned about employee motivation, we conclude the chapter by highlighting the prerequisites of successful motivational programs.

Adams's Equity Theory of Motivation

equity theory

Holds that motivation is a function of fairness in social exchanges.

Defined generally, **equity theory** is a model of motivation that explains how people strive for *fairness* and *justice* in social exchanges or give-and-take relationships. Equity theory is based on cognitive dissonance theory, developed by social psychologist Leon Festinger in the 1950s.[2]

According to Festinger's theory, people are motivated to maintain consistency between their cognitive beliefs and their behavior. Perceived inconsistencies create cognitive dissonance (or psychological discomfort), which, in turn, motivates corrective action. For example, a cigarette smoker who sees a heavy-smoking relative die of lung cancer probably would be motivated to quit smoking if he or she attributes the death to smoking. Accordingly, when victimized by unfair social exchanges, our resulting cognitive dissonance prompts us to correct the situation. Corrective action may range from a slight change in attitude or behavior to stealing to the extreme case of trying to harm someone. For example, researchers have demonstrated that people attempt to "get even" for perceived injustices by using either direct (e.g., theft, sabotage, or violence) or indirect (e.g., intentionally working slowly, giving a co-worker the silent treatment) retaliation, and the cost of this retaliation can be staggering. Experts estimate that the costs of workplace violence and employee theft, which are partly caused by feelings of inequity, is approximately $36 and $200 billion annually, respectively.[3]

Psychologist J Stacy Adams pioneered application of the equity principle to the workplace. Central to understanding Adams's equity theory of motivation is an awareness of key components of the individual–organization exchange relationship. This relationship is pivotal in the formation of employees' perceptions of equity and inequity.

The Individual–Organization Exchange Relationship

Adams points out that two primary components are involved in the employee–employer exchange, *inputs* and *outcomes*. An employee's inputs, for which he or she expects a just return, include education/training, skills, creativity, seniority, age, personality traits, effort expended, and personal appearance. On the outcome side of the exchange, the organization provides such things as pay/bonuses, fringe benefits, challenging assignments, job security, promotions, status symbols, recognition, and participation in important decisions.[4] These outcomes vary widely, depending on one's organization and rank.

Negative and Positive Inequity

On the job, feelings of inequity revolve around a person's evaluation of whether he or she receives adequate rewards to compensate for his or her contributive inputs. People perform these evaluations by comparing the perceived fairness of their employment exchange to that of relevant others. This comparative process, which is based on an equity norm, was found to generalize across countries.[5] People tend to compare themselves to other individuals with whom they have close interpersonal ties—such as friends—and/or to similar others—such as people performing the same job or individuals of the same gender or educational level—rather than dissimilar others.[6] For example, do you consider the average CEO in the US a relevant comparison person to yourself? If not, then you should not feel inequity because the average CEO makes more than 200 times as much as the average worker.[7]

Three different equity relationships are illustrated in Figure 7–1: equity, negative inequity, and positive inequity. Assume the two people in each of the equity relationships in Figure 7–1 have equivalent backgrounds (equal education, seniority, and

FIGURE 7–1 Negative and Positive Inequity

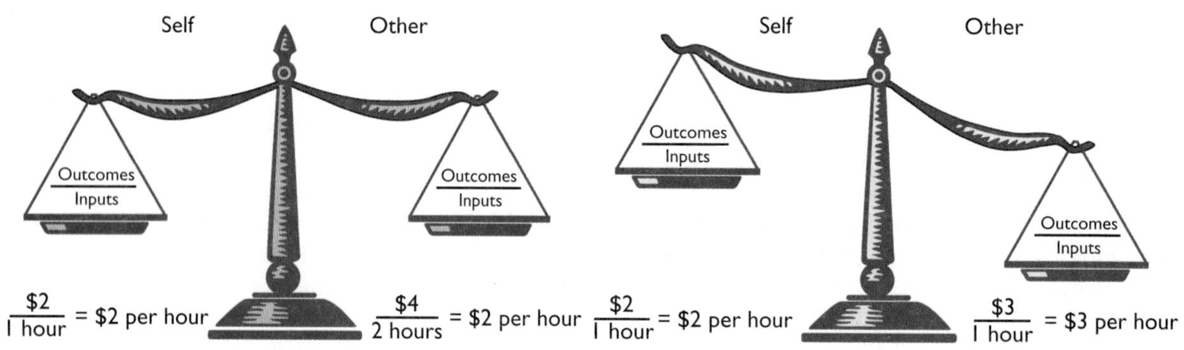

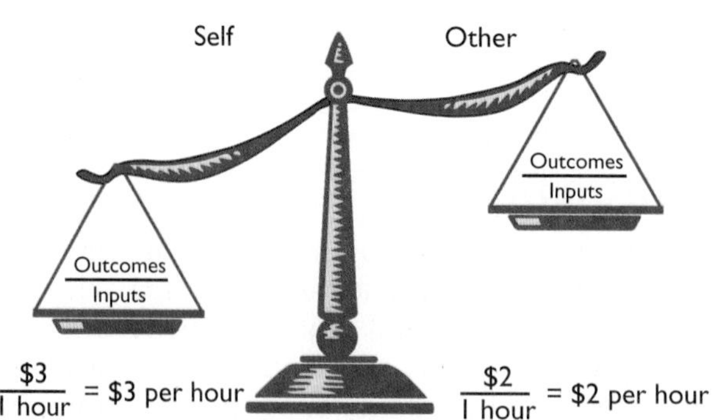

so forth) and perform identical tasks. Only their hourly pay rates differ. Equity exists for an individual when his or her ratio of perceived outcomes to inputs is equal to the ratio of outcomes to inputs for a relevant co-worker (see part A in Figure 7–1). Because equity is based on comparing *ratios* of outcomes to inputs, inequity will not necessarily be perceived just because someone else receives greater rewards. If the other person's additional outcomes are due to his or her greater inputs, a sense of equity may still exist. However, if the comparison person enjoys greater outcomes for similar inputs, **negative inequity** will be perceived (see part B in Figure 7–1). On the other hand, a person will experience **positive inequity** when his or her outcome to input ratio is greater than that of a relevant co-worker (see part C in Figure 7–1).

negative inequity

Comparison in which another person receives greater outcomes for similar inputs.

positive inequity

Comparison in which another person receives lesser outcomes for similar inputs.

Dynamics of Perceived Inequity

Managers can derive practical benefits from Adams's equity theory by recognizing that (1) people have varying sensitivities to perceived equity and inequity and (2) inequity can be reduced in a variety of ways.

Thresholds of Equity and Inequity Have you ever noticed that some people become very upset over the slightest inequity whereas others are not bothered at all? Research has shown that people respond differently to the same level of inequity due to an individual difference called equity sensitivity. **Equity sensitivity** reflects an individual's "different preferences for, tolerances for, and reactions to the level of equity associated with any given situation."[8] Equity sensitivity spans a continuum ranging from benevolents to sensitives to entitled.

equity sensitivity

An individual's tolerance for negative and positive equity.

Benevolents are people who have a higher tolerance for negative inequity. They are altruistic in the sense that they prefer their outcome/input ratio to be lower than ratios from comparison others. In contrast, equity *sensitives* are described as individuals who adhere to a strict norm of reciprocity and are quickly motivated to resolve both negative and positive inequity. Finally, *entitleds* have no tolerance for negative inequity. They actually expect to obtain greater output/input ratios than comparison others and become upset when this is not the case.[9]

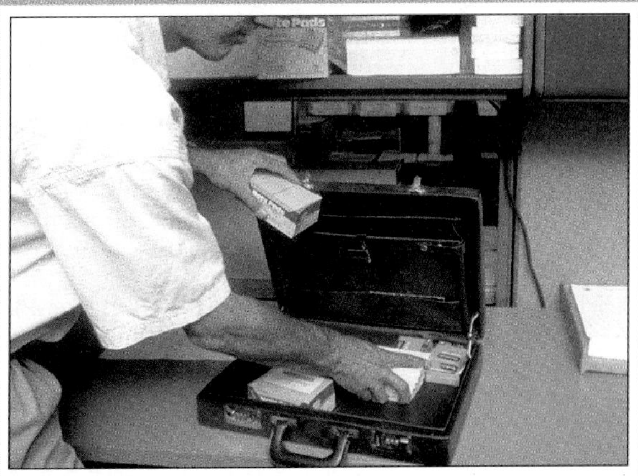

Oftentimes employees feel that "borrowing" a few office supplies from their company's inventory compensates for any perceived inequities in pay or other benefits.

Reducing Inequity Equity ratios can be changed by attempting to alter one's outcomes or adjusting one's inputs. For example, negative inequity might be resolved by asking for a raise or a promotion (i.e., raising outputs) or by reducing inputs (i.e., working fewer hours or exerting less effort). It also is important to note that equity can be restored by altering one's equity ratios behaviorally and/or cognitively. A cognitive strategy entails psychologically distorting perceptions of one's own or one's comparison person's outcomes and inputs (e.g., conclude that comparison other has more experience or works harder).

Expanding the Concept of Equity: Organizational Justice

Beginning in the later 1970s, researchers began to expand the role of equity theory in explaining employee attitudes and behavior. This led to a domain of research called *organizational justice.* Organizational justice reflects the extent to which people perceive that they are treated fairly at work. This, in turn, led to the identification of three different components of organizational justice: distributive, procedural, and interactional.[10] **Distributive justice** reflects the perceived fairness of how resources and rewards are distributed or allocated. **Procedural justice** is defined as the perceived fairness of the process and procedures used to make allocation decisions. Research shows that positive perceptions of distributive and procedural justice are enhanced by giving employees a "voice" in decisions that affect them. Voice represents the extent to which employees who are affected by a decision can present relevant information about the decision to others. Voice is analogous to asking employees for their input into the decision-making process.

distributive justice

The perceived fairness of how resources and rewards are distributed.

procedural justice

The perceived fairness of the process and procedures used to make allocation decisions.

interactional justice

Extent to which people feel fairly treated when procedures are implemented.

The last justice component, **interactional justice,** relates to the "quality of the interpersonal treatment people receive when procedures are implemented."[11] This form of justice does not pertain to the outcomes or procedures associated with decision making, but rather it focuses on whether or not people feel they are treated fairly when decisions are implemented. Fair interpersonal treatment necessitates that managers communicate truthfully and treat people with courtesy and respect. Consider the role of interactional justice in how a manager of information-management systems responded to being laid off by a New Jersey chemical company. The man gained access to the company's computer systems from home by using another executive's password and deleted critical inventory and personnel files. The sabotage ultimately caused $20 million in damage and postponed a public stock offering that had been in the works. Why would a former employee do something like this?

> An anonymous note that he wrote to the company president sheds light on his motive. "I have been loyal to the company in good and bad times for over 30 years," he wrote. "I was expecting a member of top management to come down from his ivory tower to face us with the layoff announcement, rather than sending the kitchen supervisor with guards to escort us off the premises like criminals. You will pay for your senseless behavior."[12]

This employee's direct retaliation against the company was caused by the insensitive manner—interactional justice—in which employees were notified about the layoffs.

Practical Lessons from Equity Theory

Equity theory has at least eight important practical implications. First, equity theory provides managers with yet another explanation of how beliefs and attitudes affect job performance. According to this line of thinking, the best way to manage job behavior is to adequately understand underlying cognitive processes. Indeed, we are motivated powerfully to correct a situation when our ideas of fairness and justice are offended.

Second, research on equity theory emphasizes the need for managers to pay attention to employees' perceptions of what is fair and equitable. No matter how fair management thinks the organization's policies, procedures, and reward system are, each employee's *perception* of the equity of those factors is what counts. People respond positively when they perceive organizational and interpersonal justice. For example, research demonstrates that employees' perceptions of distributive, procedural, and interactional justice are positively associated with job performance, job satisfaction, organizational commitment, and organizational citizenship behavior and negatively with intentions to quit.[13] Managers thus are encouraged to make hiring and promotion decisions on merit-based, job-related information. Moreover, because justice perceptions are influenced by the extent to which managers explain their decisions, managers are encouraged to explain the rationale behind their decisions.[14]

Third, managers benefit by allowing employees to participate in making decisions about important work outcomes. For example, employees were more satisfied with their performance appraisals and resultant outcomes when they had a "voice" during the appraisal review.[15] Fourth, employees should be given the opportunity to appeal decisions that affect their welfare. Being able to appeal a decision promotes the belief that management treats employees fairly.

Fifth, employees are more likely to accept and support organizational change when they believe it is implemented fairly and when it produces equitable outcomes.[16]

Sixth, managers can promote cooperation and teamwork among group members by treating them equitably. Research reveals that people are just as concerned with fairness in group settings as they are with their own personal interests.[17] Seventh, treating employees inequitably can lead to litigation and costly court settlements. Employees denied justice at work are more likely to file employee grievances, to seek arbitration, and to ultimately seek relief from the courts.[18] Finally, managers need to pay attention to the organization's climate for justice. For example, an organization's climate for justice was found to significantly influence employees' organizational citizenship behavior.[19] Researchers also believe that a climate of justice can significantly influence the type of customer service provided by employees. In turn, this level of service is likely to influence customers' perceptions of "fair service" and their subsequent loyalty and satisfaction.[20]

Managers can attempt to follow these practical implications by monitoring equity and justice perceptions through informal conversations, interviews, or attitude surveys. For example, researchers have developed and validated a host of surveys that can be used for this purpose. Please take a moment now to complete the Hands-On Exercise. It contains part of a survey that was developed to measure employees' perceptions of fair interpersonal treatment. If you perceive your work organization as interpersonally unfair, you are probably dissatisfied and have contemplated quitting. In contrast, your organizational loyalty and attachment are likely greater if you believe you are treated fairly at work.

Expectancy Theory of Motivation

Expectancy theory holds that people are motivated to behave in ways that produce desired combinations of expected outcomes. Perception plays a central role in expectancy theory because it emphasizes cognitive ability to anticipate likely consequences of behavior. Embedded in expectancy theory is the principle of hedonism. Hedonistic people strive to maximize their pleasure and minimize their pain. Generally, expectancy theory can be used to predict behavior in any situation in which a choice between two or more alternatives must be made.

expectancy theory

Holds that people are motivated to behave in ways that produce valued outcomes.

HANDS-ON EXERCISE

Measuring Perceived Fair Interpersonal Treatment

INSTRUCTIONS: The following survey was designed to assess the extent to which you are treated fairly at your current job: If you are not working, use a past job or your role as a student to complete the survey. There is no right or wrong answer to the statements. Circle your answers by using the rating scale provided. After evaluating each of the survey statements, complete a total score and compare your total to the arbitrary norms.

	Strongly Disagree	Disagree	Neither	Agree	Strongly Agree
1. Employees are praised for good work.	1	2	3	4	5
2. Supervisors do not yell at employees.	1	2	3	4	5
3. Employees are trusted.	1	2	3	4	5
4. Employees' complaints are dealt with effectively.	1	2	3	4	5
5. Employees are treated with respect.	1	2	3	4	5
6. Employees' questions and problems are responded to quickly.	1	2	3	4	5
7. Employees are treated fairly.	1	2	3	4	5
8. Employees' hard work is appreciated.	1	2	3	4	5
9. Employees' suggestions are used.	1	2	3	4	5
10. Employees are told the truth.	1	2	3	4	5

Total score = ________

ARBITRARY NORMS

Very fair organization = 38–50
Moderately fair organization = 24–37
Unfair organization = 10–23

SOURCE: Adapted in part from M A Donovan, F Drasgow, and L J Munson, "The Perceptions of Fair Interpersonal Treatment Scale Development and Validation of a Measure of Interpersonal Treatment in the Workplace," *Journal of Applied Psychology*, October 1998, pp 683–92.

For instance, it can be used to predict whether to quit or stay at a job; whether to exert substantial or minimal effort at a task; and whether to major in management, computer science, accounting, marketing, psychology, or communication.

This section explores Victor Vroom's version of expectancy theory. Understanding the cognitive processes underlying this theory can help managers develop organizational policies and practices that enhance employee motivation.

Vroom's Expectancy Theory

Victor Vroom formulated a mathematical model of expectancy theory in his 1964 book *Work and Motivation*. Vroom's theory has been summarized as follows:

> The strength of a tendency to act in a certain way depends on the strength of an expectancy that the act will be followed by a given consequence (or outcome) and on the value or attractiveness of that consequence (or outcome) to the actor.[21]

Motivation, according to Vroom, boils down to the decision of how much effort to exert in a specific task situation. This choice is based on a two-stage sequence of expectations (effort → performance and performance → outcome). First, motivation is affected by an individual's expectation that a certain level of effort will produce the intended performance goal. For example, if you do not believe increasing the amount of time you spend studying will significantly raise your grade on an exam, you probably will not study any harder than usual. Motivation also is influenced by the employee's perceived chances of getting various outcomes as a result of accomplishing his or her performance goal. Finally, individuals are motivated to the extent that they value the outcomes received.

Vroom used a mathematical equation to integrate these concepts into a predictive model of motivational force or strength. For our purposes, however, it is sufficient to define and explain the three key concepts within Vroom's model—*expectancy, instrumentality,* and *valence.*

Expectancy An **expectancy,** according to Vroom's terminology, represents an individual's belief that a particular degree of effort will be followed by a particular level of performance. In other words, it is an effort → performance expectation. Expectancies take the form of subjective probabilities. As you may recall from a course in statistics, probabilities range from zero to one. An expectancy of zero indicates effort has no anticipated impact on performance.

expectancy

Belief that effort leads to a specific level of performance.

For example, suppose you do not know how to type on a keyboard. No matter how much effort you exert, your perceived probability of typing 30 error-free words per minute likely would be zero. An expectancy of one suggests that performance is totally dependent on effort. If you decided to take a typing course as well as practice a couple of hours a day for a few weeks (high effort), you should be able to type 30 words per minute without any errors. In contrast, if you do not take a typing course and only practice an hour or two per week (low effort), there is a very low probability (say, a 20% chance) of being able to type 30 words per minute without any errors.

The following factors influence an employee's expectancy perceptions:

- Self-esteem.
- Self-efficacy.
- Previous success at the task.
- Help received from others.
- Information necessary to complete the task.
- Good materials and equipment to work with.[22]

Instrumentality An **instrumentality** is a performance → outcome perception. It represents a person's belief that a particular outcome is contingent on accomplishing a specific level of performance. Performance is instrumental when it leads to something else. For example, passing exams is instrumental to graduating from college.

instrumentality

A performance → outcome perception.

Instrumentalities range from −1.0 to 1.0. An instrumentality of 1.0 indicates attainment of a particular outcome is totally dependent on task performance. An instrumentality of zero indicates there is no relationship between performance and receiving an outcome. For example, most companies link the number of vacation days to seniority, not job performance. Finally, an instrumentality of −1.0 reveals

Do you think it's fair that Steve Jobs (on the right) gets a bonus regardless of Apple's performance? Do you think it's fair that Jeffrey Immelt of GE loses *all* the shares of stock that he was awarded last year based on this year's performance?

that high performance reduces the chance of obtaining an outcome while low performance increases the chance. For example, the more time you spend studying to get an A on an exam (high performance), the less time you will have for enjoying leisure activities. Similarly, as you lower the amount of time spent studying (low performance), you increase the amount of time that may be devoted to leisure activities.

The concept of instrumentality can be seen by considering the incentive programs used to pay the CEOs from General Electric, IBM, SBC Communications Inc., and Apple.

> At General Electric Co., and at IBM . . . boards have performed radical surgery to better tie pay to performance. GE's Jeffrey R. Immelt could lose all 250,000 shares of stock GE awarded him last year unless he meets performance goals. And IBM's Samuel J. Palmisano will get options, but they'll be worthless until the stock rises by 10%. . . . At SBC Communications Inc., 2003 operating income was down 25% and the stock lagged its peers. Yet CEO Edward E. Whitacre Jr. earned $19.6 million, including a $5.7 million bonus and a $7.2 million stock grant—a 93% increase over 2002. . . . At Apple, Job's $74.8 million options-for-stock swap last March came after a three-year stretch in which the stock plummeted 80%, and then barely moved. What's more, Jobs will receive them in 2006, regardless of performance."[23]

The incentive programs at GE and IBM make performance instrumental for receiving stock options, but performance is not instrumental for receiving bonuses and stock options at SBC Communications and Apple.

valence

The value of a reward or outcome.

Valence As Vroom used the term, **valence** refers to the positive or negative value people place on outcomes. Valence mirrors our personal preferences.[24] For example, most employees have a positive valence for receiving additional money or recognition. In contrast, job stress and being laid off would likely be negatively valent for most individuals. In Vroom's expectancy model, *outcomes* refer to different consequences that are contingent on performance, such as pay, promotions, or recognition. An outcome's valence depends on an individual's needs and can be measured for research purposes with scales ranging from a negative value to a positive value. For example, an individual's valence toward more recognition can be assessed on a scale ranging from −2 (very undesirable) to 0 (neutral) to +2 (very desirable).

Vroom's Expectancy Theory in Action Vroom's expectancy model of motivation can be used to analyze a real-life motivation program. Consider the following performance problem described by Frederick W Smith, founder and chief executive officer of Federal Express Corporation:

> . . . we were having a helluva problem keeping things running on time. The airplanes would come in, and everything would get backed up. We tried every kind of control mechanism that you could think of, and none of them worked. Finally, it became obvious that the underlying problem was that it was in the interest of the employees at the cargo terminal—they were college kids, mostly—to run late, because it meant that they made more money. So what we did was give them all a minimum guarantee and say, "Look, if you get through before a certain time, just go home, and you will have beat the system." Well, it was unbelievable. I mean, in the space of about 45 days, the place was way ahead of schedule. And I don't even think it was a conscious thing on their part.[25]

How did Federal Express get its college-age cargo handlers to switch from low effort to high effort? According to Vroom's model, the student workers originally exerted low effort because they were paid on the basis of time, not output. It was in their best interest to work slowly and accumulate as many hours as possible. By offering to let the student workers *go home early if and when they completed their assigned duties,* Federal Express prompted high effort. This new arrangement created two positively valued outcomes: guaranteed pay plus the opportunity to leave early. The motivation to exert high effort became greater than the motivation to exert low effort.

Research on Expectancy Theory and Managerial Implications

Many researchers have tested expectancy theory. In support of the theory, a meta-analysis of 77 studies indicated that expectancy theory significantly predicted performance, effort, intentions, preferences, and choice.[26] Another summary of 16 studies revealed that expectancy theory correctly predicted occupational or organizational choice 63.4% of the time; this was significantly better than chance predictions.[27]

Nonetheless, expectancy theory has been criticized for a variety of reasons. For example, the theory is difficult to test, and the measures used to assess expectancy, instrumentality, and valence have questionable validity.[28] In the final analysis, however, expectancy theory has important practical implications for individual managers and organizations as a whole (see Table 7–1).

Managers are advised to enhance effort → performance expectancies by helping employees accomplish their performance goals. Managers can do this by providing support and coaching and by increasing employees' self-efficacy. It also is important for managers to influence employees' instrumentalities and to monitor valences for various rewards. This raises the issue of whether organizations should use monetary

TABLE 7–1 Managerial and Organizational Implications of Expectancy Theory

Implications for Managers	Implications for Organizations
Determine the outcomes employees value.	Reward people for desired performance, and do not keep pay decisions secret.
Identify good performance so appropriate behaviors can be rewarded.	Design challenging jobs.
Make sure employees can achieve targeted performance levels.	Tie some rewards to group accomplishments to build teamwork and encourage cooperation.
Link desired outcomes to targeted levels of performance.	Reward managers for creating, monitoring, and maintaining expectancies, instrumentalities, and outcomes that lead to high effort and goal attainment.
Make sure changes in outcomes are large enough to motivate high effort.	Monitor employee motivation through interviews or anonymous questionnaires.
Monitor the reward system for inequities.	Accommodate individual differences by building flexibility into the motivation program.

rewards as the primary method to reinforce performance. Although money is certainly a positively valent reward for most people, there are three issues to consider when deciding on the relative balance between monetary and nonmonetary rewards.

First, research shows that some workers value interesting work and recognition more than money.[29] Second, extrinsic rewards can lose their motivating properties over time and may undermine intrinsic motivation.[30] This conclusion, however, must be balanced by the fact that performance is related to the receipt of financial incentives. A recent meta-analysis of 39 studies involving 2,773 people showed that financial incentives were positively related to performance quantity but not to performance quality.[31] Third, monetary rewards must be large enough to generate motivation. For example, Robert Heneman, professor of management at Ohio State University, estimates that monetary awards must be at least 7% above employees' base pay to truly motivate people.[32]

Although this percentage is well above the typical salary increase received by most employees, some organizations have designed their incentive systems with this recommendation in mind. For example, Corning Inc. created a goalsharing program in which employees can earn an annual bonus of up to 10% of salary. The bonus is based on a combination of overall corporate performance and individual performance (see Skills & Best Practices).[33] In summary, there is no one best type of reward. Individual differences and need theories tell us that people are motivated by different rewards. Managers should therefore focus on linking employee performance to valued rewards regardless of the type of reward used to enhance motivation. Managers need to be careful or thoughtful, however, when implementing this suggestion. Consider the mistake made by a *Fortune* 500 insurance firm in California when it rewarded its top salespeople with tickets to a Christmas pageant at a local cathedral.

> "The employees were upset and couldn't believe they would give them a gift like that," Davis says. [Helen Davis is president and CEO of Indaba Inc., a management consulting firm.] "What was supposed to be a reward became a disaster for the company." The workers ended up boycotting the firm for six months by bringing in only the minimum amount of sales on the insurance and investment products they sold. They wanted a formal apology from the CEO, but the executive was hoping the matter would just blow over. Although the CEO finally relented, she says, it cost the firm nearly $750,000 in sales over that period and ultimately reached a loss of $1.5 million because many top producers left the firm as a result.[34]

Can you guess what caused the problem? A third of the firm's sales force was Jewish.

There are four prerequisites to linking performance and rewards:

1. Managers need to develop and communicate performance standards to employees.
2. Managers need valid and accurate performance ratings with which to compare employees. Inaccurate ratings create perceptions of inequity and thereby erode motivation.
3. Managers need to determine the relative mix of individual versus team contribution to performance and then reward accordingly. For example, pharmaceutical giant Pharmacia designed its reward system around its belief in creating an organizational culture that reinforced collaboration, customer focus, and speed. "The company's reward system reinforced this collaborative model by explicitly linking compensation to the actions of the group. Every member's compensation would be based on the time to bring the drug to market, the time for the drug to reach peak profitable share, and total sales. The system gave group members a strong incentive to talk openly with one another and to share information freely."[35]
4. Managers should use the performance ratings to differentially allocate rewards among employees. That is, it is critical that managers allocate significantly different amounts of rewards for various levels of performance. Unfortunately, a survey by Watson Wyatt revealed that managers may not be following this suggestion. Results revealed that fewer than 40% of top-performing employees perceived that they received "moderately or significantly better pay raises, annual bonuses or total pay than do employees with average performance."[36]

SKILLS & BEST PRACTICES

Corning Inc.'s Goalsharing Program Rewards Corporate and Individual Performance

Rewarding employees for meeting important goals—whether or not the company is raking in lots of money—is the heart of the "goalsharing" program at Corning Inc. in Corning, N.Y. Started in the early 1990s, the variable pay plan can give each U.S.-based Corning employee an annual bonus of up to 10% of salary.

Employees helped develop the system, which is reviewed and adjusted annually at the business unit level by committees that include workers, managers and union representatives.

One-fourth of the bonus is based on earnings per share of company stock for the preceding year. The rest of the payment depends on how well the worker has met job performance goals established for his or her business unit over the year.

SOURCE: Excerpted from S Bates, "Goalsharing at Corning," *HR Magazine*, January 2003, p 33.

Motivation through Goal Setting

Regardless of the nature of their specific achievements, successful people tend to have one thing in common. Their lives are goal oriented. This is as true for politicians seeking votes as it is for world-class athletes. Within the context of employee motivation, this section explores the theory, research, and practice of goal setting.

Goals: Definition and Background

goal

What an individual is trying to accomplish.

Edwin Locke, a leading authority on goal setting, and his colleagues define a **goal** as "what an individual is trying to accomplish; it is the object or aim of an action."[37] The motivational effect of performance goals and goal-based reward plans has been recognized for a long time. At the turn of the century, Frederick Taylor attempted to scientifically establish how much work of a specified quality an individual should be assigned each day. He proposed that bonuses be based on accomplishing those output standards. More recently, goal setting has been promoted through a widely used management technique called management by objectives (MBO).

management by objectives

Management system incorporating participation in decision making, goal setting, and feedback.

Management by objectives is a management system that incorporates participation in decision making, goal setting, and objective feedback. A meta-analysis of MBO programs showed productivity gains in 68 of 70 different organizations. Specifically, results uncovered an average gain in productivity of 56% when top management commitment was high. The average gain was only 6% when commitment was low. A second meta-analysis of 18 studies further demonstrated that employees' job satisfaction was significantly related to top management's commitment to an MBO implementation.[38] These impressive results highlight the positive benefits of implementing MBO and setting goals. To further understand how MBO programs can increase both productivity and satisfaction, let us examine the process by which goal setting works.

How Does Goal Setting Work?

Despite abundant goal-setting research and practice, goal-setting theories are surprisingly scarce. An instructive model was formulated by Locke and his associates. According to Locke's model, goal setting has four motivational mechanisms.[39]

Goals Direct Attention Goals direct one's attention and effort toward goal-relevant activities and away from goal-irrelevant activities. If, for example, you have a term project due in a few days, your thoughts and actions tend to revolve around completing that project. Scooter Store, which was ranked as the 58th best company to work for in 2003 by *Fortune,* uses this motivational function of goal setting on a daily basis. Every morning the company's managers assemble their workers in a 14-minute huddle to discuss the day's goals.[40]

Goals Regulate Effort Not only do goals make us selectively perceptive, they also motivate us to act. The instructor's deadline for turning in your term project would prompt you to complete it, as opposed to going out with friends, watching television, or studying for another course. Generally, the level of effort expended is proportionate to the difficulty of the goal.

Goals Increase Persistence Within the context of goal setting, persistence represents the effort expended on a task over an extended period of time: It takes effort to run 100 meters; it takes persistence to run a 26-mile marathon. Persistent people tend to see obstacles as challenges to be overcome rather than as reasons to fail. A difficult goal that is important to an individual is a constant reminder to keep exerting effort in the appropriate direction. Annika Sorenstam is a great example of someone who persisted at her goal of being the best female golfer in the world. She has won 48 tournaments since starting on the LPGA tour in 1994.[41]

> She already has qualified for the LPGA and World Golf Halls of Fame, has won a career Grand Slam, shot the only round of 59 in women's pro golf and has won six Player of the Year titles.
>
> Last year, her new challenge was playing in a PGA Tour event, where she made a lasting impression but failed to make the cut. When it was over, she said she didn't care to compete in more men's tournaments but needed to move on.
>
> Moving on meant winning two more LPGA majors. Just like Tiger Woods, major titles and a single-season Grand Slam have become her new focus.
>
> "Nobody else has done it, so I think that says it all," she said. "But I like to set high goals, I like to motivate myself. If you believe it in your mind, I think you can do it."[42]

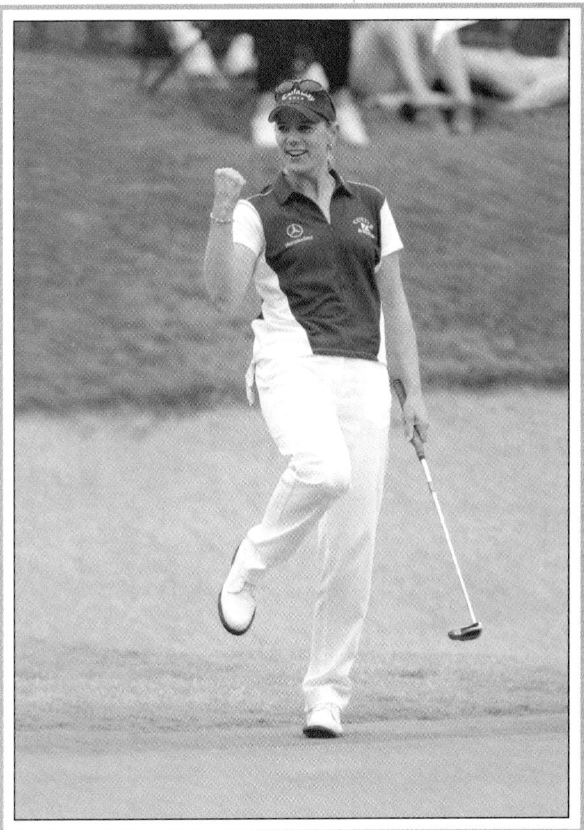

Annika Sorenstam persisted in her goal of being the best female golfer in the world.

Goals Foster the Development and Application of Task Strategies and Action Plans If you are here and your goal is out there somewhere, you face the problem of getting from here to there. For example, the person who has resolved to lose 20 pounds must develop a plan for getting from "here" (his or her present weight) to "there" (20 pounds lighter). Goals can help because they encourage people to develop strategies and action plans that enable them to achieve their goals. By virtue of setting a weight-reduction goal, the dieter may choose a strategy of exercising more, eating less, or some combination of the two. For a work-related example, consider the goals, strategies, and plans being used by Monica Luechtefeld, the executive vice president heading up Office Depot Inc.'s online business:

> Under her leadership, the Delray Beach (Fla.)-based company has quietly become the second-largest E-tailer in the world behind Amazon.com. . . . And this year [2001], online sales are expected to nearly double, to $1.5 billion, representing 20% of the company's overall sales. Now, she aims to push to 50% from 40% the number of Office Depot customers ordering online by year end. . . . To do that, she plans to offer them more than just office supplies. "I want us to serve them both as coach and trusted adviser," she says. To Luechtefeld that means expanding to include online services such as tax preparation and bookkeeping. Office Depot has no expertise in this area, so Luechtefeld is making alliances with those that do, including software giant Microsoft Corp.[43]

Insights from Goal-Setting Research

Research consistently has supported goal setting as a motivational technique. Setting performance goals increases individual, group, and organizational performance. Further, the positive effects of goal setting were found in six other countries or regions: Australia, Canada, the Caribbean, England, West Germany, and Japan. Goal setting works in different cultures. Reviews of the many goal-setting studies conducted over the past few decades have given managers five practical insights:

FIGURE 7–2
Relationship between Goal Difficulty and Performance

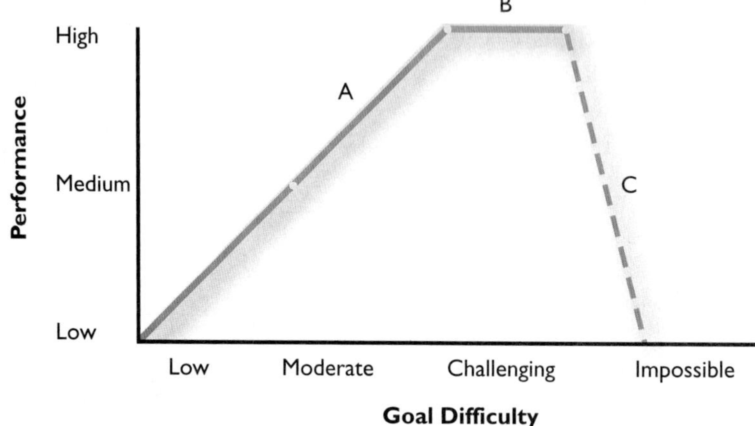

A Performance of committed individuals with adequate ability
B Performance of committed individuals who are working at capacity
C Performance of individuals who lack commitment to high goals

SOURCE: From *A Theory of Goal Setting and Task Performance,* by Locke/Latham. Copyright © 1990 Pearson Education. Reprinted by permission of Pearson Education, Inc., Upper Saddle River, NJ.

goal difficulty
The amount of effort required to meet a goal.

1. *Difficult goals lead to higher performance.* **Goal difficulty** reflects the amount of effort required to meet a goal. It is more difficult to sell nine cars a month than it is to sell three cars a month. A meta-analysis spanning 4,000 people and 65 separate studies revealed that goal difficulty was positively related to performance.[44] As illustrated in Figure 7–2, however, the positive relationship between goal difficulty and performance breaks down when goals are perceived to be impossible. Figure 7–2 reveals that performance goes up when employees are given hard goals as opposed to easy or moderate goals (section A). Performance then plateaus (section B) and drops (section C) as the difficulty of a goal goes from challenging to impossible.

goal specificity
Quantifiability of a goal.

2. *Specific, difficult goals lead to higher performance for simple rather than complex tasks.* **Goal specificity** pertains to the quantifiability of a goal. For example, a goal of selling nine cars a month is more specific than telling a salesperson to do his or her best. In an early review of goal-setting research, 99 of 110 studies (90%) found that specific, hard goals led to better performance than did easy, medium, do-your-best, or no goals. This result was confirmed in a meta-analysis of 70 studies conducted between 1966 and 1984, involving 7,407 people.[45]

In contrast to these positive effects, several recent studies demonstrated that setting specific, difficult goals leads to poorer performance under certain circumstances. For example, a meta-analysis of 125 studies indicated that goal-setting effects were strongest for easy tasks and weakest for complex tasks.[46] There are two explanations for this finding. First, employees are not likely to put forth increased effort to achieve complex goals unless they "buy-in" or support them. Thus, it is important for managers to obtain employee buy-in to the goal-setting process. Second, novel and complex tasks can make employees anxious about succeeding, which in turn causes them to develop strategies in an unsystematic way and to fail to learn what strategies or actions are effective. This can further create pressure and performance anxiety. According to Locke and his colleagues, the antidote is to set specific challenging learning goals aimed at identifying the best way to accomplish the task or goal.[47] Specific, difficult goals thus impair performance on novel, complex tasks when employees do not have clear strategies for solving these types of problems. On a positive note, however, a study demonstrated that goal setting led to gradual improvements in performance on complex tasks when people were encouraged to explicitly solve the problem at hand.[48]

3. *Feedback enhances the effect of specific, difficult goals.* Feedback plays a key role in all of our lives. For example, consider the role of feedback in bowling. Imagine going to the bowling lanes only to find that someone had hung a sheet from the ceiling to the floor in front of the pins. How likely is it that you would reach your goal score or typical bowling average? Not likely, given your inability to see the pins. Regardless of your goal, you would have to guess where to throw your second ball if you did not get a strike on your first shot. The same principles apply at work.

   Feedback lets people know if they are headed toward their goals or if they are off course and need to redirect their efforts. Goals plus feedback is the recommended approach.[49] Goals inform people about performance standards and expectations so that they can channel their energies accordingly. In turn, feedback provides the information needed to adjust direction, effort, and strategies for goal accomplishment.

4. *Participative goals, assigned goals, and self-set goals are equally effective.* Both managers and researchers are interested in identifying the best way to set goals. Should goals be participatively set, assigned, or set by the employee him- or herself? A summary of goal-setting research indicated that no single approach was consistently more effective than others in increasing performance.[50]

   Managers are advised to use a contingency approach by picking a method that seems best suited for the individual and situation at hand. For example, employees' preferences for participation should be considered. Some employees desire to participate in the process of setting goals, whereas others do not. Employees are also more likely to respond positively to the opportunity to participate in goal setting when they have greater task information, higher levels of experience and training, and greater levels of task involvement. Finally, a participative approach stimulates information exchange, which in turn results in the development of more effective task strategies and higher self-efficacy.[51]

5. *Goal commitment and monetary incentives affect goal-setting outcomes.* **Goal commitment** is the extent to which an individual is personally committed to achieving a goal. In general, an individual is expected to persist in attempts to accomplish a goal when he or she is committed to it. Researchers believe that goal commitment moderates the relationship between the difficulty of a goal and performance. That is, difficult goals lead to higher performance only when employees are committed to their goals. Conversely, difficult goals are hypothesized to lead to lower performance when people are not committed to their goals. A meta-analysis of 21 studies based on 2,360 people supported these predictions.[52] It also is important to note that people are more likely to commit to difficult goals when they have high self-efficacy

goal commitment

Amount of commitment to achieving a goal.

about successfully accomplishing their goals. Managers thus are encouraged to consider employees' self-efficacy when setting goals.

Like goal setting, the use of monetary incentives to motivate employees is seldom questioned. Unfortunately, research uncovered some negative consequences when goal achievement is linked to individual incentives. Case studies, for example, reveal that pay should not be linked to goal achievement unless (a) performance goals are under the employees' control; (b) goals are quantitative and measurable; and (c) frequent, relatively large payments are made for performance achievement.[53] Goal-based incentive systems are more likely to produce undesirable effects if these three conditions are not satisfied.

Moreover, empirical studies demonstrated that goal-based bonus incentives produced higher commitment to easy goals and lower commitment to difficult goals. People were reluctant to commit to difficult goals that were tied to monetary incentives. People with high goal commitment also offered less help to their co-workers when they received goal-based bonus incentives to accomplish difficult individual goals. Individuals neglected aspects of the job that were not covered in the performance goals.[54]

These findings underscore some of the dangers of using goal-based incentives, particularly for employees in complex, interdependent jobs requiring cooperation. Managers need to consider the advantages, disadvantages, and dilemmas of goal-based incentives prior to implementation.

Practical Application of Goal Setting

There are three general steps to follow when implementing a goal-setting program. Serious deficiencies in one step cannot make up for strength in the other two. The three steps need to be implemented in a systematic fashion.

Step I: Set Goals A number of sources can be used as input during this goal-setting stage. Time and motion studies are one source. Goals also may be based on the average past performance of job holders. Third, the employee and his or her manager may set the goal participatively, through give-and-take negotiation. Fourth, goals can be set by conducting external or internal benchmarking. Benchmarking is used when an organization wants to compare its performance or internal work processes to those of other organizations (external benchmarking) or to other internal units, branches, departments, or divisions within the organization (internal benchmarking). For example, a company might set a goal to surpass the customer service levels or profit of a benchmarked competitor. Finally, the overall strategy of a company (e.g., become the lowest-cost producer) may affect the goals set by employees at various levels in the organization.

In accordance with available research evidence, goals should be "SMART." SMART is an acronym that stands for specific, measurable, attainable, results oriented, and time bound. Table 7–2 contains a set of guidelines for writing SMART goals. There are two additional recommendations to consider

"We'd like you to be in charge of finding a goal for this project."

TABLE 7–2 Guidelines for Writing SMART Goals

Specific	Goals should be stated in precise rather than vague terms. For example, a goal that provides for 20 hours of technical training for each employee is more specific than stating that a manager should send as many people as possible to training classes. Goals should be quantified when possible.
Measurable	A measurement device is needed to assess the extent to which a goal is accomplished. Goals thus need to be measurable. It also is critical to consider the quality aspect of the goal when establishing measurement criteria. For example, if the goal is to complete a managerial study of methods to increase productivity, one must consider how to measure the quality of this effort. Goals should not be set without considering the interplay between quantity and quality of output.
Attainable	Goals should be realistic, challenging, and attainable. Impossible goals reduce motivation because people do not like to fail. Remember, people have different levels of ability and skill.
Results oriented	Corporate goals should focus on desired end-results that support the organization's vision. In turn, an individual's goals should directly support the accomplishment of corporate goals. Activities support the achievement of goals and are outlined in action plans. To focus goals on desired end-results, goals should start with the word "to," followed by verbs such as complete, acquire, produce, increase, and decrease. Verbs such as develop, conduct, implement, or monitor imply activities and should not be used in a goal statement.
Time bound	Goals specify target dates for completion.

SOURCE: A J Kinicki, *Performance Management Systems* (Superstition Mt., AZ: Kinicki and Associates Inc., 1992), pp 2–9. Reprinted with permission; all rights reserved.

when setting goals. First, for complex tasks, managers should train employees in problem-solving techniques and encourage them to develop a performance action plan. Action plans specify the strategies or tactics to be used in order to accomplish a goal.

Second, because of individual differences (recall our discussion in Chapter 5), it may be necessary to establish different goals for employees performing the same job. For example, a study of 103 undergraduate business students revealed that individuals high in conscientiousness had higher motivation, had greater goal commitment, and obtained higher grades than students low in conscientiousness.[55] An individual's goal orientation is another important individual difference to consider when setting goals. There are two types of goal orientation: a learning goal orientation and a performance goal orientation. A team of researchers described the differences and implications for goal setting in the following way:

> Individuals with a learning goal orientation are primarily concerned with developing their skills and ability. Given this focus, a difficult goal should be of interest because it provides a challenging opportunity that can lead to personal growth. In

SKILLS & BEST PRACTICES

Managerial Actions for Enhancing Goal Commitment

1. Provide valued outcomes for goal accomplishment.
2. Raise employees' self-efficacy about meeting goals by (a) providing adequate training, (b) role modeling desired behaviors and actions, and (c) persuasively communicating confidence in the employees' ability to attain the goal.
3. Have employees make a public commitment to the goal.
4. Communicate an inspiring vision and explain how individual goals relate to accomplishing the vision.
5. Allow employees to participate in setting the goals.
6. Behave supportively rather than punitively.
7. Break a long-term goal (i.e., a yearly goal) into short-term subgoals.
8. Ensure that employees have the resources required to accomplish the goal.

SOURCE: These recommendations were derived from E A Locke and G P Latham, "Building a Practically Useful Theory of Goal Setting and Task Motivation," *American Psychologist,* September 2002, pp 705–17. Copyright © 2002 by the American Psychological Association. Adapted with permission.

contrast, individuals with a performance goal orientation are concerned with obtaining positive evaluations about their ability. Given this focus, a difficult goal should be of lower interest because it provides a greater potential for failure. As goal difficulty increases, the probability of obtaining a positive evaluation through goal attainment decreases.[56]

Although some studies showed that people set higher goals, exerted more effort, and achieved higher performance when they possessed a learning orientation toward goal setting rather than a performance orientation, other research demonstrated a more complex series of relationships.[57] Specifically, performance was influenced by the interaction between an individual's goal orientation and the difficulty of the task being performed. A performance orientation had beneficial effects on performance for easy tasks, whereas a learning orientation facilitated higher performance on complex tasks.[58] In conclusion, managers should consider individual differences when setting goals.

Step 2: Promote Goal Commitment Obtaining goal commitment is important because employees are more motivated to pursue goals they view as reasonable, obtainable, and fair. Goal commitment may be increased through a variety of methods. The Skills & Best Practices, for example, presents eight managerial actions that can be used to increase employees' goal commitment.

Step 3: Provide Support and Feedback Step 3 calls for providing employees with the necessary support elements or resources to get the job done. This includes ensuring that each employee has the necessary abilities and information to reach his or her goals. As a pair of goal-setting experts succinctly stated, "Motivation without knowledge is useless."[59] Training often is required to help employees achieve difficult goals. Moreover, managers should pay attention to employees' perceptions of effort → performance expectancies, self-efficacy, and valence of rewards. Finally, as we discuss in detail in Chapter 8, employees should be provided with timely, specific feedback (knowledge of results) on how they are doing.

Putting Motivational Theories to Work

Successfully designing and implementing motivational programs is not easy. Managers cannot simply take one of the theories discussed in this book and apply it word for word. Dynamics within organizations interfere with applying motivation theories in "pure" form. According to management scholar Terence Mitchell,

> There are situations and settings that make it exceptionally difficult for a motivational system to work. These circumstances may involve the kinds of jobs or people

> present, the technology, the presence of a union, and so on. The factors that hinder the application of motivational theory have not been articulated either frequently or systematically.[60]

With Mitchell's cautionary statement in mind, this section uses Figure 6–1 (see page 150 in Chapter 6) to raise issues that need to be addressed before implementing a motivational program. Our intent is not to discuss all relevant considerations but rather to highlight a few important ones.

Assuming a motivational program is being considered to improve productivity, quality, or customer satisfaction, the first issue revolves around the difference between motivation and performance. As shown in Figure 6–1, motivation and performance are not one and the same. Motivation is only one of several factors that influence performance. For example, poor performance may be more a function of outdated or inefficient materials and machinery, not having goals to direct one's attention, a monotonous job, feelings of inequity, a negative work environment characterized by political behavior and conflict, poor supervisory support and coaching, or poor work flow. Motivation cannot make up for a deficient job context (see Figure 6–1). Managers, therefore, need to carefully consider the causes of poor performance and employee misbehavior.

Importantly, managers should not ignore the individual inputs identified in Figure 6–1. As discussed in this chapter as well as Chapters 5 and 6, individual differences are an important input that influence motivation and motivated behavior. Managers are advised to develop employees so that they have the ability and job knowledge to effectively perform their jobs. In addition, attempts should be made to nurture positive employee characteristics, such as self-esteem, self-efficacy, positive emotions, a learning goal orientation, and need for achievement.

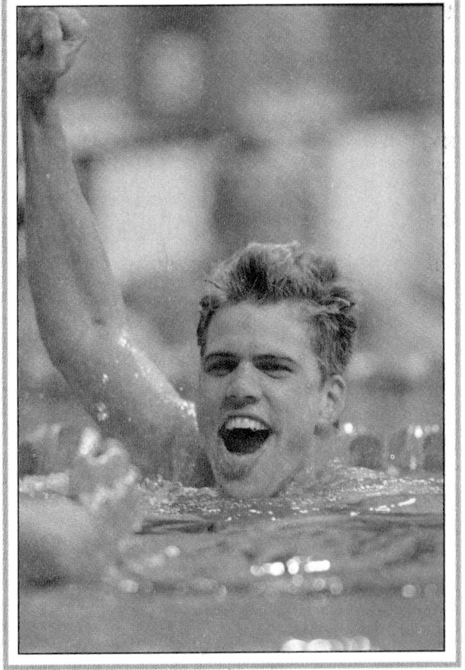

Gary Hall is a highly motivated individual. He is the most decorated American summer Olympic athlete with over eight Olympic medals.

Because motivation is goal directed, the process of developing and setting goals should be consistent with our previous discussion. Moreover, the method used to evaluate performance also needs to be considered. Without a valid performance appraisal system, it is difficult, if not impossible, to accurately distinguish good and poor performers. Consider the motivational effect of using a performance rating system in which managers are required to rank employees against each other according to some specified distribution:

> At GE, which has used the system for several years, this means that 20% of salaried, managerial, and executive employees are rated outstanding each year, 70% "high-performance middle," and 10% in need of improvement. At Enron, where some have nicknamed the system "rank and yank," employees are put in one of five categories: 5% are identified as superior, 30% excellent, 30% strong, 20% satisfactory, and 15% "needs improvement." And Ford, which began using rating systems last year, dictates that 10% of the auto maker's 18,000 managers will get A grades, 85% Bs, and 5% Cs. (Initially, it asked for 10% Cs.) Those who receive a second consecutive C can be fired.[61]

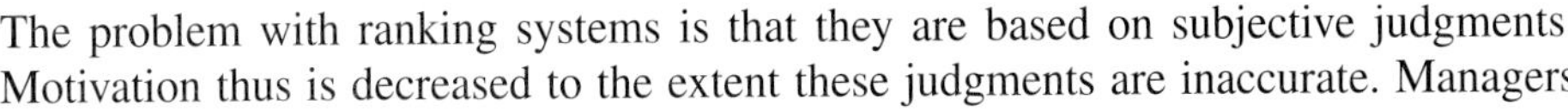

The problem with ranking systems is that they are based on subjective judgments. Motivation thus is decreased to the extent these judgments are inaccurate. Managers need to keep in mind that both equity theory and expectancy theory suggest that employee motivation is squelched by inaccurate performance ratings. Not only can inaccurate performance rating systems negatively influence motivation, but they can also lead to lawsuits. For example, employees and former employees with Microsoft, Ford, and Conoco have filed lawsuits claiming that ranking systems are biased toward some groups over others.[62]

Consistent with expectancy theory, managers should make extrinsic rewards contingent on performance. In doing so, however, it is important to consider two issues. First, managers need to ensure that performance goals are directed to achieve the "right" end-results. For example, health insurers and medical groups wrestle over the relative focus on cost savings versus patient satisfaction. Consider the case of Oakland-based Kaiser Permanente:

> Telephone clerks at California's largest HMO received bonuses for keeping calls with patients brief and limiting the number of doctor visits they set up. . . . The California Nurses Association, the union representing Kaiser's registered nurses, derided the program as deceitful and harmful to patients with serious medical problems.
>
> "Patients don't understand they're talking to a high school graduate with no nursing background," [Jim] Anderson said.
>
> The clerks, who generally have little to no medical training, answer phone calls from customers wanting to set up doctor appointments or asking simple medical questions.
>
> Cash bonuses were paid to those who made appointments for fewer than 35% of callers and spent less than an average of three minutes, 45 seconds on the phone with each patient. Clerks were also encouraged to transfer fewer than 50% of the calls to registered nurses for further evaluation.[63]

Interestingly, incentives based on quality care and patient satisfaction are twice as common as cost-cutting incentives among heath insurers across the United States.[64] Second, the promise of increased rewards will not prompt higher effort and good performance unless those rewards are clearly tied to performance and they are large enough to gain employees' interest or attention.

Moreover, equity theory tells us that motivation is influenced by employee perceptions about the fairness of reward allocations. Motivation is decreased when employees believe rewards are inequitably allocated. Rewards also need to be integrated appropriately into the appraisal system. If performance is measured at the individual level, individual achievements need to be rewarded. On the other hand, when performance is the result of group effort, rewards should be allocated to the group.[65]

Feedback also should be linked with performance. Feedback provides the information and direction needed to keep employees focused on relevant tasks, activities, and goals. Managers should strive to provide specific, timely, and accurate feedback to employees.

Finally, we end this chapter by noting that an organization's culture significantly influences employee motivation and behavior. A positive self-enhancing culture such as that at Rhino Foods, for example, is more likely to engender higher motivation and commitment than a culture dominated by suspicion, fault finding, and blame.

key terms

distributive justice 180
equity sensitivity 179
equity theory 177
expectancy 183
expectancy theory 181
goal 188
goal commitment 191
goal difficulty 190
goal specificity 190
instrumentality 183
interactional justice 180
management by objectives 188
negative inequity 179
positive inequity 179
procedural justice 180
valence 184

chapter summary

- *Discuss the role of perceived inequity in employee motivation.* Equity theory is a model of motivation that explains how people strive for fairness and justice in social exchanges. On the job, feelings of inequity revolve around a person's evaluation of whether he or she receives adequate rewards to compensate for his or her contributive inputs. People perform these evaluations by comparing the perceived fairness of their employment exchange with that of relevant others. Perceived inequity creates motivation to restore equity.
- *Describe the practical lessons derived from equity theory.* Equity theory has at least eight practical implications. First, because people are motivated to resolve perceptions of inequity, managers should not discount employees' feelings and perceptions when trying to motivate workers. Second, managers should pay attention to employees' *perceptions* of what is fair and equitable. It is the employee's view of reality that counts when trying to motivate someone, according to equity theory. Third, employees should be given a voice in decisions that affect them. Fourth, employees should be given the opportunity to appeal decisions that affect their welfare. Fifth, employees are more likely to accept and support organizational change when they believe it is implemented fairly and when it produces equitable outcomes. Sixth, managers can promote cooperation and teamwork among group members by treating them equitably. Seventh, treating employees inequitably can lead to litigation and costly court settlements. Finally, managers need to pay attention to the organization's climate for justice because it influences employee attitudes and behavior.
- *Explain Vroom's expectancy theory.* Expectancy theory assumes motivation is determined by one's perceived chances of achieving valued outcomes. Vroom's expectancy model of motivation reveals how effort $\rightarrow$ performance expectancies and performance $\rightarrow$ outcome instrumentalities influence the degree of effort expended to achieve desired (positively valent) outcomes.
- *Describe the practical implications of expectancy theory.* Managers are advised to enhance effort $\rightarrow$ performance expectancies by helping employees accomplish their performance goals. With respect to instrumentalities and valences, managers should attempt to link employee performance and valued rewards. There are four prerequisites to linking performance and rewards: (a) Managers need to develop and communicate performance standards to employees, (b) managers need valid and accurate performance ratings, (c) managers need to determine the relative mix of individual versus team contribution to performance and then reward accordingly, and (d) managers should use performance ratings to differentially allocate rewards among employees.
- *Identify five practical lessons to be learned from goal-setting research.* Difficult goals lead to higher performance than easy or moderate goals: goals should not be impossible to achieve. Specific, difficult goals lead to higher performance for simple rather than complex tasks. Third, feedback enhances the effect of specific, difficult goals. Fourth, participative goals, assigned goals, and self-set goals are equally effective. Fifth, goal commitment and monetary incentives affect goal-setting outcomes.
- *Specify issues that should be addressed before implementing a motivational program.* Managers need to consider the variety of causes of poor performance and employee misbehavior. Undesirable employee performance and behavior may be due to a host of deficient individual inputs (e.g., ability, dispositions, emotions, and beliefs) or job context factors (e.g., materials and machinery, job characteristics, reward systems, supervisory support and coaching, and social norms). The method used to evaluate performance as well as the link between performance and rewards must be examined. Performance must be accurately evaluated and rewards should be equitably distributed. Managers should also recognize that employee motivation and behavior are influenced by organizational culture.

chapter Eight

Improving Performance with Feedback, Rewards, and Positive Reinforcement

LEARNING OBJECTIVES

After reading the material in this chapter, you should be able to:

- Specify the two basic functions of feedback and three sources of feedback.
- Define upward feedback and 360-degree feedback, and summarize the general tips for giving good feedback.
- Briefly explain the four different organizational reward norms.
- Summarize the research lessons about pay for performance, and explain why rewards often fail to motivate employees.
- State Thorndike's "law of effect" and explain Skinner's distinction between respondent and operant behavior.
- Demonstrate your knowledge of positive reinforcement, negative reinforcement, punishment, and extinction, and explain behavior shaping.

THE POWER OF RESPECT

Leigh Buchanan, Senior Editor, *Harvard Business Review:* The genius of Pat McGovern is the way he makes things all about you. That impressed me hugely, because when I first met Pat back in 1989 I wasn't the sort of person *anything* was all about. I was a new copy editor at *CIO* magazine; Pat was (still is) the founder and chairman of *CIO*'s parent, International Data Group, a then $400 million technology publishing and research empire. It hadn't occurred to me that the twain would meet, so I was startled (confused, marginally freaked) when a tall, ruddy man loomed in the entrance to my cubicle a few weeks before Christmas.

Pat thanked me for my contributions. He asked how things were going and looked vaguely disappointed when all I could muster was an unilluminating "Fine." Then he complimented me on a column I had ghostwritten for some technology honcho. The column was my most substantive accomplishment to date and the thing I was proudest of. But my name didn't appear on it anywhere, so how did he know? After three or four minutes, he handed me my bonus and proceeded to the next cubicle.

The formula for Pat's Christmas calls—expression of gratitude/request for feedback/congratulations on specific achievement/delivery of loot—never varied, even as IDG grew into the $2.4 billion global behemoth it is today. To personally thank most every person in every business unit in the U.S., more than 1,500 employees, takes almost four weeks, he told me years later: Managers provide him with a list of accomplishments for all their reports, and Pat memorizes them the night before his visits. He does this because he wants employees to know that he *sees them*—really sees them—as individuals, and that he considers what they do all day to be meaningful.

Not only does Pat care about his people; he also believes in them. His commitment to decentralization has created a constellation of motivated business units that make their own decisions about everything from how to reward staff to what new businesses to launch. He also treats his end customers—the readers of such publications as *Computerworld, PC World,* and *Macworld*—with consummate respect. At IDG the quality of content is sacrosanct, a tough ideal to sustain when advertising pays so many of the bills.

Did I mention that he's giving $350 million to MIT to create an institute for brain research? Maybe I shouldn't: I don't want to lay it on too thick.

Another small-company tradition Pat has kept up

over the years is taking each employee out for a meal at the Ritz on his or her 10th anniversary with IDG. I left *CIO* after only seven years (to work for *Inc.*, where I could write about people like Pat and not just work for them), so I never got my anniversary dinner. Too bad—it would have been a class act. And I'm not talking about the restaurant.[1]

FOR DISCUSSION

What do you like most about Pat McGovern's management style? Why? For an interpretation of this case and additional comments, visit our Online Learning Center:

www.mhhe.com/kinickiob2e

PRODUCTIVITY AND QUALITY IMPROVEMENT EXPERTS tell us we need to work smarter, not harder. While it is true that a sound education and appropriate skill training are needed if one is to work smarter, the process does not end there. Today's employees need instructive and supportive feedback and desired rewards if they are to translate their knowledge into improved productivity and superior quality. This point was reinforced by a recent survey of 2,600 employees in the United States. Forty-two percent reported getting regular feedback on their job performance and only 29% said they were rewarded for good work. Worse yet, 29% claimed poor performers in their department were not managed appropriately.[2] Figure 8–1 illustrates a learning- and development-focused cycle in which feedback enhances ability, encourages effort, and acknowledges results. Rewards and reinforcement, in turn, motivate effort and compensate results.

This chapter concludes our coverage of individual behavior by discussing the effects of feedback, rewards, and positive reinforcement on behavior and by integrating those insights with what you have learned about perception, individual differences, and various motivational tools such as goal setting.

Providing Effective Feedback

Numerous surveys tell us employees have a hearty appetite for feedback.[3] So also do achievement-oriented students. Following a difficult exam, for instance, students want to know two things: how they did and how their peers did. By letting students know how their work measures up to grading and competitive standards, an instructor's feedback permits the students to adjust their study habits so they can reach their goals. Likewise, managers in well-run organizations follow up goal setting with a feedback program to provide a rational basis for adjustment and improvement. For example, notice the importance

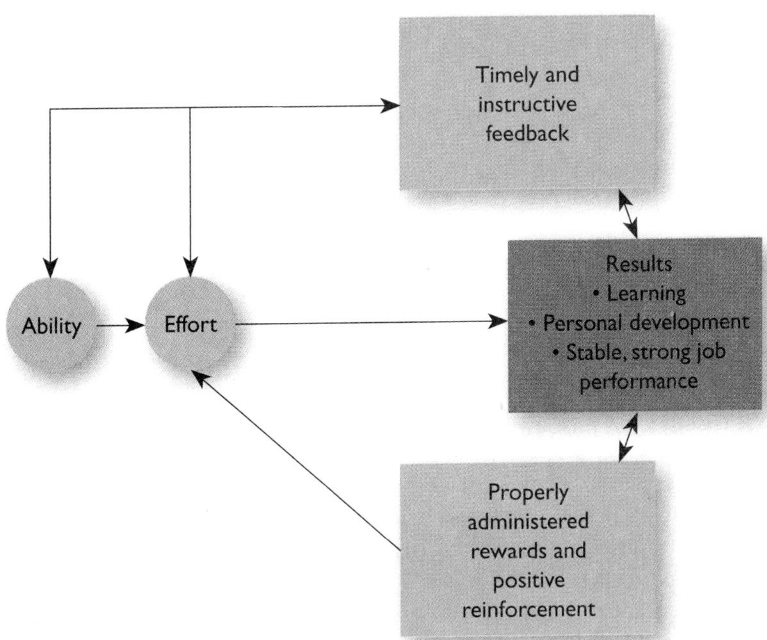

FIGURE 8–1 Bolstering the Job Performance Cycle with Feedback, Rewards, and Reinforcement

Fred Smith, the founder and head of Federal Express, places on feedback when outlining his philosophy of leadership:

> When people walk in the door, they want to know: What do you expect out of me? What's in this deal for me? What do I have to do to get ahead? Where do I go in this organization to get justice if I'm not treated appropriately? They want to know how they're doing. They want some feedback. And they want to know that what they are doing is important.
>
> If you take the basic principles of leadership and answer those questions over and over again, you can be successful dealing with people.[4]

Feedback too often gets shortchanged. In fact, "poor or insufficient feedback" was the leading cause of deficient performance in a survey of US and European companies.[5]

feedback

Objective information about performance.

As the term is used here, **feedback** is objective information about individual or collective performance shared with those in a position to improve the situation. Subjective assessments such as, "You're doing a poor job," "You're too lazy," or "We really appreciate your hard work" do not qualify as objective feedback. But hard data such as units sold, days absent, dollars saved, projects completed, customers satisfied, and quality rejects are all candidates for objective feedback programs. Management consultants Chip Bell and Ron Zemke offered this helpful perspective of feedback:

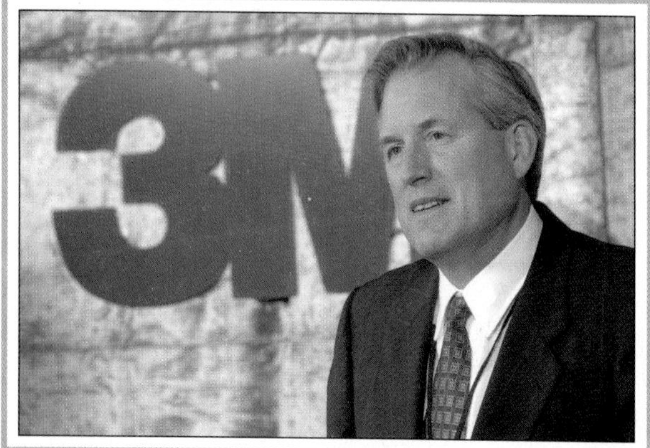

CEOs can have just as much trouble getting quality feedback as the middle manager. Being the new "leader" at a new company means patience in getting people to do what you want. 3M CEO Jim McNerney calls it "personal engagement." "I want a lot of feedback on how to run this company. The trick for me is to create an environment where I get honest feedback. That's the hard part. The natural tendency for people is to say, Jim, what a great idea!" (Business Week Online, "The Hard Work in Leadership," 4/12/04.)

> Feedback is, quite simply, any information that answers those "How am I doing?" questions. *Good* feedback answers them truthfully and productively. It's information people can use either to confirm or correct their performance.
>
> Feedback comes in many forms and from a variety of sources. Some is easy to get and requires hardly any effort to understand. The charts and graphs tracking group and individual performance that are fixtures in many workplaces are an example of this variety. Performance feedback—the numerical type at least—is at the heart of most approaches to total quality management.
>
> Some feedback is less accessible. It's tucked away in the heads of customers and managers. But no matter how well-hidden the feedback, if people need it to keep their performance on track, we need to get it to them—preferably while it's still fresh enough to make an impact.[6]

Two Functions of Feedback

Experts say feedback serves two functions for those who receive it; one is *instructional* and the other *motivational.* Feedback instructs when it clarifies roles or teaches new behavior. For example, an assistant accountant might be advised to handle a certain entry as a capital item rather than as an expense item. On the other hand, feedback motivates when it serves as a reward or promises a reward.[7] Having the boss tell you that a grueling project you worked on earlier has just been completed can be a rewarding piece of news. As documented in one study, the motivational function of feedback can be significantly enhanced by pairing *specific,* challenging goals with *specific* feedback about results.[8]

Three Sources of Feedback: Others, Task, and Self

It almost goes without saying that employees receive objective feedback from *others* such as peers, supervisors, lower-level employees, and outsiders. Perhaps less obvious is the fact that the *task* itself is a ready source of objective feedback.[9] Anyone who has spent hours on a "quick" Internet search can appreciate the power of task-provided feedback. Similarly, skilled tasks such as computer programming or landing a jet airplane provide a steady stream of feedback about how well or poorly one is doing. A third source of feedback is *oneself,* but self-serving bias and other perceptual problems can contaminate this source. Those high in self-confidence tend to rely on personal feedback more than those with low self-confidence. Although circumstances vary, an employee can be bombarded by feedback from all three sources simultaneously. This is where the gatekeeping functions of perception and cognitive evaluation are needed to help sort things out.

The Recipient's Perspective of Feedback

The need for feedback is variable, across both individuals and situations[10] (see Hands-On Exercise). Feedback can be positive or negative. Generally, people tend to perceive and recall positive feedback more accurately than they do negative feedback.[11] But negative feedback (e.g., being told your performance is below average) can have a *positive* motivational effect. In fact, in one study, those who were told they were below average on a creativity test subsequently outperformed those who were led to believe their results were above average. The subjects apparently took the negative feedback as a challenge and set and pursued higher goals. Those receiving positive feedback apparently were less motivated to do better.[12] Nonetheless, feedback with a negative message or threatening content needs to be administered carefully to avoid creating insecurity and defensiveness.[13] Self-efficacy also can be damaged by negative feedback, as discovered in a pair of experiments with business students. The researchers concluded, "To facilitate the development of strong efficacy beliefs, managers should be careful about the provision of negative feedback. Destructive criticism by managers which attributes the cause of poor performance to internal factors reduces both the beliefs of self-efficacy and the self-set goals of recipients."[14]

Upon receiving feedback, people cognitively evaluate factors such as its accuracy, the credibility of the source, the fairness of the system (e.g., performance appraisal system), their performance-reward expectancies, and the reasonableness of the standards. Any feedback that fails to clear one or more of these cognitive hurdles will be rejected or downplayed. Personal experience largely dictates how these factors are weighed.

Behavioral Outcomes of Feedback

In Chapter 7, we discussed how goal setting gives behavior direction, increases expended effort, and fosters persistence. Because feedback is intimately related to the goal-setting process, it involves the same behavioral outcomes: direction, effort, and persistence. However, while the fourth outcome of goal setting involves formulating goal-attainment strategies, the fourth possible outcome of feedback is *resistance.* Feedback schemes that smack of manipulation or fail one or more of the perceptual and cognitive evaluation tests mentioned above breed resistance.[15]

HANDS-ON EXERCISE

Measuring Your Desire for Performance Feedback

INSTRUCTIONS: Circle one number indicating the strength of your agreement or disagreement with each statement. Total your responses, and compare your score with our arbitrary norms.

	Disagree				Agree
1. As long as I think that I have done something well, I am not too concerned about how other people think I have done.	**5**	**4**	**3**	**2**	**1**
2. How other people view my work is not as important as how I view my own work.	**5**	**4**	**3**	**2**	**1**
3. It is usually better not to put much faith in what others say about your work, regardless of whether it is complimentary or not.	**5**	**4**	**3**	**2**	**1**
4. If I have done something well, I know it without other people telling me so.	**5**	**4**	**3**	**2**	**1**
5. I usually have a clear idea of what I am trying to do and how well I am proceeding toward my goal.	**5**	**4**	**3**	**2**	**1**
6. I find that I am usually a pretty good judge of my own performance.	**5**	**4**	**3**	**2**	**1**
7. It is very important to me to know what people think of my work.	**1**	**2**	**3**	**4**	**5**
8. It is a good idea to get someone to check on your work before it's too late to make changes.	**1**	**2**	**3**	**4**	**5**
9. Even though I may think I have done a good job, I feel a lot more confident of it after someone else tells me so.	**1**	**2**	**3**	**4**	**5**
10. Since one cannot be objective about their own performance, it is best to listen to the feedback provided by others.	**1**	**2**	**3**	**4**	**5**

Total score = ____________

ARBITRARY NORMS
10–23 = Low desire for feedback
24–36 = Moderate desire for feedback
37–50 = High desire for feedback

SOURCE: Excerpted and adapted from D M Herold, C K Parsons, and R B Rensvold, "Individual Differences in the Generation and Processing of Performance Feedback," *Educational and Psychological Measurement*, February 1996, Table 1, p 9.

Nontraditional Upward Feedback and 360-Degree Feedback

Traditional top-down feedback programs have given way to some interesting variations in recent years. Two newer approaches, discussed in this section, are upward feedback and so-called 360-degree feedback. Aside from breaking away from a strict superior-to-subordinate feedback loop, these newer approaches are different because they typically involve *multiple sources* of feedback.[16] Instead of getting feedback from one boss, often during an annual performance appraisal, more and more managers are getting structured feedback from superiors, lower-level employees, peers, and even outsiders such as customers. Nontraditional feedback is growing in popularity for at least six reasons:

1. Traditional performance appraisal systems have created widespread dissatisfaction.
2. Team-based organization structures are replacing traditional hierarchies. This trend requires managers to have good interpersonal skills that are best evaluated by team members.
3. Multiple-rater systems are said to make feedback more valid than single-source feedback.[17]
4. Advanced computer network technology (the Internet and company intranets) greatly facilitates multiple-rater systems.[18]
5. Bottom-up feedback meshes nicely with the trend toward participative management and employee empowerment.
6. Co-workers and lower-level employees are said to know more about a manager's strengths and limitations than the boss.[19]

Together, these factors make a compelling case for looking at better ways to give and receive performance feedback.

upward feedback
Employees evaluate their boss.

Upward Feedback **Upward feedback** stands the traditional approach on its head by having lower-level employees provide feedback on a manager's style and performance. This type of feedback is generally anonymous. Most students are familiar with upward feedback programs from years of filling out anonymous teacher evaluation surveys. Early adopters of upward evaluations include AT&T, General Mills, Motorola, and Procter & Gamble.[20]

Managers often resist upward feedback programs because they believe it erodes their authority. Other critics say anonymous upward feedback can become little more than a personality contest or, worse, be manipulated by managers who make promises or threats. What does the research literature tell us about upward feedback?

Studies with diverse samples have given us these useful insights:

- The question of whether upward feedback should be *anonymous* was addressed by a study at a large US insurance company. All told, 183 employees rated the skills and effectiveness of 38 managers. Managers who received anonymous upward feedback received *lower* ratings and liked the process *less* than did those receiving feedback from identifiable employees. This finding confirmed the criticism that employees will tend to go easier on their boss when not protected by confidentiality.[21]
- A large-scale study at the US Naval Academy, where student leaders and followers live together day and night, discovered a positive impact of upward feedback on leader behavior.[22]
- In a field study of 238 corporate managers, upward feedback had a positive impact on the performance of low-to-moderate performers.[23]

360-degree feedback
Comparison of anonymous feedback from one's superior, subordinates, and peers with self-perceptions.

360-Degree Feedback Letting individuals compare their own perceived performance with behaviorally specific (and usually anonymous) performance information from their manager, subordinates, and peers is known as **360-degree feedback.** Even outsiders may be involved in what is sometimes called full-circle feedback. The idea is to let the individual know how their behavior affects others, with the goal of motivating change. Consider this manager's story, for example:

> Lydia Whitefield, vice president of corporate marketing at Avaya, has received dozens of performance reviews from dozens of bosses during her 10-year career in telecommunications. But the one review she never forgot, the one that pushed her to alter her management style, came from an employee.
>
> "He told me, 'You're angry a lot,'" says Ms. Whitefield. "I was stunned, because what he and other employees saw as anger, I saw as my passion." She subsequently learned to be more contained when discussing assignments with staff and to avoid reacting vehemently.
>
> "That feedback was a life-altering experience for me," says Ms. Whitefield, who currently supervises about 75 people. She believes in the need for appraisals by employees of their bosses. "They can sting, but they are always instructive," she says.[24]

In a 360-degree feedback program, a given manager will play different roles, including focal person, superior, subordinate, and peer. Of course, the focal person role is played only once. The other roles are played more than once for various other focal persons. As a barometer of popularity, the Society for Human Resource Management found 32% of the companies it surveyed in 2000 using 360-degree feedback.[25]

Because upward feedback is a part of 360-degree feedback programs, the evidence reviewed earlier applies here as well. As with upward feedback, peer- and self-evaluations, central to 360-degree feedback programs, also are a significant affront to tradition.[26] But advocates say co-workers and managers themselves are appropriate performance evaluators because they are closest to the action. Generally, research builds a stronger case for peer appraisals than for self-appraisals.[27] Self-serving bias, discussed in Chapter 4, is a problem.

Rigorous research evidence of 360-degree feedback programs is scarce. A two-year study of 48 managers given 360-degree feedback in a large US public utility company led to these somewhat promising results. According to the researchers, "The group as a whole developed its skills, but there was substantial variability among individuals in how much change occurred."[28] Thus, as with any feedback, individuals vary in their response to 360-degree feedback. This problem was addressed in a recent field study of 20 managers and 67 employees at a manufacturing company. In addition to receiving 360-degree feedback, the managers were coached to enhance their self-awareness and employ the self-management techniques we discussed in Chapter 5. According to the researchers, "this feedback-coaching resulted in improved manager and employee satisfaction, commitment, intentions to turnover, and at least indirectly, this firm's performance."[29]

SKILLS & BEST PRACTICES

How to Make Sure Feedback Gets Results

- Relate feedback to existing performance *goals* and clear *expectations*.
- Give *specific* feedback tied to observable behavior or measurable results.
- Channel feedback toward *key result areas*.
- Give feedback as *soon* as possible.
- Give positive feedback for *improvement*, not just final results.
- Focus feedback on *performance*, not personalities.
- Base feedback on *accurate* and *credible* information.

Practical Recommendations Research evidence on upward and 360-degree feedback leads us to *favor* anonymity and *discourage* use for pay and promotion decisions. Otherwise, managerial resistance and self-serving manipulation would prevail.[30] We enthusiastically endorse the use of upward and/or 360-degree feedback for management development and training purposes.

Why Feedback Often Fails

Experts on the subject cite the following six common trouble signs for organizational feedback systems:

1. Feedback is used to punish, embarrass, or put down employees.
2. Those receiving the feedback see it as irrelevant to their work.
3. Feedback information is provided too late to do any good.
4. People receiving feedback believe it relates to matters beyond their control.
5. Employees complain about wasting too much time collecting and recording feedback data.
6. Feedback recipients complain about feedback being too complex or difficult to understand.[31]

Managers can provide effective feedback by consciously avoiding these pitfalls and following the practical tips in Skills & Best Practices.

Organizational Reward Systems

Rewards are an ever-present and always controversial feature of organizational life.[32] Some employees see their job as the source of a paycheck and little else. Others derive great pleasure from their job and association with co-workers. Even volunteers who donate their time to charitable organizations, such as the Red Cross, walk away with rewards in the form of social recognition and pride of having given unselfishly of their time. Hence, the subject of organizational rewards includes, but goes far beyond, monetary compensation.[33] This section examines key components of organizational reward systems.

Despite the fact that reward systems vary widely, it is possible to identify and interrelate some common components. The model in Figure 8–2 focuses on four important components: (1) types of rewards, (2) reward norms, (3) distribution criteria, and (4) desired outcomes. Let us examine these components.

Types of Rewards

Including the usual paycheck, the variety and magnitude of organizational rewards boggles the mind—from subsidized day care to college tuition reimbursement to stock options.[34] A US Bureau of Labor Statistics economist offered the following historical perspective of employee compensation:

> One of the more striking developments . . . over the past 75 years has been the growing complexity of employee compensation. Limited at the outbreak of World War I largely to straight-time pay for hours worked, compensation now includes a variety of employer-financed benefits, such as health and life insurance, retirement income, and paid time off. Although the details of each vary widely, these benefits are today standard components of the compensation package, and workers generally have come to expect them.[35]

Today, it is common for nonwage benefits to be 50% or more of total compensation.

In addition to the obvious pay and benefits, there are less obvious social and psychic rewards. Social rewards include praise and recognition from others both inside and outside the organization. Psychic rewards come from personal feelings of self-esteem, self-satisfaction, and accomplishment.

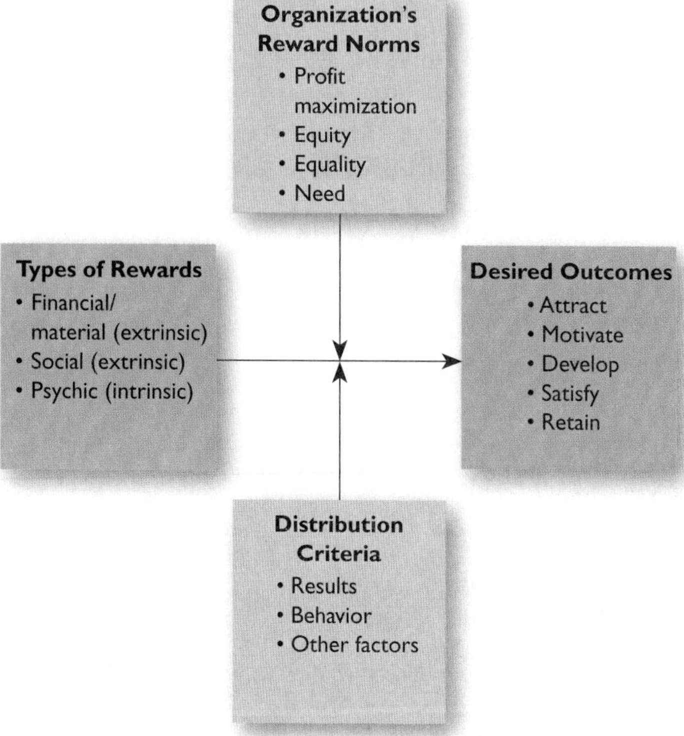

FIGURE 8–2 Key Factors in Organizational Reward Systems

extrinsic rewards
Financial, material, or social rewards from the environment.

intrinsic rewards
Self-granted, psychic rewards.

An alternative typology for organizational rewards is the distinction between extrinsic and intrinsic rewards. Financial, material, and social rewards qualify as **extrinsic rewards** because they come from the environment. Psychic rewards, however, are **intrinsic rewards** because they are self-granted. An employee who works to obtain extrinsic rewards, such as money or praise, is said to be extrinsically motivated. As we discussed in Chapter 6, one who derives pleasure from the task itself or experiences a sense of competence or self-determination is said to be intrinsically motivated.[36] The relative importance of extrinsic and intrinsic rewards is a matter of culture and personal tastes.

Organizational Reward Norms

As discussed in Chapter 7 under the heading of equity theory, the employer–employee linkage can be viewed as an exchange relationship. Employees exchange their time and talent for rewards. Ideally, four alternative norms dictate the nature of this exchange. In pure form, each would lead to a significantly different reward distribution system. They are as follows:

- *Profit maximization.* The objective of each party is to maximize its net gain, regardless of how the other party fares. A profit-maximizing company would attempt to pay the least amount of wages for maximum effort. Conversely, a profit-maximizing employee would seek maximum rewards, regardless of the organization's financial well-being, and leave the organization for a better deal.

- *Equity.* According to the **reward equity norm,** rewards should be allocated proportionate to contributions. Those who contribute the most should be rewarded the most. A cross-cultural study of American, Japanese, and Korean college students led the researchers to the following conclusion: "Equity is probably a phenomenon common to most cultures, but its strength will vary."[37] Basic principles of fairness and justice, evident in most cultures, drive the equity norm. However, pay equity between women and men in the United States remains an unresolved issue.[38]

reward equity norm
Rewards should be tied to contributions.

- *Equality.* The **reward equality norm** calls for rewarding all parties equally, regardless of their comparative contributions. Because absolute equality does not exist in today's hierarchical organizations, researchers explored the impact of pay *inequality.* They looked at *pay dispersion* (the pay gap between high-level and low-level employees). Result: The smaller the pay gap, the better the individual and organizational performance.[39] Thus, the outlandish compensation packages for many of today's top executives is not only a widely debated moral issue, it is a productivity issue as well.[40]

reward equality norm
Everyone should get the same rewards.

- *Need.* This norm calls for distributing rewards according to employees' needs, rather than their contributions.[41]

A pair of researchers concluded that these contradictory norms are typically intertwined:

> We propose that employer–employee exchanges are governed by the contradictory norms of profit maximization, equity, equality, and need. These norms can coexist; what varies is the extent to which the rules for correct application of a norm are clear and the relative emphasis different managements will give to certain norms in particular allocations.[42]

"Oh yeah? Well my dad has more employee awards than your dad."

Conflict and ethical debates often arise over the perceived fairness of reward allocations because of disagreement about reward norms. Stockholders might prefer a profit-maximization norm, while technical specialists would like an equity norm, and unionized hourly workers would argue for a pay system based on equality. A reward norm anchored to need might prevail in a family owned and operated business. Effective reward systems are based on clear and consensual exchange norms.

Distribution Criteria

According to one expert on organizational reward systems, three general criteria for the distribution of rewards are as follows:

- *Performance: results.* Tangible outcomes such as individual, group, or organization performance; quantity and quality of performance.
- *Performance: actions and behaviors.* Such as teamwork, cooperation, risk taking, creativity.

SKILLS & BEST PRACTICES

Profit Sharing and Pay for Performance Pay Off for this Canadian Steelmaker

It's a line that most CEOs routinely insert into their annual reports: "Our employees are our most important asset." . . . Dofasco's unique relationship with its employees makes it more than a line. In the steel industry, Dofasco is one of the only mills without a union—and its employees like it that way: Turnover at the company's primary facility in Hamilton is less than 1%. (The company also has operations in Ohio and in Monterrey, Mexico.)

Part of the reason for the low rate is Dofasco's approach to compensation. All of the company's employees receive equal bonuses based on 14% of the company's pre-tax income. In 1999, employees split a record pot of $36 million. And in 1996, Dofasco added a variable-compensation plan [that ties pay to job performance]. Every employee, from the cafeteria cooks to the senior managers, has a percentage of their salary that is variable pay.

SOURCE: Excerpted from C Dahle, "A Steelmaker's Heart of Gold," *Fast Company,* June 2003, p 46.

- *Nonperformance considerations.* Customary or contractual, where the type of job, nature of the work, equity, tenure, level in hierarchy, etc., are rewarded.[43]

As illustrated in the following example, the trend today is toward *performance* criteria and away from nonperformance criteria:

> Del Wallick wears his pride under his sleeve. A handshake reveals his prized wristwatch, given to mark his 25th anniversary with Timken Co. "I only take it off to shower and sleep," he says.
>
> The hallways of Mr. Wallick's home in Canton, Ohio, are filled with an array of certificates marking the milestones in his 31-year career as a Timken steel-mill worker. Down in his rec room, a mantel clock that he and his wife picked out from a Timken gift catalog rests atop the family television.
>
> But these days, once-paternal companies like Timken are trying to move away from rewarding employees for long service. Many are reducing service-award programs—and a few are eliminating them entirely. Besides wanting to save money, these companies hope to tilt recognition more toward performance and away from years of loyal service.[44]

We turn our attention to pay for performance after rounding out the reward system model in Figure 8–2.

Desired Outcomes

As listed in Figure 8–2, a good reward system should attract talented people and motivate and satisfy them once they have joined the organization.[45] Further, a good reward system should foster personal growth and development and keep talented people from leaving. A prime example is Dofasco Inc., the Canadian steel company based in Hamilton, Ontario (see Skills & Best Practices).

Pay for Performance

pay for performance

Monetary incentives tied to one's results or accomplishments.

Pay for performance is the popular term for monetary incentives linking at least some portion of the paycheck directly to results or accomplishments. Many refer to it simply as *incentive pay,* while others call it *variable pay.*[46] The general idea behind pay-for-performance schemes—including but not limited to merit pay, bonuses, and profit sharing—is to give employees an incentive for working harder or smarter. Pay for performance is something extra, compensation above and beyond basic wages and salaries. Proponents of incentive compensation say something extra is needed because hourly wages and fixed salaries do little more than motivate people to show up at work and put in the required hours.[47] The most basic form of pay for performance is the traditional piece-rate plan, whereby the employee is paid a specified amount of money for each unit of work. For example, 2,500 artisans at Longaberger's, in Frazeyburg, Ohio, are paid a fixed amount for each handcrafted wooden basket they weave. Together, they produce 40,000 of the prized maple baskets daily.[48] Sales

TABLE 8–1 The Use and Effectiveness of Modern Incentive Pay Plans

Plan Type	Presently Have	Rated Highly Effective
Annual bonus	74%	20%
Special one-time spot awards (after the fact)	42	38
Individual incentives	39	27
Long-term incentives (executive level)	32	44
Lump-sum merit pay	28	19
Competency-based pay	22	31
Profit-sharing (apart from retirement program)	22	43
Profit-sharing (as part of retirement program)	22	46
ESOP* stock plan	21	33
Suggestion/proposal programs	17	19
Team-based pay	15	29
Long-term incentives (below executive levels)	13	43
Skill-/knowledge-based pay	12	58
Group incentives (not team-based)	11	24
Pay for quality	9	29
Gainsharing	8	38
Special key-contributor programs (before the fact)	7	55

*Employee stock ownership plan.

SOURCE: Adapted from "Incentive Pay Plans: Which Ones Work . . . and Why," *HR Focus,* April 2001, p 3.

commissions, whereby a salesperson receives a specified amount of money for each unit sold, are another long-standing example of pay for performance. Today's service economy is forcing management to creatively adapt and go beyond piece rate and sales commission plans to accommodate greater emphasis on product and service quality, interdependence, and teamwork.

Current Practices For an indication of current practices, see Table 8–1, which is based on a survey of 156 US executives. The lack of clear patterns in Table 8–1 is indicative of the still experimental nature of incentive compensation today. Much remains to be learned from research and practice.

Research Insights According to available expert opinion and research results, pay for performance too often falls short of its goal of improved job performance. "Experts say that roughly half the incentive plans they see don't work, victims of poor design and administration."[49] In fact, one study documented how incentive pay had a *negative* effect on the performance of 150,000 managers from 500 financially distressed companies.[50] A meta-analysis of 39 studies found only a modest positive correlation between financial incentives and performance *quantity* and no impact on performance *quality.*[51] Other researchers have found only a weak statistical link between large executive bonuses paid out in good years and subsequent improvement in corporate profitability.[52] Also, in a survey of small business owners, more than half

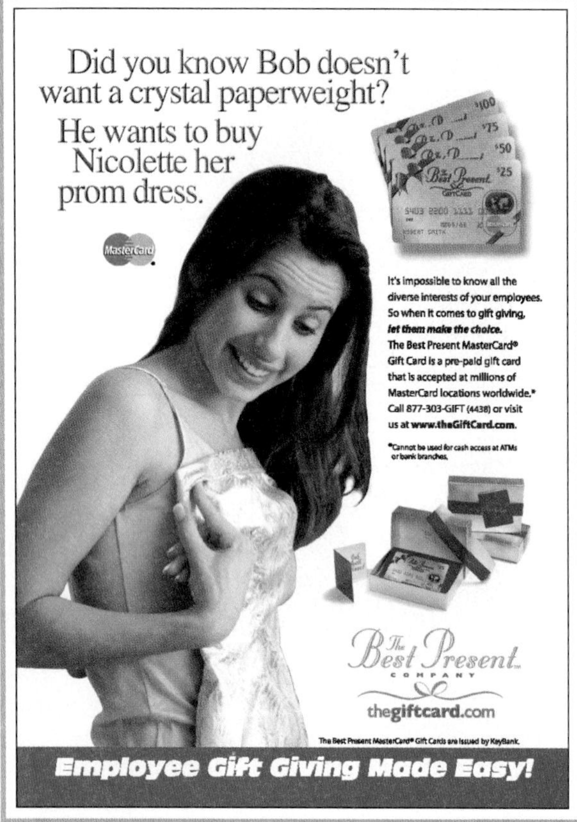

Did you know Bob doesn't want a crystal paperweight?
He wants to buy Nicolette her prom dress.
It's impossible to know all the diverse interests of your employees. So when it comes to gift giving, let them make the choice.
The Best Present MasterCard® Gift Card is a pre-paid gift card that is accepted at millions of MasterCard locations worldwide.* Call 877-303-GIFT (4438) or visit us at www.theGiftCard.com.
*Cannot be used for cash access at ATMs or bank branches.
The Best Present Company
thegiftcard.com
Employee Gift Giving Made Easy!

This ad touts the benefits of giving employees a choice in regard to the reward they receive. By getting a gift card, Bob is able to buy his daughter's prom dress, rather than getting a useless, dust-gathering, crystal paperweight.

said their commission plans failed to motivate extra effort from their salespeople.[53] Linking teachers' merit pay to student performance, an exciting school reform idea, turned out to be a big disappointment: "The bottom line is that despite high hopes, none of the 13 districts studied was able to use teacher pay incentives to achieve significant, lasting gains in student performance."[54] Clearly, the pay-for-performance area is still very much up in the air.

Why Rewards Often Fail to Motivate

Despite huge investments of time and money for organizational reward systems, the desired motivational effect often is not achieved. A management consultant/writer recently offered these eight reasons:

1. Too much emphasis on monetary rewards.
2. Rewards lack an "appreciation effect."
3. Extensive benefits become entitlements.
4. Counterproductive behavior is rewarded. (For example, "a pizza delivery company focused its rewards on the on-time performance of its drivers, only to discover that it was inadvertently rewarding reckless driving."[55])
5. Too long a delay between performance and rewards.
6. Too many one-size-fits-all rewards.
7. Use of one-shot rewards with a short-lived motivational impact.
8. Continued use of demotivating practices such as layoffs, across-the-board raises and cuts, and excessive executive compensation.[56]

These stubborn problems have fostered a growing interest in more effective reward and compensation practices.[57]

Positive Reinforcement

Feedback and reward programs all too often are ineffective because they are administered in haphazard ways. For example, consider these scenarios:

respondent behavior
Skinner's term for unlearned stimulus–response reflexes.

operant behavior
Skinner's term for learned, consequence-shaped behavior.

- A young programmer stops E-mailing creative suggestions to his boss because she never responds.
- The office politician gets a great promotion while her more skilled co-workers scratch their heads and gossip about the injustice.

In the first instance, a productive behavior faded away for lack of encouragement. In the second situation, unproductive behavior was unwittingly rewarded. Feedback and rewards need to be handled more precisely. Fortunately, the field of behavioral psychology can help. Thanks to the pioneering work of Edward L Thorndike, B F Skinner, and many others, a behavior modification technique called *positive reinforcement* helps managers achieve needed discipline and desired effect when providing feedback and granting rewards.[58]

Thorndike's Law of Effect

law of effect

Behavior with favorable consequences is repeated; behavior with unfavorable consequences disappears.

During the early 1900s, Edward L Thorndike observed in his psychology laboratory that a cat would behave randomly and wildly when placed in a small box with a secret trip lever that opened a door. However, once the cat accidentally tripped the lever and escaped, the animal would go straight to the lever when placed back in the box. Hence, Thorndike formulated his famous **law of effect,** which says *behavior with favorable consequences tends to be repeated, while behavior with unfavorable consequences tends to disappear.*[59] This was a dramatic departure from the prevailing notion a century ago that behavior was the product of inborn instincts.

Renowned behavioral psychologist B F Skinner and your co-author Bob Kreitner met and posed for a snapshot at an Academy of Management meeting in Boston. As a behaviorist, Skinner preferred to deal with observable behavior and its antecedents and consequences in the environment rather than with inner states such as attitudes and cognitive processes. The late professor Skinner was a fascinating man who left a permanent mark on modern psychology.

Skinner's Operant Conditioning Model

Skinner refined Thorndike's conclusion that behavior is controlled by its consequences. Skinner's work became known as *behaviorism* because he dealt strictly with observable behavior.[60] As a behaviorist, Skinner believed it was pointless to explain behavior in terms of unobservable inner states such as needs, drives, attitudes, or thought processes.[61] He similarly put little stock in the idea of self-determination.

In his 1938 classic, *The Behavior of Organisms,* Skinner drew an important distinction between two types of behavior: respondent and operant behavior.[62] He labeled unlearned reflexes or stimulus–response (S–R) connections **respondent behavior.** This category of behavior was said to describe a very small proportion of adult human behavior. Examples of respondent behavior would include shedding tears while peeling onions and reflexively withdrawing one's hand from a hot stove.[63] Skinner attached the label **operant behavior** to behavior that is learned when one "operates on" the environment to produce desired consequences. Some call this the response–stimulus (R–S) model. Years of controlled experiments with pigeons in "Skinner boxes" helped Skinner develop a sophisticated technology of behavior control, or operant conditioning. For example, he taught pigeons how to pace figure eights and how to bowl by reinforcing the underweight (and thus hungry) birds with food whenever they more closely approximated target behaviors. Skinner's work has significant implications for OB because the vast majority of organizational behavior falls into the operant category.[64]

Contingent Consequences

Contingent consequences, according to Skinner's operant theory, control behavior in four ways: positive reinforcement, negative reinforcement, punishment, and extinction.[65] The term *contingent* means there is a systematic if-then linkage between the

FIGURE 8–3 Contingent Consequences in Operant Conditioning

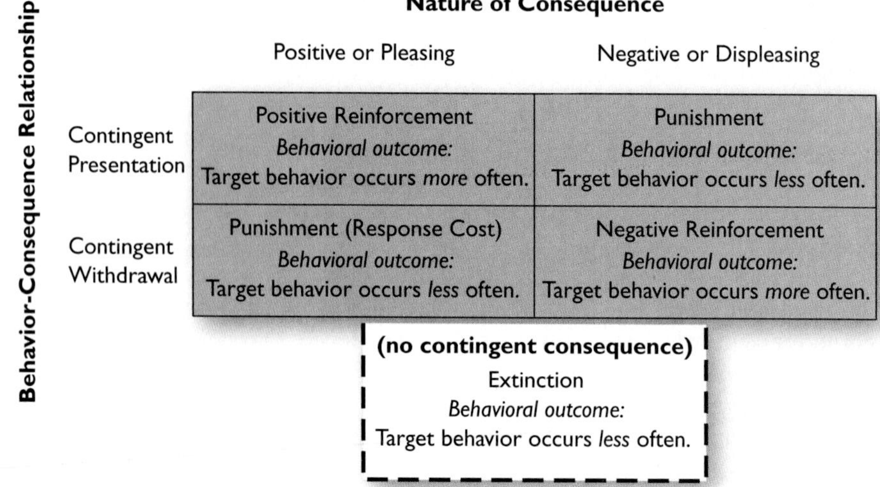

target behavior and the consequence. Remember Mom (and Pink Floyd) saying something to this effect: "If you don't finish your dinner, you don't get dessert" (see Figure 8–3)? To avoid the all-too-common mislabeling of these consequences, let us review some formal definitions.

positive reinforcement
Making behavior occur more often by contingently presenting something positive.

Positive Reinforcement Strengthens Behavior **Positive reinforcement** is the process of strengthening a behavior by contingently presenting something pleasing. (Importantly, a behavior is strengthened when it increases in frequency and weakened when it decreases in frequency.) The watchwords for using positive reinforcement are "catch them doing something *right*!"[66] For example, good-performance awards are handed out by the thousands each year to employees at Baptist Health Care Hospital in Pensacola, Florida. A $15 gift certificate goes to anyone accumulating five of the awards.[67]

negative reinforcement
Making behavior occur more often by contingently withdrawing something negative.

punishment
Making behavior occur less often by contingently presenting something negative or withdrawing something positive.

Negative Reinforcement Also Strengthens Behavior **Negative reinforcement** is the process of strengthening a behavior by contingently withdrawing something displeasing. For example, an army sergeant who stops yelling when a recruit jumps out of bed has negatively reinforced that particular behavior. Similarly, the behavior of clamping our hands over our ears when watching a jumbo jet take off is negatively reinforced by relief from the noise. Negative reinforcement is often confused with punishment. But the two strategies have opposite effects on behavior. Negative reinforcement, as the word *reinforcement* indicates, strengthens a behavior because it provides relief from an unpleasant situation.

Punishment Weakens Behavior **Punishment** is the process of weakening behavior through either the contingent presentation of something displeasing or the contingent withdrawal of something positive. A manager assigning a tardy employee to a dirty job exemplifies the first type of punishment. Docking a tardy employee's pay is an example of the second type of punishment, called "response cost" punishment. Legal fines involve response cost punishment. Sales people who must make up any cash register shortages out of their own pockets are being managed through response cost punishment. Ethical questions can and should be raised about this type of on-the-job punishment.[68]

extinction

Making behavior occur less often by ignoring or not reinforcing it.

Extinction Also Weakens Behavior

Extinction is the weakening of a behavior by ignoring it or making sure it is not reinforced. Getting rid of a former boyfriend or girlfriend by refusing to return their phone calls is an extinction strategy. A good analogy for extinction is to imagine what would happen to your houseplants if you stopped watering them. Like a plant without water, a behavior without occasional reinforcement eventually dies. Although very different processes, both punishment and extinction have the same weakening effect on behavior.

At Granite Construction in Watsonville, California, 20% of every manager's bonus depends on the person's "people skills." For most of its 80 years, a call from the boss's office meant bad news. "Employees were only contacted when something went wrong," says division manager Bruce McGowan, a 20-year veteran who oversees a staff of 700. Now the emphasis is on positive reinforcement.

Schedules of Reinforcement

As just discussed, contingent consequences are an important determinant of future behavior. The *timing* of behavioral consequences can be even more important. Based on years of tedious laboratory experiments with pigeons in highly controlled environments, Skinner and his colleagues discovered distinct patterns of responding for various schedules of reinforcement.[69] Although some of their conclusions can be generalized to negative reinforcement, punishment, and extinction, it is best to think only of positive reinforcement when discussing schedules.

Continuous Reinforcement As indicated in Table 8–2, every instance of a target behavior is reinforced when a **continuous reinforcement** (CRF) schedule is in effect. For instance, when your television set is operating properly, you are reinforced with a picture every time you turn it on (a CRF schedule). But, as with any CRF schedule of reinforcement, the behavior of turning on the television will undergo rapid extinction if the set breaks.

continuous reinforcement

Reinforcing every instance of a behavior.

intermittent reinforcement

Reinforcing some but not all instances of behavior.

Intermittent Reinforcement Unlike CRF schedules, **intermittent reinforcement** involves reinforcement of some but not all instances of a target behavior. Four subcategories of intermittent schedules, described in Table 8–2, are fixed and variable ratio schedules and fixed and variable interval schedules. Reinforcement in *ratio* schedules is contingent on the number of responses emitted. *Interval* reinforcement is tied to the passage of time. Some common examples of the four types of intermittent reinforcement are as follows:

- *Fixed ratio*—piece-rate pay; bonuses tied to the sale of a fixed number of units.
- *Variable ratio*—slot machines that pay off after a variable number of lever pulls; lotteries that pay off after the purchase of a variable number of tickets.

TABLE 8–2 Schedules of Reinforcement

Schedule	Description	Probable Effects on Responding
Continuous (CRF)	Reinforcer follows every response.	Steady high rate of performance as long as reinforcement continues to follow every response. High frequency of reinforcement may lead to early satiation. Behavior weakens rapidly (undergoes extinction) when reinforcers are withheld. Appropriate for newly emitted, unstable, or low-frequency responses.
Intermittent	Reinforcer does not follow every response.	Capable of producing high frequencies of responding. Low frequency of reinforcement precludes early satiation. Appropriate for stable or high-frequency responses.
Fixed ratio (FR)	A fixed number of responses must be emitted before reinforcement occurs.	A fixed ratio of 1:1 (reinforcement occurs after every response) is the same as a continuous schedule. Tends to produce a high rate of response, which is vigorous and steady.
Variable ratio (VR)	A varying or random number of responses must be emitted before reinforcement occurs.	Capable of producing a high rate of response, which is vigorous, steady, and resistant to extinction.
Fixed interval (FI)	The first response after a specific period of time has elapsed is reinforced.	Produces an uneven response pattern varying from a very slow, unenergetic response immediately following reinforcement to a very fast, vigorous response immediately preceding reinforcement.
Variable interval (VI)	The first response after varying or random periods of time have elapsed is reinforced.	Tends to produce a high rate of response, which is vigorous, steady, and resistant to extinction.

SOURCE: F Luthans and R Kreitner, *Organizational Behavior Modification and Beyond: An Operant and Social Learning Approach* (Glenview, IL: Scott, Foresman, 1985), p 58. Used with permission of the authors.

- *Fixed interval*—hourly pay; annual salary paid on a regular basis.
- *Variable interval*—random supervisory praise and pats on the back for employees who have been doing a good job.

Proper Scheduling Is Important The schedule of reinforcement can more powerfully influence behavior than the magnitude of reinforcement. Although this proposition grew out of experiments with pigeons, subsequent on-the-job research confirmed it. Consider, for example, a field study of 12 unionized beaver trappers employed by a lumber company to keep the large rodents from eating newly planted tree seedlings.[70]

The beaver trappers were randomly divided into two groups that alternated weekly between two different bonus plans. Under the first schedule, each trapper earned his regular $7 per hour wage plus $1 for each beaver caught. Technically, this bonus was paid on a CRF schedule. The second bonus plan involved the regular $7 per hour wage plus a one-in-four chance (as determined by rolling the dice) of receiving $4 for each beaver trapped. This second bonus plan qualified as a variable ratio (VR-4) schedule. In the long run, both incentive schemes averaged out to a $1-per-beaver bonus. Surprisingly, however, when the trappers were under the VR-4 schedule, they were 58% more productive than under the CRF schedule, despite the fact that the net amount of pay averaged out the same for the two groups during the 12-week trapping season.

Work Organizations Typically Rely on the Weakest Schedule Generally, variable ratio and variable interval schedules of reinforcement produce the strongest behavior that is most resistant to extinction. As gamblers will attest, variable schedules hold the promise of reinforcement after the next target response. For example, the following drama at a Laughlin, Nevada, gambling casino is one more illustration of the potency of variable ratio reinforcement:

> An elderly woman with a walker had lost her grip on the slot [machine] handle and had collapsed on the floor.
>
> "Help," she cried weakly.
>
> The woman at the machine next to her interrupted her play for a few seconds to try to help her to her feet, but all around her the army of slot players continued feeding coins to the machines.
>
> A security man arrived to soothe the woman and take her away.
>
> "Thank you," she told him appreciatively.
>
> "But don't forget my winnings."[71]

Organizations without at least some variable reinforcement are less likely to prompt this type of dedication to task. Despite the trend toward pay-for-performance, time-based pay schemes such as hourly wages and yearly salaries that rely on the weakest schedule of reinforcement (fixed interval) are still the rule in today's workplaces.

Shaping Behavior with Positive Reinforcement

Have you ever wondered how trainers at aquarium parks manage to get bottle-nosed dolphins to do flips, killer whales to carry people on their backs, and seals to juggle balls? The results are seemingly magical. Actually, a mundane learning process called shaping is responsible for the animals' antics.

SKILLS & BEST PRACTICES

How to Effectively Shape Job Behavior

1. *Accommodate the process of behavioral change.* Behaviors change in gradual stages, not in broad, sweeping motions.
2. *Define new behavior patterns specifically.* State what you wish to accomplish in explicit terms and in small amounts that can be easily grasped.
3. *Give individuals feedback on their performance.* A once-a-year performance appraisal is not sufficient.
4. *Reinforce behavior as quickly as possible.*
5. *Use powerful reinforcement.* To be effective, rewards must be important to the employee—not to the manager.
6. *Use a continuous reinforcement schedule.* New behaviors should be reinforced every time they occur. This reinforcement should continue until these behaviors become habitual.
7. *Use a variable reinforcement schedule for maintenance.* Even after behavior has become habitual, it still needs to be rewarded, though not necessarily every time it occurs.
8. *Reward teamwork—not competition.* Group goals and group rewards are one way to encourage cooperation in situations in which jobs and performance are interdependent.
9. *Make all rewards contingent on performance.*
10. *Never take good performance for granted.* Even superior performance, if left unrewarded, will eventually deteriorate.

SOURCE: Adapted from A T Hollingsworth and D Tanquay Hoyer, "How Supervisors Can Shape Behavior," *Personnel Journal*, May 1985, pp 86, 88.

Two-ton killer whales, for example, have a big appetite, and they find buckets of fish very reinforcing. So if the trainer wants to ride a killer whale, he or she reinforces very basic behaviors that will eventually lead to the whale being ridden. The killer whale is contingently reinforced with a few fish for coming near the trainer, then for being touched, then for putting its nose in a harness, then for being straddled, and eventually for swimming with the trainer on its back. In effect, the trainer systematically raises the behavioral requirement for reinforcement. Thus, **shaping** is defined as the process of reinforcing closer and closer approximations to a target behavior.

shaping

Reinforcing closer and closer approximations to a target behavior.

Shaping works very well with people, too, especially in training and quality programs involving continuous improvement. Praise, recognition, and instructive and credible feedback cost managers little more than moments of their time.[72] Yet, when used in conjunction with a behavior-shaping program, these consequences can efficiently foster significant improvements in job performance.[73] The key to successful behavior shaping lies in reducing a complex target behavior to easily learned steps and then faithfully (and patiently) reinforcing any improvement. For example, Continental Airlines used a cash bonus program to improve its on-time arrival record from one of the worst in the industry to one of the best. Employees originally were promised a $65 bonus each month Continental earned a top-five ranking. Now it takes a second- or third-place ranking to earn the $65 bonus and a $100 bonus awaits employees when they achieve a No. 1 ranking.[74] The airline handed out a total of $47 million in on-time bonuses in 2002.[75] (Skills & Best Practices lists practical tips on shaping.)

key terms

chapter summary

- *Specify the two basic functions of feedback and three sources of feedback.* Feedback, in the form of *objective* information about performance, both instructs and motivates. Individuals receive feedback from others, the task, and from themselves.
- *Define upward feedback and 360-degree feedback, and summarize the general tips for giving good feedback.* Lower-level employees provide upward feedback (usually anonymous) to their managers. A focal person receives 360-degree feedback from subordinates, the manager, peers, and selected others such as customers or suppliers. Good feedback is tied to performance *goals* and clear *expectations*, linked with *specific* behavior and/or results, reserved for *key result areas*, given as *soon* as possible, provided for *improvement* as well as for final results, focused on *performance* rather than on personalities, and based on *accurate* and *credible* information.

- *Briefly explain the four different organizational reward norms.* Maximizing individual gain is the object of the *profit maximization* reward norm. The *equity* norm calls for distributing rewards proportionate to contributions (those who contribute the most should earn the most). Everyone is rewarded equally when the *equality* reward norm is in force. The *need* reward norm involves distributing rewards based on employees' needs.
- *Summarize the research lessons about pay for performance, and explain why rewards often fail to motivate employees.* Research on pay for performance has yielded mixed results, with no clear pattern of effectiveness. Reward systems can fail to motivate employees for these reasons: overemphasis on money, no appreciation effect, benefits become entitlements, wrong behavior is rewarded, rewards are delayed too long, use of one-size-fits-all rewards, one-shot rewards with temporary effect, and demotivating practices such as layoffs.
- *State Thorndike's "law of effect," and explain Skinner's distinction between respondent and operant behavior.* According to Edward L Thorndike's law of effect, behavior with favorable consequences tends to be repeated, while behavior with unfavorable consequences tends to disappear. B F Skinner called unlearned stimulus–response reflexes *respondent behavior.* He applied the term *operant behavior* to all behavior learned through experience with environmental consequences.
- *Demonstrate your knowledge of positive reinforcement, negative reinforcement, punishment, and extinction, and explain behavior shaping.* Positive and negative reinforcement are consequence management strategies that strengthen behavior, whereas punishment and extinction weaken behavior. These strategies need to be defined objectively in terms of their actual impact on behavior frequency, not subjectively on the basis of intended impact. Behavior shaping occurs when closer and closer approximations of a target behavior are reinforced. In effect, the standard for reinforcement is made more difficult as the individual learns. The process begins with continuous reinforcement, which gives way to intermittent reinforcement when the target behavior becomes strong and habitual.

discussion questions

1. What specific roles did feedback, rewards, and positive reinforcement play in the chapter-opening vignette?
2. How has feedback instructed or motivated you lately?
3. How would you summarize the practical benefits and drawbacks of 360-degree feedback?
4. How would you respond to a manager who said, "Employees cannot be motivated with money"?
5. What real-life examples of positive reinforcement, negative reinforcement, both forms of punishment, and extinction can you draw from your recent experience? Were these strategies appropriately or inappropriately used?

ethical dilemma

CEO Pay: Welcome to the Twilight Zone between Need and Greed

As a matter of basic fairness, Plato posited that no one in a community should earn more than five times the wages of the ordinary worker. Management guru Peter F. Drucker has long warned that the growing pay gap between CEOs and workers could threaten the very credibility of leadership. He argued in the mid-1980s that no leader should earn more than 20 times the company's lowest-paid employee. His reasoning: If the CEO took too large a share of the rewards, it would make a mockery of the contributions of all the other employees in a successful organization.

After massive increases in compensation, Drucker's suggested standard looks quaint. CEOs of large corporations . . . [in 2001] made 411 times as much as the average factory worker. In the past decade, as rank-and-file wages increased 36%, CEO pay climbed 340%, to $11 million.[76]

What Is Your Ethical Interpretation of This Situation?

1. CEO pay these days is obscene and unethical. Explain why.
2. CEOs deserve whatever they get because of the pressures and demands of their jobs and their many years of dedication and hard work. Explain.
3. CEOs should be paid no more than ______ times the company's lowest-paid employee. Explain your choice. How will this limit be enforced?
4. Like top athletes and Hollywood actors, CEOs should be paid whatever the market dictates. Explain.
5. CEOs should voluntarily cap their compensation at reasonable and fair levels. What's reasonable and fair?
6. Something needs to be done to curb CEO compensation because it is eroding employee trust and loyalty. Suggestions?
7. Invent other options (but not stock options). Discuss.

For an interpretation of this situation, visit our Web site, www.mhhe.com/kininckiob2e.

If you're looking for additional study materials, be sure to check out the Online Learning Center at

www.mhhe.com/kinickiob2e

for more information and interactivities that correspond to this chapter.

part Three

Making Decisions and Managing Social Processes

chapter
Nine

Making Decisions

LEARNING OBJECTIVES

After reading the material in this chapter, you should be able to:

- Compare and contrast the rational model of decision making and Simon's normative model.
- Discuss knowledge management and techniques used by companies to increase knowledge sharing.
- Explain the model of decision-making styles and the stages of the creative process.
- Summarize the pros and cons of involving groups in the decision-making process.
- Explain how participative management affects performance.
- Contrast brainstorming, the nominal group technique, the Delphi technique, and computer-aided decision making.

IDEO USES ITS CREATIVE PRODUCT DESIGN PROCESS TO HELP COMPANIES IMPROVE CUSTOMER SERVICE

From its inception, IDEO has been a force in the world of design. It has designed hundreds of products and won more design awards over the past decade than any other firm. . . . Now, IDEO is transferring its ability to create consumer products into designing consumer experiences in services, from shopping and banking to health care and wireless communication.

Yet by showing global corporations how to change their organizations to focus on the consumer, IDEO is becoming much more than a design company. Indeed, it is now a rival to the traditional purveyors of corporate advice: the management consulting companies such as McKinsey, Boston Consulting, and Bain. . . .

And IDEO works fast. That's because the company requires its clients to participate in virtually all the consumer research, analysis, and decisions that go into developing solutions. When the process is complete, there's no need for a buy-in: Clients already know what to do—and how to do it quickly. Unlike traditional consultants, IDEO shares its innovative process with its customers through projects, workshops, and IDEO U, its customized teaching program. In IDEO-speak, this is "open-source innovation." . . .

Corporate execs probably have the most fun simply participating in the IDEO Way, the design firm's disciplined yet wild-and-woolly five-step process that emphasizes empathy with the consumer, anything-is-possible brainstorming, visualizing solutions by creating actual prototypes, using technology to find creative solutions, and doing it all with incredible speed.

Here's how it works: A company goes to IDEO with a problem. It wants a better product, service, or space—no matter. IDEO puts together an eclectic team composed of members from the client company and its own experts who go out to observe and document the consumer experience. Often, IDEO will have top executives play the roles of their own customers. Execs from food and clothing companies shop for their own stuff in different retail stores and on the Web. Health-care managers get care in different hospitals. Wireless providers use their own—and competing—services.

The next stage is brainstorming. IDEO mixes designers, engineers, and social scientists with its clients in a room where they intensely scrutinize a given problem and suggest possible solutions. It is managed chaos: a dozen or so very smart people examining data, throwing out ideas, writing potential solutions on big Post-its that are ripped off and attached to the wall.

IDEO designers then mock up working models of the best concepts that emerge. Rapid prototyping has always been a hallmark of the company. Seeing ideas in working, tangible form is a far more powerful mode of explanation than simply reading about them off a page. IDEO uses inexpensive prototyping tools—Apple-based iMovies to portray consumer experiences and cheap cardboard to mock up examination rooms or fitting rooms. . . .

Like a law firm, IDEO specializes in different practices. The "TEX"—or technology-enabled experiences—aims to take new high-tech products that first appeal only to early adopters and remake them for a mass consumer audience. IDEO's success with the Palm V led AT&T Wireless to call for help on its mMode consumer wireless platform. The company launched mMode in 2002 to allow AT&T Wireless mobile-phone customers to access e-mail and instant messaging, play games, find local restaurants, and connect to sites for news, stocks, weather, and other information. Techies liked mMode, but average consumers were not signing up. "We asked [IDEO] to redesign the interface so someone like my mother who isn't Web savvy can use the phone to navigate how to get the weather or where to shop," says mMode's Hall.

IDEO's GAME PLAN: It immediately sent AT&T Wireless managers on an actual scavenger hunt in San Francisco to see the world from their customers' perspective. They were told to find a CD by a certain Latin singer that was available at only one small music store, find a Walgreen's that sold its own brand of ibuprofen, and get a Pottery Barn catalog. They discovered that it was simply too difficult to find these kinds of things with their mMode service and wound up using the newspaper or the phone directory instead. IDEO and AT&T Wireless teams also went to AT&T Wireless stores and videotaped people using mMode. They saw that consumers couldn't find the sites they wanted. It took too many steps and clicks. "Even teenagers didn't get it," says Duane Bray, leader of the TEX practice at IDEO.

After dozens of brainstorming sessions and many prototypes, IDEO and AT&T Wireless came up with a new mMode wireless service platform. The opening page starts with "My mMode" which is organized like a Web browser's favorites list and can be managed on a Web site. A consumer can make up an individualized selection of sites, such as ESPN or Sony Pictures Entertainment, and ring tones. Nothing is more than two clicks away.

An mMode Guide on the page allows people to list five places—a restaurant, coffee shop, bank, bar, and retail store—that GPS location finders can identify in various cities around the U.S. Another feature spotlights the five nearest movie theaters that still have seats available within the next hour. Yet another, My Locker, lets users store a large number of photos and ring tones with AT&T Wireless. The whole design process took only 17 weeks. "We are thrilled with the results," says Hall. "We talked to frog design, Razorfish, and other design firms, and they thought this was a Web project that needed flashy graphics. IDEO knew it was about making the cell phone experience better."[1]

FOR DISCUSSION

Describe IDEO's creative design process. For an interpretation of this case and additional comments, visit our Online Learning Center:

www.mhhe.com/kinickiob2e

DECISION MAKING is one of the primary responsibilities of being a manager. The quality of a manager's decisions is important for two principal reasons. First, the quality of a manager's decisions directly affects his or her career opportunities, rewards, and job satisfaction. Second, managerial decisions contribute to the success or failure of an organization.

In Part Two, we studied individual and personal factors within organizational settings. Now, in Part Three, our attention turns to the collective or social dimensions of organizational behavior. We begin this new focus by examining individual and group decision making.

The chapter-opening vignette is a good illustration of creative decision making in action. It also highlights that decision making is a means to an end. Specifically, AT&T Wireless used IDEO's problem-solving process as a vehicle to redesign its mMode wireless platform with the goal of increasing customer subscriptions.

Decision making entails identifying and choosing alternative solutions that lead to a desired state of affairs. The process begins with a problem and ends when a solution has been chosen. To gain an understanding of how managers can make better decisions, this chapter focuses on (1) models of decision making, (2) the dynamics of decision making, and (3) group decision making.

Models of Decision Making

There are two fundamental models of decision making: (1) the rational model and (2) Simon's normative model. Each is based on a different set of assumptions and offers unique insights into the decision-making process.

decision making

Identifying and choosing solutions that lead to a desired end result.

The Rational Model

The **rational model** proposes that managers use a rational, four-step sequence when making decisions: (1) identifying the problem, (2) generating alternative solutions, (3) selecting a solution, and (4) implementing and evaluating the solution. According to this model, managers are completely objective and possess complete information to make a decision. Despite criticism for being unrealistic, the rational model is instructive because it analytically breaks down the decision-making process and serves as a conceptual anchor for newer models.[2] Let us now consider each of these four steps.

rational model

Logical four-step approach to decision making.

Identifying the Problem A **problem** exists when the actual situation and the desired situation differ. For example, a problem exists when you have to pay rent at the end of the month and don't have enough money. Your problem is not that you have to pay rent. Your problem is obtaining the needed funds. Consider the situation faced by Jean-Pierre Garnier, CEO of GlaxoSmithKline, after the merger of the top two pharmaceutical companies in Great Britain—Glaxo Wellcome and SmithKline Beecham:

problem

Gap between an actual and desired situation.

> Although their combined revenue is more than $30 billion, accounting for 7% of the world drug market, their pipelines were essentially empty. In the years running up to the deal the companies' laboratories had failed to come up with new drugs to replace the household names—Augmentin (antibiotic), Paxil (antidepressant), and Flixonase (intranasal anti-inflammatory)—nearing the end of their patents. Little known to the outside world: By the end of 2001, 22% of GSK's sales would be exposed to generic competition.[3]

Garnier's problem was the lack of new drugs being developed at GlaxoSmithKline. Potential causes of the problem included poor drug discovery facilities and processes, lack of resources for research and development, and lack of inventors.

Generating Solutions After identifying a problem, the next logical step is generating alternative solutions. For repetitive and routine decisions such as deciding when to send customers a bill, alternatives are readily available through decision rules. For example, a company might routinely bill customers three days after shipping a product. This is not the case for novel and unstructured decisions. Because there are no simple procedures for dealing with novel problems, managers must creatively generate alternative solutions. Managers can use a number of techniques to stimulate creativity.

Selecting a Solution Optimally, decision makers want to choose the alternative with the greatest value. Decision theorists refer to this as maximizing the expected utility of an outcome. This is no easy task. First, assigning values to alternatives is complicated and prone to error. Not only are values subjective, but they also vary according to the preferences of the decision maker. Eric Schmidt, CEO and chairman of Google, attempts to overcome this limitation by requiring two people to agree on solutions for every important decision. Schmidt told a reporter from *The Wall Street Journal,* "I really, really like this approach. It typically means that you get a kind of check and balance in the decision-making process. . . . The other thing that happens is decisions are made in front of people. We don't like people to go off and make a decision. We try to make decisions in as large a group as possible by as few people as possible."[4] Further, evaluating alternatives assumes they can be judged according to some standards or criteria. This further assumes that (1) valid criteria exist, (2) each alternative can be compared against these criteria, and (3) the decision maker actually uses the criteria. As you know from making your own key life decisions, people frequently violate these assumptions. Finally, it is important to consider whether or not the solution is ethical (see Skills & Best Practices). While the questions listed in the Skills & Best Practices are not meant to be exhaustive, yes answers indicate that you are off to a good start.

SKILLS & BEST PRACTICES

Diagnostic Questions to Assess Whether or Not Your Decisions Are Ethical

1. Am I being honest—telling the truth, the whole truth?
2. Does the decision parallel my personal values?
3. Will I be keeping all promises, commitments, contracts, etc.?
4. Is my decision permitting me to remain faithful?
5. Would I have the other person (entity, etc.) do this to me?
6. Am I willing to accept responsibility for this decision?
7. Is it safe—that is, safe from liability, safe from physical or emotional hurt, safe from danger?
8. Does it promote excellence?
9. Is it fair?
10. Is my decision a result of genuine concern for someone else?

SOURCE: These questions were taken from S Jackson, R Dooley, and D Lacy, "Substance Abuse, Ethics, Intermittent Leave," *HR Magazine,* July 2003, pp 41–42.

Implementing and Evaluating the Solution Once a solution is chosen, it needs to be implemented. After a solution is implemented, the evaluation phase is used to assess its effectiveness. If the solution is effective, it should reduce the difference between the actual and desired states that created the problem. If the gap is not closed, the implementation was not successful, and one of the following is true: Either the problem was incorrectly identified, or the solution was inappropriate.

Summarizing the Rational Model

The rational model is based on the premise that managers optimize when they make decisions. **Optimizing** involves solving problems by producing the best possible solution. As noted by Herbert Simon, a decision theorist who in 1978 earned the Nobel Prize for his work on decision making, "The assumptions of perfect rationality are contrary to fact. It is not a question of approximation; they do not even remotely describe the processes that human beings use for making decisions in complex situations."[5] Thus, the rational model is at best an instructional tool. Since decision makers do not follow these rational procedures, Simon proposed a normative model of decision making.

"Our task, then, is to decide how to decide how to decide."

Simon's Normative Model

This model attempts to identify the process that managers actually use when making decisions. The process is guided by a decision maker's bounded rationality. **Bounded rationality** represents the notion that decision makers are "bounded" or restricted by a variety of constraints when making decisions. These constraints include any personal or environmental characteristics that reduce rational decision making. Examples are the limited capacity of the human mind, problem complexity and uncertainty, amount and timeliness of information at hand, criticality of the decision, and time demands.[6]

optimizing
Choosing the best possible solution.

bounded rationality
Constraints that restrict decision making.

As opposed to the rational model, Simon's normative model suggests that decision making is characterized by (1) limited information processing, (2) the use of judgmental heuristics, and (3) satisficing. Each of these characteristics is now explored.

Limited Information Processing Managers are limited by how much information they process because of bounded rationality. This results in the tendency to acquire manageable rather than optimal amounts of information. In turn, this practice makes it difficult for managers to identify all possible alternative solutions. In the long run, the constraints of bounded rationality cause decision makers to fail to evaluate all potential alternatives.

Judgmental Heuristics **Judgmental heuristics** represent rules of thumb or shortcuts that people use to reduce information processing demands.[7] Research also shows that we tend to use these heuristics when confronted with excessive amounts of choice or information, and we use them without conscious awareness.[8] The use of heuristics helps decision makers to reduce the uncertainty inherent within the decision-making process. Because these shortcuts represent knowledge gained from past experience, they can help decision makers evaluate current problems. But they also

judgmental heuristics
Rules of thumb or shortcuts that people use to reduce information-processing demands.

Changing a flat by putting your car's spare tire on is a wise move if you're far from home or a repair shop. Changing a tire, however, can be very dangerous when done on the side of a freeway or interstate. How do the representativeness heuristic and satisficing influence an individual's decision to change a tire on the side of a freeway or interstate?

can lead to systematic errors that erode the quality of decisions. There are two common categories of heuristics that are important to consider: the availability heuristic and the representativeness heuristic.

The **availability heuristic** represents a decision maker's tendency to base decisions on information that is readily available in memory. Information is more accessible in memory when it involves an event that recently occurred, when it is salient (e.g., a plane crash), and when it evokes strong emotions (e.g., a high school student shooting other students). This heuristic is likely to cause people to overestimate the occurrence of unlikely events such as a plane crash or a high school shooting. This bias also is partially responsible for the recency effect discussed in Chapter 4. For example, a manager is more likely to give an employee a positive performance evaluation if the employee exhibited excellent performance over the last few months.

The **representativeness heuristic** is used when people estimate the probability of an event occurring. It reflects the tendency to assess the likelihood of an event occurring based on one's impressions about similar occurrences. A manager, for example, may hire a graduate from a particular university because the past three people hired from this university turned out to be good performers. In this case, the "school attended" criterion is used to facilitate complex information processing associated with employment interviews. Unfortunately, this shortcut can result in a biased decision. Similarly, an individual may believe that he or she can master a new software package in a short period of time because he or she was able to learn how to use a different type of software. This estimate may or may not be accurate. For example, it may take the individual a much longer period of time to learn the new software because it requires the person to learn a new programming language.

availability heuristic
Tendency to base decisions on information readily available in memory.

representativeness heuristic
Tendency to assess the likelihood of an event occurring based on impressions about similar occurrences.

satisficing
Choosing a solution that meets a minimum standard of acceptance.

Satisficing People satisfice because they do not have the time, information, or ability to handle the complexity associated with following a rational process. This is not necessarily undesirable. **Satisficing** consists of choosing a solution that meets some minimum qualifications, one that is "good enough." Satisficing resolves problems by producing solutions that are satisfactory, as opposed to optimal. Finding a radio station to listen to in your car is a good example of satisficing. You cannot optimize because it is impossible to listen to all stations at the same time. You thus stop searching for a station when you find one playing a song you like or do not mind hearing.

Dynamics of Decision Making

Decision making is part science and part art. Accordingly, this section examines four dynamics of decision making—knowledge management, decision-making styles, escalation of commitment, and creativity—that affect the "science" component. An understanding of these dynamics can help managers make better decisions.

Improving Decision Making through Effective Knowledge Management

Have you ever had to make a decision without complete information? If you have, then you know the quality of a decision is only as good as the information used to make the decision. The same is true for managerial decision making. In this case, however, managers frequently need information or knowledge possessed by people working in other parts of the organization. This realization has spawned a growing interest in the concept of knowledge management. **Knowledge management** (KM) is "the development of tools, processes, systems, structures, and cultures explicitly to improve the creation, sharing, and use of knowledge critical for decision making."[9] The effective use of KM helps organizations improve the quality of their decision making and correspondingly reduce costs and increase efficiency.[10] In contrast, ineffective use of knowledge management can be very costly. For example, experts estimate that *Fortune* 500 companies lose at least $31.5 billion a year by failing to share knowledge.[11]

knowledge management

Implementing systems and practices that increase the sharing of knowledge and information throughout an organization.

This section explores the fundamentals of KM so that you can use them to improve your decision making.

Knowledge Comes in Different Forms There are two types of knowledge that impact the quality of decisions: tacit knowledge and explicit knowledge. **Tacit knowledge** "entails information that is difficult to express, formalize, or share. It . . . is unconsciously acquired from the experiences one has while immersed in an environment."[12] Many skills, for example, such as swinging a golf club or writing a speech, are difficult to describe in words because they involve tacit knowledge. Tacit knowledge is intuitive and is acquired by having considerable experience and expertise at some task or job. Although some people joke about the role of intuition or gut feelings when making decisions, executive testimonies and research results increasingly reveal that the intuitive component of tacit knowledge is a key component of effective decision making. Consider the opinions of Ralph Larsen, former chair and CEO of Johnson & Johnson, and Richard Abdoo, chair and CEO of Wisconsin Energy Corporation, for example:

tacit knowledge

Information gained through experience that is difficult to express and formalize.

> "Often there is absolutely no way that you could have the time to thoroughly analyze every one of the options or alternatives available to you," says Larsen. "So you have to rely on your business judgment." Richard Abdoo . . . agrees. . . . "We now have to make decisions in a timely manner. And that means that we process the best information that's available and infer from it and use our intuition to make a decision." . . . Larsen says that one thing his experience has taught him is to listen to his instincts. "Ignoring them has led to some bad decisions," he notes. Adds Abdoo, "You end up consuming more Rolaids, but you have to learn to trust your intuition. Otherwise, at the point when you've gathered enough data to be 99.99% certain that the decision you're about to make is the correct one, that decision has become obsolete."[13]

Larsen and Abdoo reinforce the importance of intuition in decision making. Don't underestimate its value.[14]

SKILLS & BEST PRACTICES

Partners HealthCare Uses Medically Based Knowledge Management Software to Save Lives and Money

To help physicians keep up with 10,000 diseases and syndromes, 3,000 medications and 400,000 articles added to biomedical literature each year, Partners HealthCare in Boston imbeds knowledge into the workflow of its physicians through an online patient order management system. The system links constantly updated clinical knowledge and the patient's history to the IT systems. At any point, it may question the actions of physicians, who then must enter a reason for their decision into the computer. Doctors still have the ability to override the system. The power of such knowledge-based systems is that they operate in real time, says Davenport of Babson [Thomas Davenport is a professor at Babson College in Wellesley, Mass.].

A study found the system reduced medication errors by 55 percent. When Partners established that a new drug was particularly beneficial for heart problems, orders jumped from 12 percent to 81 percent. When the system began recommending a cancer drug be given fewer times each day because the lower dosage had the same effect as the higher one, orders for the lower frequency rose from 6 percent to 75 percent. Likewise, when it began to remind physicians that patients requiring bed rest also needed the blood thinner heparin to help prevent strokes, prescriptions rose from 24 percent to 54 percent.

Davenport says such a system can save lives and money and can offer quantifiable results often missing from other knowledge management endeavors.

"Everybody's busy these days, and nobody seems to have the time to browse through repositories anymore," he says. "So I think the only answer is embedding knowledge into the work itself."

SOURCE: Excerpted from P Babcock, "Shedding Light on Knowledge Management," *HR Magazine,* May 2004, p 50.

explicit knowledge

Information that can be easily put into words and shared with others.

In contrast, **explicit knowledge** can easily be put into words and explained to others. This type of knowledge is shared verbally or in written documents or numerical reports. In summary, tacit knowledge represents private information that is difficult to share, whereas explicit knowledge is external or public and is more easily communicated. Although both types of knowledge affect decision making, experts suggest competitive advantages are created when tacit knowledge is shared among employees.[15] Let us now examine how companies foster this type of information sharing.

Knowledge Sharing Organizations increasingly rely on sophisticated KM software to share explicit knowledge. This software allows companies to amass large amounts of information that can be accessed quickly from around the world. For example, Skills & Best Practices illustrates how KM software is being used by Partners HealthCare to help doctors provide better care and treatment for their patients. In contrast, tacit knowledge is shared most directly by observing, participating, or working with experts or coaches. Mentoring, which was discussed in Chapter 3, is another method for spreading tacit knowledge. Finally, informal networking, periodic meetings, and the design of office space can be used to facilitate KM. Alcoa, for example, designed its headquarters with the aim of increasing information sharing among its executives:

> Alcoa, the world's leading producer of aluminum, wanted to improve access between its senior executives. When designing their new headquarters they focused on open offices, family-style kitchens in the center of each floor, and plenty of open spaces. Previously, top executives would only interact with a couple of people in the elevator and those they had scheduled meetings with. Now, executives bump into each other more often and are more accessible for serendipitous conversations. This change in space has increased general accessibility as well as narrowed the gap between top executives and employees.[16]

It is important to remember that the best-laid plans for increasing KM are unlikely to succeed without the proper organizational culture. Effective KM requires a knowledge-sharing culture that both encourages and reinforces the spread of tacit knowledge. IBM Global Services has taken this recommendation to heart:

> IBM Global Services has incorporated knowledge creation, sharing, and reuse measurements into performance metrics. Performance metrics and incentives, particularly at the executive rank, have driven

collaborative behavior into the day-to-day work practices of executive networks. Further, knowledge sharing has been incorporated into personal business commitments, which are required for certification and affect promotion decisions. This encourages employees at all levels to be collaborative with and accessible to each other.[17]

General Decision-Making Styles

This section focuses on how an individual's decision-making style affects his or her approach to decision making. A **decision-making style** reflects the combination of how an individual perceives and comprehends stimuli and the general manner in which he or she chooses to respond to such information.[18] A team of researchers developed a model of decision-making styles that is based on the idea that styles vary along two different dimensions: value orientation and tolerance for ambiguity.[19] *Value orientation* reflects the extent to which an individual focuses on either task and technical concerns or people and social concerns when making decisions. The second dimension pertains to a person's *tolerance for ambiguity.* This individual difference indicates the extent to which a person has a high need for structure or control in his or her life. When the dimensions of value orientation and tolerance for ambiguity are combined, they form four styles of decision making (see Figure 9–1): directive, analytical, conceptual, and behavioral.

decision-making style

A combination of how individuals perceive and respond to information.

Directive People with a directive style have a low tolerance for ambiguity and are oriented toward task and technical concerns when making decisions. They are efficient, logical, practical, and systematic in their approach to solving problems. People with this style are action oriented and decisive and like to focus on facts. In their pursuit of speed and results, however, these individuals tend to be autocratic, exercise power and control, and focus on the short run. Consider how Mario Monti's directive style influences his behavior and the administrative practices he recommended as the former head of the European Union's antitrust department:

> EU antitrust agents can walk without warning into any company doing business in the 15-nation union to look for whatever they think might be proof of illegal activity. Then they can use the evidence to levy fines as steep as 10% of a company's worldwide revenue. . . . Now Mr Monti is taking big steps to expand this controversial

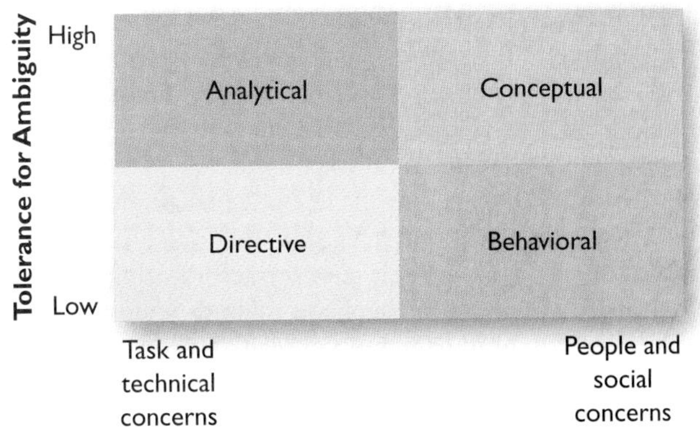

FIGURE 9–1 Decision-Making Styles

SOURCE: Based on discussion contained in A J Rowe and R O Mason, *Managing with Style: A Guide to Understanding, Assessing, and Improving Decision Making* (San Francisco: Jossey-Bass, 1987), pp 1–17.

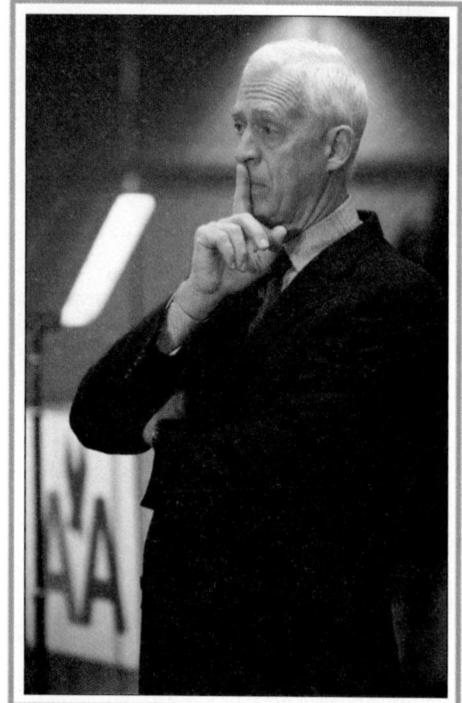

In early 2003, Don Carty, then CEO of American Airlines, made the decision to ask its union employees to accept annual concessions in pay and benefits in order to keep American solvent. During this same time, it came to light that executive-retention bonuses and pension protections were to remain intact. Which type of decision-making style was Carty using when he asked the unions to assume the brunt of the cost of keeping American Airlines solvent?

practice [dawn raids in which investigators show up unannounced]. Currently, his investigators are limited to searching corporate offices for evidence of price fixing and abuse of market power, but he is pushing to extend raids to executives' homes. He is also seeking the power to interrogate employees about antitrust violations without guaranteeing they would be entitled to consult a lawyer. "We must make the commission's inspection powers more biting," the 58-year-old former economics professor said in a speech in Stockholm.[20]

Analytical This style has a much higher tolerance for ambiguity and is characterized by the tendency to overanalyze a situation. People with this style like to consider more information and alternatives than do directives. Analytic individuals are careful decision makers who take longer to make decisions but who also respond well to new or uncertain situations. They can often be autocratic.

Conceptual People with a conceptual style have a high tolerance for ambiguity and tend to focus on the people or social aspects of a work situation. They take a broad perspective to problem solving and like to consider many options and future possibilities. Conceptual types adopt a long-term perspective and rely on intuition and discussions with others to acquire information. They also are willing to take risks and are good at finding creative solutions to problems. On the downside, however, a conceptual style can foster an idealistic and indecisive approach to decision making.

Behavioral People with this style work well with others and enjoy social interactions in which opinions are openly exchanged. Behavioral types are supportive, receptive to suggestions, show warmth, and prefer verbal to written information. Although they like to hold meetings, people with this style have a tendency to avoid conflict and to be too concerned about others. This can lead behavioral types to adopt a "wishy-washy" approach to decision making, to have a hard time saying no to others, and to have a hard time making difficult decisions.

Research and Practical Implications Please take a moment now to complete the Hands-On Exercise. It assesses your decision-making style. How do your scores compare with the following norms: directive (75), analytical (90), conceptual (80), and behavioral (55)?[21] What do the differences between your scores and the survey norms suggest about your decision-making style?

Research shows that very few people have only one dominant decision-making style. Rather, most managers have characteristics that fall into two or three styles. Studies also show that decision-making styles vary across occupations, job level, and countries.[22] You can use knowledge of decision-making styles in three ways. First, knowledge of styles helps you to understand yourself. Awareness of your style assists you in identifying your strengths and weaknesses as a decision maker and facilitates the potential for self-improvement. Second, you can increase your ability to influence others by being aware of styles. For example, if you are dealing with an analytical person, you should provide as much information as possible to support your ideas. This same approach is more likely to frustrate a directive type. Finally,

HANDS-ON EXERCISE

What Is Your Decision-Making Style?

INSTRUCTIONS: This survey consists of 20 questions, each with four responses. You must consider each possible response for a question and then rank them according to how much you prefer each response. Because many of the questions are anchored to how individuals make decisions at work, you can feel free to use your student role as a frame of reference to answer the questions. For each question, use the space on the survey to rank the four responses with either a 1, 2, 4, or 8. Use the number 8 for the responses that are **most** like you, a 4 for those that are **moderately** like you, a 2 for those that are **slightly** like you, and a 1 for the responses that are **least** like you. For example, a question could be answered [8], [4], [2], [1]. Do not repeat any number when answering a question, and place the numbers in the boxes next to each of the answers. Once all of the responses for the 20 questions have been ranked, total the scores in each of the four columns. The total score for column one represents your directive style, column two your analytical style, column three your conceptual style, and column four your behavioral style.

1. My prime objective in life is to:	have a position with status	☐	be the best in whatever I do	☐	be recognized for my work	☐	feel secure in my job	☐
2. I enjoy work that:	is clear and well defined	☐	is varied and challenging	☐	lets me act independently	☐	involves people	☐
3. I expect people to be:	productive	☐	capable	☐	committed	☐	responsive	☐
4. My work lets me:	get things done	☐	find workable approaches	☐	apply new ideas	☐	be truly satisfied	☐
5. I communicate best by:	talking with others	☐	putting things in writing	☐	being open with others	☐	having a group meeting	☐
6. My planning focuses on:	current problems	☐	how best to meet goals	☐	future opportunities	☐	needs of people in the organization	☐
7. I prefer to solve problems by:	applying rules	☐	using careful analysis	☐	being creative	☐	relying on my feelings	☐
8. I prefer information:	that is simple and direct	☐	that is complete	☐	that is broad and informative	☐	that is easily understood	☐
9. When I'm not sure what to do:	I rely on my intuition	☐	I search for alternatives	☐	I try to find a compromise	☐	I avoid making a decision	☐
10. Whenever possible, I avoid:	long debates	☐	incomplete work	☐	technical problems	☐	conflict with others	☐
11. I am really good at:	remembering details	☐	finding answers	☐	seeing many options	☐	working with people	☐
12. When time is important, I:	decide and act quickly	☐	apply proven approaches	☐	look for what will work	☐	refuse to be pressured	☐
13. In social settings, I:	speak with many people	☐	observe what others are doing	☐	contribute to the conversation	☐	want to be part of the discussion	☐
14. I always remember:	people's names	☐	places I have been	☐	people's faces	☐	people's personalities	☐
15. I prefer jobs where I:	receive high rewards	☐	have challenging assignments	☐	can reach my personal goals	☐	am accepted by the group	☐
16. I work best with people who:	are energetic and ambitious	☐	are very competent	☐	are open minded	☐	are polite and understanding	☐
17. When I am under stress, I:	speak quickly	☐	try to concentrate on the problem	☐	become frustrated	☐	worry about what I should do	☐
18. Others consider me:	aggressive	☐	disciplined	☐	imaginative	☐	supportive	☐
19. My decisions are generally:	realistic and direct	☐	systematic and logical	☐	broad and flexible	☐	sensitive to the other's needs	☐
20. I dislike:	losing control	☐	boring work	☐	following rules	☐	being rejected	☐

Total score ________

SOURCE: © Dr. Alan J Rowe, Distinguished Emeritus Professor. Revised 12/18/98. Reprinted with permission.

knowledge of styles gives you an awareness of how people can take the same information and yet arrive at different decisions by using a variety of decision-making strategies. It is important to conclude with the caveat that there is not a best decision-making style that applies in all situations.

Escalation of Commitment

Escalation situations involve circumstances in which things have gone wrong but where the situation can possibly be turned around by investing additional time, money, or effort.[23] **Escalation of commitment** refers to the tendency to stick to an ineffective course of action when it is unlikely that the bad situation can be reversed. Personal examples include investing more money into an old or broken car, waiting an extremely long time for a bus to take you somewhere that you could have walked just as easily, or trying to save a disruptive interpersonal relationship that has lasted 10 years. Case studies also indicate that escalation of commitment is partially responsible for some of the worst financial losses experienced by organizations. For example, from 1966 to 1989 the Long Island Lighting Company's investment in the Shoreham nuclear power plant escalated from $65 million to $5 billion, despite a steady flow of negative feedback. The plant was never opened.[24]

escalation of commitment
Sticking to an ineffective course of action too long.

OB researchers Jerry Ross and Barry Staw identified four reasons for escalation of commitment. They involve psychological and social determinants, organizational determinants, project characteristics, and contextual determinants.[25]

Psychological and Social Determinants Ego defense and individual motivations are the key psychological contributors to escalation of commitment. Individuals "throw good money after bad" because they tend to (1) bias facts so that they support previous decisions, (2) take more risks when a decision is stated in negative terms (to recover losses) rather than positive ones (to achieve gains), and (3) get too ego-involved with the project. Because failure threatens an individual's self-esteem or ego, people tend to ignore negative signs and push forward.

Social pressures can make it difficult for a manager to reverse a course of action. For instance, peer pressure makes it difficult for an individual to drop a course of action when he or she publicly supported it in the past. Further, managers may continue to support bad decisions because they don't want their mistakes exposed to others.

Organizational Determinants Breakdowns in communication, workplace politics, and organizational inertia cause organizations to maintain bad courses of action.

Project Characteristics Project characteristics involve the objective features of a project. They have the greatest impact on escalation decisions. For example, because most projects do not reap benefits until some delayed time period, decision makers are motivated to stay with the project until the end.[26] Thus, there is a tendency to attribute setbacks to temporary causes that are correctable with additional expenditures. Moreover, escalation is related to whether the project has clearly defined goals and whether people receive clear feedback about performance. One study, for instance, revealed that escalation was fueled by ambiguous performance feedback and the lack of performance standards.[27]

Contextual Determinants These causes of escalation are due to forces outside an organization's control. For instance, research showed that a manager's national culture influenced the amount of escalation in decision making. Samples of decision makers in Mexico and the United States revealed that Mexican managers exhibited more escalation than US managers.[28] External political forces also represent a contextual determinant. The continuance of the previously discussed Shoreham nuclear power plant, for example, was partially influenced by pressures from other public utilities interested in nuclear power, representatives of the nuclear power industry, and people in the federal government pushing for the development of nuclear power.[29]

Reducing Escalation of Commitment It is important to reduce escalation of commitment because it leads to poor decision making for both individuals and groups. Barry Staw and Jerry Ross, the researchers who originally identified the phenomenon of escalation, recommended several ways to reduce it (see Skills & Best Practices).

SKILLS & BEST PRACTICES

Recommendations to Reduce Escalation of Commitment

- Set minimum targets for performance, and have decision makers compare their performance with these targets.
- Have different individuals make the initial and subsequent decisions about a project.
- Encourage decision makers to become less ego-involved with a project.
- Provide more frequent feedback about project completion and costs.
- Reduce the risk or penalties of failure.
- Make decision makers aware of the costs of persistence.

Creativity

In light of today's need for fast-paced decisions, an organization's ability to stimulate the creativity and innovation of its employees is becoming increasingly important. Although many definitions have been proposed, **creativity** is defined here as the process of using intelligence, imagination, and skill to develop a new or novel product, object, process, or thought.[30] It can be as simple as locating a new place to hang your car keys or as complex as developing a pocket-size microcomputer. This definition highlights three broad types of creativity. One can create something new (creation), one can combine or synthesize things (synthesis), or one can improve or change things (modification).

creativity
Process of developing something new or unique.

Researchers are not absolutely certain how creativity takes place. Nonetheless, we do know that creativity involves "making remote associations" between unconnected events, ideas, information stored in memory (recall our discussion in Chapter 4), or physical objects. Consider how biologist Napoleone Ferrara's remote association led to the creation of a new type of cancer therapy that extends cancer patients' lives:

> Twenty years ago biologist Napoleone Ferrara discovered a mysterious protein in the pituitary gland of cows that seemed to make blood vessels grow. He foresaw a new weapon against cancer—block the protein and tumors may be unable to proliferate—but the finding was so obscure that even his boss was skeptical. Last month the drug that resulted from Ferrara's work began to look like a success: Genentech unveiled trial results that showed it extended colon cancer patients' lives by a median of five months, or 30%, one of the biggest advances in years.[31]

Dr. Ferrara obviously associated the characteristics of a cow protein with a solution for stopping the growth of cancerous tumors. Researchers, however, have identified five stages underlying the creative process: preparation, concentration, incubation, illumination, and verification. Let us consider these stages.

The *preparation* stage reflects the notion that creativity starts from a base of knowledge. Experts suggest that creativity involves a convergence between tacit or implied knowledge and explicit knowledge. During the *concentration* stage, an individual focuses on the problem at hand. Research shows that creative ideas at work are often triggered by work-related problems, incongruities, or failures.[32] Eli Lilly

SKILLS & BEST PRACTICES

Avoid These Creativity Killers

1. Lack of discretion and autonomy.
2. Fragmented work schedule in which people are frequently interrupted.
3. Insufficient resources to get the job done.
4. A focus on short-term goals.
5. Time pressures.
6. A lack of collaboration and coordination among employees.

SOURCE: These ideas were taken from S Dingfelder, "Creativity on the Clock," *Monitor on Psychology,* November 2003, pp 56–57. Copyright © 2003 by the American Psychological Association. Adapted with permission.

& Company, for example, uses this awareness to fuel the development of new drug discoveries:

> Lilly has long had a culture that looks at failure as an inevitable part of discovery and encourages scientists to take risks. If a new drug doesn't work out for its intended use, Lilly scientists are taught to look for new uses for a drug. In the early 1990s, W Leigh Thompson, Lilly's chief scientific officer, initiated "failure parties" to commemorate excellent scientific work, done efficiently, that nevertheless resulted in failure.
>
> Other drug companies are also seeing the importance of tolerating—and learning from—failure, a valuable strategy since about 90% of experimental drugs in the industry fail. For example, Pfizer Inc. originally developed the blockbuster impotence drug Viagra to treat angina, or severe heart pain.[33]

Interestingly, Japanese companies are noted for encouraging this stage as part of a quality improvement process more than American companies. For example, the average number of ideas per employee was 37.4 for Japanese workers versus .12 for US workers.[34]

Incubation is done unconsciously. During this stage, people engage in daily activities while their minds simultaneously mull over information and make remote associations. These associations ultimately are generated in the *illumination* stage. Finally, *verification* entails going through the entire process to verify, modify, or try out the new idea.

Let us examine the stages of creativity to determine why Japanese organizations propose and implement more ideas than do American companies. To address this issue, a creativity expert visited and extensively interviewed employees from five major Japanese companies. He observed that Japanese firms have created a management infrastructure that encourages and reinforces creativity. People were taught to identify problems (discontents) on their first day of employment. In turn, discontents were referred to as "golden eggs" to reinforce the notion that it is good to identify problems.

These organizations also promoted the stages of incubation, illumination, and verification through teamwork and incentives. For example, some companies posted the golden eggs on large wall posters in the work area; employees were then encouraged to interact with each other to execute the final three stages of the creative process. Employees eventually received monetary awards for any suggestions that passed all five phases of this process.[35] This research underscores the conclusion that creativity can be enhanced by effectively managing the creativity process and by fostering a positive and supportive work environment.[36] See the Skills & Best Practices for a list of work-environment factors found to kill creativity.

Group Decision Making

This section explores issues associated with group decision making. Specifically, we discuss (1) group involvement in decision making, (2) advantages and disadvantages of group-aided decision making, (3) participative management, and (4) group problem-solving techniques.

Group Involvement in Decision Making

Whether groups assemble in face-to-face meetings or rely on other technologically based methods to communicate, they can contribute to each stage of the decision-making process. In order to maximize the value of group-aided decision making, however, it is important to create an environment in which group members feel free to participate and express their opinions. A study sheds light on how managers can create such an environment.

A team of researchers conducted two studies to determine whether a group's innovativeness was related to *minority dissent,* defined as the extent to which group members feel comfortable disagreeing with other group members, and a group's level of participation in decision making. Results showed that the most innovative groups possessed high levels of both minority dissent and participation in decision making.[37] These findings encourage managers to seek divergent views from group members during decision making. They also support the practice of not seeking compliance from group members or punishing group members who disagree with majority opinion. Take a moment now to complete the Hands-On Exercise on page 240. It assesses the amount of minority dissent and participation in group decision making for a group project you have completed or are currently working on in school or on the job. Is your satisfaction with the group related to minority dissent and participation in decision making? If not, what might explain this surprising result?

The previously discussed study about minority dissent reinforces the notion that the quality of group decision making varies across groups. This in turn raises the issue of how to best assess a group's decision-making effectiveness. Although experts do not agree on the one "best" criterion, there is agreement that groups need to work through various aspects of decision making in order to be effective. One expert proposed that decision-making effectiveness in a group is dependent on successfully accomplishing the following:[38]

1. Developing a clear understanding of the decision situation.
2. Developing a clear understanding of the requirements for an effective choice.
3. Thoroughly and accurately assessing the positive qualities of alternative solutions.
4. Thoroughly and accurately assessing the negative qualities of alternative solutions.

To increase the probability of groups making high-quality decisions, managers, team leaders, and individual group members are encouraged to focus on satisfying these four requirements.[39]

Advantages and Disadvantages of Group-Aided Decision Making

Including groups in the decision-making process has both pros and cons (see Table 9–1). On the positive side, groups contain a greater pool of knowledge, provide more varied perspectives, create more comprehension of decisions, increase decision acceptance, and create a training ground for inexperienced employees. These advantages must be balanced, however, with the disadvantages listed in Table 9–1. In doing so, managers need to determine the extent to which the advantages and disadvantages apply to the decision situation. The following three guidelines may then be applied to help decide whether groups should be included in the decision-making process:

HANDS-ON EXERCISE

Assessing Participation in Group Decision Making

INSTRUCTIONS: The following survey measures minority dissent, participation in group decision making, and satisfaction with a group. For each of the items, use the rating scale shown below to circle the answer that best represents your feelings based on a group project you were or currently are involved in. Next, use the scoring key to compute scores for the levels of minority dissent, participation in decision making, and satisfaction with the group.

1 = Strongly disagree
2 = Disagree
3 = Neither agree nor disagree
4 = Agree
5 = Strongly agree

1. Within my team, individuals disagree with one another.	**1**	**2**	**3**	**4**	**5**
2. Within my team, individuals do not go along with majority opinion.	**1**	**2**	**3**	**4**	**5**
3. Within my team, individuals voice their disagreement of majority opinion.	**1**	**2**	**3**	**4**	**5**
4. Within my team, I am comfortable voicing my disagreement of the majority opinion.	**1**	**2**	**3**	**4**	**5**
5. Within my team, individuals do not immediately agree with one another.	**1**	**2**	**3**	**4**	**5**
6. As a team member, I have a real say in how work is carried out.	**1**	**2**	**3**	**4**	**5**
7. Within my team, most members have a chance to participate in decisions.	**1**	**2**	**3**	**4**	**5**
8. My team is designed so that everyone has the opportunity to participate in decisions.	**1**	**2**	**3**	**4**	**5**
9. I am satisfied with my group.	**1**	**2**	**3**	**4**	**5**
10. I would like to work with this group on another project.	**1**	**2**	**3**	**4**	**5**

SCORING KEY

Minority dissent (add scores for items 1, 2, 3, 4, 5): __________

Participation in decision making (add scores for items 6, 7, 8): __________

Satisfaction (add scores for items 9, 10): __________

ARBITRARY NORMS

Low minority dissent = 5–15

High minority dissent = 16–25

Low participation in decision making = 3–8

High participation in decision making = 9–15

Low satisfaction = 2–5

High satisfaction = 6–10

SOURCE: The items in the survey were developed from C K W De Dreu and M A West, "Minority Dissent and Team Innovation: The Importance of Participation in Decision Making," *Journal of Applied Psychology,* December 2001, pp 119–201.

TABLE 9–1 Advantages and Disadvantages of Group-Aided Decision Making

Advantages	Disadvantages
1. *Greater pool of knowledge.* A group can bring much more information and experience to bear on a decision or problem than can an individual acting alone.	1. *Social pressure.* Unwillingness to "rock the boat" and pressure to conform may combine to stifle the creativity of individual contributors.
2. *Different perspectives.* Individuals with varied experience and interests help the group see decision situations and problems from different angles.	2. *Domination by a vocal few.* Sometimes the quality of group action is reduced when the group gives in to those who talk the loudest and longest.
3. *Greater comprehension.* Those who personally experience the give-and-take of group discussion about alternative courses of action tend to understand the rationale behind the final decision.	3. *Logrolling.* Political wheeling and dealing can displace sound thinking when an individual's pet project or vested interest is at stake.
4. *Increased acceptance.* Those who play an active role in group decision making and problem solving tend to view the outcome as "ours" rather than "theirs."	4. *Goal displacement.* Sometimes secondary considerations such as winning an argument, making a point, or getting back at a rival displace the primary task of making a sound decision or solving a problem.
5. *Training ground.* Less experienced participants in group action learn how to cope with group dynamics by actually being involved.	5. *"Groupthink."* Sometimes cohesive "in-groups" let the desire for unanimity override sound judgment when generating and evaluating alternative courses of action. (Groupthink is discussed in Chapter 10.)

SOURCE: R Kreitner, *Management,* 7th ed (Boston: Houghton Mifflin, 1998), p 234.

1. If additional information would increase the quality of the decision, managers should involve those people who can provide the needed information.
2. If acceptance is important, managers need to involve those individuals whose acceptance and commitment are important.
3. If people can be developed through their participation, managers may want to involve those whose development is most important.[40]

Group versus Individual Performance Before recommending that managers involve groups in decision making, it is important to examine whether groups perform better or worse than individuals. After reviewing 61 years of relevant research, a decision-making expert concluded that "Group performance was generally qualitatively and quantitatively superior to the performance of the average individual."[41] Although subsequent research of small-group decision making generally supported this conclusion, additional research suggests that managers should use a contingency approach when determining whether to include others in the decision-making process. Let us now consider these contingency recommendations.

Practical Contingency Recommendations If the decision occurs frequently, such as deciding on promotions or who qualifies for a loan, use groups because they tend to produce more consistent decisions than do individuals. Given time constraints, let the most competent individual, rather than a group, make the decision. In the face of environmental threats such as time pressure and the potentially serious effects of a decision, groups use less information and fewer communication channels. This increases the probability of a bad decision.[42] This conclusion underscores a general recommendation that managers should keep in mind: Because the quality of communication strongly affects a group's productivity, on complex tasks it is essential to devise mechanisms to enhance communication effectiveness.

Participative Management

An organization needs to maximize its workers' potential if it wants to successfully compete in the global economy. Participative management and employee empowerment, which is discussed in Chapter 13, are highly touted methods for meeting this productivity challenge. Interestingly, employees also seem to desire or recognize the need for participative management. A nationwide survey of 2,408 employees, for example, revealed that almost 66% desired more influence or decision-making power in their jobs.[43]

Confusion exists about the exact meaning of participative management (PM). One management expert clarified this situation by defining **participative management** as the process whereby employees play a direct role in (1) setting goals, (2) making decisions, (3) solving problems, and (4) making changes in the organization. Without question, participative management entails much more than simply asking employees for their ideas or opinions.

participative management
Involving employees in various forms of decision making.

Advocates of PM claim employee participation increases employee satisfaction, commitment, and performance. To get a fuller understanding of how and when participative management works, we begin by discussing a model of participative management.

A Model of Participative Management Consistent with both Maslow's need theory and the job characteristics model of job design (see Chapter 6), participative management is predicted to increase motivation because it helps employees fulfill three basic needs: (1) autonomy, (2) meaningfulness of work, and (3) interpersonal contact. Satisfaction of these needs enhances feelings of acceptance and commitment, security, challenge, and satisfaction. In turn, these positive feelings supposedly lead to increased innovation and performance.[44]

Participative management does not work in all situations. The design of work, the level of trust between management and employees, and the employees' competence and readiness to participate represent three factors that influence the effectiveness of PM. With respect to the design of work, individual participation is counterproductive when employees are highly interdependent on each other, as on an assembly line. The problem with individual participation in this case is that interdependent employees generally do not have a broad understanding of the entire production process. Participative management also is less likely to succeed when employees do not trust management. Finally, PM is more effective when employees are competent, prepared, and interested in participating. Northwest Airlines is a good case in point. Employees responded very positively to the company's new employee suggestion system because they were motivated to help the airline reduce operating costs in order to save jobs. The suggestion system resulted in $6 million in annual savings from workers' ideas. "A flight attendant, for instance, noticed that too many coffeepots were being boarded on planes, so Northwest cut back and now saves $120,000 a year. A customer-service agent suggested that blanket folding and washing be done in-house, for savings of $205,000 annually. A manager in Minneapolis had an idea that resulted in an annual saving of $916,000 on maintenance on DC-10 thrust reversers."[45]

Research and Practical Suggestions for Managers Participative management can significantly increase employee job involvement, organizational commitment, creativity, and perceptions of procedural justice and personal control.[46] Two meta-analyses provided additional support for the value of participative management. Results from a meta-analysis involving 27 studies and 6,732 individuals revealed that employee participation in the performance appraisal process was positively related to an employee's satisfaction with his or her performance review, perceived value of the appraisal, motivation to improve performance following a performance review, and perceived fairness of the appraisal process.[47] A second meta-analysis of 86 studies involving 18,872 people further demonstrated that participation had a small but significant effect on job performance and a moderate relationship with job satisfaction.[48] This later finding questions the widespread conclusion that participative management should be used to increase employee performance.

So what is a manager to do? We believe that PM is not a quick-fix solution for low productivity and motivation, as some enthusiastic supporters claim. Nonetheless, because participative management is effective in certain situations, managers can increase their chances of obtaining positive results by using once again a contingency approach. For example, the effectiveness of participation depends on the type of interactions between managers and employees as they jointly solve problems. Effective participation requires a constructive interaction that fosters cooperation and respect, as opposed to competition and defensiveness. Managers are advised not to use participative programs when they have destructive interpersonal interactions with their employees.

Experiences of companies implementing participative management programs suggest three additional practical recommendations. First, supervisors and middle managers tend to resist participative management because it reduces their power and authority. It thus is important to gain the support and commitment from employees who have managerial responsibility. This conclusion was supported by results from a 15-year study of 41,000 middle and upper-level managers: 35% of the managers surveyed between 1985 and 1987 preferred to make decisions autocratically versus 31% between 1997 and 1999.[49] Second, a longitudinal study of *Fortune* 1000 firms in 1987, 1990, and 1993 indicated that employee involvement was more effective when it was implemented as part of a broader total quality management program.[50] This study suggests that organizations should use participative management and employee involvement as vehicles to help them meet their strategic and operational goals as opposed to using these techniques as ends in and of themselves. Third, the process of implementing participative management must be firmly supported and monitored by top management.[51]

Group Problem-Solving Techniques

Using groups to make decisions generally requires that they reach a consensus. According to a decision-making expert, a **consensus** "is reached when all members can say they either agree with the decision or have had their 'day in court' and were unable to convince the others of their viewpoint. In the final analysis, everyone agrees to support the outcome."[52] This definition indicates that consensus does not require unanimous agreement because group members may still disagree with the final decision but are willing to work toward its success.

consensus
Presenting opinions and gaining agreement to support a decision.

Groups can experience roadblocks when trying to arrive at a consensus decision. For one, groups may not generate all relevant alternatives to a problem because an individual dominates or intimidates other group members. This is both overt and/or subtle. For instance, group members who possess power and authority, such as a CEO, can be intimidating, regardless of interpersonal style, simply by being present in the room. Moreover, shyness inhibits the generation of alternatives. Shy or socially anxious individuals may withhold their input for fear of embarrassment or lack of confidence. Satisficing is another hurdle to effective group decision making. As previously noted, groups satisfice due to limited time, information, or ability to handle large amounts of information.[53] A management expert offered the following "do's" and "don'ts" for successfully achieving consensus: Groups should use active listening skills, involve as many members as possible, seek out the reasons behind arguments, and dig for the facts. At the same time, groups should not horse trade (I'll support you on this decision because you supported me on the last one), vote, or agree just to avoid "rocking the boat."[54] Voting is not encouraged because it can split the group into winners and losers.

Decision-making experts have developed three group problem-solving techniques—brainstorming, the nominal group technique, and the Delphi technique—to reduce the above roadblocks. Knowledge of these techniques can help current and future managers to more effectively use group-aided decision making. Further, the advent of computer-aided decision making enables managers to use these techniques to solve complex problems with large groups of people.

brainstorming

Process to generate a quantity of ideas.

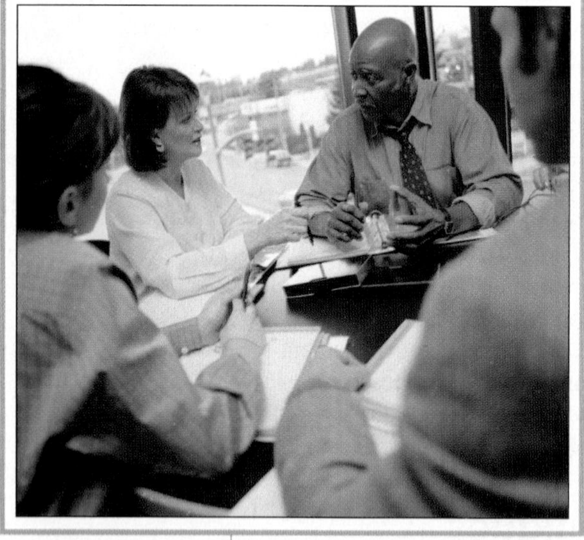

Brainstorming is a technique used to generate as many ideas as possible to solve a problem. You have probably engaged in brainstorming sessions for various class or work projects. Which of the seven rules for brainstorming do you think is most important?

Brainstorming Brainstorming was developed by A F Osborn, an advertising executive, to increase creativity.[55] **Brainstorming** is used to help groups generate multiple ideas and alternatives for solving problems. This technique is effective because it helps reduce interference caused by critical and judgmental reactions to one's ideas from other group members.

When brainstorming, a group is convened, and the problem at hand is reviewed. Individual members then are asked to silently generate ideas/alternatives for solving the problem. Silent idea generation is recommended over the practice of having group members randomly shout out their ideas because it leads to a greater number of unique ideas. Next, these ideas/alternatives are solicited and written on a board or flip chart. A recent study suggests that managers or team leaders may want to collect the brainstormed ideas anonymously. Results demonstrated that more controversial ideas and more nonredundant ideas were generated by anonymous than nonanonymous brainstorming groups.[56] Finally, a second session is used to critique and evaluate the alternatives. Managers are advised to follow the seven rules for brainstorming used by IDEO, the product design company featured in the chapter-opening vignette:[57]

1. *Defer judgment.* Don't criticize during the initial stage of idea generation. Phrases such as "we've never done it that way," "it won't work," "it's too expensive," and "our manager will never agree" should not be used.

2. *Build on the ideas of others.* Encourage participants to extend others' ideas by avoiding "buts" and using "ands."
3. *Encourage wild ideas.* Encourage out-of-the-box thinking. The wilder and more outrageous the ideas, the better.
4. *Go for quantity over quality.* Participants should try to generate and write down as many new ideas as possible. Focusing on quantity encourages people to think beyond their favorite ideas.
5. *Be visual.* Use different colored pens (e.g., red, purple, blue) to write on big sheets of flip chart paper, white boards, or poster board that are put on the wall.
6. *Stay focused on the topic.* A facilitator should be used to keep the discussion on target.
7. *One conversation at a time.* The ground rules are that no one interrupts another person, no dismissing of someone's ideas, no disrespect, and no rudeness.

Brainstorming is an effective technique for generating new ideas/alternatives. It is not appropriate for evaluating alternatives or selecting solutions.

The Nominal Group Technique The **nominal group technique** (NGT) helps groups generate ideas and evaluate and select solutions. NGT is a structured group meeting that follows this format:[58] A group is convened to discuss a particular problem or issue. After the problem is understood, individuals silently generate ideas in writing. Each individual, in round-robin fashion, then offers one idea from his or her list. Ideas are recorded on a blackboard or flip chart; they are not discussed at this stage of the process. Once all ideas are elicited, the group discusses them. Anyone may criticize or defend any item. During this step, clarification is provided as well as general agreement or disagreement with the idea. The "30-second soap box" technique, which entails giving each participant a maximum of 30 seconds to argue for or against any of the ideas under consideration, can be used to facilitate this discussion. Finally, group members anonymously vote for their top choices with a weighted voting procedure (e.g., 1st choice = 3 points; 2nd choice = 2 points; 3rd choice = 1 point). Alternatively, group members can vote by placing colored dots next to their top choices. The group leader then adds the votes to determine the group's choice. Prior to making a final decision, the group may decide to discuss the top ranked items and conduct a second round of voting.

nominal group technique
Process to generate ideas and evaluate solutions.

The nominal group technique reduces the roadblocks to group decision making by (1) separating brainstorming from evaluation, (2) promoting balanced participation among group members, and (3) incorporating mathematical voting techniques in order to reach consensus. NGT has been successfully used in many different decision-making situations, and has been found to generate more ideas than a standard brainstorming session.[59]

The Delphi Technique This problem-solving method was originally developed by the Rand Corporation for technological forecasting.[60] It now is used as a multipurpose planning tool. The **Delphi technique** is a group process that anonymously generates ideas or judgments from physically dispersed experts. Unlike the NGT, experts' ideas are obtained from questionnaires or via the Internet as opposed to face-to-face group discussions.

Delphi technique
Process to generate ideas from physically dispersed experts.

A manager begins the Delphi process by identifying the issue(s) he or she wants to investigate. For example, a manager might want to inquire about customer demand, customers' future preferences, or the effect of locating a plant in a certain region of the country. Next, participants are identified and a questionnaire is developed. The questionnaire is sent to participants and returned to the manager. In today's computer-networked environments, this often means that the questionnaires are E-mailed to participants. The manager then summarizes the responses and sends feedback to the participants. At this stage, participants are asked to (1) review the feedback, (2) prioritize the issues being considered, and (3) return the survey within a specified time period. This cycle repeats until the manager obtains the necessary information.

The Delphi technique is useful when face-to-face discussions are impractical, when disagreements and conflict are likely to impair communication, when certain individuals might severely dominate group discussion, and when groupthink is a probable outcome of the group process.[61]

Computer-Aided Decision Making The purpose of computer-aided decision making is to reduce consensus roadblocks while collecting more information in a shorter period of time. There are two types of computer-aided decision making systems: chauffeur driven and group driven.[62] Chauffeur-driven systems ask participants to answer predetermined questions on electronic keypads or dials. Live television audiences on shows such as "Who Wants to Be a Millionaire" are frequently polled with this system. The computer system tabulates participants' responses in a matter of seconds.

Group-driven electronic meetings are conducted in one of two major ways. First, managers can use E-mail systems, which are discussed in Chapter 12, or the Internet to collect information or brainstorm about a decision that must be made. For example, MedPanel, a Cambridge, MA, medical consulting company, uses E-mail to obtain information and feedback from medical doctors around the country about new and existing drugs. Consider how MedPanel's system works:

> A client contracts with MedPanel for a research project—looking for, perhaps, advice on how to structure clinical trials for a cancer drug. MedPanel consults its database of participating physicians and E-mails invitations to the most appropriate doctors. The doctors who sign up (earning a fee for their time) log onto www.medpanel.com, type in a password, and call up a screen that looks a lot like a bulletin-board-style discussion group. Individual messages are listed in chronological order. A moderator poses questions and helps guide the discussion. Doctors drop in whenever they can, catch up on recent postings, and type their own messages. It's simple technology, but the results can be powerful.[63]

MedPanel has found that it can collect information faster and cheaper using its electronic system of data collection.

The second method of computer-aided, group-driven meetings are conducted in special facilities equipped with individual workstations that are networked to each other. Instead of talking, participants type their input, ideas, comments, reactions, or evaluations on their keyboards. The input simultaneously appears on a large projector screen at the front of the room, thereby enabling all participants to see all input. This computer-driven process reduces consensus roadblocks because input is anonymous, everyone gets a chance to contribute, and no one can dominate the process. Research demonstrated that computer-aided decision making produced greater quality and quantity of ideas than either traditional brainstorming or the nominal group technique for both small and large groups of people.[64]

Interestingly, however, another recent study suggests caution when determining what forms of computer-aided decision making to use. This meta-analysis of 52 studies compared the effectiveness of face-to-face decision-making groups with "chat" groups. Results revealed that the use of chat groups led to decreased group effectiveness and member satisfaction and increased time to complete tasks compared to face-to-face groups.[65] These findings underscore the need to use a contingency approach for selecting the best method of computer-aided decision making in a given situation.

key terms

chapter summary

- *Compare and contrast the rational model of decision making and Simon's normative model.* The rational decision-making model consists of identifying the problem, generating alternative solutions, evaluating and selecting a solution, and implementing and evaluating the solution. Research indicates that decision makers do not follow the series of steps outlined in the rational model.

  Simon's normative model is guided by a decision maker's bounded rationality. Bounded rationality means that decision makers are bounded or restricted by a variety of constraints when making decisions. The normative model suggests that decision making is characterized by (a) limited information processing, (b) the use of judgmental heuristics, and (c) satisficing.
- *Discuss knowledge management and techniques used by companies to increase knowledge sharing.* Knowledge management involves the implementation of systems and practices that increase the sharing of knowledge and information throughout an organization. There are two types of knowledge that impact the quality of decisions: tacit knowledge and explicit knowledge. Organizations use computer systems to share explicit knowledge. Tacit knowledge is shared by observing, participating, or working with experts or coaches. Mentoring, informal networking, meetings, and design of office space also influence knowledge sharing.
- *Explain the model of decision-making styles and the stages of the creative process.* The model of decision-making styles is based on the idea that styles vary along two different dimensions: value orientation and tolerance for ambiguity. When these two dimensions are combined, they form four styles of decision making: directive, analytical, conceptual, and behavioral. People with a directive style have a low tolerance for ambiguity and are oriented toward task and technical concerns. Analytics have a higher tolerance for ambiguity and are characterized by a tendency to overanalyze a situation. People with a conceptual style have a high threshold for ambiguity and tend to focus on people or social aspects of a work situation. The behavioral style is the most people oriented of the four styles.

  Creativity is defined as the process of using intelligence, imagination, and skill to develop a new or novel product, object, process, or thought. There are five stages of the creative process: preparation, concentration, incubation, illumination, and verification.

- *Summarize the pros and cons of involving groups in the decision-making process.* There are both pros and cons to involving groups in the decision-making process (see Table 9–1). Although research shows that groups typically outperform the average individual, managers need to use a contingency approach when determining whether to include others in the decision-making process.
- *Explain how participative management affects performance.* Participative management reflects the extent to which employees participate in setting goals, making decisions, solving problems, and making changes in the organization. Participative management is expected to increase motivation because it helps employees fulfill three basic needs: (a) autonomy, (b) meaningfulness of work, and (c) interpersonal contact. Participative management does not work in all situations.The design of work and the level of trust between management and employees influence the effectiveness of participative management.
- *Contrast brainstorming, the nominal group technique, the Delphi technique, and computer-aided decision making.* Group problem-solving techniques facilitate better decision making within groups. Brainstorming is used to help groups generate multiple ideas and alternatives for solving problems. The nominal group technique assists groups both to generate ideas and to evaluate and select solutions. The Delphi technique is a group process that anonymously generates ideas or judgments from physically dispersed experts. The purpose of computer-aided decision making is to reduce consensus roadblocks while collecting more information in a shorter period of time.

discussion questions

1. To what extent does IDEO use the five stages of the creative process? Explain.
2. Do you think knowledge management will become more important in the future? Explain your rationale.
3. Why would decision-making styles be a source of interpersonal conflict?
4. Describe a situation in which you exhibited escalation of commitment. Why did you escalate a losing situation?
5. Given the intuitive appeal of participative management, why do you think it fails as often as it succeeds? Explain.

ethical dilemma

Are Lawyers at Vinson & Elkins Partly Responsible for Enron's Collapse?[66]

Early in the morning . . . [on] October 23, [2001,] Ronald Astin, a partner at the Houston law firm Vinson & Elkins, joined Enron Corp. executives in a meeting room next to Chairman Kenneth Lay's office. A conference call with analysts was about to begin, and the group needed to script an explanation for Enron's unfolding troubles, which included mysterious partnerships that appeared to be keeping big chunks of debt hidden away.

The tense mood soon grew worse. Mr Astin had drafted a section saying that Enron Chief Financial Officer Andrew Fastow initially presented the idea of the partnerships to the board. According to people at the meeting, Mr Fastow began shouting that he wasn't responsible for forming the partnerships.

It was the climax of a beneath-the-surface struggle between the outside lawyer and the Enron executive. Over five years, as Mr Fastow structured ever-more-complex deals for the big energy and trading company, Mr Astin and other Vinson & Elkins lawyers sometimes objected, saying the deals posed conflicts of interest or weren't in Enron's best interests.

But Vinson & Elkins didn't blow the whistle. Again and again, its lawyers backed down when rebuffed by Mr Fastow or his lieutenants, expressing their unease to Enron's in-house attorneys but not to its most senior executives or to its board. And when asked to assess Enron manager Sherron Watkins' warning to Mr Lay last summer of potential accounting scandals, Vinson & Elkins delivered to Enron a report that largely downplayed the risks.

Now, deals that troubled some Vinson & Elkins lawyers are central to investigations of the collapse of Enron. But while the mantle of heroine has fallen on Ms

Watkins, Vinson & Elkins is on the defensive. One of the country's most powerful law firms, with some 850 lawyers in nine cities, Vinson & Elkins now faces lawsuits from Enron shareholders and Enron employees. And a report of a special investigation done for Enron's board has criticized the law firm for an "absence" of "objective and critical professional advice."

The firm's bind casts a stark light on the central issue law firms face when they represent large corporations: Just what are their obligations to the client and the client's shareholders? In terms of legal ethics, outside lawyers have a clear ethical duty to withdraw from transactions in which clients are obviously breaking the law. But many situations are murkier. At what point should the lawyers speak up, and to whom, when the legality of planned corporate moves is merely questionable? And what about when individual executives are planning steps that appear not in the interests of the client company itself?

Vinson & Elkins' managing partner, Joseph Dilg, has told a congressional panel probing Enron that so long as a transaction isn't illegal and has been approved by the client company's management, outside lawyers may advise on the transaction. "In doing so, the lawyers are not approving the business decisions that were made by their clients," he said.

But others, such as Boston University law professor Susan Koniak, say lawyers must do more. They have a duty to make sure a client's managers aren't "breaching their duties to the corporation," says Ms Koniak, who testified before a Senate hearing on Enron and accountability issues in February [2002]. She believes Vinson & Elkins lawyers should have taken their concerns to Enron directors.

What Should Lawyers at Vinson & Elkins Have Done in This Case?

1. The lawyers are not responsible for the acts of Enron's management. Lawyers are paid to advise their clients, and it is up to the clients to take or ignore this advice.
2. Blow the whistle and let legal authorities know about Enron's mysterious partnerships. Explain your rationale and discuss the ramifications of this choice.
3. Take your concerns to Enron's board of directors. Explain your rationale and discuss the ramifications of this choice.
4. Invent other options. Discuss.

For an interpretation of this situation, visit our Web site, www.mhhe.com/kinickiob2e.

If you're looking for additional study materials, be sure to check out the Online Learning Center at

www.mhhe.com/kinickiob2e

for more information and interactivities that correspond to this chapter.

chapter Ten

Effective Groups and Teamwork

LEARNING OBJECTIVES

After reading the material in this chapter, you should be able to:

- Describe the five stages of Tuckman's theory of group development.
- Contrast roles and norms, and specify four reasons why norms are enforced in organizations.
- Explain how a work group becomes a team, and identify five teamwork competencies.
- List at least four things managers can do to build trust.
- Describe self-managed teams and virtual teams.
- Describe groupthink, and identify at least four of its symptoms.

TEAMING UP TO LEARN AT GERMANY'S SIEMENS

A start-up company that needs entrepreneurial managers can go out and hire them as it builds its organization. By contrast, established companies like Siemens, a worldwide provider of everything from mobile phones to gas turbines, already have tens of thousands of managers around the world and have no choice but to find ways to make its old managers into new ones. So collaboration became the central goal of an in-house management development program at Siemens. The program was created . . . in the late 1990s.

Many companies have established "active learning" curricula focused on the study of cases and other real-life problems. But we realized that changing people's behavior is less about intellectual learning than it is about blasting them loose from nearly impenetrable, self-imposed—and often company-rewarded—boundaries. We started our people off with some classroom teaching, but the bulk of the program put them in teams working on actual projects.

These "business impact projects" had to show measurable results and typically lasted about four months. It wasn't enough for a team to recommend a new marketing strategy or propose a new procedure for product development. We didn't want the end result to be a paper no one would read. Instead, we wanted people to get their hands dirty in the real work of organizational maneuvering and achievement.

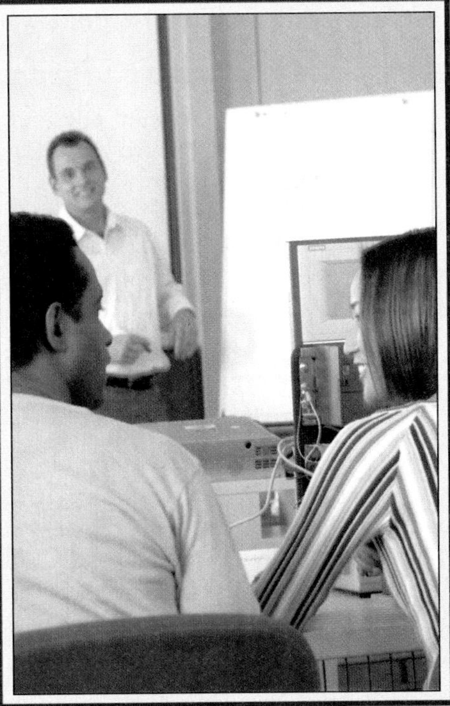

Once a team settled on an opportunity to pursue, they had to recruit a "coach," usually a high-level executive in the business area that the team was focusing on. Executives were free to decline these requests; some teams had to try several times. . . .

In each case, it helped that the teams consisted of people from different product areas, functions, and geographies. But diverse teammates and their existing contact networks weren't enough; the projects wouldn't work without each team figuring out how to win support from people who had little interest in—or who even felt threatened by—the team's efforts.

In interviews after the projects ended, nearly all the participants reported a new perspective on their organizational comfort zones.

At first, they said, they had felt liberated by their status in the program—as though they were immune from risk. But in retrospect, they came to understand that the program conferred no special status on them at all; their previous hesitation toward risk-taking had been largely self-imposed. The management program had given them the unique sense of "permission" to venture that they had actually had all along.[1]

FOR DISCUSSION

Why is this a good "team-building" exercise? For an interpretation of this case and additional comments, visit our Online Learning Center:

www.mhhe.com/kinickiob2e

BOTH DAILY EXPERIENCE and research reveal the importance of social skills for individual and organizational success. An ongoing study by the Center for Creative Leadership (involving diverse samplings from Belgium, France, Germany, Italy, the United Kingdom, the United States, and Spain) found four stumbling blocks that tend to derail executives' careers. According to the researchers, "A derailed executive is one who, having reached the general manager level, finds that there is little chance of future advancement due to a misfit between job requirements and personal skills."[2] The four stumbling blocks, consistent across the cultures studied, are as follows:

1. Problems with interpersonal relationships.
2. Failure to meet business objectives.
3. Failure to build and lead a team.
4. Inability to change or adapt during a transition.[3]

Notice how both the first and third career stumbling blocks involve interpersonal skills—the ability to get along and work effectively with others. Managers with interpersonal problems typically were described as manipulative and insensitive. Interestingly, two-thirds of the derailed European managers studied had problems with interpersonal relationships. That same problem reportedly plagued one-third of the derailed US executives.[4] Management, as defined in Chapter 1, involves getting things done with and through others. The job is simply too big to do it alone.[5]

The purpose of this chapter is to shift the focus from individual behavior to collective behavior. We explore groups and teams, key features of modern life, and discuss how to make them effective while avoiding common pitfalls. Among the interesting variety of topics in this chapter are group development, trust, self-managed teams, virtual teams, and groupthink.

Fundamentals of Group Behavior

group
Two or more freely interacting people with shared norms and goals and a common identity.

Drawing from the field of sociology, we define a **group** as two or more freely interacting individuals who share collective norms and goals and have a common identity.[6] Organizational psychologist Edgar Schein shed additional light on this concept by drawing instructive distinctions between a group, a crowd, and an organization:

> The size of a group is thus limited by the possibilities of mutual interaction and mutual awareness. Mere aggregates of people do not fit this definition because they do not interact and do not perceive themselves to be a group even if they are aware of each other as, for instance, a crowd on a street corner watching some event. A total department, a union, or a whole organization would not be a group in spite of thinking of themselves as "we," because they generally do not all interact and are not all aware of each other. However, work teams, committees, subparts of departments, cliques, and various other informal associations among organizational members would fit this definition of a group.[7]

Take a moment now to think of various groups of which you are a member. Does each of your "groups" satisfy the four criteria in our definition?

Formal and Informal Groups

Individuals join groups, or are assigned to groups, to accomplish various purposes. If the group is formed by a manager to help the organization accomplish its goals, then it qualifies as a **formal group.** Formal groups typically wear such labels as work group, team, committee, or task force. An **informal group** exists when the members' overriding purpose of getting together is friendship.[8] Formal and informal groups often overlap, such as when a team of corporate auditors heads for the tennis courts after work. A recent survey of 1,385 office workers in the US found 71% had attended important events with co-workers, such as weddings and funerals.[9] The desirability of overlapping formal and informal groups is problematic. Some managers firmly believe personal friendship fosters productive teamwork on the job while others view workplace "bull sessions" as a serious threat to productivity. Both situations are common, and it is the manager's job to strike a workable balance, based on the maturity and goals of the people involved.

formal group
Formed by the organization.

informal group
Formed by friends.

Functions of Formal Groups

Researchers point out that formal groups fulfill two basic functions: *organizational* and *individual.*[10] The various functions are listed in Table 10–1. Complex combinations of these functions can be found in formal groups at any given time.

For example, consider what Mazda's new American employees experienced when they spent a month working in Japan before the opening of the firm's Flat Rock, Michigan, plant:

> After a month of training in Mazda's factory methods, whipping their new Japanese buddies at softball and sampling local watering holes, the Americans were fired up. . . . [A maintenance manager] even faintly praised the Japanese practice of holding group calisthenics at the start of each working day: "I didn't think I'd like doing exercises every morning, but I kind of like it."[11]

While Mazda pursued the organizational functions it wanted—interdependent teamwork, creativity, coordination, problem solving, and training—the American workers benefited from the individual functions of formal groups. Among those benefits were affiliation with new friends, enhanced self-esteem, exposure to the Japanese social reality, and reduction of anxieties about working for a foreign-owned company. In

Formal Groups Fulfill Organizational and Individual Functions **TABLE 10–1**

Organizational Functions	Individual Functions
1. Accomplish complex, interdependent tasks that are beyond the capabilities of individuals.	1. Satisfy the individual's need for affiliation.
2. Generate new or creative ideas and solutions.	2. Develop, enhance, and confirm the individual's self-esteem and sense of identity.
3. Coordinate interdepartmental efforts.	3. Give individuals an opportunity to test and share their perceptions of social reality.
4. Provide a problem-solving mechanism for complex problems requiring varied information and assessments.	4. Reduce the individual's anxieties and feelings of insecurity and powerlessness.
5. Implement complex decisions.	5. Provide a problem-solving mechanism for personal and interpersonal problems.
6. Socialize and train newcomers.	

SOURCE: Adapted from E H Schein, *Organizational Psychology,* 3rd ed (Englewood Cliffs. NJ: Prentice-Hall, 1980), pp 149–51.

short, Mazda created a workable blend of organizational and individual group functions by training its newly hired American employees in Japan.

The Group Development Process

Groups and teams in the workplace go through a maturation process, such as one would find in any life-cycle situation (e.g., humans, organizations, products). While there is general agreement among theorists that the group development process occurs in identifiable stages, they disagree about the exact number, sequence, length, and nature of those stages.[12] One oft-cited model is the one proposed in 1965 by educational psychologist Bruce W Tuckman. His original model involved only four stages (forming, storming, norming, and performing). The five-stage model in Figure 10–1 evolved when Tuckman and a doctoral student added "adjourning" in 1977.[13] A word of caution is in order. Somewhat akin to Maslow's need hierarchy theory, Tuckman's theory has been repeated and taught so often and for so long that many have come to view it as documented fact, not merely a theory. Even today, it is good to remember Tuckman's own caution that his group development model was derived more from group therapy sessions than from natural-life groups. Still, many in the OB field like Tuckman's five-stage model of group development because of its easy-to-remember labels and commonsense appeal.

Let us briefly examine each of the five stages in Tuckman's model. Notice in Figure 10–1 how individuals give up a measure of their independence when they join

FIGURE 10–1 Tuckman's Five-Stage Theory of Group Development

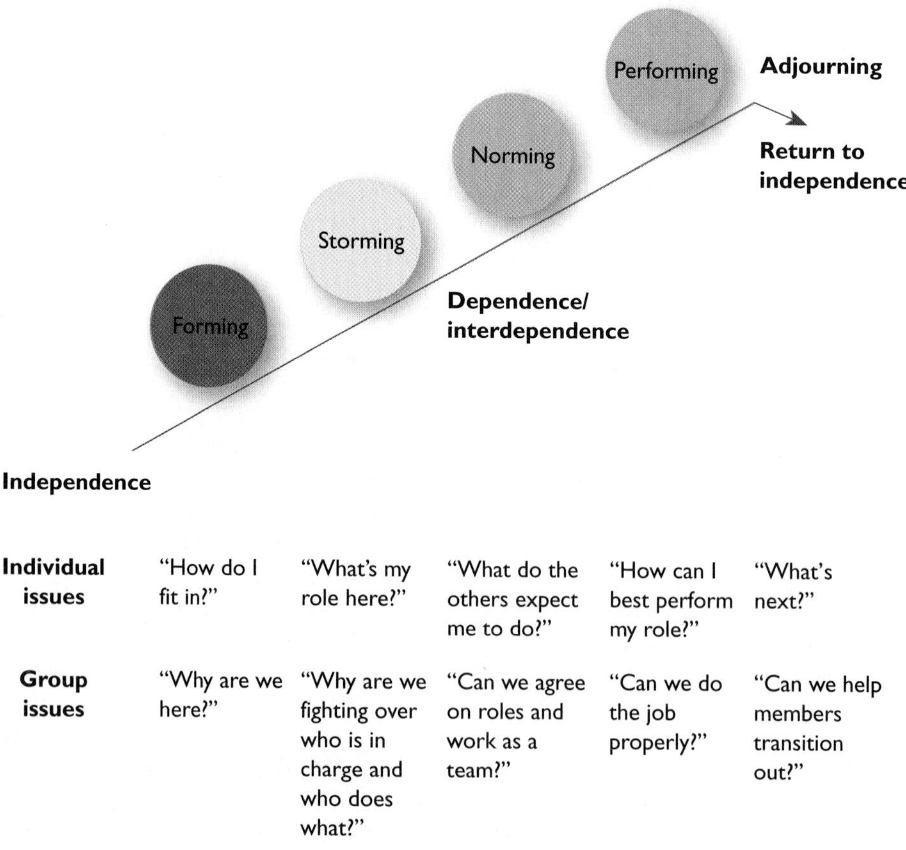

Individual issues	"How do I fit in?"	"What's my role here?"	"What do the others expect me to do?"	"How can I best perform my role?"	"What's next?"
Group issues	"Why are we here?"	"Why are we fighting over who is in charge and who does what?"	"Can we agree on roles and work as a team?"	"Can we do the job properly?"	"Can we help members transition out?"

and participate in a group. Also, the various stages are not necessarily of the same duration or intensity. For instance, the storming stage may be practically nonexistent or painfully long, depending on the goal clarity and the commitment and maturity of the members. You can make this process come to life by relating the various stages to your own experiences with work groups, committees, athletic teams, social or religious groups, or class project teams. Some group happenings that surprised you when they occurred may now make sense or strike you as inevitable when seen as part of a natural development process.

Group cohesiveness or a "we feeling" can help groups develop through the norming stage.

Stage 1: Forming During this "ice-breaking" stage, group members tend to be uncertain and anxious about such things as their roles, who is in charge, and the group's goals. Mutual trust is low, and there is a good deal of holding back to see who takes charge and how. If the formal leader (e.g., a supervisor) does not assert his or her authority, an emergent leader will eventually step in to fulfill the group's need for leadership and direction. Leaders typically mistake this honeymoon period as a mandate for permanent control. But later problems may force a leadership change.

Stage 2: Storming This is a time of testing. Individuals test the leader's policies and assumptions as they try to determine how they fit into the power structure.[14] Subgroups take shape, and subtle forms of rebellion, such as procrastination, occur. Many groups stall in stage 2 because power politics erupts into open rebellion.

Stage 3: Norming Groups that make it through stage 2 generally do so because a respected member, other than the leader, challenges the group to resolve its power struggles so something can be accomplished. Questions about authority and power are resolved through unemotional, matter-of-fact group discussion. A feeling of team spirit is experienced because members believe they have found their proper roles. **Group cohesiveness,** defined as the "we feeling" that binds members of a group together, is the principal by-product of stage 3.[15]

group cohesiveness
A "we feeling" binding group members together.

Stage 4: Performing Activity during this vital stage is focused on solving task problems. As members of a mature group, contributors get their work done without hampering others. There is a climate of open communication, strong cooperation, and lots of helping behavior. Conflicts and job boundary disputes are handled constructively and efficiently. Cohesiveness and personal commitment to group goals help the group achieve more than could any one individual acting alone.

Stage 5: Adjourning The work is done; it is time to move on to other things. Having worked so hard to get along and get something done, many members feel a compelling sense of loss. The return to independence can be eased by rituals celebrating "the end" and "new beginnings." Parties, award ceremonies, graduations, or mock funerals can provide the needed punctuation at the end of a significant group project. Leaders need to emphasize valuable lessons learned in group dynamics to prepare everyone for future group and team efforts.

Group Member Roles

Four centuries have passed since William Shakespeare had his character Jaques speak the following memorable lines in Act II of *As You Like It:* "All the world's a stage, And all the men and women merely players; They have their exits and their entrances; And one man in his time plays many parts. . . ." This intriguing notion of all people as actors in a universal play was not lost on 20th-century sociologists who developed a complex theory of human interaction based on roles. According to an OB scholar, "**roles** are sets of behaviors that persons expect of occupants of a position."[16] As described in Table 10–2, both task and maintenance roles need to be performed if a work group is to accomplish anything.[17]

roles

Expected behaviors for a given position.

task roles

Task-oriented group behavior.

Task versus Maintenance Roles **Task roles** enable the work group to define, clarify, and pursue a common purpose. Meanwhile,

TABLE 10–2 Task and Maintenance Roles

Task Roles	Description
Initiator	Suggests new goals or ideas.
Information seeker/giver	Clarifies key issues.
Opinion seeker/giver	Clarifies pertinent values.
Elaborator	Promotes greater understanding through examples or exploration of implications.
Coordinator	Pulls together ideas and suggestions.
Orienter	Keeps group headed toward its stated goal(s).
Evaluator	Tests group's accomplishments with various criteria such as logic and practicality.
Energizer	Prods group to move along or to accomplish more.
Procedural technician	Performs routine duties (e.g., handing out materials or rearranging seats).
Recorder	Performs a "group memory" function by documenting discussion and outcomes.
Maintenance Roles	**Description**
Encourager	Fosters group solidarity by accepting and praising various points of view.
Harmonizer	Mediates conflict through reconciliation or humor.
Compromiser	Helps resolve conflict by meeting others "half way."
Gatekeeper	Encourages all group members to participate.
Standard setter	Evaluates the quality of group processes.
Commentator	Records and comments on group processes/dynamics.
Follower	Serves as a passive audience.

SOURCE: Adapted from discussion in K D Benne and P Sheats, "Functional Roles of Group Members," *Journal of Social Issues,* Spring 1948, pp 41–49.

maintenance roles foster supportive and constructive interpersonal relationships. In short, task roles keep the group *on track* while maintenance roles keep the group *together*. A project team member is performing a task function when he or she says at an update meeting, "What is the real issue here? We don't seem to be getting anywhere." Another individual who says, "Let's hear from those who oppose this plan," is performing a maintenance function. Importantly, each of the various task and maintenance roles may be played in varying combinations and sequences by either the group's leader or any of its members.

maintenance roles

Relationship-building group behavior.

Checklist for Managers The task and maintenance roles listed in Table 10–2 can serve as a handy checklist for managers and group leaders who wish to ensure proper group development. Roles that are not always performed when needed, such as those of coordinator, evaluator, and gatekeeper, can be performed in a timely manner by the formal leader or assigned to other members. The task roles of initiator, orienter, and energizer are especially important because they are *goal-directed* roles. Research studies on group goal setting confirm the motivational power of challenging goals. As with individual goal setting (in Chapter 7), difficult but achievable goals are associated with better group results.[18] Also in line with individual goal-setting theory and research, group goals are more effective if group members clearly understand them and are both individually and collectively committed to achieving them. Initiators, orienters, and energizers can be very helpful in this regard.

International managers need to be sensitive to cultural differences regarding the relative importance of task and maintenance roles. In Japan, for example, cultural tradition calls for more emphasis on maintenance roles, especially the roles of harmonizer and compromiser:

> Courtesy requires that members not be conspicuous or disputatious in a meeting or classroom. If two or more members discover that their views differ—a fact that is tactfully taken to be unfortunate—they adjourn to find more information and to work toward a stance that all can accept. They do not press their personal opinions through strong arguments, neat logic, or rewards and threats. And they do not hesitate to shift their beliefs if doing so will preserve smooth interpersonal relations. (To lose is to win.)[19]

Norms

Norms are more encompassing than roles. While roles involve behavioral expectations for specific positions, norms help organizational members determine right from wrong and good from bad. According to one respected team of management consultants: "A **norm** is an attitude, opinion, feeling, or action—shared by two or more people—that guides their behavior."[20] Although norms are typically unwritten and seldom discussed openly, they have a powerful influence on group and organizational behavior.[21] PepsiCo Inc., for instance, has evolved a norm that equates corporate competitiveness with physical fitness. According to observers,

norm

Shared attitudes, opinions, feelings, or actions that guide social behavior.

> Leanness and nimbleness are qualities that pervade the company. When Pepsi's brash young managers take a few minutes away from the office, they often head straight for the company's physical fitness center or for a jog around the museum-quality sculptures outside of PepsiCo's Purchase, New York, headquarters.[22]

At PepsiCo and elsewhere, group members positively reinforce those who adhere to current norms with friendship and acceptance. On the other hand, nonconformists experience criticism and even **ostracism,** or rejection by group members. Anyone who has experienced the "silent treatment" from a group of friends knows what a potent social weapon ostracism can be.[23] Norms can be put into proper perspective by understanding how they develop and why they are enforced.

ostracism

Rejection by other group members.

How Norms Are Developed Experts say norms evolve in an informal manner as the group or organization determines what it takes to be effective. Generally speaking, norms develop in various combinations of the following four ways:

1. *Explicit statements by supervisors or co-workers.* For instance, a group leader might explicitly set norms about not drinking alcohol at lunch.
2. *Critical events in the group's history.* At times there is a critical event in the group's history that establishes an important precedent. (For example, a key recruit may have decided to work elsewhere because a group member said too many negative things about the organization. Hence, a norm against such "sour grapes" behavior might evolve.)
3. *Primacy.* The first behavior pattern that emerges in a group often sets group expectations. For example, this is how Paul Pressler set the norm for informality, creativity, and questioning when he recently took over as CEO of Gap Inc., the clothing retailer that owns the Old Navy and Banana Republic stores: "On his first day at work, speaking to 400 employees in Gap's first-floor auditorium, Pressler said, 'I've got a gazillion ideas, many of which are really stupid. But what the hell—you'll let me know!'"[24]
4. *Carryover behaviors from past situations.* Such carryover of individual behaviors from past situations can increase the predictability of group members' behaviors in new settings and facilitate task accomplishment. For instance, students and professors carry fairly constant sets of expectations from class to class.[25]

We would like you to take a few moments and think about the norms that are currently in effect in your classroom. List the norms on a sheet of paper. Do these norms help or hinder your ability to learn? Norms can affect performance either positively or negatively.

Why Norms Are Enforced Norms tend to be enforced by group members when they

- Help the group or organization survive.
- Clarify or simplify behavioral expectations.
- Help individuals avoid embarrassing situations.
- Clarify the group's or organization's central values and/or unique identity.[26]

Teams, Trust, and Teamwork

The team approach to managing organizations is having diverse and substantial impacts on organizations and individuals. Teams promise to be a cornerstone of progressive management for the foreseeable future.

General Electric's CEO, Jeffrey Immelt, offers this blunt overview: "You lead today by building teams and placing others first. It's not about you."[27] This means virtually all employees will need to polish their team skills. Southwest Airlines, a company that credits a strong team spirit for its success, puts team skills above all else. Case in point:

> Southwest rejected a top pilot from another airline who did stunt work for movie studios because he was rude to a receptionist. Southwest believes that technical skills are easier to acquire than a teamwork and service attitude.[28]

Fortunately, the trend toward teams has a receptive audience today. Both women and younger employees, according to research, thrive in team-oriented organizations.[29]

In this section, we define the term *team,* look at teamwork competencies, discuss trust as a key to real teamwork, and explore two evolving forms of teamwork—self-managed teams and virtual teams.

A Team Is More Than Just a Group

Jon R Katzenbach and Douglas K Smith, management consultants at McKinsey & Company, say it is a mistake to use the terms *group* and *team* interchangeably. After studying many different kinds of teams—from athletic to corporate to military—they concluded that successful teams tend to take on a life of their own. Katzenbach and Smith define a **team** as "a small number of people with complementary skills who are committed to a common purpose, performance goals, and approach for which they hold themselves mutually accountable."[30]

team

Small group with complementary skills who hold themselves mutually accountable for common purpose, goals, and approach.

Thus, a group becomes a team when the following criteria are met:

1. *Leadership* becomes a shared activity.
2. *Accountability* shifts from strictly individual to both individual and collective.
3. The group develops its own *purpose* or mission.
4. *Problem solving* becomes a way of life, not a part-time activity.
5. *Effectiveness* is measured by the group's collective outcomes and products.[31]

Relative to Tuckman's theory of group development covered earlier—forming, storming, norming, performing, and adjourning—teams are task groups that have matured to the *performing* stage. Because of conflicts over power and authority and unstable interpersonal relations, many work groups never qualify as a real team.[32] Katzenbach and Smith clarified the distinction this way: "The essence of a team is common commitment. Without it, groups perform as individuals; with it, they become a powerful unit of collective performance."[33]

When Katzenbach and Smith refer to "a small number of people" in their definition, they mean between 2 and 25 team members. They found effective teams to typically have fewer than 10 members. This conclusion was echoed in a survey of 400 workplace team members in the United States and Canada: "The average North American team consists of 10 members. Eight is the most common size."[34]

Developing Teamwork Competencies

Forming workplace teams and urging employees to be good team players are good starting points on the road to effective teams. But they are not enough today.

SKILLS & BEST PRACTICES

How Strong Are Your Teamwork Competencies?

Orients Team to Problem-Solving Situation
Assists the team in arriving at a common understanding of the situation or problem. Determines the important elements of a problem situation. Seeks out relevant data related to the situation or problem.

Organizes and Manages Team Performance
Helps team establish specific, challenging, and accepted team goals. Monitors, evaluates, and provides feedback on team performance. Identifies alternative strategies or reallocates resources to address feedback on team performance.

Promotes a Positive Team Environment
Assists in creating and reinforcing norms of tolerance, respect, and excellence. Recognizes and praises other team members' efforts. Helps and supports other team members. Models desirable team member behavior.

Facilitates and Manages Task Conflict
Encourages desirable and discourages undesirable team conflict. Recognizes the type and source of conflict confronting the team and implements an appropriate resolution strategy. Employs "win–win" negotiation strategies to resolve team conflicts.

Appropriately Promotes Perspective
Defends stated preferences, argues for a particular point of view, and withstands pressure to change position for another that is not supported by logical or knowledge-based arguments. Changes or modifies position if a defensible argument is made by another team member. Projects courtesy and friendliness to others while arguing position.

SOURCE: G Chen, L M Donahue, and R I Klimoski, "Training Undergraduates to Work in Organizational Teams," *Academy of Management Learning and Education,* March 2004, Appendix A, p 40.

Teamwork skills and competencies need to be role modeled and taught (see Skills & Best Practices). Notice the importance of group problem solving, mentoring, and conflict management skills, in addition to emotional intelligence. Teamwork competencies should be rewarded, too. For example, consider what has taken place at Internet equipment maker Cisco Systems:

> [CEO John] Chambers took . . . steps to rein in Cisco's Wild West culture during 2002. Most pointedly, he made teamwork a critical part of top execs' bonus plans. He told them 30% of their bonuses for the 2003 fiscal year would depend on how well they collaborated with others. "It tends to formalize the discussion around how can I help you and how can you help me," says Sue Bostrom, head of Cisco's Internet consulting group.[35]

Trust: A Key Ingredient of Teamwork

These have not been good times for trust in the corporate world. Years of mergers, layoffs, bloated executive bonuses, and corporate criminal proceedings have left many of us justly cynical about trusting management. "In Harris Interactive's 2004 Annual Corporation Reputation Survey, 74% say corporate America's reputation is 'not good' or 'terrible.'"[36] While challenging readers of *Harvard Business Review* to do a better job of investing in social capital, experts offered this constructive advice:

> No one can manufacture trust or mandate it into existence. When someone says, "You can trust me," we usually don't, and rightly so. But leaders can make deliberate investments in trust. They can give people reasons to trust one another instead of reasons to watch their backs. They can refuse to reward successes that are built on untrusting behavior. And they can display trust and trustworthiness in their own actions, both personally and on behalf of the company.[37]

trust
Reciprocal faith in others' intentions and behavior.

Three Dimensions of Trust

Trust is defined as reciprocal faith in others' intentions and behavior.[38] Experts on the subject explain the reciprocal (give-and-take) aspect of trust as follows:

> When we see others acting in ways that imply that they trust us, we become more disposed to reciprocate by trusting in them more. Conversely, we come to distrust those whose actions appear to violate our trust or to distrust us.[39]

In short, we tend to give what we get: trust begets trust; distrust begets distrust.

Trust is expressed in different ways. Three dimensions of trust are *overall trust* (expecting fair play, the truth, and empathy), *emotional trust* (having faith that someone will not misrepresent you to others or betray a confidence), and *reliableness* (believing that promises and appointments will be kept and commitments met).[40] These different dimensions contribute to a wide and complex range of trust, from very low to very high.

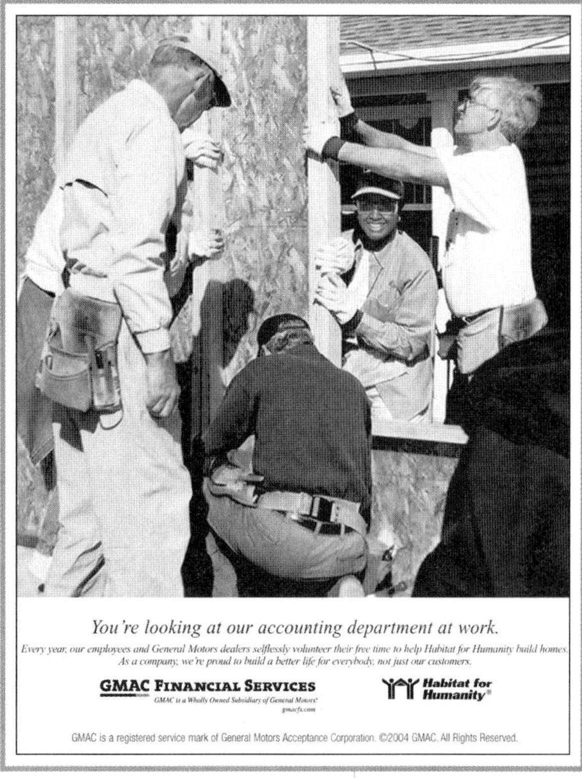

Habitat for Humanity builds homes in partnership with low-income families by bringing together volunteers who are relative strangers. How do you suppose group leaders build trust in such a short time frame?

How to Build Trust Management professor/consultant Fernando Bartolomé offers the following six guidelines for building and maintaining trust:

1. *Communication.* Keep team members and employees informed by explaining policies and decisions and providing accurate feedback. Be candid about one's own problems and limitations. Tell the truth.[41]
2. *Support.* Be available and approachable. Provide help, advice, coaching, and support for team members' ideas.
3. *Respect.* Delegation, in the form of real decision-making authority, is the most important expression of managerial respect. Actively listening to the ideas of others is a close second. (Empowerment is not possible without trust.)[42]
4. *Fairness.* Be quick to give credit and recognition to those who deserve it. Make sure all performance appraisals and evaluations are objective and impartial.
5. *Predictability.* Be consistent and predictable in your daily affairs. Keep both expressed and implied promises.
6. *Competence.* Enhance your credibility by demonstrating good business sense, technical ability, and professionalism.[43]

Trust needs to be earned; it cannot be demanded.

Self-Managed Teams

Have you ever thought you could do a better job than your boss? Well, if the trend toward self-managed work teams continues to grow as predicted, you just may get your chance. Entrepreneurs and artisans often boast of not having a supervisor. The same generally cannot be said for employees working in offices and factories. But things are changing. In fact, an estimated half of the employees at *Fortune* 500 companies are working on teams.[44] A growing share of those teams are self-managing. For example, "At a General Mills cereal plant in Lodi,

This group of people is learning the basic rule of trusting fellow colleagues: Trust must be earned, not demanded.

California, teams . . . schedule, operate, and maintain machinery so effectively that the factory runs with no managers present during the night shift."[45] More typically, managers are present to serve as trainers and facilitators. Self-managed teams come in every conceivable format today, some more autonomous than others (see Hands-On Exercise).

self-managed teams

Groups of employees granted administrative oversight for their work.

Self-managed teams are defined as groups of workers who are given administrative oversight for their task domains. Administrative oversight involves delegated activities such as planning, scheduling, monitoring, and staffing. These are chores normally performed by managers. In short, employees in these unique work groups act as their own supervisor. Accountability is maintained *indirectly* by outside managers and leaders. According to a recent study of a company with 300 self-managed teams, 66 "team advisors" relied on these four indirect influence tactics:

- *Relating* (understanding the organization's power structure, building trust, showing concern for individual team members)
- *Scouting* (seeking outside information, diagnosing teamwork problems, facilitating group problem solving)
- *Persuading* (gathering outside support and resources, influencing team to be more effective and pursue organizational goals)
- *Empowering* (delegating decision-making authority, facilitating team decision-making process, coaching).[46]

Self-managed teams are variously referred to as semiautonomous work groups, autonomous work groups, and superteams.

HANDS-ON EXERCISE

How Autonomous Is Your Work Group?

INSTRUCTIONS: Think of your current (or past) job and work group. Characterize the group's situation by circling one number on the following scale for each statement. Add your responses for a total score:

Strongly Disagree						**Strongly Agree**
1	2	3	4	5	6	7

Work Method Autonomy

1. My work group decides how to get the job done. ______
2. My work group determines what procedures to use. ______
3. My work group is free to choose its own methods when carrying out its work. ______

Work Scheduling Autonomy

4. My work group controls the scheduling of its work. ______
5. My work group determines how its work is sequenced. ______
6. My work group decides when to do certain activities. ______

Work Criteria Autonomy

7. My work group is allowed to modify the normal way it is evaluated so some of our activities are emphasized and some deemphasized. ______
8. My work group is able to modify its objectives (what it is supposed to accomplish). ______
9. My work group has some control over what it is supposed to accomplish. ______

Total score = ______

NORMS

9–26 = Low autonomy
27–45 = Moderate autonomy
46–63 = High autonomy

SOURCE: Adapted from an individual autonomy scale in J A Breaugh, "The Work Autonomy Scales: Additional Validity Evidence," *Human Relations,* November 1989, pp 1033–56.

Managerial Resistance Something much more complex is involved than this apparently simple label suggests. The term *self-managed* does not mean simply turning workers loose to do their own thing. Indeed, an organization embracing self-managed teams should be prepared to undergo revolutionary changes in management philosophy, structure, staffing and training practices, and reward systems. Moreover, the traditional notions of managerial authority and control are turned on their heads. Not surprisingly, many managers strongly resist giving up the reins of power to people they view as subordinates. They see self-managed teams as a threat to their job security.

Cross-Functionalism A common feature of self-managed teams, particularly among those above the shop-floor or clerical level, is **cross-functionalism.**[47] In other words, specialists from different areas are put on the same team. Mark Stefik, a manager at the world-renowned Palo Alto Research Center in California, explains the wisdom of cross-functionalism:

cross-functionalism
Team made up of technical specialists from different areas.

> Something magical happens when you bring together a group of people from different disciplines with a common purpose. It's a middle zone, the breakthrough zone. The idea is to start a team on a problem—a hard problem, to keep people motivated. When there's an obstacle, instead of dodging it, bring in another point of view: an electrical engineer, a user interface expert, a sociologist, whatever spin on the market is needed. Give people new eyeglasses to cross-pollinate ideas.[48]

SKILLS & BEST PRACTICES

Cross-Functional Studies Take Root at Carnegie Mellon University

Back in early 2001, Kenneth B Dunn set himself a tough goal: to restore Carnegie Mellon University's business school to its once-lofty stature of the 1980s and early 1990s. He talked to students, consulted with professors, studied the school's course requirements, and benchmarked its offerings and resources against those of competitors. By the time he was done with fact-finding, Dunn had developed a strategy for the school to "own the space where business and technology intersect." . . .

The new dean needed all the goodwill he could garner, given the curriculum overhaul he had in mind. Early on, Dunn replaced the school's generic approach with courses that included classwork outside the B-school, thus giving MBA candidates exposure beyond the staples of finance, management, and strategy. One example: The Integrated Product Development class brings professors and students from the business school together with those in engineering and fine arts to create products. Most recently they focused on Ford Motor Co.'s small SUV, the Escape. "They were simulating a practice that was very similar to the real world process at Ford where marketing people, technical people, designers, and engineers all come together to design a product the customer wants," says Stephen Lesh, Ford's program supervisor for the Escape. Ford has applied for patents for three products developed in last year's class—all having to do with interior components, says Lesh.

SOURCE: Excerpted from J Merritt, "How to Rebuild a B-School," *Business Week*, March 29, 2004, pp 90–91. Reprinted with permission.

Cross-functionalism is seeping down into university programs to help students see the big picture and polish their team skills (see Skills & Best Practices).

Are Self-Managed Teams Effective? The Research Evidence Among companies with self-managed teams, the most commonly delegated tasks are work scheduling and dealing directly with outside customers. The least common team chores are hiring and firing.[49] Most of today's self-managed teams remain bunched at the shop-floor level in factory settings. Experts predict growth of the practice in the managerial ranks and in service operations.[50]

Much of what we know about self-managed teams comes from testimonials and case studies. Fortunately, a body of higher quality field research is slowly developing. A review of three meta-analyses covering 70 individual studies concluded that self-managed teams had

- A positive effect on productivity.
- A positive effect on specific attitudes relating to self-management (e.g., responsibility and control).
- No significant effect on general attitudes (e.g., job satisfaction and organizational commitment).
- No significant effect on absenteeism or turnover.[51]

Although encouraging, these results do not qualify as a sweeping endorsement of self-managed teams. Nonetheless, experts say the trend toward self-managed work teams will continue upward in North America because of a strong cultural bias in favor of direct participation. Managers need to be prepared for the resulting shift in organizational administration.

Virtual Teams

Virtual teams are a product of modern times. They take their name from *virtual reality* computer simulations, where "it's almost like the real thing." Thanks to evolving information technologies such as the Internet, E-mail, videoconferencing, groupware, and fax machines, you can be a member of a work team without really being there.[52] Traditional team meetings are location specific. Team members are either physically present or absent. Virtual teams, in contrast, convene electronically with members reporting in from different locations, different organizations, and even different time zones.

virtual team

Information technology allows group members in different locations to conduct business.

Because virtual teams are so new, there is no consensual definition. Our working definition of a **virtual team** is a physically dispersed task group that conducts its business through modern information technology.[53] Advocates say virtual teams are very flexible and efficient because they are driven by information and skills, not by time and location.[54] People with needed information and/or skills can be team members, regardless of where or when they actually do their work. For example, Volvo's new station wagon grew out of a global collaboration among designers in Sweden, Spain, and the United States:

In today's "wired workplaces," it is possible to be a member of a virtual team while working alone.

> Using software called Alias, designers in Sweden and Detroit can change the curve of a fender or the shape of a headlight in real time. And if they want the big picture, they don 3-D goggles in special theaters that can project a full-size image of the car in two places at once. When Volvo's European designers put down their laser pens for the day, their counterparts in Irvine, Calif., pick up their pens and keep going. "We have almost 24-hour design," says [chief designer Peter] Horbury.[55]

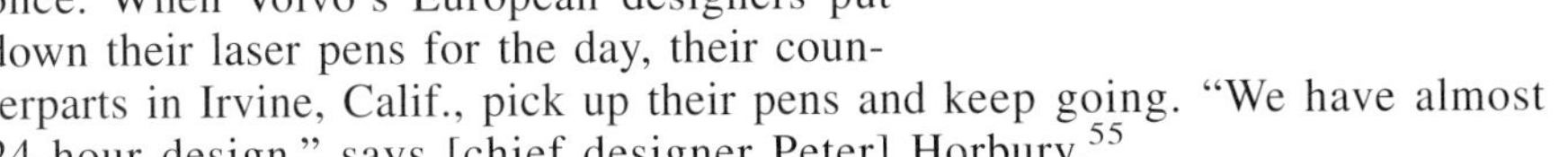

On the negative side, lack of face-to-face interaction can weaken trust, communication, and accountability.

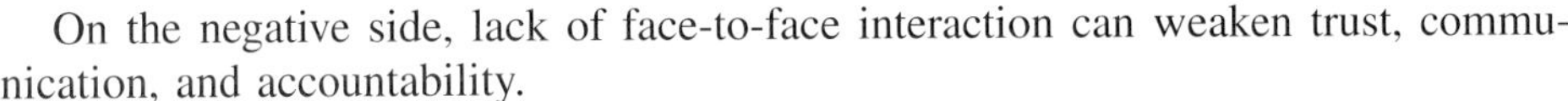

Research Insights As one might expect with a new and ill-defined area, research evidence to date is a bit spotty. Here is what we have learned so far from recent studies of computer-mediated groups:

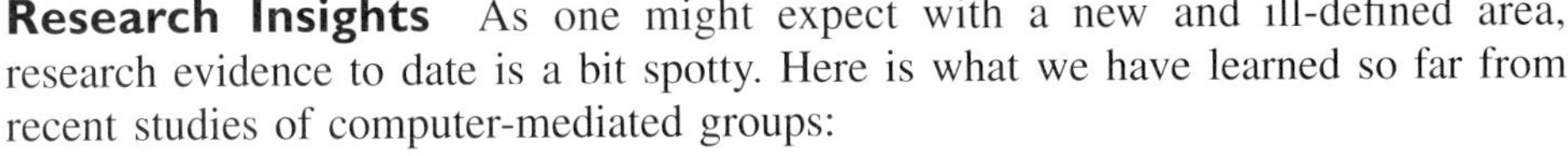

- Virtual groups formed over the Internet follow a group development process similar to that for face-to-face groups.[56]
- Internet chat rooms create more work and yield poorer decisions than face-to-face meetings and telephone conferences.[57]
- Successful use of groupware (software that facilitates interaction among virtual group members) requires training and hands-on experience.[58]
- Inspirational leadership has a positive impact on creativity in electronic brainstorming groups.[59]

Practical Considerations Virtual teams may be in fashion, but they are not a cure-all. In fact, they may be a giant step backward for those not well versed in modern information technology and group dynamics.[60] Managers who rely on virtual teams agree on one point: *Meaningful face-to-face contact, especially during early phases of the group development process, is absolutely essential.* Virtual group members need "faces" in their minds to go with names and electronic messages.[61] Additionally, virtual teams cannot succeed without some old-fashioned factors such as top-management support, hands-on training, a clear mission and specific objectives, effective leadership, and schedules and deadlines.[62]

Threats to Group and Team Effectiveness

No matter how carefully managers staff and organize task groups, group dynamics can still go haywire. Forehand knowledge of two major threats to group effectiveness—groupthink and social loafing—can help managers and team members alike take necessary preventive steps.

Groupthink

Systematic analysis of the decision-making processes underlying the war in Vietnam and other US foreign policy fiascoes prompted Yale University's Irving Janis to coin the term *groupthink*.[63] Modern managers can all too easily become victims of groupthink, just like professional politicians, if they passively ignore the danger.

groupthink

Janis's term for a cohesive in-group's unwillingness to realistically view alternatives.

Janis defines **groupthink** as "a mode of thinking that people engage in when they are deeply involved in a cohesive in-group, when members' strivings for unanimity override their motivation to realistically appraise alternative courses of action."[64] He adds, "Groupthink refers to a deterioration of mental efficiency, reality testing, and moral judgment that results from in-group pressures."[65] Members of groups victimized by groupthink tend to be friendly and tightly knit.

According to Janis's model, there are eight classic symptoms of groupthink. The greater the number of symptoms, the higher the probability of groupthink:

1. *Invulnerability:* An illusion that breeds excessive optimism and risk taking.
2. *Inherent morality:* A belief that encourages the group to ignore ethical implications.
3. *Rationalization:* Protects pet assumptions.
4. *Stereotyped views of opposition:* Cause group to underestimate opponents.
5. *Self-censorship:* Stifles critical debate.
6. *Illusion of unanimity:* Silence interpreted to mean consent.
7. *Peer pressure:* Loyalty of dissenters is questioned.
8. *Mindguards:* Self-appointed protectors against adverse information.[66]

These symptoms thrive in the sort of climate outlined in the following critique of corporate directors in the United States:

> Many directors simply don't rock the boat. "No one likes to be the skunk at the garden party," says [management consultant] Victor H Palmieri. . . . "One does not make friends and influence people in the boardroom or elsewhere by raising hard questions that create embarrassment or discomfort for management."[67]

In short, policy- and decision-making groups can become so cohesive that strong-willed executives are able to gain unanimous support for poor decisions.[68]

Janis believes that prevention is better than cure when dealing with groupthink (see Skills & Best Practices for his preventive measures).

How to Prevent Groupthink

1. Each member of the group should be assigned the role of critical evaluator. This role involves actively voicing objections and doubts.
2. Top-level executives should not use policy committees to rubber-stamp decisions that have already been made.
3. Different groups with different leaders should explore the same policy questions.
4. Subgroup debates and outside experts should be used to introduce fresh perspectives.
5. Someone should be given the role of devil's advocate when discussing major alternatives. This person tries to uncover every conceivable negative factor.
6. Once a consensus has been reached, everyone should be encouraged to rethink their position to check for flaws.

SOURCE: Adapted from discussion in I L Janis, *Groupthink*, 2nd ed. (Boston: Houghton Mifflin, 1982), ch 11.

SKILLS & BEST PRACTICES

Social Loafing

Is group performance less than, equal to, or greater than the sum of its parts? Can three people, for example, working together accomplish less than, the same as, or more than they would working separately? An interesting study conducted more than a half century ago by a French agricultural engineer named Ringelmann found the answer to be "less than."[69] In a rope-pulling exercise, Ringlemann reportedly found that three people pulling together could achieve only two and a half times the average individual rate. Eight pullers achieved less than four times the individual rate. This tendency for individual effort to decline as group size increases has come to be called **social loafing.**[70] Let us briefly analyze this threat to group effectiveness and synergy with an eye toward avoiding it.

social loafing
Decrease in individual effort as group size increases.

Social Loafing Theory and Research Among the theoretical explanations for the social loafing effect are (1) equity of effort ("Everyone else is goofing off, so why shouldn't I?"), (2) loss of personal accountability ("I'm lost in the crowd, so who cares?"), (3) motivational loss due to the sharing of rewards ("Why should I work harder than the others when everyone gets the same reward?"), and (4) coordination loss as more people perform the task ("We're getting in each other's way.").

Laboratory studies refined these theories by identifying situational factors that moderated the social loafing effect. Social loafing occurred when

- The task was perceived to be unimportant, simple, or not interesting.[71]
- Group members thought their individual output was not identifiable.[72]
- Group members expected their co-workers to loaf.[73]

But social loafing did *not* occur when group members in two laboratory studies expected to be evaluated.[74] Also, research suggests that self-reliant "individualists" are more prone to social loafing than are group-oriented "collectivists." But individualists can be made more cooperative by keeping the group small and holding each member personally accountable for results.[75]

Practical Implications These findings demonstrate that social loafing is not an inevitable part of group effort. Management can curb this threat to group effectiveness by making sure the task is challenging and perceived as important. Additionally, it is a good idea to hold group members personally accountable for identifiable portions of the group's task.[76] (Recall our discussion of the power of goal-setting in Chapter 7.)

key terms

chapter summary

- *Describe the five stages of Tuckman's theory of group development.* The five stages in Tuckman's theory are *forming* (the group comes together), *storming* (members test the limits and each other), *norming* (questions about authority and power are resolved as the group becomes more cohesive), *performing* (effective communication and cooperation help the group get things done), and *adjourning* (group members go their own way).
- *Contrast roles and norms, and specify four reasons why norms are enforced in organizations.* While roles are specific to the person's position, norms are shared attitudes that differentiate appropriate from inappropriate behavior in a variety of situations. Norms evolve informally and are enforced because they help the group or organization survive, clarify behavioral expectations, help people avoid embarrassing situations, and clarify the group's or organization's central values.
- *Explain how a work group becomes a team, and identify five teamwork competencies.* A team is a mature group where leadership is shared, accountability is both individual and collective, the members have developed their own purpose, problem solving is a way of life, and effectiveness is measured by collective outcomes. Five teamwork competencies are (1) orients team to problem-solving situations; (2) organizes and manages team performance; (3) promotes a positive team environment; (4) facilitates and manages task conflict; and (5) appropriately promotes perspective.
- *List at least four things managers can do to build trust.* Six recommended ways to build trust are through communication, support, respect (especially delegation), fairness, predictability, and competence.
- *Describe self-managed teams and virtual teams.* Self-managed teams are groups of workers who are given administrative oversight for various chores normally performed by managers—such as planning, scheduling, monitoring, and staffing. They are typically cross-functional, meaning they are staffed with a mix of specialists from different areas. Self-managed teams vary widely in the autonomy or freedom they enjoy. A virtual team is a physically dispersed task group that conducts its business through modern information technology such as the Internet. Periodic and meaningful face-to-face contact seems to be crucial for virtual team members, especially during the early stages of group development.
- *Describe groupthink, and identify at least four of its symptoms.* Groupthink plagues cohesive in-groups that shortchange moral judgment while putting too much emphasis on unanimity. Symptoms of groupthink include invulnerability, inherent morality, rationalization, stereotyped views of opposition, self-censorship, illusion of unanimity, peer pressure, and mindguards. Critical evaluators, outside expertise, and devil's advocates are among the preventive measures recommended by Irving Janis, who coined the term *groupthink.*

discussion questions

1. What role, if any, did trust likely play in the success of the teams discussed in the chapter-opening vignette?
2. What is your opinion about managers being friends with the people they supervise (in other words, overlapping formal and informal groups)?

3. In your personal relationships, how do you come to trust someone? How fragile is that trust? Explain.
4. Are virtual teams likely to be a passing fad? Why or why not?
5. Have you ever witnessed groupthink or social loafing firsthand? Explain the circumstances and how things played out.

ethical dilemma

Do Things My Way, or Hit the Highway!

Dr. Kerry J Sulkowicz, a psychiatrist, psychoanalyst, and author of *Fast Company* magazine's "The Corporate Shrink" column, recently fielded this question:

> I'm a lawyer, and I have just joined my first corporate board. The chairman, a client of mine, runs meetings as if only his ideas matter; he seems more interested in impressing us rather than in using our counsel. How do I handle this?[77]

What Course of Action Would You Recommend?

1. You're too new to "rock the boat." Be quiet and observe the group dynamics of the board until you *really* understand what is going on.
2. Quit the board before you get involved in a bad situation.
3. There is no ethical issue here until an unethical decision is made. Only then will it be time to do something. Do what?
4. The chairman needs to learn something about trust. What would you tell him (or have an influential board member tell him)?
5. This creates a climate for groupthink. Preventive steps should be taken *now*. What steps?
6. Invent other interpretations or options. Discuss.

For an interpretation of this situation, visit our Web site, www.mhhe.com/kinickiob2e.

If you're looking for additional study materials, be sure to check out the Online Learning Center at

www.mhhe.com/kinickiob2e

for more information and interactivities that correspond to this chapter.

agreed to immediately pay all expenses so she could complete graduate school. Official policy partly covered tuition after six months' service. She also got time off to study. "It was a mutual gain for both of us," said Ms. Regan, now 39.

Some women tend to accept extra work without negotiating fewer regular duties or higher pay because they don't want to appear pushy, Dr. Kolb observed. "Never make a unilateral concession," she suggested. "Say, 'At what price?'"[1]

FOR DISCUSSION

Are you a good negotiator? If you are, what are your secrets to success? If not, what causes you problems? For an interpretation of this case and additional comments, visit our Online Learning Center:

www.mhhe.com/kinickiob2e

MAKE NO MISTAKE about it. Conflict is an unavoidable aspect of modern life. These major trends conspire to make *organizational* conflict inevitable:

- Constant change.
- Greater employee diversity.
- More teams (virtual and self-managed).
- Less face-to-face communication (more electronic interaction).
- A global economy with increased cross-cultural dealings.

Dean Tjosvold, from Canada's Simon Fraser University, notes that "Change begets conflict, conflict begets change"[2] and challenges us to do better with this sobering global perspective:

> Learning to manage conflict is a critical investment in improving how we, our families, and our organizations adapt and take advantage of change. Managing conflicts well does not insulate us from change, nor does it mean that we will always come out on top or get all that we want. However, effective conflict management helps us keep in touch with new developments and create solutions appropriate for new threats and opportunities.
>
> Much evidence shows we have often failed to manage our conflicts and respond to change effectively. High divorce rates, disheartening examples of sexual and physical abuse of children, the expensive failures of international joint ventures, and bloody ethnic violence have convinced many people that we do not have the abilities to cope with our complex interpersonal, organizational, and global conflicts.[3]

But respond we must. As outlined in this chapter, tools and solutions are available, if only we develop the ability and will to use them persistently. The choice is ours: Be active managers of conflict and effective negotiators, or be managed by conflict.[4]

A Modern View of Conflict

A comprehensive review of the conflict literature yielded this consensus definition: "**conflict** is a process in which one party perceives that its interests are being opposed or negatively affected by another party."[5] The word *perceives* reminds us that sources of conflict and issues can be real or imagined. The resulting conflict is the same. Conflict can escalate (strengthen) or deescalate (weaken) over time. "The conflict process unfolds in a context, and whenever conflict, escalated or not, occurs the disputants or third parties can attempt to manage it in some manner."[6] Consequently, current and future managers need to understand the dynamics of conflict and know how to handle it effectively (both as disputants and as third parties).

conflict

One party perceives its interests are being opposed or set back by another party.

A Conflict Continuum

Ideas about managing conflict underwent an interesting evolution during the 20th century. Initially, scientific management experts such as Frederick W Taylor believed all conflict ultimately threatened management's authority and thus had to be avoided or quickly resolved.[7] Later, human relationists recognized the inevitability of conflict and advised managers to learn to live with it. Emphasis remained on resolving conflict whenever possible, however. Beginning in the 1970s, OB specialists realized conflict had both positive and negative outcomes, depending on its nature and intensity. This perspective introduced the revolutionary idea that organizations could suffer from *too little* conflict.

Work groups, departments, or organizations experiencing too little conflict tend to be plagued by apathy, lack of creativity, indecision, and missed deadlines. Excessive conflict, on the other hand, can erode organizational performance because of political infighting, dissatisfaction, lack of teamwork, and turnover. Workplace aggression and violence can be manifestations of excessive conflict.[8] Appropriate types and levels of conflict energize people in constructive directions.[9]

Functional versus Dysfunctional Conflict

functional conflict
Serves organization's interests.

dysfunctional conflict
Threatens organization's interests.

The distinction between **functional conflict** and **dysfunctional conflict** pivots on whether the organization's interests are served. According to one conflict expert,

> Some [types of conflict] support the goals of the organization and improve performance; these are functional, constructive forms of conflict. They benefit or support the main purposes of the organization. Additionally, there are those types of conflict that hinder organizational performance; these are dysfunctional or destructive forms. They are undesirable and the manager should seek their eradication.[10]

Functional conflict is commonly referred to in management circles as constructive or cooperative conflict.[11]

Often, a simmering conflict can be defused in a functional manner or driven to dysfunctional proportions, depending on how it is handled. For example, consider these two very different outcomes at Southwest Airlines and Gateway, the computer maker with the familiar black-and-white cow shipping boxes:

> Recently tensions broke out between flight attendants and their schedulers (the ones with the sorry job of telling flight attendants they have to work on a day off). The flight attendants believed the schedulers were overworking them; the schedulers claimed the attendants were hostile and uncooperative. The solution was very, well, Southwest: Both sides had to switch jobs for a day and see how difficult the other side had it. For now, at least, the tactic has eased tensions.[12]

Meanwhile, trouble was brewing at Gateway, where sales were off sharply. Company founder Ted Waitt had retired one year earlier when his hand-picked successor, Jeff Weitzen, took over after being hired from AT&T. *Fortune* magazine followed the action:

> It all came to a head at Gateway's Jan. 17 [2001] board meeting. In a hostile and combative proceeding, insiders say, Waitt and the board interrogated Weitzen relentlessly. At one point, after Weitzen had finished talking about his plans to improve customer service, one board member snapped, "Why should we believe you?"
>
> After the meeting Weitzen was furious. Stewing all weekend, he confronted Waitt the following Monday. High-level insiders say they argued for hours behind locked doors over how and by whom Gateway should be run. Waitt told Weitzen that he wanted him to stay on as CEO while Waitt took a more active role as chairman. For Weitzen, this arrangement—effectively a demotion—was unacceptable. Weitzen delivered an ultimatum: Back off or he was quitting.
>
> Taking a day to think about it, Waitt decided he wasn't backing off.[13]

A few days later, Weitzen and most of his top-management team were gone and Waitt's brief retirement was over.

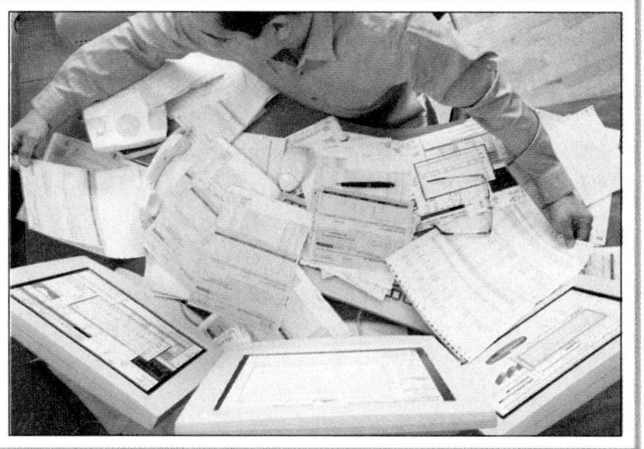

Layoff survivors typically complain about being overworked, thus paving the way for stress and conflict.

Antecedents of Conflict

Certain situations produce more conflict than others. By knowing the antecedents of conflict, managers are better able to anticipate conflict and take steps to resolve it if it becomes dysfunctional. Among the situations that tend to produce either functional or dysfunctional conflict are

- Incompatible personalities or value systems.
- Overlapping or unclear job boundaries.
- Competition for limited resources.
- Interdepartment/intergroup competition.
- Inadequate communication.
- Interdependent tasks (e.g., one person cannot complete his or her assignment until others have completed their work).
- Organizational complexity (conflict tends to increase as the number of hierarchical layers and specialized tasks increase).
- Unreasonable or unclear policies, standards, or rules.
- Unreasonable deadlines or extreme time pressure.
- Collective decision making (the greater the number of people participating in a decision, the greater the potential for conflict).
- Decision making by consensus.
- Unmet expectations (employees who have unrealistic expectations about job assignments, pay, or promotions are more prone to conflict).
- Unresolved or suppressed conflicts.[14]

Proactive managers carefully read these early warnings and take appropriate action (See Hands-On Exercise). For example, group conflict sometimes can be reduced by making decisions on the basis of majority approval rather than striving for a consensus.

Why People Avoid Conflict

Are you uncomfortable in conflict situations? Do you go out of your way to avoid conflict? If so, you're not alone. Many of us avoid conflict for a variety of both good and bad reasons. Tim Ursiny, in his entertaining and instructive book, *The Coward's Guide to Conflict,* contends that we avoid conflict because we fear various combinations of the following things: "harm"; "rejection"; "loss of relationship"; "anger"; "being seen as selfish"; "saying the wrong thing"; "failing"; "hurting someone else"; "getting what you want"; and "intimacy."[15] This list is self-explanatory, except for the fear of "getting what you want." By this, Ursiny is referring to those who, for personal reasons, feel undeserving and/or fear the consequences of success

HANDS-ON EXERCISE

The Conflict Iceberg

INSTRUCTIONS: This is a useful tool for understanding the full context of an interpersonal or intergroup conflict. First, identify a conflict situation that has involved and perhaps frustrated you lately (such as a broken friendship, a disagreement at school or work, or a family feud). Next, work your way down the conflict iceberg by writing some brief notes about the apparent issue, the personalities involved, relevant emotions, and so forth. The goal is to achieve "awareness of interconnection." In the spirit of functional or cooperative conflict, see if the other party to the conflict would be willing to complete this exercise from his or her perspective. Use the information gathered from one or both parties to move toward some sort of resolution. Importantly, be very honest with yourself because *you* may be a major obstacle or problem in the conflict situation. How can a similar conflict be avoided in the future?

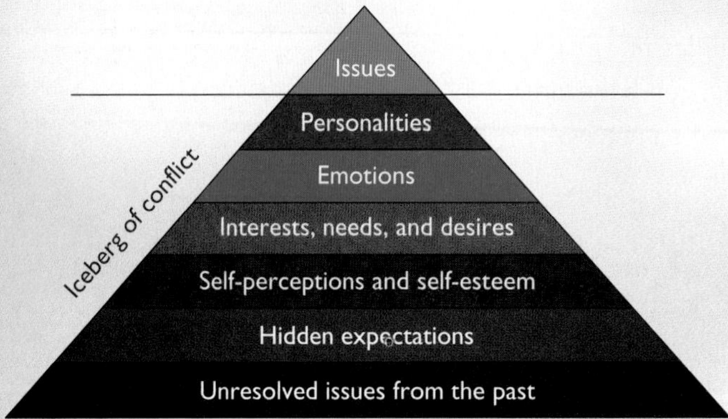

Awareness of interconnection
(The potential to move above and beyond the conflict, to have genuine empathy for others)

SOURCE: From K Cloke and J Goldsmith, *Resolving Conflicts at Work: A Complete Guide for Everyone on the Job* (San Francisco: Jossey-Bass, 2000), p 114. Copyright © 2000 Jossey-Bass, Inc. This material is used by permission of John Wiley & Sons, Inc.

(so they tend to sabotage themselves). For our present purposes, it is sufficient to become consciously aware of our fears and practice overcoming them. Reading, understanding, and acting upon the material in this chapter are steps in a positive direction.

Desired Outcomes of Conflict

Within organizations, conflict management is more than simply a quest for agreement. If progress is to be made and dysfunctional conflict minimized, a broader agenda is in order. Tjosvold's cooperative conflict model calls for three desired outcomes:

1. *Agreement.* But at what cost? Equitable and fair agreements are best. An agreement that leaves one party feeling exploited or defeated will tend to breed resentment and subsequent conflict.
2. *Stronger relationships.* Good agreements enable conflicting parties to build bridges of goodwill and trust for future use. Moreover, conflicting parties who trust each other are more likely to keep their end of the bargain.

3. *Learning.* Functional conflict can promote greater self-awareness and creative problem solving. Like the practice of management itself, successful conflict handling is learned primarily by doing. Knowledge of the concepts and techniques in this chapter is a necessary first step, but there is no substitute for hands-on practice. In a contentious world, there are plenty of opportunities to practice conflict management.[16]

Major Forms of Conflict

Certain antecedents of conflict deserve a closer look. This section explores the nature and organizational implications of three common forms of conflict: personality conflict, intergroup conflict, and cross-cultural conflict. Our discussion of each type of conflict includes some practical tips.

Personality Conflicts

As discussed in Chapter 5, your *personality* is the package of stable traits and characteristics creating your unique identity. According to experts on the subject:

> Each of us has a unique way of interacting with others. Whether we are seen as charming, irritating, fascinating, nondescript, approachable, or intimidating depends in part on our personality, or what others might describe as our style.[17]

personality conflict

Interpersonal opposition driven by personal dislike or disagreement.

Given the many possible combinations of personality traits, it is clear why personality conflicts are inevitable. We define a **personality conflict** as interpersonal opposition based on personal dislike and/or disagreement. This is an important topic, as evidenced by a recent survey of 173 managers in the US. When the managers were asked what makes them most uncomfortable, an overwhelming 73% said, "Building relationships with people I dislike." "Asking for a raise" (25%) and "speaking to large audiences" (24%) were the distant second and third responses.[18]

Workplace Incivility: The Seeds of Personality Conflict Somewhat akin to physical pain, chronic personality conflicts often begin with seemingly insignificant irritations. For instance, a manager can grow to deeply dislike someone in the next cubicle who persistently whistles off-key while drumming his foot on the side of a filing cabinet. Sadly, grim little scenarios such as this are all too common today, given the steady erosion of civility in the workplace. Researchers recently noted how increased informality, pressure for results, and employee diversity have fostered an "anything goes" atmosphere in today's workplaces. They view incivility as a self-perpetuating vicious cycle that can end in violence.[19] A new

"Lewis, we called your mother because you haven't been working well with others."

What does the body language in this photo tell you about workplace conflict? It underscores the importance of following the general guideline to "focus on problems and performance, not personalities." When managers wrongly attack an employee's personality, integrity, or character, job performance and morale tend to suffer.

survey of 632 employees indicates the nature and extent of workplace incivility in the US:

> Ethnic and racial slurs each declined by 2 points from the previous year, from about 29 percent to 27 percent. The biggest declines, about 4 points each, were in ridicule based on sexual orientation (from 24.4 percent to 20.2 percent) and disability (from 7.2 percent to 3.2 percent). Ridicule based on age declined by 1 point.
>
> Sexually inappropriate remarks were most often heard in the workplace by U.S. employees for the second year in a row—remaining steady at 34 percent in 2002 and 2003.[20]

The need for diversity training and penalties for misconduct remains high.

Vicious cycles of incivility need to be avoided (or broken early) with an organizational culture that places a high value on respect for co-workers. This requires managers and leaders to act as caring and courteous role models. A positive spirit of cooperation, as opposed to one based on negativism and aggression, also helps. Some organizations have resorted to workplace etiquette training.[21] More specifically, constructive feedback and skillful positive reinforcement can keep a single irritating behavior from precipitating a full-blown personality conflict (or worse).

Dealing with Personality Conflicts Personality conflicts are a potential minefield for managers. Let us frame the situation. Personality traits, by definition, are stable and resistant to change. Moreover, according to the American Psychiatric Association's *Diagnostic and Statistical Manual of Mental Disorders,* there are 410 psychological disorders that can and do show up in the workplace.[22] This brings up legal issues. Employees in the United States suffering from psychological disorders such as depression and mood-altering diseases such as alcoholism are protected from discrimination by the Americans with Disabilities Act.[23] (Other nations have similar laws.) Also, sexual harassment and other forms of discrimination can grow out of apparent personality conflicts.[24] Finally, personality conflicts can spawn workplace aggression and violence.[25]

Traditionally, managers dealt with personality conflicts by either ignoring them or transferring one party.[26] In view of the legal implications, just discussed, both of these options may be open invitations to discrimination lawsuits. Skills & Best Practices presents practical tips for both nonmanagers and managers who are involved in or affected by personality conflicts. Our later discussions of handling dysfunctional conflict and alternative dispute resolution techniques also apply.

Intergroup Conflict

Conflict among work groups, teams, and departments is a common threat to organizational competitiveness. For example, when Michael Volkema became CEO of Herman Miller in the mid-1990s, he found an inward-focused company with divisions fighting over budgets. He has since curbed intergroup conflict at the Michigan-based furniture maker by emphasizing collaboration and redirecting everyone's attention outward, to the customer.[27] Managers who understand the mechanics of intergroup conflict are better equipped to face this sort of challenge.

In-Group Thinking: The Seeds of Intergroup Conflict As we discussed in the previous chapter, *cohesiveness*—a "we feeling" binding group members together—can be a good or bad thing. A certain amount of cohesiveness can turn a group of individuals into a smooth-running team. Too much cohesiveness, however, can breed groupthink because a desire to get along pushes aside critical thinking. The study of in-groups by small group researchers has revealed a whole package of changes associated with increased group cohesiveness. Specifically,

- Members of in-groups view themselves as a collection of unique individuals, while they stereotype members of other groups as being "all alike."
- In-group members see themselves positively and as morally correct, while they view members of other groups negatively and as immoral.
- In-groups view outsiders as a threat.
- In-group members exaggerate the differences between their group and other groups. This typically involves a distorted perception of reality.[28]

Avid sports fans who simply can't imagine how someone would support the opposing team exemplify one form of in-group thinking. Also, this pattern of behavior is a form of ethnocentrism, discussed as a cross-cultural barrier in Chapter 3. Reflect for a moment on evidence of in-group behavior in your life. Does your circle of friends make fun of others because of their race, gender, nationality, weight, sexual preference, or major in college?[29]

In-group thinking is one more fact of organizational life that virtually guarantees conflict. Managers cannot eliminate in-group thinking, but they certainly should not ignore it when handling intergroup conflicts.

Research Lessons for Handling Intergroup Conflict Sociologists have long recommended the contact hypothesis for reducing intergroup conflict. According to the *contact hypothesis,* the more the members of different groups interact, the less intergroup conflict they will experience. Those interested in improving race, international, and union-management relations typically encourage cross-group

SKILLS & BEST PRACTICES

How to Deal with Personality Conflicts

Tips for Employees Having a Personality Conflict	Tips for Third-Party Observers of a Personality Conflict	Tips for Managers Whose Employees Are Having a Personality Conflict
• All employees need to be familiar with and *follow* company policies for diversity, antidiscrimination, and sexual harassment.		
• Communicate directly with the other person to resolve the perceived conflict (emphasize problem solving and common objectives, not personalities). • Avoid dragging co-workers into the conflict. • If dysfunctional conflict persists, seek help from direct supervisors or human resource specialists.	• Do not take sides in someone else's personality conflict. • Suggest the parties work things out themselves in a constructive and positive way. • If dysfunctional conflict persists, refer the problem to the parties' direct supervisors.	• Investigate and document conflict. • If appropriate, take corrective action (e.g., feedback or behavior modification). • If necessary, attempt informal dispute resolution. • Refer difficult conflicts to human resource specialists or hired counselors for formal resolution attempts and other interventions.

Conflicts can arise for any group—the trick is to make them productive. This ad promotes the American Arbitration Association's mission to train professionals on how to effectively minimize and manage conflict—"before the mud starts flying."

interaction. The hope is that *any* type of interaction, short of actual conflict, will reduce stereotyping and combat in-group thinking. But research has shown this approach to be naive and limited. For example, one study of 83 health center employees (83% female) at a midwest US university probed the specific nature of intergroup relations and concluded:

> The number of *negative* relationships was significantly related to higher perceptions of intergroup conflict. Thus, it seems that negative relationships have a salience that overwhelms any possible positive effects from friendship links across groups.[30]

Intergroup friendships are still desirable, as documented in many studies,[31] but they are readily overpowered by negative intergroup interactions. Thus, *priority number 1 for managers faced with intergroup conflict is to identify and root out specific negative linkages between (or among) groups.* A single personality conflict, for instance, may contaminate the entire intergroup experience. The same goes for an employee who voices negative opinions or spreads negative rumors about another group. Our updated contact model in Figure 11–1 is based on this and other recent research insights, such as the need to foster positive attitudes toward other groups.[32] Also, notice how conflict within the group and negative gossip from third parties are threats that need to be neutralized if intergroup conflict is to be minimized.

Cross-Cultural Conflict

Doing business with people from different cultures is commonplace in our global economy where cross-border mergers, joint ventures, and alliances are the order of the day.[33] Because of differing assumptions about how to think and act, the potential for cross-cultural conflict is both immediate and huge.[34] Success or failure, when conducting business across cultures, often hinges on avoiding and minimizing actual or perceived conflict. For example, consider this cultural mismatch:

> Mexicans place great importance on saving face, so they tend to expect any conflicts that occur during negotiations to be downplayed or kept private. The prevailing attitude in the [United States], however, is that conflict should be dealt with directly and publicly to prevent hard feelings from developing on a personal level.[35]

This is not a matter of who is right and who is wrong; rather it is a matter of accommodating cultural differences for a successful business transaction. Awareness of the cross-cultural differences we discussed in Chapter 3 is an important first step. Beyond that, cross-cultural conflict can be moderated by using international consultants and building cross-cultural relationships.

FIGURE 11–1 Minimizing Intergroup Conflict: An Updated Contact Model

Level of perceived intergroup conflict tends to increase when:

- Conflict within the group is high.
- There are negative interactions between groups (or between members of those groups).
- Influential third-party gossip about other group is negative.

→

Recommended actions:

- Work to eliminate *specific negative* interactions between groups (and members).
- Conduct team building to reduce *intra*group conflict and prepare employees for cross-functional teamwork.
- Encourage personal friendships and good working relationships across groups and departments.
- Foster positive attitudes toward members of other groups (empathy, compassion, sympathy).
- Avoid or neutralize negative gossip across groups or departments.

SOURCE: Based on research evidence in G Labianca, D J Brass, and B Gray, "Social Networks and Perceptions of Intergroup Conflict: The Role of Negative Relationships and Third Parties," *Academy of Management Journal*, February 1998, pp 55–67; C D Batson et al., "Empathy and Attitudes: Can Feeling for a Member of a Stigmatized Group Improve Feelings toward the Group?" *Journal of Personality and Social Psychology*, January 1997, pp 105–18; and S C Wright et al., "The Extended Contact Effect: Knowledge of Cross-Group Friendships and Prejudice," *Journal of Personality and Social Psychology*, July 1997, pp 73–90.

Using International Consultants In response to broad demand, there is a growing army of management consultants specializing in cross-cultural relations. Competency and fees vary widely, of course. But a carefully selected cross-cultural consultant can be helpful, as this illustration shows:

> Last year, when electronics-maker Canon planned to set up a subsidiary in Dubai through its Netherlands division, it asked consultant Sahid Mirza of Glocom, based in Dubai, to find out how the two cultures would work together.
>
> Mirza sent out the test questionnaires and got a sizable response. "The findings were somewhat surprising," he recalls. "We found that, at the bedrock level, there were relatively few differences. Many of the Arab businessmen came from former British colonies and viewed business in much the same way as the Dutch."
>
> But at the level of behavior, there was a real conflict. "The Dutch are blunt and honest in expression, and such expression is very offensive to Arab sensibilities." Mirza offers the example of a Dutch executive who says something like, "We can't

SKILLS & BEST PRACTICES

How to Build Cross-Cultural Relationships

Behavior	Rank
Be a good listener	1
Be sensitive to needs of others	2 (Tie)
Be cooperative, rather than overly competitive	2 (Tie)
Advocate inclusive (participative) leadership	3
Compromise rather than dominate	4
Build rapport through conversations	5
Be compassionate and understanding	6
Avoid conflict by emphasizing harmony	7
Nurture others (develop and mentor)	8

SOURCE: Adapted from R L Tung, "American Expatriates Abroad: From Neophytes to Cosmopolitans," *Journal of World Business*, Summer 1998, Table 6, p 136.

Racial, ethnic, and religious differences can make cross-cultural conflict all the more challenging.

meet the deadline." Such a negative expression—true or not—would be gravely offensive to an Arab. As a result of Mirza's research, Canon did start the subsidiary in Dubai, but it trained both the Dutch and the Arab executives first.[36]

Consultants also can help untangle possible personality, value, and intergroup conflicts from conflicts rooted in differing national cultures. Note: Although we have discussed basic types of conflict separately, they typically are encountered in complex, messy bundles.

Building Relationships across Cultures Rosalie L Tung's study of 409 expatriates from US and Canadian multinational firms is very instructive.[37] Her survey sought to pinpoint success factors for the expatriates (14% female) who were working in 51 different countries worldwide. Nine specific ways to facilitate interaction with host-country nationals, as ranked from most useful to least useful by the respondents, are listed in Skills & Best Practices on page 283. Good listening skills topped the list, followed by sensitivity to others and cooperativeness rather than competitiveness. Interestingly, US managers often are culturally characterized as just the opposite: poor listeners, blunt to the point of insensitivity, and excessively competitive. Some managers need to add self-management to the list of ways to minimize cross-cultural conflict.

Managing Conflict

As we have seen, conflict has many faces and is a constant challenge for managers who are responsible for reaching organizational goals. Our attention now turns to the active management of both functional and dysfunctional conflict. We discuss how to stimulate functional conflict, how to handle dysfunctional conflict, and how third parties can deal effectively with conflict.

Programming Functional Conflict

Sometimes committees and decision-making groups become so bogged down in details and procedures that nothing substantive is accomplished. Carefully monitored functional conflict can help get the creative juices flowing once again. Managers basically have two options. They can fan the fires of naturally occurring conflict—although this approach can be unreliable and slow. Alternatively, managers can resort to programmed conflict. Experts in the field define **programmed conflict** as "conflict that raises different opinions *regardless of the personal feelings of the managers.*"[38] The trick is to get contributors to either defend or criticize ideas based on relevant facts rather than on the basis of personal preference or political interests. This requires disciplined role playing and effective leadership. Two programmed conflict techniques with proven track records are devil's advocacy and the dialectic method. Let us explore these two ways of stimulating functional conflict.

programmed conflict

Encourages different opinions without protecting management's personal feelings.

Devil's Advocacy This technique gets its name from a traditional practice within the Roman Catholic Church. When someone's name came before the College of Cardinals for elevation to sainthood, it was absolutely essential to ensure that he or she had a spotless record. Consequently, one individual was assigned the role of *devil's advocate* to uncover and air all possible objections to the person's canonization. In accordance with this practice, **devil's advocacy** in today's organizations involves assigning someone the role of critic.[39] Recall from Chapter 10, Irving Janis recommended the devil's advocate role for preventing groupthink.

devil's advocacy

Assigning someone the role of critic.

In the left half of Figure 11–2, note how devil's advocacy alters the usual decision-making process in steps 2 and 3. This approach to programmed conflict is intended to generate critical thinking and reality testing.[40] It is a good idea to rotate the job of devil's advocate so no one person or group develops a strictly negative reputation. Moreover, periodic devil's advocacy role-playing is good training for developing analytical and communication skills and emotional intelligence.

The Dialectic Method Like devil's advocacy, the dialectic method is a time-honored practice. This particular approach to programmed conflict traces back to the dialectic school of philosophy in ancient Greece. Plato and his followers attempted to synthesize truths by exploring opposite positions (called *thesis* and *antithesis*). Court systems in the United States and elsewhere rely on directly opposing points of view for determining guilt or innocence. Accordingly, today's **dialectic method** calls for managers to foster a structured debate of opposing viewpoints prior to making a decision.[41] Steps 3 and 4 in the right half of Figure 11–2 set the dialectic approach apart from the normal decision-making process. Here is how Anheuser-Busch's corporate policy committee uses the dialectic method:

dialectic method

Fostering a debate of opposing viewpoints to better understand an issue.

> When the policy committee . . . considers a major move—getting into or out of a business, or making a big capital expenditure—it sometimes assigns teams to make the case for each side of the question. There may be two teams or even three. Each is knowledgeable about the subject; each has access to the same information. Occasionally someone in favor of the project is chosen to lead the dissent, and an opponent to argue for it. Pat Stokes, who heads the company's beer empire, describes the result: "We end up with decisions and alternatives we hadn't thought of previously," sometimes representing a synthesis of the opposing views. "You become a lot more anticipatory, better able to see what might happen, because you have thought through the process."[42]

A major drawback of the dialectic method is that "winning the debate" may overshadow the issue at hand. Also, the dialectic method requires more skill training than

FIGURE 11–2 Techniques for Stimulating Functional Conflict: Devil's Advocacy and the Dialectic Method

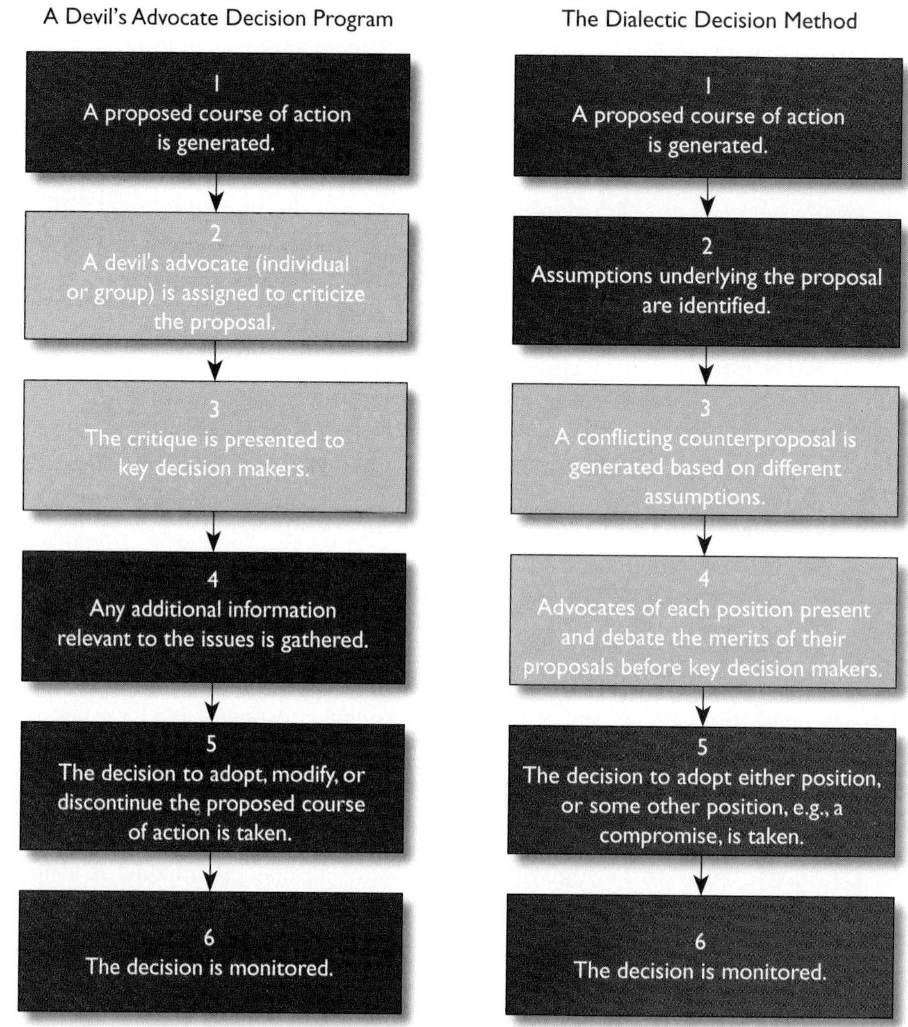
A Devil's Advocate Decision Program
1
A proposed course of action is generated.
2
A devil's advocate (individual or group) is assigned to criticize the proposal.
3
The critique is presented to key decision makers.
4
Any additional information relevant to the issues is gathered.
5
The decision to adopt, modify, or discontinue the proposed course of action is taken.
6
The decision is monitored.
The Dialectic Decision Method
1
A proposed course of action is generated.
2
Assumptions underlying the proposal are identified.
3
A conflicting counterproposal is generated based on different assumptions.
4
Advocates of each position present and debate the merits of their proposals before key decision makers.
5
The decision to adopt either position, or some other position, e.g., a compromise, is taken.
6
The decision is monitored.

SOURCE: R A Cosier and C R Schwenk, "Agreement and Thinking Alike: Ingredients for Poor Decisions," *Academy of Management Executive: The Thinking Manager's Source,* February 1990, pp 72–73. Copyright 1990 by Academy of Management. Reproduced with permission of Academy of Management via Copyright Clearance Center.

does devil's advocacy. Regarding the comparative effectiveness of these two approaches to stimulating functional conflict, however, a laboratory study ended in a tie. Compared with groups that strived to reach a consensus, decision-making groups using either devil's advocacy or the dialectic method yielded equally higher quality decisions.[43] But, in a more recent laboratory study, groups using devil's advocacy produced more potential solutions and made better recommendations for a case problem than did groups using the dialectic method.[44]

In light of this mixed evidence, managers have some latitude in using either devil's advocacy or the dialectic method for pumping creative life back into stalled deliberations.[45] Personal preference and the role players' experience may well be the deciding factors in choosing one approach over the other. The important thing is to actively stimulate functional conflict when necessary, such as when the risk of blind conformity or groupthink is high. Joseph M Tucci, CEO of EMC, a leading data storage equipment company, fosters functional conflict by creating a supportive climate for dissent:

> Good leaders always leave room for debate and different opinions. . . .
>
> The team has to be in harmony. But before you move out, there needs to be a debate. Leadership is not a right. You have to earn it.
>
> . . . [E]very company needs a healthy paranoia. It's the CEO's job to keep it on the edge, to put tension in the system. You have to do the right thing for the right circumstances.[46]

This meshes well with the results of a pair of recent laboratory studies that found a positive relationship between the degree of minority dissent and team innovation, *but only when participative decision making was used.*[47]

Alternative Styles for Handling Dysfunctional Conflict

People tend to handle negative conflict in patterned ways referred to as *styles.* Several conflict styles have been categorized over the years. According to conflict specialist Afzalur Rahim's model, five different conflict-handling styles can be plotted on a 2 × 2 grid. High to low concern for *self* is found on the horizontal axis of the grid while low to high concern for *others* forms the vertical axis (see Figure 11–3). Various combinations of these variables produce the five different conflict-handling styles: integrating, obliging, dominating, avoiding, and compromising.[48] There is no single best style; each has strengths and limitations and is subject to situational constraints.

Integrating (Problem Solving) In this style, interested parties confront the issue and cooperatively identify the problem, generate and weigh alternative solutions, and select a solution. Integrating is appropriate for complex issues plagued by misunderstanding. However, it is inappropriate for resolving conflicts rooted in opposing value systems. Its primary strength is its longer lasting impact because it deals with the underlying problem rather than merely with symptoms. The primary weakness of this style is that it is very time-consuming.

Obliging (Smoothing) "An obliging person neglects his or her own concern to satisfy the concern of the other party."[49] This style, often called smoothing, involves playing down differences while emphasizing commonalities. Obliging may be an appropriate conflict-handling strategy when it is possible to eventually get something in return. But it is inappropriate for complex or worsening problems. Its

Five Conflict-Handling Styles **FIGURE 11–3**

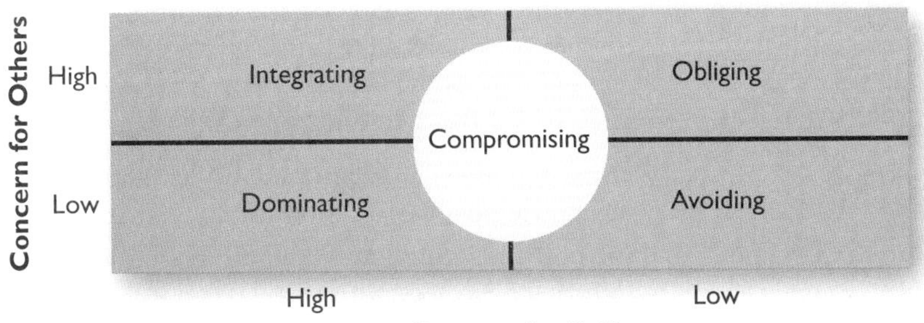

SOURCE: Reprinted by permission of Sage Publications Ltd from M A Rahim, "A Strategy for Managing Conflict in Complex Organizations," *Human Relations,* January 1985, p 84. Copyright © 1985 The Tavistock Institute.

primary strength is that it encourages cooperation. Its main weakness is that it's a temporary fix that fails to confront the underlying problem.

Dominating (Forcing) High concern for self and low concern for others encourages "I win, you lose" tactics. The other party's needs are largely ignored. This style is often called forcing because it relies on formal authority to force compliance. Dominating is appropriate when an unpopular solution must be implemented, the issue is minor, or a deadline is near. It is inappropriate in an open and participative climate. Speed is its primary strength. The primary weakness of this domineering style is that it often breeds resentment.[50]

Avoiding This tactic may involve either passive withdrawal from the problem or active suppression of the issue. Avoidance is appropriate for trivial issues or when the costs of confrontation outweigh the benefits of resolving the conflict. It is inappropriate for difficult and worsening problems. The main strength of this style is that it buys time in unfolding or ambiguous situations. The primary weakness is that the tactic provides a temporary fix that sidesteps the underlying problem.

Compromising This is a give-and-take approach involving moderate concern for both self and others. Compromise is appropriate when parties have opposite goals or possess equal power. But compromise is inappropriate when overuse would lead to inconclusive action (e.g., failure to meet production deadlines). The primary strength of this tactic is that everyone gets something, but it's a temporary fix that can stifle creative problem solving.[51]

Third-Party Interventions: Alternative Dispute Resolution

Disputes between employees, between employees and their employer, and between companies too often end up in lengthy and costly court battles. A more constructive, less expensive approach called alternative dispute resolution has enjoyed enthusiastic growth in recent years.[52] In fact, the widely imitated "People's Court"–type television shows operating outside the formal judicial system are part of this trend toward what one writer calls "do-it-yourself justice."[53] **Alternative dispute resolution** (ADR), according to a pair of Canadian labor lawyers, "uses faster, more user-friendly methods of dispute resolution, instead of traditional, adversarial approaches (such as unilateral decision making or litigation)."[54] The following ADR techniques represent a progression of steps third parties can take to resolve organizational conflicts.[55] They are ranked from easiest and least expensive to most difficult and costly. A growing number of organizations have formal ADR policies involving an established sequence of various combinations of these techniques:

alternative dispute resolution
Avoiding costly lawsuits by resolving conflicts informally or through mediation or arbitration.

- *Facilitation.* A third party, usually a manager, informally urges disputing parties to deal directly with each other in a positive and constructive manner.
- *Conciliation.* A neutral third party informally acts as a communication conduit between disputing parties. This is appropriate when conflicting parties refuse to meet face to face. The immediate goal is to establish direct communication, with the broader aim of finding common ground and a constructive solution.

- *Peer review.* A panel of trustworthy co-workers, selected for their ability to remain objective, hears both sides of a dispute in an informal and confidential meeting. Any decision by the review panel may or may not be binding, depending on the company's ADR policy. Membership on the peer review panel often is rotated among employees.[56]
- *Ombudsman.* Someone who works for the organization, and is widely respected and trusted by his or her co-workers, hears grievances on a confidential basis and attempts to arrange a solution. This approach, more common in Europe than North America, permits someone to get help from above without relying on the formal hierarchy chain.
- *Mediation.* "The mediator—a trained, third-party neutral—actively guides the disputing parties in exploring innovative solutions to the conflict. Although some companies have in-house mediators who have received ADR training, most also use external mediators who have no ties to the company."[57] Unlike an arbitrator, a mediator does *not* render a decision. It is up to the disputants to reach a mutually acceptable decision.
- *Arbitration.* Disputing parties agree ahead of time to accept the decision of a neutral arbitrator in a formal courtlike setting, often complete with evidence and witnesses. Statements are confidential. Decisions are based on legal merits. Trained arbitrators, typically from outside agencies such as the American Arbitration Association, are versed in relevant laws and case precedents. Historically, employee participation in arbitration was voluntary. A 2001 US Supreme Court decision changed things. As part of the employment contract with nonunion workers, employers in the United States now have the legal right to insist upon *mandatory* arbitration in lieu of a court battle. A vigorous debate now rages over the fairness and quality of mandatory arbitration.[58]

Negotiating

Formally defined, **negotiation** is a give-and-take decision-making process involving interdependent parties with different preferences.[59] Common examples include labor-management negotiations over wages, hours, and working conditions and negotiations between supply chain specialists and vendors involving price, delivery schedules, and credit terms. Self-managed work teams with overlapping task boundaries also need to rely on negotiated agreements. Negotiating skills are more important than ever today.[60]

negotiation

Give-and-take process between conflicting interdependent parties.

Two Basic Types of Negotiation

Negotiation experts distinguish between two types of negotiation—*distributive* and *integrative*. Understanding the difference requires a change in traditional "fixed-pie" thinking:

> A *distributive* negotiation usually involves a single issue—a "fixed-pie"—in which one person gains at the expense of the other. For example, haggling over the price of a rug in a bazaar is a distributive negotiation. In most conflicts, however, more than one issue is at stake, and each party values the issues differently. The outcomes available are no longer a fixed-pie divided among all parties. An agreement can be found that is better for both parties than what they would have reached through distributive negotiation. This is an *integrative* negotiation.

SKILLS & BEST PRACTICES

Seven Steps to Negotiating Your Salary

1. **Know the going rate.** You probably won't get very far by telling your boss that competitors pay better than he does (unless one has made you an offer). But knowing your potential value can help steel you to ask for what you're really worth. . . .
2. **Don't fudge your past compensation.** Potential employers occasionally ask for a W-2, so be honest about what you're earning now.
3. **Present cold, hard proof of your value.** Remember, you're selling your boss on a hot productivity tool: you. So provide concrete, quantifiable examples of how you made previous bosses look good and saved them effort. . . .
4. **Let the other party name a figure first.** You don't want to show your hand. If pressed, suggest a salary range instead of a number. Career coach Lenore Mewton suggests upping what you think is a fair range by as much as 10 percent. "Notch it up a little without being unrealistic," she says. You can always come down later if you need to.
5. **Don't nickel-and-dime.** Set a fairly high target, but once the company has agreed on a number within a range that you deem acceptable, don't nitpick—you might seem not to be a person of your word. . . .
6. **Avoid extravagant extras.** This economic environment is no time to ask for expensive perks. "I'd be embarrassed to ask for first-class travel or a fancy office," says Andy Ellenthal, a senior vice president at PointRoll. . . . "It leaves the impression that you want to sit around on your butt all day."
7. **Seek incentives and practical perks.** In lieu of luxuries—or if you're stonewalled on a salary demand—request benefits that cost your employer little and suggest that they be contingent on how well you do your job.

Source: B Brophy, "Bargaining for Bigger Bucks: A Step-by-Step Guide to Negotiating Your Salary," *Business 2.0,* May 2004, p 107.

However, parties in a negotiation often don't find these beneficial trade-offs because each *assumes* its interests *directly* conflict with those of the other party. "What is good for the other side must be bad for us" is a common and unfortunate perspective that most people have. This is the mind-set we call the *mythical* "fixed-pie."[61]

Distributive negotiation involves traditional win-lose thinking. Integrative negotiation calls for a progressive win–win strategy.[62]

Added-Value Negotiation

One practical application of the integrative approach is **added-value negotiation** (AVN). During AVN, the negotiating parties cooperatively develop multiple deal packages while building a productive long-term relationship. AVN consists of these five steps:

1. *Clarify interests.* After each party identifies its tangible and intangible needs, the two parties meet to discuss their respective needs and find *common ground* for negotiation.
2. *Identify options.* A *marketplace of value* is created when the negotiating parties discuss desired elements of value (such as property, money, behavior, rights, and risk reduction).
3. *Design alternative deal packages.* While aiming for *multiple deals,* each party mixes and matches elements of value from both parties in workable combinations.
4. *Select a deal.* Each party analyzes deal packages proposed by the other party. Jointly, the parties discuss and select from feasible deal packages, with a spirit of *creative agreement.*
5. *Perfect the deal.* Together the parties discuss unresolved issues, develop a written agreement, and *build relationships* for future negotiations.[63]

Applying What You Have Learned: How to Negotiate Your Pay and Benefits

Our opening vignette for this chapter illustrated the importance of being able to negotiate fair compensation on the job. Women and other minorities too often come up short in this regard, in addition to being *under*-represented in top-management positions. *Harvard Business Review* recently offered this interpretation:

Research has shown that both conscious and subconscious biases contribute to this problem. But we've discovered another, subtler source of inequality: Women often don't get what they want and deserve because they don't ask for it. In three separate studies, we found that men are more likely than women to negotiate for what they want. . . .

Women are less likely than men to negotiate for themselves for several reasons. First, they often are socialized from an early age not to promote their own interests and to focus instead on the needs of others. . . . Women tend to assume that they will be recognized and rewarded for working hard and doing a good job. Unlike men, they haven't been taught that they can ask for more.

Second, many companies' cultures penalize women when they do ask—further discouraging them from doing so.[64]

added-value negotiation

Cooperatively developing multiple-deal packages while building a long-term relationship.

Consequently, women (and any other employees) who feel they are being shortchanged in pay and/or promotions need to polish their integrative negotiation skills (see Skills & Best Practices). Employers, meanwhile, need to cultivate a diversity ethic, grant rewards equitably, and foster a culture of dignity and fair play.

key terms

chapter summary

- *Define the term* conflict, *distinguish between functional and dysfunctional conflict, and identify three desired outcomes of conflict.* Conflict is a process in which one party perceives that its interests are being opposed or negatively affected by another party. It is inevitable and not necessarily destructive. Too little conflict, as evidenced by apathy or lack of creativity, can be as great a problem as too much conflict. Functional conflict enhances organizational interests while dysfunctional conflict is counterproductive. Three desired conflict outcomes are agreement, stronger relationships, and learning.
- *Define* personality conflicts, *and explain how they should be managed.* Personality conflicts involve interpersonal opposition based on personal dislike and/or disagreement (or as an outgrowth of workplace incivility). Care needs to be taken with personality conflicts in the workplace because of the legal implications of diversity, discrimination, and sexual harassment. Managers should investigate and document personality conflicts, take corrective actions such as feedback or behavior modification if appropriate, or attempt informal dispute resolution. Difficult or persistent personality conflicts need to be referred to human resource specialists or counselors.
- *Discuss the role of in-group thinking in intergroup conflict, and explain what can be done to avoid cross-cultural conflict.* Members of in-groups tend to see themselves as unique individuals who are more moral than outsiders, whom they view as a threat and stereotypically as all alike. In-group thinking is associated with ethnocentric behavior. International consultants can prepare people from different cultures to work effectively together. Cross-cultural conflict can be minimized by having expatriates build strong cross-cultural relationships with their hosts (primarily by being good listeners, being sensitive to others, and being more cooperative than competitive).
- *Explain how managers can program functional conflict, and identify the five conflict-handling styles.* Functional conflict can be stimulated by permitting antecedents of conflict to persist or programming conflict during decision making with devil's advocates or the dialectic method. The five conflict-handling styles are integrating (problem solving), obliging (smoothing), dominating (forcing), avoiding, and compromising. There is no single best style.

- *Identify and describe at least four alternative dispute resolution (ADR) techniques.* Alternative dispute resolution (ADR) involves avoiding costly court battles with more informal and user-friendly techniques such as facilitation, conciliation, peer review, ombudsman, mediation, and arbitration.
- *Draw a distinction between distributive and integrative negotiation, and explain the concept of added-value negotiation.* Distributive negotiation involves fixed-pie and win-lose thinking. Integrative negotiation is a win-win approach to better results for both parties. The five steps in added-value negotiation are as follows: Step 1, clarify interests; Step 2, identify options; Step 3, design alternative deal packages; Step 4, select a deal; and Step 5, perfect the deal. Elements of value, multiple deals, and creative agreement are central to this approach.

discussion questions

1. Relative to the chapter-opening vignette, what steps should companies take to close the gender pay gap?
2. What examples of functional and dysfunctional conflict have you observed in organizations lately? What were the outcomes? What caused the dysfunctional conflict?
3. Which of the five conflict-handling styles is your strongest? Your weakest? How can you improve your ability to handle conflict?
4. Which of the six ADR techniques appeals the most to you? Why?
5. How could added-value negotiation make your life a bit easier? Explain in terms of a specific problem, conflict, or deadlock.

ethical dilemma

A Matter of Style at German Software Giant SAP

While [Co-Founder and Chairman Hasso] Plattner believes in obtaining consensus among his lieutenants, he doesn't care how much he irritates people along the way. In fact, his confrontational style is deliberate. "He creates stressful situations. He fuels the discussions with provocative statements. Sometimes he's rigid, even rude. But it's about getting people engaged so they can be creative," says Wolfgang Kemna, CEO of SAP America, a 13-year SAP veteran. Co-CEO Henning Kagermann, whom Plattner elevated to work alongside him in 1998, is his counterweight in the organization—calm and efficient.[65]

Is Plattner's Heavy-handed Management Style an Ethical Issue?

1. No, not if he effectively stimulates creativity and functional conflict. Explain.
2. Yes, his abrasive personality will intimidate some coworkers and possibly even promote blind obedience or groupthink. Explain.
3. Yes, his intimidating management style could create a hostile work environment where sexual harassment might thrive. Explain.
4. Maybe. It depends upon the circumstances and individuals involved. Explain.
5. Not in this situation, because his tough ways are counterbalanced by his CEO's calm style. Explain.
6. Invent other options. Discuss.

For an interpretation of this situation, visit our Web site, www.mhhe.com/kinickiob2e.

If you're looking for additional study materials, be sure to check out the Online Learning Center at

www.mhhe.com/kinickiob2e

for more information and interactivities that correspond to this chapter.

part Four

Managing Organizational Processes

chapter Twelve

Communicating in the Internet Age

LEARNING OBJECTIVES

After reading the material in this chapter, you should be able to:

- Describe the perceptual process model of communication.
- Demonstrate your familiarity with four antecedents of communication distortion between managers and employees.
- Contrast the communication styles of assertiveness, aggressiveness, and nonassertiveness.
- Discuss the primary sources of nonverbal communication and 10 keys to effective listening.
- Explain the information technology of Internet/intranet/extranet, e-mail, videoconferencing, and collaborative computing, and explain the related use of telecommuting.
- Describe the process, personal, physical, and semantic barriers to effective communication.

INFORMATION TECHNOLOGY: HELP OR HINDRANCE?

Vickie Farrell had an e-mail account before most people were using desktop computers. Since 1979, when she was a manager at Digital Equipment Corp. in Boston, she has watched e-mail evolve "from an experimental novelty to a significant productivity-improvement tool, to a mainstream work mode enabling people to communicate globally 24/7."

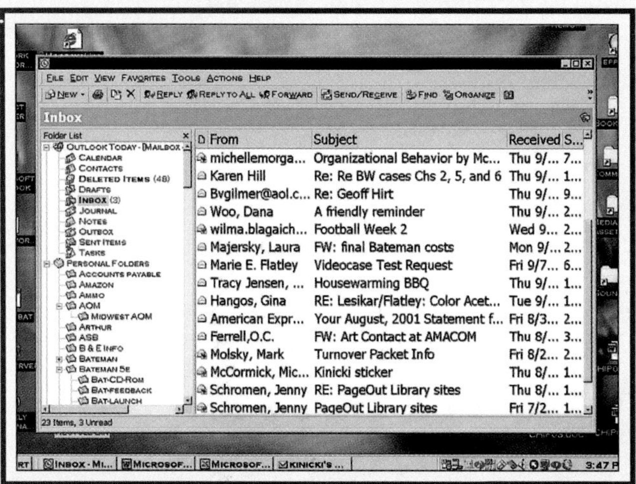

Today, Ms. Farrell, now a vice president at Teradata, a unit of NCR Corp., sees e-mail becoming a counter-productive intrusion in the workplace. She, like other managers, are turning off, or ignoring, their e-mail in an effort to get some work accomplished. They've reached the breaking point, where even attempts to put messages in priority or to use filtering systems to delete junk e-mail aren't helping enough.

Managers complain that the relentless flow of computer messages disrupts thought processes and kills creativity. There is no quiet time available during the workday, or even after office hours, to digest information, to ponder fresh ideas, to concentrate wholeheartedly on a difficult problem, or even to daydream. Instead, the expectation that messages from colleagues, bosses, customers and suppliers will be answered promptly requires that employees think only in short bursts, moving quickly from one topic to another.

"The messages keep coming and coming," says Ms. Farrell, who recalls how when she first used e-mail she received just three or four messages a day. "Now it has gotten to the point where you can spend your entire day doing nothing but answering e-mail. It's intrusive and disruptive." . . .

As a result, we are losing the ability to initiate work independently and cope with the frustration of not getting answers immediately. The more we are encouraged to remain perpetually logged on, the more we fear separation. We become unable to detach long enough to create a new idea or devise an answer to a complex problem.

Now, Ms. Farrell logs off her e-mail for at least two hours a day to grant herself time to write long memos and reports—and think. She also avoids checking her e-mail when she is working away from the office or at a conference. "Some people think that because I have my laptop with me, I should stay connected, but that would prevent me from meeting potential customers, and defeat the purpose of being at the conference," she says.

Even when she is online, she doesn't read or answer every e-mail. Instead, she tells colleagues to phone her when they send an important e-mail, so that she can quickly handle it.

Jeff Phelps, chief operating officer and senior vice president at ABE Services, Sonoma, Calif., a consulting firm for independent-contractor employment, agrees that the pressure many employees feel to keep up with e-mail traffic undermines their work. "It's like being on a production line and having to plow through the next set of messages, knowing more are coming right behind," he says. "There's no time to think about providing truly thoughtful information."

He understands the value of e-mail when needing to address several people, but he says he is copied on far too many messages. He misses the days when it was acceptable not to respond to an office memo or a letter for at least 24 hours. That interval allowed time to ponder a topic and originate some new ideas.

Mr. Phelps also resents the intrusion of e-mail into his personal life, and refuses to get a BlackBerry. "If I had a BlackBerry, I'd be on line all the time and never get a break or a chance to have another form of engagement," he says.[1]

FOR DISCUSSION

How can managers increase their time to think while managing the deluge of e-mail messages? Explain. For an interpretation of this case and additional comments, visit our Online Learning Center:

www.mhhe.com/kinickiob2e

MANAGEMENT IS COMMUNICATION. Every managerial function and activity involves some form of direct or indirect communication. Whether planning and organizing or directing and leading, managers find themselves communicating with and through others. Managerial decisions and organizational policies are ineffective unless they are understood by those responsible for enacting them. Consider, for example, how the communication process within Adecco SA, the world's largest temporary help company, negatively affected the company's stock price:

> Eight days ago, the Swiss-based concern announced it wouldn't be able to release its year-end results on schedule in February and warned of "material weaknesses with internal controls" at its North American staffing business. But Adecco officials refused to elaborate on the terse statement, citing legal constraints. At the time, they wouldn't even confirm the identity of an independent counsel that Adecco's board has appointed to conduct its own investigation.
>
> The company's bunker mentalilty stirred anxiety among investors, who quickly dumped Adecco shares. Within a few hours, the company lost 35% of its market capitalization.[2]

Ineffective communication clearly contributed to the drop in Adecco's share price.

Moreover, effective communication is critical for employee motivation and job satisfaction. For example, a study of 274 students revealed that student motivation was positively related to the quality of student-faculty communication in the instructor's office. Another study involving 65 savings and loan employees and 110 manufacturing employees revealed that employee satisfaction with organizational communication was positively and significantly correlated with job satisfaction and performance.[3]

This chapter will help you better understand how managers can both improve their communication skills and design more effective communication programs. We discuss (1) basic dimensions of the communication process, (2) interpersonal communication, (3) communication in the computerized age, and (4) communication barriers.

Basic Dimensions of the Communication Process

Communication is defined as "the exchange of information between a sender and a receiver, and the inference (perception) of meaning between the individuals involved."[4] Analysis of this exchange reveals that communication is a two-way process consisting of consecutively linked elements (see Figure 12–1). Managers who understand this process can analyze their own communication patterns as well as design communication programs that fit organizational needs. This section reviews a perceptual process model of communication and discusses communication distortion.

communication

Interpersonal exchange of information and understanding.

A Perceptual Process Model of Communication

As we all know, communicating is not that simple or clear-cut. Communication is fraught with miscommunication. In recognition of this, researchers have begun to examine communication as a form of social information processing (recall the discussion in Chapter 4) in which receivers interpret messages by cognitively processing information. This view led to development of a perceptual model of communication that depicts communication as a process in which receivers create meaning in their

FIGURE 12–1 A Perceptual Model of Communication

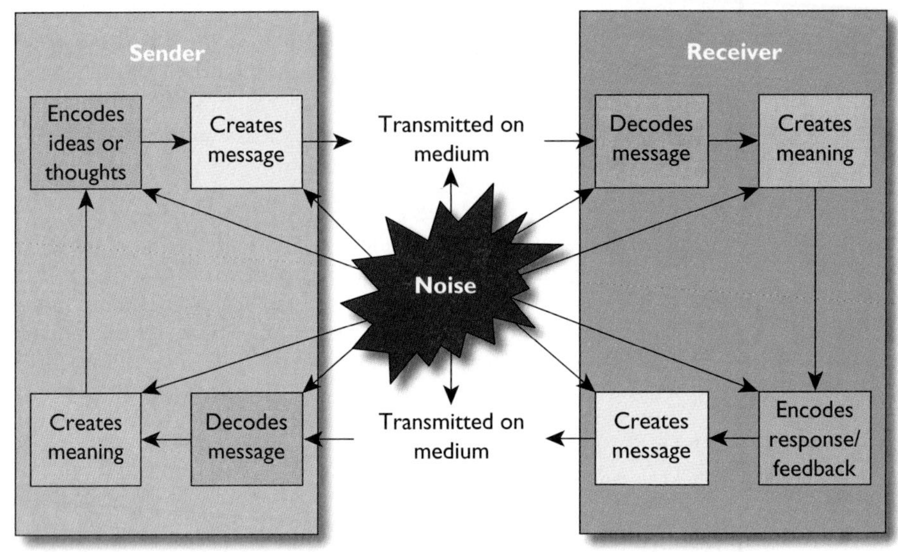

own minds. Let us briefly examine the elements of the perceptual process model shown in Figure 12–1.

Sender The sender is an individual, group, or organization that desires or attempts to communicate with a particular receiver. Receivers may be individuals, groups, or organizations.

Encoding Communication begins when a sender encodes an idea or thought. Encoding translates mental thoughts into a code or language that can be understood by others. Managers typically encode using words, numbers, gestures, nonverbal cues such as facial expressions, or pictures. Moreover, different methods of encoding can be used to portray similar ideas.

The Message The output of encoding is a message. There are two important points to keep in mind about messages. First, they contain more than meets the eye. Messages may contain hidden agendas as well as trigger affective or emotional reactions. Second, messages need to match the medium used to transmit them. How would you evaluate the match between the message of letting someone know they have been laid off and the communication medium used in the following example?

> Six months ago [January 2002], Tower Snow was chairman of Brobeck, Phleger & Harrison, one of the nation's premier law firms. Late Friday, as he got off a United Airlines flight in San Francisco, a gate agent handed him an envelope. Inside: notice that Brobeck had fired him.[5]

How would you feel if this happened to you? Surely there is a better way to let someone know he or she is being fired. This example illustrates how thoughtless managers can be when they do not carefully consider the interplay between a message and the medium used to convey it.

Selecting a Medium Managers can communicate through a variety of media. Potential media include face-to-face conversations, telephone calls, electronic mail, voice mail, videoconferencing, written memos or letters, photographs or drawings,

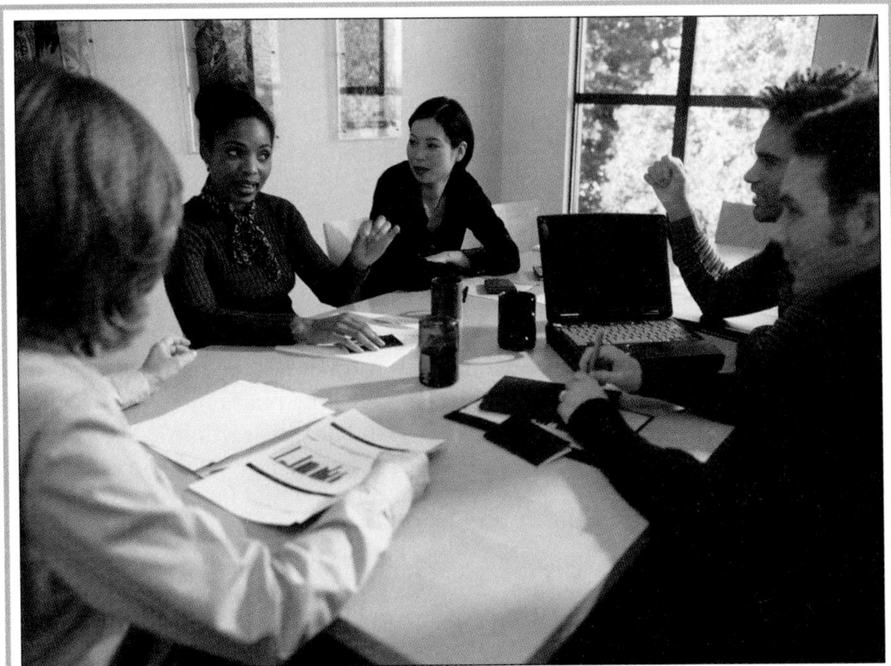

Although managers can communicate through a variety of media, face-to-face communication is useful for delivering sensitive or important issues that require feedback, intensive interaction, or nonverbal cues.

meetings, bulletin boards, computer output, and charts or graphs. Choosing the appropriate media depends on many factors, including the nature of the message, its intended purpose, the type of audience, proximity to the audience, time horizon for disseminating the message, personal preferences, and the complexity of the problem/situation at hand.

All media have advantages and disadvantages and should be used in different situations. Face-to-face conversations, for example, are useful for communicating about sensitive or important issues that require feedback and intensive interaction. In contrast, telephones are convenient, fast, and private, but lack nonverbal information. Although writing memos or letters is time-consuming, it is a good medium when it is difficult to meet with the other person, when formality and a written record are important, and when face-to-face interaction is not necessary to enhance understanding. Electronic communication, which is discussed later in this chapter, can be used to communicate with a large number of dispersed people and is potentially a very fast medium when recipients of messages regularly check their e-mail.[6]

Decoding Decoding is the receiver's version of encoding. Decoding consists of translating verbal, oral, or visual aspects of a message into a form that can be interpreted. Receivers rely on social information processing to determine the meaning of a message during decoding. Decoding is a key contributor to misunderstanding in interracial and intercultural communication because decoding by the receiver is subject to social values and cultural values that may not be understood by the sender.

Creating Meaning The perceptual model of communication is based on the belief that a receiver creates the meaning of a message in his or her head. A receiver's interpretation of a message can thus differ from that intended by the sender. In turn, receivers act according to their own interpretations, not the communicator's.

Feedback The receiver's response to a message is the crux of the feedback loop. At this point in the communication process, the receiver becomes a sender. Specifically, the receiver encodes a response and then transmits it to the original sender. This new message is then decoded and interpreted. As you can see from this discussion, feedback is used as a comprehension check. It gives senders an idea of how accurately their message is understood.

noise

Interference with the transmission and understanding of a message.

Noise **Noise** represents anything that interferes with the transmission and understanding of a message. It affects all linkages of the communication process. Sue Weidemann, director of research for a consulting company, investigated the impact of noise at a large law firm. Her results indicated that "the average number of times that people were interrupted by noise, visual distractions and chatty visitors prairie-dogging over a cube wall was 16 a day—or 21 a day including work-related distractions." She concluded that it takes 2.9 minutes to recover concentration after these disruptions, "meaning people spend more than an hour a day trying to refocus. And that doesn't even count the time drain of the distraction itself."[7] Noise includes factors such as a speech impairment, poor telephone connections, illegible handwriting, inaccurate statistics in a memo or report, poor hearing and eyesight, and physical distance between sender and receiver. Managers can improve communication by reducing noise.

Communication Distortion between Managers and Employees

communication distortion

Purposely modifying the content of a message.

Communication distortion occurs when an employee purposely modifies the content of a message, thereby reducing the accuracy of communication between managers and employees. Employees tend to engage in this practice because of workplace politics, a desire to manage impressions, or fear of how a manager might respond to a message.[8] Communication experts point out the organizational problems caused by distortion:

> Distortion is an important problem in organizations because modifications to messages cause misdirectives to be transmitted, nondirectives to be issued, incorrect information to be passed on, and a variety of other problems related to both the quantity and quality of information.[9]

Knowledge of the antecedents or causes of communication distortion can help managers avoid or limit these problems.

Studies have identified four situational antecedents of distortion in upward communication (see Figure 12–2). Distortion tends to increase when supervisors have high upward influence and/or power. Employees also tend to modify or distort information when they aspire to move upward and when they do not trust their supervisors.[10] Because managers generally do not want to reduce their upward influence or curb their direct reports' desire for upward mobility, they can reduce distortion in several ways:

1. Managers can deemphasize power differences between themselves and their direct reports.
2. They can enhance trust through a meaningful performance review process that rewards actual performance.
3. Managers can encourage staff feedback by conducting smaller, more informal meetings. This is precisely what the Lodge at Vail did to improve

Situational Antecedents			Pattern of Distortion in Upward Communication
1. Supervisor's upward influence	Low →	**High**	Increased distortion because employees send more favorable information and withhold useful information.
2. Supervisor's power	Low →	**High**	Increased distortion because employees screen out information detrimental to their welfare.
3. Subordinate's aspiration for upward mobility	Low →	**High**	Less accuracy because employees tend to pass along information that helps their cause.
4. Subordinate's trust in the supervisor	**Low** →	High	Considerable distortion because employees do not pass up all information they receive.

SOURCE: Adapted in part from J Fulk and S Mani, "Distortion of Communication in Hierarchical Relationships," in *Communication Yearbook 9,* ed M L McLaughlin (Beverly Hills, CA: Sage Publications, 1986).

FIGURE 12–2
Sources of Distortion in Upward Communication

upward communication. The company implemented a "lunch with the boss" program in which groups of employees meet with the hotel manager Wolfgang Triebnig for lunch in the hotel's five-star restaurant. "The lunch discussion is freewheeling, with no agenda. Triebnig asks participants to introduce themselves and to share any comments or concerns. . . . 'We've learned to let the employees lead,' [Mandy] Wulfe [HR director] says. 'Some come prepared with questions, some come because they were invited and prefer to listen quietly, and some are moved to ask questions because of what they are hearing.'"[11]

4. Managers can establish performance goals that encourage employees to focus on problems rather than personalities.
5. Distortion can be limited by encouraging dialogue between those with opposing viewpoints.

Interpersonal Communication

The quality of interpersonal communication within an organization is very important. People with good communication skills helped groups to make more innovative decisions and were promoted more frequently than individuals with less developed abilities.[12] Although there is no universally accepted definition of **communication competence,** it is a performance-based index of an individual's abilities to effectively use communication behaviors in a given context.[13] Business etiquette, for example, is one component of communication competence. At this time we would like you to complete the business etiquette test in the Hands-On Exercise on page 301. How did you score?

communication competence
Ability to effectively use communication behaviors in a given context.

Communication competence is determined by three components: communication abilities and traits, situational factors, and the individuals involved in the interaction (see Figure 12–3). Cross-cultural awareness, for instance, is an important communication ability/trait. Individuals involved in an interaction also affect communication

FIGURE 12–3 Communication Competence Affects Upward Mobility

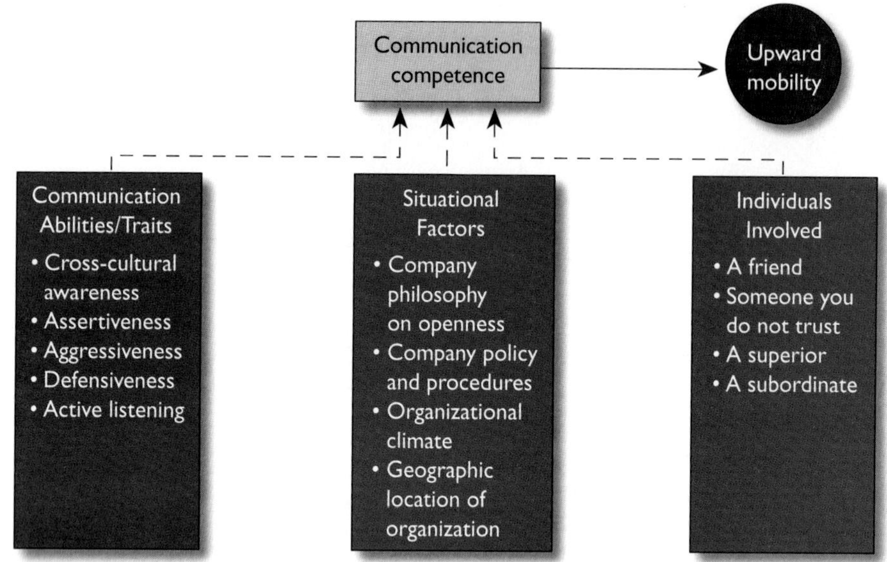

competence. People are likely to withhold information and react emotionally or defensively when interacting with someone they dislike or do not trust. You can improve your communication competence through five communication styles/abilities/traits under your control: assertiveness, aggressiveness, nonassertiveness, nonverbal communication, and active listening. We conclude this section by discussing gender differences in communication.

Assertiveness, Aggressiveness, and Nonassertiveness

The saying "You can attract more flies with honey than with vinegar" captures the difference between using an assertive communication style and an aggressive style. Research studies indicate that assertiveness is more effective than aggressiveness in both work-related and consumer contexts.[15] An **assertive style** is expressive and self-enhancing and is based on the "ethical notion that it is not right or good to violate our own or others' basic human rights, such as the right to self-expression or the right to be treated with dignity and respect."[16] In contrast, an **aggressive style** is expressive and self-enhancing and strives to take unfair advantage of others. A **nonassertive style** is characterized by timid and self-denying behavior. Nonassertiveness is ineffective because it gives the other person an unfair advantage.

assertive style
Expressive and self-enhancing, but does not take advantage of others.

aggressive style
Expressive and self-enhancing, but takes unfair advantage of others.

nonassertive style
Timid and self-denying behavior.

Managers may improve their communication competence by trying to be more assertive and less aggressive or nonassertive. This can be achieved by using the appropriate nonverbal and verbal behaviors listed in Table 12–1. For instance, managers should attempt to use the nonverbal behaviors of good eye contact, a strong, steady, and audible voice, and selective interruptions. They should avoid nonverbal behaviors such as glaring or little eye contact, threatening gestures, slumped posture, and a weak or whiny voice. Appropriate verbal behaviors include direct and unambiguous language and

HANDS-ON EXERCISE

What Is Your Business Etiquette?

INSTRUCTIONS: Business etiquette is one component of communication competence. Test your business etiquette by answering the following questions. After circling your response for each item, calculate your score by reviewing the correct answers listed in note 14 in the Endnotes section of the book. Next, use the norms at the end of the test to interpret your results.

1. The following is an example of a proper introduction: "Ms Boss, I'd like you to meet our client, Mr Smith."
True False

2. If someone forgets to introduce you, you shouldn't introduce yourself you should just let the conversation continue.
True False

3. If you forget someone's name, you should keep talking and hope no one will notice. This way you don't embarrass yourself or the person you are talking to.
True False

4. When shaking hands, a man should wait for a woman to extend her hand.
True False

5. Who goes through a revolving door first?
a. Host *b.* Visitor

6. It is all right to hold private conversations, either in person or on a cell phone in office bathrooms, elevators, and other public spaces.
True False

7. When two US businesspeople are talking to one another, the space between them should be approximately
a. 1.5 feet *b.* 3 feet *c.* 7 feet

8. Business casual attire requires socks for men and hose for women.
True False

9. To signal that you do not want a glass of wine, you should turn your wine glass upside down.
True False

10. If a call is disconnected, it's the caller's responsibility to redial.
True False

11. When using a speakerphone, you should tell the caller if there is anyone else in the room.
True False

12. You should change your voicemail message if you are going to be out of the office.
True False

ARBITRARY NORMS

Low business etiquette (0–4 correct): Consider buying an etiquette book or hiring a coach to help you polish your professional image.
Moderate business etiquette (5–8 correct): Look for a role model or mentor, and look for ways you can improve your business etiquette.
High business etiquette (9–12 correct): Good for you. You should continue to practice good etiquette and look for ways to maintain your professional image.

SOURCE: This test was adapted from material contained in M Brody, "Test Your Etiquette," *Training & Development*, February 2002, pp 64–66.

TABLE 12–1 Communication Styles

Communication Style	Description	Nonverbal Behavior Pattern	Verbal Behavior Pattern
Assertive	Pushing hard without attacking; permits others to influence outcome; expressive and self-enhancing without intruding on others	Good eye contact Comfortable but firm posture Strong, steady, and audible voice Facial expressions matched to message Appropriately serious tone Selective interruptions to ensure understanding	Direct and unambiguous language No attributions or evaluations of others' behavior Use of "I" statements and cooperative "we" statements
Aggressive	Taking advantage of others; expressive and self-enhancing at others' expense	Glaring eye contact Moving or leaning too close Threatening gestures (pointed finger; clenched fist) Loud voice Frequent interruptions	Swear words and abusive language Attributions and evaluations of others' behavior Sexist or racist terms Explicit threats or put-downs
Nonassertive	Encouraging others to take advantage of us; inhibited; self-denying	Little eye contact Downward glances Slumped posture Constantly shifting weight Wringing hands Weak or whiny voice	Qualifiers ("maybe"; "kind of") Fillers ("uh," "you know," "well") Negaters ("It's not really that important"; "I'm not sure")

SOURCE: Adapted in part from J A Waters, "Managerial Assertiveness," *Business Horizons*, September–October 1982, pp 24–29.

the use of "I" messages instead of "you" statements. For example, when you say, "Mike, I was disappointed with your report because it contained typographical errors," rather than "Mike, your report was poorly done," you reduce defensiveness. "I" statements describe your feelings about someone's performance or behavior instead of laying blame on the person.

Sources of Nonverbal Communication

nonverbal communication
Messages sent outside of the written or spoken word.

Nonverbal communication is "Any message, sent or received independent of the written or spoken word . . . [It] includes such factors as use of time and space, distance between persons when conversing, use of color, dress, walking behavior, standing, positioning, seating arrangement, office locations and furnishings."[17]

Experts estimate that 90% of every conversation is nonverbal.[18] Because of the prevalence of nonverbal communication and its significant effect on organizational behavior (including, but not limited to, perceptions of others, hiring decisions, work attitudes, turnover, and the acceptance of one's ideas in a presentation), it is important that managers become consciously aware of the sources of nonverbal communication.

Body Movements and Gestures Body movements, such as leaning forward or backward, and gestures, such as pointing, provide additional nonverbal information that can either enhance or detract from the communication process. Open body positions, such as leaning backward, communicate *immediacy,* a term used to represent openness, warmth, closeness, and availability for communication. *Defensiveness* is communicated by gestures such as folding arms, crossing hands, and crossing one's legs. Although it is both easy and fun to interpret body movements and gestures, it is important to remember that body-language analysis is subjective, easily misinterpreted, and highly dependent on the context and cross-cultural differences.[19] Thus, managers need to be careful when trying to interpret body movements. Inaccurate interpretations can create additional "noise" in the communication process.

Touch Touching is another powerful nonverbal cue. People tend to touch those they like. A meta-analysis of gender differences in touching indicated that women do more touching during conversations than men.[20] Touching conveys an impression of warmth and caring and can be used to create a personal bond between people. Be careful about touching people from diverse cultures, however, as norms for touching vary significantly around the world.[21]

Facial Expressions Facial expressions convey a wealth of information. Smiling, for instance, typically represents warmth, happiness, or friendship, whereas frowning conveys dissatisfaction or anger. Do you think these interpretations apply to different cross-cultural groups? A summary of relevant research revealed that the association between facial expressions and emotions varies across cultures.[22] A smile, for example, does not convey the same emotion in different countries. Therefore, managers need to be careful in interpreting facial expressions among diverse groups of employees.

Eye Contact Eye contact is a strong nonverbal cue that varies across cultures. Westerners are taught at an early age to look at their parents when spoken to. In contrast, Asians are taught to avoid eye contact with a parent or superior in order to show obedience and subservience.[23] Once again, managers should be sensitive to different orientations toward maintaining eye contact with diverse employees.

Practical Tips It is important to have good nonverbal communication skills in light of the fact that they are related to the development of positive interpersonal relationships. The Skills & Best Practices offers insights into improving your nonverbal communication skills. Practice these tips by turning the sound

SKILLS & BEST PRACTICES

Advice to Improve Nonverbal Communication Skills

Positive nonverbal actions include the following:

- Maintain eye contact.
- Nod your head to convey that you are listening or that you agree.
- Smile and show interest.
- Lean forward to show the speaker you are interested.
- Use a tone of voice that matches your message.

Negative nonverbal behaviors include the following:

- Avoiding eye contact and looking away from the speaker.
- Closing your eyes or tensing your facial muscles.
- Excessive yawning.
- Using body language that conveys indecisiveness or lack of confidence (e.g., slumped shoulders, head down, flat tones, inaudible voice).
- Speaking too fast or too slow.

off while watching television and then trying to interpret emotions and interactions. Honest feedback from your friends about your nonverbal communication style also may help.

Active Listening

Some communication experts contend that listening is the keystone communication skill for employees involved in sales, customer service, or management. In support of this conclusion, listening effectiveness was positively associated with success in sales and obtaining managerial promotions.[24]

Listening involves much more than hearing a message. Hearing is merely the physical component of listening. **Listening** is the process of *actively* decoding and interpreting verbal messages. Listening requires cognitive attention and information processing; hearing does not. With these distinctions in mind, we examine listening styles and offer some practical advice for becoming a more effective listener.

listening
Actively decoding and interpreting verbal messages.

Listening Styles Communication experts believe that people listen with a preferred listening style. While people may lean toward one dominant listening style, we tend to use a combination of two or three. There are five dominant listening styles: appreciative, empathetic, comprehensive, discerning, and evaluative.[25] Let us consider each style.

An *appreciative* listener listens in a relaxed manner, preferring to listen for pleasure, entertainment, or inspiration. He or she tends to tune out speakers who provide no amusement or humor in their communications. *Empathetic* listeners interpret messages by focusing on the emotions and body language being displayed by the speaker as well as the presentation media. They also tend to listen without judging. A *comprehensive* listener makes sense of a message by first organizing specific thoughts and actions and then integrates this information by focusing on relationships among ideas. These listeners prefer logical presentations without interruptions. *Discerning* listeners attempt to understand the main message and determine important points. They like to take notes and prefer logical presentations. Finally, *evaluative* listeners listen analytically and continually formulate arguments and challenges to what is being said. They tend to accept or reject messages based on personal beliefs, ask a lot of questions, and can become interruptive.

You can improve your listening skills by first becoming aware of the effectiveness of the different listening styles you use in various situations. This awareness can then help you to modify your style to fit a specific situation. For example, if you are listening to a presidential debate, you may want to focus on using a comprehensive and discerning style. In contrast, an evaluative style may be more appropriate if you are listening to a sales presentation.

Becoming a More Effective Listener Effective listening is a learned skill that requires effort and motivation. That's right, it takes energy and desire to really listen to others. Unfortunately, it may seem like there are no rewards for listening, but there are negative consequences when we don't. Think of a time, for example, when someone did not pay attention to you by looking at his or her watch or doing some other activity such as typing on a keyboard. How did you feel? You may have felt put down, unimportant, or offended. In turn, such feelings can erode the quality of interpersonal relationships as well as fuel job dissatisfaction, lower productivity, and poor

TABLE 12–2 The Keys to Effective Listening

Keys to Effective Listening	The Bad Listener	The Good Listener
1. Capitalize on thought speed	Tends to daydream	Stays with the speaker, mentally summarizes the speaker, weighs evidence, and listens between the lines
2. Listen for ideas	Listens for facts	Listens for central or overall ideas
3. Find an area of interest	Tunes out dry speakers or subjects	Listens for any useful information
4. Judge content, not delivery	Tunes out dry or monotone speakers	Assesses content by listening to entire message before making judgments
5. Hold your fire	Gets too emotional or worked up by something said by the speaker and enters into an argument	Withholds judgment until comprehension is complete
6. Work at listening	Does not expend energy on listening	Gives the speaker full attention
7. Resist distractions	Is easily distracted	Fights distractions and concentrates on the speaker
8. Hear what is said	Shuts out or denies unfavorable information	Listens to both favorable and unfavorable information
9. Challenge yourself	Resists listening to presentations of difficult subject matter	Treats complex presentations as exercise for the mind
10. Use handouts, overheads, or other visual aids	Does not take notes or pay attention to visual aids	Takes notes as required and uses visual aids to enhance understanding of the presentation

SOURCES: Derived from N Skinner, "Communication Skills," *Selling Power,* July/August 1999, pp 32–34; and G Manning, K Curtis, and S McMillen, *Building the Human Side of Work Community* (Cincinnati, OH: Thomson Executive Press, 1996), pp 127–54.

customer service. Listening is an important skill that can be improved by avoiding the 10 habits of bad listeners while cultivating the 10 good listening habits (see Table 12–2).[26] Stephen Covey, author of the bestseller *The 7 Habits of Highly Effective People,* offers another good piece of advice about becoming a more effective listener. He concludes that we should "seek first to understand, then to be understood."[27] In conclusion, it takes awareness, effort, and practice to improve one's listening comprehension. Listening is not a skill that will improve on its own. Is anyone listening?

Women and Men Communicate Differently

Women and men have communicated differently since the dawn of time. Gender-based differences in communication are partly caused by linguistic styles commonly used by women and men. Deborah Tannen, a communication expert, defines **linguistic style** as follows:

linguistic style
A person's typical speaking pattern.

> Linguistic style refers to a person's characteristic speaking pattern. It includes such features as directness or indirectness, pacing and pausing,

> word choice, and the use of such elements as jokes, figures of speech, stories, questions, and apologies. In other words, linguistic style is a set of culturally learned signals by which we not only communicate what we mean but also interpret others' meaning and evaluate one another as people.[28]

Linguistic style not only helps explain communication differences between women and men, but it also influences our perceptions of others' confidence, competence, and abilities. Increased awareness of linguistic styles can thus improve communication accuracy and your communication competence. This section strives to increase your understanding of interpersonal communication between women and men by discussing alternative explanations for differences in linguistic styles, various communication differences between women and men, and recommendations for improving communication between the sexes.

Why Linguistic Styles Vary between Women and Men Although researchers do not completely agree on the cause of communication differences between women and men, there are two competing explanations that involve the well-worn debate between *nature* and *nurture.* Some researchers believe that interpersonal differences between women and men are due to inherited biological differences between the sexes. More specifically, this perspective, which also is called the "Darwinian perspective" or "evolutionary psychology," attributes gender differences in communication to drives, needs, and conflicts associated with reproductive strategies used by women and men. For example, proponents would say that males communicate more aggressively, interrupt others more than women, and hide their emotions because they have an inherent desire to possess features attractive to females in order to compete with other males for purposes of mate selection. Although males are certainly not competing for mate selection during a business meeting, evolutionary psychologists propose that men cannot turn off the biologically based determinants of their behavior.[29]

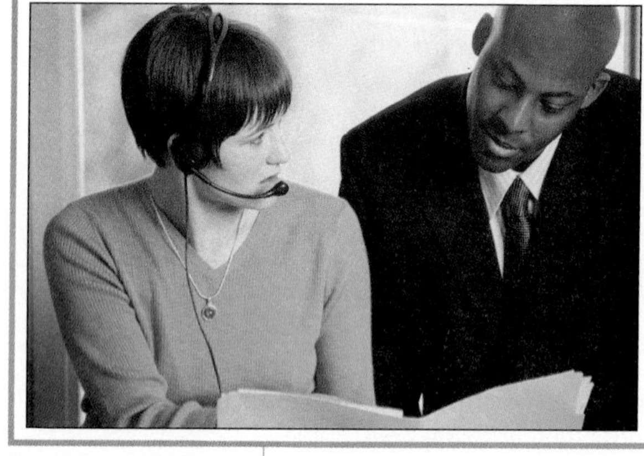

Research reveals that men and women possess different communication styles. For example, men are more boastful about their accomplishments whereas women are more modest. How might differences in male and female communication patterns affect how men and women are perceived during group problem-solving meetings?

In contrast, social role theory is based on the idea that females and males learn ways of speaking as children growing up. Research shows that girls learn conversational skills and habits that focus on rapport and relationships, whereas boys learn skills and habits that focus on status and hierarchies. Accordingly, women come to view communication as a network of connections in which conversations are negotiations for closeness. This orientation leads women to seek and give confirmation and support more so than men. Men, on the other hand, see conversations as negotiations in which people try to achieve and maintain the upper hand. It thus is important for males to protect themselves from others' attempts to put them down or push them around. This perspective increases a male's need to maintain independence and avoid failure.[30]

Gender Differences in Communication Research demonstrates that women and men communicate differently in a number of ways.[31] Women, for example, are more likely to share credit for success, to ask questions for clarification, to tactfully give feedback by mitigating criticism with praise, and to indirectly tell others what to do. In contrast, men are more likely to boast about themselves, to bluntly give feedback, and to withhold compliments, and are less likely to ask questions and to admit fault or weaknesses.

There are two important issues to keep in mind about these trends. First, the trends identified cannot be generalized to include all women and men. Some men are less likely to boast about their achievements while some women are less likely to share the credit. The point is that there are always exceptions to the rule. Second, your linguistic style influences perceptions about your confidence, competence, and authority. These judgments may, in turn, affect your future job assignments and subsequent promotability.

Improving Communications between the Sexes Deborah Tannen recommends that everyone needs to become aware of how linguistic styles work and how they influence our perceptions and judgments. She believes that knowledge of linguistic styles helps to ensure that people with valuable insights or ideas get heard. Consider how gender-based linguistic differences affect who gets heard at a meeting:

> Those who are comfortable speaking up in groups, who need little or no silence before raising their hands, or who speak out easily without waiting to be recognized are far more likely to get heard at meetings. Those who refrain from talking until it's clear that the previous speaker is finished, who wait to be recognized, and who are inclined to link their comments to those of others will do fine at a meeting where everyone else is following the same rules but will have a hard time getting heard in a meeting with people whose styles are more like the first pattern. Given the socialization typical of boys and girls, men are more likely to have learned the first style and women the second, making meetings more congenial for men than for women.[32]

Knowledge of these linguistic differences can assist managers in devising methods to ensure that everyone's ideas are heard and given fair credit both in and out of meetings. Furthermore, it is useful to consider the organizational strengths and limitations of your linguistic style. You may want to consider modifying a linguistic characteristic that is a detriment to perceptions of your confidence, competence, and authority. In conclusion, communication between the sexes can be improved by remembering that women and men have different ways of saying the same thing.

Communication in the Computerized Information Age

Organizations are increasingly using information technology as a lever to improve productivity and customer and employee satisfaction. In turn, communication patterns at work are radically changing. Consider the use of high-speed wireless Internet access, known as Wi-Fi, at BJ's Wholesale Club, which operates 141 warehouse stores in the United States:

> The stores measure more than 100,000 square feet each, and they used to have only a few wired telephones, usually in the front office. Every time a manager

> got a phone call from a customer, a supplier, or the boss at headquarters, he or she would have to hustle across the store to get on the line. Voiceover Wi-Fi, which the company began implementing three years ago, has changed that. Each store has about four Symbol handsets, enough for every manager on duty (who passes the phone to the manager on the next shift). The time savings have been considerable.[33]

The use of Wi-Fi has helped BJ's Wholesale Club to increase productivity and customer satisfaction while decreasing costs.

While you may not own a Wi-Fi, the computerized information age is radically changing communication patterns in both our personal and work lives. For example, a national survey indicated that 58% of all Americans were connected to the Internet in 2003.[34] Interestingly, some people use the Internet with such frequency that they become dependent on it. For example, a recent study of 1,300 students at eight colleges revealed that nearly 10% were dependent on the Internet and that their Internet usage affected their academics, ability to meet new people, and sleep patterns.[35] This section explores five key components of information technology that influence communication patterns and management within a computerized workplace: Internet/intranet/extranet, electronic mail, videoconferencing, collaborative computing, and telecommuting.

Internet/Intranet/Extranet

Internet
A global network of computer networks.

intranet
An organization's private Internet.

extranet
Connects internal employees with selected customers, suppliers, and strategic partners.

The Internet, or more simply "the Net," is more than a computer network. It is a network of computer networks. The **Internet** is a global network of independently operating, but interconnected computers. The Internet connects everything from supercomputers, to large mainframes contained in businesses, government, and universities, to the personal computers in our homes and offices. An **intranet** is nothing more than an organization's private Internet. Intranets also have *firewalls* that block outside Internet users from accessing internal information. This is done to protect the privacy and confidentiality of company documents. More than half of companies with more than 500 employees have corporate intranets according to Information Data Corporation.[36] In contrast to the internal focus of an intranet, an **extranet** is an extended intranet in that it connects internal employees with selected customers, suppliers, and other strategic partners. Ford Motor Company, for instance, has an extranet that connects its dealers worldwide. Ford's extranet was set up to help support the sales and servicing of cars and to enhance customer satisfaction.

The primary benefit of the Internet, intranets, and extranets is that they can enhance the ability of employees to find, create, manage, and distribute information. The effectiveness of these systems, however, depends on how organizations set up and manage their intranet/extranet and how employees use the acquired information because information by itself cannot solve or do anything; information is knowledge or a thing. For example, communication effectiveness actually can decrease if a corporate intranet becomes a dumping ground of unorganized information. In this case, employees will find themselves flailing in a sea of information. To date, however, no rigorous research studies have been conducted that directly demonstrate productivity increases from using the Internet, intranets, or extranets. But there are case studies that reveal other organizational benefits. For example, IBM saved $1 million in costs in 2000 by asking 140,000 employees located in Armonk, New York, to enroll for employee benefits on the company's intranet: 80% enrolled electronically.[37] United Parcel Service also estimated that productivity increased 35% after the implementation of Wi-Fi.[38]

In contrast to these positive case studies, a survey conducted by Vault.com revealed that one out of every eight workers spent more than two hours a day corresponding via e-mail, shopping on the Web, or searching for information related to personal interests. All told, International Data Corp. estimated personal use of the Internet during work hours contributes to a 30 to 40% decrease in productivity.[39] Organizations are taking these statistics to heart and are attempting to root out cyberslackers by tracking employee behavior with electronic monitoring. A recent survey of more than 700 companies by the Society for Human Resource Management revealed that almost 75% of those companies monitored their employees' use of the Internet and checked their e-mail.[40] Only the future will tell whether the Internet is more useful as a marketing/sales tool, a device to conduct personal transactions such as banking or ordering movies, or a management vehicle that enhances employee motivation and productivity.

Electronic Mail

Electronic mail or e-mail uses the Internet/intranet to send computer-generated text and documents between people. The use of e-mail is on the rise throughout the world. For example, surveys reveal that US employees receive somewhere between 20 to 30 e-mail messages per day.[41] E-mail is becoming a major communication medium because of four key benefits:[42]

electronic mail

Uses the Internet/intranet to send computer-generated text and documents.

1. E-mail reduces the cost of distributing information to a large number of employees.
2. E-mail is a tool for increasing teamwork. It enables employees to quickly send messages to colleagues on the next floor, in another building, or in another country.
3. E-mail reduces the costs and time associated with print duplication and paper distribution. One management expert estimated that these savings can total $9,000 a year per employee.[43]
4. E-mail fosters flexibility. This is particularly true for employees with a portable computer because they can log onto e-mail whenever and wherever they want.

In spite of these positive benefits, there are four key drawbacks to consider. First, sending and receiving e-mail can lead to a lot of wasted time and effort, or it can distract employees from completing critical job duties. For example, a national survey of US workers indicated that between 33% and 50% of their e-mail messages were unimportant.[44] Second, the system itself may be cumbersome and ineffective. Consider what happened at AOL Time Warner when the company adopted a new e-mail system.

> In a humbling reversal, AOL Time Warner Inc. is retreating from a top-level directive that required the divisions of the old Time Warner to convert to an

SKILLS & BEST PRACTICES

Managing Your E-Mail

1. Scan first, read second.
2. Learn to delete without reading. Over time, you will get a sense for low-value messages and you should be able to delete messages from unrecognizable addresses.
3. Group messages by topic. Read the first message in a series and then go to the most recent. This enables you to save time by skipping e-mails between the first and last message.
4. Once steps 1–3 are complete, prioritize your inbox and respond in order of a message's importance.
5. Stop the madness by asking people to stop sending you unimportant messages.
6. Rather than continuing to engage in ping-pong e-mailing, determine if a phone call can get to the heart of the matter.
7. Get off cc lists. Ask to be removed from distribution lists.
8. Only respond to a message when it is absolutely required.
9. Keep messages brief and clear. Use clear subject headings and state the purpose of your e-mail in the first sentence or paragraph.
10. Avoid the "reply to all" feature.
11. If the message concerns a volatile or critical matter, e-mail is probably the wrong medium to use. Consider using the phone.

SOURCE: These recommendations were taken from C Cavanagh, *Managing Your E-Mail: Thinking Outside the Inbox*.

e-mail system based on AOL software and run by America Online's giant public server computers in Virginia. . . .

Instead, management got months of complaints from both senior and junior executives in the divisions involved, who said the e-mail system, initially designed for consumers, wasn't appropriate for business use. Among the problems cited: The e-mail software frequently crashed, staffers weren't able to send messages with large attachments, they were often kicked offline without warning, and if they tried to send messages to large groups of users they were labeled as spammers and locked out of the system. Sometimes, e-mails were just plain lost in the AOL etherworld and never found. And if there was an out-of-office reply function, most people couldn't find it.[45]

Information overload is the third problem associated with the increased use of e-mail: Skills & Best Practices contains suggestions for managing e-mail overload. People tend to send more messages to others, and there is a lot of "spamming" going on: sending junk mail, bad jokes, chain letters, or irrelevant memos (e.g., the "cc" of e-mail). A recent study by Nucleus documented the extent of this problem. Results revealed that companies are expected to receive about 7,500 spam messages per employee in 2004, up from 3,500 per employee in 2003. Nucleus estimated that this increased spam results in a direct cost of $1,934 per employee and an additional average loss in productivity of 3.1%.[46]

Finally, preliminary evidence suggests that people are using electronic mail to communicate when they should be using other media. This practice can result in reduced communication effectiveness. A four-year study of communication patterns within a university demonstrated that the increased use of electronic mail was associated with decreased face-to-face interactions and with a drop in the overall amount of organizational communication. Employees also expressed a feeling of being less connected and less cohesive as a department as the amount of e-mails increased.[47] This interpersonal "disconnection" may be caused by the trend of replacing everyday face-to-face interactions with electronic messages. It is important to remember that employees' social needs are satisfied through the many different interpersonal interactions that occur at work.

There are three additional issues to consider when using e-mail: (1) E-mail only works when the party you desire to communicate with also uses it. E-mail may not be a viable communication medium in all cases. (2) The speed of getting a response to an e-mail message is dependent on how frequently the receiver examines his or her messages. It is important to consider this issue when picking a communication medium. (3) Many companies do not have policies for using e-mail, which can lead to misuse and potential legal liability. For instance, four female employees working at Chevron filed a suit claiming that they were sexually harassed through e-mail. The company settled for $2.2 million, plus legal fees and court costs. Do not assume that your e-mail messages are private and confidential. Organizations are advised to develop policies regarding the use of e-mail.[48]

"You have one phone message and twelve zillion kabillion infinitillion emails."

Videoconferencing

Videoconferencing, also known as teleconferencing, uses video and audio links along with computers to enable people in different locations to see, hear, and talk with one another. This enables people from many locations to conduct a meeting without having to travel. Consider the following applications of videoconferencing:

> At Harken Energy Corp., an oil and gas exploration company in Houston, engineers use video capabilities to share seismic graphs and other geological displays and data from offices in Latin America. The Department of Labor uses videoconferencing to impart basic computer, financial, and résumé-writing skills to citizens. The potential uses of the technology seem even brighter, particularly in marketing and community outreach efforts. . . . Video also is a critical component of eGetgoing's virtual therapy offering. "Treatment requires the participants to see the reaction of the counselor in order to create an emotional bond," says [Barry] Karlin, who notes that the one-way streaming video eGetgoing uses contains the benefit of maintaining anonymity among the 10 patients in each single-group session.[49]

Videoconferencing thus can significantly reduce an organization's travel expenses. Many organizations set up special videoconferencing rooms or booths with specially equipped television cameras. More recent equipment enables people to attach small cameras and microphones to their desks or computer monitors. This enables employees to conduct long-distance meetings and training classes without leaving their office or cubicle.

Collaborative Computing

Collaborative computing entails using state-of-the-art computer software and hardware to help people work better together. Collaborative systems enable people to share information without the constraints of time and space. This is accomplished by utilizing computer networks to link people across a room or across the globe. Collaborative applications include messaging and e-mail systems, calendar management, videoconferencing,

collaborative computing

Using computer software and hardware to help people work better together.

A BlackBerry represents a technological advancement because one handheld device offers a tri-band phone, e-mail, Internet access, and text messaging. There is no question that a BlackBerry gives us more opportunity to communicate with others across different media 24 hours a day. On the negative side, more and more people use BlackBerrys during meetings to communicate with others outside the meeting. Does this behavior impact the quality of a meeting?

computer teleconferencing, electronic whiteboards, and the type of computer-aided decision-making systems discussed in Chapter 9.

Organizations that use full-fledged collaborative systems have the ability to create virtual teams or to operate as a virtual organization: Virtual organizations are discussed in Chapter 15. You may recall from Chapter 10 that a virtual team represents a physically dispersed task group that conducts its business by using the types of information technology currently being discussed. Specifically, virtual teams tend to use Internet/intranet systems, collaborative software systems, and videoconferencing systems. These real-time systems enable people to communicate with anyone at anytime.

It is important to keep in mind that modern-day information technology only enables people to interact virtually; it doesn't guarantee effective communication. Interestingly, there are a whole host of unique communication problems associated with using the information technology needed to operate virtually.[50]

Telecommuting

Telecommuting is a work practice in which an employee does part of his or her job in a remote location using a variety of information technologies. Examples include "wireless e-mail from Starbucks, videoconferencing from Kinko's and home, and even telework centers in remote villages in India, served by wireless computer links."[51] As you can see from these examples, telecommuting involves receiving and sending work from a remote location via some form of information technology such as wireless devices, fax, or a home computer that is linked via modem to an office computer. Telecommuting is more common for jobs involving computer work, writing, and phone work that require concentration and limited interruptions. The International Telework Association and Council estimated that 23.5 million US workers telecommuted in 2003, and an additional 23.4 million self-employed individuals telecommuted.[52] Potential benefits of telecommuting include:

1. *Reduction of capital costs.* Sun Microsystems reported saving $50 million in 2002 by letting employees work from home.
2. *Increased flexibility and autonomy for workers.*
3. *Competitive edge in recruitment.* Arthur Andersen, Merrill Lynch, and Cisco used telecommuting to increase their ability to keep and attract qualified personnel.
4. *Increased job satisfaction and lower turnover.* Employees like telecommuting because it helps resolve work–family conflicts. AT&T's telecommuters had less absenteeism than traditional employees.

5. *Increased productivity.* Telecommuting resulted in productivity increases of 25% and 35% for FourGen Software and Continental Traffic Services, respectively.
6. *Tapping nontraditional labor pools* (such as prison inmates and homebound disabled persons).[53]

telecommuting

Doing work that is generally performed in the office away from the office using different information technologies.

Although telecommuting represents an attempt to accommodate employee needs and desires, it requires adjustments and is not for everybody. Many people thoroughly enjoy the social camaraderie that exists within an office setting. These individuals probably would not like to telecommute. Others lack the self-motivation needed to work at home. Finally, organizations must be careful to implement telecommuting in a nondiscriminatory manner. Organizations can easily and unknowingly violate one of several antidiscrimination laws.[54]

Barriers to Effective Communication

Communication noise is a barrier to effective communication because it interferes with the accurate transmission and reception of a message. Management awareness of these barriers is a good starting point to improve the communication process. There are four key barriers to effective communication: (1) process barriers, (2) personal barriers, (3) physical barriers, and (4) semantic barriers.

Process Barriers

Every element of the perceptual model of communication shown in Figure 12–1 is a potential process barrier. Consider the following examples:

1. *Sender barrier.* A customer gets incorrect information from a customer service agent because he or she was recently hired and lacks experience.
2. *Encoding barrier.* An employee for whom English is a second language has difficulty explaining why a delivery was late.
3. *Message barrier.* An employee misses a meeting for which he or she never received a confirmation memo.
4. *Medium barrier.* A salesperson gives up trying to make a sales call when the potential customer fails to return three previous phone calls.
5. *Decoding barrier.* An employee does not know how to respond to a manager's request to stop exhibiting "passive aggressive" behavior.
6. *Receiver barrier.* A student who is talking to his or her friend during a lecture asks the professor the same question that was just answered.
7. *Feedback barrier.* The nonverbal head nodding of an interviewer leads an interviewee to think that he or she is doing a great job answering questions.

Barriers in any of these process elements can distort the transfer of meaning. Reducing these barriers is essential but difficult given the current diversity of the workforce.

Personal Barriers

There are many personal barriers to communication. We highlight eight of the more common ones. The first is our *ability to effectively communicate.* As highlighted throughout this chapter, people possess varying levels of communication skills. The *way people process and interpret information* is a second barrier. Chapter 4 highlighted the fact that people use different frames of reference and experiences to interpret the world around them. We also learned that people selectively attend to various stimuli. All told, these differences affect both what we say and what we think we hear. Third, the *level of interpersonal trust between people* can either be a barrier or enabler of effective communication. Communication is more likely to be distorted when people do not trust each other. *Stereotypes and prejudices* are a fourth barrier. They can powerfully distort what we perceive about others. Our *egos* are a fifth barrier. Egos can cause political battles, turf wars, and pursuit of power, credit, and resources. Egos influence how people treat each other as well as our receptiveness to being influenced by others. *Poor listening skills* are a sixth barrier.[55]

Carl Rogers, a renowned psychologist, identified the seventh and eighth barriers that interfere with interpersonal communication.[56] The seventh barrier is a *natural tendency to evaluate or judge a sender's message.* To highlight the natural tendency to evaluate, consider how you might respond to the statement "I like the book you are reading." What would you say? Your likely response is to approve or disapprove the statement. You may say, "I agree," or alternatively, "I disagree, the book is boring." The point is that we all tend to evaluate messages from our own point of view or frame of reference. The tendency to evaluate messages is greatest when one has strong feelings or emotions about the issue being discussed. An *inability to listen with understanding* is the eighth personal barrier to effective communication. Listening with understanding occurs when a receiver can "see the expressed idea and attitude from the other person's point of view, to sense how it feels to him, to achieve his frame of reference in regard to the thing he is talking about."[57] Listening with understanding reduces defensiveness and improves accuracy in perceiving a message.

Physical Barriers

The distance between employees can interfere with effective communication. It is hard to understand someone who is speaking to you from 20 yards away. Time zone differences between the East and West Coasts also represent physical barriers. Work and office noise are additional barriers. The quality of telephone lines or crashed computers represent physical barriers that impact our ability to communicate with information technology.

In spite of the general acceptance of physical barriers, they can be reduced. For example, employees on the East Coast can agree to call their West Coast peers prior to leaving for lunch. Distracting or inhibiting walls also can be torn down. It is important that managers attempt to manage this barrier by choosing a medium that optimally reduces the physical barrier at hand.

Semantic Barriers

Semantics is the study of words. Semantic barriers show up as encoding and decoding errors because these phases of communication involve transmitting and receiving words and symbols. Consider the semantic barriers experienced by Indians working in India's call centers as they try to communicate with English-speaking customers:

> According to Sabira Merchant, speech-voice consultant, "Indians have excellent control over written English, yet when it comes to pronunciation, we do not always sound right. The problem is while Americans think in English, we think in our mother tongue and translate it while speaking. As a nation we do speak good English. That is why most Indians score easily over people of other nationalities. But it will still take time for Indians to speak with a polished accent and fluency."[58]

Semantic barriers also are related to the choice of words we use when communicating. Consider the following statement: Crime is ubiquitous.

Do you understand this message? Even if you do, would it not be simpler to say that "crime is all around us" or "crime is everywhere"? Choosing our words more carefully is the easiest way to reduce semantic barriers. This barrier can also be decreased by attentiveness to mixed messages and cultural diversity. Mixed messages occur when a person's words imply one message while his or her actions or nonverbal cues suggest something different. Obviously, understanding is enhanced when a person's actions and nonverbal cues match the verbal message.

key terms

aggressive style 300
assertive style 300
collaborative computing 311
communication 295
communication competence 299
communication distortion 298
electronic mail 309
extranet 308
Internet 308
intranet 308
linguistic style 305
listening 304
noise 298
nonassertive style 300
nonverbal communication 302
telecommuting 312

chapter summary

- *Describe the perceptual process model of communication.* Communication is a process of consecutively linked elements. This model of communication depicts receivers as information processors who create the meaning of messages in their own mind. Because receivers' interpretations of messages often differ from those intended by senders, miscommunication is a common occurrence.
- *Demonstrate your familiarity with four antecedents of communication distortion between managers and employees.* Communication distortion is a common problem that consists of modifying the content of a message. Employees distort upward communication when their supervisor has high upward influence and/or power. Distortion also increases when employees aspire to move upward and when they do not trust their supervisor.
- *Contrast the communication styles of assertiveness, aggressiveness, and nonassertiveness.* An assertive style is expressive and self-enhancing but does not violate others' basic human rights. In contrast, an aggressive style is expressive and self-enhancing but takes unfair advantage of others. A nonassertive style is characterized by timid and self-denying behavior. An assertive communication

style is more effective than either an aggressive or nonassertive style.

- *Discuss the primary sources of nonverbal communication and 10 keys to effective listening.* There are several identifiable sources of nonverbal communication effectiveness. Body movements and gestures, touch, facial expressions, and eye contact are important nonverbal cues. The interpretation of these nonverbal cues significantly varies across cultures. Good listeners use the following 10 listening habits: (a) capitalize on thought speed by staying with the speaker and listening between the lines, (b) listen for ideas rather than facts, (c) identify areas of interest between the speaker and listener, (d) judge content and not delivery, (e) do not judge until the speaker has completed his or her message, (f) put energy and effort into listening, (g) resist distractions, (h) listen to both favorable and unfavorable information, (i) read or listen to complex material to exercise the mind, and (j) take notes when necessary and use visual aids to enhance understanding.
- *Explain the information technology of Internet/intranet/extranet, e-mail, videoconferencing, and collaborative computing, and explain the related use of telecommuting.* The Internet is a global network of computer networks. An intranet is an organization's private Internet. It contains a firewall that blocks outside Internet users from accessing private internal information. An extranet connects an organization's internal employees with selected customers, suppliers, and strategic partners. The primary benefit of these "nets" is that they can enhance the ability of employees to find, create, manage, and distribute information. E-mail uses the Internet/intranet/extranet to send computer-generated text and documents between people. Videoconferencing uses video and audio links along with computers to enable people located at different locations to see, hear, and talk with one another. Collaborative computing entails using state-of-the-art computer software and hardware to help people work better together. Information is shared across time and space by linking people with computer networks. Telecommuting involves doing work that is generally performed in the office away from the office using a variety of information technologies.
- *Describe the process, personal, physical, and semantic barriers to effective communication.* Every element of the perceptual model of communication is a potential process barrier. There are eight personal barriers that commonly influence communication: (a) the ability to effectively communicate, (b) the way people process and interpret information, (c) the level of interpersonal trust between people, (d) the existence of stereotypes and prejudices, (e) the egos of the people communicating, (f) the ability to listen, (g) the natural tendency to evaluate or judge a sender's message, and (h) the inability to listen with understanding. Physical barriers pertain to distance, physical objects, time, and work and office noise. Semantic barriers show up as encoding and decoding errors because these phases of communication involve transmitting and receiving words and symbols. Cultural diversity is a key contributor to semantic barriers.

discussion questions

1. Which of the four barriers to effective communication is affecting Vickie Farrell and Jeff Phelps? Explain your rationale.
2. What are some sources of noise that interfere with communication during a class lecture, an encounter with a professor in his or her office, or a movie?
3. Have you ever distorted upward communication? What was your reason? Was it related to one of the four antecedents of communication distortion? Explain.
4. Which of the keys to effective listening are most difficult to follow when listening to a class lecture? Explain.
5. Which barrier to effective communication is most difficult to reduce? Explain.

ethical dilemma

Are Camera Cellphones Creating Ethical Problems?[59]

Although camera phones have been broadly available for only a few months in the United States, more than 25 million of the devices are out on the streets of Japan. . . .

Now that cellphones with little digital cameras have spread throughout Asia, so have new brands of misbehavior. Some people are secretly taking photos up women's skirts and down into bathroom stalls. Others are avoiding buying books by snapping free shots of desired pages.

"The problem with a new technology is that society has yet to come up with a common understanding about appropriate behavior," said Mizuko Ito, an expert on mobile phone culture at Keio University Tokyo.

Samsung Electronics is banning their use in semiconductor and research facilities, hoping to stave off industrial espionage. Samsung, a leading maker of cellphones, is taking a low-tech approach: requiring employees and visitors to stick tape over the handset's camera lens.

Solving the Dilemma

You are the manager of a large bookstore. You have a camera phone as do several of your employees. You have seen customers use their camera phones to take pictures of one another in the store. Yesterday, for the first time, you observed a customer taking photos of 10 pages of material from a cookbook. Although you did not say anything to this customer, you are wondering what should be done in the future. Select one of the following options.

1. Place a sign on the door asking customers to mind their "cellphone manners." This way you don't have to prevent anyone from using their phone; you can rely on common decency.
2. Ask customers to leave their camera cellphones with an employee at the front of the store. The employee will give the customer a claim check and they can retrieve their phones once they finish shopping.
3. Station an employee at the front of the store who places tape over the lens of camera phones as customers come in.
4. Don't do anything. There is nothing wrong with people taking pictures of materials out of a book.
5. Invent other options. Discuss.

If you're looking for additional study materials, be sure to check out the Online Learning Center at

www.mhhe.com/kinickiob2e

for more information and interactivities that correspond to this chapter.

chapter Thirteen

Influence, Power, and Politics: An Organizational Survival Kit

LEARNING OBJECTIVES

After reading the material in this chapter, you should be able to:

- Name five "soft" and four "hard" influence tactics, and summarize the practical lessons from influence research.
- Identify and briefly describe French and Raven's five bases of power.
- Define the term *empowerment,* and explain how to make it succeed.
- Define *organizational politics,* explain what triggers it, and specify the three levels of political action in organizations.
- Distinguish between favorable and unfavorable impression management tactics.
- Explain how to manage organizational politics.

A FIRM BUT NURTURING STYLE GETS RESULTS AT 3M

Jim McNerney was one of those boys: up early in the morning climbing trees while everybody else in the family was in bed, rousing his three younger brothers to play two-on-two hockey in their basement, running his high school's boys club, and pitching on the varsity baseball team. And he grew up to be one of those men: For three decades, Walter James McNerney Jr. has climbed the corporate ladder without a pause, uprooting his family every two to three years since earning his master's degree from Harvard Business School in 1975. He job-hopped from Procter & Gamble to McKinsey & Co. and then up through General Electric. On Jan. 1, 2001, after losing a three-way race to succeed John F. Welch as chief executive, he moved on yet again to become chairman and CEO of 3M, the first outsider to head the Saint Paul (Minn.) company in its century-long history. . . .

But 3M Co. had begun to drift. Its vaunted research facilities were turning out fewer and fewer commercial hits, and quarterly results were underwhelming. While 3M still draws many of the world's best chemical engineers, the company's labs haven't had a hit like Post-it Notes since, well, Post-it Notes first came out almost a quarter-century ago. Managers at 3M seemed to know instinctively what they needed, and they found it in McNerney: a strong outsider who could restore discipline and focus. It helped that he started in the midst of a recession, when making painful decisions was easier. After rounds of cost-cutting, layoffs, and smart repositioning of the company into more-promising fields such as health care, 3M recently announced its best results ever. . . .

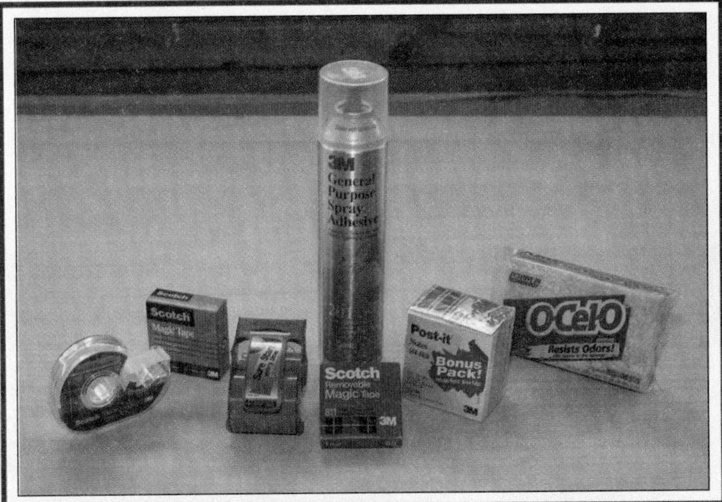

McNerney's secret to success is elementary. He sets high goals that can be measured, such as business-unit sales or the rate of product introductions, and demands that his managers meet them. Granted, many CEOs do that today. But like a dedicated teacher or coach, McNerney also works with his team day in, day out, to help them make the grade. "Some people think you either have a demanding, command-and-control management style or you have a nurturing, encouraging style," he says. "I believe you can't have one without the other."

Unusual in this age of celebrity CEOs, and especially for somebody who is so far untouched by scandal or intrigue, McNerney is also one of Corporate America's lowest-profile execs. He has largely ducked the outside world since taking over at 3M. He usually dispatches Chief Financial Officer Patrick D. Campbell to speak for the company, and you can count his national TV appearances on one hand.

His shy-guy public persona is at odds with his image inside the company. There, McNerney is praised as an inspirational leader comfortable speaking to big groups or conversing one-on-one. "He's personable," says Charles Reich, executive vice-president of 3M's health-care business. "He really engages people." Yet family and friends say McNerney genuinely thinks it would be unseemly to draw attention to himself. "It's all about me? No, it's all about my people," says Charles S. Lauer, publisher of *Modern Healthcare* magazine and a neighbor who has known the McNerney family since the 1960s. "That's Jimmy, the captain of the team. He's got his head screwed on straight." . . .

Sitting at a conference table in his 14th-floor office suite, McNerney seems to be enjoying himself. He wears a sports jacket and a polo shirt, his usual work attire. He is quick to attribute 3M's achievements to the entire organization and praises 3Mers for their work ethic. "My experience is that if people are convinced they're growing as they pursue company goals, that's when you get ignition," he says. He is also disciplined and direct: He makes his points and doesn't utter a word more. When the allotted time for the appointment ends, he stands up and retreats to his inner office. Back to work. . . .

Today, McNerney figures he spends most of his time on personnel. Every other week, he addresses groups of employees at company headquarters. He begins the two-hour sessions with an update on 3M's numbers and a progress report on Six Sigma [a quality improvement program] and his other initiatives. Then, for the last hour and a half, he takes questions. He does the same thing while visiting 3M's far-flung facilities around the world. McNerney also is a regular instructor at 3M's leadership-development institute, another program he has borrowed from GE. In between, he monitors how members of his operating committee—3M's top 15 executives—are doing, often swinging by their offices for a chat. If a manager isn't measuring up, McNerney probably won't raise his voice. But he will expect a solution, pronto. "I think all of us are working harder than we've ever worked before," says David W. Powell, 3M's senior vice-president of marketing.[1]

FOR DISCUSSION

What is there about McNerney's management style that has restored trust and commitment at 3M? Explain. For an interpretation of this case and additional comments, visit our Online Learning Center:

www.mhhe.com/kinickiob2e

IN A PERFECT WORLD, individual and collective interests would be closely aligned and everyone would move forward as one. Instead, we typically find a rather messy situation in which self-interests often override the collective mission. Personal hidden agendas are pursued, political coalitions are formed, false impressions are made, and people end up working at cross purposes. Managers need to be able to guide diverse individuals, who are often powerfully motivated to put their own self-interests first, to pursue common objectives. At stake in this tug-of-war between individual and collective interests is no less than the ultimate survival of the organization.

The purpose of this chapter is to give you a survival kit for the rough-and-tumble side of organizational life. We do so by exploring the interrelated topics of organizational influence, social power, employee empowerment, organizational politics, and impression management.

Influencing Others

How do you get others to carry out your wishes? Do you simply tell them what to do? Or do you prefer a less direct approach, such as promising to return the favor? Whatever approach you use, the crux of the issue is *social influence*. A large measure of interpersonal interaction involves attempts to influence others, including parents, bosses, co-workers, spouses, teachers, friends, and children.

Let's start sharpening your influence skills with a familiarity of the following research insights.

Nine Generic Influence Tactics

A particularly fruitful stream of research, initiated by David Kipnis and his colleagues in 1980, reveals how people influence each other in organizations. The Kipnis methodology involved asking employees how they managed to get either their bosses, co-workers, or subordinates to do what they wanted them to do.[2] Statistical refinements and replications by other researchers over a 13-year period eventually yielded nine influence tactics. The nine tactics, ranked in diminishing order of use in the workplace are as follows:

1. *Rational persuasion.* Trying to convince someone with reason, logic, or facts.
2. *Inspirational appeals.* Trying to build enthusiasm by appealing to others' emotions, ideals, or values.
3. *Consultation.* Getting others to participate in planning, making decisions, and changes.
4. *Ingratiation.* Getting someone in a good mood prior to making a request; being friendly, helpful, and using praise or flattery.
5. *Personal appeals.* Referring to friendship and loyalty when making a request.
6. *Exchange.* Making express or implied promises and trading favors.
7. *Coalition tactics.* Getting others to support your effort to persuade someone.
8. *Pressure.* Demanding compliance or using intimidation or threats.
9. *Legitimating tactics.* Basing a request on one's authority or right, organizational rules or policies, or express or implied support from superiors.[3]

These approaches can be considered *generic* influence tactics because they characterize social influence in all directions. Researchers have found this ranking to be fairly consistent regardless of whether the direction of influence is downward, upward, or lateral.[4]

Some call the first five influence tactics—rational persuasion, inspirational appeals, consultation, ingratiation, and personal appeals—"soft" tactics because they are friendlier and not as coercive as the last four tactics. Exchange, coalition, pressure, and legitimating tactics accordingly are called "hard" tactics because they involve more overt pressure.

Three Influence Outcomes

According to researchers, an influence attempt has three possible outcomes:

1. *Commitment*: Substantial agreement followed by initiative and persistence in pursuit of common goals.
2. *Compliance*: Reluctant or insincere agreement requiring subsequent prodding to satisfy minimum requirements.
3. *Resistance*: Stalling, unproductive arguing, or outright rejection.[5]

Commitment is the best outcome in the workplace because the target person's intrinsic motivation will energize good performance. Consider, for instance, how one CEO recently got what he wanted from a valued colleague:

> Lots of executives at Johnson & Johnson have stories about William C. Weldon's powers of persuasion. The onetime drug salesman who now leads the health-care giant is famed for his ability to convince, cajole, or sometimes just sweet-talk colleagues into seeing things his way. A couple of years ago, Dr. Per A. Peterson, the chief of pharmaceutical research and development, was fed up with personnel headaches and told Weldon he was thinking of leaving the company. The next morning, Peterson, who lives minutes from Weldon in central New Jersey, got a call from the boss at 5:30, inviting him over for breakfast. As Weldon tended to the skillet, the two men discussed Peterson's concerns. And then they talked some more: Their conversation lasted well into the afternoon. Eventually, Peterson agreed to stay, and within a week Weldon had made the changes Peterson sought. "What else can you say to a guy who cooks you an omelette at six in the morning?" says Peterson with a laugh. "You say yes."[6]

Two keys to this successful influence attempt were (1) a personal one-on-one meeting; and (2) quick follow-up on promises made. Too often in today's hectic workplaces managers must settle for compliance or face resistance because they do not invest themselves in the situation, as Weldon did.

Practical Research Insights

Laboratory and field studies have taught us useful lessons about the relative effectiveness of influence tactics along with other instructive insights:

- Commitment is more likely when people rely on consultation, strong rational persuasion, and inspirational appeals and *do not* rely on pressure and coalition tactics.[7] Interestingly, in one study, managers were not very effective at *downward* influence. They relied most heavily on inspiration (an effective tactic), ingratiation (a moderately effective tactic), and pressure (an ineffective tactic).[8]
- A review of 69 studies suggests ingratiation (making the boss feel good) can slightly improve your performance appraisal results and make your boss like you significantly more.[9]
- Commitment is more likely when the influence attempt involves something *important* and *enjoyable* and is based on a *friendly* relationship.[10]

- Credible (believable and trustworthy) people tend to be the most persuasive.[11]
- In a survey, 214 employed MBA students (55% female) tended to perceive their superiors' "soft" influence tactics as fair and "hard" influence tactics as unfair. *Unfair* influence tactics were associated with greater *resistance* among employees.[12]

Strategic Alliances and Reciprocity

In their book, *Influence without Authority,* Allan R Cohen and David L Bradford extended the concept of corporate strategic alliances to interpersonal influence.[13] Hardly a day goes by without another mention in the business press of a new strategic alliance between two global companies intent on staying competitive. These win-win relationships are based on complementary strengths. According to Cohen and Bradford, managers need to follow suit by forming some strategic alliances of their own with anyone who has a stake in their area. This is particularly true given today's rapid change, cross-functional work teams, and diminished reliance on traditional authority structures.

While admitting the task is not an easy one, Cohen and Bradford recommend the tips in Skills & Best Practices for dealing with potential allies: True, these tactics involve taking some personal risks. But the effectiveness of interpersonal strategic alliances is anchored to the concept of reciprocity. "**Reciprocity** is the almost universal belief that people should be paid back for what they do—that one good (or bad) turn deserves another."[14] In short, people tend to get what they give when attempting to influence others.

By demonstrating the rich texture of social influence, the foregoing research evidence and practical advice whet our appetite for learning more about how today's managers can and do reconcile individual and organizational interests. Let us focus on social power.

SKILLS & BEST PRACTICES

How to Turn Your Co-Workers into Strategic Allies

1. ***Mutual respect.*** Assume they are competent and smart.
2. ***Openness.*** Talk straight to them. It isn't possible for any one person to know everything, so give them the information they need to know to help you better.
3. ***Trust.*** Assume that no one will take any action that is purposely intended to hurt another, so hold back no information that the other could use, even if it doesn't help your immediate position.
4. ***Mutual benefit.*** Plan every strategy so that both parties win. If that doesn't happen over time, the alliance will break up. When dissolving a partnership becomes necessary as a last resort, try to do it in a clean way that minimizes residual anger. Some day, you may want a new alliance with that person.

SOURCE: Excerpted from A R Cohen and D L Bradford, *Influence without Authority* (New York: John Wiley & Sons, 1990), pp 23–24.

reciprocity

Widespread belief that people should be paid back for their positive and negative acts.

Social Power and Empowerment

The term *power* evokes mixed and often passionate reactions. To skeptics, Lord Acton's time-honored declaration that "power corrupts and absolute power corrupts absolutely" is truer than ever.[15] However, OB specialists remind us that, like it or not, power is a fact of life in modern organizations. According to one management writer:

> Power must be used because managers must influence those they depend on. Power also is crucial in the development of managers' self-confidence and willingness to support subordinates. From this perspective, power should be accepted as a natural part of any organization. Managers should recognize and develop their own power to coordinate and support the work of subordinates; it is powerlessness, not power, that undermines organizational effectiveness.[16]

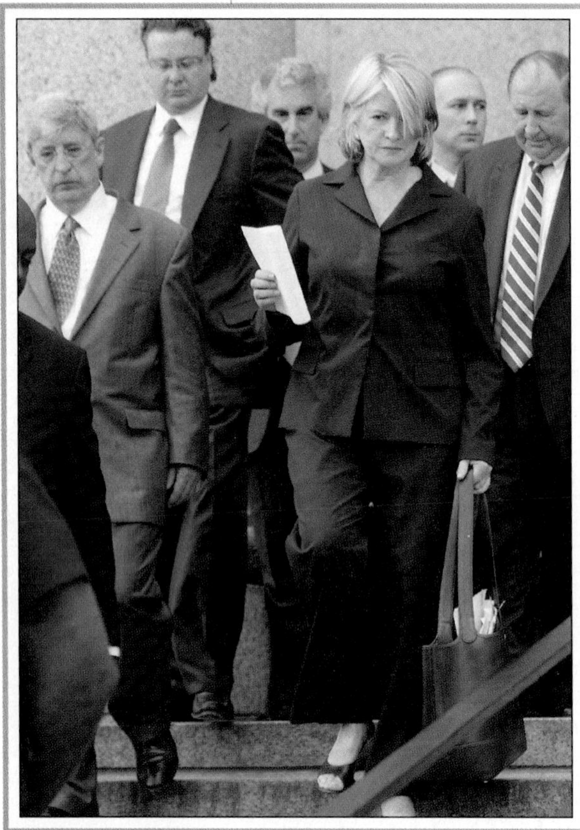

Many would say that Martha Stewart was queen of the creative, stylish life. At the helm of a thriving multimedia company, she was an inspiration to homemakers and businesswomen alike. Which bases of power did she likely wield during her rise to the top? What bases of power do you think she lost when she was convicted in 2004 for lying about a stock sale and sentenced to five months in prison?

Thus, power is a necessary and generally positive force in organizations.[17] As the term is used here, **social power** is defined as "the ability to marshal the human, informational, and material resources to get something done."[18]

Importantly, the exercise of social power in organizations is not necessarily a downward proposition. Employees can and do exercise power upward and laterally. An example of an upward power play occurred at Alberto-Culver Company, the personal care products firm. Leonard Lavin, founder of the company, was under pressure to revitalize the firm because key employees were departing for more innovative competitors such as Procter & Gamble. Lavin's daughter Carol Bernick, and her husband Howard, both long-time employees, took things into their own hands. As *Business Week* reported:

> Even the Bernicks were thinking of jumping ship. Instead, in September 1994, they marched into Lavin's office and presented him with an ultimatum: Either hand over the reins as CEO or run the company without them. It was a huge blow for Lavin, forcing him to face selling his company to outsiders or ceding control to the younger generation. Unwilling to sell, he reluctantly stepped down, though he remains chairman.
>
> How does it feel to push aside your own father and wrest operating control of the company he created? "It isn't an easy thing to do with the founder of any company, whether he's your father or not," says Carol Bernick, 46, now vice-chairman and president of Alberto-Culver North America.[19]

Howard Bernick became CEO, the firm's top-down management style was scrapped in favor of a more open culture, and Lavin reportedly is happy with how things have turned out.

Five Bases of Power

A popular classification scheme for social power traces back to the landmark work of John French and Bertram Raven. They proposed that power arises from five different bases: reward power, coercive power, legitimate power, expert power, and referent power.[20] Each involves a different approach to influencing others. Each has advantages and drawbacks.

Reward Power Managers have **reward power** if they can obtain compliance by promising or granting rewards. Pay-for-performance plans and positive reinforcement programs attempt to exploit reward power.

Coercive Power Threats of punishment and actual punishment give an individual **coercive power.** Richard M. Scrushy, the former head of HealthSouth now facing federal fraud charges, reportedly relied heavily on coercive power. According to *Business Week:*

HANDS-ON EXERCISE

How Much Power Do You Have?

INSTRUCTIONS: Score your various bases of power for your current (or former) job, using the following scale:

1 = Strongly disagree
2 = Disagree
3 = Slightly agree
4 = Agree
5 = Strongly agree

Reward Power Score = ________

1. I can reward persons at lower levels. ________
2. My review actions affect the rewards gained at lower levels. ________
3. Based on my decisions, lower level personnel may receive a bonus. ________

Coercive Power Score = ________

1. I can punish employees at lower levels. ________
2. My work is a check on lower level employees. ________
3. My diligence reduces error. ________

Legitimate Power Score = ________

1. My position gives me a great deal of authority. ________
2. The decisions made at my level are of critical importance. ________
3. Employees look to me for guidance. ________

Expert Power Score = ________

1. I am an expert in this job. ________
2. My ability gives me an advantage in this job. ________
3. Given some time, I could improve the methods used on this job. ________

Referent Power Score = ________

1. I attempt to set a good example for other employees. ________
2. My personality allows me to work well in this job. ________
3. My fellow employees look to me as their informal leader. ________

Arbitrary norms for each of the five bases of power are: 3–6 = Weak power base; 7–11 = Moderate power base; 12–15 = Strong power base.

SOURCE: Adapted and excerpted in part from D L Dieterly and B Schneider, "The Effect of Organizational Environment on Perceived Power and Climate: A Laboratory Study." *Organizational Behavior and Human Performance,* June, 1974, pp 316–37.

> As he assumed the trappings of wealth, Scrushy became an increasingly imperious leader, say insiders. He publicly berated financial analysts who dared to challenge his forecasts of continued growth. Staffers feared him, too. Scrushy would pop up unannounced at his rehab centers for surprise inspections. Like a drill sergeant, he would run a finger along the tops of a picture frame, then wipe it on the blazer of the center's administrator. Any visible mark meant points deducted—and possible dismissal.[21]

How would you respond to this management style?

Legitimate Power This base of power is anchored to one's formal position or authority. Thus, managers who obtain compliance primarily because of their formal authority to make decisions have **legitimate power.** Legitimate power may be expressed either positively or negatively. Positive legitimate power focuses constructively on job performance. Negative legitimate power tends to be threatening and demeaning to those being influenced. Its main purpose is to build the power holder's ego.

social power
Ability to get things done with human, informational, and material resources.

reward power
Obtaining compliance with promised or actual rewards.

coercive power
Obtaining compliance through threatened or actual punishment.

legitimate power
Obtaining compliance through formal authority.

Getting the point across in today's hectic workplaces requires a delicate balance between expertise and charisma.

expert power
Obtaining compliance through one's knowledge or information.

referent power
Obtaining compliance through charisma or personal attraction.

empowerment
Sharing varying degrees of power with lower-level employees to better serve the customer.

Expert Power Valued knowledge or information gives an individual **expert power** over those who need such knowledge or information. The power of supervisors is enhanced because they know about work assignments and schedules before their employees do. Skillful use of expert power played a key role in the effectiveness of team leaders in a study of three physician medical diagnosis teams.[22] Knowledge *is* power in today's high-tech workplaces.

Referent Power Also called charisma, **referent power** comes into play when one's personality becomes the reason for compliance. Role models have referent power over those who identify closely with them.[23]

To further your understanding of these five bases of power, take a moment to complete the questionnaire in the Hands-On Exercise on page 327. What is your power profile? Where do you need improvement?

Practical Lessons from Research

Researchers have identified the following relationships between power bases and work outcomes such as job performance, job satisfaction, and turnover:

- Expert and referent power had a generally positive effect.
- Reward and legitimate power had a slightly positive effect.
- Coercive power had a slightly negative effect.[24]

A follow-up study involving 251 employed business seniors looked at the relationship between influence styles and bases of power. This was a bottom-up study. In other words, employee perceptions of managerial influence and power were examined. Rational persuasion was found to be a highly acceptable managerial influence tactic. Why? Because employees perceived it to be associated with the three bases of power they viewed positively: legitimate, expert, and referent.[25]

In summary, expert and referent power appear to get the best *combination* of results and favorable reactions from lower-level employees.[26]

Employee Empowerment

An exciting trend in today's organizations centers on giving employees a greater say in the workplace. This trend wears various labels, including "participative management" and "open-book management."[27] Regardless of the label one prefers, it is all about empowerment. One management writer defines **empowerment** in terms of serving the customer:

> Empowerment quite simply means granting supervisors or workers permission to give the customer priority over other issues in the operation. In practical terms, it relates to the resources, skill, time and support to become leaders rather than controllers or mindless robots.[28]

Steve Kerr, a pioneer in employee empowerment, explains: "We say empowerment is moving decision making down to the lowest level *where a competent decision can be made*."[29] Of course, it is naive and counterproductive to hand power over to unwilling and/or unprepared employees.

The concept of empowerment requires some adjustment in traditional thinking (see Skills & Best Practices). First and foremost, power is *not* a zero-sum situation where one person's gain is another's loss. Social power is unlimited. This requires win–win thinking. Frances Hesselbein, the woman credited with modernizing the Girl Scouts of the USA, put it this way: "The more power you give away, the more you have."[30] Authoritarian managers who view employee empowerment as a threat to their personal power are missing the point because of their win–lose thinking.[31]

Making Empowerment Work

We believe empowerment has good promise if managers go about it properly. Empowerment is a sweeping concept with many different definitions. Consequently, researchers use inconsistent measurements, and cause-effect relationships are fuzzy.[32] Managers committed to the idea of employee empowerment need to follow the path of continuous improvement, learning from their successes and

SKILLS & BEST PRACTICES

Empowerment in Action from Wall Street to Brazil

Citigroup (banking and financial services)
Debby Hopkins, head of corporate strategy and chief operations and technology officer:
"The key thing I've learned is that the most powerful thing you can do is listen. You don't have to have the last word. You don't have to get credit for anything. I've always led in groups—you know, get people around the table to discuss an issue. But now I hold back what I think. I say to myself, 'Not now, not now! Wait, wait!' This new approach has changed my life."

Amazon.com (online books and retailing)
One of Amazon's most prestigious awards is called a Just Do It—the winners are employees who do something they think will help Amazon *without* getting their boss's permission. It has to be well thought through, but it doesn't have to succeed. There are risks to rewarding such behavior, [founder and CEO Jeff] Bezos agrees, but "the cure—to encourage people to always ask for permission—is worse than the disease."

Harley-Davidson (motorcycle manufacturing)
The last time Cathy Pasbrig shut down the production line at Harley-Davidson, it wasn't because of a malfunctioning part or a dangerous leak. She saw a blemish on a shiny chrome chain guard, and "I put the line down in a heartbeat," says the eight-year Harley veteran. "I wouldn't want to put anything on the market that I wouldn't buy myself."

Semco (industrial and environmental consulting in Brazil)
Ricardo Semler, CEO, who allows his 3,000 employees to work whenever and wherever they choose:
"We negotiate with our employees for a final result and let them figure out how they'll achieve the desired result. So let's say I need you to sell 512 widgets. We agree that that is a realistic expectation. Now it's up to you. Maybe you do paperwork on a rainy Sunday and golf or pick up your kids from school on Tuesday—as long as you sell the 512 widgets and our customers are happy, why do I care? . . .

SOURCES: Excerpted from P Sellers, "Power: Do Women Really Want It?" *Fortune,* October 13, 2003, p 88; F Vogelstein, "Mighty Amazon," *Fortune,* May 26, 2003, p 70; R Levering and M Moskowitz, "2004 Special report: The 100 Best Companies to Work For," *Fortune,* January 12, 2004, p 76; and B Wieners, "Extreme Flextime," *Inc.,* April 2004, p 91.

FIGURE 13–1 Randolph's Empowerment Model

The Empowerment Plan

Share Information

- Share company performance information.
- Help people understand the business.
- Build trust through sharing sensitive information.
- Create self-monitoring possibilities.

Create Autonomy through Structure

- Create a clear vision and clarify the little pictures.
- Create new decision-making rules that support empowerment.
- Clarify goals and roles collaboratively.
- Establish new empowering performance management processes.
- Use heavy doses of training.

Let Teams Become the Hierarchy

- Provide direction and training for new skills.
- Provide encouragement and support for change.
- Gradually have managers let go of control.
- Work through the leadership vacuum stage.
- Acknowledge the fear factor.

Remember: Empowerment is not magic; it consists of a few simple steps and a lot of persistence.

SOURCE: Reprinted from *Organizational Dynamics*, W Alan Randolph, "Navigating the Journey to Empowerment," Spring 1995. Copyright © 1995, with permission from Elsevier.

failures. Eight years of research with 10 "empowered" companies led consultant W Alan Randolph to formulate the three-pronged empowerment plan in Figure 13–1. Notice how open-book management and active information sharing are needed to build the necessary foundation of trust. Beyond that, clear goals and lots of relevant training are needed. While noting that the empowerment process can take several years to unfold, Randolph offered this perspective:

> While the keys to empowerment may be easy to understand, they are hard to implement. It takes tremendous courage to start sharing sensitive information. It takes true strength to build more structure just at the point when people want more freedom of action. It takes real growth to allow teams to take over the management decision-making process. And above all, it takes perseverance to complete the empowerment process.[33]

Organizational Politics and Impression Management

Most students of OB find the study of organizational politics intriguing. Perhaps this topic owes its appeal to the antics of Hollywood's corporate villains and contestants on *The Apprentice* stepping on each other to avoid Donald Trump's dreaded words, "You're fired!"[34] As we will see, however, organizational politics includes, but is not limited to, dirty dealing. Organizational politics is an ever-present and sometimes annoying feature of modern work life.

"According to 150 executives from large US companies, office politics wastes an average of 20% of their time; that's 10 weeks a year."[35] On the other hand, organizational politics is often a positive force in modern work organizations. Skillful and well-timed politics can help you get your point across, neutralize resistance to a key project, relieve stress, or get a choice job assignment.[36]

We explore this important and interesting area by (1) defining the term *organizational politics,* (2) identifying three levels of political action, (3) discussing eight specific political tactics, (4) considering a related area called *impression management,* and (5) discussing how to curb organizational politics.

Definition and Domain of Organizational Politics

"**Organizational politics** involves intentional acts of influence to enhance or protect the self-interest of individuals or groups."[37] An emphasis on *self-interest* distinguishes this form of social influence. Managers are endlessly challenged to achieve a workable balance between employees' self-interests and organizational interests, as discussed at the beginning of this chapter. When a proper balance exists, the pursuit of self-interest may serve the organization's interests. Political behavior becomes a negative force when self-interests erode or defeat organizational interests. For example, researchers have documented the political tactic of filtering and distorting information flowing up to the boss. This self-serving practice put the reporting employees in the best possible light.[38]

organizational politics

Intentional enhancement of self-interest.

Political Behavior Triggered by Uncertainty Political maneuvering is triggered primarily by *uncertainty*. Five common sources of uncertainty within organizations are

1. Unclear objectives.
2. Vague performance measures.
3. Ill-defined decision processes.
4. Strong individual or group competition.[39]
5. Any type of change.

Regarding this last source of uncertainty, organization development specialist Anthony Raia noted, "Whatever we attempt to change, the political subsystem becomes active. Vested interests are almost always at stake and the distribution of power is challenged."[40]

We would expect a field sales representative, striving to achieve an assigned quota, to be less political than a management trainee working on a variety of projects. While some management trainees stake their career success on hard work, competence, and a bit of luck, many do not. These people attempt to gain a competitive edge through some combination of the political tactics discussed below. Meanwhile, the salesperson's performance is measured in actual sales, not in terms of being friends with the boss or taking credit for others' work. Thus, the management trainee would tend to be more political than the field salesperson because of greater uncertainty about management's expectations.

Because employees generally experience greater uncertainty during the earlier stages of their careers, are junior employees more political than more senior ones?

FIGURE 13–2 Levels of Political Action in Organizations

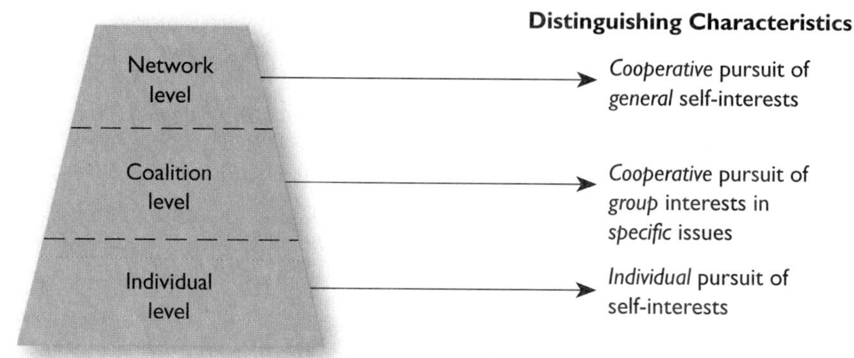

The answer is yes, according to a survey of 243 employed adults in upstate New York. In fact, one senior employee nearing retirement told the researcher: "I used to play political games when I was younger. Now I just do my job."[41]

Three Levels of Political Action Although much political maneuvering occurs at the individual level, it also can involve group or collective action. Figure 13–2 illustrates three different levels of political action: the individual level, the coalition level, and the network level.[42] Each level has its distinguishing characteristics. At the individual level, personal self-interests are pursued by the individual. The political aspects of coalitions and networks are not so obvious, however.

coalition Temporary groupings of people who actively pursue a single issue.

People with a common interest can become a political coalition by fitting the following definition. In an organizational context, a **coalition** is an informal group bound together by the *active* pursuit of a *single* issue. Coalitions may or may not coincide with formal group membership. When the target issue is resolved (a sexually harassing supervisor is fired, for example), the coalition disbands. Experts note that political coalitions have "fuzzy boundaries," meaning they are fluid in membership, flexible in structure, and temporary in duration.[43]

Coalitions are a potent political force in organizations. During the 1990s, coalitions on the corporate boards of American Express, IBM, and General Motors ousted the heads of those giant companies.

A third level of political action involves networks.[44] Unlike coalitions, which pivot on specific issues, networks are loose associations of individuals seeking social support for their general self-interests. Politically, networks are people oriented, while coalitions are issue oriented. Networks have broader and longer term agendas than do coalitions. For instance, Avon's Hispanic and Latino employees have built a network to enhance the members' career opportunities.

Eight Political Tactics Anyone who has worked in an organization has firsthand knowledge of blatant politicking. Blaming someone else for your mistake is an obvious political ploy. So are these self-serving games, as reported in *The Wall Street Journal:*

> A former Wall Street analyst, a veteran of several investment banks who knows the value of that most ludicrous of achievements—performing "better than expected"—advises us to list easy goals and just make them sound hard. That way next year you can say you "achieved 100% of goals" last year.

> All year long, she would collect kudos as ammo, dumping them into folders she named "Success" and "Yay." The latter was for praise from colleagues. "Getting messages from my boss's boss—or anyone else he respected and was also slightly intimidated by—was even better," she confides.
>
> Brownie points, we all know, come from personally saving a few pennies. "Point out in the review—not in writing!—that the rest of the team stayed at the Four Seasons and flew American," the analyst says. Then, wipe your fingerprints from the knives you stuck in everyone's backs.[45]

But other political tactics are more subtle. Researchers have identified a range of political behavior.

One landmark study, involving in-depth interviews with 87 managers from 30 electronics companies in Southern California, identified eight political tactics. Top-, middle-, and low-level managers were represented about equally in the sample. According to the researchers: "Respondents were asked to describe organizational political tactics and personal characteristics of effective political actors based upon their accumulated experience in *all* organizations in which they had worked."[46] Listed in descending order of occurrence, the eight political tactics that emerged were

1. Attacking or blaming others.
2. Using information as a political tool.
3. Creating a favorable image. (Also known as *impression management.*)[47]
4. Developing a base of support.
5. Praising others (ingratiation).
6. Forming power coalitions with strong allies.
7. Associating with influential people.
8. Creating obligations (reciprocity).

The researchers distinguished between reactive and proactive political tactics. Some of the tactics, such as scapegoating, were *reactive* because the intent was to *defend* one's self-interest. Other tactics, such as developing a base of support, were *proactive* because they sought to *promote* the individual's self-interest.

Impression Management

impression management
Getting others to see us in a certain manner.

Impression management is defined as "the process by which people attempt to control or manipulate the reactions of others to images of themselves or their ideas."[48] This encompasses how one talks, behaves, and looks. Most impression management attempts are directed at making a *good* impression on relevant others. But, as we will see, some employees strive to make a *bad* impression. For purposes of conceptual clarity, we will focus on *upward* impression management (trying to impress one's immediate supervisor) because it is most relevant for managers. Still, it is good to remember that *anyone* can be the intended target of impression management. Parents, teachers, peers, employees, and customers are all fair game when it comes to managing the impressions of others.

Good Impressions If you "dress for success," project an upbeat attitude at all times, and avoid offending others, you are engaging in favorable impression management—particularly so if your motive is to improve your chances of getting what you want in life.[49] There are questionable ways to create a good impression,

"Fine presentation, Matthews, but lose the wiggle dance."

as well. For instance, Stewart Friedman, director of the University of Pennsylvania's Leadership Program, offered this gem:

> Last year, I was doing some work with a large bank. The people there told me a story that astounded me: After 7 PM, people would open the door to their office, drape a spare jacket on the back of their chair, lay a set of glasses down on some reading material on their desk—and then go home for the night. The point of this elaborate gesture was to create the illusion that they were just out grabbing dinner and would be returning to burn the midnight oil.[50]

Impression management often strays into unethical territory.

A statistical factor analysis of the influence attempts reported by a sample of 84 bank employees (including 74 women) identified three categories of favorable upward impression management tactics.[51] Favorable upward impression management tactics can be *job-focused* (manipulating information about one's job performance), *supervisor-focused* (praising and doing favors for one's supervisor), and *self-focused* (presenting oneself as a polite and nice person). A moderate amount of upward impression management is a necessity for the average employee today. Too little, and busy managers are liable to overlook some of your valuable contributions when they make job assignment, pay, and promotion decisions. Too much, and you run the risk of being branded a "schmoozer," a "phony," and other unflattering things by your co-workers.[52] Excessive flattery and ingratiation can backfire by embarrassing the target person and damaging one's credibility. Also, the risk of unintended insult is very high when impression management tactics cross gender, racial, ethnic, and cultural lines.[53] International management experts warn:

> The impression management tactic is only as effective as its correlation to accepted norms about behavioral presentation. In other words, slapping a Japanese

subordinate on the back with a rousing "Good work, Hiro!" will not create the desired impression in Hiro's mind that the expatriate intended. In fact, the behavior will likely create the opposite impression.[54]

Each year, *Fortune* magazine tracks the progress of powerful businesswomen. Making the recent list for the first time is Myrtle Potter, chief operating officer and executive vice president of Genentech, a leading biotechnology firm. She built her resume, skill portfolio, and power base at pharmaceutical giants Merck and Bristol-Myers Squibb. As the head of Genentech's marketing efforts, Potter wields significant power and influence at a company with a very unique power—the power to heal and save lives.

Bad Impressions At first glance, the idea of consciously trying to make a bad impression in the workplace seems absurd.[55] But an interesting new line of impression management research has uncovered both motives and tactics for making oneself look *bad*. In a survey of the work experiences of business students at a large northwestern US university, more than half "reported witnessing a case of someone intentionally looking bad at work."[56] Why? Four motives came out of the study:

> (1) *Avoidance:* Employee seeks to avoid additional work, stress, burnout, or an unwanted transfer or promotion. (2) *Obtain concrete rewards:* Employee seeks to obtain a pay raise or a desired transfer, promotion, or demotion. (3) *Exit:* Employee seeks to get laid off, fired, or suspended, and perhaps also to collect unemployment or workers' compensation. (4) *Power:* Employee seeks to control, manipulate, or intimidate others, get revenge, or make someone else look bad.[57]

Within the context of these motives, *unfavorable* upward impression management makes sense.

Five unfavorable upward impression management tactics identified by the researchers are as follows:

- *Decreasing performance*—restricting productivity, making more mistakes than usual, lowering quality, neglecting tasks.
- *Not working to potential*—pretending ignorance, having unused capabilities.
- *Withdrawing*—being tardy, taking excessive breaks, faking illness.
- *Displaying a bad attitude*—complaining, getting upset and angry, acting strangely, not getting along with co-workers.
- *Broadcasting limitations*—letting co-workers know about one's physical problems and mistakes (both verbally and nonverbally).[58]

Recommended ways to manage employees who try to make a bad impression can be found throughout this book. They include more challenging work, greater autonomy, better feedback, supportive leadership, clear and reasonable goals, and a less stressful work setting.[59]

Keeping Organizational Politics in Check

Organizational politics cannot be eliminated. A manager would be naive to expect such an outcome. But political maneuvering can and should be managed to keep it constructive and within reasonable bounds. Harvard's Abraham Zaleznik put the issue this way: "People can focus their attention on only so many things. The more

SKILLS & BEST PRACTICES

How to Keep Organizational Politics within Reasonable Bounds

- Screen out overly political individuals at hiring time.
- Create an open-book management system.
- Make sure every employee knows how the business works and has a personal line of sight to key results with corresponding measureable objectives for individual accountability.
- Have nonfinancial people interpret periodic financial and accounting statements for all employees.
- Establish formal conflict resolution and grievance processes.
- As an ethics filter, do only what you would feel comfortable doing on national television.
- Publicly recognize and reward people who get real results without political games.

SOURCE: Adapted in part from discussion in LB MacGregor Server, "The End of Office Politics as Usual" (New York: American Management Association, 2002), pp 184–99.

it lands on politics, the less energy—emotional and intellectual—is available to attend to the problems that fall under the heading of real work."[60]

An individual's degree of politicalness is a matter of personal values, ethics, and temperament. People who are either strictly nonpolitical or highly political generally pay a price for their behavior. The former may experience slow promotions and feel left out, while the latter may run the risk of being called self-serving and lose their credibility. People at both ends of the political spectrum may be considered poor team players. A moderate amount of prudent political behavior generally is considered a survival tool in complex organizations. Experts remind us that

> . . . political behavior has earned a bad name only because of its association with politicians. On its own, the use of power and other resources to obtain your objectives is not inherently unethical. It all depends on what the preferred objectives are.[61]

With this perspective in mind, the practical steps in Skills & Best Practices are recommended. Notice the importance of reducing uncertainty through clear performance-reward linkages. Measurable objectives are management's first line of defense against negative expressions of organizational politics.[62]

key terms

coalition 330
coercive power 324
empowerment 327
expert power 326
impression management 331
legitimate power 325
organizational politics 329
reciprocity 323
referent power 326
reward power 324
social power 324

chapter summary

- *Name five "soft" and four "hard" influence tactics, and summarize the practical lessons from influence research.* Five soft influence tactics are rational persuasion, inspirational appeals, consultation, ingratiation, and personal appeals. They are more friendly and less coercive than the four hard influence tactics: exchange, coalition tactics, pressure, and legitimating tactics. According to research, soft tactics are better for generating commitment and are perceived as more fair than hard tactics.
- *Identify and briefly describe French and Raven's five bases of power.* French and Raven's five bases of power are reward power (rewarding compliance), coercive power

(punishing noncompliance), legitimate power (relying on formal authority), expert power (providing needed information), and referent power (relying on personal attraction).

- *Define the term* empowerment, *and explain how to make it succeed.* Empowerment involves sharing varying degrees of power and decision-making authority with lower-level employees to better serve the customer. According to Randolph's model, empowerment requires active sharing of key information, structure that encourages autonomy, transfer of control from managers to teams, and persistence. Trust and training also are very important.
- *Define* organizational politics, *explain what triggers it, and specify the three levels of political action in organizations.* Organizational politics is defined as intentional acts of influence to enhance or protect the self-interests of individuals or groups. Uncertainty triggers most politicking in organizations. Political action occurs at individual, coalition, and network levels. Coalitions are informal, temporary, and single-issue alliances.
- *Distinguish between favorable and unfavorable impression management tactics.* Favorable upward impression management can be job-focused (manipulating information about one's job performance), supervisor-focused (praising or doing favors for the boss), or self-focused (being polite and nice). Unfavorable upward impression management tactics include decreasing performance, not working to potential, withdrawing, displaying a bad attitude, and broadcasting one's limitations.
- *Explain how to manage organizational politics.* Although organizational politics cannot be eliminated, managers can keep it within reasonable bounds. Measurable objectives for personal accountability are key. Participative management also helps, especially in the form of open-book management. Formal conflict resolution and grievance programs are helpful. Overly political people should not be hired, and employees who get results without playing political games should be publicly recognized and rewarded. The "how-would-it-look-on-TV" ethics test can limit political maneuvering.

discussion questions

1. Based on the chapter-opening vignette about 3M, what would likely happen to a highly political executive reporting to McNerney? Explain.
2. Before reading this chapter, did the term *power* have a negative connotation for you? Do you view it differently now? Explain.
3. In your opinion, how much empowerment is too much in today's workplaces?
4. Why do you think organizational politics is triggered primarily by uncertainty?
5. How much impression management do you see in your classroom or workplace today? Citing specific examples, are those tactics effective?

ethical dilemma

Your Job: Up in Smoke?

Smokers have been banned from lighting up on airplanes, at work, and in restaurants. Now, a nicotine habit could cost a smoker a job. As of March 25, [2002,] St. Cloud, Florida (population 19,000), requires applicants for city jobs to swear they've been tobacco-free for a year. New hires can't smoke or dip and can be tested to make sure they're not cheating. (Current employees are exempt.)

Other Florida cities have similar laws, but none go as far: North Miami bans smokers from applying for city jobs, too, but relents after they're hired; Coral Gables won't let smokers be cops.

Boosters say the restrictions mean fewer lost workdays, higher productivity, and lower health-insurance costs. Eric Nieves, St. Cloud's human-resources director, says 6% to 12% of the $1.3 million the city spends on health insurance is tobacco-related.

But civil-rights advocates say saving money is not worth the loss of privacy. Smoking is a health risk, "but so is high blood pressure and cholesterol," says Angie Brooks of the American Civil Liberties Union, which is considering whether to file suit. "It's a very slippery slope."

And some say the law will make hiring harder. Says public works director Bob MacKichan: "I could have the most qualified person there is, but now I don't even get to see the application."[63]

What Is Your Position on This Ethically Charged Workplace Power Play?

1. Smoking is hazardous to all involved and should be discouraged in every possible way. Explain.
2. This is an abuse of power. Smokers have rights, too. Explain.
3. Current no-smoking policies in most workplaces are strict enough already. Explain.
4. Exempting current employees from a tobacco-free policy for new hires is an unacceptable double standard that could hurt morale and productivity. Explain.
5. Employees in each particular organization should be allowed to vote on tobacco-free hiring. Explain.
6. Invent other options. Discuss.

For an interpretation of this situation, visit our Web site, www.mhhe.com/kinickiob2e.

If you're looking for additional study materials, be sure to check out the Online Learning Center at

www.mhhe.com/kinickiob2e

for more information and interactivities that correspond to this chapter.

chapter Fourteen

Leadership

LEARNING OBJECTIVES

After reading the material in this chapter, you should be able to:

- Review trait theory research, and discuss the idea of one best style of leadership, using the Ohio State studies and the Leadership Grid® as points of reference.
- Explain, according to Fiedler's contingency model, how leadership style interacts with situational control.
- Discuss House's revised path–goal theory and Hersey and Blanchard's situational leadership theory.
- Describe the difference between transactional and transformational leadership and discuss how transformational leadership transforms followers and work groups.
- Explain the leader–member exchange (LMX) model of leadership and the concept of shared leadership.
- Review the principles of servant leadership and discuss Level 5 leadership.

ANN FUDGE LEAVES EARLY RETIREMENT TO TAKE OVER THE REINS AT YOUNG & RUBICAM BRANDS

In February, 2001, Ann Fudge did something that has become achingly common among high-powered career women. She quit. After a quarter-century as a rising star in Corporate America and just one year after she had been promoted to run a $5 billion division of Kraft Foods Inc., Fudge walked away. She didn't do it for her two sons, who were already grown and embarked on careers of their own. She didn't do it to accept another turnaround challenge, building on her reputation for reviving brands from Minute Rice to Maxwell House. Like a number of her peers, she simply wanted to define herself by more than her professional status, considerable as it was, and financial rewards, sizable as they were. "It was definitely not dissatisfaction," says Fudge, now 52. "It was more about life." . . .

Well, not quite. About two years into her sojourn, Fudge got a call from Martin Sorrell, chief executive of Britain's advertising conglomerate, WPP Group PLC. He wasn't interested in seeking her reflections on retirement. If anything, he says, "I thought, what a waste." If everybody followed Fudge's lead, he argues, "look at the damage to the economy to have all these talented 50-year-olds out." No, Sorrell called to tempt Fudge back in with an offer to run Young & Rubicam Inc., the distressed advertising and communications giant that he had bought for $4.7 billion in 2000. He thought that Fudge, with her marketing expertise and renowned people skills, could rescue a company that two CEOs in three years couldn't. And he certainly wasn't oblivious to the buzz that hiring a prominent black woman would create. Besides, the notoriously hands-on boss contends, "women are better managers than men."

What an offer, though: Fudge would take over a company with about 40% of the revenues of the unit she ran at Kraft, a company that a former Y&R client calls "distracted and uninspired" in an industry worried about becoming irrelevant. All at a time when Fudge was dreaming of starting her own children's media venture. But here was a chance to make a difference in a hurry. As CEO, she could alter the way that business was done—turning the company from an insular idea factory stymied by its own turf battles to a truly client-focused and efficient operation. Her ideal: a collaborative family in which independent businesses work together to diagnose and solve customers' problems. This was a company where she could put her marketing savvy and management ideas into practice, a company that needed her, a company of her own. And so in May, 2003, she became chairman and chief executive of what is now called Young

& Rubicam Brands, as well as Y&R, its flagship ad agency. . . .

At Young & Rubicam, she has been welcomed with as much skepticism as enthusiasm. Fudge was an unconventional choice as chief executive, and she is taking an unconventional approach—importing a management rigor and an inclusive style rarely associated with advertising. Fudge's leadership could result in dramatic improvements or end in very public failure.

Fudge traded her enlightened early retirement and entrepreneurial plans for a daunting challenge. She has thrust her newly centered self smack in the middle of a company that has endured neglect, executive greed, and a messy merger. . . .

Some employees are bitter. And now many are peeved to have a consumer-products executive who espouses management principles like "Lean Six Sigma" at the helm of an ad agency, where a modicum of chaos is thought to be necessary for creativity. To them, it's an awkward match.

The new CEO acknowledges that it'll take time to create goodwill among a group of people who have been so disillusioned for the past few years.

But it is Fudge's vision for how Y&R should operate that really puts her at odds with some of her new colleagues. She brings a client's perspective to the job in a way that is fundamentally different from the usual ad agency ethos. In Fudge's world, creativity is only worthwhile if the client appreciates it. That's practically heresy to some. As an experienced marketing executive, she knows all too well the limits of the traditional 30-second commercial. When clients approach her agency for help selling a product, she believes the response should be to find the best possible combination of services, drawing on all the far-flung units in the empire. To underscore this, she launched the Young & Rubicam Brands name for the group's family of companies. That's a difficult mind shift for a confederation of businesses used to working independently and even competing against one another. Meanwhile, many insiders complain that despite the change in nomenclature, Fudge has failed to give Y&R the dynamic, fresh identity it needs to draw customers and talent back into the fold. Instead, from her open cubicle at Madison Avenue, she has focused on meeting with customers and encouraging her employees to unite in giving them better service. Her goal: more revenue from existing clients, rather than the buzz of new business. Y&R Vice-Chairman Stephanie Kugelman calls the griping "old world ad-speak," arguing that marshaling resources for clients trumps fresh slogans. "This is what you have to do these days," says Kugelman. "The whole business has changed."

Fudge may not have won the hearts and minds of all her staffers, but at least some clients are in sync with the kinds of changes she's trying to make. "Too many people add a lot of cost and not a lot of value," says M. Carl Johnson III, chief strategy officer at client Campbell Soup Co. "They have to stop doing stuff that's stupid." Fudge's first big success was Microsoft Corp.'s recent decision to give roughly $250 million of its customer-relationship management business to Y&R. "If it wasn't for her leadership, we wouldn't have been able to close the deal," says John B. Kahan, Microsoft's general manager of corporate customer-relationship management.

"Most agencies come to the table with: 'Here's what I did for other customers.' She says: 'What does it take to delight your customer?' " . . .

Such observations underline two obvious characteristics that set Fudge apart: She is female, and she is black. That may account for the preponderance of adjectives like "lovely," "nurturing," and "nice" that get thrown at her. It may also explain why Fudge says she is used to being underestimated. On a recent business trip, someone mixed up Fudge and a junior associate, who is white. "I almost think it's funny," says Fudge, noting that she has experienced racism every day of her life. When her sons were teenagers, she used to tell them not to put their hands in their pockets, in case people thought they were carrying guns. "It's not different for any person who grows up black in this country. You understand who you are. You deal with it." The bigger issue, she says, is "the challenge of being questioned all the time."[1]

FOR DISCUSSION

How would you describe Ann Fudge's leadership style? For an interpretation of this case and additional comments, visit our Online Learning Center (OLC):

www.mhhe.com/kinickiob2e

SOMEONE ONCE OBSERVED THAT a leader is a person who finds out which way the parade is going, jumps in front, and yells "Follow me!" The plain fact is that this approach to leadership has little chance of working in today's rapidly changing world. As illustrated in the chapter's opening vignette, leadership involves more than simply taking charge. Ann Fudge not only had to deal with negative employee emotions and questions about her ability to lead an advertising agency, she also needed to focus on client relationships and operational issues. In short, successful leaders are those individuals who can step into a difficult situation and make a noticeable difference. But how much of a difference can leaders make in modern organizations?

OB researchers have discovered that leaders can make a difference. One study, for instance, revealed that leadership was positively associated with net profits from 167 companies over a time span of 20 years.[2] Research also showed that a coach's leadership skills affected the success of his or her team. Specifically, teams in both Major League Baseball and college basketball won more games when players perceived the coach to be an effective leader.[3] Rest assured, leadership make a difference!

After formally defining the term *leadership*, this chapter focuses on the following areas: (1) trait and behavioral approaches to leadership, (2) alternative situational theories of leadership, (3) charismatic leadership, and (4) additional perspectives on leadership. Because there are many different leadership theories within each of these areas, it is impossible to discuss them all. This chapter reviews those theories with the most research support.

What Does Leadership Involve?

Disagreement about the definition of leadership stems from the fact that it involves a complex interaction among the leader, the followers, and the situation. For example, some researchers define leadership in terms of personality and physical traits, while others believe leadership is represented by a set of prescribed behaviors. In contrast, other researchers believe that leadership is a temporary role that can be filled by anyone. There is a common thread, however, among the different definitions of leadership. The common thread is social influence.

leadership

Influencing employees to voluntarily pursue organizational goals.

As the term is used in this chapter, **leadership** is defined as "a social influence process in which the leader seeks the voluntary participation of subordinates in an effort to reach organizational goals."[4] This definition implies that leadership involves more than wielding power and exercising authority and is exhibited on different levels. At the individual level, for example, leadership involves mentoring, coaching, inspiring, and motivating. Leaders build teams, create cohesion, and resolve conflict at the group level. Finally, leaders build culture and create change at the organizational level.[5]

There are two components of leadership missing from the above definition: the moral and follower perspectives. Leadership is not a moral concept. History is filled with examples of great leaders who were killers, corrupt, and morally bankrupt. Barbara Kellerman, a leadership expert, commented on this notion by concluding "Leaders are like the rest of us: trustworthy and deceitful, cowardly and brave, greedy and generous. To assume that all good leaders are good people is to be willfully blind to the reality of the human condition, and it more severely limits our scope for becoming more effective at leadership."[6] The point is that good leaders develop a keen sense of their strengths and weaknesses and build on their positive attributes.[7]

Moreover, research on the follower perspective reveals that people seek, admire, and respect leaders who foster three emotional responses in others. Followers want organizational leaders to create feelings of *significance* (what one does at work is important and meaningful), *community* (a sense of unity encourages people to treat others with respect and dignity and to work together in pursuit of organizational goals), and *excitement* (people are engaged and feel energy at work).[8]

Trait and Behavioral Theories of Leadership

This section examines the two earliest approaches used to explain leadership. Trait theories focused on identifying the personal traits that differentiated leaders from followers. Behavioral theorists examined leadership from a different perspective. They tried to uncover the different kinds of leader behaviors that resulted in higher work group performance. Both approaches to leadership can teach current and future managers valuable lessons about leading.

leader trait

Personal characteristic that differentiates leaders from followers.

Sports teams, like leaders, have followers that respond to the behaviors of television and cable networks that broadcast their favorite teams. When the father and son team of Cablevision Systems Corporation, Chairman Charles F. Dolan and CEO James L. Dolan, decided not to include the New York Yankees Entertainment & Sports Network as part of its basic offerings, diehard Yankees fans said, "Na na na na, hey hey hey, good-bye." As the Dolans found out, a leader's decisions clearly affect the attitudes and behaviors of followers.

Trait Theory

Trait theory is the successor to what was called the "great man" theory of leadership. This approach was based on the assumption that leaders such as Abraham Lincoln, Martin Luther King, or Jack Welch were born with some inborn ability to lead. In contrast, trait theorists believed that leadership traits were not innate, but could be developed through experience and learning. A **leader trait** is a physical or personality characteristic that can be used to differentiate leaders from followers.

Before World War II, hundreds of studies were conducted to pinpoint the traits of successful leaders. Dozens of leadership traits were identified. During the postwar period, however, enthusiasm was replaced by widespread criticism. Researchers simply were unable to uncover a consistent set of traits that accurately predicted which individuals became leaders in organizations.

Contemporary Trait Research Two OB researchers concluded in 1983 that past trait data may have been incorrectly analyzed. By applying modern statistical techniques to an old database, they demonstrated that the majority of a leader's behavior could be attributed to stable underlying traits.[9] Unfortunately, their methodology did not single out specific traits.

More recently, results from three separate meta-analyses shed light on important leadership traits. The first was conducted in 1986 by Robert Lord and his associates. Based on a reanalysis of past studies, Lord concluded that people have leadership *prototypes* that affect our perceptions of who is and who is not an effective leader. Your **leadership prototype** is a mental representation of the traits and behaviors that you believe are possessed by leaders. We thus tend to perceive that someone is a leader when he or she exhibits traits or behaviors that are consistent with our prototypes.[10] Lord's research demonstrated that people are perceived as being leaders when they exhibit the traits associated with intelligence, masculinity, and dominance. Another study of 6,052 middle-level managers from 22 European countries revealed that leadership prototypes are culturally based. In

leadership prototype

Mental representation of the traits and behaviors possessed by leaders.

other words, leadership prototypes are influenced by national cultural values.[11] Researchers have not yet identified a set of global leadership prototypes.

The next two meta-analyses were completed by Timothy Judge and his colleagues. The first examined the relationship among the Big Five personality traits (see Table 5–2 for a review of these traits) and leadership emergence and effectiveness in 94 studies. Results revealed that extraversion was most consistently and positively related to both leadership emergence and effectiveness. Conscientiousness and openness to experience also were positively correlated with leadership effectiveness.[12] Judge's second meta-analysis involved 151 samples and demonstrated that intelligence was modestly related to leadership effectiveness. Judge concluded that personality is more important than intelligence when selecting leaders.[13]

This conclusion is supported by research that examined the causes of leadership failures. Findings revealed that managers who failed exhibited several personality flaws including being overly controlling, irritable, exploitative, arrogant, abrasive, selfish, and lacking emotional intelligence (recall our discussion in Chapter 5).[14] Consider the case of Steven Heyer:

> In less than three years at Coca-Cola, Steven J. Heyer has shaken up a struggling corporate giant and added some much-needed new fizz. But last week, when Chairman Douglas Daft announced his plans to step down, the board decided that Mr. Heyer, the current No. 2, might not be the man it wants.
>
> While few question the former entertainment and advertising executive's dedication and intelligence, directors wonder whether he fits their vision of a world-class leader. . . . To many board members, the ideal Coke chairman and CEO is a visionary who commands admiration, delegates easily and communicates well with Coke's 50,000 or so employees and the public.
>
> Blunt, assertive and at times acerbic, Mr. Heyer strikes many observers as a much-needed tonic in Coke's staid corporate culture. But some company insiders criticize his sharp tongue and what they see as self-promotion.[15]

A reporter at *Business Week* concluded that Heyer is not ready to be a CEO. He noted that Heyer's confrontational style, including a habit of belittling other executives and staffers, is not characteristic of an effective leader.[16] Apparently this reporter was correct because E. Neville Isdell was selected over Heyer to be the next CEO of Coke.

Gender and Leadership The increase of women in the workforce has generated much interest in understanding the similarities and differences in female and male leaders. Research uncovered the following differences: (1) Men and women were seen as displaying more task and social leadership, respectively;[17] (2) women used a more democratic or participative style than men, and men used a more autocratic and directive style than women;[18] (3) men and women were equally assertive;[19] (4) women executives, when rated by their peers, managers, and direct reports, scored higher than their male counterparts on a variety of effectiveness criteria;[20] and (5) men displayed more laissez-faire leadership (i.e., a general failure to take responsibility for managing).[21]

In spite of these positive results, the same behavior by a male and female can be interpreted differently and lead to opposite consequences. Consider the case of Deborah Hopkins, former chief financial officer at Lucent Technologies:

> Ms Hopkins, 46 years old and widely viewed as one of America's hottest female executives, had been at the maker of phone-industry equipment just over a year. . . . Ms Hopkins's management technique, which earned her the nickname "Hurricane

> Debby," fell flat at Lucent. There, she was known for unforgiving candor, in which she typically cut off colleagues in midsentence. . . . Being a women didn't help, say people close to Ms Hopkins. Indeed, she was the fourth high-ranking female executive to leave Lucent, starting with Ms Fiorina [Carly Fiorina is CEO of Hewlett-Packard] in 1999. And while traits such as candor and abrasiveness can be considered good qualities in male chief executives in a tough turnaround situation, Ms Hopkins was criticized for her personality.[22]

Trait Theory in Perspective We can no longer afford to ignore the implications of leadership traits. Traits play a central role in how we perceive leaders and a central role in determining the characteristics of effective leaders. As done by the board of directors at Coca-Cola, organizations should consider selected leadership traits when choosing among candidates for leadership positions. Gender and race should not be used as any of these traits.

Behavioral Styles Theory

This phase of leadership research began during World War II as part of an effort to develop better military leaders. It was an outgrowth of two events: the seeming inability of trait theory to explain leadership effectiveness and the human relations movement, an outgrowth of the Hawthorne Studies. The thrust of early behavioral leadership theory was to focus on leader behavior, instead of on personality traits. It was believed that leader behavior directly affected work group effectiveness. This led researchers to identify patterns of behavior (called leadership styles) that enabled leaders to effectively influence others.

The Ohio State Studies Researchers at Ohio State University began by generating a list of behaviors exhibited by leaders. Ultimately, the Ohio State researchers concluded there were only two independent dimensions of leader behavior: consideration and initiating structure. **Consideration** involves leader behavior associated with creating mutual respect or trust and focuses on a concern for group members' needs and desires. **Initiating structure** is leader behavior that organizes and defines what group members should be doing to maximize output. These two dimensions of leader behavior were oriented at right angles to yield four behavioral styles of leadership: low structure–high consideration, high structure–high consideration, low structure–low consideration, and high structure–low consideration.

consideration

Creating mutual respect and trust with followers.

initiating structure

Organizing and defining what group members should be doing.

It initially was hypothesized that a high-structure–high-consideration style would be the one best style of leadership. Through the years, the effectiveness of the high–high style has been tested many times. Overall, results have been mixed. Researchers thus concluded that there is not one best style of leadership. Rather, it is argued that effectiveness of a given leadership style depends on situational factors.

University of Michigan Studies As in the Ohio State studies, this research sought to identify behavioral differences between effective and ineffective leaders. Researchers identified two different styles of leadership: one was employee centered, the other was job centered. These behavioral styles parallel the consideration and initiating-structure styles identified by the Ohio State group.

The Leadership Grid® Developed by Robert Blake and Jane Srygley Mouton, the Leadership Grid® is based on the idea that there is one best style of leadership.

SKILLS & BEST PRACTICES

Peter Drucker's Tips for Improving Leadership Effectiveness

1. Determine what needs to be done.
2. Determine the right thing to do for the welfare of the entire enterprise or organization.
3. Develop action plans that specify desired results, probable restraints, future revisions, check-in points, and implications for how one should spend his or her time.
4. Take responsibility for decisions.
5. Take responsibility for communicating action plans and give people the information they need to get the job done.
6. Focus on opportunities rather than problems. Do not sweep problems under the rug, and treat change as an opportunity rather than a threat.
7. Run productive meetings. Different types of meetings require different forms of preparation and different results. Prepare accordingly.
8. Think and say "we" rather than "I." Consider the needs and opportunities of the organization before thinking of your own opportunities and needs.
9. Listen first, speak last.

SOURCE: Reprinted by permission of *Harvard Business Review*. These recommendations were derived from P F Drucker, "What Makes an Effective Executive," *Harvard Business Review*, June 2004, pp 58–63.

The Grid is formed by the intersection of two dimensions of leader behavior. On the horizontal axis is "concern for production" and "concern for people" is on the vertical axis. By scaling each axis of the grid from 1 (Low) to 9 (High), Blake and Mouton were able to plot five leadership styles. The styles are impoverished management (1, 1), country club management (1, 9), authority-compliance (9, 1), middle-of-the-road management (5, 5), and team management (9, 9). The team management style is considered to be the best style regardless of the situation.

Behavioral Styles Theory in Perspective By emphasizing leader *behavior,* something that is learned, the behavioral style approach makes it clear that leaders are made, not born. Given what we know about behavior shaping and model-based training, leader *behaviors* can be systematically improved and developed.[23]

Behavioral styles research also revealed that there is no one best style of leadership. The effectiveness of a particular leadership style depends on the situation at hand. For instance, employees prefer structure over consideration when faced with role ambiguity.[24] Finally, research also reveals that it is important to consider the difference between how frequently and how effectively managers exhibit various leader behaviors. For example, a manager might ineffectively display a lot of considerate leader behaviors. Such a style is likely to frustrate employees and possibly result in lowered job satisfaction and performance. Because the frequency of exhibiting leadership behaviors is secondary in importance to effectiveness, managers are encouraged to concentrate on improving the effective execution of their leader behaviors.[25] Finally, Peter Drucker, an internationally renowned management expert and consultant, recommended a set of nine behaviors (see Skills & Best Practices) managers can focus on to improve their leadership effectiveness. The first two practices provide the knowledge leaders need. The next four help leaders convert knowledge into effective action, and the following two ensure that the whole organization feels responsible and accountable. Drucker refers to the last recommendation as a managerial rule.

Situational Theories

situational theories

Propose that leader styles should match the situation at hand.

Situational leadership theories grew out of an attempt to explain the inconsistent findings about traits and styles. **Situational theories** propose that the effectiveness of a particular style of leader behavior depends on the situation. As situations change, different styles become appropriate. This directly challenges the idea of one best style of leadership. Let us closely examine three alternative situational theories of leadership that reject the notion of one best leadership style.

Fiedler's Contingency Model

Fred Fiedler, an OB scholar, developed a situational model of leadership. It is the oldest and one of the most widely known models of leadership. Fiedler's model is based on the following assumption:

> The performance of a leader depends on two interrelated factors: (1) the degree to which the situation gives the leader control and influence—that is, the likelihood that [the leader] can successfully accomplish the job; and (2) the leader's basic motivation—that is, whether [the leader's] self-esteem depends primarily on accomplishing the task or on having close supportive relations with others.[26]

With respect to a leader's basic motivation, Fiedler believes that leaders are either task motivated or relationship motivated. These basic motivations are similar to initiating structure/concern for production and consideration/concern for people.

Fiedler's theory also is based on the premise that leaders have one dominant leadership style that is resistant to change. He suggests that leaders must learn to manipulate or influence the leadership situation in order to create a "match" between their leadership style and the amount of control within the situation at hand. After discussing the components of situational control and the leadership matching process, we review relevant research and managerial implications.[27]

Situational Control Situational control refers to the amount of control and influence the leader has in her or his immediate work environment. Situational control ranges from high to low. High control implies that the leader's decisions will produce predictable results because the leader has the ability to influence work outcomes. Low control implies that the leader's decisions may not influence work outcomes because the leader has very little influence. There are three dimensions of situational control: leader–member relations, task structure, and position power. These dimensions vary independently, forming eight combinations of situational control (see Figure 14–1).

The three dimensions of situational control are defined as follows:

- *Leader–member relations* reflect the extent to which the leader has the support, loyalty, and trust of the work group.
- *Task structure* is concerned with the amount of structure contained within tasks performed by the work group.
- *Position power* refers to the degree to which the leader has formal power to reward, punish, or otherwise obtain compliance from employees.

Linking Leadership Motivation and Situational Control Fiedler's complete contingency model is presented in Figure 14–1. The last row under the Situational Control column shows that there are eight different leadership situations. Each situation represents a unique combination of leader–member relations, task structure, and position power. Situations I, II, and III represent high control situations. Figure 14–1 shows that task-motivated leaders are hypothesized to be most effective in situations of high control. Under conditions of moderate control (situations IV, V, VI, and VII), relationship-motivated leaders are expected to be more effective. Finally, the results orientation of task-motivated leaders is predicted to be more effective under the condition of very low control (situation VIII).

Research and Managerial Implications Research has provided mixed support for Fiedler's model, suggesting that the model needs theoretical refinement.[28]

FIGURE 14–1 Representation of Fiedler's Contingency Model

Situational Control	High Control Situations			Moderate Control Situations				Low Control Situations
Leader–member relations	Good	Good	Good	Good	Poor	Poor	Poor	Poor
Task structure	High	High	Low	Low	High	High	Low	Low
Position power	Strong	Weak	Strong	Weak	Strong	Weak	Strong	Weak
Situation	I	II	III	IV	V	VI	VII	VIII
Optimal Leadership Style	**Task-Motivated Leadership**			**Relationship-Motivated Leadership**				**Task-Motivated Leadership**

SOURCE: Adapted from F E Fiedler, "Situational Control and a Dynamic Theory of Leadership," in *Managerial Control and Organizational Democracy*, eds B King, S Streufert, and F E Fiedler (New York: John Wiley & Sons, 1978), p 114.

That said, the major contribution of Fiedler's model is that it prompted others to examine the contingency nature of leadership. This research, in turn, reinforced the notion that there is no one best style of leadership. Leaders are advised to alter their task and relationship orientation to fit the demands of the situation at hand. Consider, for example, the different leadership styles of IBM's current CEO—Sam Palmisano—and former CEO—Lou Gerstner:

> His aw-schucks nature, coupled with Palmisano's ability to chat up just about anyone he meets, makes him approachable for customers and employees. . . . He's constantly on the phone, calling all over the world: "How's your quarter?" "Did we close this deal?" . . . Software chief Steve Mills calls Palmisano an "execution maniac." . . . This single-mindedness about results is a big reason Palmisano was selected by Gerstner to take over IBM two years ago. Says Merrill Lynch security analyst . . . Steve Milunovich: "Sam is the right guy to run IBM right now. He's great externally and a hard-charging Marine internally."
>
> Palmisano's style is a big departure from that of the gruff and intimidating Gerstner. But then Gerstner's role wasn't to be nice; it was to keep IBM from disintegrating. He took over just as it was about to split itself up into 13 distinct, loosely affiliated entities.[29]

Sam Palmisano and Lou Gerstner used different leadership styles to successfully lead employees within IBM. As suggested by Fiedler, they both were effective because their respective leadership styles were appropriate for the situation at the time.

Path–Goal Theory

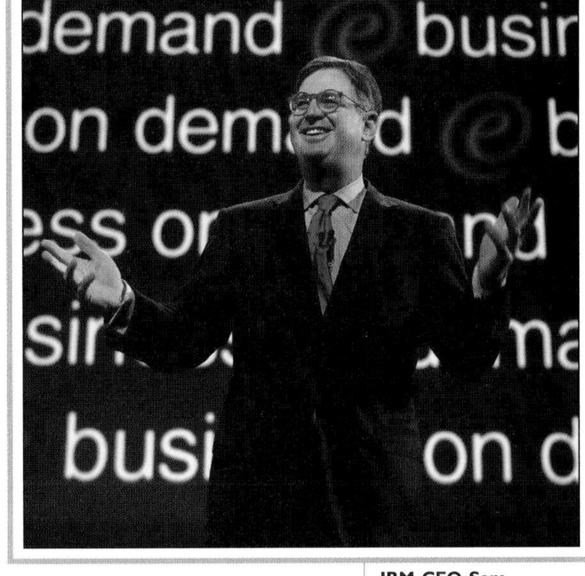

IBM CEO Sam Palmisano, since taking the reins in 2002, has offered a good chunk of his own bonus to stake a performance-based bonus for 20 top executives, dissolved a committee consisting of 300 members that had been in place for generations, and placed a new emphasis on teams with his "on-demand" strategy. Palmisano has a vision of remaking IBM into the powerhouse it once was.

Path–goal theory was originally proposed by Robert House in the 1970s.[30] He developed a model that describes how leadership effectiveness is influenced by the interaction between four leadership styles (directive, supportive, participative, and achievement-oriented) and a variety of contingency factors. **Contingency factors** are situational variables that cause one style of leadership to be more effective than another. Path–goal theory has two groups of contingency variables. They are employee characteristics and environmental factors. Five important employee characteristics are locus of control, task ability, need for achievement, experience, and need for clarity. Two relevant environmental factors are task structure (independent versus interdependent tasks) and work group dynamics. In order to gain a better understanding of how these contingency factors influence leadership effectiveness, we illustratively consider locus of control (see Chapter 5), task ability and experience, and task structure.

Employees with an internal locus of control are more likely to prefer participative or achievement-oriented leadership because they believe they have control over the work environment. Such individuals are unlikely to be satisfied with directive leader behaviors that exert additional control over their activities. In contrast, employees with an external locus tend to view the environment as uncontrollable, thereby preferring the structure provided by supportive or directive leadership. An employee with high task ability and experience is less apt to need additional direction and thus would respond negatively to directive leadership. This person is more likely to be motivated and satisfied by participative and achievement-oriented leadership. Oppositely, an inexperienced employee would find achievement-oriented leadership overwhelming as he or she confronts challenges associated with learning a new job. Supportive and directive leadership would be helpful in this situation. Finally, directive and supportive leadership should help employees experiencing role ambiguity. However, directive leadership is likely to frustrate employees working on routine and simple tasks. Supportive leadership is most useful in this context.

contingency factors
Variables that influence the appropriateness of a leadership style.

There have been about 50 studies testing various predictions derived from House's original model. Results have been mixed, with some studies supporting the theory and others not.[31] House thus proposed a new version of path–goal theory in 1996 based on these results and the accumulation of new knowledge about OB.

A Reformulated Theory The revised theory is presented in Figure 14–2.[32] There are three key changes in the new theory. First, House now believes that leadership is more complex and involves a greater variety of leader behavior. He thus identifies eight categories of leadership styles or behavior (see Table 14–1). The need for an expanded list of leader behaviors is supported by current research and

FIGURE 14–2
A General Representation of House's Revised Path–Goal Theory

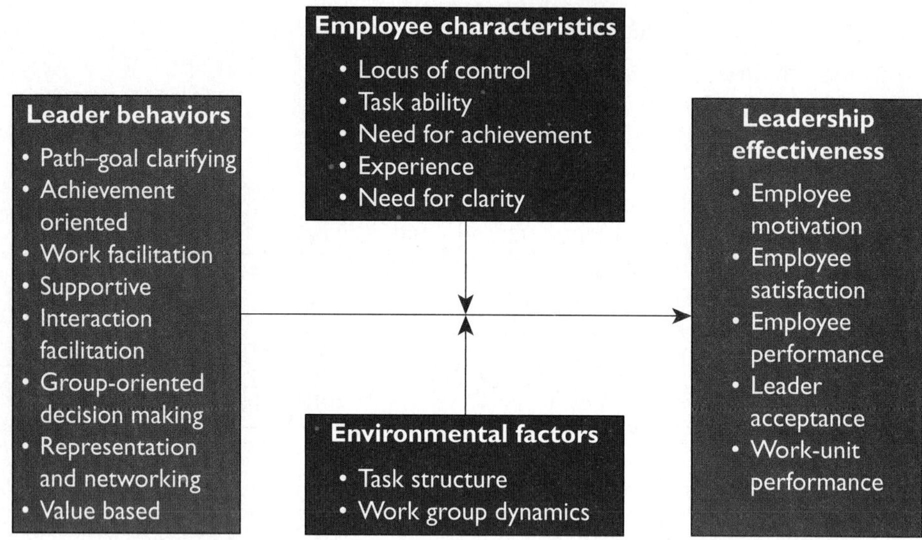

descriptions of business leaders.[33] Consider the different leader behaviors exhibited by Carly Fiorina, CEO of Hewlett-Packard Company:

> She's a well-rehearsed businesswoman with a buttoned-down message to customers that echoes HP's new marketing theme: "Demand more." . . . But the words could also describe Fiorina's own management style. Opinions vary on the stylish 48-year-old with the multimillion-dollar paycheck, who has been described as everything from brilliant and visionary to arrogant and self-serving, but on one point people agree. Carly Fiorina—who rises at 4:30 A.M. and routinely puts in 16-hour workdays—is a furiously driven executive who expects the very best from herself and her 141,000 employees.
>
> "She's not in our offices every day beating on us, but she expects us to be on top of what we're doing," says Shane Robison, executive vice president and chief strategy and technology officer. "She believes our culture should be based on performance, self-motivation and high-achievement." . . .[34]

Carly Fiorina exhibited path–goal clarifying behaviors, achievement-oriented behaviors, work facilitation behaviors, representation and networking behaviors, and value-based behaviors.

The second key change involves the role of intrinsic motivation (discussed in Chapter 6) and empowerment (discussed in Chapter 13) in influencing leadership effectiveness. House places much more emphasis on the need for leaders to foster intrinsic motivation through empowerment. Shared leadership represents the final change in the revised theory. That is, path–goal theory is based on the premise that an employee does not have to be a supervisor or manager to engage in leader behavior. Rather, House believes that leadership is shared among all employees within an organization. More is said about shared leadership in the final section of this chapter.

Research and Managerial Implications There are not enough direct tests of House's revised path–goal theory using appropriate research methods and

TABLE 14–1 Categories of Leader Behavior within the Revised Path–Goal Theory

Category of Leader Behavior	Description of Leader Behaviors
Path–goal clarifying behaviors	Clarifying employees' performance goals; providing guidance on how employees can complete tasks; clarifying performance standards and expectations; use of positive and negative rewards contingent on performance
Achievement-oriented behaviors	Setting challenging goals; emphasizing excellence; demonstrating confidence in employees' abilities
Work facilitation behaviors	Planning, scheduling, organizing, and coordinating work; providing mentoring, coaching, counseling, and feedback to assist employees in developing their skills; eliminating roadblocks; providing resources; empowering employees to take actions and make decisions
Supportive behaviors	Showing concern for the well-being and needs of employees; being friendly and approachable; treating employees as equals
Interaction facilitation behaviors	Resolving disputes; facilitating communication; encouraging the sharing of minority opinions; emphasizing collaboration and teamwork; encouraging close relationships among employees
Group-oriented decision-making behaviors	Posing problems rather than solutions to the work group; encouraging group members to participate in decision making; providing necessary information to the group for analysis; involving knowledgeable employees in decision making
Representation and networking behaviors	Presenting the work group in a positive light to others; maintaining positive relationships with influential others; participating in organizationwide social functions and ceremonies; doing unconditional favors for others
Value-based behaviors	Establishing a vision, displaying passion for it, and supporting its accomplishment; demonstrating self-confidence; communicating high performance expectations and confidence in others' abilities to meet their goals; giving frequent positive feedback

SOURCE: Descriptions were adapted from R J House, "Path–Goal Theory of Leadership: Lessons, Legacy, and a Reformulated Theory," *Leadership Quarterly*, 1996, pp 323–52.

statistical procedures to draw overall conclusions. Future research is clearly needed to assess the accuracy of this model. That said, there still are two important managerial implications. First, effective leaders possess and use more than one style of leadership. Managers are encouraged to familiarize themselves with the different categories of leader behavior outlined in path–goal theory and to try new behaviors when the situation calls for them. Second, a small set of employee characteristics (i.e., ability, experience, and need for independence) and environmental factors (task characteristics of autonomy, variety, and significance) are relevant contingency factors.[35] Managers are advised to modify their leadership style to fit these various employee and task characteristics.

Hersey and Blanchard's Situational Leadership Theory

readiness

Follower's ability and willingness to complete a task.

Situational leadership theory (SLT) was developed by management writers Paul Hersey and Kenneth Blanchard.[36] According to the theory, effective leader behavior depends on the readiness level of a leader's followers. **Readiness** is defined as the extent to which a follower possesses the ability and willingness to complete a task. Willingness is a combination of confidence, commitment, and motivation.

The SLT model is summarized in Figure 14–3. The appropriate leadership style is found by cross-referencing follower readiness, which varies from low to high, with one of four leadership styles. The four leadership styles represent combinations of task and relationship-oriented leader behaviors (S_1 to S_4). Leaders are encouraged to use a "telling style" for followers with low readiness. This style combines high task-oriented leader behaviors, such as providing instructions, with low relationship-oriented behaviors, such as close supervision (see Figure 14–3). As follower readiness increases, leaders are advised to gradually

FIGURE 14–3 Situational Leadership Model

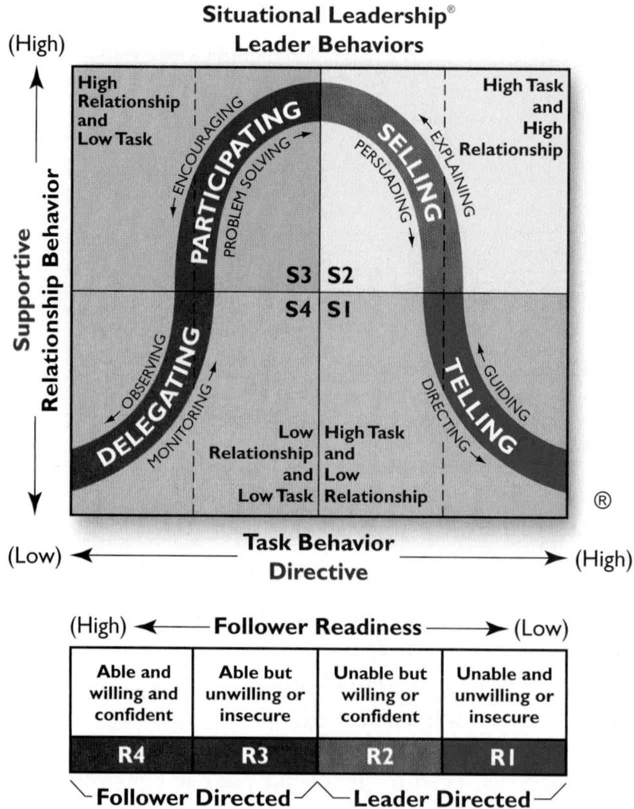

SOURCE: Paul Hersey, *The Management of Organizational Behavior: Utilizing Human Resources*, Center for Leadership Studies, Escondido, CA, 1984. Reprinted with permission. Situational Leadership® is a registered trademark of the Center for Leadership Studies, Inc.

move from a telling, to a selling, to a participating, and, ultimately, to a delegating style.[37]

Although SLT is widely used as a training tool, it is not strongly supported by scientific research. Finally, researchers have concluded that the self-assessment instrument used to measure leadership style and follower readiness is inaccurate and should be used with caution.[38] In summary, managers should exercise discretion when using prescriptions from SLT.

The Full-Range Theory of Leadership: From Transactional to Transformational Leadership

One of the most recent approaches to leadership is referred to as a full-range theory of leadership.[39] The authors of this theory, Bernard Bass and Bruce Avolio, proposed that leadership behavior varied along a continuum from laissez-faire leadership (i.e., a general failure to take responsibility for leading) to transactional leadership to transformational leadership. Of course, laissez-faire leadership is a terrible way for any manger to behave and should be avoided. In contrast, transactional and transformational leadership are both positively related to a variety of employee attitudes and behaviors and represent different aspects of being a good leader. Let us consider these two important dimensions of leadership.

transactional leadership Focuses on clarifying employees' roles and providing rewards contingent on performance.

Transactional leadership focuses on clarifying employees' role and task requirements and providing followers with positive and negative rewards contingent on performance. Further, transactional leadership encompasses the fundamental managerial activities of setting goals, monitoring progress toward goal achievement, and rewarding and punishing people for their level of goal accomplishment.[40] You can see from this description that transactional leadership is based on using extrinsic motivation (recall our discussion in Chapter 6) to increase employee productivity. Consider how Jim McNerney, chairman and CEO of 3M, uses transactional leadership to improve organizational performance.

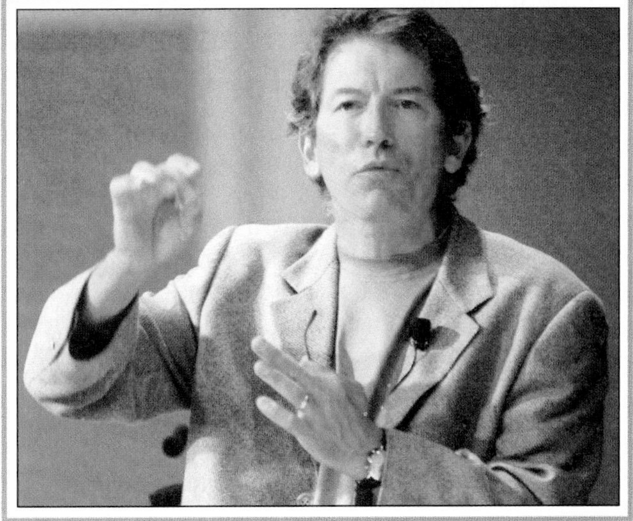

Thomas Siebel, founder and CEO of Siebel Systems, is a good example of a transactional leader. He motivates his employees by linking measures of customer satisfaction with employees' bonuses and commissions. Will this type of leadership continue to motivate employees in the long term?

> McNerney's secret to success is elementary. He sets high goals that can be measured, such as business-unit sales or the rate of product introductions, and demands that his managers meet them. Granted, many CEOs do that today. But like a dedicated teacher or coach, McNerney also works with his team day in, day out, to help them make the grade.[41]

In contrast, **transformational leaders** "engender trust, seek to develop leadership in others, exhibit self-sacrifice and serve as moral agents, focusing themselves and followers on objectives that transcend the more immediate needs of the work group."[42] Transformational leaders can produce significant organizational change and

transformational leadership

Transforms employees to pursue organizational goals over self-interests.

results because this form of leadership fosters higher levels of intrinsic motivation, trust, commitment, and loyalty from followers than does transactional leadership. That said, however, it is important to note that transactional leadership is an essential prerequisite to effective leadership, and that the best leaders learn to display both transactional and transformational leadership to various degrees. In support of this proposition, research reveals that transformational leadership leads to superior performance when it "augments" or adds to transactional leadership.[43] Let us return to the example of Jim McNerney, CEO of 3M, to see how he augments transactional leadership with transformational leadership:

> "Some people think you either have a demanding, command-and-control management style or you have a nurturing, encouraging style," he says. "I believe you can't have one without the other." . . . McNerney is praised as an inspirational leader comfortable speaking to big groups or conversing one-on-one. . . . He is quick to attribute 3M's achievement to the entire organization and praises 3Mers for their work ethic. "My experience is that if people are convinced they're growing as they pursue company goals, that's when you get ignition," he says."[44]

We now turn our attention to examining the process by which transformational leadership influences followers.

How Does Transformational Leadership Transform Followers?

Transformational leaders transform followers by creating changes in their goals, values, needs, beliefs, and aspirations. They accomplish this transformation by appealing to followers' self-concepts—namely their values and personal identity. Figure 14–4 presents a model of how leaders accomplish this transformation process.

Figure 14–4 shows that transformational leader behavior is first influenced by various individual and organizational characteristics. For example, research reveals that transformational leaders tend to have personalities that are more extraverted, agreeable, and proactive than nontransformational leaders, and female leaders use transformational leadership more than male leaders.[45] Organizational culture also influences the extent to which leaders are transformational. Cultures that are adaptive and flexible rather than rigid and bureaucratic are more likely to create environments that foster the opportunity for transformational leadership to be exhibited.

Transformational leaders engage in four key sets of leader behavior (see Figure 14–4).[46] The first set, referred to as *inspirational motivation,* involves establishing an attractive vision of the future, the use of emotional arguments, and exhibition of optimism and enthusiasm. A vision is "a realistic, credible, attractive future for your organization."[47] According to Burt Nanus, a leadership expert, the "right" vision unleashes human potential because it serves as a beacon of hope and common purpose. It does this by attracting commitment, energizing workers, creating meaning in employees' lives, establishing a standard of excellence, promoting high ideals, and bridging the gap between an organization's present problems and its future goals and aspirations. Ed Zander, Motorola's CEO, understands the importance of using a vision to energize his workforce. He has been talking to employees, customers, and suppliers in pursuit of information to create a vision for

A Transformational Model of Leadership **FIGURE 14–4**

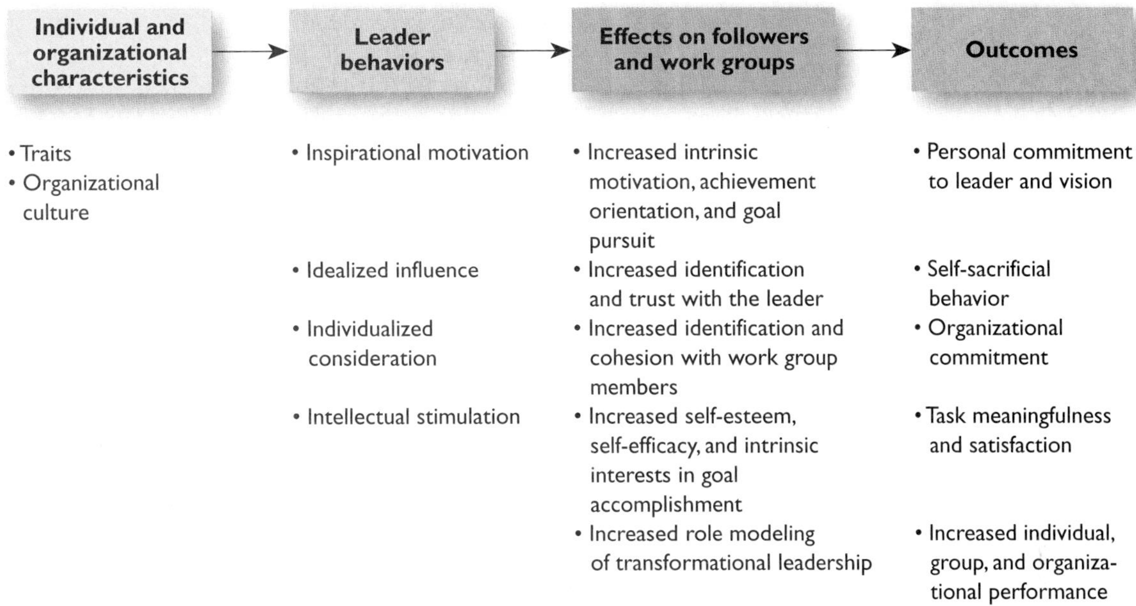

SOURCE: Based in part on D A Waldman and F J Yammarino, "CEO Charismatic Leadership: Levels-of-Management and Levels-of-Analysis Effects," *Academy of Management Review,* April 1999, pp 266–85; and B Shamir, R J House, and M B Arthur, "The Motivational Effects of Charismatic Leadership: A Self-Concept Based Theory," *Organization Science,* November 1993, pp 577–94.

Motorola. He feels this is necessary because customers and employees told him that the company "does too many things—and not enough of them well."[48] A good vision will enable Zander to marshal the company's efforts and resources toward a common long-term goal.

Idealized influence, the second set of leader behaviors, includes behaviors such as sacrificing for the good of the group, being a role model, and displaying high ethical standards. Through their actions, transformational leaders model the desired values, traits, beliefs, and behaviors needed to realize the vision. The third set, *individualized consideration,* entails behaviors associated with providing support, encouragement, empowerment, and coaching to employees. *Intellectual stimulation,* the fourth set of leadership behaviors, involves behaviors that encourage employees to question the status quo and to seek innovative and creative solutions to organizational problems.

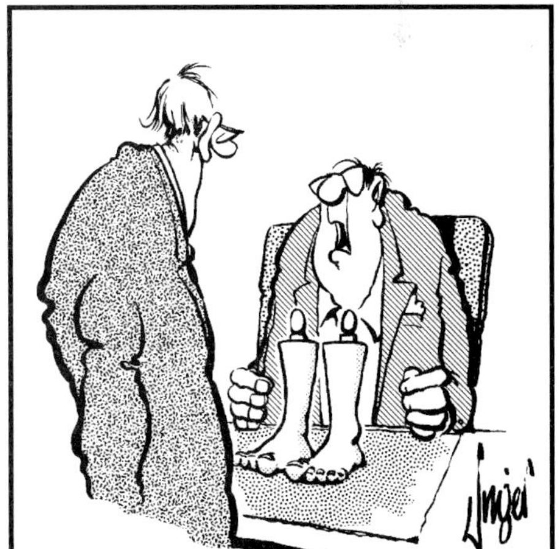

"You've got the job. Now, take these home and practice kissing them."

© Jim Unger/HERMAN reprinted by permission of Newspaper Enterprise Association, Inc.

Research and Managerial Implications

Components of the transformational model of leadership have been the most widely researched leadership topic over the last decade. Overall, the relationships outlined in Figure 14–4 generally were supported by previous research. For example, transformational leader behaviors were positively associated with the extent to which employees identified with both their leaders and immediate work groups.[49] Followers of transformational leaders also were found to set goals that were consistent with those of the leader, to be more engaged in their work, to have higher levels of intrinsic motivation, and to have higher levels of group cohesion.[50] With respect to the direct relationship between transformational leadership and work outcomes, a meta-analysis of 49 studies indicated that transformational leadership was positively associated with measures of leadership effectiveness and employees' job satisfaction.[51] At the organizational level, a second meta-analysis demonstrated that transformational leadership was positively correlated with organizational measures of effectiveness.[52]

These results underscore four important managerial implications. First, the best leaders are not just transformational; they are both transactional and transformational. Leaders should attempt to use these two types of leadership while avoiding a "laissez-faire" or "wait-and-see" style.

Second, transformational leadership not only affects individual-level outcomes like job satisfaction, organizational commitment, and performance, but it also influences group dynamics and group-level outcomes. Managers can thus use the four types of transformational leadership shown in Figure 14–4 as a vehicle to improve group dynamics and work-unit outcomes. This is important in today's organizations because most employees do not work in isolation. Rather, people tend to rely on the input and collaboration of others, and many organizations are structured around teams. The key point to remember is that transformational leadership transforms individuals as well as teams and work groups. We encourage you to use this to your advantage.

Third, employees at any level in an organization can be trained to be more transactional and transformational.[53] This reinforces the organizational value of developing and rolling out a combination of transactional and transformational leadership training for all employees. These programs, however, should be based on an overall corporate philosophy that constitutes the foundation of leadership development. Johnson & Johnson Company, for example, implemented an extensive process of leadership development that was based on seven principles of leadership development (see Skills & Best Practices).[54]

Fourth, transformational leaders can be ethical or unethical. Whereas ethical transformational leaders enable employees to enhance their self-concepts, unethical ones select or produce obedient, dependent, and compliant followers. Top management can create and maintain ethical transformational leadership by

1. Creating and enforcing a clearly stated code of ethics.
2. Recruiting, selecting, and promoting people who display ethical behavior.

SKILLS & BEST PRACTICES

Johnson & Johnson Company Bases Its Leadership Development around Seven Guiding Principles

1. Leadership development is a key business strategy.
2. Leadership excellence is a definable set of standards.
3. People are responsible for their own development.
4. Johnson & Johnson executives are accountable for developing leaders.
5. Leaders are developed primarily on the job.
6. People are an asset of the corporation; leadership development is a collaborative, corporation-wide process.
7. Human resources is vital to the success of leadership development.

SOURCE: Excerpted from R M Fulmer, "Johnson & Johnson: Framework for Leadership," *Organizational Dynamics*, Winter 2001, p 214.

3. Developing performance expectations around the treatment of employees—these expectations can then be assessed in the performance appraisal process.
4. Training employees to value diversity.
5. Identifying, rewarding, and publicly praising employees who exemplify high moral conduct.[55]

Additional Perspectives on Leadership

This section examines four additional perspectives to leadership: leader–member exchange theory, shared leadership, servant-leadership, and level 5 leadership. We spend more time discussing leader–member exchange theory because it has been more thoroughly investigated.

The Leader–Member Exchange (LMX) Model of Leadership

The leader–member exchange model of leadership revolves around the development of dyadic relationships between managers and their direct reports. This model is quite different from those previously discussed in that it focuses on the quality of relationships between managers and subordinates as opposed to the behaviors or traits of either leaders or followers. It also is different in that it does not assume that leader behavior is characterized by a stable or average leadership style as does the Leadership Grid® and Fiedler's contingency theory. In other words, these models assume a leader treats all employees in about the same way. In contrast, the LMX model is based on the assumption that leaders develop unique one-to-one relationships with each of the people reporting to them. Behavioral scientists call this sort of relationship a *vertical dyad.* The forming of vertical dyads is said to be a naturally occurring process, resulting from the leader's attempt to delegate and assign work roles. As a result of this process, two distinct types of leader–member exchange relationships are expected to evolve.[56]

One type of leader–member exchange is called the **in-group exchange.** In this relationship, leaders and followers develop a partnership characterized by reciprocal influence, mutual trust, respect and liking, and a sense of common fates. In the second type of exchange, referred to as an **out-group exchange,** leaders are characterized as overseers who fail to create a sense of mutual trust, respect, or common fate.[57]

in-group exchange
A partnership characterized by mutual trust, respect, and liking.

out-group exchange
A partnership characterized by a lack of mutual trust, respect, and liking.

Research Findings If the leader–member exchange model is correct, there should be a significant relationship between the type of leader–member exchange and job-related outcomes. Research supports this prediction. For example, a positive leader–member exchange was positively associated with job satisfaction, job performance, goal commitment, trust between managers and employees, work climate, and satisfaction with leadership.[58] The type of leader–member exchange also was found to predict not only turnover among nurses and computer analysts, but also career outcomes, such as promotability, salary level, and receipt of bonuses over a seven-year period.[59] Finally, studies also have identified a variety of variables that influence the quality of an LMX. For example, LMX was related to personality similarity and demographic similarity.[60] Further, the quality of an LMX was positively related with the extent to which leaders and followers like each other, the leaders' positive expectations of their subordinates, and the frequency of communications between managers and their direct reports.[61]

Managerial Implications There are three important implications associated with the LMX model of leadership. First, leaders are encouraged to establish high-performance expectations for all of their direct reports because setting high-performance standards fosters high-quality LMXs. Second, because personality and demographic similarity between leaders and followers is associated with higher LMXs, managers need to be careful that they don't create a homogeneous work environment in the spirit of having positive relationships with their direct reports. Our discussion of diversity in Chapter 4 clearly documented that there are many positive benefits of having a diverse workforce. The third implication pertains to those of us who find ourselves in a poor LMX. Before providing advice about what to do in this situation, we would like you to assess the quality of your current leader–member exchange. The Hands-On Exercise contains a measure of leader–member exchange that segments an LMX into four subdimensions: mutual affection, loyalty, contribution to work activities, and professional respect.

What is the overall quality of your LMX? Do you agree with this assessment? Which subdimensions are high and low? If your overall LMX and associated subdimensions are all high, you should be in a very good situation with respect to the relationship between you and your manager. Having a low LMX overall score or a low dimensional score, however, reveals that part of the relationship with your manager may need improvement. A management consultant offers the following tips for improving the quality of leader–member exchanges.[62]

1. Stay focused on your department's goals and remain positive about your ability to accomplish your goals. An unsupportive boss is just another obstacle to be overcome.
2. Do not fall prey to feeling powerless, and empower yourself to get things done.
3. Exercise the power you have by focusing on circumstances you can control and avoid dwelling on circumstances you cannot control.
4. Work on improving your relationship with your manager. Begin by examining the level of trust between the two of you and then try to improve it by frequently and effectively communicating. You can also increase trust by following through on your commitments and achieving your goals.
5. Use an authentic, respectful, and assertive approach to resolve differences with your manager. It also is useful to use a problem-solving approach when disagreements arise.

Shared Leadership

A pair of OB scholars noted that "there is some speculation, and some preliminary evidence, to suggest that concentration of leadership in a single chain of command

HANDS-ON EXERCISE

Assessing Your Leader–Member Exchange

INSTRUCTIONS: For each of the items shown below, use the following scale to circle the answer that best represents how you feel about the relationship between you and your current manager/supervisor. If you are not currently working, complete the survey by thinking about a previous manager. Remember, there are no right or wrong answers. After circling a response for each of the 12 items, use the scoring key to compute scores for the subdimensions within your leader–member exchange.

1 = Strongly disagree
2 = Disagree
3 = Neither agree nor disagree
4 = Agree
5 = Strongly agree

1.	I like my supervisor very much as a person.	1 2 3 4 5
2.	My supervisor is the kind of person one would like to have as a friend.	1 2 3 4 5
3.	My supervisor is a lot of fun to work with.	1 2 3 4 5
4.	My supervisor defends my work actions to a superior, even without complete knowledge of the issue in question.	1 2 3 4 5
5.	My supervisor would come to my defense if I were "attacked" by others.	1 2 3 4 5
6.	My supervisor would defend me to others in the organization if I made an honest mistake.	1 2 3 4 5
7.	I do work for my supervisor that goes beyond what is specified in my job description.	1 2 3 4 5
8.	I am willing to apply extra efforts, beyond those normally required, to meet my supervisor's work goals.	1 2 3 4 5
9.	I do not mind working my hardest for my supervisor.	1 2 3 4 5
10.	I am impressed with my supervisor's knowledge of his/her job.	1 2 3 4 5
11.	I respect my supervisor's knowledge of and competence on the job.	1 2 3 4 5
12.	I admire my supervisor's professional skills.	1 2 3 4 5

SCORING KEY

Mutual affection (add items 1–3) __________

Loyalty (add items 4–6) __________

Contribution to work activities (add items 7–9) __________

Professional respect (add items 10–12) __________

Overall score (add all 12 items) __________

ARBITRARY NORMS

Low mutual affection = 3–9
High mutual affection = 10–15
Low loyalty = 3–9
High loyalty = 10–15
Low contribution to work activities = 3–9
High contribution to work activities = 10–15
Low professional respect = 3–9
High professional respect = 10–15
Low overall leader–member exchange = 12–38
High overall leader–member exchange = 39–60

SOURCE: Reprinted from *Journal of Management*, R C Liden and J M Maslyn, "Multidimensionality of Leader–Member Exchange: An Empirical Assessment through Scale Development," p 56, Vol 24, No 1. Copyright © 1998, with permission from Elsevier.

may be less optimal than shared leadership responsibility among two or more individuals in certain task environments."[63] This perspective is quite different from the previous theories and models discussed in this chapter, which assume that leadership is a vertical, downward-flowing process. In contrast, the notion of shared leadership is based on the idea that people need to share information and collaborate to get things done at work. This in turn underscores the need for employees to adopt a horizontal process of influence or leadership. **Shared leadership** entails a simultaneous, ongoing, mutual influence process in which individuals share responsibility for leading regardless of formal roles and titles.

shared leadership
Simultaneous, ongoing, mutual influence process in which people share responsibility for leading.

Shared leadership is most likely to be needed when people work in teams, when people are involved in complex projects, and when people are doing knowledge work—work that requires voluntary contributions of intellectual capital by skilled professionals.[64] Consider how Bill Ford, CEO of Ford Motor Company, is using shared leadership to run the auto company:

> They [Bill Ford, Jim Padilla (chief operating officer), and Nick Scheele (president)] are also the core of the office of the chairman and chief executive (OCCE), a ten-member group that meets once a week to review operations. . . . As the first-quarter results show, Ford's management by committee is remarkably effective. The OCCE is described as an open forum that encourages free-flowing discussion, with Bill Ford getting the last word. Says Padilla: "Bill's style is to get a lot of input and triangulate. He doesn't like a big meeting with a lot of railbirds. He's not a command-and-control CEO. He's a good listener and manages by consensus. Bill is very involved. There is not a decision that goes forward without his input and knowledge. He leaves it to the operating people to do the work.[65]

Researchers are just now beginning to explore the process of shared leadership, and results are promising. For example, shared leadership in teams was positively associated with group cohesion, group citizenship, and group effectiveness.[66] Table 14–2 contains a list of key questions and answers that managers should consider when determining how they can develop shared leadership.

Servant-Leadership

Servant-leadership is more a philosophy of managing than a testable theory. The term *servant-leadership* was coined by Robert Greenleaf in 1970. Greenleaf believes that great leaders act as servants, putting the needs of others, including employees, customers, and community, as their first priority. **Servant-leadership** focuses on increased service to others rather than to oneself.[67] George Merck II, who was Merck & Co.'s CEO in the 1950s, is a good example of a servant-leader. He also was recognized by *Fortune* as being the fourth greatest CEO of all time in 2003. He made a point of instilling a sense of servant-leadership in his employees while running the company. He also found that this leadership philosophy was very profitable.

servant-leadership
Focuses on increased service to others rather than to oneself.

> "Medicine is for people, not for profits," George Merck II declared on the cover of Time in August 1952—a rule his company observed in dispensing streptomycin to Japanese children following World War II. Yet fuzzy-headed moralistic fervor wasn't George Merck. Austere and patrician, he simply believed that the purpose of a corporation is to do something useful, and to do it very well. "And if we have remembered that, the profits have never failed to appear," he explained. "The better we remembered, the larger they have been."[68]

Merck's approach to leadership served his shareholders very well because he served others first.

TABLE 14–2 Key Questions and Answers to Consider When Developing Shared Leadership

Key Questions	Answers
What task characteristics call for shared leadership?	Tasks that are highly *interdependent.* Tasks that require a great deal of *creativity.* Tasks that are highly *complex.*
What is the role of the leader in developing shared leadership?	*Designing the team,* including clarifying purpose, securing resources, articulating vision, selecting members, and defining team processes. *Managing the boundaries* of the team.
How can organizational systems facilitate the development of shared leadership?	*Training and development systems* can be used to prepare both designated leaders and team members to engage in shared leadership. *Reward systems* can be used to promote and reward shared leadership. *Cultural systems* can be used to articulate and to demonstrate the value of shared leadership.
What vertical and shared leadership behaviors are important to team outcomes?	*Directive leadership* can provide task-focused directions. *Transactional leadership* can provide both personal and material rewards based on key performance metrics. *Transformational leadership* can stimulate commitment to a team vision, emotional engagement, and fulfillment of higher-order needs. *Empowering leadership* can reinforce the importance of self-motivation.
What are the ongoing responsibilities of the vertical leader?	The vertical leader needs to be able to step in and *fill voids* in the team. The vertical leader needs to continue to *emphasize the importance of the shared leadership approach,* given the task characteristics facing the team.

Source: C L Pearce, "The Future of Leadership: Combining Vertical and Shared Leadership to Transform Knowledge Work," *Academy of Management Executive: The Thinking Manager's Source,* February 2004, p 48.

According to Jim Stuart, co-founder of the leadership circle in Tampa, Florida, "Leadership derives naturally from a commitment to service. You know that you're practicing servant-leadership if your followers become wiser, healthier, more autonomous—and more likely to become servant-leaders themselves."[69] Servant-leadership is not a quick-fix approach to leadership. Rather, it is a long-term, transformational approach to life and work. Table 14–3 presents 10 characteristics possessed by servant-leaders. One can hardly go wrong by trying to adopt these characteristics.

Level 5 Leadership

This model of leadership was not derived from any particular theory or model of leadership. Rather, it was developed from a longitudinal research study attempting to answer the following question: Can a good company become a great company and, if so, how? The study was conducted by a research team headed by Jim Collins, a former university professor who started his own research-based consulting company. He summarized his work in the best seller *Good to Great.*[70]

To answer the research question, Collins identified a set of companies that shifted from good performance to great performance. Great performance was defined as

Nelson Mandela struggled for years against the racism and apartheid in South Africa. Jailed for nearly three decades for his political activism, he emerged in 1990 to continue leading the fight against oppression and racism. He has sacrificed his private life and his youth for his people, and remains South Africa's best known and loved hero. But as Mandela himself claims, "I was not a messiah, but an ordinary man who had become a leader because of extraordinary circumstances." He is a true servant-leader.

TABLE 14–3 Characteristics of the Servant-Leader

Servant-Leadership Characteristics	Description
1. Listening	Servant-leaders focus on listening to identify and clarify the needs and desires of a group.
2. Empathy	Servant-leaders try to empathize with others' feelings and emotions. An individual's good intentions are assumed even when he or she performs poorly.
3. Healing	Servant-leaders strive to make themselves and others whole in the face of failure or suffering.
4. Awareness	Servant-leaders are very self-aware of their strengths and limitations.
5. Persuasion	Servant-leaders rely more on persuasion than positional authority when making decisions and trying to influence others.
6. Conceptualization	Servant-leaders take the time and effort to develop broader based conceptual thinking. Servant-leaders seek an appropriate balance between a short-term, day-to-day focus and a long-term, conceptual orientation.
7. Foresight	Servant-leaders have the ability to foresee future outcomes associated with a current course of action or situation.
8. Stewardship	Servant-leaders assume that they are stewards of the people and resources they manage.
9. Commitment to the growth of people	Servant-leaders are committed to people beyond their immediate work role. They commit to fostering an environment that encourages personal, professional, and spiritual growth.
10. Building community	Servant-leaders strive to create a sense of community both within and outside the work organization.

SOURCE: These characteristics and descriptions were derived from L C Spears, "Introduction: Servant-Leadership and the Greenleaf Legacy," in *Reflections on Leadership: How Robert K Greenleaf's Theory of Servant-Leadership Influenced Today's Top Management Thinkers,* ed L C Spears (New York: John Wiley & Sons, 1995), pp 1–14.

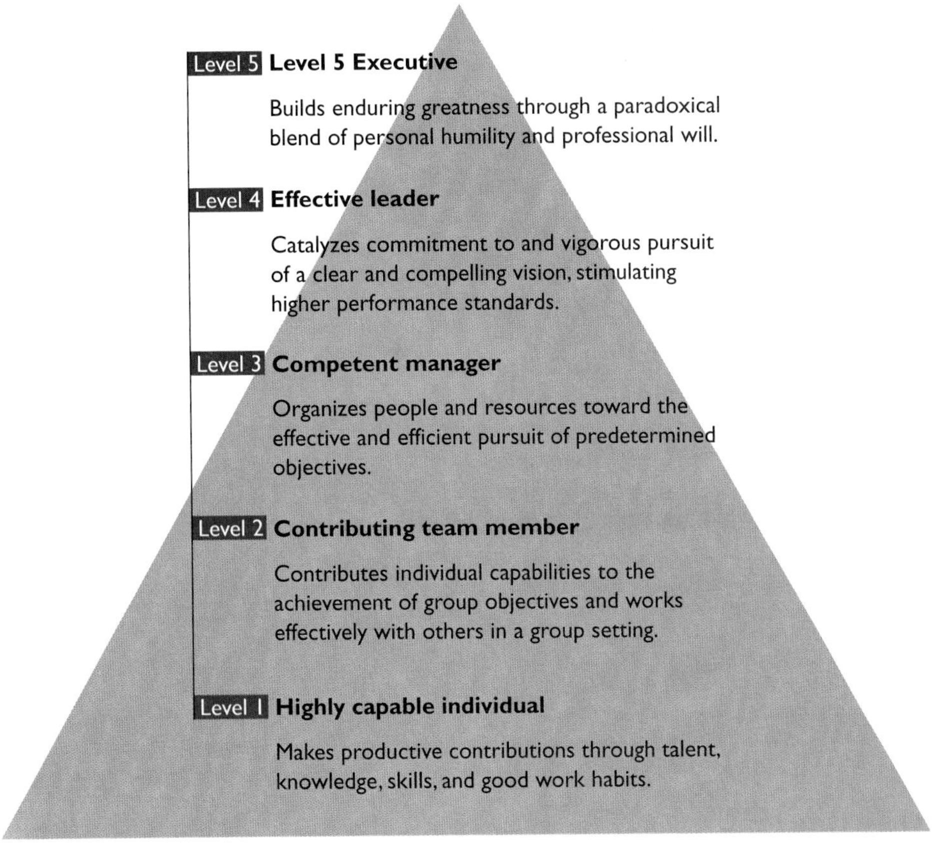

FIGURE 14–5
The Level 5 Hierarchy

Level 5 **Level 5 Executive**
Builds enduring greatness through a paradoxical blend of personal humility and professional will.
Level 4 **Effective leader**
Catalyzes commitment to and vigorous pursuit of a clear and compelling vision, stimulating higher performance standards.
Level 3 **Competent manager**
Organizes people and resources toward the effective and efficient pursuit of predetermined objectives.
Level 2 **Contributing team member**
Contributes individual capabilities to the achievement of group objectives and works effectively with others in a group setting.
Level 1 **Highly capable individual**
Makes productive contributions through talent, knowledge, skills, and good work habits.

SOURCE: Figure from *Good to Great: Why Some Companies Make the Leap and Others Don't* by J Collins. Copyright © 2001 by J Collins. Reprinted by permission of HarperCollins Publishers, Inc.

"cumulative stock returns at or below the general stock market for 15 years, punctuated by a transition point, then cumulative returns at least three times the market over the next 15 years."[71] Beginning with a sample of 1,435 companies on the *Fortune* 500 from 1965 to 1995, he identified 11 good-to-great companies: Abbot, Circuit City, Fannie Mae, Gillette, Kimberly-Clark, Kroger, Nucor, Philip Morris, Pitney Bowes, Walgreens, and Wells Fargo. His next step was to compare these 11 companies with a targeted set of direct comparison companies. This comparison enabled him to uncover the drivers of good-to-great transformations. One of the key drivers was called Level 5 leadership (see Figure 14–5). In other words, every company that experienced good-to-great performance was led by an individual possessing the characteristics associated with Level 5 leadership. Let us consider this leadership hierarchy.

Figure 14–5 reveals that a Level 5 leader possesses the characteristics of humility and a fearless will to succeed. American president Abraham Lincoln is an example of such an individual. Although he was soft-spoken and shy, he possessed great will to accomplish his goal of uniting his country during the Civil War in the 1860s. This determination resulted in the loss of 250,000 Confederates, 360,000 Union soldiers, and ultimately to a united country. Being humble and determined, however, was not enough for Lincoln to succeed at his quest. Rather, a Level 5 leader must also possess the capabilities associated with the other levels in the hierarchy. Although an individual does not move up the hierarchy in a stair-step fashion, a Level 5 leader must possess the capabilities contained in Levels 1–4 before he or she can use the Level 5 characteristics to transform an organization.

It is important to note the overlap between the capabilities represented in this model and the previous leadership theories discussed in this chapter. For example, Level 1 is consistent with research on trait theory. Trait research tells us that leaders are intelligent and possess the personality characteristics of extraversion, conscientiousness, and openness to experience. Levels 3 and 4 also seem to contain behaviors associated with transactional and transformational leadership. The novel and unexpected component of this theory revolves around the conclusion that good-to-great leaders are not only transactional and transformational, but most importantly, they are humble and fiercely determined.

There are three points to keep in mind about Level 5 leadership. First, Collins notes that there are additional drivers for taking a company from good to great other than being a Level 5 leader.[72] Level 5 leadership enables the implementation of these additional drivers. Second, to date there has not been any additional research testing Collins's conclusions. Future research is clearly needed to confirm the Level 5 hierarchy. Finally, Collins believes that some people will never become Level 5 leaders because their narcissistic and boastful tendencies do not allow them to subdue their own ego and needs for the greater good of others.

key terms

consideration 345
contingency factors 349
in-group exchange 357
initiating structure 345
leader trait 343
leadership 342
leadership prototype 344
out-group exchange 357
readiness 352
servant-leadership 360
shared leadership 360
situational theories 346
transactional leadership 353
transformational leadership 354

chapter summary

- *Review trait theory research, and discuss the idea of one best style of leadership, using the Ohio State studies and the Leadership Grid® as points of reference.* Historical leadership research did not support the notion that effective leaders possessed unique traits from followers. However, teams of researchers reanalyzed this historical data with modern-day statistical procedures. Results revealed that individuals tend to be perceived as leaders when they possess one or more of the following traits: intelligence, dominance, and masculinity. Research also showed that the personality traits of extraversion, conscientiousness, and openness to experience were positively correlated with leadership effectiveness. Intelligence also was modestly related to leadership effectiveness. Research further examined the relationship between gender and leadership. Results demonstrated that (a) leadership styles varied by gender, (b) men and women were equally assertive, and (c) women scored higher than their male counterparts on a variety of effectiveness criteria. The Ohio State studies revealed that there were two key independent dimensions of leadership behavior: consideration and initiating structure. Authors of the Leadership Grid® proposed that leaders should adopt a style that demonstrates high concern for production and people. Research did not support the premise that there is one best style of leadership.
- *Explain, according to Fiedler's contingency model, how leadership style interacts with situational control.* Fiedler believes leader effectiveness depends on an appropriate match between leadership style and situational control. Leaders are either task motivated or relationship motivated. Situation control is composed of leader–member relations, task structure,

and position power. Task-motivated leaders are effective under situations of both high and low control. Relationship-motivated leaders are more effective when they have moderate situational control.

- *Discuss House's revised path–goal theory and Hersey and Blanchard's situational leadership theory.* There are three key changes in the revised path–goal theory. Leaders now are viewed as exhibiting eight categories of leader behavior (see Table 14–1) instead of four. In turn, the effectiveness of these styles depends on various employee characteristics and environmental factors. Second, leaders are expected to spend more effort fostering intrinsic motivation through empowerment. Third, leadership is not limited to people in managerial roles. Rather, leadership is shared among all employees within an organization. According to situational leadership theory (SLT), effective leader behavior depends on the readiness level of a leader's followers. As follower readiness increases, leaders are advised to gradually move from a telling to a selling to a participating and, finally, to a delegating style. Research does not support SLT.
- *Describe the difference between transactional and transformational leadership and discuss how transformational leadership transforms followers and work groups.* There is an important difference between transactional and transformational leadership. Transactional leaders focus on clarifying employees' role and task requirements and provide followers with positive and negative rewards contingent on performance. Transformational leaders motivate employees to pursue organizational goals over their own self-interests. Both forms of leadership are important for organizational success. Individual characteristics and organizational culture are key precursors of transformational leadership, which is comprised of four sets of leader behavior. These leader behaviors, in turn, positively affect followers' and work groups' goals, values, beliefs, aspirations, and motivation. These positive effects are then associated with a host of preferred outcomes.
- *Explain the leader–member exchange (LMX) model of leadership and the concept of shared leadership.* The LMX model revolves around the development of dyadic relationships between managers and their direct reports. These leader–member exchanges qualify as either in-group or out-group relationships. Research supports this model of leadership. Shared leadership involves a simultaneous, ongoing, mutual influence process in which individuals share responsibility for leading regardless of formal roles and titles. This type of leadership is most likely to be needed when people work in teams, when people are involved in complex projects, and when people are doing knowledge work.
- *Review the principles of servant-leadership and discuss Level 5 leadership.* Servant-leadership is more a philosophy than a testable theory. It is based on the premise that great leaders act as servants, putting the needs of others, including employees, customers, and community, as their first priority. Level 5 leadership represents a hierarchy of leadership capabilities that are needed to lead companies in transforming from good to great.

discussion questions

1. Citing examples, which different leadership traits and styles were displayed by Ann Fudge?
2. Is everyone cut out to be a leader? Explain.
3. Does it make more sense to change a person's leadership style or the situation? How would Fred Fiedler and Robert House answer this question?
4. Have you ever worked for a transformational leader? Describe how she or he transformed followers.
5. In your view, which leadership theory has the greatest practical application? Why?

ethical dilemma

You are a manager at a call center and are faced with the difficult task of having to lay off a friend who works for the company. This employee has performed wonderfully in the past and you would hate to see him go. Nonetheless, your company lost a contract with a major client and his position is obsolete. You are aware that this employee has been building a house and is 10 days from closing. He has sold his other home and now is living with his in-laws. The employee has come to you and is asking for a favor. He wants you to extend his employment for 10 more days so that he can qualify for the loan for his new home. Unfortunately, you do not have the authority to do so, and you told him you cannot grant this favor. He then told you that the mortgage company will be calling sometime soon to get a verbal confirmation of his employment. This confirmation is an essential prerequisite in order for your friend to obtain the loan for his new home. Because you can't extend his employment, he now is asking for another favor. He wants you to tell the mortgage company that he is still employed.

Solving the Dilemma

As a manager at this call center, what would you do?

1. Tell the mortgage company he is still working for the company. Your friend needs a break and you are confident that he'll find a job in the near future.
2. Refuse to lie. It is unethical to falsify information regarding employment.
3. Simply avoid the mortgage company's phone call.
4. Invent other options. Discuss.

If you're looking for additional study materials, be sure to check out the Online Learning Center at

www.mhhe.com/kinickiob2e

for more information and interactivities that correspond to this chapter.

part Five

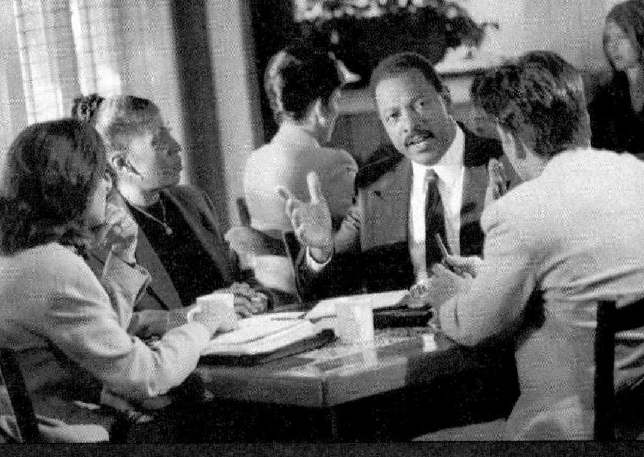

Managing Evolving Organizations

chapter Fifteen

Designing Effective Organizations

LEARNING OBJECTIVES

After reading the material in this chapter, you should be able to:

- Describe the four characteristics common to all organizations.
- Explain the difference between closed and open systems, and contrast the military/mechanical, biological, and cognitive systems metaphors for organizations.
- Describe the four generic organizational effectiveness criteria.
- Explain what the contingency approach to organization design involves.
- Discuss Burns and Stalker's findings regarding mechanistic and organic organizations.
- Describe new-style and old-style organizations, and list three keys to managing geographically dispersed employees in virtual organizations.

THE TWO FACES OF WAL-MART

There is an evil company in Arkansas, some say. It's a discount store—a very, very big discount store—and it will do just about anything to get bigger. You've seen the headlines. Illegal immigrants mopping its floors. Workers locked inside overnight. A big gender discrimination suit. Wages low enough to make *other* companies' workers go on strike. And we know what it does to weaker suppliers and competitors. Crushing the dream of the independent proprietor—an ideal as American as Thomas Jefferson—it is the enemy of all that's good and right in our nation.

There is another big discount store in Arkansas, yet this one couldn't be more different from the first. Founded by a folksy entrepreneur whose notions of thrift, industry, and the square deal were pure Ben Franklin, this company is not a tyrant but a servant. Passing along the gains of its brilliant distribution system to consumers, its farsighted managers have done nothing less than democratize the American dream. Its low prices are spurring productivity and helping win the fight against inflation. It is America's most admired company.

Weirdest part is, both these companies are named Wal-Mart Stores Inc.

The more America talks about Wal-Mart, it seems, the more polarized its image grows. Its executives are credited with the most expansive of visions and the meanest of intentions; its CEO is presumed to be in league with Lex Luthor *and* St. Francis of Assisi. It's confusing. Which should we believe in: good Wal-Mart or evil Wal-Mart?

Some of the allegations—and Wal-Mart was sued more than 6,000 times in 2002—certainly seem damning. Yet there's an important piece of context: Wal-Mart employs 1.4 million people. That's three times as many as the nation's next biggest employer and 56 times as many as the average FORTUNE 500 company. Meaning that all things being equal, a bad event is 5,500% more likely to happen at Wal-Mart than at Borders.

One consistent refrain is that Wal-Mart squeezes its suppliers to death—and you don't have to do much digging to find horror stories. But while Wal-Mart's reputation for penny-pinching is well deserved, so is its reputation for straightforwardness—none of the slotting fees, rebates, or other game playing that many merchants engage in. . . .

Another rap on Wal-Mart—that it stomps competitors to dust through sheer brute force—seems undeniable: Studies have indicated a decline in the life expectancy of local businesses after Wal-Mart moves in. But this morality play is missing some key characters—namely, you and me. The scene where we drop into Wal-Mart to pick up a case of Coke, for instance, has been conveniently cut. No small omission, since the main reason we can't shop at Ed's Variety Store anymore is that we stopped shopping at Ed's Variety Store.

Evil Wal-Mart's original sin, then, was to open stores that sold things for less. This was a powerful idea but hardly a new one. . . .

Not surprisingly, that's how the people running Good Wal-Mart see their story. They cast their jobs in almost missionary terms—"to lower the world's cost of living"—and in this, they have succeeded spectacularly. One consultancy estimates that Wal-Mart saves consumers $20 billion a year. Its constant push for low prices, meanwhile, puts the heat on suppliers and competitors to offer better deals.

That's a good thing, right? If a company achieves its lower prices by finding better and smarter ways of doing things, then yes, everybody wins. But if it cuts costs by cutting pay and benefits—or by sending production to China—then not everybody wins. And here's where the story of Good Wal-Mart starts to falter. Just as its Everyday Low Prices benefit shoppers who've never come near a Wal-Mart, there are mounting signs that its Everyday Low Pay (Wal-Mart's full-time hourly employees average $9.76 an hour) is hurting some workers who have never worked there. . . .

Where you stand on Wal-Mart, then, seems to depend on where you sit. If you're a consumer, Wal-Mart is good for you. If you're a wage earner, there's a good chance it's bad. If you're a Wal-Mart shareholder, you want the company to grow. If you're a citizen, you probably don't want it growing in your backyard. So, which one are you?

And that's the point: Chances are, you're more than one. And you may think each role is important. Yet America has elevated one above the rest. . . .

Wal-Mart swore fealty to the consumer and rode its coattails straight to the top. Now we have more than just a big retailer on our hands, though. We have a servant-king—one powerful enough to place everyone else in servitude to the consumer too. Gazing up at this new order, we wonder if our original choices made so much sense after all. . . .

Now Wal-Mart has been brought face to face with its own contradiction: Its promises of the good life threaten to ring increasingly hollow if it doesn't pay its workers enough to have that good life.

It's important that this debate continue. But in holding the mirror up to Wal-Mart, we would do well to turn it back on ourselves. Sam Walton created Wal-Mart. But we created it, too.[1]

FOR DISCUSSION

Is Wal-Mart an organizational "good guy" or a "bad guy"? Explain. For an interpretation of this case and additional comments, visit our Online Learning Center:

www.mhhe.com/kinickiob2e

VIRTUALLY EVERY ASPECT OF LIFE is affected at least indirectly by some type of organization.[2] We look to organizations to feed, clothe, house, educate, and employ us. Organizations attend to our needs for entertainment, police and fire protection, insurance, recreation, national security, transportation, news and information, legal assistance, and health care. Many of these organizations seek a profit, others do not. Some are extremely large, others are tiny mom-and-pop operations. Despite this mind-boggling diversity, modern organizations have one basic thing in common. They are the primary context for *organizational* behavior. In a manner of speaking, organizations are the chessboard upon which the game of organizational behavior is played. Therefore, present and future managers need a working knowledge of modern organizations to improve their chances of making the right moves when managing people at work.

This chapter explores the effectiveness, design, and future of today's organizations. We begin by defining the term *organization,* discussing important dimensions of organization charts, and examining alternative organizational metaphors. Our attention then turns to criteria for assessing organizational effectiveness. Next, we discuss the contingency approach to designing organizations. We conclude with a profile of new-style organizations, with special attention to Internet-age *virtual* organizations.

Organizations: Definition and Dimensions

As a necessary springboard for this chapter, we need to formally define the term *organization* and clarify the meaning of organization charts.

What Is an Organization?

According to Chester I Barnard's classic definition, an **organization** is "a system of consciously coordinated activities or forces of two or more persons."[3] Embodied in the *conscious coordination* aspect of this definition are four common denominators of all organizations: coordination of effort, a common goal, division of labor, and a hierarchy of authority.[4] Organization theorists refer to these factors as the organization's *structure.*

organization

System of consciously coordinated activities of two or more people.

Coordination of effort is achieved through formulation and enforcement of policies, rules, and regulations. Division of labor occurs when the common goal is pursued by individuals performing different but related tasks. The hierarchy of authority, also called the chain of command, is a control mechanism dedicated to making sure the right people do the right things at the right time. Historically, managers have maintained the integrity of the hierarchy of authority by adhering to the unity of command principle. The **unity of command principle** specifies that each employee should report to only one manager. Otherwise, the argument goes, inefficiency would prevail because of conflicting orders and lack of personal accountability. (Indeed, these are problems in today's more fluid and flexible organizations based on innovations such as cross-functional and self-managed teams.) Managers in the hierarchy of authority also administer rewards and punishments. When operating in concert, the four definitional factors—coordination of effort, a common goal, division of labor, and a hierarchy of authority—enable an *organization* to exist.

unity of command principle

Each employee should report to a single manager.

Organization Charts

organization chart

Boxes-and-lines illustration showing chain of formal authority and division of labor.

An **organization chart** is a graphic representation of formal authority and division of labor relationships. To the casual observer, the term *organization chart* means the family tree–like pattern of boxes and lines posted on workplace walls. Within each box one usually finds the names and titles of current position holders. To organization theorists, however, organization charts reveal much more. The partial organization chart in Figure 15–1 reveals four basic dimensions of organizational structure: (1) hierarchy of authority (who reports to whom), (2) division of labor, (3) spans of control, and (4) line and staff positions.

Hierarchy of Authority As Figure 15–1 illustrates, there is an unmistakable hierarchy of authority.[5] Working from bottom to top, the 10 directors report to the two executive directors who report to the president who reports to the chief executive officer. Ultimately, the chief executive officer answers to the hospital's board of directors. The chart in Figure 15–1 shows strict unity of command up

FIGURE 15–1 Sample Organization Chart for a Hospital (executive and director levels only)

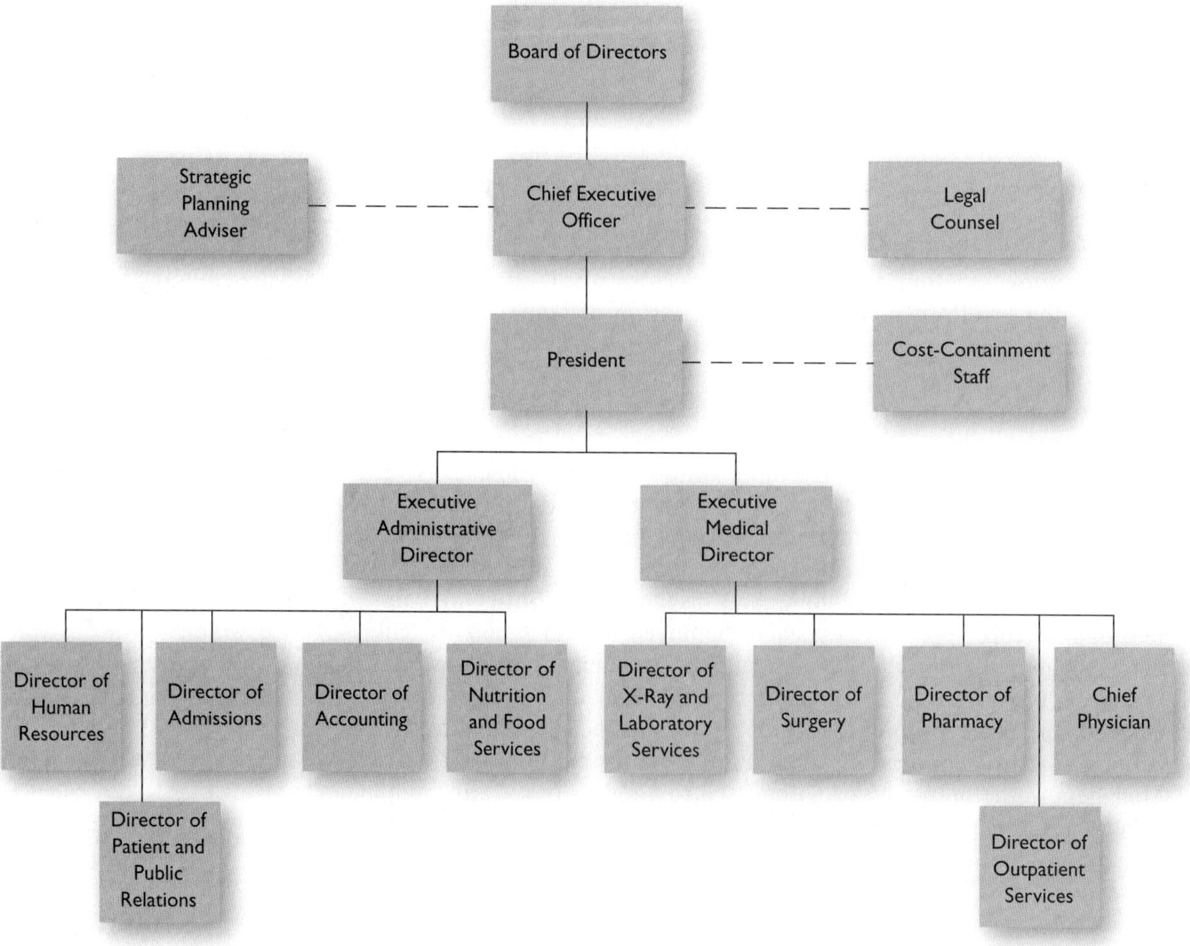

and down the line. A formal hierarchy of authority also delineates the official communication network.

Division of Labor In addition to showing the chain of command, the sample organization chart indicates extensive division of labor. Immediately below the hospital's president, one executive director is responsible for general administration while another is responsible for medical affairs. Each of these two specialties is further subdivided as indicated by the next layer of positions. At each successively lower level in the organization, jobs become more specialized.

Spans of Control The **span of control** refers to the number of people reporting directly to a given manager.[6] Spans of control can range from narrow to wide. For example, the president in Figure 15–1 has a narrow span of control of two. (Staff assistants usually are not included in a manager's span of control.) The executive administrative director in Figure 15–1 has a wider span of control of five. Spans of control exceeding 30 can be found in assembly-line operations where machine-paced and repetitive work substitutes for close supervision. Historically, spans of five to six were considered best. Despite years of debate, organization theorists have not arrived at a consensus regarding the ideal span of control.

span of control
The number of people reporting directly to a given manager.

Generally, the narrower the span of control, the closer the supervision and the higher the administrative costs as a result of a higher manager-to-worker ratio. Recent emphasis on leanness and administrative efficiency dictates spans of control as wide as possible but guarding against inadequate supervision and lack of coordination. Wider spans also complement the trend toward greater worker autonomy and empowerment.

Line and Staff Positions The organization chart in Figure 15–1 also distinguishes between line and staff positions. Line managers such as the president, the two executive directors, and the various directors occupy formal decision-making positions within the chain of command. Line positions generally are connected by solid lines on organization charts. Dotted lines indicate staff relationships. **Staff personnel** do background research and provide technical advice and recommendations to their **line managers,** who have the authority to make decisions. For example, the cost-containment specialists in the sample organization chart merely advise the president on relevant matters. Apart from supervising the work of their own staff assistants, they have no line authority over other organizational members. Modern trends such as cross-functional teams and reengineering are blurring the distinction between line and staff.

staff personnel
Provide research, advice, and recommendations to line managers.

line managers
Have authority to make organizational decisions.

According to a study of 207 police officers in Israel, line personnel exhibited greater job commitment than did their staff counterparts.[7] This result was anticipated because the line managers' decision-making authority empowered them and gave them comparatively more control over their work situations.

Organizational Metaphors

The complexity of modern organizations makes them somewhat difficult to describe. Consequently, organization theorists have resorted to the use of metaphors.[8] A *metaphor* is a figure of speech that characterizes one object in terms of another object. Good metaphors help us comprehend complicated things by describing them in everyday terms. For example, organizations are often likened to

"YOU KNOW, EVER SINCE I STARTED WORKING HERE, I'VE HAD THIS CRAVING FOR CHEESE."

Reprinted by permission of Dave Carpenter from *Harvard Business Review,* April 2004.

an orchestra. OB scholar Kim Cameron sums up the value of organizational metaphors as follows: "Each time a new metaphor is used, certain aspects of organizational phenomena are uncovered that were not evident with other metaphors. In fact, the usefulness of metaphors lies in their possession of some degree of falsehood so that new images and associations emerge."[9] With the orchestra metaphor, for instance, one could come away with an exaggerated picture of harmony in large and complex organizations. On the other hand, it realistically encourages us to view managers as facilitators rather than absolute dictators.

Early managers and management theorists used military units and machines as metaphors for organizations. These rigid models gave way to more dynamic and realistic metaphors. Today's organizational metaphors require *open-system* thinking.

Needed: Open-System Thinking

closed system
A relatively self-sufficient entity.

open system
Organism that must constantly interact with its environment to survive.

A **closed system** is said to be a self-sufficient entity. It is "closed" to the surrounding environment. In contrast, an **open system** depends on constant interaction with the environment for survival. The distinction between closed and open systems is a matter of degree. Because every worldly system is partly closed and partly open, the key question is: How great a role does the environment play in the functioning of the system? For instance, a battery-powered clock is a relatively closed system. Once the battery is inserted, the clock performs its time-keeping function hour after hour until the battery goes dead. The human body, on the other hand, is a highly open system because it requires a constant supply of life-sustaining oxygen from the environment. Nutrients also are imported from the environment. Open systems are capable of self-correction, adaptation, and growth, thanks to characteristics such as homeostasis and feedback control.

The traditional military/mechanical metaphor, discussed next, is a closed system model because it largely ignores environmental influences. It gives the impression that organizations are self-sufficient entities. Conversely, the biological and cognitive metaphors emphasize interaction between organizations and their environments. These newer models are based on open-system assumptions. They reveal instructive insights about organizations and how they work. Each of the three metaphorical perspectives offers something useful.

Organizations as Military/ Mechanical Bureaucracies

A major by-product of the Industrial Revolution was the factory system of production. People left their farms and cottage industries to operate steam-powered machines in centralized factories. The social unit of production evolved from the family to formally managed organizations encompassing hundreds or even thousands of people. Managers sought to maximize the economic efficiency of large factories and offices by structuring them according to military principles. At the turn of the 20th century, a German sociologist, Max Weber, formulated what he termed the most rationally efficient form of organization.[10] He patterned his ideal organization after the vaunted Prussian army and called it **bureaucracy.**

bureaucracy

Max Weber's idea of the most rationally efficient form of organization.

Weber's Bureaucracy According to Weber's theory, the following four factors should make bureaucracies the epitome of efficiency:

1. Division of labor (people become proficient when they perform standardized tasks over and over again).
2. A hierarchy of authority (a formal chain of command ensures coordination and accountability).
3. A framework of rules (carefully formulated and strictly enforced rules ensure predictable behavior).
4. Administrative impersonality (personnel decisions such as hiring and promoting should be based on competence, not favoritism).[11]

How the Term *Bureaucracy* Became a Synonym for Inefficiency All organizations possess varying degrees of these characteristics. Thus, every organization is a bureaucracy to some extent. In terms of the ideal metaphor, a bureaucracy should run like a well-oiled machine, and its members should perform with the precision of a polished military unit. But practical and ethical problems arise when bureaucratic characteristics become extreme or dysfunctional. For example, extreme expressions of specialization, rule following, and impersonality can cause a bureaucrat to treat a client as a number rather than as a person.[12]

Weber probably would be surprised and dismayed that his model of rational efficiency has become a synonym for inefficiency.[13] Today, bureaucracy stands for being put on hold, waiting in long lines, and getting shuffled from one office to the next. This irony can be explained largely by the fact that organizations with excessive or dysfunctional bureaucratic tendencies become rigid, inflexible, and resistant to environmental demands and influences.[14]

Organizations as Biological Systems

Drawing upon the field of general systems theory that emerged during the 1950s,[15] organization theorists suggested a more dynamic model for modern organizations. This metaphor likens organizations to the human body. Hence, it has been labeled the *biological model.* In his often-cited organization theory text, *Organizations in Action,* James D Thompson explained the biological model of organizations in the following terms:

> Approached as a natural system, the complex organization is a set of interdependent parts which together make up a whole because each contributes something and receives something from the whole, which in turn is interdependent with some larger environment. Survival of the system is taken to be the goal, and the parts and their relationships presumably are determined through evolutionary processes. . . .
>
> Central to the natural-system approach is the concept of homeostasis, or self-stabilization, which spontaneously, or naturally, governs the necessary relationships among parts and activities and thereby keeps the system viable in the face of disturbances stemming from the environment.[16]

FIGURE 15–2 The Organization as an Open System: The Biological Model

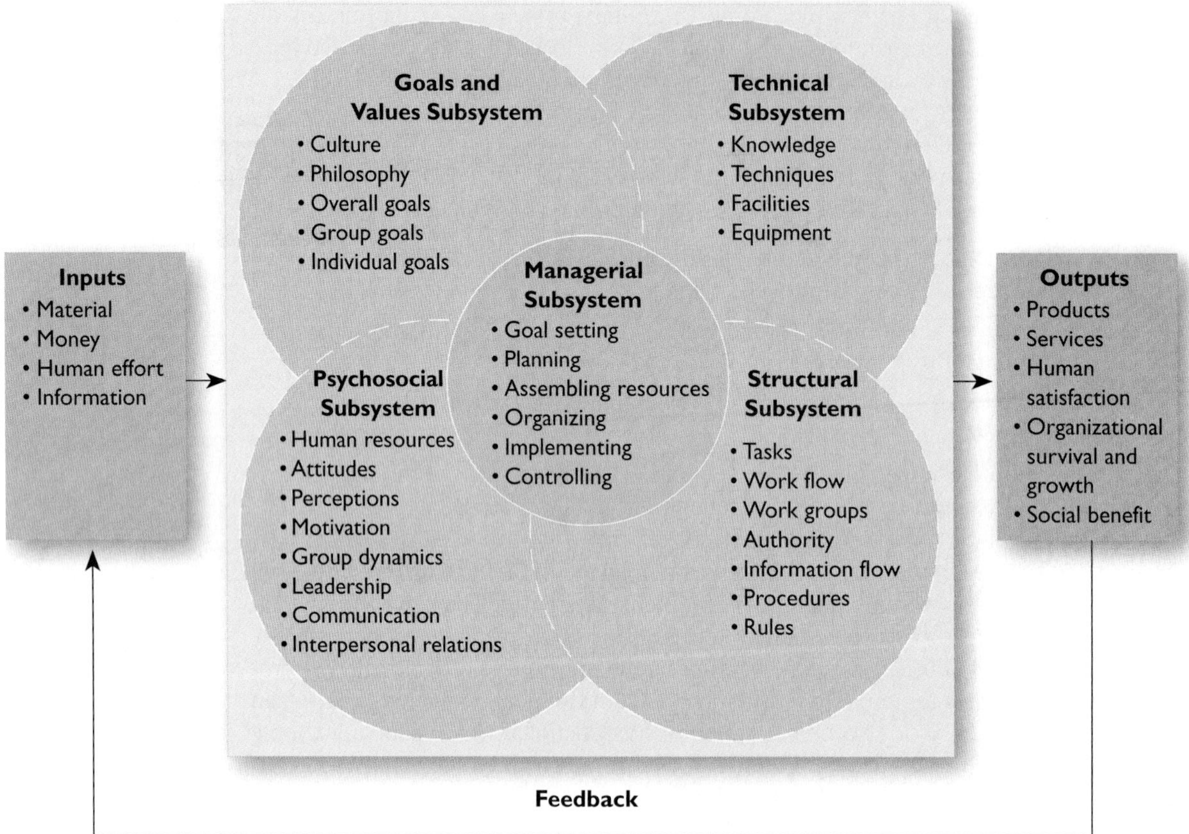

SOURCE: This model is a combination of Figures 5–2 and 5–3 in F E Kast and J E Rosenzweig, *Organization and Management: A Systems and Contingency Approach,* 4th ed (New York: McGraw-Hill, 1986), pp 112, 114. Copyright © 1986 by the McGraw-Hill Companies. Reprinted with permission.

Unlike the traditional military/mechanical theorists who downplayed the environment, advocates of the biological model stress organization–environment interaction. As Figure 15–2 illustrates, the biological model characterizes the organization as an open system that transforms inputs into various outputs. The outer boundary of the organization is permeable. People, information, capital, and goods and services move back and forth across this boundary. Moreover, each of the five organizational subsystems—goals and values, technical, psychosocial, structural, and managerial—is dependent on the others. Feedback about such things as sales and customer satisfaction or dissatisfaction enables the organization to self-adjust and survive despite uncertainty and change.[17] In effect, the organization is alive.

Organizations as Cognitive Systems

A more recent metaphor characterizes organizations in terms of mental functions. According to respected organization theorists Richard Daft and Karl Weick,

> This perspective represents a move away from mechanical and biological metaphors of organizations. Organizations are more than transformation

processes or control systems. To survive, organizations must have mechanisms to interpret ambiguous events and to provide meaning and direction for participants. Organizations are meaning systems, and this distinguishes them from lower-level systems. . . .

Almost all outcomes in terms of organization structure and design, whether caused by the environment, technology, or size, depend on the interpretation of problems or opportunities by key decision makers. Once interpretation occurs, the organization can formulate a response.[18]

Nokia changed its organizational structure in 2002 in response to saturation and a shifting marketplace. CEO Jorma Ollila broke down the company into nine business units, each with its own defined market segment. One unit concentrated on phones for corporate customers, another unit focused on camera phones and their colorful screens and software, and yet another unit was dedicated to high technology phones for data processing and video imaging. Ollila felt the break-up was necessary in order to maintain the "entrepreneurial thrust" it had in the 1990s.

This interpretation process, as it migrates throughout the organization, leads to organizational *learning* and adaptation.[19]

In fact, the concept of the *learning organization,*[20] discussed in Chapter 16, is popular in management circles these days. Great Harvest Bread Co., based in Dillon, Montana, is an inspiring case in point (annual revenue for the company's 137 retail franchises, where grains are fresh-ground daily, exceeds $60 million):

While most franchisors dictate everything about their franchisees' operations in order to ensure a predictable experience for customers everywhere, Great Harvest doesn't even require that its franchisees use the same bread recipes. . . . Instead, Great Harvest sets its franchisees free after a one-year apprenticeship to run their stores in the time-honored mom-and-pop way. Be unique, the company tells them; be yourselves, and experiment. . . .

In other words, Great Harvest says to its bakery owners, *Do whatever you want.* Except in one respect, which makes all the difference: Every owner in the chain is encouraged to be part of Great Harvest's "learning community." Those who join (and most have) must share information, financial results, observations, and ideas. If asked questions, they must give answers. They must keep no secrets.[21]

Thus, it takes a cooperative culture, mutual trust, and lots of internal cross communication to fully exploit the organization as a cognitive system (or learning organization).

Striving for Organizational Effectiveness

Assessing organizational effectiveness is an important topic for an array of people, including managers, stockholders, government agencies, and OB specialists. The purpose of this section is to introduce a widely applicable and useful model of organizational effectiveness.

Generic Effectiveness Criteria

A good way to better understand this complex subject is to consider four generic approaches to assessing an organization's effectiveness (see Figure 15–3). These effectiveness criteria apply equally well to large or small and profit or not-for-profit organizations. Moreover, as denoted by the overlapping circles in Figure 15–3, the four effectiveness criteria can be used in various combinations. The key thing to

FIGURE 15–3 Four Dimensions of Organizational Effectiveness

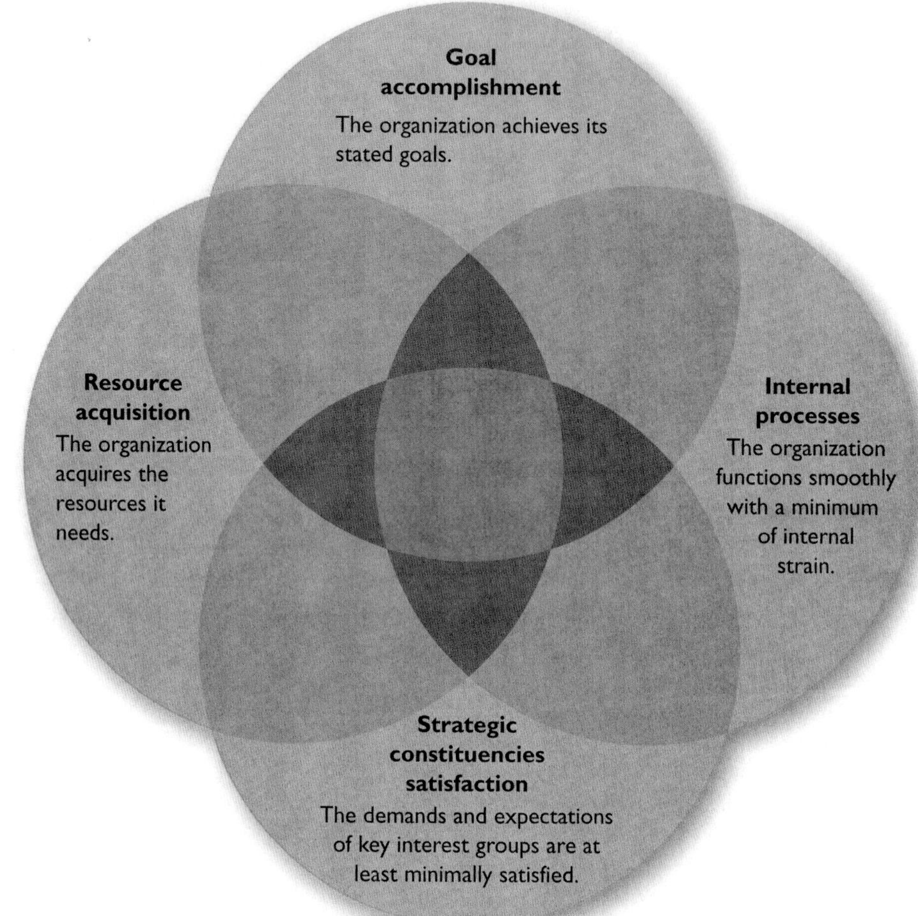
Goal accomplishment
The organization achieves its stated goals.
Resource acquisition
The organization acquires the resources it needs.
Internal processes
The organization functions smoothly with a minimum of internal strain.
Strategic constituencies satisfaction
The demands and expectations of key interest groups are at least minimally satisfied.

SOURCES: Adapted from discussion in K Cameron, "Critical Questions in Assessing Organizational Effectiveness," *Organizational Dynamics*, Autumn 1980, pp 66–80; and K S Cameron, "Effectiveness as Paradox: Consensus and Conflict in Conceptions of Organizational Effectiveness," *Management Science*, May 1986. pp 539–53.

remember is "no single approach to the evaluation of effectiveness is appropriate in all circumstances or for all organization types."[22] What do Coca-Cola and France Télécom, for example, have in common, other than being large profit-seeking corporations? Because a multidimensional approach is required, we need to look more closely at each of the four generic effectiveness criteria.

Goal Accomplishment Goal accomplishment is the most widely used effectiveness criterion for organizations. Key organizational results or outputs are compared with previously stated goals or objectives. Deviations, either plus or minus, require corrective action. This is simply an organizational variation of the personal goal-setting process discussed in Chapter 7.[23] Effectiveness, relative to the criterion of goal accomplishment, is gauged by how well the organization meets or exceeds its goals.

Productivity improvement, involving the relationship between inputs and outputs, is a common organization-level goal.[24] Goals also may be set for organizational efforts such as minority recruiting, pollution prevention, and quality improvement. Given today's competitive pressures and E-commerce revolution, *innovation* and *speed* are very important organizational goals worthy of measurement and monitoring.[25] Toyota gave a powerful indicator of where things are going in this regard. The Japanese automaker announced it could custom-build a car in just five days! A customer's new Toyota would roll off the Ontario, Canada, assembly line just five days after the order was placed. A 30-day lag was the industry standard at the time.[26]

Southwest Airlines is the envy of the beleaguered commercial airline industry because it is consistently effective at turning a profit by satisfying its customers and employees with a low-cost, on-time strategy and a no-layoff policy.

Resource Acquisition This second criterion relates to inputs rather than outputs. An organization is deemed effective in this regard if it acquires necessary factors of production such as raw materials, labor, capital, and managerial and technical expertise. Charitable organizations such as the Salvation Army judge their effectiveness in terms of how much money they raise from private and corporate donations.

Internal Processes Some refer to this third effectiveness criterion as the "healthy systems" approach. An organization is said to be a healthy system if information flows smoothly and if employee loyalty, commitment, job satisfaction, and trust prevail. Goals may be set for any of these internal processes. Healthy systems, from a behavioral standpoint, tend to have a minimum of dysfunctional conflict and destructive political maneuvering. M Scott Peck, the physician who wrote the highly regarded book, *The Road Less Traveled,* characterizes healthy organizations in ethical terms:

> A healthy organization, Peck says, is one that has a genuine sense of community: It's a place where people are emotionally present with one another, and aren't afraid to talk about fears and disappointments—because that's what allows us to care for one another. It's a place where there is authentic communication, a willingness to be vulnerable, a commitment to speaking frankly and respectfully—and a commitment not to walk away when the going gets tough.[27]

Strategic Constituencies Satisfaction Organizations both depend on people and affect the lives of people. Consequently, many consider the satisfaction of key interested parties to be an important criterion of organizational effectiveness.

> A **strategic constituency** is any group of individuals who have some stake in the organization—for example, resource providers, users of the organization's products or services, producers of the organization's output, groups whose cooperation is essential for the organization's survival, or those whose lives are significantly affected by the organization.[28]

strategic constituency

Any group of people with a stake in the organization's operation or success.

Strategic constituencies (or *stakeholders*) generally have competing or conflicting interests.[29] This forces executives to do some strategic juggling to achieve workable balances. In a recent *Business Week* interview, Microsoft's CEO, Steve Ballmer, offered this perspective:

> When you have gone through the kind of experience that we went through with government authorities, it really does cause you to step back and reflect: Who are we, what are we doing? The expectation bar, be it from government, be it from customers, be it from industry partners, is different, and the bar is higher. How do you hit the balance between being forceful and aggressive and still [having the] right level of cooperation [with our industry and] with government? We have worked hard on that theme of responsible leadership.[30]

Mixing Effectiveness Criteria: Practical Guidelines

Experts on the subject recommend a multidimensional approach to assessing the effectiveness of modern organizations. This means no single criterion is appropriate for all stages of the organization's life cycle. Nor will a single criterion satisfy competing stakeholders. Well-managed organizations mix and match effectiveness criteria to fit the unique requirements of the situation.[31] Managers need to identify and seek input from strategic constituencies. This information, when merged with the organization's stated mission and philosophy, enables management to derive an appropriate *combination* of effectiveness criteria. The following guidelines are helpful in this regard:

- *The goal accomplishment approach* is appropriate when "goals are clear, consensual, time-bounded, measurable."[32]
- *The resource acquisition approach* is appropriate when inputs have a traceable effect on results or output. For example, the amount of money the American Red Cross receives through donations dictates the level of services provided.
- *The internal processes approach* is appropriate when organizational performance is strongly influenced by specific processes (e.g., cross-functional teamwork).
- *The strategic constituencies approach* is appropriate when powerful stakeholders can significantly benefit or harm the organization.[33]

See Skills & Best Practices for Federal Express's formula for long-term organizational effectiveness.

SKILLS & BEST PRACTICES

How FedEx Continues to Deliver Organizational Effectiveness

Fred Smith, Federal Express founder and CEO: We do three things that are very important to keeping any company successful over time.

- **Promote change.** When I first wrote our managers' guide, I put in a quote from Marcus Aurelius about the inevitability of change. We hammer home that not to change is to be in the process of dying, of not meeting the market as it is. We applaud people who instigate change. We don't hang people who try something new that doesn't work out, because that's the easiest way to ossify an organization—to crucify the people who are trying to innovate.
- **Have a clear strategy and communicate it.** We have meetings each year to review our strategy, to make sure we're not drifting out of our core competencies, and to make sure we're correctly seeing where the markets are going. Once we've bought into that as a senior management team, we then communicate that in every way we can think of. We put it in the mission statement. We put it in the employee handbooks. We tie our business plans to it. We tie our incentive plans to it. We have one of the biggest industrial TV networks in the world and we use it to make sure our employees understand what we're trying to do and why we're trying to do it.
- **Make sure management is disciplined.** No employee wants to be treated like an automaton. You have to train them and tell them what's expected of them. You've got to let them express their views about how the business is being run. We make our managers treat our employees and contractors with dignity. They're sure not going to deliver the kind of service that FedEx is known for unless you deal with them on that basis.

SOURCE: Excerpt from "How To Keep Your Company's Edge," *Business 2.0*, December 2003, p 93.

The Contingency Approach to Designing Organizations

According to the **contingency approach to organization design,** organizations tend to be more effective when they are structured to fit the demands of the situation.[34] The purpose of this section is to introduce you to the contingency approach to organization design by reviewing a landmark study, drawing a distinction between centralized and decentralized decision making, contrasting new-style and old-style organizations, and discussing today's virtual organizations.

contingency approach to organization design
Creating an effective organization–environment fit.

Mechanistic versus Organic Organizations

A landmark contingency design study was reported by a pair of British behavioral scientists, Tom Burns and G M Stalker. In the course of their research, they drew a very instructive distinction between what they called mechanistic and organic organizations. **Mechanistic organizations** are rigid bureaucracies with strict rules, narrowly defined tasks, and top-down communication. Ironically, it is at the cutting edge of technology that this seemingly out-of-date approach has found a home. In the highly competitive business of Web hosting—running clients' Web sites in high-security facilities humming with Internet servers—speed and reliability are everything. Enter military-style managers who require strict discipline, faithful adherence to thick rule books, and flawless execution. But, as *Business Week* observed, "The regimented atmosphere and military themes . . . may be tough to stomach for skilled workers used to a more free-spirited atmosphere."[35]

mechanistic organizations
Rigid, command-and-control bureaucracies.

Oppositely, **organic organizations** are flexible networks of multitalented individuals who perform a variety of tasks.[36] W L Gore & Associates, the Newark, Delaware, maker of waterproof Gore-Tex fabric, is a highly organic organization because it lacks job descriptions and a formalized hierarchy and deemphasizes titles and status.[37]

organic organizations
Fluid and flexible network of multitalented people.

A Matter of Degree Importantly, as illustrated in the Hands-On Exercise on page 385, each of the mechanistic-organic characteristics is a matter of degree. Organizations tend to be *relatively* mechanistic or *relatively* organic. Pure types are rare because divisions, departments, or units in the same organization may be more or less mechanistic or organic. From an employee's standpoint, which organization structure would you prefer?

Different Approaches to Decision Making Decision making tends to be centralized in mechanistic organizations and decentralized in organic organizations. **Centralized decision making** occurs when key decisions are made by top management. **Decentralized decision making** occurs when important decisions are made by middle- and lower-level managers. Generally, centralized organizations are more tightly controlled while decentralized organizations are more adaptive to changing situations.[38] Each has its appropriate use (see Skills & Best Practices).

centralized decision making
Top managers make all key decisions.

decentralized decision making
Lower-level managers are empowered to make important decisions.

SKILLS & BEST PRACTICES

Centralization Works for Nissan while Decentralization Reigns at Johnson & Johnson

Nissan: To reduce the potential for . . . unpleasant surprises, [CEO Carlos] Ghosn has reorganized Nissan's product-development system and put himself at the center of it. Before Ghosn, Nissan's design studios around the world competed among themselves to create new models, a chaotic system that executives now say hadn't worked for 20 years. Ghosn hired a new designer from Isuzu, Shiro Nakamura, to run the studios and report to a management committee that Ghosn heads. Ghosn also chairs monthly product-planning meetings and chooses among competing design proposals. "He's by far the smartest guy in the room," says Tom Semple, president of Nissan Design America. "He can make a $3 billion decision in 20 minutes."

Ghosn says he put himself in charge to ensure an orderly evaluation process. "I approve designs not because I think I am more gifted or somebody who can see ahead three or four years from now," he says, "but just to make sure that the design is a logical, rational decision, taken after analyzing pros and cons." "When the CEO makes a decision, people don't come back on it," Ghosn says. "When I come to a design decision, people know that is that."

Johnson & Johnson: The 117-year-old company is an astonishingly complex enterprise, made up of 204 different businesses organized into three divisions: drugs, medical devices and diagnostics, and consumer products. . . .

Each of its far-flung units operates pretty much as an independent enterprise. Businesses set their own strategies; they have their own finance and human resources departments, for example. While this degree of decentralization makes for relatively high overhead costs, no chief executive, [CEO William] Weldon included, has thought that too high a price to pay. Johnson & Johnson has been able to turn itself into a powerhouse precisely because the businesses it buys, and the ones it starts, are given near-total autonomy. That independence fosters an entrepreneurial attitude that has kept J & J intensely competitive as others around it have faltered.

SOURCES: Excerpt from A Taylor III, "Nissan Shifts into Higher Gear," *Fortune,* July 21, 2003, pp 98–104, Copyright © 2003 Time Inc. All rights reserved. And A Barrett, "Staying on Top," *Business Week,* May 5, 2003, pp 60–68.

Experts on the subject warn against extremes of centralization or decentralization. The challenge is to achieve a workable balance between the two extremes. A management consultant put it this way:

> The modern organization in transition will recognize the pull of two polarities: a need for greater centralization to create low-cost shared resources; and, a need to improve market responsiveness with greater decentralization. Today's winning organizations are the ones that can handle the paradox and tensions of both pulls. These are the firms that analyze the optimum organizational solution in each particular circumstance, without prejudice for one type of organization over another. The result is, almost invariably, a messy mixture of decentralized units sharing cost-effective centralized resources.[39]

Centralization and decentralization are not an either-or proposition; they are an *and-also* balancing act.

Practical Research Insights When they classified a sample of actual companies as either mechanistic or organic, Burns and Stalker discovered one type was not superior to the other. Each type had its appropriate place, depending on the environment. When the environment was relatively *stable and certain,* the successful organizations tended to be *mechanistic. Organic* organizations tended to be the successful ones when the environment was *unstable and uncertain.*[40]

In a more recent study of 103 department managers from eight manufacturing firms and two aerospace organizations, managerial skill was found to have a greater impact on a global measure of department effectiveness in organic departments than in mechanistic departments. This led the researchers to recommend the following contingencies for management staffing and training:

> If we have two units, one organic and one mechanistic, and two potential applicants differing in overall managerial ability, we might want to assign the more competent to the organic unit since in that situation there are few structural aids available to the manager in performing required responsibilities. It is also possible that managerial training is especially needed by managers being groomed to take over units that are more organic in structure.[41]

Another interesting finding comes from a study of 42 voluntary church organizations. As the organizations became more mechanistic (more bureaucratic) the intrinsic motivation of their members decreased.

HANDS-ON EXERCISE

Mechanistic or Organic?

INSTRUCTIONS: Think of your present (or a past) place of employment and rate it on the following eight factors. Calculate a total score and compare it to the scale.

Characteristics									
1. Task definition and knowledge required	Narrow, technical	1	2	3	4	5	6	7	Broad; general
2. Linkage between individual's contribution and organization's purpose	Vague or indirect	1	2	3	4	5	6	7	Clear or direct
3. Task flexibility	Rigid; routine	1	2	3	4	5	6	7	Flexible; varied
4. Specification of techniques, obligations, and rights	Specific	1	2	3	4	5	6	7	General
5. Degree of hierarchical control	High	1	2	3	4	5	6	7	Low (self-control emphasized)
6. Primary communication pattern	Top-down	1	2	3	4	5	6	7	Lateral (between peers)
7. Primary decision-making style	Authoritarian	1	2	3	4	5	6	7	Democratic; participative
8. Emphasis on obedience and loyalty	High	1	2	3	4	5	6	7	Low

Total score = ________

Scale

8–24 = Relatively mechanistic
25–39 = Mixed
40–56 = Relatively organic

SOURCE: Adapted from discussion in T Burns and G M Stalker, *The Management of Innovation* (London: Tavistock, 1961), pp 119–25.

Mechanistic organizations apparently undermined the volunteers' sense of freedom and self-determination. Additionally, the researchers believe their findings help explain why bureaucracy tends to feed on itself: "A mechanistic organizational structure may breed the need for a more extremely mechanistic system because of the reduction in intrinsically motivated behavior."[42] Thus, bureaucracy begets greater bureaucracy.

Most recently, field research in two factories, one mechanistic and the other organic, found expected communication patterns. Command-and-control (downward) communication characterized the mechanistic factory. Consultative or participative (two-way) communication prevailed in the organic factory.[43]

Both Mechanistic and Organic Structures Have Their Places

Although achievement-oriented students of OB typically express a distaste for mechanistic organizations, not all organizations or subunits can or should be organic. For

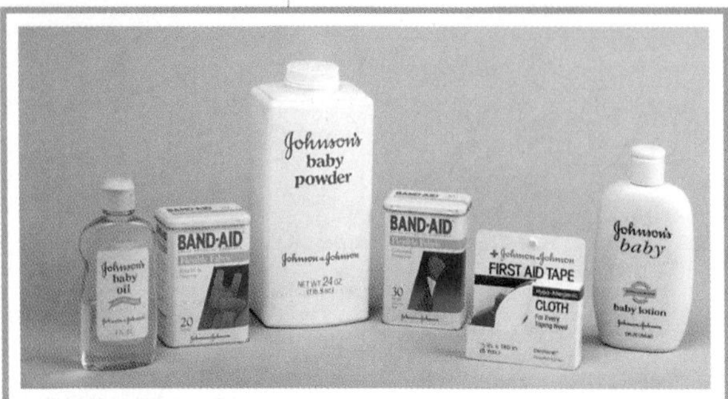

Johnson & Johnson's decentralization traces to the very beginnings of the company. The new bride of a J & J cotton mill worker kept cutting and burning her hand while learning to cook. Her husband came up with makeshift bandages, using the gauze they made at the mill and adhesive tape. He took his idea to J & J management, and after a few tweaks, the Band-Aid bandage was born. No top-down management here—innovation comes from all over the company to this day.

example, McDonald's could not achieve its admired quality and service standards without extremely mechanistic restaurant operations. Imagine the food and service you would get if McDonald's employees used their own favorite ways of doing things and worked at their own pace! On the other hand, mechanistic structure alienates some employees because it erodes their sense of self-control.

New-Style versus Old-Style Organizations

Organization theorists Jay R Galbraith and Edward E Lawler III have called for a "new logic of organizing."[44] They recommend a whole new set of adjectives to describe organizations (see Table 15–1). Traditional pyramid-shaped organizations, conforming to the old-style pattern, tend to be too slow and inflexible today. Leaner, more organic organizations increasingly are needed to accommodate today's strategic balancing act between cost, quality, and speed. These new-style organizations embrace the total quality management (TQM) principles discussed in Chapter 1. This means they are customer focused, dedicated to continuous improvement and learning, and structured around teams. These qualities, along with computerized information technology, hopefully enable big organizations to mimic the speed and flexibility of small organizations.

Virtual Organizations

Like virtual teams, discussed in Chapter 10, modern information technology allows people in virtual organizations to get something accomplished despite being geographically dispersed.[45] Instead of relying heavily on face-to-face meetings,

TABLE 15–1 New-Style versus Old-Style Organizations

New	Old
Dynamic, learning	Stable
Information rich	Information is scarce
Global	Local
Small and large	Large
Product/customer oriented	Functional
Skills oriented	Job oriented
Team oriented	Individual oriented
Involvement oriented	Command/control oriented
Lateral/networked	Hierarchical
Customer oriented	Job requirements oriented

SOURCE: From J R Galbraith and E E Lawler III, "Effective Organizations: Using the New Logic of Organizing," p 298 in *Organizing for the Future: The New Logic for Managing Complex Organizations,* eds J R Galbraith, E E Lawler III, and Associates. Copyright © 1993 Jossey-Bass Inc. Reprinted with permission of John Wiley & Sons, Inc.

The US military used decentralized command during the second war in Iraq. Marine commanders gave colonels unprecendented autonomy as long as they achieved results. Shifting this power down enabled colonels to make decisions within the heat of battle. In relation to business, Jason Santamaria, a former Marine and author of *The Marine Corps Way: Using Maneuver Warfare to Lead a Winning Organization,* says "you want to push the decision making onto the people with interaction in the market." *Inc.*, May 2004, p 24.

members of virtual organizations send e-mail and voice-mail messages, exchange project information over the Internet, and convene videoconferences among far-flung participants. In addition, cellular phones and the wireless Internet have made the dream of doing business from the beach a reality. This disconnection between work and location is causing managers to question traditional assumptions about centralized offices and factories. Various configurations have emerged. For example, consider *Business Week*'s recent description of JetBlue Airways Corp.:

> Look no further than JetBlue's 700-person reservation center in Salt Lake City. You don't see it? That's because its sales agents all work from their homes. They're linked by an Internet telephone system in which e-mail, chat, Web searches, and phone calls all pour through the same pipes.[46]

A more controversial form of virtual organization involves "offshoring" jobs to lower-wage countries. Sapient, a consulting firm based in Cambridge, Massachusetts, is a case in point:

> About half its 700 employees are in India. Via broadband, employees there and in Cambridge share electronic documents in real time and scribble to each other on virtual white boards.
>
> Broadband makes it possible, says Vice President Alan Wexler. "It's almost as if the work is being done in one physical place."[47]

Yet another form of virtual organization is not a single organization, but rather a *network* of several organizations linked together contractually and electronically. Why own a computer factory when contract-manufacturer Solectron will do the job for you? Why own warehouses and fleets of delivery trucks when UPS and FedEx can provide a complete supply chain? These different types of virtual organization—and the E-leadership challenges listed in Chapter 1—require new thinking about how to manage people who are out of sight, but not out of mind[48] (see Skills & Best Practices).

SKILLS & BEST PRACTICES

How to Manage Geographically Dispersed Employees

*The three keys are **sharing knowledge, building trust, and maintaining connectedness.*** Other steps include:

Hire carefully: People working in remote locations, especially at home, need to be self-starters who are well-organized, self-motivated, and effective communicators.

Communicate regularly: Daily e-mails and weekly phone conversations, at a minimum, help nip problems in the bud, address complaints, and build strong working relationships.

Practice "management by wandering around": Get out of the home office and regularly visit remote employees on their turf to get a first-hand view of what is happening. These visits also afford opportunities for coaching, feedback, and positive reinforcement.

Conduct regular audits: Formal audits ensure compliance with company policies, legal requirements, and ethical standards.

Use technology as a tool, not a weapon: Rely on cost-effective new technologies to enhance productivity. Be sensitive to privacy rights and employee morale when engaging in electronic performance monitoring (e.g., videotaping, monitoring e-mail and Internet use, and counting keystrokes).

Achieve a workable balance between online and live training. Live face-to-face training is expensive, but can build trust and teamwork.

SOURCE: Adapted from J W Janove, "Management by Remote Control," *HR Magazine,* April 2004, pp 119–24.

Gazing into the Crystal Ball Here is how we envision life in the emerging virtual organizations and organizational networks. Things will be very interesting and profitable for the elite core of entrepreneurs and engineers who hit on the right business formula. Turnover among the financial and information "have nots"—data entry, customer service, and production employees—will be high because of glaring inequities and limited opportunities for personal fulfillment and growth. Telecommuters who work from home will feel liberated and empowered (and sometimes lonely). Commitment, trust, and loyalty could erode badly if managers do not heed this caution by Charles Handy, a British management expert. According to Handy: "A shared commitment still requires personal contact to make the commitment feel real. *Paradoxically, the more virtual an organization becomes the more its people need to meet in person.*"[49] Independent contractors, both individuals and organizations, will participate in many different organizational networks and thus have diluted loyalty to any single one. Substandard working conditions and low pay at some smaller contractors will make them little more than Internet-age sweat shops.[50] Companies living from one contract to another will offer little in the way of job security and benefits. Offshoring of jobs in both the manufacturing and service sectors, despite being a politically charged issue, will continue as long as consumers demand low-cost (and often foreign-sourced) goods and services.[51] Opportunities to start new businesses will be numerous, but prolonged success could prove elusive at Internet speed.[52]

Needed: Self-Starting Team Players The only certainty about tomorrow's organizations is they will produce a lot of surprises. Only flexible, adaptable people who see problems as opportunities, are self-starters capable of teamwork, and are committed to lifelong learning will be able to handle whatever comes their way.

key terms

chapter summary

- *Describe the four characteristics common to all organizations.* They are coordination of effort (achieved through policies and rules), a common goal (a collective purpose), division of labor (people performing different but related tasks), and a hierarchy of authority (the chain of command).
- *Explain the difference between closed and open systems, and contrast the military/mechanical, biological, and cognitive systems metaphors for organizations.* Closed systems, such as a battery-powered clock, are relatively self-sufficient. Open systems, such as the human body, are highly dependent on the environment for survival. In the past, the military/mechanical metaphor characterized organizations as self-sufficient closed systems. Newer biological and cognitive metaphors view the organization as an open system. The biological metaphor views the organization as a living organism striving to survive in an uncertain environment. In terms of the cognitive metaphor, an organization is like the human mind, capable of interpreting and learning from uncertain and ambiguous situations.
- *Describe the four generic organizational effectiveness criteria.* They are goal accomplishment (satisfying stated objectives), resource acquisition (gathering the necessary productive inputs), internal processes (building and maintaining healthy organizational systems), and strategic constituencies satisfaction (achieving at least minimal satisfaction for all key stakeholders).
- *Explain what the contingency approach to organization design involves.* The contingency approach to organization design calls for fitting the organization to the demands of the situation.
- *Discuss Burns and Stalker's findings regarding mechanistic and organic organizations.* British researchers Burns and Stalker found that mechanistic (bureaucratic, centralized) organizations tended to be effective in stable situations. In unstable situations, organic (flexible, decentralized) organizations were more effective. These findings underscored the need for a contingency approach to organization design.
- *Describe new-style and old-style organizations, and list three keys to managing geographically dispersed employees in virtual organizations.* New-style organizations are characterized as dynamic and learning, information rich, global, small and large, product/customer oriented, skills oriented, team oriented, involvement oriented, lateral/networked, and customer oriented. Old-style organizations are characterized as stable, information is scarce, local, large, functional, job oriented, individual oriented, command/control oriented, hierarchical, and job requirements oriented. The three keys to effectively managing people geographically dispersed throughout a virtual organization are sharing knowledge, building trust, and maintaining connectedness.

discussion questions

1. How would you interpret Wal-Mart's effectiveness in terms of Figure 15–3? Explain.
2. What would an organization chart of your current (or last) place of employment look like? Does the chart you have drawn reveal the hierarchy (chain of command), division of labor, span of control, and line–staff distinctions? Does it reveal anything else? Explain.
3. Why is it appropriate to view modern organizations as open systems?
4. In a nutshell, what does contingency organization design entail?
5. If organic organizations are popular with most employees, why can't all organizations be structured in an organic fashion?

ethical dilemma

Close Supervision or Unethical "Snoopervision"?

If your employees are working outside your line of sight, how do you know they're working at all?

The days when managers could check up on their minions by looking out over rows of desks are over. More and more workers are toiling far away from their bosses' gaze—at home, in hotel rooms or in other remote locations. So, how is a supervisor to know whether they're really laboring at the monthly report and not shopping on eBay or watching Oprah?

Many managers may find comfort in the fact that the very technology that allows employees to work anywhere also enables companies to monitor their actions. In fact, a wealth of high-tech tools make it possible to keep a closer eye on employees than could ever be done when everybody was on the same floor. Some software can monitor whether employees are logged on to their computers, or working in particular applications. Other programs can track each keystroke or block access to undesirable Web sites. Web-connected video cameras can even watch workers at their desks.[53]

How Much Electronic Surveillance in the Workplace Is Too Much?

1. Electronic surveillance signals a distrust in employees, erodes morale, and ultimately hampers productivity. Explain your rationale.
2. Employers sign the paychecks and own the equipment, so they have the right to make sure they are getting their money's worth and their equipment is being used properly. Explain.
3. This sort of "snoopervision" creates a cat-and-mouse game in which "beating the system" becomes more important than productivity. Explain.
4. Electronic surveillance is unnecessary if properly trained and equipped employees are held accountable for meeting challenging but fair performance goals. Explain your rationale.
5. No amount of electronic performance monitoring can make up for poor hiring decisions, inadequate training, a weak performance-reward system, and inept supervision. Explain.
6. Invent other interpretations or options. Discuss.

For an interpretation of this situation, visit our Web site, www.mhhe.com/kinickiob2e.

If you're looking for additional study materials, be sure to check out the Online Learning Center at

www.mhhe.com/kinickiob2e

for more information and interactivities that correspond to this chapter.

chapter Sixteen

Managing Change and Organizational Learning

LEARNING OBJECTIVES

After reading the material in this chapter, you should be able to:

- Discuss the external and internal forces that create the need for organizational change.
- Describe Lewin's change model and the systems model of change.
- Explain Kotter's eight steps for leading organizational change.
- Review the 10 reasons employees resist change.
- Identify alternative strategies for overcoming resistance to change.
- Discuss the process organizations use to build their learning capabilities.

PEPSICO AGGRESSIVELY CHANGES ITS PRODUCTS TO ACCOMMODATE CONSUMERS' PREFERENCES

Few companies seem as pained by the thought of missing a customer as PepsiCo. Every year, the food and beverage giant adds more than 200 product variations to its vast global portfolio—which ranges from Quaker Soy Crisps to Gatorade Xtremo Thirst Quencher. Steven S. Reinemund, chairman and chief executive officer, believes that constant quest for change, more than even quality and value, is what has driven the Purchase (N.Y.) company to consistent double-digit earnings growth. As Reinemund has put it: "Innovation is what consumers are looking for, particularly in the small, routine things of their life."

What distinguishes PepsiCo from some competitors is an intense lack of sentimentality about its principal brands. Sure, it continues to hawk core products such as Pepsi cola and Lay's potato chips, adding flavors and doing targeted marketing campaigns every year to jazz up consumer interest. But Reinemund & Co. seem far more obsessed with understanding and catering to changing tastes than in trying to shape them. To capitalize on the growing market for New Age herbally enhanced beverages, for example, the company acquired SoBe Beverages for $370 million in 2001. Since then, the company has extended the brand with such offerings as the energy drink SoBe No Fear, SoBe Synergy targeted at the school-aged market with 50% juice, and SoBe Fuerte, aimed at the Hispanic market. . . .

"They have an exceptional ability to face the facts and adapt products to them," says UBS Investment Bank analyst Caroline Levy. Such innovation is a big reason PepsiCo sales jumped 7% last year, to $27 billion, while earnings grew 19%, to $3.6 billion—numbers that rated the No. 44 spot on *Business Week's* list of the 50 best-performing large public companies. . . .

In one of its more daring moves, the company reached south of the border two years ago to bring in four popular brands from its $1 billion Mexican subsidiary, Sabritas. The motive was to win over the foreign-born segment of the 46 million-strong Hispanic market that wasn't warming to Latin-flavored versions of Lay's and Doritos chips. . . .

The risk of importing foreign brands was that they might cannibalize Frito-Lay's core U.S. lines. So the company limited the distribution of products like Sabritones chile and lime puffed wheat snacks to smaller mom-and-pop retail operations in Mexican-dominated areas.

The gamble paid off. Despite no advertising and minimal distribution, U.S. sales of Sabritas brands are expected to exceed $100 million this year—double what they generated in 2002. Sabritas can now be found in markets covering roughly one-third of the U.S. population, up from 10% coverage two years ago. . . .

By defining its mission as serving the customer rather than protecting its venerable brands, PepsiCo is hoping to stave off a stagnant middle age. And if it has to tap its international portfolio for ideas or snap up products in hot new niches to do so, it will. There's nothing more American, after all, than giving consumers what they want.[1]

FOR DISCUSSION

Why is PepsiCo's approach to product development so successful? For an interpretation on this case and additional comments, visit our Online Learning Center:

www.mhhe.com/kinickiob2e

STEVEN REINEMUND'S EXPERIENCES AT PepsiCo are not the exception. Increased global competition, startling breakthroughs in information technology, changes in consumer preferences, and calls for greater corporate ethics are forcing companies to change the way they do business. Employees want satisfactory work environments, customers are demanding greater value, and investors want more integrity in financial disclosures. The rate of organizational and societal change is clearly accelerating.

As exemplified by PepsiCo in the opening vignette, organizations must change in order to satisfy customers and shareholders. The PepsiCo case also illustrates a subtle and important aspect about any type of change, whether it be product driven, personal, or organizational. Change is more likely to succeed when it is proactive rather than reactive. Peter Senge, a well-known expert on the topic of organizational change, made the following comment about organizational change during an interview with *Fast Company* magazine:

> When I look at efforts to create change in big companies over the past 10 years, I have to say that there's enough evidence of success to say that change is possible—and enough evidence of failure to say that it isn't likely.[2]

If Senge is correct, then it is all the more important for current and future managers to learn how they can successfully implement organizational change. This final chapter was written to help managers navigate the journey of change.

Specifically, we discuss the forces that create the need for organization change, models of planned change, resistance to change, and creating a learning organization.

Forces of Change

How do organizations know when they should change? What cues should an organization look for? Although there are no clear-cut answers to these questions, the "cues" that signal the need for change are found by monitoring the forces for change.

Organizations encounter many different forces for change. These forces come from external sources outside the organization and from internal sources. This section examines the forces that create the need for change. Awareness of the forces of change can help managers determine when they should consider implementing an organizational change.

External Forces

External forces for change originate outside the organization. Because these forces have global effects, they may cause an organization to question the essence of what business it is in and the process by which products and services are produced. There are four key external forces for change: demographic characteristics, technological advancements, market changes, and social and political pressures. Each is now discussed.

external forces for change

Originate outside the organization.

Demographic Characteristics Chapter 4 provided a detailed discussion of the demographic changes occurring in the US workforce. We concluded that organizations need to effectively manage diversity if they are to receive maximum contribution and commitment from employees. Consider the implications associated with hiring the 80 million people dubbed the Net or Echo-Boom Generation—people born between 1977 and 1997:

> Employers will have to face the new realities of the Net Generation's culture and values, and what it wants from work if they expect to attract and retain those talents and align them with corporate goals. . . . The new wave of 80 million young people entering the workforce during the next 20 years are technologically equipped and, therefore, armed with the most powerful tools for business. That makes their place in history unique: No previous generation has grown up understanding, using, and expanding on such a pervasive instrument as the PC.[3]

The organizational challenge will be to motivate and utilize this talented pool of employees to its maximum potential.

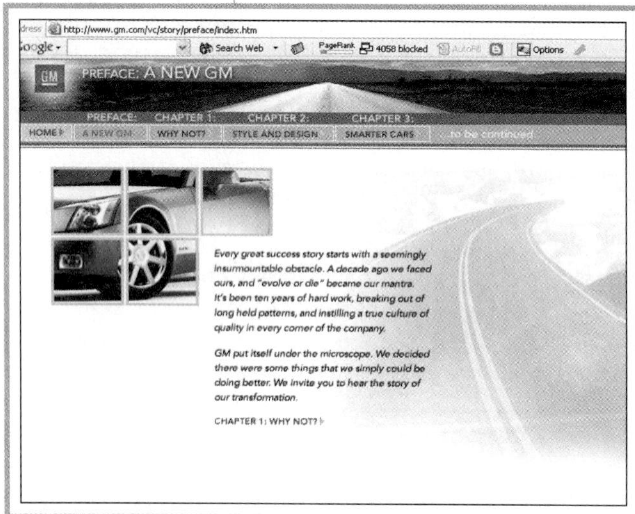

In June 2003, GM ran special "Road to Redemption" ads, aimed at overhauling their corporate image with customers who had given up on the automaker or on US-made cars in general. Creating a new mantra, "evolve or die," employees at GM had to rethink every facet of their day-to-day business practices. The full story can be found on the GM Web site at http://www.gm.com/vc/story/preface/index.htm.

Technological Advancements Both manufacturing and service organizations are increasingly using technology as a means to improve productivity and market competitiveness. Development and use of information technologies is probably one of the biggest forces for change. Organizations, large and small, private and public, for profit and not for profit, all must adapt to using a host of information technologies. For example, Wal-Mart, the world's largest retailer, is requiring its top 100 suppliers to implement radio-frequency identification (RFID) technology by January 2005. By placing small electronic tags on products or shipping crates, RFID will enable Wal-Mart to track everything that happens to its supplies, thereby reducing distribution time and costs. Analysts estimate that RFID will reduce Wal-Mart's distribution costs by $8 billion in 2005 if the January deadline is met.[4] Experts also predict that E-business will continue to create evolutionary change in organizations around the world.

Customer and Market Changes Increasing customer sophistication is requiring organizations to deliver higher value in their products and services. Customers are simply demanding more now than they did in the past. Moreover, customers are more likely to shop elsewhere if they do not get what they want because of lower customer switching costs. For example, Verizon lost nearly 2 million lines in 2002 as customers switched to alternatives such as wireless and telephone service via cable-TV wires.[5]

With respect to market changes, service companies are experiencing increased pressure to obtain more productivity because competition is fierce and prices have remained relatively stable.[6] Further, the emergence of a global economy is forcing companies to change the way they do business. US companies have been forging new partnerships and alliances with their suppliers and potential competitors in order to gain advantages in the global marketplace.

Social and Political Pressures These forces are created by social and political events. For example, tobacco companies are experiencing a lot of pressure to alter the way they market their products within the United States. This pressure is being exerted through legislative bodies that represent the American populace. Political events can create substantial change. For instance, the collapse of communism in Russia created many new business opportunities. Although it is difficult for organizations to predict changes in political forces, many organizations hire lobbyists and consultants to help them detect and respond to social and political changes.

Internal Forces

internal forces for change

Originate inside the organization.

Internal forces for change come from inside the organization. These forces can be subtle, such as low job satisfaction, or can manifest in outward signs, such as low productivity or high turnover and conflict. Internal forces for change come from both human resource problems and managerial behavior/decisions. For example, Glenn Tilton, CEO of United Airlines, is creating much-needed change at the airline in order to help the company navigate through its 18-month stay in bankruptcy court. He has cut the workforce, asked employees for wage concessions, and instituted a bonus system that rewards the company's 63,000 employees for achieving the company's goals for on-time flight departures and for customer intent to fly United. These changes seem to be working as employees across the board have made concessions and United's customer service ratings have gone from nearly the worst to among the best in the industry.[7]

Models of Planned Change

American managers are criticized for emphasizing short-term, quick-fix solutions to organizational problems. When applied to organizational change, this approach is doomed from the start. Quick-fix solutions do not really solve underlying causes of problems and they have little staying power. Researchers and managers alike have thus tried to identify effective ways to manage the change process. This section reviews three models of planned change—Lewin's change model, a systems model of change, and Kotter's eight steps for leading organizational change—and organizational development.

Lewin's Change Model

Most theories of organizational change originated from the landmark work of social psychologist Kurt Lewin. Lewin developed a three-stage model of planned change which explained how to initiate, manage, and stabilize the change process.[8] The three stages are unfreezing, changing, and refreezing.

Unfreezing The focus of this stage is to create the motivation to change. In so doing, individuals are encouraged to replace old behaviors and attitudes with those desired by management. Managers can begin the unfreezing process by disconfirming the usefulness or appropriateness of employees' present behaviors or attitudes. In other words, employees need to become dissatisfied with the old way of doing things. Glenn Tilton attempted to unfreeze employees for change at United Airlines by traveling around the country and talking to employees about what was needed to help the company recover from bankruptcy. One of his goals in these talks was to get employees to think about solving problems rather than blaming others for what was wrong in the company. He wanted to eliminate a "blame" mentality. To do this, Mr. Tilton used one ground rule with employees. "They could ask any question as long as they didn't blame their colleagues, supervisors, unions, or management for the airline's plight. In a meeting where a burly male ground worker started blaming other employees for the airline's woes, Mr. Tilton stopped the man and told him to leave the room."[9]

Benchmarking is a technique that can be used to help unfreeze an organization. **Benchmarking** "describes the overall process by which a company compares its performance with that of other companies, then learns how the strongest-performing companies achieve their results."[10] For example, one company for which we consulted discovered through benchmarking that their costs to develop software were twice as high as the best companies in the industry, and the time it took to get a new product to market was four times longer than the benchmarked organizations. These data were ultimately used to unfreeze employees' attitudes and motivate people to change the organization's internal processes in order to remain competitive. Managers also need to devise ways to reduce the barriers to change during this stage.

benchmarking

Process by which a company compares its performance with that of high-performing organizations.

Changing Because change involves learning, this stage entails providing employees with new information, new behavioral models, or new ways of looking at things. The purpose is to help employees learn new concepts or points of view. Consider, for example, the organizational changes implemented by KPMG Consulting as it transforms itself from an organization run by a partnership to one that is publicly held and focuses on meeting financial goals:

> The massive mahogany desks and expansive offices once occupied by KPMG's venerated partners have given way to cookie-cutter work spaces, pint-size offices, and managing directors. . . . KPMG Consulting has already laid off 800 of its 10,000 employees in the past 16 months, for which it will take a $15 million to $20 million charge. . . . Those who are left have had to adapt to an environment in which the focus is firmly on the numbers. Instead of measuring profitability once a year—standard operating procedure in the partnership—the company now monitors financials constantly. Every Friday, Senior Vice President Kenneth C Taormina grills his sales force on every would-be client: "I go through every single deal [asking] 'What do we need to get it done?'" Even the office kitty that partners dipped into freely for morale-building activities such as staff dinners is now under scrutiny.[11]

Directors at KPMG are clearly trying to get employees to become more customer focused and cost conscious. During the change process like that at KPMG, organizations use role models, mentors, consultants, benchmarking results, and training to facilitate change. Experts recommend that it is best to convey the idea that change is a continuous learning process rather than a one-time event.

Refreezing Change is stabilized during refreezing by helping employees integrate the changed behavior or attitude into their normal way of doing things. This is accomplished by first giving employees the chance to exhibit the new behaviors or attitudes. Once exhibited, positive reinforcement is used to reinforce the desired change. Additional coaching and modeling also are used at this point to reinforce the stability of the change. Returning to the example of United Airlines, the company used a new incentive system to refreeze employee behavior regarding productivity and customer service. United paid out $26 million under the bonus plan in the first quarter of 2004 after the company exceeded its goals. This example highlights the power of using monetary incentives to reinforce behavioral change.

A Systems Model of Change

A systems approach takes a "big picture" perspective of organizational change. It is based on the notion that any change, no matter how large or small, has a cascading effect throughout an organization. For example, promoting an individual to a new work group affects the group dynamics in both the old and new groups. Similarly, creating project or work teams may necessitate the need to revamp compensation practices. These examples illustrate that change creates additional change. Today's solutions are tomorrow's problems. A systems model of change offers managers a framework to understand the broad complexities of organizational change.[12] The three main components of a systems model are inputs, target elements of change, and outputs (see Figure 16–1).

A Systems Model of Change **FIGURE 16–1**

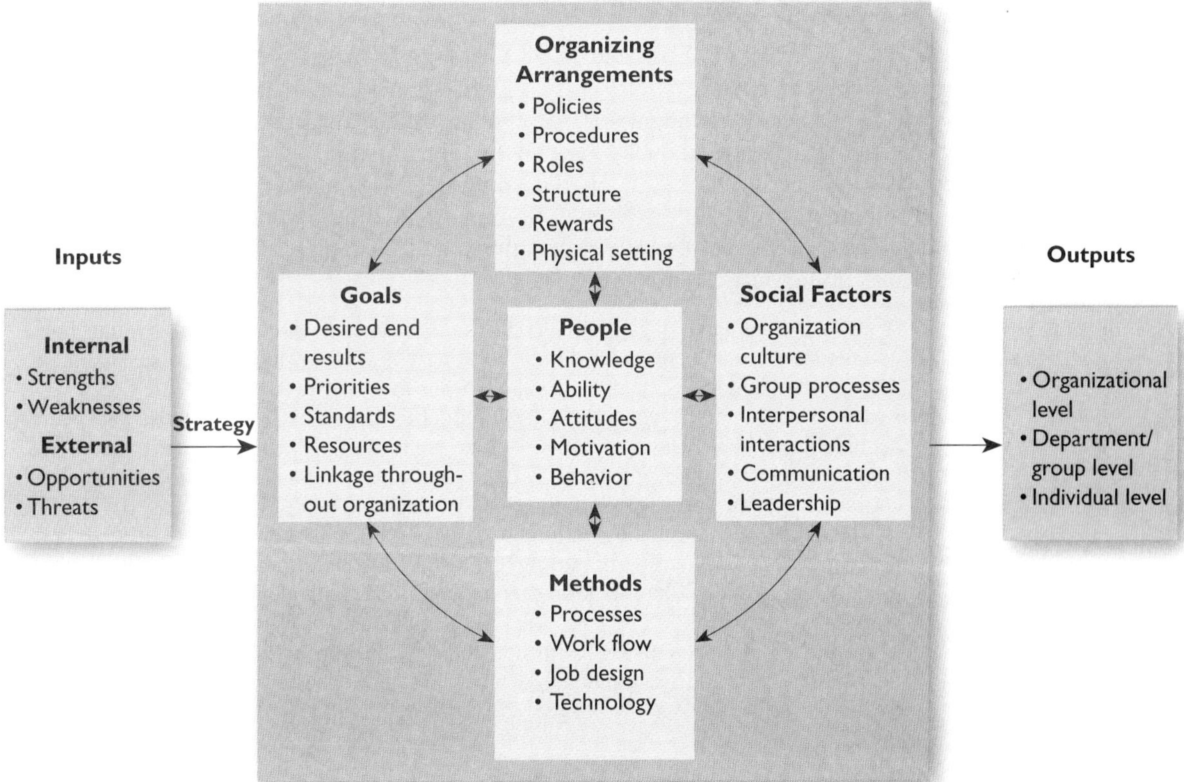

SOURCES: Adapted from D R Fuqua and D J Kurpius, "Conceptual Models in Organizational Consultation," *Journal of Counseling & Development,* July/August 1993, pp 602–18; and D A Nadler and M L Tushman, "Organizational Frame Bending: Principles for Managing Reorientation," *Academy of Management Executive,* August 1989, pp 194–203.

mission statement

Summarizes "why" an organization exists.

strategic plan

A long-term plan outlining actions needed to achieve planned results.

target elements of change

Components of an organization that may be changed.

Inputs All organizational changes should be consistent with an organization's mission, vision, and resulting strategic plan. A **mission statement** represents the "reason" an organization exists, and an organization's *vision* is a long-term goal that describes "what" an organization wants to become. Consider how the difference between mission and vision affects organizational change. Your university probably has a mission to educate people. This mission does not necessarily imply anything about change. It simply defines the university's overall purpose. In contrast, the university may have a vision to be recognized as the "best" university in the country. This vision requires the organization to benchmark itself against other world-class universities and to create plans for achieving the vision. While vision statements point the way, strategic plans contain the detail needed to create organizational change.

A **strategic plan** outlines an organization's long-term direction and actions necessary to achieve planned results. Strategic plans are based on considering an organization's strengths and weaknesses relative to its environmental opportunities and threats. This comparison results in developing an organizational strategy to attain desired outputs such as profits, customer satisfaction, quality, adequate return on investment, and acceptable levels of turnover and employee commitment (see Figure 16–1). In summary, organizations tend to commit resources to counterproductive or conflicting activities when organizational changes are not consistent with its strategic plan.

Target Elements of Change **Target elements of change** represent the components of an organization that may be changed. As shown in Figure 16–1, change can be directed at realigning organizing arrangements, social factors, methods, goals, and people.[13] The choice is based on the strategy being pursued or the organizational problem at hand. For example, Southwest Airlines is targeting technological changes in order to improve productivity and customer service while simultaneously cutting costs.

> High-tech is already paying dividends for Southwest, which gets more than half its customer revenue from its online booking site, www.southwest.com. That's an industry benchmark.
>
> But in other areas, such as its maintenance operations, Southwest has been decidedly low-tech. Until recently, each airplane repair created a huge paper trail, forcing mechanics and managers to manually enter loads of data into an outdated computer system and sort through reams of data. . . .
>
> To make the system more efficient, [Gary] Kelley [chief financial officer] and Vice President Jim Wimberly, Southwest's chief of operations, have installed computer programs that keep track of scheduled maintenance for the carrier's 390 planes.
>
> Southwest now spends \$400 million to \$450 million a year on its maintenance operations. The carrier estimates the computers could shave 10% or more from that total.[14]

Outputs Outputs represent the desired end results of a change. Once again, these end results should be consistent with an organization's strategic plan. Figure 16–1 indicates that change may be directed at the organizational level, department/group level, or individual level. Change efforts are more complicated and difficult to manage when they are targeted at the organizational level. This occurs because organizational-level changes are more likely to affect multiple target elements of change shown in the model.

Kotter's Eight Steps for Leading Organizational Change

John Kotter, an expert in leadership and change management, believes that organizational change typically fails because senior management makes a host of implementation errors. Kotter recommends that organizations should follow eight sequential steps to overcome these implementation problems (see Table 16–1).[15]

These steps also subsume Lewin's model of change. The first four steps represent Lewin's "unfreezing" stage. Steps 5, 6, and 7 represent "changing," and step 8 corresponds to "refreezing." The value of Kotter's steps is that they provide specific recommendations about behaviors that managers need to exhibit to successfully lead

Steps to Leading Organizational Change TABLE 16–1

Step	Description
1. Establish a sense of urgency	Unfreeze the organization by creating a compelling reason for why change is needed.
2. Create the guiding coalition	Create a cross-functional, cross-level group of people with enough power to lead the change.
3. Develop a vision and strategy	Create a vision and strategic plan to guide the change process.
4. Communicate the change vision	Create and implement a communication strategy that consistently communicates the new vision and strategic plan.
5. Empower broad-based action	Eliminate barriers to change, and use target elements of change to transform the organization. Encourage risk taking and creative problem solving.
6. Generate short-term wins	Plan for and create short-term "wins" or improvements. Recognize and reward people who contribute to the wins.
7. Consolidate gains and produce more change	The guiding coalition uses credibility from short-term wins to create more change. Additional people are brought into the change process as change cascades throughout the organization. Attempts are made to reinvigorate the change process.
8. Anchor new approaches in the culture	Reinforce the changes by highlighting connections between new behaviors and processes and organizational success. Develop methods to ensure leadership development and succession.

SOURCE: The steps were developed by J P Kotter, *Leading Change* (Boston: Harvard Business School Press, 1996).

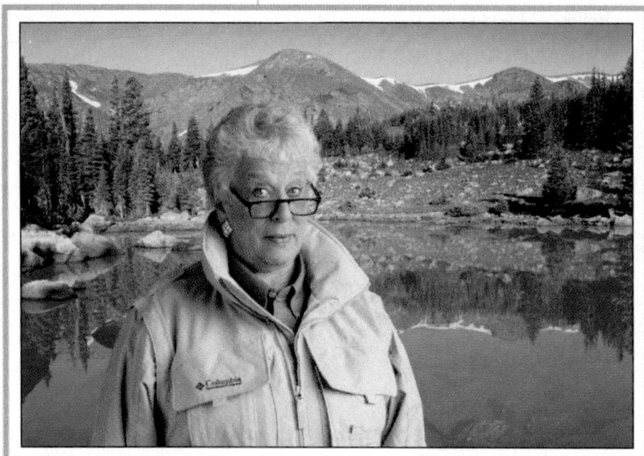

When Gert Boyle's husband suddenly died of a heart attack, he left her with a debt-ridden company, and no knowledge of how to run it. This created a clear sense of urgency that change was needed. Thirty-two years later, she and her son Tim Boyle have turned Columbia Sportswear Company into a successful outerwear company. Her first decisions were difficult ones, including firing nearly all of her roughly 55 employees, but Gert and Tim focused on listening to customers and innovating. Since 1984, sales have grown from $3 million to nearly $1 billion. Change can sometimes lead to very good things.

organizational change. It is important to remember that Kotter's research reveals that it is ineffective to skip steps and that successful organizational change is 70% to 90% leadership and only 10% to 30% management. Senior managers are thus advised to focus on leading rather than managing change.[16]

Organization Development

Organization development (OD) is an applied field of study and practice. A pair of OD experts defined **organization development** as follows:

> Organization development is concerned with helping managers plan change in organizing and managing people that will develop requisite commitment, coordination, and competence. Its purpose is to enhance both the effectiveness of organizations and the well-being of their members through planned interventions in the organization's human processes, structures, and systems, using knowledge of behavioral science and its intervention methods.[17]

As you can see from this definition, OD constitutes a set of techniques or interventions that are used to implement organizational change. These techniques can be targeted to change individual attitudes and behavior, group dynamics, and organizations as a whole. Large scale organizational development that attempts to change an entire organization is commonly referred to as *organizational transformation*. Further, these techniques or interventions apply to each of the change models discussed in this section. For example, OD is used during Lewin's "changing" stage. It also is used to identify and implement targeted elements of change within the systems model of change. Finally, OD might be used during Kotter's steps 1, 3, 5, 6, and 7. In this section, we briefly review the four identifying characteristics of OD and its research and practical implications.[18]

OD Involves Profound Change Change agents using OD generally desire deep and long-lasting improvement. OD consultant Warner Burke, for example, who strives for fundamental *cultural* change, wrote: "By fundamental change, as opposed to fixing a problem or improving a procedure, I mean that some significant aspect of an organization's culture will never be the same."[19]

organization development

A set of techniques or tools that are used to implement organizational change.

OD Is Value Loaded Owing to the fact that OD is rooted partially in humanistic psychology, many OD consultants carry certain values or biases into the client organization. They prefer cooperation over conflict, self-control over institutional control, and democratic and participative management over autocratic management. In addition to OD being driven by a consultant's values, OD practitioners now believe that there is a broader "value perspective" that should underlie any organizational change. Specifically, OD should always be customer focused and it should help an organization achieve its vision and strategic goals. This approach implies that organizational interventions should be aimed at helping to satisfy customers' needs and thereby provide enhanced value of an organization's products and services.

TABLE 16–2 Some OD Interventions for Implementing Change

- **Survey feedback:** A questionnaire is distributed to employees to ascertain their perceptions and attitudes. The results are then shared with them. The questionnaire may ask about such matters as group cohesion, job satisfaction, and managerial leadership. Once the survey is done, meaningful results can be communicated with employees so that they can then engage in problem solving and constructive changes.
- **Process consultation:** An OD consultant observes the communication process—interpersonal-relations, decision-making, and conflict-handling patterns—occurring in work groups and provides feedback to the members involved. In consulting with employees (particularly managers) about these processes, the change agent hopes to give them the skills to identify and improve group dynamics on their own.
- **Team building:** Work groups are made to become more effective by helping members learn to function as a team. For example, members of a group might be interviewed independently by the OD change agent to establish how they feel about the group, then a meeting may be held away from their usual workplace to discuss the issues. To enhance team cohesiveness, the OD consultant may have members work together on a project such as rock climbing, with the consultant helping with communication and conflict resolution. The objective is for members to see how they can individually contribute to the group's goals and efforts.
- **Intergroup development:** Intergroup development resembles team building in many of its efforts. However, intergroup development attempts to achieve better cohesiveness among several work groups, not just one. During the process, the change agent tries to elicit misperceptions and stereotypes that the groups have for each other so that they can be discussed, leading to better coordination among them.
- **Technostructural activities:** Technostructural activities are interventions concerned with improving the work technology or organizational design with people on the job. An intervention involving a work-technology change might be the introduction of e-mail to improve employee communication. An intervention involving an organizational-design change might be making a company less centralized in its decision making.

SOURCE: A Kinicki and B Williams, *Management: A Practical Introduction* (Burr Ridge: IL: McGraw-Hill/Irwin, 2003) p 330.

OD Is a Diagnosis/Prescription Cycle OD theorists and practitioners have long adhered to a medical model of organization. Like medical doctors, internal and external OD consultants approach the "sick" organization, "diagnose" its ills, "prescribe" and implement an intervention, and "monitor" progress. Table 16–2 presents a list of several different OD interventions that can be used to change individual, group, or organizational behavior as whole.[20]

OD Is Process Oriented Ideally, OD consultants focus on the form and not the content of behavioral and administrative dealings. For example, product design engineers and market researchers might be coached on how to communicate more effectively with one another without the consultant knowing the technical details of their conversations. In addition to communication, OD specialists focus on other processes, including problem solving, decision making, conflict handling, trust, power sharing, and career development.

OD Research and Practical Implications Before discussing OD research, it is important to note that many of the topics contained in this book are used during OD interventions. Team building, for example, is commonly used as an OD technique. It is used to improve the functioning of work groups. The point is that OD research has practical implications for a variety of OB applications previously discussed. OD-related interventions produced the following insights:

- A meta-analysis of 18 studies indicated that employee satisfaction with change was higher when top management was highly committed to the change effort.[21]
- A meta-analysis of 52 studies provided support for the systems model of organizational change. Specifically, varying one target element of change created changes in other target elements. Also, there was a positive relationship between individual behavior change and organizational-level change.[22]
- A meta-analysis of 126 studies demonstrated that multifaceted interventions using more than one OD technique were more effective in changing job attitudes and work attitudes than interventions that relied on only one human-process or technostructural approach.[23]
- A survey of 1,700 firms from China, Japan, the United States, and Europe revealed that (1) US and European firms used OD interventions more frequently than firms from China and Japan and (2) some OD interventions are culture free and some are not.[24]

There are four practical implications derived from this research. First, planned organizational change works. However, management and change agents are advised to rely on multifaceted interventions. As indicated elsewhere in this book, goal setting, feedback, recognition and rewards, training, participation, and challenging job design have good track records relative to improving performance and satisfaction. Second, change programs are more successful when they are geared toward meeting both short-term and long-term results. Managers should not engage in organizational change for the sake of change. Change efforts should produce positive results. Third, organizational change is more likely to succeed when top management is truly committed to the change process and the desired goals of the change program. This is particularly true when organizations pursue large-scale transformation. Finally, the effectiveness of OD interventions is affected by cross-cultural considerations. Managers and OD consultants should not blindly apply an OD intervention that worked in one country to a similar situation in another country.

Understanding and Managing Resistance to Change

We are all creatures of habit. It generally is difficult for people to try new ways of doing things. It is precisely because of this basic human characteristic that most employees do not have enthusiasm for change in the workplace. Rare is the manager who does not have several stories about carefully cultivated changes that died on the vine because of resistance to change. It is important for managers to learn to manage resistance because failed change efforts are costly. Costs include decreased employee loyalty, lowered probability of achieving corporate goals, waste of money and resources, and difficulty in fixing the failed change effort. This section examines employee resistance to change and practical ways of dealing with the problem.

Copyright © 2002 Ted Goff. Reprinted with permission.

Why People Resist Change in the Workplace

No matter how technically or administratively perfect a proposed change may be, people make or break it. Individual and group behavior following an organizational change can take many forms. The extremes range from acceptance to active resistance. **Resistance to change** is an emotional/behavioral response to real or imagined threats to an established work routine. Resistance can be as subtle as passive resignation and as overt as deliberate sabotage. Let us now consider the reasons employees resist change in the first place. Ten of the leading reasons are listed here:[25]

1. *An individual's predisposition toward change.* This predisposition is highly personal and deeply ingrained. It is an outgrowth of how one learns to handle change and ambiguity as a child. While some people are distrustful and suspicious of change, others see change as a situation requiring flexibility, patience, and understanding.[26]
2. *Surprise and fear of the unknown.* When innovative or radically different changes are introduced without warning, affected employees become fearful of the implications. Grapevine rumors fill the void created by a lack of official announcements. Harvard's Rosabeth Moss Kanter recommends appointing a transition manager charged with keeping all relevant parties adequately informed.[27]
3. *Climate of mistrust.* Trust, as discussed in Chapter 10, involves reciprocal faith in others' intentions and behavior. Mutual mistrust can doom to failure an otherwise well-conceived change. Mistrust encourages secrecy, which begets deeper mistrust. Managers who trust their employees make the change process an open, honest, and participative affair. Employees who, in turn, trust management are more willing to expend extra effort and take chances with something different.
4. *Fear of failure.* Intimidating changes on the job can cause employees to doubt their capabilities. Self-doubt erodes self-confidence and cripples personal growth and development.
5. *Loss of status and/or job security.* Administrative and technological changes that threaten to alter power bases or eliminate jobs generally trigger strong resistance. For example, most corporate restructuring involves the elimination of managerial jobs. One should not be surprised when middle managers resist restructuring and participative management programs that reduce their authority and status.
6. *Peer pressure.* Someone who is not directly affected by a change may actively resist it to protect the interest of his or her friends and co-workers.

resistance to change
Emotional/behavioral response to real or imagined work changes.

7. *Disruption of cultural traditions and/or group relationships.* Whenever individuals are transferred, promoted, or reassigned, cultural and group dynamics are thrown into disequilibrium.
8. *Personality conflicts.* Just as a friend can get away with telling us something we would resent hearing from an adversary, the personalities of change agents can breed resistance.
9. *Lack of tact and/or poor timing.* Undue resistance can occur because changes are introduced in an insensitive manner or at an awkward time.
10. *Nonreinforcing reward systems.* Individuals resist when they do not foresee positive rewards for changing. For example, an employee is unlikely to support a change effort that is perceived as requiring him or her to work longer with more pressure.

Alternative Strategies for Overcoming Resistance to Change

Before recommending specific approaches to overcome resistance, there are five key conclusions that should be kept in mind. First, an organization must be ready for change. Just as a table must be set before you can eat, so must an organization be ready for change before it can be effective.[28] Second, people are more likely to resist change when they do not agree on the causes of current problems and the need for change. This is a "cognitive" hurdle that must be overcome by increasing employees' commitment to change.[29] **Commitment to change** is defined as a mind-set "that binds an individual to a course of action deemed necessary for the successful implementation of a change initiative."[30] In order to bring this concept to life, we would like you to complete a shortened version of a commitment to change instrument presented in the Hands-On Exercise on page 405. Were you committed to the change? Did this level of commitment affect your behavioral support for what management was trying to accomplish?

commitment to change

A mind-set of doing whatever it takes to effectively implement change.

Third, organizational change is less successful when top management fails to keep employees informed about the process of change. Fourth, do not assume that people are consciously resisting change. Managers are encouraged to use a systems model of change to identify the obstacles that are affecting the implementation process. Fifth, employees' perceptions or interpretations of a change significantly affect resistance. Employees are less likely to resist when they perceive that the benefits of a change overshadow the personal costs. At a minimum then, managers are advised to (1) provide as much information as possible to employees about the change, (2) inform employees about the reasons/rationale for the change, (3) conduct meetings to address employees' questions regarding the change, and (4) provide employees the opportunity to discuss how the proposed change might affect them.[31] These recommendations underscore the importance of communicating with employees throughout the process of change.

In addition to communication, employee participation in the change process is another generic approach for reducing resistance. That said, however, organizational change experts have criticized the tendency to treat participation as a cure-all for

HANDS-ON EXERCISE

Does Your Commitment to a Change Initiative Predict Your Behavioral Support for the Change?

INSTRUCTIONS: First, think of a time in which a previous or current employer was undergoing a change initiative that required you to learn something new or to discontinue an attitude, behavior, or organizational practice. Next, evaluate your commitment to this change effort by indicating the extent to which you agree with the following survey items. Use the rating scale shown below. Finally, assess your behavioral support for the change.

1 = Strongly disagree
2 = Disagree
3 = Neither agree nor disagree
4 = Agree
5 = Strongly agree

1. I believe in the value of this change	1——2——3——4——5
2. This change serves an important purpose	1——2——3——4——5
3. This change is a good strategy for the organization	1——2——3——4——5
4. I have no choice but to go along with this change	1——2——3——4——5
5. It would be risky to speak out against this change	1——2——3——4——5
6. It would be too costly for me to resist this change	1——2——3——4——5
7. I feel a sense of duty to work toward this change	1——2——3——4——5
8. It would be irresponsible of me to resist this change	1——2——3——4——5
9. I feel obligated to support this change	1——2——3——4——5

Total score = ________

ARBITRARY NORMS

9–18 = Low commitment
19–35 = Moderate commitment
36–45 = High commitment

BEHAVIORAL SUPPORT FOR THE CHANGE

Overall, I modified my attitudes and behavior in line with what management was trying to accomplish	1——2——3——4——5

SOURCE: Survey items were obtained from L Herscovitch and J P Meyer, "Commitment to Organizational Change: Extension of a Three-Component Model," *Journal of Applied Psychology,* June 2002, p 477.

resistance to change. They prefer a contingency approach because resistance can take many forms and, furthermore, because situational factors vary (see Table 16–3). As seen in Table 16–3, Participation + Involvement does have its place, but it takes time that is not always available. Also as indicated in Table 16–3, each of the other five methods has its situational niche, advantages, and drawbacks. In short, there is no universal strategy for overcoming resistance to change. Managers need a complete repertoire of change strategies.

TABLE 16–3 Six Strategies for Overcoming Resistance to Change

Approach	Commonly Used in Situations	Advantages	Drawbacks
Education + Communication	Where there is a lack of information or inaccurate information and analysis.	Once persuaded, people will often help with the implementation of the change.	Can be very time consuming if lots of people are involved.
Participation + Involvement	Where the initiators do not have all the information they need to design the change and where others have considerable power to resist.	People who participate will be committed to implementing change, and any relevant information they have will be integrated into the change plan.	Can be very time consuming if participators design an inappropriate change.
Facilitation + Support	Where people are resisting because of adjustment problems.	No other approach works as well with adjustment problems.	Can be time consuming, expensive, and still fail.
Negotiation + Agreement	Where someone or some group will clearly lose out in a change and where that group has considerable power to resist.	Sometimes it is a relatively easy way to avoid major resistance.	Can be too expensive in many cases if it alerts others to negotiate for compliance.
Manipulation + Co-optation	Where other tactics will not work or are too expensive.	It can be a relatively quick and inexpensive solution to resistance problems.	Can lead to future problems if people feel manipulated.
Explicit + Implicit coercion	Where speed is essential and where the change initiators possess considerable power.	It is speedy and can overcome any kind of resistance.	Can be risky if it leaves people angry at the initiators.

SOURCE: Reprinted by permission of the *Harvard Business Review.* An exhibit from "Choosing Strategies for Change" by J P Kotter and L A Schlesinger (March/April 1979).

Creating a Learning Organization

Organizations are finding that yesterday's competitive advantage is becoming the minimum entrance requirement for staying in business. This puts tremendous pressure on organizations to learn how best to improve and stay ahead of competitors. In fact, both researchers and practicing managers agree that an organization's capability to learn is a key strategic weapon. It thus is important for organizations to enhance and nurture their capability to learn.

So what is organizational learning and how do organizations become learning organizations? To help clarify what this process entails, this section begins by defining organizational learning and a learning organization. We then present a model of organizational learning and conclude by reviewing new roles and skills required of leaders to create a learning organization.

Defining Organizational Learning and a Learning Organization

Organizational learning (OL) and a learning organization (LO) are not the same thing. Susan Fisher and Margaret White, experts on organizational change and learning, define organizational learning as follows:

> Organizational learning is a reflective process, played out by members at all levels of the organization, that involves the collection of information from both the external and internal environments. This information is filtered through a collective sensemaking process, which results in shared interpretations that can be used to instigate actions resulting in enduring changes to the organization's behavior and theories in use.[32]

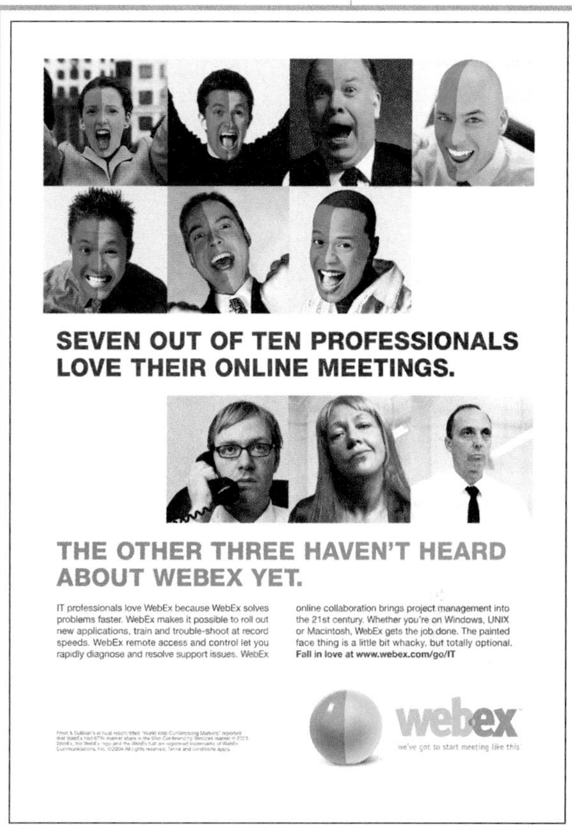

SEVEN OUT OF TEN PROFESSIONALS LOVE THEIR ONLINE MEETINGS.
THE OTHER THREE HAVEN'T HEARD ABOUT WEBEX YET.
IT professionals love WebEx because WebEx solves problems faster. WebEx makes it possible to roll out new applications, train and trouble-shoot at record speeds. WebEx remote access and control let you rapidly diagnose and resolve support issues. WebEx online collaboration brings project management into the 21st century. Whether you're on Windows, UNIX or Macintosh, WebEx gets the job done. The painted face thing is a little bit whacky, but totally optional.
Fall in love at www.webex.com/go/IT
webex
we've got to start meeting like this

Employees are often resistant to change, especially when it involves new technologies or systems changes. WebEx offers a new way of communicating, featuring online meetings, live training, and seminars.

This definition highlights that organizational learning represents a process by which information is gathered and then interpreted through a cognitive, social process. The accumulated information from this interpretative process represents an organization's knowledge base. This knowledge in turn is stored in organizational "memory," which consists of files, records, procedures, policies, and organizational culture. In contrast, learning organizations use organizational knowledge to foster innovation and organizational effectiveness.

Peter Senge, a professor at the Massachusetts Institute of Technology, popularized the term *learning organization* in his best-selling book entitled *The Fifth Discipline.* He described a learning organization as "a group of people working together to collectively enhance their capacities to create results that they truly care about."[33] A practical interpretation of these ideas results in the following definition. A **learning organization** is one that proactively creates, acquires, and transfers knowledge and that changes its behavior on the basis of new knowledge and insights.

By breaking this definition into its three component parts, we can clearly see the characteristics of a learning organization. First, new ideas are a prerequisite for learning. Learning organizations actively try to infuse their organizations with new ideas and information. They do this by constantly scanning their external environments, hiring new talent and expertise when needed, and devoting significant resources to train and develop their employees. Second, new knowledge must be transferred throughout the organization. Learning organizations strive to reduce structural, process, and interpersonal barriers to the sharing of information, ideas, and knowledge among organizational members. Finally, behavior must change as a result of new knowledge. Learning organizations are results oriented. They foster an environment in which employees are encouraged to use new behaviors and operational processes to achieve corporate goals.[34]

learning organization
Proactively creates, acquires, and transfers knowledge throughout the organization.

FIGURE 16–2 Building an Organization's Learning Capability

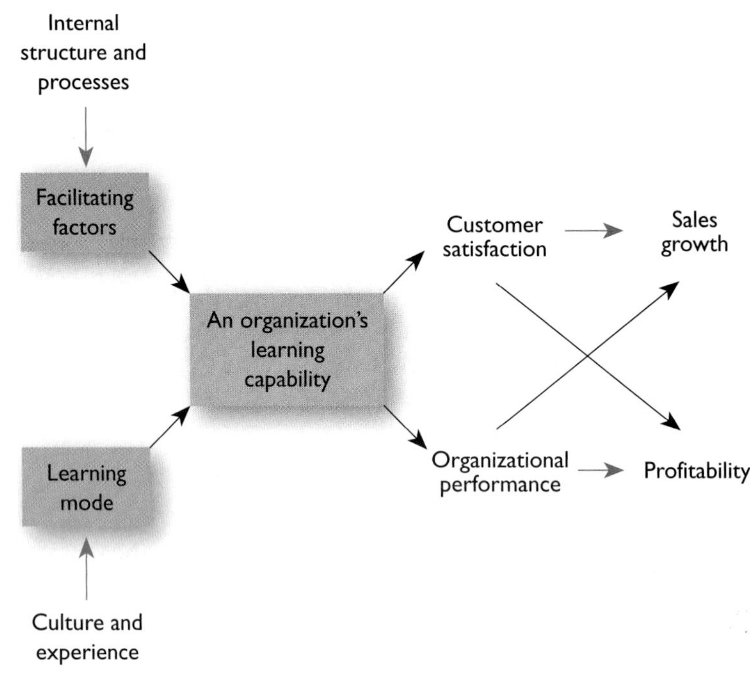

Building an Organization's Learning Capability

learning capabilities The set of core competencies and internal processes that enable an organization to adapt to its environment.

Figure 16–2 presents a model of how organizations build and enhance their learning capability. **Learning capabilities** represent the set of core competencies, which are defined as the special knowledge, skills, and technological know-how that differentiate an organization from its competitors, and processes that enable an organization to adapt to its environment.[35] The general idea underlying Figure 16–2 is that learning capabilities are the fuel for organizational success. Just like gasoline enables a car's engine to perform, learning capabilities equip an organization to foresee and respond to internal and external changes. This capability, in turn, increases the chances of satisfying customers and boosting sales and profitability.[36] Let us now consider the two major contributors to an organization's learning capability: facilitating factors and learning mode.

Facilitating Factors *Facilitating factors* represent "the internal structure and processes that affect how easy or hard it is for learning to occur and the amount of effective learning that takes place."[37] Table 16–4 contains a list of 10 key facilitating factors. Keep in mind as you read them that these factors can either enable or impede an organization's ability to respond to its environment. Consider, for example, the "concern for measurement" factor. A national survey of 203 executives compared companies that did and did not focus on measurement-management. Results revealed that those companies that focused on measurement-management were identified as industry leaders, had financial performance that put them in the top third of their industry, and were more successful at implementing and managing major change initiatives.[38] This study suggests that concern for measurement enhanced these organizations' learning capabilities.

Factors That Facilitate Organizational Learning Capabilities TABLE 16–4

1. Scanning imperative	Interest in external happenings and in the nature of one's environment. Valuing the processes of awareness and data generation. Curious about what is "out there" as opposed to "in here."
2. Performance gap	Shared perception of a gap between actual and desired state of performance. Disconfirming feedback interrupts a string of successes. Performance shortfalls are seen as opportunities for learning.
3. Concern for measurement	Spend considerable effort in defining and measuring key factors when venturing into new areas; strive for specific, quantifiable measures; discourse over metrics is seen as a learning activity.
4. Experimental mind-set	Support for trying new things; curiosity about how things work; ability to "play" with things. Small failures are encouraged, not punished. See changes in work processes, policies, and structures as a continuous series of graded tryouts.
5. Climate of openness	Accessibility of information; relatively open boundaries. Opportunities to observe others; problems/errors are shared, not hidden; debate and conflict are acceptable.
6. Continuous education	Ongoing commitment to education at all levels; support for growth and development of members.
7. Operational variety	Variety exists in response modes, procedures, systems; significant diversity in personnel. Pluralistic rather than monolithic definition of valued internal capabilities.
8. Multiple advocates	Top-down and bottom-up initiatives are possible; multiple advocates and gatekeepers exist.
9. Involved leadership	Leadership at significant levels articulates vision and is very actively engaged in its actualization; takes ongoing steps to implement vision; "hands-on" involvement in educational and other implementation steps.
10. Systems perspective	Strong focus on how parts of the organization are interdependent; seek optimization of organizational goals at the highest levels; see problems and solutions in terms of systemic relationships.

SOURCE: Reprinted by permission of Sage Publications Ltd. from B Moingeon and A Edmondson, in *Organizational Learning and Competitive Advantage* (Thousand Oaks, CA: Sage, © 1996), p 43.

learning modes The various ways in which organizations attempt to create and maximize their learning.

Learning Mode **Learning modes** represent the various ways in which organizations attempt to create and maximize their learning. Figure 16–2 shows that learning modes are directly influenced by an organization's culture and experience or past history.[39] The Men's Wearhouse, for example, is highly committed to organizational learning. The company sends all employees on average to 40 hours of training a year. Consider how the organizational culture affects this commitment to training:

> "We know that the only constant is change," says Eric Anderson, Men's Wearhouse's director of training. "We have said for a long time that we are in the people business, not the men's clothing business. We happen to sell men's clothing, but by recognizing what is really important—the people—we have a different paradigm than many other businesses. In order of priority, our employees, our customers, our vendors, our communities in which we do business, and our stockholders are our key stakeholders."

> Anderson says his challenge has been to create an environment where employees want to bring the best of themselves to work so that the business achieves positive results. "How do you nurture creativity, empowerment, responsibility, trust, and excitement?" he asks. "We try to recognize and nurture the potential in people. Because we are in the people business, training permeates our company culture."[40]

OB researcher Danny Miller reviewed the literature on organizational learning and identified six dominant modes of learning:[41]

1. *Analytic learning.* Learning occurs through systematic gathering of internal and external information. Information tends to be quantitative and analyzed via formal systems. The emphasis is on using deductive logic to numerically analyze objective data.
2. *Synthetic learning.* Synthetic learning is more intuitive and generic than the analytic mode. It emphasizes the synthesis of large amounts of complex information by using systems thinking. That is, employees try to identify interrelationships between issues, problems, and opportunities.
3. *Experimental learning.* This mode is a rational methodological approach that is based on conducting small experiments and monitoring the results.
4. *Interactive learning.* This mode involves learning-by-doing. Rather than using systematic methodological procedures, learning occurs primarily through the exchange of information. Learning is more intuitive and inductive.
5. *Structural learning.* This mode is a methodological approach that is based on the use of organizational routines. Organizational routines represent standardized processes and procedures that specify how to carry out tasks and roles. People learn from routines because they direct attention, institutionalize standards, and create consistent vocabularies.
6. *Institutional learning.* This mode represents an inductive process by which organizations share and model values, beliefs, and practices either from their external environments or from senior executives. Employees learn by observing environmental examples or senior executives. Socialization and mentoring play a significant role in institutional learning.

Leadership Is the Foundation of a Learning Organization

Leadership is the key to fostering organizational learning and the creation of a learning organization. The most effective leaders are those who use both transactional and transformational leadership (recall our discussion in Chapter 14) to facilitate organizational learning.[42] To make this happen, however, leaders must adopt new roles and associated activities. Specifically, leaders perform three key functions in building a learning organization: (1) building a commitment to learning, (2) working to generate ideas with impact, and (3) working to generalize ideas with impact.[43]

Building a Commitment to Learning Leaders need to instill an intellectual and emotional commitment to learning. Thomas Tierney, CEO of Bain & Company, proposes that leaders foster this commitment by building a culture that promotes the concept of "teacher-learners." His concept is based on the idea that organizational learning and innovation are enhanced when employees behave like both teachers and learners (see Skills & Best Practices). Of course, leaders also need to invest the financial resources needed to create a learning infrastructure.

Working to Generate Ideas with Impact

Ideas with impact are those that add value to one or more of an organization's three key stakeholders: employees, customers, and shareholders. Experts suggest the following ways to generate ideas with impact:

- Implement continuous improvement programs.
- Increase employee competence through training, or buy talent from outside the organization.
- Experiment with new ideas, processes, and structural arrangements.
- Go outside the organization to identify world-class ideas and processes.
- Instill systems thinking throughout the organization.

Working to Generalize Ideas with Impact

Leaders must make a concerted effort to reduce interpersonal, group, and organizational barriers to learning. This can be done by creating a learning infrastructure.[44] This is a large-scale effort that includes the following activities:

- Measuring and rewarding learning.
- Increasing open and honest dialogue among organizational members.
- Reducing conflict.
- Increasing horizontal and vertical communication.
- Promoting teamwork.
- Rewarding risk taking and innovation.
- Reducing the fear of failure.
- Increasing the sharing of successes, failures, and best practices across organizational members.
- Reducing stressors and frustration.
- Reducing internal competition.
- Increasing cooperation and collaboration.
- Creating a psychologically safe and comforting environment.[45]

SKILLS & BEST PRACTICES

Characteristics of Teacher-Learners

1. Being actively engaged in teaching, probing, and learning simultaneously.
2. Demonstrating care for their colleagues and making intellectual and emotional connections in and beyond their circle of peers.
3. Relating to as many people from different backgrounds, experience, maturity levels, and positions as possible.
4. Reflecting on what they learn as well as how they learn. After learning or teaching, teacher-learners ask themselves, "What have I learned about learning? What should I explore to enrich my own learning as a result of that interaction?"
5. Keeping their receiver-transmitters on at all times. Teacher-learners possess a child's mind: They don't presuppose; they listen.

SOURCE: Excerpted from J C Meister, "The CEO-Driven Learning Culture," *Training & Development,* June 2000, p 54.

Unlearning the Organization

In addition to implementing the ideas discussed earlier, organizations must concurrently unlearn organizational practices and paradigms that made them successful. Quite simply, traditional organizations and the associated organizational behaviors they created have outlived their usefulness. Management must seriously question and challenge the ways of thinking that worked in the past if they want to create a learning organization.[46] For example, the old management paradigm of planning, organizing, and control might be replaced with one of vision, values, and empowerment. The time has come for management and employees to think as owners, not as "us" and "them" adversaries.

key terms

chapter summary

- *Discuss the external and internal forces that create the need for organizational change.* Organizations encounter both external and internal forces for change. There are four key external forces for change: demographic characteristics, technological advancements, customer and market changes, and social and political pressures. Internal forces for change come from both human resource problems and managerial behavior/decisions.
- *Describe Lewin's change model and the systems model of change.* Lewin developed a three-stage model of planned change that explained how to initiate, manage, and stabilize the change process. The three stages were *unfreezing,* which entails creating the motivation to change, *changing,* and stabilizing change through *refreezing.* A systems model of change takes a big picture perspective of change. It focuses on the interaction among the key components of change. The three main components of change are inputs, target elements of change, and outputs. The target elements of change represent the components of an organization that may be changed. They include organizing arrangements, social factors, methods, goals, and people.
- *Discuss Kotter's eight steps for leading organizational change.* John Kotter believes that organizational change fails for one or more of eight common errors. He proposed eight steps that organizations should follow to overcome these errors. The eight steps are as follows: (a) establish a sense of urgency, (b) create the guiding coalition, (c) develop a vision and strategy, (d) communicate the change vision, (e) empower broad-based action, (f) generate short-term wins, (g) consolidate gains and produce more change, and (h) anchor new approaches in the culture.
- *Discuss the 10 reasons employees resist change.* Resistance to change is an emotional/behavioral response to real or imagined threats to an established work routine. Ten reasons employees resist change are (a) an individual's predisposition toward change, (b) surprise and fear of the unknown, (c) climate of mistrust, (d) fear of failure, (e) loss of status and/or job security, (f) peer pressure, (g) disruption of cultural traditions and/or group relationships, (h) personality conflicts, (i) lack of tact and/or poor timing, and (j) nonreinforcing reward systems.
- *Identify alternative strategies for overcoming resistance to change.* Organizations must be ready for change. Assuming an organization is ready for change, the alternative strategies for overcoming resistance to change are education + communication, participation + involvement, facilitation + support, negotiation + agreement, manipulation + co-operation, and explicit + implict coercion. Each has its situational appropriateness and advantages and drawbacks.
- *Discuss the process organizations use to build their learning capabilities.* Learning capabilities represent the set of core competencies and processes that enable an organization to adapt to its environment. Learning capabilities are directly affected by organizational facilitating factors and learning modes. Facilitating factors constitute the internal structure and processes that either encourage or impede learning within an organization. Learning modes represent the various ways by which organizations attempt to create and maximize their learning. Researchers believe that there is some type of optimal matching between the facilitating factors and learning modes that affects learning capability.

discussion questions

1. Which of the external and internal forces for changes are influencing PepsiCo's product development strategy? Explain.
2. How would you respond to a manager who made the following statement? "Unfreezing is not important; employees will follow my directives."

3. Have you ever gone through a major organizational change at work? If yes, what type of organizational development intervention was used? Was it effective? Explain.
4. Which source of resistance to change do you think is the most common? Which is the most difficult for management to deal with?
5. How would you assess the extent to which an organization is truly a learning organization? Discuss different alternative methods.

ethical dilemma

What Is More Important? Your Manager's Advice or Your Customer's Needs?

You are a broker for a trusted brokerage firm. Part of your job is to offer advice to clients concerning their mutual funds. A client's mutual fund was not performing very well and she was losing money. As her broker, you advised her to sell. Your client was happy but you were called into your boss's office where he questioned your advice. He informs you that your brokerage firm receives hefty incentives from that mutual fund company in exchange for favoring its funds. Your boss tells you that the practice is known as "revenue sharing"—mutual fund companies give brokers a cut of their management fees to get them to sell their products. He also tells you that the mutual fund company pays for cruises and other lavish vacations for brokers who meet sales goals and since you just advised your client to sell, you probably won't be on that list.

Solving the Dilemma

As a broker for this firm what should you do?

1. If it is the firm's policy that you recommend certain mutual funds over others, then this is the policy you will follow from here on out. Besides, you want a chance to win a cruise or some other lavish vacation.
2. Even though you might receive certain perks for recommending a specific mutual fund over others, your client sees you as an objective advisor and you will continue to base your decisions on her best interests rather than a managerial edict or incentives.
3. Because it is the firm's policy to recommend certain mutual funds over others, you will follow this practice. However, you make sure you advise your clients that you are paid an incentive if they purchase a specific mutual fund.
4. Invent other options. Discuss.

(SOURCE: This case was based on material contained in L Johannes and J Hechinger, "Conflicting Interests: Why a Brokerage Giant Pushes Some Mediocre Mutual Funds," *The Wall Street Journal,* January 9, 2004, pp A1, A5.)

If you're looking for additional study materials, be sure to check out the Online Learning Center at

www.mhhe.com/kinickiob2e

for more information and interactivities that correspond to this chapter.

ENDNOTES

Chapter 1

[1] From P Burrows, "Architects of the Info. Age," *Business Week,* March 29, 2004, p 22. Reprinted with permission.
[2] Excerpted from J R Healey, D Kiley, and E Eldridge, "Auto Execs Shed Game Faces to Answer 3 Tough Questions," *USA Today,* January 19, 2004, p 4B.
[3] Data from "Fortune 500 Largest U.S. Corporations," *Fortune,* April 5, 2004, p F-58.
[4] J Pfeffer and J F Veiga, "Putting People First for Organizational Success," *Academy of Management Executive,* May 1999, p 37.
[5] Adapted from ibid. Also see J K Harter, F L Schmidt, and T L Hayes, "Business-Unit-Level Relationship Between Employee Satisfaction, Employee Engagement, and Business Outcomes: A Meta-Analysis," *Journal of Applied Psychology,* April 2002, pp 268–79.
[6] See, for instance, "HR Executives Embrace Outplacement Assistance Efforts," *HR Magazine,* March 2004, p 12; and D Jones, "When You're Smiling, Are You Seething Inside?" *USA Today,* April 12, 2004, pp 1B–2B.
[7] Data from Pfeffer and Veiga, "Putting People First for Organizational Success," p 47.
[8] S Zuboff, "From Subject to Citizen," *Fast Company,* May 2004, p 104.
[9] For inspiring discussion and examples, see S Bates, "Getting Engaged," *HR Magazine,* February 2004, pp 44–51; R B Bowen "Today's Workforce Requires New Age Currency," *HR Magazine,* March 2004, pp 101–6; H R Nalbantian and A Szostak, "How Fleet Bank Fought Employee Flight," *Harvard Business Review,* April 2004, pp 116–25; K Maney, "SAS Workers Won When Greed Lost," *USA Today,* April 22, 2004, pp 1B–2B; and C Salter, "And Now the Hard Part," *Fast Company,* May 2004, pp 66–75.
[10] R Levering and M Moskowitz, "2004 Special Report: The 100 Best Companies to Work For," *Fortune,* January 12, 2004, p 76.
[11] See I S Fulmer, B Gerhart, and K S Scott, "Are the 100 Best Better? An Empirical Investigation of the Relationship Between Being a 'Great Place to Work' and Firm Performance," *Personnel Psychology,* Winter 2003, pp 965–93.
[12] H Mintzberg, "The Manager's Job: Folklore and Fact," *Harvard Business Review,* July–August 1975, p 61. Also see M M Clark, "NLRB General Counsel's Office Issues Liberal Criteria for Defining 'Supervisor,'" *HR Magazine,* February 2004, p 30.
[13] See, for example, H Mintzberg, "Managerial Work: Analysis from Observation," *Management Science,* October 1971, pp B97–B110; and F Luthans, "Successful vs. Effective Real Managers," *Academy of Management Executive,* May 1988, pp 127–32. For an instructive critique of the structured observation method, see M J Martinko and W L Gardner, "Beyond Structured Observation: Methodological Issues and New Directions," *Academy of Management Review,* October 1985, pp 676–95. Also see N Fondas, "A Behavioral Job Description for Managers," *Organizational Dynamics,* Summer 1992, pp 47–58.
[14] See L B Kurke and H E Aldrich, "Mintzberg Was Right! A Replication and Extension of *The Nature of Managerial Work," Management Science,* August 1983, pp 975–84.
[15] For example, see N H Woodward, "The Coming of the X Managers," *HR Magazine,* March 1999, pp 74–80; and J Gosling and H Mintzberg, "The Five Minds of a Manager," *Harvard Business Review,* November 2003, pp 54–63.
[16] Validation studies can be found in E Van Velsor and J B Leslie, *Feedback to Managers, Volume II: A Review and Comparison of Sixteen Multi-Rater Feedback Instruments* (Greensboro, NC: Center for Creative Leadership, 1991); F Shipper, "A Study of the Psychometric Properties of the Managerial Skill Scales of the Survey of Management Practices," *Educational and Psychological Measurement,* June 1995, pp 468–79; and C L Wilson, *How and Why Effective Managers Balance Their Skills: Technical, Teambuilding, Drive* (Columbia, MD: Rockatech Multimedia Publishing, 2003).
[17] For example, see J Sandberg, "Understanding Competence at Work," *Harvard Business Review,* March 2001, pp 24–28.
[18] See F Shipper, "Mastery and Frequency of Managerial Behaviors Relative to Sub-Unit Effectiveness," *Human Relations,* April 1991, pp 371–88.
[19] Ibid; and Wilson, *How and Why Effective Managers Balance Their Skills.*
[20] Data from F Shipper, "A Study of Managerial Skills of Women and Men and Their Impact on Employees' Attitudes and Career Success in a Nontraditional Organization," paper presented at the Academy of Management Meeting, August 1994, Dallas, Texas. The same outcome for on-the-job studies is reported in A H Eagly and B T Johnson, "Gender and Leadership Style: A Meta-Analysis," *Psychological Bulletin,* September 1990, pp 233–56.
[21] For instance, see J B Rosener, "Ways Women Lead," *Harvard Business Review,* November–December 1990, pp 119–25; C Lee, "The Feminization of Management," *Training,* November 1994, pp 25–31; and A Fels, "Do Women Lack Ambition?" *Harvard Business Review,* April 2004, pp 50–60.
[22] See T W Malone, *The Future of Work: How the New Order of Business Will Shape Your Organization, Your Management Style, and Your Life* (Boston: Harvard Business School Press, 2004).
[23] Essential sources on reengineering are M Hammer and J Champy, *Reengineering the Corporation: A Manifesto for Business Revolution* (New York: HarperCollins, 1993); and J Champy, *Reengineering Management: The Mandate for New Leadership* (New York: HarperCollins, 1995). Also see "Anything Worth Doing Is Worth Doing from Scratch," *Inc.,* May 18, 1999 (20th Anniversary Issue), pp 51–52.
[24] See R J Trent, "Becoming an Effective Teaming Organization," *Business Horizons,* March–April 2004, pp 33–40; D D Davis, "The Tao of Leadership in Virtual Teams," *Organizational Dynamics,* no 1, 2004, pp 47–62; and N Heintz, "Smells Like Team Spirit," *Inc.,* May 2004, p 58.
[25] For more, see S Ghoshal and H Bruch, "Going Beyond Motivation to the Power of Volition," *MIT Sloan Management Review,* Spring 2003, pp 51–57; L Grensing-Pophal, "Involve Your Employees in Cost Cutting," *HR Magazine,* November 2003, pp 52–56; and P T Coleman, "Implicit Theories of Organizational Power and Priming Effects on Managerial Power-Sharing Decisions: An Experimental Study," *Journal of Applied Social Psychology,* February 2004, pp 297–321.
[26] See K Carnes, D Cottrell, and M C Layton, *Management Insights: Discovering the Truths to Management Success* (Dallas: CornerStone Leadership Institute, 2004).
[27] For details, see J B Miner, "The Rated Importance, Scientific Validity, and Practical Usefulness of Organizational Behavior Theories: A Quantitative Review," *Academy of Management Learning and Education,* September 2003, pp 250–68.
[28] B S Lawrence, "Historical Perspective: Using the Past to Study the Present," *Academy of Management Review,* April 1984, p 307. Also see H Rubin, "Past Track to the Future," *Fast Company,* May 2001, pp 166–73.
[29] Evidence indicating that the original conclusions of the famous Hawthorne studies were unjustified may be found in R G Greenwood, A A Bolton, and R A Greenwood, "Hawthorne a Half Century Later: Relay Assembly Participants Remember," *Journal of Management,* Fall–Winter 1983, pp 217–31; and R H Franke and J D Kaul, "The Hawthorne Experiments: First Statistical Interpretation," *American Sociological Review,* October 1978, pp 623–43. For a positive interpretation of the Hawthorne studies, see J A Sonnenfeld, "Shedding Light on the Hawthorne Studies," *Journal of Occupational Behaviour,* April 1985, pp 111–30.
[30] See M Parker Follett, *Freedom and Coordination* (London: Management Publications Trust, 1949).
[31] See D McGregor, *The Human Side of Enterprise* (New York: McGraw-Hill, 1960). Also see D Jacobs, "Book Review Essay: Douglas McGregor—The Human Side of Enterprise in Peril," *Academy of Management Review,* April 2004, pp 293–96.

[32] J Hall, "Americans Know How to Be Productive If Managers Will Let Them," *Organizational Dynamics,* Winter 1994, p 38.
[33] See, for example, R Zemke, "TQM: Fatally Flawed or Simply Unfocused?" *Training,* October 1992, p 8.
[34] L Wah, "The Almighty Customer," *Management Review,* February 1999, p 17.
[35] Data from "AMA Global Survey on Key Business Issues," *Management Review,* December 1998, p 30. Also see "1999 Annual Survey: Corporate Concerns," *Management Review,* March 1999, pp 55–56.
[36] Instructive background articles on TQM are R Zemke, "A Bluffer's Guide to TQM," *Training,* April 1993, pp 48–55; R R Gehani, "Quality Value-Chain: A Meta-Synthesis of Frontiers of Quality Movement," *Academy of Management Executive,* May 1993, pp 29–42; P Mears, "How to Stop Talking About, and Begin Progress Toward, Total Quality Management," *Business Horizons,* May–June 1993, pp 11–14; and the Total Quality Special Issue of *Academy of Management Review,* July 1994.
[37] M Sashkin and K J Kiser, *Putting Total Quality Management to Work* (San Francisco: Berrett-Koehler, 1993), p 39.
[38] R J Schonberger, "Total Quality Management Cuts a Broad Swath—Through Manufacturing and Beyond," *Organizational Dynamics,* Spring 1992, p 18. Other quality-related articles include H Liao and A Chuang, "A Multilevel Investigation of Factors Influencing Employee Service Performance and Customer Outcomes," *Academy of Management Journal,* February 2004, pp 41–58; L Heuring, "Six Sigma in Sight," *HR Magazine,* March 2004, pp 76–80; N Brodsky, "You're Fired!" *Inc.,* May 2004, pp 51–52; and D McDonald, "Roll Out the Blue Carpet," *Business 2.0,* May 2004, pp 53–54.
[39] Deming's landmark work is W E Deming, *Out of the Crisis* (Cambridge, MA: MIT, 1986).
[40] See M Trumbull, "What Is Total Quality Management?" *The Christian Science Monitor,* May 3, 1993, p 12; and J Hillkirk, "World-Famous Quality Expert Dead at 93," *USA Today,* December 21, 1993, pp 1B–2B.
[41] Based on discussion in M Walton, *Deming Management at Work* (New York: Putnam/Perigee, 1990).
[42] Ibid., p 20.
[43] Adapted from D E Bowen and E E Lawler III, "Total Quality-Oriented Human Resources Management," *Organizational Dynamics,* Spring 1992, pp 29–41. Also see P B Seybold, "Get Inside the Lives of Your Customers," *Harvard Business Review,* May 2001, pp 80–89.
[44] As quoted in P LaBarre, "The Industrialized Revolution," *Fast Company,* November 2003, pp 116, 118.
[45] B E Becker, M A Huselid, and D Ulrich, *The HR Scorecard: Linking People, Strategy, and Performance* (Boston: Harvard Business School Press, 2001), p 4.
[46] See L Bassi and D McMurrer, "How's Your Return on People?" *Harvard Business Review,* March 2004, p 18; B Hall, "Here Comes Human Capital Management," *Training,* March 2004, pp 16–17; and "Employers Say Measuring Is Vital But Still Don't Do It," *HR Magazine,* April 2004, p 18.
[47] For details, see www.intel.com; select "Intel Innovation in Education" under the heading "About Intel."
[48] Data from "The 100 Best Companies to Work For," *Fortune,* February 4, 2002, p 84. Also see G Anders, "The Reeducation of Silicon Valley," *Fast Company,* April 2002, pp 100–8.
[49] Inspired by P S Adler and S Kwon, "Social Capital: Prospects for a New Concept," *Academy of Management Review,* January 2002, pp 17–40. Also see "Social Capitalists: The Top 20 Groups That Are Changing the World," *Fast Company,* January 2004, pp 45–57; and J Allik and Anu Realo, "Individualism-Collectivism and Social Capital," *Journal of Cross-Cultural Psychology,* January 2004, pp 29–49.
[50] L Prusak and D Cohen, "How to Invest in Social Capital," *Harvard Business Review,* June 2001, p 93.
[51] Data from "What Makes a Job OK," *USA Today,* May 15, 2002, p 1B.
[52] L D Tyson, "Good Works—With a Business Plan," *Business Week,* May 3, 2004, p 32.
[53] M E P Seligman and M Csikszentmihalyi, "Positive Psychology: An Introduction," *American Psychologist,* January 2000, p 5. Also see the other 15 articles in the January 2000 issue of *American Psychologist;* and M Elias, "What Makes People Happy; Psychologists Now Know," *USA Today,* December 9, 2002, pp 1A–2A.
[54] See F Luthans, K W Luthans, and B C Luthans, "Positive Psychological Capital: Beyond Human and Social Capital," *Business Horizons,* January–February 2004, pp 45–50.
[55] F Luthans, "The Need for and Meaning of Positive Organizational Behavior," *Journal of Organizational Behavior,* September 2002, p 698. Also see T A Wright, "Positive Organizational Behavior: An Idea Whose Time Has Truly Come," *Journal of Organizational Behavior,* June 2003, pp 437–42.
[56] Levering and Moskowitz, "2004 Special Report: The 100 Best Companies to Work For," p 78.
[57] Ibid., p 76.
[58] See K Maney, "Once-Wild Net World Enters Calmer Second Generation," *USA Today,* June 23, 2003, pp 1B–2B.
[59] See J O'C Hamilton, "The Harder They Fall," *Business Week* **E.BIZ,** May 14, 2002, pp EB14, EB16.
[60] B Elgin, "Google," *Business Week,* May 3, 2004, pp 82–90. Also see S Levy, "All Eyes on Google," *Newsweek,* March 29, 2004, pp 48–58.
[61] Data from K Maney, "The Economy According to eBay," *USA Today,* December 29, 2003, pp 1B–2B.
[62] As quoted in K Maney, "Chambers, Cisco Born Again," *USA Today,* January 21, 2004, p 2B.
[63] R D Hof, "How E-Biz Rose, Fell, and Will Rise Anew," *Business Week,* May 13, 2002, p 67.
[64] See M Athitakis, "How to Make Money on the Net," *Business 2.0,* May 2003, pp 83–90; L Buchanan, "Working Wonders on the Web," *Inc.,* November 2003, pp 76–84, 104; L W Lam and L J Harrison-Walker, "Toward an Objective-Based Typology of E-Business Models," *Business Horizons,* November–December 2003, pp 17–26; and J Reingold, "What We Learned in the New Economy," *Fast Company,* March 2004, pp 56–68.
[65] M J Mandel and R D Hof, "Rethinking the Internet," *Business Week,* March 26, 2001, p 118.
[66] "The Comeback Kids," *Business Week,* September 29, 2003, p 116.
[67] Six implications excerpted from B J Avolio and S S Kahai, "Adding the 'E' to E-Leadership: How It May Impact Your Leadership," *Organizational Dynamics,* no. 4, 2003, p 333.
[68] W Echikson, "Nestlé: An Elephant Dances," *Business Week* **E.BIZ,** December 11, 2000, pp EB47–EB48. Also see B Sosnin, "Digital Newsletters 'E-volutionize' Employee Communications," *HR Magazine,* May 2001, pp 99–107.
[69] For more, see G Meyer, "eWorkbench: Real-Time Tracking of Synchronized Goals," *HR Magazine,* April 2001, pp 115–18.
[70] See A Majchrzak, A Malhotra, J Stamps, and J Lipnack, "Can Absence Make a Team Grow Stronger?" *Harvard Business Review,* May 2004, pp 131–37.
[71] R Moss Kanter, *Evolve! Succeeding in the Digital Culture of Tomorrow* (Boston: Harvard Business School Press, 2001), p 206. Also see R Moss Kanter, "You Are Here," *Inc.,* February 2001, pp 84–90.
[72] Data from "Hurry Up and Decide!" *Business Week,* May 14, 2001.
[73] See M Hequet, "The State of the E-Learning Market," *Training,* September 2003, pp 24–29; J Barbian, "High-Tech Times," *Training,* November 2003, pp 52–55; and H Dolezalek, "Dose of Reality," *Training,* April 2004, pp 28–34.
[74] G Johnson, "Uncharted Territory," *Training,* September 2003, p 24.
[75] B Hall, "The Time Is Now," *Training,* February 2004, p 16.
[76] See B Lessard and S Baldwin, *Net Slaves: True Tales of Working the Web* (New York: McGraw-Hill, 2000); P Babcock, "America's Newest Export: White-Collar Jobs," *HR Magazine,* April 2004, pp 50–57; B W Hornaday, "Conseco Shows Outsourcing Is Not Always Best Call," *USA Today,* April 26, 2004, p 10B; and D Altman, "A More Productive Outsourcing Debate," *Business 2.0,* May 2004, p 39.
[77] J Merritt, "You Mean Cheating Is Wrong?" *Business Week,* December 9, 2002, p 8.

Ethics Learning Module

[1] Excerpted from Ellen E Schultz and Theo Francis, "Financial Surgery: How Cuts in Retiree Benefits Fatten Companies' Bottom Lines," *The Wall Street Journal,* Eastern Edition, March 16, 2004, p A1. Copyright 2004 by Dow Jones & Co. Inc. Reproduced with permission of Dow Jones & Co. Inc. via Copyright Clearance Center.

[2] These statistics are reported in Susan Pulliam, Almar Latour, and Ken Brown, "Reaching the Top: U.S. Indicts WorldCom Chief Ebbers," *The Wall Street Journal,* March 3, 2004, pp A1, A12.
[3] Details of these examples can be found in See L Wah, "Lip-Service Ethics Programs Prove Ineffective," *Management Review,* June 1999, p 9; and Jennifer Schramm, "A Return to Ethics?" *HR Magazine,* July 2003, p 144.
[4] Results can be found in Matthew Boyle, "By the Numbers: Liarliar!" *Fortune,* May 26, 2003, p 44.
[5] R Lieber, "New Hidden Fees Hit Overseas Travel," *The Wall Street Journal,* April 23, 2001, p D1.
[6] See C Gilligan, "In a Different Voice: Women's Conceptions of Self and Morality," *Harvard Educational Review,* November 1977, pp 481–517.
[7] The following discussion is based on A J Daboub, A M A Rasheed, R L Priem, and D A Gray, "Top Management Team Characteristics and Corporate Illegal Activity," *Academy of Management Review,* January 1995, pp 138–70.
[8] L Simpson, "Taking the High Road," *Training,* January 2002, p 38.
[9] Excerpted from Mark Gimein, "What Did Joe Know?" *Fortune,* May 12, 2003, pp 122, 124.
[10] For more details, see Steve Hamm, "Probes: Charges for Computer Associates?" *Business Week,* May 17, 2004, p 11.
[11] Results can be found in T Jackson, "Cultural Values and Management Ethics: A 10-Nation Study," *Human Relations,* October 2001, pp 1267–1302.
[12] The following discussion is based on Daboub et al., "Top Management Team Characteristics and Corporate Illegal Activity."
[13] This discussion is based on Constance E Bagley, "The Ethical Leader's Decision Tree," *Harvard Business Review,* February 2003, pp 18–19.
[14] For a thorough discussion of this issue, see Schultz and Francis, "Financial Surgery: How Cuts in Retiree Benefits Fatten Companies' Bottom Lines."
[15] T Gutner, "Blowing Whistles—and Being Ignored," *Business Week,* March 18, 2002, p 107.
[16] Results are discussed in ibid.
[17] C Gilligan and J Attanucci, "Two Moral Orientations: Gender Differences and Similarities," *Merril-Palmer Quarterly,* July 1988, pp 224–25.
[18] Results can be found in S Jaffee and J Hyde, "Gender Differences in Moral Orientation: A Meta-Analysis," *Psychological Bulletin,* September 2000, pp 703–26.
[19] Ibid, p 719.
[20] See Ch. 6 in K Hodgson, *A Rock and a Hard Place: How to Make Ethical Business Decisions When the Choices Are Tough* (New York: AMACOM, 1992), pp 66–77.
[21] Excerpted from Peter Asmus, "100 Best Corporate Citizens for 2004: Companies that Serve a Variety of Stakeholders Well," http://www.business-ethics.com/100best.htm, May 5, 2004, p. 3.
[22] Adapted from W E Stead, D L Worrell, and J Garner Stead, "An Integrative Model for Understanding and Managing Ethical Behavior in Business Organizations," *Journal of Business Ethics,* March 1990, pp 233–42.
[23] For an excellent review of integrity testing, see D S Ones and C Viswesvaran, "Integrity Testing in Organizations," in *Dysfunctional Behavior in Organizations: Violent and Deviant Behavior,* eds R W Griffin et al. (Stamford, CT: JAI Press, 1998), pp 243–76.
[24] Guidelines for conducting ethics training are discussed by Holly Dolezalek, "When It Comes to Ethics Training, You Have to Keep Your Eye on the Unintentional as well as the Underhanded," *Training,* November 2003, pp 43–45.
[25] For details regarding Boeing, see "Boeing Hires Outsider to Monitor Its Ethics," *The Arizona Republic,* May 5, 2004, p d5; and J Lynn Lunsford and Anne Marie Squeo, "Boeing Dismisses Two Executives for Violating Ethical Standards," *The Wall Street Journal,* November 25, 2003, pp A1, A8.
[26] These scenarios were excerpted from L M Dawson, "Women and Men, Morality, and Ethics," *Business Horizons,* July–August 1995, pp 62, 65.
[27] Comparative norms were obtained from Dawson, "Women and Men, Morality and Ethics." Scenario 1: would sell (28% males, 57% females); would not sell (66% males, 28% females); unsure (6% males, 15% females). Scenario 2: would consult (84% males, 32% females); would not consult (12% males, 62% females); unsure (4% males, 6% females).
[28] The following trends were taken from Dawson, "Women and Men, Morality and Ethics." Women were likely to primarily respect feelings, ask "who will be hurt?", avoid being judgmental, search for compromise, seek solutions that minimize hurt, rely on communication, believe in contextual relativism, be guided by emotion, and challenge authority. Men were likely to primarily respect rights, ask "who is right?", value decisiveness, make unambiguous decisions, seek solutions that are objectively fair, rely on rules, believe in blind impartiality, be guided by logic, and accept authority.

Chapter 2

[1] Excerpted from John Helyar, "The Only Company Wal-Mart Fears," *Fortune,* November 24, 2003, pp 160, 164, 166. Copyright © 2003 Time Inc. All rights reserved.
[2] For details on Costco's effectiveness, see Stanley Holmes and Wendy Zellner, "The Costco Way," *Business Week,* April 12, 2004, p 76.
[3] E H Schein, "Culture: The Missing Concept in Organization Studies," *Administrative Science Quarterly,* June 1996, p 236.
[4] This figure and related discussion are based on C Ostroff, A Kinicki, and M Tamkins, "Organizational Culture and Climate," in *Handbook of Psychology,* vol. 12, eds W C Borman, D R Ilgen, and R J Klimoski (New York: Wiley & Sons, 2003), pp 565–93.
[5] This discussion is based on E H Schein, *Organizational Culture and Leadership,* 2nd ed (San Francisco: Jossey-Bass, 1992), pp 16–48.
[6] S H Schwartz, "Universals in the Content and Structure of Values: Theoretical Advances and Empirical Tests in 20 Countries," in *Advances in Experimental Social Psychology,* ed M P Zanna (New York: Academic Press, 1992), p 4.
[7] Julia Boorstin, "The 100 Best Companies to Work For," *Fortune,* January 12, 2004, p 58.
[8] Excerpted from C Terhune, "Home Depot's Home Improvement," *The Wall Street Journal,* March 8, 2001, pp B1, B4.
[9] Results can be found in S Clarke, "Perceptions of Organizational Safety: Implications for the Development of Safety Culture," *Journal of Organizational Behavior,* March 1999, pp 185–98.
[10] See Terhune, "Home Depot's Home Improvement."
[11] Adapted from L Smircich, "Concepts of Culture and Organizational Analysis," *Administrative Science Quarterly,* September 1983, pp 339–58.
[12] Statistics and data contained in the Southwest Airlines example can be found in the "Southwest Airlines Fact Sheet," May 2004 (www.southwest.com).
[13] K D Godsey, "Slow Climb to New Heights," *Success,* October 1996, p 21.
[14] Southwest's mission statement can be found in "Customer Service Commitment," May 2004 (www.southwest.com).
[15] See Ostroff, Kinicki, and Tamkins, "Organizational Culture and Climate."
[16] The validity of these cultural types was summarized and supported by R A Cooke and J L Szumal, "Using the Organizational Culture Inventory to Understand the Operating Cultures of Organizations," in *Handbook of Organizational Culture and Climate,* eds N M Ashkanasy, C P M Wilderom, and M F Peterson (Thousand Oaks, CA: Sage Publications, 2000), pp 147–62.
[17] Brian Bremner and Gail Edmondson, "Japan: A Tale of Two Mergers," *Business Week,* May 10, 2004, p 42.
[18] Mark Gimein, "What Did Joe Know?" *Fortune,* May 12, 2003, p 124.
[19] Subcultures were examined by G Hofstede, "Identifying Organizational Subcultures: An Empirical Approach," *Journal of Management Studies,* January 1998, pp 1–12.
[20] Results can be found in R Cooke and J Szumal, "Measuring Normative Beliefs and Shared Behavioral Expectations in Organizations: The Reliability and Validity of the Organizational Culture Inventory," *Psychological Reports,* June 1993, pp 1299–330.
[21] Supportive results can be found in D C Cable and D S DeRue, "The Convergent and Discriminant Validity of Subjective Fit Perceptions," *Journal of Applied Psychology,* October 2002, pp 875–84; and A L Kristof-Brown and A E Colbert, "A Policy-Capturing Study of the Simultaneous Effects of Fit with Jobs, Groups, and Organizations," *Journal of Applied Psychology,* October 2002, pp 985–93.

[22] See C Wilderom, U Glunk, and R Maslowski, "Organizational Culture as a Predictor of Organizational Performance," in *Handbook of Organizational Culture & Climate,* eds N Ashkanasy, C Wilderom, and M Peterson (Thousand Oaks, CA: Sage, 2000), pp 193–210.
[23] Results can be found in J P Kotter and J L Heskett, *Corporate Culture and Performance* (New York: The Free Press, 1992).
[24] The success rate of mergers is discussed in M J Epstein, "The Drivers of Success in Post-Merger Integration," *Organizational Dynamics,* May 2004, pp 174–89.
[25] The mechanisms were based on material contained in E H Schein, "The Role of the Founder in Creating Organizational Culture," *Organizational Dynamics,* Summer 1983, pp 13–28.
[26] Wal-Mart's values can be found at www.walmart.com.
[27] Excerpted from Faith Arner and Lauren Young, "Can This Man Save Putnam?" *Business Week,* April 19, 2004, p 103.
[28] This example can be found in Barbara Kaufman, "Stories That Sell, Stories That Tell," *Journal of Business Strategy,* March/April 2003, p 15.
[29] Excerpted from Moon Ihlwan, Larry Armstrong, and Michael Eidam, "Hyundai: Kissing Clunkers Goodbye," *Business Week,* May 17, 2004, p 45.
[30] J Van Maanen, "Breaking In: Socialization to Work," in *Handbook of Work, Organization, and Society,* ed R Dubin (Chicago: Rand-McNally, 1976), p 67.
[31] For an instructive capsule summary of the five different organizational socialization models, see J P Wanous, A E Reichers, and S D Malik, "Organizational Socialization and Group Development: Toward an Integrative Perspective," *Academy of Management Review,* October 1984, pp 670–83, Table 1.
[32] Excerpted from T Galvin, "Birds of a Feather," *Training,* March 2001, p 60.
[33] Reprinted by permission of *Harvard Business Review*. From "No Ordinary Boot Camp" by N M Tichy, April 2001. Copyright © 2001 by the Harvard Business School Publishing Corporation; all rights reserved.
[34] Results can be found in H Klein and N Weaver, "The Effectiveness of an Organizational-Level Orientation Training Program in the Socialization of New Hires," *Personnel Psychology,* Spring 2000, pp 47–66.
[35] See D Cable and C Parsons, "Socialization Tactics and Person-Organization Fit," *Personnel Psychology,* Spring 2001, pp 1–23.
[36] Excerpted from "Workforce: Optimas Awards 2003," *Workforce,* March 2003, p 46.
[37] See A M Saks and B E Ashforth, "Proactive Socialization and Behavioral Self-Management," *Journal of Vocational Behavior,* June 1996, pp 301–23.
[38] For a thorough review of research on the socialization of diverse employees with disabilities see A Colella, "Organizational Socialization of Newcomers with Disabilities: A Framework for Future Research," in *Research in Personnel and Human Resources Management,* ed G R Ferris (Greenwich, CT: JAI Press, 1996), pp 351–417.
[39] This definition is based on the network perspective of mentoring proposed by M Higgins and K Kram, "Reconceptualizing Mentoring at Work: A Development Network Perspective," *Academy of Management Review,* April 2001, pp 264–88.
[40] Supportive results can be found in Monica L Forret and Thomas W Dougherty, "Networking Behaviors and Career Outcomes: Differences for Men and Women?" *Journal of Organizational Behavior,* May 2004, pp 419–37; and L Eby, M Butts, A Lockwood, and S A Simon, "Proteges' Negative Mentoring Experiences: Construct Development and Nomological Validation," *Personnel Psychology,* Summer 2004, pp 411–47.
[41] Career functions are discussed in detail in K Kram, *Mentoring of Work: Developmental Relationships in Organizational Life* (Glenview, IL: Scott, Foresman, 1985).
[42] Excerpted from Kris Maher, "The Jungle: Focus on Retirement, Pay and Getting Ahead," *The Wall Street Journal,* February 24, 2004, p B8.
[43] This discussion is based on Higgins and Kram, "Reconceptualizing Mentoring at Work."
[44] This discussion is based on Higgins and Kram, "Reconceptualizing Mentoring at Work."
[45] Supportive results can be found in T Allen, M Poteet, and J Russell, "Protégé Selection by Mentors: What Makes the Difference?" *Journal of Organizational Behavior,* May 2000, pp 271–82.
[46] Excerpted from "Best Practice: Mentoring—Blue Cross and Blue Shield of North Carolina," *Training,* March 2004, p 62.
[47] K Brown and J Weil, "How Andersen's Embrace of Consulting Altered the Culture of the Auditing Firm," *The Wall Street Journal,* Eastern Edition, March 12, 2002, pp C1, C16. Copyright 2002 by Dow Jones & Co. Inc. Reproduced with permission of Dow Jones & Co. Inc. via Copyright Clearance Center.

Chapter 3

[1] Excerpted from M Kripalani and P Engardio, "The Rise of India," *Business Week,* December 8, 2003, pp 66, 68.
[2] R Levering and M Moskowitz, "2004 Special Report: The 100 Best Companies to Work For," *Fortune,* January 12, 2004, p 70.
[3] G Barrett, "Made in America? Not Likely," *USA Today,* December 15, 2003, p 1B.
[4] Data from N Knox, "EU Expansion Brings USA Opportunities," *USA Today,* April 27, 2004, pp 1B–2B.
[5] P Coy, "The Future of Work," *Business Week,* March 22, 2004, p 52 (emphasis added). Also see S Bates, "Overseas Outsourcing: How Big a Threat?" *HR Magazine,* September 2003, pp 12, 14; and S Baker and M Kripalani, "Software," *Business Week,* March 1, 2004, pp 84–94.
[6] J Shinal, "Can Mike Volpi Make Cisco Sizzle Again?" *Business Week,* February 26, 2001, p 104.
[7] See S Meisinger, "Going Global: A Smart Move for HR Professionals," *HR Magazine,* March 2004, p 6.
[8] See Y Kashima, "Conceptions of Culture and Person for Psychology," *Journal of Cross-Cultural Psychology,* January 2000, pp 14–32.
[9] "How Cultures Collide," *Psychology Today,* July 1976, p 69. Also see E T Hall, *The Hidden Dimension* (Garden City, NY: Doubleday, 1966).
[10] F Trompenaars and C Hampden-Turner, *Riding the Waves of Culture: Understanding Cultural Diversity in Global Business,* 2nd ed (New York: McGraw-Hill, 1998), pp 6–7.
[11] See M Mendenhall, "A Painless Approach to Integrating 'International' into OB, HRM, and Management Courses," *Organizational Behavior Teaching Review,* no. 3 (1988–89), pp 23–27.
[12] See C L Sharma, "Ethnicity, National Integration, and Education in the Union of Soviet Socialist Republics," *The Journal of East and West Studies,* October 1989, pp 75–93; and R Brady and P Galuszka, "Shattered Dreams," *Business Week,* February 11, 1991, pp 38–42.
[13] J Main, "How to Go Global—And Why," *Fortune,* August 28, 1989, p 73.
[14] An excellent contrast between French and American values can be found in C Gouttefarde, "American Values in the French Workplace," *Business Horizons,* March–April 1996, pp 60–69.
[15] See M R Testa, S L Mueller, and A S Thomas, "Cultural Fit and Job Satisfaction in a Global Service Environment," *Management International Review,* April 2003, pp 129–148; R E Nelson and S Gopalan, "Do Organizational Cultures Replicate National Cultures? Isomorphism, Rejection and Reciprocal Opposition in the Corporate Values of Three Countries," *Organization Studies,* September 2003, pp 1115–51; and P B Smith, "Nations, Cultures, and Individuals," *Journal of Cross-Cultural Psychology,* January 2004, pp 6–12.
[16] W D Marbach, "Quality: What Motivates American Workers?" *Business Week,* April 12, 1993, p 93.
[17] See G A Sumner, *Folkways* (New York: Ginn, 1906). Also see J G Weber, "The Nature of Ethnocentric Attribution Bias: Ingroup Protection or Enhancement?" *Journal of Experimental Social Psychology,* September 1994, pp 482–504.
[18] E Thomas, J Barry, and C Caryl, "A War in the Dark," *Newsweek,* November 10, 2003, p 30.
[19] D A Heenan and H V Perlmutter, *Multinational Organization Development* (Reading, MA: Addison-Wesley, 1979), p 17.
[20] Data from R Kopp, "International Human Resource Policies and Practices in Japanese, European, and United States Multinationals," *Human Resource Management,* Winter 1994, pp 581–99.
[21] See D Doke, "Shipping Diversity Abroad," *HR Magazine,* November 2003, pp 58–64.
[22] Data from B Hagerty, "Trainers Help Expatriate Employees Build Bridges to Different Cultures," *The Wall Street Journal,* June 14, 1993, pp B1, B3. Also see A Weiss, "Global Doesn't Mean 'Foreign' Anymore," *Training,* July 1998, pp 50–55; and G Dutton, "Do You Think Globally?" *Management Review,* February 1999, p 6.

[23] C M Farkas and P De Backer, "There Are Only Five Ways to Lead," *Fortune,* January 15, 1996, p 111. The shortage of global managers is discussed in L K Stroh and P M Caligiuri, "Increasing Global Competitiveness through Effective People Management," *Journal of World Business,* Spring 1998, pp 1–16.
[24] For complete details, see G Hofstede, *Culture's Consequences: International Differences in Work-Related Values,* abridged ed (Newbury Park, CA: Sage Publications, 1984); G Hofstede, "The Interaction between National and Organizational Value Systems," *Journal of Management Studies,* July 1985, pp 347–57; and G Hofstede, "Management Scientists Are Human," *Management Science,* January 1994, pp 4–13. Also see M H Hoppe, "Introduction: Geert Hofstede's *Culture's Consequences: International Differences in Work-Related Values,*" *Academy of Management Executive,* February 2004, pp 73–74; M H Hoppe, "An Interview with Geert Hofstede," *Academy of Management Executive,* February 2004, pp 75–79; J W Bing, "Hofstede's Consequences: The Impact of His Work on Consulting and Business Practices," *Academy of Management Executive,* February 2004, pp 80–87; and H C Triandis, "The Many Dimensions of Culture," *Academy of Management Executive,* February 2004, pp 88–93.
[25] A similar conclusion is presented in the following replication of Hofstede's work: A Merritt, "Culture in the Cockpit: Do Hofstede's Dimensions Replicate?" *Journal of Cross-Cultural Psychology,* May 2000, pp 283–301. Another extension of Hofstede's work can be found in S M Lee and S J Peterson, "Culture, Entrepreneurial Orientation, and Global Competitiveness," *Journal of World Business,* Winter 2000, pp 401–16.
[26] Based on discussion in P R Harris and R T Moran, *Managing Cultural Differences,* 3rd ed (Houston: Gulf Publishing, 1991) p 12. Also see "Workers' Attitudes Similar Worldwide," *HR Magazine,* December 1998, pp 28–30; and C Comeau-Kirschner, "It's a Small World," *Management Review,* March 1999, p 8.
[27] For background, see Javidan and House, "Cultural Acumen for the Global Manager," pp 289–305; and the entire Spring 2002 issue of *Journal of World Business.*
[28] R House, M Javidan, P Hanges, and P Dorfman, "Understanding Cultures and Implicit Leadership Theories across the Globe: An Introduction to Project GLOBE," *Journal of World Business,* Spring 2002, p 4.
[29] See J C Kennedy, "Leadership in Malaysia: Traditional Values, International Outlook," *Academy of Management Executive,* August 2002, pp 15–26; M Javidan and A Dastmalchian, "Culture and Leadership in Iran: The Land of Individual Achievers, Strong Family Ties, and Powerful Elite," *Academy of Management Executive,* November 2003, pp 127–42; and R J House, P J Hanges, M Javidan, P W Dorfman, and V Gupta, eds, *Culture, Leadership, and Organizations: The Globe Study of 62 Societies* (Thousand Oaks, Calif.: Sage Publications, 2004). For updates, visit the GLOBE project's Web site: www.ucalgary.ca/mg/GLOBE/public/publications_2001.html
[30] Adapted from the list in House, Javidan, Hanges, and Dorfman, "Understanding Cultures and Implicit Leadership Theories across the Globe," pp 5–6.
[31] M Irvine, "Young Workers Saving to Retire," *The Arizona Republic,* December 28, 2003, p D5.
[32] Data from Trompenaars and Hampden-Turner, *Riding the Waves of Culture: Understanding Cultural Diversity in Global Business,* Ch 5. For relevant research evidence, see S Wang and C S Tamis-LeMonda, "Do Child-Rearing Values in Taiwan and the United States Reflect Cultural Values of Collectivism and Individualism?" *Journal of Cross-Cultural Psychology,* November 2003, pp 629–42; and J Allik and A Realo, "Individualism-Collectivism and Social Capital," *Journal of Cross-Cultural Psychology,* January 2004, pp 29–49.
[33] See J A Vandello and D Cohen, "Patterns of Individualism and Collectivism across the United States," *Journal of Personality and Social Psychology,* August 1999, pp 279–92.
[34] As quoted in E E Schultz, "Scudder Brings Lessons to Navajo, Gets Some of Its Own," *The Wall Street Journal,* April 29, 1999, p C12.
[35] Trompenaars and Hampden-Turner, *Riding the Waves of Culture: Understanding Cultural Diversity in Global Business,* p 56. The importance of "relationships" in Eastern and Western cultures is explored in S H Ang, "The Power of Money: A Cross-Cultural Analysis of Business-Related Beliefs," *Journal of World Business,* Spring 2000, pp 43–60.
[36] See M Munter, "Cross-Cultural Communication for Managers," *Business Horizons,* May–June 1993, pp 69–78.
[37] I Adler, "Between the Lines," *Business Mexico,* October 2000, p 24.
[38] See C Saunders, C Van Slyke, and D R Vogel, "My Time or Yours? Managing Time Visions in Global Virtual Teams," *Academy of Management Executive,* February 2004, pp 19–31.
[39] For a comprehensive treatment of time, see J E McGrath and J R Kelly, *Time and Human Interaction: Toward a Social Psychology of Time* (New York: Guilford Press, 1986). Also see L A Manrai and A K Manrai, "Effects of Cultural-Context, Gender, and Acculturation on Perceptions of Work versus Social/Leisure Time Usage," *Journal of Business Research,* February 1995, pp 115–28.
[40] A good discussion of doing business in Mexico is G K Stephens and C R Greer, "Doing Business in Mexico: Understanding Cultural Differences," *Organizational Dynamics,* Summer 1995, pp 39–55.
[41] R W Moore, "Time, Culture, and Comparative Management: A Review and Future Direction," in *Advances in International Comparative Management,* vol. 5, ed S B Prasad (Greenwich, CT: JAI Press, 1990), pp 7–8.
[42] See A C Bluedorn, C F Kaufman, and P M Lane, "How Many Things Do You Like to Do at Once? An Introduction to Monochronic and Polychronic Time," *Academy of Management Executive,* November 1992, pp 17–26.
[43] "Multitasking" term drawn from S McCartney, "The Breaking Point: Multitasking Technology Can Raise Stress and Cripple Productivity," *The Arizona Republic,* May 21, 1995, p D10.
[44] O Port, "You May Have To Reset This Watch—In a Million Years," *Business Week,* August 30, 1993, p 65.
[45] For details, see D Hartog, et al., "Emics and Etics of Culturally-Endorsed Implicit Leadership Theories: Are Attributes of Charismatic/Transformational Leadership Universally Endorsed?" *Leadership Quarterly,* in press. This paper is available on the Web at: www.ucalgary.ca/mg/GLOBE/public/publications_2001.html
[46] For example, see M F R Kets de Vries, "A Journey into the 'Wild East': Leadership Style and Organizational Practices in Russia," *Organizational Dynamics,* Spring 2000, pp 67–81; and F C Brodbeck, M Frese, and M Javidan, "Leadership Made in Germany: Low on Comparison, High on Performance," *Academy of Management Executive,* February 2002, pp 16–29.
[47] M Vande Berg, "Siemens: Betting That Big Is Once Again Beautiful," *Milken Institute Review,* Second Quarter 2002, p 47.
[48] J S Black and H B Gregersen, "The Right Way to Manage Expats," *Harvard Business Review,* March–April 1999, p 53. A more optimistic picture is presented in R L Tung, "American Expatriates Abroad: From Neophytes to Cosmopolitans," *Journal of World Business,* Summer 1998, pp 125–44.
[49] Adapted from R L Tung, "Expatriate Assignments: Enhancing Success and Minimizing Failure," *Academy of Management Executive,* May 1987, pp 117–26. Also see G S Insch and J D Daniels, "Causes and Consequences of Declining Early Departures from Foreign Assignments," *Business Horizons,* November–December 2002, pp 39–48.
[50] S Dallas, "Rule No. 1: Don't Diss the Locals," *Business Week,* May 15, 1995, p 8.
[51] See B A Anderson, "Expatriate Management: An Australian Tri-Sector Comparative Study," *Thunderbird International Business Review,* January–February 2001, pp 33–51.
[52] These insights come from Tung, "American Expatriates Abroad: From Neophytes to Cosmopolitans"; P M Caligiuri and W F Cascio, "*Can We Send Her There?* Maximizing the Success of Western Women on Global Assignments," *Journal of World Business,* Winter 1998, pp 394–416; T L Speer, "Gender Barriers Crumbling, Traveling Business Women Report," *USA Today,* March 16, 1999, p 5E; G Koretz, "A Woman's Place Is . . . ," *Business Week,* September 13, 1999, p 28; and L K Stroh, A Varma, and S J Valy-Durbin, "Why Are Women Left at Home: Are They Unwilling to Go on International Assignments?" *Journal of World Business,* Fall 2000, pp 241–55. Also see S Bates, "Are Women Better for International Assignments?" *HR Magazine,* December 2003, p 16.
[53] An excellent reference book on this topic is J S Black, H B Gregersen, and M E Mendenhall, *Global Assignments: Successfully Expatriating and*

Repatriating International Managers (San Francisco: Jossey-Bass, 1992). Also see M B Hess and P Linderman, *The Expert Expatriate: Your Guide to Successful Relocation Abroad* (Yarmouth, Maine: Intercultural Press, 2002); and E Gundling, *Working GlobeSmart: 12 People Skills for Doing Business across Borders* (Palo Alto, CA: Davies-Black Publishing, 2003).
[54] See K Roberts, E E Kossek, and C Ozeki, "Managing the Global Workforce: Challenges and Strategies," *Academy of Management Executive,* November 1998, pp 93–106.
[55] J S Lublin, "Younger Managers Learn Global Skills," *The Wall Street Journal,* March 31, 1992, p B1.
[56] See P C Earley, "Intercultural Training for Managers: A Comparison of Documentary and Interpersonal Methods," *Academy of Management Journal,* December 1987, pp 685–98; and J S Black and M Mendenhall, "Cross-Cultural Training Effectiveness: A Review and a Theoretical Framework for Future Research," *Academy of Management Review,* January 1990, pp 113–36. Also see M R Hammer and J N Martin, "The Effects of Cross-Cultural Training on American Managers in a Japanese-American Joint Venture," *Journal of Applied Communication Research,* May 1992, pp 161–81; and J K Harrison, "Individual and Combined Effects of Behavior Modeling and the Cultural Assimilator in Cross-Cultural Management Training," *Journal of Applied Psychology,* December 1992, pp 952–62.
[57] See K Tyler, "I Say Potato, You Say *Patata,*" *HR Magazine,* January 2004, pp 85–87.
[58] See D Stamps, "Welcome to America: Watch Out for Culture Shock," *Training,* November 1996, pp 22–30; L Glanz, R Williams, and L Hoeksema, "Sensemaking in Expatriation—A Theoretical Basis," *Thunderbird International Business Review,* January–February 2001, pp 101–19; and E Marx, *Breaking Through Culture Shock: What You Need to Succeed in International Business* (London: Nicholas Brealey Publishing, 2001).
[59] S Armour, "For Chao, It's a Labor of Love As She Initiates Big Changes," *USA Today,* August 29, 2003, p 2B.
[60] S Tully, "The Modular Corporation," *Fortune,* February 8, 1993, pp 108, 112.
[61] See H H Nguyen, L A Messe, and G E Stollak, "Toward a More Complex Understanding of Acculturation and Adjustment," *Journal of Cross-Cultural Psychology,* January 1999, pp 5–31.
[62] K L Miller, "How a Team of Buckeyes Helped Honda Save a Bundle," *Business Week,* September 13, 1993, p 68.
[63] For more, see S Overman, "Mentors Without Borders," *HR Magazine,* March 2004, pp 83–86.
[64] B Newman, "For Ira Caplan, Re-Entry Has Been Strange," *The Wall Street Journal,* December 12, 1995, p A12.
[65] See Black, Gregersen, and Mendenhall, *Global Assignments: Successfully Expatriating and Repatriating International Managers,* p 227. Also see H B Gregersen, "Commitments to a Parent Company and a Local Work Unit During Repatriation," *Personnel Psychology,* Spring 1992, pp 29–54; and H B Gregersen and J S Black, "Multiple Commitments upon Repatriation: The Japanese Experience," *Journal of Management,* no. 2, 1996, pp 209–29.
[66] Ibid., pp 226–27.
[67] See J R Engen, "Coming Home," *Training,* March 1995, pp 37–40; and L K Stroh, H B Gregersen, and J S Black, "Closing the Gap: Expectations versus Reality among Repatriates," *Journal of World Business,* Summer 1998, pp 111–24.
[68] Excerpted from M V Gratchev, "Making the Most of Cultural Differences," *Harvard Business Review,* October 2001, pp 28, 30.

Chapter 4

[1] Excerpted from C Hymowitz, "Top Executives Chase Youthful Appearance, But Miss Real Issue." *The Wall Street Journal,* February 17, 2004, p B1. From *Wall Street Journal,* Eastern Edition. Copyright 2004 by Dow Jones & Co. Inc. Reproduced with permission of Dow Jones & Co. Inc. via Copyright Clearance Center.
[2] Excerpted from C Daniels, "Women vs. Wal-Mart," *Fortune,* July 21, 2003, p 80.
[3] The negativity bias was examined and supported by O Ybarra and W G Stephan, "Misanthropic Person Memory," *Journal of Personality and Social Psychology,* April 1996, pp 691–700; and Y Ganzach, "Negativity (and Positivity) in Performance Evaluation: Three Field Studies," *Journal of Applied Psychology,* August 1995, pp 491–99.
[4] E Rosch, C B Mervis, W D Gray, D M Johnson, and P Boyes-Braem, "Basic Objects in Natural Categories," *Cognitive Psychology,* July 1976, p 383.
[5] For a thorough discussion of the role of schema during encoding, see S T Fiske and S E Taylor, *Social Cognition,* 2nd ed (Reading, MA: Addison-Wesley, 1991).
[6] The use of stereotypes is discussed by Z Kunda and S J Spencer, "When Do Stereotypes Come to Mind and When Do They Color Judgment? A Goal-Based Theoretical Framework for Stereotype Activation and Application," *Psychological Bulletin,* June 2003, pp 522–44.
[7] C M Judd and B Park, "Definition and Assessment of Accuracy in Social Stereotypes," *Psychological Review,* January 1993, p 110.
[8] Results can be found in E H James, "Race-Related Differences in Promotions and Support: Underlying Effects of Human and Social Capital," *Organization Science,* September–October 2000, pp 493–508.
[9] Results are reported in C Daniels, "Young, Gifted, Black—and Out of Here," *Fortune,* May 3, 2004, p 48.
[10] This study was conducted by K S Lyness and D E Thompson, "Climbing the Corporate Ladder: Do Female and Male Executives Follow the Same Route?" *Journal of Applied Psychology,* February 2000, pp 86–101.
[11] The process of stereotype formation and maintenance is discussed by M Biernat, "Toward a Broader View of Social Stereotyping," *American Psychologist,* December 2003, pp 1019–27.
[12] This discussion is based on material presented in G V Bodenhausen, C N Macrae, and J W Sherman, "On the Dialectics of Discrimination," in *Dual-Process Theories in Social Psychology,* eds S Chaiken and Y Trope (New York: Guilford Press, 1999) pp 271–90.
[13] For a thorough discussion about the structure and organization of memory, see L R Squire, B Knowlton, and G Musen, "The Structure and Organization of Memory," in *Annual Review of Psychology,* eds L W Porter and M R Rosenzweig (Palo Alto, CA: Annual Reviews Inc., 1993), vol. 44, pp 453–95.
[14] Event memory is discussed by D Zohar and G Luria, "Organizational MetaScripts as a Source of High Reliability: The Case of an Army Armored Brigade," *Journal of Organizational Behavior,* November 2003, pp 837–59.
[15] A thorough discussion of the reasoning process used to make judgments and decisions is provided by S A Sloman, "The Empirical Case for Two Systems of Reasoning," *Psychological Bulletin,* January 1996, pp 3–22.
[16] Results can be found in C M Marlowe, S L Schneider, and C E Nelson, "Gender and Attractiveness Biases in Hiring Decisions: Are More Experienced Managers Less Biased?" *Journal of Applied Psychology,* February 1996, pp 11–21.
[17] Details of this study can be found in C K Stevens, "Antecedents of Interview Interactions, Interviewers' Ratings, and Applicants' Reactions," *Personnel Psychology,* Spring 1998, pp 55–85.
[18] See R C Mayer and J H Davis, "The Effect of the Performance Appraisal System on Trust for Management: A Field Quasi-Experiment," *Journal of Applied Psychology,* February 1999, pp 123–36.
[19] Results can be found in W H Bommer, J L Johnson, G A Rich, P M Podsakoff, and S B Mackenzie, "On the Interchangeability of Objective and Subjective Measures of Employee Performance: A Meta-Analysis," *Personnel Psychology,* Autumn 1995, pp 587–605.
[20] The effectiveness of rater training was supported by D V Day and L M Sulsky, "Effects of Frame-of-Reference Training and Information Configuration on Memory Organization and Rating Accuracy," *Journal of Applied Psychology,* February 1995, pp 158–67.
[21] Results can be found in J S Phillips and R G Lord, "Schematic Information Processing and Perceptions of Leadership in Problem-Solving Groups," *Journal of Applied Psychology,* August 1982, pp 486–92.
[22] B Yost, "Office Duds: Clothes That Don't Work Jeopardize 'Casual Friday,'" *Arizona Republic,* March 5, 2004, p E1.
[23] Kelley's model is discussed in detail in H H Kelley, "The Processes of Causal Attribution," *American Psychologist,* February 1973, pp 107–28.

[24] For examples, see J Susskind, K Maurer, V Thakkar, D L Hamilton, and J W Sherman, "Perceiving Individuals and Groups: Expectancies, Dispositional Inferences, and Causal Attributions," *Journal of Personality and Social Psychology,* February 1999, pp 181–91; and J McClure, "Discounting Causes of Behavior: Are Two Reasons Better than One?" *Journal of Personality and Social Psychology,* January 1998, pp 7–20.
[25] Results from these studies can be found in D A Hofmann and A Stetzer, "The Role of Safety Climate and Communication in Accident Interpretation: Implications for Learning from Negative Events," *Academy of Management Journal,* December 1998, pp 644–57; and I Choi, R E Nisbett, and A Norenzayan, "Causal Attribution across Cultures: Variation and Universality," *Psychological Bulletin,* January 1999, pp 47–63.
[26] D Bickley, "Russians Won't Stop Whining," *Arizona Republic,* February 23, 2002, p C1.
[27] Details may be found in S E Moss and M J Martinko, "The Effects of Performance Attributions and Outcome Dependence on Leader Feedback Behavior Following Poor Subordinate Performance," *Journal of Organizational Behavior,* May 1998, pp 259–74; and E C Pence, W C Pendelton, G H Dobbins, and J A Sgro, "Effects of Causal Explanations and Sex Variables on Recommendations for Corrective Actions Following Employee Failure," *Organizational Behavior and Human Performance,* April 1982, pp 227–40.
[28] See D Konst, R Vonk, and R V D Vlist, "Inferences about Causes and Consequences of Behavior of Leaders and Subordinates," *Journal of Organizational Behavior,* March 1999, pp 261–71.
[29] See J Silvester, F Patterson, E Ferguson, "Comparing Two Attributional Models of Job Performance in Retail Sales: A Field Study," *Journal of Occupational and Organizational Psychology,* March 2003, pp 115–32.
[30] K Somers, "A Proven Record of Success," *Arizona Republic,* January 10, 2004, p C1.
[31] Definitions of diversity are discussed by A Wellner, "How Do You Spell Diversity?" *Training,* April 2000, pp 34–38; and R R Thomas, Jr, *Redefining Diversity* (New York: AMACOM, 1996), pp 4–9.
[32] The following discussion is based on L Gardenswartz and A Rowe, *Diverse Teams at Work* (New York: McGraw-Hill, 1994), pp 31–57.
[33] This distinction is made by M Loden, *Implementing Diversity* (Chicago: Irwin, 1996).
[34] H Collingwood, "Who Handles a Diverse Work Force Best?" *Working Women,* February 1996, p 25.
[35] See A Karr, "Work Week: A Special News Report about Life on the Job—and Trends Taking Shape There," *The Wall Street Journal,* June 1, 1999, p A1.
[36] A description of Ford's program can be found in E Garsten, "Ford Muslim Workers Organize 'Islam,'" *Arizona Republic,* December 13, 2001, p D2.
[37] Excerpted from "Workforce Optimas Awards 2003," *Workforce,* March 2003, p 47.
[38] F J Crosby, A Iyer, S Clayton, and R A Downing, "Affirmative Action: Psychological Data and the Policy Debates," *American Psychologist,* February 2003, p 94.
[39] See M Frase-Blunt, "Thwarting the Diversity Backlash," *HR Magazine,* June 2003, pp 137–44.
[40] See D A Kravitz and S L Klinberg, "Reactions to Two Versions of Affirmative Action among Whites, Blacks, and Hispanics," *Journal of Applied Psychology,* August 2000, pp 597–611.
[41] See Crosby, Iyer, Clayton, and Downing, "Affirmative Action: Psychological Data and the Policy Debates," pp 93–115.
[42] A M Morrison, *The New Leaders: Guidelines on Leadership Diversity in America* (San Francisco: Jossey-Bass, 1992), p 78.
[43] See K Blanton, "More Women in Top-Tier Jobs Earn 6 Figures," *Arizona Republic,* March 11, 2004, pp D1, D5.
[44] Results can be found in K S Lyness and D E Thompson, "Above the Glass Ceiling: A Comparison of Matched Samples of Female and Male Executives," *Journal of Applied Psychology,* June 1997, pp 359–75.
[45] This study was conducted by K S Lyness and M K Judiesch, "Are Women More Likely to Be Hired or Promoted into Management Positions?" *Journal of Vocational Behavior,* February 1999, pp 158–73.
[46] See fortune.com, May 19, 2004.
[47] These statistics are reported in C Hymowitz, "Women Put Noses to the Grindstone, and Miss Opportunities," *The Wall Street Journal,* February 3, 2004, p B1.
[48] Here are the ranks for each career strategy: Strategy 1 = 12; Strategy 2 = 6; Strategy 3 = 5; Strategy 4 = 11; Strategy 5 = 9; Strategy 6 = 3; Strategy 7 = 10; Strategy 8 = 1; Strategy 9 = 7; Strategy 10 = 8; Strategy 11 = 4; Strategy 12 = 2; and Strategy 13 = 13.
[49] Details of this study can be found in B R Ragins, B Townsend, and M Mattis, "Gender Gap in the Executive Suite: CEOs and Female Executives Report on Breaking the Glass Ceiling," *Academy of Management Executive,* February 1998, pp 28–42.
[50] See G C Armas, "Almost Half of U.S. Likely to be Minorities by 2050," *Arizona Republic,* March 18, 2004, p A5.
[51] These statistics were obtained from "Race-Based Charges: FY 1992–FY 2003," http://www.eeoc.gov/stats/race.html, last modified on March 8, 2004.
[52] These statistics were obtained from "Income of Households by Race and Hispanic Origin Using 2- and 3-Year Averages: 2000–2002," http://www.census.gov, last revised May 13, 2004.
[53] For a review of this research, see L Roberson and C J Block, "Racioethnicity and Job Performance: A Review and Critique of Theoretical Perspectives on the Causes of Group Differences," in *Research in Organizational Behavior,* vol 23, eds B M Staw and R I Sutton (New York: JAI Press, 2001), pp 247–326.
[54] See "USA Statistics in Brief—Law, Education, Communications, Transportation, Housing," http://www.census.gov, last revised March 16, 2004.
[55] See D Dooley and J Prause, "Underemployment and Alcohol Misuse in the National Longitudinal Survey of Youth," *Journal of Studies on Alcohol,* November 1998, pp 669–80; and D C Feldman, "The Nature, Antecedents and Consequences of Underemployment," *Journal of Management,* 1966, pp 385–407.
[56] See "Unemployment and Earnings for Workers Age 25 and Over, by Educational Attainment," http://www.bls.gov/emp, last modified August 7, 2003.
[57] These statistics were obtained from "Summary Measures of Educational Attainment of the U.S. Population: March 2002," http://www/census.gov/Press-Release/www/2003/cb03-51.html, last revised March 21, 2003; and "Fast Facts on Literacy," http://www.svcs.net/wpci/litfacts.htm, last revised April 26, 2000.
[58] "Fast Facts on Literacy."
[59] See H London, "The Workforce, Education, and the Nation's Future," www.hudson.org/american_outlook/articles_sm98/ london.htm, Summer 1998.
[60] S Armour, "Welcome Mat Rolls Out for Hispanic Workers: Corporate America Cultivates Talent as Ethnic Population Booms," *USA Today,* April 12, 2001, pp 1B, 2B.
[61] Excerpted from K Tyler, "I Say Potato, You Say Patata," *HR Magazine,* January 2004, pp 85–86.
[62] Approaches for handling elder care are discussed by T F Shea, "Help with Elder Care," *HR Magazine,* September 2003, pp 113–14, 116, 118.
[63] Managerial issues and solutions for an aging workforce are discussed by M M Greller and L K Stroh, "Making the Most of 'Late-Career' for Employers and Workers Themselves: Become Elders Not Relics," *Organizational Dynamics,* May 2004, pp 202–14.
[64] These barriers were taken from discussions in Loden, *Implementing Diversity;* E E Spragins, "Benchmark: The Diverse Work Force," *Inc.,* January 1993, p 33; and Morrison, *The New Leaders: Guidelines on Leadership Diversity in America.*
[65] See the related discussion in A Fels, "Do Women Lack Ambition?" *Harvard Business Review,* April 2004, pp 50–60.
[66] For complete details and results from this study, see A M Morrison, *The New Leaders: Guidelines on Leadership Diversity in America* (San Francisco: Jossey-Bass, 1992).
[67] Excerpted from "The Diversity Factor," *Fortune,* October 13, 2003, p S4.
[68] Excerpted from R Koonce, "Redefining Diversity," *Training & Development,* December 2001, pp 24, 26.
[69] Excerpted from J Leopold, "En-Ruse? Workers at Enron Say They Posed as Busy Traders to Impress Visiting Analysts," *The Wall Street Journal,* February 17, 2002, p C1.

Chapter 5

[1] Excerpted from Michelle Conlin, "I'm a Bad Boss? Blame My Dad," *Business Week,* May 10, 2004, pp 60–61. Reprinted with permission.
[2] D Seligman, "The Trouble with Buyouts," *Fortune,* November 30, 1992, p 125.
[3] See R Rodriguez, "Tapping the Hispanic Labor Pool," *HR Magazine,* April 2003, pp 72–79; J Barthold, "Waiting in the Wings," *HR Magazine,* April 2004, pp 88–95; S Armour, "Gay Marriage Debate Moves into Workplace," *USA Today,* April 14, 2004, pp 1B–2B; and C Daniels, "Young, Gifted, Black—and Out of Here," *Fortune,* May 3, 2004, p 48.
[4] Data from "If We Could Do It Over Again," *USA Today,* February 19, 2001, p 4D.
[5] V Gecas, "The Self-Concept," in *Annual Review of Sociology,* eds R H Turner and J F Short, Jr. (Palo Alto, CA: Annual Reviews Inc., 1982), vol. 8, p 3. Also see A P Brief and R J Aldag, "The 'Self' in Work Organizations: A Conceptual Review," *Academy of Management Review,* January 1981, pp 75–88; J J Sullivan, "Self Theories and Employee Motivation," *Journal of Management,* June 1989, pp 345–63; P Cushman, "Why the Self Is Empty," *American Psychologist,* May 1990, pp 599–611; and L Gaertner, C Sedikides, and K Graetz, "In Search of Self-Definition: Motivational Primacy of the Individual Self, Motivational Primacy of the Collective Self, or Contextual Primacy?" *Journal of Personality and Social Psychology,* January 1999, pp 5–18.
[6] L Festinger, *A Theory of Cognitive Dissonance* (Stanford, CA: Stanford University Press, 1957), p 3.
[7] A Canadian versus Japanese comparison of self-concept can be found in J D Campbell, P D Trapnell, S J Heine, I M Katz, L F Lavallee, and D R Lehman, "Self-Concept Clarity: Measurement, Personality Correlates, and Cultural Boundaries," *Journal of Personality and Social Psychology,* January 1996, pp 141–56. Also see R W Tafarodi, C Lo, S Yamaguchi, W W S Lee, and H Katsura, "The Inner Self in Three Countries," *Journal of Cross-Cultural Psychology,* January 2004, pp 97–117.
[8] See D C Barnlund, "Public and Private Self in Communicating with Japan," *Business Horizons,* March–April 1989, pp 32–40; and the section on "Doing Business with Japan" in P R Harris and R T Moran, *Managing Cultural Differences,* 4th ed (Houston: Gulf Publishing, 1996), pp 267–76.
[9] J Champy, "The Hidden Qualities of Great Leaders," *Fast Company,* November 2003, p 135.
[10] Based in part on a definition found in Gecas, "The Self-Concept." Also see N Branden, *Self-Esteem at Work: How Confident People Make Powerful Companies* (San Francisco: Jossey-Bass, 1998).
[11] H W Marsh, "Positive and Negative Global Self-Esteem: A Substantively Meaningful Distinction or Artifacts?" *Journal of Personality and Social Psychology,* April 1996, p 819.
[12] Ibid.
[13] For related research, see R C Liden, L Martin, and C K Parsons, "Interviewer and Applicant Behaviors in Employment Interviews," *Academy of Management Journal,* April 1993, pp 372–86; M B Setterlund and P M Niedenthal, " 'Who Am I? Why Am I Here?': Self-Esteem, Self-Clarity, and Prototype Matching," *Journal of Personality and Social Psychology,* October 1993, pp 769–80; and G J Pool, W Wood, and K Leck, "The Self-Esteem Motive in Social Influence: Agreement with Valued Majorities and Disagreement with Derogated Minorities," *Journal of Personality and Social Psychology,* October 1998, pp 967–75.
[14] E Diener and M Diener, "Cross-Cultural Correlates of Life Satisfaction and Self-Esteem," *Journal of Personality and Social Psychology,* April 1995, p 662. For cross-cultural evidence of a similar psychological process for self-esteem, see T M Singelis, M H Bond, W F Sharkey, and C S Y Lai, "Unpackaging Culture's Influence on Self-Esteem and Embarrassability," *Journal of Cross-Cultural Psychology,* May 1999, pp 315–41.
[15] See C Kobayashi and J D Brown, "Self-Esteem and Self-Enhancement in Japan and America," *Journal of Cross-Cultural Psychology,* September 2003, pp 567–80.
[16] Based on data in F L Smoll, R E Smith, N P Barnett, and J J Everett, "Enhancement of Children's Self-Esteem through Social Support Training for Youth Sports Coaches," *Journal of Applied Psychology,* August 1993, pp 602–10.
[17] W J McGuire and C V McGuire, "Enhancing Self-Esteem by Directed-Thinking Tasks: Cognitive and Affective Positivity Asymmetries," *Journal of Personality and Social Psychology,* June 1996, p 1124.
[18] S Begley, "Real Self-Esteem Builds on Achievement, Not Praise for Slackers," *The Wall Street Journal,* April 18, 2003, p B1. Also see A Dijksterhuis, "I Like Myself But I Don't Know Why: Enhancing Implicit Self-Esteem by Subliminal Evaluative Conditioning," *Journal of Personality and Social Psychology,* February 2004, pp 345–55.
[19] M E Gist, "Self-Efficacy: Implications for Organizational Behavior and Human Resource Management," *Academy of Management Review,* July 1987, p 472. Also see A Bandura, "Self-Efficacy: Toward a Unifying Theory of Behavioral Change," *Psychological Review,* March 1977, pp 191–215; M E Gist and T R Mitchell, "Self-Efficacy: A Theoretical Analysis of Its Determinants and Malleability," *Academy of Management Review,* April 1992, pp 183–211; and T J Maurer and K D Andrews, "Traditional, Likert, and Simplified Measures of Self-Efficacy," *Educational and Psychological Measurement,* December 2000, pp 965–73.
[20] D Rader, "I Always Believed There Was a Place for Me," *Parade Magazine,* May 21, 2000, p 6.
[21] Based on D H Lindsley, D A Brass, and J B Thomas, "Efficacy-Performance Spirals: A Multilevel Perspective," *Academy of Management Review,* July 1995, pp 645–78.
[22] See, for example, V Gecas, "The Social Psychology of Self-Efficacy," in *Annual Review of Sociology,* eds W R Scott and J Blake (Palo Alto, CA: Annual Reviews, Inc., 1989), vol. 15, pp 291–316; C K Stevens, A G Bavetta, and M E Gist, "Gender Differences in the Acquisition of Salary Negotiation Skills: The Role of Goals, Self-Efficacy, and Perceived Control," *Journal of Applied Psychology,* October 1993, pp 723–35; and D Eden and Y Zuk, "Seasickness as a Self-Fulfilling Prophecy: Raising Self-Efficacy to Boost Performance at Sea," *Journal of Applied Psychology,* October 1995, pp 628–35.
[23] For more on learned helplessness, see Gecas, "The Social Psychology of Self-Efficacy"; M J Martinko and W L Gardner, "Learned Helplessness: An Alternative Explanation for Performance Deficits," *Academy of Management Review,* April 1982, pp 195–204; and C R Campbell and M J Martinko, "An Integrative Attributional Perspective of Empowerment and Learned Helplessness: A Multimethod Field Study," *Journal of Management,* no. 2, 1998, pp 173–200. Also see A Dickerson and M A Taylor, "Self-Limiting Behavior in Women: Self-Esteem and Self-Efficacy as Predictors," *Group & Organization Management,* June 2000, pp 191–210.
[24] For an update on Bandura, see D Smith, "The Theory Heard 'Round the World," *Monitor on Psychology,* October 2002, pp 30–32.
[25] Research on this connection is reported in R B Rubin, M M Martin, S S Bruning, and D E Powers, "Test of a Self-Efficacy Model of Interpersonal Communication Competence," *Communication Quarterly,* Spring 1993, pp 210–20.
[26] Excerpted from T Petzinger Jr, "Bob Schmonsees Has a Tool for Better Sales, and It Ignores Excuses," *The Wall Street Journal,* March 26, 1999, p B1.
[27] Data from A D Stajkovic and F Luthans, "Self-Efficacy and Work-Related Performance: A Meta-Analysis," *Psychological Bulletin,* September 1998, pp 240–61.
[28] Based in part on discussion in Gecas, "The Social Psychology of Self-Efficacy."
[29] See S K Parker, "Enhancing Role Breadth Self-Efficacy: The Roles of Job Enrichment and Other Organizational Interventions," *Journal of Applied Psychology,* December 1998, pp 835–52.
[30] The positive relationship between self-efficacy and readiness for retraining is documented in L A Hill and J Elias, "Retraining Midcareer Managers: Career History and Self-Efficacy Beliefs," *Human Resource Management,* Summer 1990, pp 197–217. Also see A M Saks, "Longitudinal Field Investigation of the Moderating and Mediating Effects of Self-Efficacy on the Relationship between Training and Newcomer Adjustment," *Journal of Applied Psychology,* April 1995, pp 211–25.
[31] See A D Stajkovic and Fred Luthans, "Social Cognitive Theory and Self-Efficacy: Going beyond Traditional Motivational and Behavioral Approaches," *Organizational Dynamics,* Spring 1998, pp 62–74.

[32] See P C Earley and T R Lituchy, "Delineating Goal and Efficacy Effects: A Test of Three Models," *Journal of Applied Psychology,* February 1991, pp 81–98.
[33] See P Tierney and S M Farmer, "Creative Self-Efficacy: Its Potential Antecedents and Relationship to Creative Performance," *Academy of Management Journal,* December 2002, pp 1137–48.
[34] See W S Silver, T R Mitchell, and M E Gist, "Response to Successful and Unsuccessful Performance: The Moderating Effect of Self-Efficacy on the Relationship between Performance and Attributions," *Organizational Behavior and Human Decision Processes,* June 1995, pp 286–99; R Zemke, "The Corporate Coach," *Training,* December 1996, pp 24–28; and J P Masciarelli, "Less Lonely at the Top," *Management Review,* April 1999, pp 58–61.
[35] For a comprehensive update, see S W Gangestad and M Snyder, "Self-Monitoring: Appraisal and Reappraisal," *Psychological Bulletin,* July 2000, pp 530–55.
[36] M Snyder and S Gangestad, "On the Nature of Self-Monitoring: Matters of Assessment, Matters of Validity," *Journal of Personality and Social Psychology,* July 1986, p 125.
[37] Data from M Kilduff and D V Day, "Do Chameleons Get Ahead? The Effects of Self-Monitoring on Managerial Careers," *Academy of Management Journal,* August 1994, pp 1047–60.
[38] Data from D B Turban and T W Dougherty, "Role of Protege Personality in Receipt of Mentoring and Career Success," *Academy of Management Journal,* June 1994, pp 688–702.
[39] See F Luthans, "Successful vs. Effective Managers," *Academy of Management Executive,* May 1988, pp 127–32.
[40] See A Bandura, *Social Learning Theory* (Englewood Cliffs, NJ: Prentice Hall, 1977). A further refinement is reported in A D Stajkovic and F Luthans, "Social Cognitive Theory and Self-Efficacy: Going Beyond Traditional Motivational and Behavioral Approaches," *Organizational Dynamics,* Spring 1998, pp 62–74. Also see M Uhl-Bien and G B Graen, "Individual Self-Management: Analysis of Professionals' Self-Managing Activities in Functional and Cross-Functional Work Teams," *Academy of Management Journal,* June 1998, pp 340–50.
[41] Bandura, *Social Learning Theory,* p 13.
[42] For related research, see M Castaneda, T A Kolenko, and R J Aldag, "Self-Management Perceptions and Practices: A Structural Equations Analysis," *Journal of Organizational Behavior,* January 1999, pp 101–20. An alternative model is discussed in K M Sheldon, D B Turban, K G Brown, M R Barrick, and T M Judge, "Applying Self-Determination Theory to Organizational Research," in *Research in Personnel and Human Resources Management,* vol 22, eds J J Martocchio and G R Ferris (New York: Elsevier, 2003), pp 357–93.
[43] "Career Self-Management," *Industry Week,* September 5, 1994, p 36.
[44] See L Nash and H Stevenson, "Success That Lasts," *Harvard Business Review,* February 2004, pp 102–9.
[45] S R Covey, *The 7 Habits of Highly Effective People* (New York: Simon & Schuster, 1989), p 42. Also see J Hillkirk, "Golden Rules Promoted for Work Success," *USA Today,* August 20, 1993, pp 1B–2B; L Bongiorno, "Corporate America, Dr. Feelgood Will See You Now," *Business Week,* December 6, 1993, p 52; T K Smith, "What's So Effective about Stephen Covey?" *Fortune,* December 12, 1994, pp 116–26; E Brown, "Stephen Covey's New One-Day Seminar," *Fortune,* February 1, 1999, pp 138–40; and "Put More Passion in Your Life," *Nonprofit World,* May–June 2000, p 39.
[46] "Labor Letter: A Special News Report on People and Their Jobs in Offices, Fields, and Factories," *The Wall Street Journal,* October 15, 1985, p 1.
[47] J Chatzky, "The 4 Steps to Setting Goals & 6 Keys to Achieving Them," *Money,* November 2003, pp 111, 113.
[48] R McGarvey, "Rehearsing for Success," *Executive Female,* January/February 1990, p 36.
[49] See W P Anthony, R H Bennett, III, E N Maddox, and W J Wheatley, "Picturing the Future: Using Mental Imagery to Enrich Strategic Environmental Assessment," *Academy of Management Executive,* May 1993, pp 43–56.
[50] D S Looney, "Mental Toughness Wins Out," *The Christian Science Monitor,* July 31, 1998, p B4.
[51] For excellent tips on self-management, see C P Neck, "Managing Your Mind," *Internal Auditor,* June 1996, pp 60–63.
[52] C Zastrow, *Talk to Yourself: Using the Power of Self-Talk* (Englewood Cliffs, NJ: Prentice Hall, 1979), p 60. Also see C C Manz and C P Neck, "Inner Leadership: Creating Productive Thought Patterns," *Academy of Management Executive,* August 1991, pp 87–95; C P Neck and R F Ashcraft, "Inner Leadership: Mental Strategies for Nonprofit Staff Members," *Nonprofit World,* May–June 2000, pp 27–30; and T C Brown, "The Effect of Verbal Self-Guidance Training on Collective Efficacy and Team Performance," *Personnel Psychology,* Winter 2003, pp 935–64.
[53] E Franz, "Private Pep Talk," *Selling Power,* May 1996, p 81.
[54] Drawn from discussion in A Bandura, "Self-Reinforcement: Theoretical and Methodological Considerations," *Behaviorism,* Fall 1976, pp 135–55.
[55] R Kreitner and F Luthans, "A Social Learning Approach to Behavioral Management: Radical Behaviorists 'Mellowing Out,' " *Organizational Dynamics,* Autumn 1984, p 63.
[56] See K Painter, "We Are Who We Are, or Are We?" *USA Today,* October 3, 2002, p 9; and S Begley, "In the Brave Guppy and Hyper Octopus, Clues to Personality," *The Wall Street Journal,* October 10, 2003, p B1.
[57] The landmark report is J M Digman, "Personality Structure: Emergence of the Five-Factor Model," *Annual Review of Psychology,* vol. 41, 1990, pp 417–40. Also see C Viswesvaran and D S Ones, "Measurement Error in 'Big Five Factors' Personality Assessment: Reliability Generalization across Studies and Measures," *Educational and Psychological Measurement,* April 2000, pp 224–35; and S J T Branje, C F M van Lieshout, and M A G van Aken, "Relations between Big Five Personality Characteristics and Perceived Support in Adolescents' Families," *Journal of Personality and Social Psychology,* April 2004, pp 615–28. An alternative 6-factor personality structure is discussed in M C Ashton, et al., "A Six-Factor Structure of Personality-Descriptive Adjectives: Solutions from Psycholexical Studies in Seven Languages," *Journal of Personality and Social Psychology,* February 2004, pp 356–66.
[58] See K M DeNeve and H Cooper, "The Happy Personality: A Meta-Analysis of 137 Personality Traits and Subjective Well-Being," *Psychological Bulletin,* September 1998, pp 197–229; D P Skarlicki, R Folger, and P Tesluk, "Personality as a Moderator in the Relationship between Fairness and Retaliation," *Academy of Management Journal,* February 1999, pp 100–8; and R E Lucas and B M Baird, "Extraversion and Emotional Reactivity," *Journal of Personality and Social Psychology,* March 2004, pp 473–85.
[59] Data from S V Paunonen et al., "The Structure of Personality in Six Cultures," *Journal of Cross-Cultural Psychology,* May 1996, pp 339–53. Also see C Ward, C Leong, and M Low, "Personality and Sojourner Adjustment: An Exploration of the Big Five and the Cultural Fit Proposition," *Journal of Cross-Cultural Psychology,* March 2004, pp 137–51.
[60] J Allik and R R McCrae, "Toward a Geography of Personality Traits: Patterns of Profiles across 36 Cultures," *Journal of Cross-Cultural Psychology,* January 2004, p 13.
[61] See M R Barrick and M K Mount, "The Big Five Personality Dimensions and Job Performance: A Meta-Analysis," *Personnel Psychology,* Spring 1991, pp 1–26. Also see R P Tett, D N Jackson, and M Rothstein, "Personality Measures as Predictors of Job Performance: A Meta-Analytic Review," *Personnel Psychology,* Winter 1991, pp 703–42; and S E Seibert and M L Kraimer, "The Five-Factor Model of Personality and Career Success," *Journal of Vocational Behavior,* February 2001, pp 1–21.
[62] Barrick and Mount, "The Big Five Personality Dimensions and Job Performance: A Meta-Analysis," p 18. See O Behling, "Employee Selection: Will Intelligence and Conscientiousness Do the Job?" *Academy of Management Executive,* February 1998, pp 77–86; J A Lepine and L Van Dyne, "Peer Responses to Low Performers: An Attributional Model of Helping in the Context of Groups," *Academy of Management Review,* January 2001, pp 67–84; and J F Salgado, "Predicting Job Performance Using FFM and non-FFM Personality Measures," *Journal of Occupational and Organizational Psychology,* September 2003, pp 323–46.
[63] Barrick and Mount, "The Big Five Personality Dimensions and Job Performance: A Meta-Analysis," p 21. Also see D M Tokar, A R Fischer, and L M Subich, "Personality and Vocational Behavior: A Selective Review of the Literature, 1993–1997," *Journal of Vocational Behavior,* October 1998, pp 115–53; and K C Wooten, T A Timmerman, and

R Folger, "The Use of Personality and the Five-Factor Model to Predict New Business Ventures: From Outplacement to Start-up," *Journal of Vocational Behavior,* February 1999, pp 82–101.

[64] For details, see L A Witt and G R Ferris, "Social Skill as Moderator of the Conscientiousness-Performance Relationship: Convergent Results across Four Studies," *Journal of Applied Psychology,* October 2003, pp 809–20. Also see H Liao and A Chuang, "A Multilevel Investigation of Factors Influencing Employee Service Performance and Customer Outcomes," *Academy of Management Journal,* February 2004, pp 41–58.

[65] Lead researcher William Fleeson, as quoted in M Dittmann, "Acting Extraverted Spurs Positive Feelings, Study Finds," *Monitor on Psychology,* April 2003, p 17.

[66] J M Crant, "Proactive Behavior in Organizations," *Journal of Management,* no. 3, 2000, p 439.

[67] Ibid., pp 439–41.

[68] B Hagenbaugh, "Economics Majors Build Brand Name with Unmentionables," *USA Today,* May 20, 2002, p 3B.

[69] See S B Gustafson and M D Mumford, "Personal Style and Person-Environment Fit: A Pattern Approach," *Journal of Vocational Behavior,* April 1995, pp 163–88.

[70] For an instructive update, see J B Rotter, "Internal versus External Control of Reinforcement: A Case History of a Variable," *American Psychologist,* April 1990, pp 489–93. A critical review of locus of control and a call for a meta-analysis can be found in R W Renn and R J Vandenberg, "Differences in Employee Attitudes and Behaviors Based on Rotter's (1966) Internal-External Locus of Control: Are They All Valid?" *Human Relations,* November 1991, pp 1161–77.

[71] For an overall review of research on locus of control, see P E Spector, "Behavior in Organizations as a Function of Employee's Locus of Control," *Psychological Bulletin,* May 1982, pp 482–97; the relationship between locus of control and performance and satisfaction is examined in D R Norris and R E Niebuhr, "Attributional Influences on the Job Performance–Job Satisfaction Relationship," *Academy of Management Journal,* June 1984, pp 424–31; salary differences between internals and externals were examined by P C Nystrom, "Managers' Salaries and Their Beliefs about Reinforcement Control," *Journal of Social Psychology,* August 1983, pp 291–92. Also see S S K Lam and J Schaubroeck, "The Role of Locus of Control in Reactions to Being Promoted and to Being Passed Over: A Quasi Experiment," *Academy of Management Journal,* February 2000, pp 66–78.

[72] See S R Hawk, "Locus of Control and Computer Attitude: The Effect of User Involvement," *Computers in Human Behavior,* no. 3, 1989, pp 199–206. Also see A S Phillips and A G Bedeian, "Leader-Follower Exchange Quality: The Role of Personal and Interpersonal Attributes," *Academy of Management Journal,* August 1994, pp 990–1001.

[73] These recommendations are from Spector, "Behavior in Organizations as a Function of Employee's Locus of Control."

[74] M Fishbein and I Ajzen, *Belief, Attitude, Intention and Behavior: An Introduction to Theory and Research* (Reading, MA: Addison-Wesley Publishing, 1975), p 6. For more, see D Andrich and I M Styles, "The Structural Relationship between Attitude and Behavior Statements from the Unfolding Perspective," *Psychological Methods,* December 1998, pp 454–69; A P Brief, *Attitudes in and around Organizations* (Thousand Oaks, CA: Sage Publications, 1998); and "Tips to Pick the Best Employee," *Business Week,* March 1, 1999, p 24.

[75] See B M Staw and J Ross, "Stability in the Midst of Change: A Dispositional Approach to Job Attitudes," *Journal of Applied Psychology,* August 1985, pp 469–80. Also see J Schaubroeck, D C Ganster, and B Kemmerer, "Does Trait Affect Promote Job Attitude Stability?" *Journal of Organizational Behavior,* March 1996, pp 191–96.

[76] Data from P S Visser and J A Krosnick, "Development of Attitude Strength over the Life Cycle: Surge and Decline," *Journal of Personality and Social Psychology,* December 1998, pp 1389–1410.

[77] For interesting reading on intelligence, see J R Flynn, "Searching for Justice: The Discovery of IQ Gains over Time," *American Psychologist,* January 1999, pp 5–20; and E Benson, "Intelligent Intelligence Testing," *Monitor on Psychology,* February 2003, pp 48–54.

[78] For an excellent update on intelligence, including definitional distinctions and a historical perspective of the IQ controversy, see R A Weinberg, "Intelligence and IQ," *American Psychologist,* February 1989, pp 98–104. Genetics and intelligence are discussed in R Plomin and F M Spinath, "Intelligence: Genetics, Genes, and Genomics," *Journal of Personality and Social Psychology,* January 2004, pp 112–29.

[79] Ibid. Also see M Elias, "Mom's IQ, Not Family Size, Key to Kids' Smarts," *USA Today,* June 12, 2000, p 1D; and R Sapolsky, "Score One for Nature—or Is It Nurture?" *USA Today,* June 21, 2000, p 17A.

[80] S L Wilk, L Burris Desmarais, and P R Sackett, "Gravitation to Jobs Commensurate with Ability: Longitudinal and Cross-Sectional Tests," *Journal of Applied Psychology,* February 1995, p 79.

[81] B Azar, "People Are Becoming Smarter—Why?" *APA Monitor,* June 1996, p 20. Also see " 'Average' Intelligence Higher than It Used to Be," *USA Today,* February 18, 1997, p 6D.

[82] See D Lubinski, "Introduction to the Special Section on Cognitive Abilities: 100 Years after Spearman's (1904) 'General Intelligence,' Objectively Determined and Measured," *Journal of Personality and Social Psychology,* January 2004, pp 96–111.

[83] See F L Schmidt and J E Hunter, "Employment Testing: Old Theories and New Research Findings," *American Psychologist,* October 1981, p 1128; and N R Kuncel, S A Hezlett, and D S Ones, "Academic Performance, Career Potential, Creativity, and Job Performance: Can One Construct Predict Them All?" *Journal of Personality and Social Psychology,* January 2004, pp 148–61. A brief overview of the foregoing study can be found in M Greer, "General Cognition Also Makes the Difference on the Job, Study Finds," *Monitor on Psychology,* April 2004, p 12. Also see F L Schmidt and J Hunter, "General Mental Ability in the World of Work: Occupational Attainment and Job Performance," *Journal of Personality and Social Psychology,* January 2004, pp 162–73.

[84] A Reinhardt, "I've Left a Few Dead Bodies," *Business Week,* January 31, 2000, p 69. Also see K Tyler, "Helping Employees Cope with Grief," *HR Magazine,* September 2003, pp 54–58; and L W Andrews, "Aftershocks of War," *HR Magazine,* April 2004, pp 64–70.

[85] Quoted in B Schlender, "Why Andy Grove Can't Stop," *Fortune,* July 10, 1995, p 91.

[86] D Lieberman, "Fear of Failing Drives Diller," *USA Today,* February 10, 1999, p 3B.

[87] R S Lazarus, *Emotion and Adaptation* (New York: Oxford University Press, 1991), p 6. Also see, J A Russell and L F Barrett, "Core Affect, Prototypical Emotional Episodes, and Other Things Called *Emotion:* Dissecting the Elephant," *Journal of Personality and Social Psychology,* May 1999, pp 805–19; S Fineman, *Understanding Emotion at Work* (Thousand Oaks, CA: Sage, 2003); and D DeSteno, R E Petty, D D Rucker, D T Wegener, and J Braverman, "Discrete Emotions and Persuasion: The Role of Emotion-Induced Expectancies," *Journal of Personality and Social Psychology,* January 2004, pp 43–56.

[88] Based on discussion in R D Arvey, G L Renz, and T W Watson, "Emotionality and Job Performance: Implications for Personnel Selection," in *Research in Personnel and Human Resources Management,* vol. 16, ed G R Ferris (Stamford, CT: JAI Press, 1998), pp 103–47. Also see L A King, "Ambivalence over Emotional Expression and Reading Emotions," *Journal of Personality and Social Psychology,* March 1998, pp 753–62; and J L Tsai and Y Chentsova-Dutton, "Variation among European Americans in Emotional Facial Expression," *Journal of Cross-Cultural Psychology,* November 2003, pp 650–57.

[89] Data from S D Pugh, "Service with a Smile: Emotional Contagion in the Service Encounter," *Academy of Management Journal,* October 2001, pp 1018–27.

[90] Drawn from P Totterdell, S Kellett, K Teuchmann, and R B Briner, "Evidence of Mood Linkage in Work Groups," *Journal of Personality and Social Psychology,* June 1998, pp 1504–15. Also see C D Fisher, "Mood and Emotions while Working: Missing Pieces of Job Satisfaction," *Journal of Organizational Behavior,* March 2000, pp 185–202; K M Lewis, "When Leaders Display Emotion: How Followers Respond to Negative Emotional Expression of Male and Female Leaders," *Journal of Organizational Behavior,* March 2000, pp 221–34; and A Singh-Manoux and C Finkenauer, "Cultural Variations in Social Sharing of Emotions: An Intercultural Perspective," *Journal of Cross-Cultural Psychology,* November 2001, pp 647–61.

[91] As quoted in D Jones, "Music Director Works to Blend Strengths," *USA Today,* October 27, 2003, p 6B.

[92] N M Ashkanasy and C S Daus, "Emotion in the Workplace: The New Challenge for Managers," *Academy of Management Executive,* February 2002, p 79. Also see J Schaubroeck and J R Jones, "Antecedents of Workplace Emotional Labor Dimensions and Moderators of Their Effects on Physical Symptoms," *Journal of Organizational Behavior,* March 2000, pp 163–83; "The Killer Smile: The Cost of Service at Any Cost," *Training,* May 2000, p 22; A A Grandey, "When 'The Show Must Go On': Surface Acting and Deep Acting as Determinants of Emotional Exhaustion and Peer-Rated Service Delivery," *Academy of Management Journal,* February 2003, pp 86–96; C M Brotheridge and R T Lee, "Development and Validation of the Emotional Labour Scale," *Journal of Occupational and Organizational Psychology,* September 2003, pp 365–79; and Y Guerrier and A Adib, "Work at Leisure and Leisure at Work: A Study of the Emotional Labour of Tour Reps," *Human Relations,* November 2003, pp 1399–1417.

[93] Data from A M Kring and A H Gordon, "Sex Differences in Emotions: Expression, Experience, and Physiology," *Journal of Personality and Social Psychology,* March 1998, pp 686–703.

[94] D Goleman, *Emotional Intelligence* (New York: Bantam Books, 1995), p 34. For more, see Q N Huy, "Emotional Capability, Emotional Intelligence, and Radical Change," *Academy of Management Review,* April 1999, pp 325–45; V U Druskat and S B Wolff, "Building the Emotional Intelligence of Groups," *Harvard Business Review,* March 2001, pp 80–90; M Dittmann, "How 'Emotional Intelligence' Emerged," *Monitor on Psychology,* October 2003, p 64; and M M Tugade and B L Fredrickson, "Resilient Individuals Use Positive Emotions to Bounce Back from Negative Emotional Experiences," *Journal of Personality and Social Psychology,* February 2004, pp 320–33.

[95] See the box titled "Get Happy Carefully" on p 49 of D Goleman, R Boyatzis, and A McKee, "Primal Leadership: The Hidden Driver of Great Performance," *Harvard Business Review,* Special Issue: Breakthrough Leadership, December 2001, pp 43–51.

[96] J S Lublin, "Surviving the Pressure with a Ready Plan or, Literally, a Script," *The Wall Street Journal,* March 2, 2004, p B1.

[97] M N Martinez, "The Smarts That Count," *HR Magazine,* November 1997, pp 72–78.

[98] "What's Your EQ at Work?" *Fortune,* October 26, 1998, p 298.

[99] Based on M Davies, L Stankov, and R D Roberts, "Emotional Intelligence: In Search of an Elusive Construct," *Journal of Personality and Social Psychology,* October 1998, pp 989–1015; and K A Barchard, "Does Emotional Intelligence Assist in the Prediction of Academic Success?" *Educational and Psychological Measurement,* October 2003, pp 840–58.

[100] A Fisher, "Success Secret: A High Emotional IQ," *Fortune,* October 26, 1998, p 294. Also see Daniel Goleman, "Never Stop Learning," *Harvard Business Review,* Special Issue: Inside the Mind of the Leader," January 2004, pp 28–29.

[101] Excerpted from J Macht, "To Get Ahead, Get Mad," *Business 2.0,* May 2002, p 94. © Time, Inc. All rights reserved.

Chapter 6

[1] Excerpted from S Bates, "Getting Engaged," *HR Magazine,* February 2004, pp 49–50. Copyright 2004 by Society for Human Resource Management. Reproduced with permission of Society for Human Resource Management via Copyright Clearance Center.

[2] T R Mitchell, "Motivation: New Direction for Theory, Research, and Practice," *Academy of Management Review,* January 1982, p 81.

[3] This discussion is based on T R Mitchell and D Daniels, "Motivation," in *Handbook of Psychology* (Vol 12), eds W C Borman, D R Ilgen, and R J Klimoski (Hoboken, NJ: John Wiley & Sons, Inc., 2003), pp 225–54.

[4] Excerpted from S Greengard, "What's in Store for 2004," *Workforce Management,* December 2003, p 36.

[5] See J Mehring, "What's Lifting Productivity," *Business Week,* May 24, 2004, p 32.

[6] For a complete description of Maslow's theory, see A H Maslow, "A Theory of Human Motivation," *Psychological Review,* July 1943, pp 370–96.

[7] H R Nalbantian and A Szostak, "How Fleet Bank Fought Employee Flight," *Harvard Business Review,* April 2004, p 116.

[8] Excerpted from K Tyler, "A Roof Over Their Heads," *HR Magazine,* February 2001, p 41.

[9] H A Murray, *Explorations in Personality* (New York: John Wiley & Sons, 1938), p 164.

[10] See K G Shaver, "The Entrepreneurial Personality Myth," *Business and Economic Review,* April/June 1995, pp 20–23.

[11] See the following series of research reports: D K McNeese-Smith, "The Relationship between Managerial Motivation, Leadership, Nurse Outcomes and Patient Satisfaction," *Journal of Organizational Behavior,* March 1999, pp 243–59; A M Harrell and M J Stahl, "A Behavioral Decision Theory Approach for Measuring McClelland's Trichotomy of Needs," *Journal of Applied Psychology,* April 1981, pp 242–47; and M J Stahl, "Achievement, Power and Managerial Motivation: Selecting Managerial Talent with the Job Choice Exercise," *Personnel Psychology,* Winter 1983, pp 775–89.

[12] For a review of the foundation of achievement motivation training, see D C McClelland, "Toward a Theory of Motive Acquisition," *American Psychologist,* May 1965, pp 321–33. Evidence for the validity of motivation training can be found in H Heckhausen and S Krug, "Motive Modification," in *Motivation and Society,* ed A J Stewart (San Francisco: Jossey-Bass, 1982).

[13] Results can be found in D B Turban and T L Keon, "Organizational Attractiveness: An Interactionist Perspective," *Journal of Applied Psychology,* April 1993, pp 184–93.

[14] See D Steele Johnson and R Perlow, "The Impact of Need for Achievement Components on Goal Commitment and Performance," *Journal of Applied Social Psychology,* November 1992, pp 1711–20.

[15] J L Bowditch and A F Buono, *A Primer on Organizational Behavior* (New York: John Wiley & Sons, 1985), p 210.

[16] This framework was proposed by M A Campion and P W Thayer, "Development and Field Evaluation of an Interdisciplinary Measure of Job Design," *Journal of Applied Psychology,* February 1985, pp 29–43.

[17] These outcomes are discussed by J R Edwards, J A Scully, and M D Brtek, "The Nature and Outcomes of Work: A Replication and Extension of Interdisciplinary Work-Design Research," *Journal of Applied Psychology,* December 2000, pp 860–68.

[18] Supportive results can be found in S K Parker, "Longitudinal Effects of Lean Production on Employee Outcomes and the Mediating Role of Work Characteristics," *Journal of Applied Psychology,* August 2003, pp 620–34; and B Melin, U Lundberg, J Söderlund, and M Granqvist, "Psychological and Physiological Stress Reactions of Male and Female Assembly Workers: A Comparison between Two Different Forms of Work Organization," *Journal of Organizational Behavior,* January 1999, pp 47–61.

[19] See Edwards, Scully, and Brtek, "The Nature and Outcomes of Work: A Replication and Extension of Interdisciplinary Work-Design Research."

[20] This type of program was developed and tested by M A Campion and C L McClelland, "Follow-Up and Extension of the Interdisciplinary Costs and Benefits of Enlarged Jobs," *Journal of Applied Psychology,* June 1993, pp 339–51.

[21] Excerpted from R J Grossman, "Putting HR in Rotation," *HR Magazine,* March 2003, p 53.

[22] See F Herzberg, B Mausner, and B B Snyderman, *The Motivation to Work* (New York: John Wiley & Sons, 1959).

[23] Excerpted from M Conlin and A Bernstein, "Working . . . and Poor," *Business Week,* May 31, 2004, p 60.

[24] F Herzberg, "One More Time: How Do You Motivate Employees?" *Harvard Business Review,* January/February 1968, p 56.

[25] For a thorough review of research on Herzberg's theory, see C C Pinder, *Work Motivation: Theory, Issues, and Applications* (Glenview, IL: Scott, Foresman, 1984).

[26] J R Hackman, G R Oldham, R Janson, and K Purdy, "A New Strategy for Job Enrichment," *California Management Review,* Summer 1975, p 58.

[27] Definitions of the job characteristics were adapted from J R Hackman and G R Oldham, "Motivation through the Design of Work: Test of a Theory," *Organizational Behavior and Human Performance,* August 1976, pp 250–79.

[28] A review of this research can be found in M L Ambrose and C T Kulik, "Old Friends, New Faces: Motivation Research in the 1990s," *Journal of Management,* 1999, pp 231–92.

[29] For details see "The 100 Best Companies to Work For," *Fortune,* January 12, 2004, pp 61, 70.
[30] Results can be found in M R Kelley, "New Process Technology, Job Design, and Work Organization: A Contingency Model," *American Sociological Review,* April 1990, pp 191–208.
[31] Productivity studies are reviewed in R E Kopelman, *Managing Productivity in Organizations* (New York: McGraw-Hill, 1986).
[32] The turnover meta-analysis was conducted by R W Griffeth, P W Hom, and S Gaertner, "A Meta-Analysis of Antecedents and Correlates of Employee Turnover: Update, Moderator Tests, and Research Implications for the Next Millennium," *Journal of Management,* 2000, pp 463–88. Absenteeism results are discussed in Y Fried and G R Ferris, "The Validity of the Job Characteristics Model: A Review and Meta-Analysis," *Personnel Psychology,* Summer 1987, pp 287–322.
[33] See K Dobbs, "Knowing How to Keep Your Best and Brightest," *Workforce,* April 2001, pp 557–60.
[34] A thorough discussion of reengineering and associated outcomes can be found in J Champy, *Reengineering Management: The Mandate for New Leadership* (New York: Harper Business, 1995).
[35] See J D Jonge and W B Schaufeli, "Job Characteristics and Employee Well-Being: A Test of Warr's Vitamin Model in Health Care Workers Using Structural Equation Modelling," *Journal of Organizational Behavior,* July 1998, pp 387–407; and D C Ganster and D J Dwyer, "The Effects of Understaffing on Individual and Group Performance in Professional and Trade Occupations," *Journal of Management,* 1995, pp 175–90.
[36] This description was taken from Edwards, Scully, and Brtek, "The Nature and Outcomes of Work."
[37] S Armour, "Young Tech Workers Face Crippling Injuries," *USA Today,* February 9, 2001, p 2B.
[38] This description was taken from Edwards, Scully, and Brtek, "The Nature and Outcomes of Work."
[39] These descriptions were excerpted from J Prichard, "Reinventing the Office," *Arizona Republic,* January 16, 2002, p D1.
[40] Armour, "Young Tech Workers Face Crippling Injuries," p 2B.
[41] The guidelines are summarized in "How to Cope with the New Standard," *HR Focus,* January 2001, pp 1, 13, 14.
[42] The descriptions of employee engagement were taken from D Welch, "Mutual of Omaha's Healthy Preocupation with Talent," *Gallup Management Journal,* May 13, 2004, http://gmj.gallup.com/content/default.asp?ci=11608.
[43] See A Gopal, "Disengaged Employees Cost Singapore $4.9 Billion," *The Gallup Management Journal,* October 9, 2003, http://gmj.gallup.com/content/default.asp?ci=1207.
[44] The definition and discussion of intrinsic motivation were drawn from R M Ryan and E L Deci, "Intrinsic and Extrinsic Motivations: Classic Definitions and New Directions," *Contemporary Educational Psychology,* January 2000, pp 54–67.
[45] The definition and discussion of extrinsic motivation were drawn from ibid.
[46] See K W Thomas, E Jansen, and W G Tymon, Jr, "Navigating in the Realm of Theory: An Empowering View of Construct Development," in *Research in Organizational Change and Development,* vol. 10, eds W A Pasmore and R W Woodman (Greenwich, CT: JAI Press, 1997), pp 1–30.
[47] See E L Deci and R M Ryan, "The 'What' and 'Why' of Goal Pursuits: Human Needs and Self-Determination of Behavior," *Psychological Inquiry*. December 2000, pp 227–68.
[48] Thomas, *Intrinsic Motivation at Work,* p 44.
[49] Results are presented in J Barbian, "In the Battle to Attract Talent, Companies Are Finding New Ways to Keep Employees Smiling," *Training,* January 2001, pp 93–96.
[50] Thomas, *Intrinsic Motivation at Work,* p 44.
[51] See "The 100 Best Companies to Work For," p 78.
[52] Thomas, *Intrinsic Motivation at Work,* p 44.
[53] Thomas, *Intrinsic Motivation at Work,* p 44.
[54] Preliminary supportive results can be found in N W Van Yperen and M Hagedoorn, "Do High Job Demands Increase Intrinsic Motivation or Fatigue or Both? The Role of Job Control and Job Social Support," *Academy of Management Journal,* June 2003, pp 339–48; and F K Lee, K M Sheldon, and D B Turban, "Personality and the Goal-Striving Process: The Influence of Achievement Goal Patterns, Goal Level, and Mental Focus on Performance and Enjoyment," *Journal of Applied Psychology,* April 2003, pp 256–65.
[55] See the related discussion in A Fisher, "Turning Clock-Watchers Into Stars," *Fortune,* March 22, 2004, p 60.
[56] C Taylor, "On-the-Spot Incentives," *HR Magazine,* May 2004, p 82.
[57] Excerpted from S Nearman, "The Simple Billionaire," *Selling Power,* June 1999, p 48.
[58] For norms on this survey, see D J Weiss, R V Dawis, G W England, and L H Lofquist, *Manual for the Minnesota Satisfaction Questionnaire* (Minneapolis: Industrial Relations Center, University of Minnesota, 1967).
[59] Results are reported in M Boyle, "Happiness Index: Nothing Is Rotten in Denmark," *Fortune,* February 19, 2001, p 242.
[60] For a review of these models, see A P Brief, *Attitudes In and Around Organizations* (Thousand Oaks, CA: Sage Publications, 1998).
[61] See A R Karr, "Work Week: A Special News Report about Life on the Job—And Trends Taking Shape There," *The Wall Street Journal,* June 29, 1999, p A1.
[62] For a review of need satisfaction models, see E F Stone, "A Critical Analysis of Social Information Processing Models of Job Perceptions and Job Attitudes," in *Job Satisfaction: How People Feel about Their Jobs and How It Affects Their Performance,* eds C J Cranny, P Cain Smith, and E F Stone (New York: Lexington Books, 1992), pp 21–52.
[63] See J P Wanous, T D Poland, S L Premack, and K S Davis, "The Effects of Met Expectations on Newcomer Attitudes and Behaviors: A Review and Meta-Analysis," *Journal of Applied Psychology,* June 1992, pp 288–97.
[64] A complete description of this model is provided by E A Locke, "Job Satisfaction," in *Social Psychology and Organizational Behavior,* eds M Gruneberg and T Wall (New York: John Wiley & Sons, 1984).
[65] For a test of the value fulfillment value, see W A Hochwarter, P L Perrewe, G R Ferris, and R A Brymer, "Job Satisfaction and Performance: The Moderating Effects of Value Attainment and Affective Disposition," *Journal of Vocational Behavior,* April 1999, pp 296–313.
[66] Results can be found in J Cohen-Charash and P E Spector, "The Role of Justice in Organizations: A Meta-Analysis." *Organizational Behavior and Human Decision Processes,* November 2001, pp 278–321.
[67] A thorough discussion of this model is provided by C L Hulin, and T A Judge, "Job Attitudes," in *Handbook of Psychology* (Vol 12), eds W C Borman, D R Ilgen, and R J Klimoski (Hoboken, NJ: John Wiley & Sons, Inc., 2003), pp 255–76.
[68] Supportive results can be found in R Ilies and T A Judge, "On the Heritability of Job Satisfaction: The Mediating Role of Personality," *Journal of Applied Psychology,* August 2003, pp 750–59; and B M Staw and J Ross, "Stability in the Midst of Change: A Dispositional Approach to Job Attitudes," *Journal of Applied Psychology,* August 1985, pp 69–80.
[69] See R D Arvey, T J Bouchard, Jr, N L Segal, and L M Abraham, "Job Satisfaction: Environmental and Genetic Components," *Journal of Applied Psychology,* April 1989, pp 187–92.
[70] See C Dormann and D Zapf, "Job Satisfaction: A Meta-Analysis of Stabilities," *Journal of Organizational Behavior,* August 2001, pp 483–504.
[71] Results can be found in A J Kinicki, F M McKee-Ryan, C A Schriesheim, and K P Carson, "Assessing the Construct Validity of the Job Descriptive Index (JDI): A Review and Analysis," *Journal of Applied Psychology,* February 2002, pp 14–32.
[72] See S P Brown, "A Meta-Analysis and Review of Organizational Research on Job Involvement," *Psychological Bulletin,* September 1996, pp 235–55.
[73] D W Organ, "The Motivational Basis of Organizational Citizenship Behavior," in *Research in Organizational Behavior,* eds B M Staw and L L Cummings (Greenwich, CT: JAI Press, 1990), p 46.
[74] Results can be found in J A LePine, A Erez, and D E Johnson, "The Nature and Dimensionality of Organizational Citizenship Behavior: A Critical Review and Meta-Analysis," *Journal of Applied Psychology,* February 2002, pp 52–65.
[75] Supportive results can be found in P M Podsakoff, S B MacKenzie, J B Paine, and D G Bachrach, "Organizational Citizenship Behaviors: A Critical Review of the Theoretical and Empirical Literature and Suggestions for Future Research," *Journal of Management,* 2000, pp 513–63.

[76] Supportive findings are presented in ibid; and LePine, Erez, and Johnson, "The Nature and Dimensionality of Organizational Citizenship Behavior."
[77] Results can be found in D J Koys, "The Effects of Employee Satisfaction, Organizational Citizenship Behavior, and Turnover on Organizational Effectiveness: A Unit-Level, Longitudinal Study," *Personnel Psychology,* Spring 2001, pp 101–14.
[78] See R P Tett and J P Meyer, "Job Satisfaction, Organizational Commitment, Turnover Intention, and Turnover: Path Analysis Based on Meta-Analytic Findings," *Personnel Psychology,* Summer 1993, pp 259–93.
[79] See R D Hackett, "Work Attitudes and Employee Absenteeism: A Synthesis of the Literature," *Journal of Occupational Psychology,* 1989, pp 235–48.
[80] The results can be found in R W Griffeth, P W Hom, and S Gaertner, "A Meta-Analysis of Antecedents and Correlates of Employee Turnover: Update, Moderator Tests, and Research Implications for the Next Millennium," *Journal of Management,* 2000, pp 463–88.
[81] See P W Hom and R W Griffeth, *Employee Turnover* (Cincinnati, OH: SouthWestern, 1995), pp 35–50; and C Kalb and A Rogers, "Stress," *Newsweek,* June 14, 1999, pp 56–63.
[82] Results can be found in M A Blegen, "Nurses' Job Satisfaction: A Meta-Analysis of Related Variables," *Nursing Research,* January/February 1993, pp 36–41.
[83] The various models are discussed in T A Judge, C J Thoresen, J E Bono, and G K Patton, "The Job Satisfaction–Job Performance Relationship: A Qualitative and Quantitative Review," *Psychological Bulletin,* May 2001, pp 376–407.
[84] Results can be found in ibid.
[85] One example is provided by D J Schleicher, J D Watt, and G J Greguras, "Reexamining the Job Satisfaction–Performance Relationship: The Complexity of Attitudes," *Journal of Applied Psychology,* February 2004, pp 165–77.
[86] These issues are discussed by C Ostroff, "The Relationship between Satisfaction, Attitudes, and Performance: An Organizational Level Analysis," *Journal of Applied Psychology,* December 1992, pp 963–74.
[87] Results can be found in J K Harter, F L Schmidt, and T L Hayes, "Business-Unit-Level Relationship between Employee Satisfaction, Employee Engagement, and Business Outcomes: A Meta-Analysis," *Journal of Applied Psychology,* April 2002, pp 268–79.
[88] For a thorough discussion, see J R Edwards and N P Rothbard, "Mechanisms Linking Work and Family: Clarifying the Relationship between Work and Family Constructs," *Academy of Management Review,* January 2000, pp 178–99; and S C Clark, "Work/Family Border Theory: A New Theory of Work/Family Balance," *Human Relations,* 2000, pp 747–70.
[89] The meta-analysis was conducted by M Tait, M Y Padgett, and T T Baldwin, "Job and Life Satisfaction: A Reevaluation of the Strength of the Relationship and Gender Effects as a Function of the Date of the Study," *Journal of Applied Psychology,* June 1989, pp 502–7.
[90] C Hymowitz, "In the Lead: More Managers Allow Workers to Multitask as Jobs and Home Blur," *The Wall Street Journal,* October 28, 2003, p B1.
[91] See B R Baltes, H A Heddens-Gahir, "Reduction of Work–Family Conflict through the Use of Selection, Optimization, and Compensation Behaviors," *Journal of Applied Psychology,* December 2003, pp 1005–18.
[92] See A Geller, "Worker Flexibility Takes a Hit," *Arizona Republic,* November 3, 2003, pp D1, D4.
[93] R Rapoport, L Bailyn, J K Fletcher, and B H Pruitt, *Beyond Work–Family Balance: Advancing Gender Equity and Workplace Performance* (San Francisco: Jossey-Bass, 2002), p 36.

Chapter 7

[1] Excerpted from J Sandberg, "Counting Pizza Slices, Cutting Water Cups—You Call This a Budget?" *The Wall Street Journal,* Eastern Edition, January 21, 2004, p B1. Copyright 2004 by Dow Jones & Co. Inc. Reproduced with permission of Dow Jones & Co. Inc. via Copyright Clearance Center.
[2] See L Festinger, *A Theory of Cognitive Dissonance* (Stanford, CA: Stanford University Press, 1957).
[3] See S A Feeney, "The High Cost of Employee Violence," *Workforce Management,* August 2003, pp 23–24; and B P Niehoff and R J Paul, "Causes of Employee Theft and Strategies That HR Managers Can Use for Prevention," *Human Resource Management,* Spring 2000, pp 51–64.
[4] Inputs and outputs are discussed by J S Adams, "Toward an Understanding of Inequity," *Journal of Abnormal and Social Psychology,* November 1963, pp 422–36.
[5] The generalizability of the equity norm was examined by L K Scheer, N A Kumar, J-B E M Steenkamp, "Reactions to Perceived Inequity in U.S. and Dutch Interorganizational Relationships," *Academy of Management Journal,* June 2003, pp 303–16.
[6] The choice of a comparison person is discussed by E E Umphress, G Labianca, D J Brass, E Kass, and L Scholten, "The Role of Instrumental and Expressive Social Ties in Employees' Perceptions of Organizational Justice," *Organization Science,* November–December 2003, pp 738–53.
[7] CEO salaries are discussed by L Lavelle, F F Jespersen, S Ante, and J Kerstetter, "Executive Pay," *Business Week,* April 21, 2003, pp 86–90.
[8] M N Bing and S M Burroughs, "The Predictive and Interactive Effects of Equity Sensitivity in Teamwork-Oriented Organizations," *Journal of Organizational Behavior,* May 2001, p 271.
[9] Types of equity sensitivity are discussed by ibid., pp 271–90; and K S Sauley and A G Bedeian, "Equity Sensitivity: Construction of a Measure and Examination of Its Psychometric Properties," *Journal of Management,* 2000, pp 885–910.
[10] For a thorough review of organizational justice theory and research, see R Cropanzano, D E Rupp, C J Mohler, and M Schminke, "Three Roads to Organizational Justice," in *Research in Personnel and Human Resources Management* vol. 20, eds G R Ferris (New York: JAI Press, 2001), pp 269–329.
[11] J A Colquitt, D E Conlon, M J Wesson, C O L H Porter, and K Y Ng, "Justice at the Millennium: A Meta-Analytic Review of 25 Years of Organizational Justice Research," *Journal of Applied Psychology,* June 2001, p 426.
[12] E Tahmincioglu, "Electronic Workplace Vulnerable to Revenge," *Arizona Republic,* August 6, 2001, p D1.
[13] Supportive results can be found in M Ambrose and R Cropanzano, "A Longitudinal Analysis of Organizational Fairness: An Examination of Reactions to Tenure and Promotion Decisions," *Journal of Applied Psychology,* April 2003, pp 266–75; S J Farmer, T A Beehr, and K G Love, "Becoming an Undercover Police Officer: A Note on Fairness Perceptions, Behavior, and Attitudes," *Journal of Organizational Behavior,* June 2003, pp 373–87; and B J Tepper and E C Taylor, "Relationship among Supervisors' and Subordinates' Procedural Justice Perceptions and Organizational Citizenship Behaviors," *Academy of Management Journal,* February 2003, pp 97–105.
[14] See C R Wanberg, L W Bunce, and M B Gavin, "Perceived Fairness of Layoffs among Individuals Who Have Been Laid Off: A Longitudinal Study," *Personnel Psychology,* Spring 1999, pp 59–84.
[15] See Korsgaard, Roberson, and Rymph, "What Motivates Fairness? The Role of Subordinate Assertive Behavior on Managers' Interactional Fairness."
[16] The role of equity in organizational change is thoroughly discussed by A T Cobb, R Folger, and K Wooten, "The Role Justice Plays in Organizational Change," *Public Administration Quarterly,* Summer 1995, pp 135–51.
[17] Group level effects of justice were examined by S E Naumann and N Bennett, "A Case for Procedural Justice Climate: Development and Test of a Multilevel Model," *Academy of Management Journal,* October 2000, pp 881–89.
[18] See W R Boswell and J B Olson-Buchanan, "Experiencing Mistreatment at Work: the Role of Grievance Filing, Nature of Mistreatment, and Employee Withdrawal," *Academy of Management Journal,* February 2004, pp 129–39.
[19] Results can be found in M G Ehrhart, "Leadership and Procedural Justice Climate as Antecedents of Unit-Level Organizational Citizenship Behavior," *Personnel Psychology,* Spring 2004, pp 61–94.
[20] The relationship between organizational justice and customer service is investigated by T Simons and Q Roberson, "Why Managers Should Care about Fairness: The Effects of Aggregate Justice Perceptions on Organizational Outcomes," *Journal of Applied Psychology,* June 2003, pp 432–43.

[21] For a complete discussion of Vroom's theory, see V H Vroom, *Work and Motivation* (New York: John Wiley & Sons, 1964).
[22] See J Chowdhury, "The Motivational Impact of Sales Quotas on Effort," *Journal of Marketing Research,* February 1993, pp 28–41; and C C Pinder, *Work Motivation* (Glenview, IL: Scott, Foresman, 1984), ch 7.
[23] Excerpted from L Lavelle and D Brady, "The Gravy Train May Be Drying Up," *Business Week,* April 5, 2004, pp 52–53.
[24] The measurement and importance of valence was investigated by N T Feather, "Values, Valences, and Choice: The Influence of Values on the Perceived Attractiveness and Choice of Alternatives," *Journal of Personality and Social Psychology,* June 1995, pp 1135–51.
[25] Excerpted from "Federal Express's Fred Smith," *Inc.,* October 1986, p 38.
[26] Results can be found in W van Eerde and H Thierry, "Vroom's Expectancy Models and Work-Related Criteria: A Meta-Analysis," *Journal of Applied Psychology,* October 1996, pp 575–86.
[27] See J P Wanous, T L Keon, and J C Latack, "Expectancy Theory and Occupational/Organizational Choices: A Review and Test," *Organizational Behavior and Human Performance,* August 1983, pp 66–86.
[28] See the discussion in T R Mitchell and D Daniels, "Motivation," in *Handbook of Psychology,* vol. 12, eds W C Borman, D R Ilgen, and R J Klimoski (Hoboken, NJ: John Wiley & Sons, Inc., 2003), pp 225–54.
[29] Supportive results are presented in L Morris, "Employees Not Encouraged to Go Extra Mile," *Training & Development,* April 1996, pp 59–60.
[30] See D R Spitzer, "Power Rewards: Rewards That Really Motivate," *Management Review,* May 1996, pp 45–50; and A Kohn, *Punished by Rewards: The Trouble with Gold Stars, Incentive Plans, A's, Praise, and Other Bribes* (Boston: Houghton Mifflin, 1993).
[31] Result can be found in G D Jenkins, Jr, A Mitra, N Gupta, and J D Shaw, "Are Financial Incentives Related to Performance? A Meta-Analytic Review of Empirical Research," *Journal of Applied Psychology,* October 1998, pp 777–87.
[32] See S Bates, "Top Pay for Best Performance," *HR Magazine,* January 2003, pp 31–38.
[33] Details of this program can be found in S Bates, "Goalsharing at Corning," *HR Magazine,* January 2003, p 33.
[34] Excerpted from E Tahmincioglu, "Gifts That Gall," *Workforce Management,* April 2004, p 44.
[35] R Charan, "Conquering a Culture of Indecision," *Harvard Business Review,* April 2001, pp 75–82.
[36] Bates, "Top Pay for Best Performance," p 36.
[37] E A Locke, K N Shaw, L M Saari, and G P Latham, "Goal Setting and Task Performance: 1969–1980," *Psychological Bulletin,* July 1981, p 126.
[38] Results from both studies can be found in R Rodgers and J E Hunter, "Impact of Management by Objectives on Organizational Productivity," *Journal of Applied Psychology,* April 1991, pp 322–36; and R Rodgers, J E Hunter, and D L Rogers, "Influence of Top Management Commitment on Management Program Success," *Journal of Applied Psychology,* February 1993, pp 151–55.
[39] The following discussion is based on E A Locke and G P Latham, "Building a Practically Useful Theory of Goal Setting and Task Motivation," *American Psychologist,* September 2002, pp 705–17.
[40] See "100 Best Companies to Work For," *Fortune,* January 12, 2004, p 70.
[41] Annika Sorenstam's biography can be found at www.lpga.com/player-career.aspx?id=29, last updated May 2004.
[42] J Davis, "For Now, Sorenstam Feels She Still Has Peaks to Scale," *Arizona Republic,* March 18, 2004, p C14.
[43] Excerpted from "Empire Builders," *Business Week,* May 14, 2001, p EB 28.
[44] Results can be found in P M Wright, "Operationalization of Goal Difficulty as a Moderator of the Goal Difficulty–Performance Relationship," *Journal of Applied Psychology,* June 1990, pp 227–34.
[45] See Locke, Shaw, Saari, and Latham, "Goal Setting and Task Performance: 1969–1980"; and A J Mento, R P Steel, and R J Karren, "A Meta-Analytic Study of the Effects of Goal Setting on Task Performance: 1966–1984," *Organizational Behavior and Human Decision Processes,* February 1987, pp 52–83.
[46] Results from the meta-analysis can be found in R E Wood, A J Mento, and E A Locke, "Task Complexity as a Moderator of Goal Effects: A Meta-Analysis," *Journal of Applied Psychology,* August 1987, pp 416–25.
[47] See Locke and Latham, "Building a Practically Useful Theory of Goal Setting and Task Motivation."
[48] See R P DeShon and R A Alexander, "Goal Setting Effects on Implicit and Explicit Learning of Complex Tasks," *Organizational Behavior and Human Decision Processes,* January 1996, pp 18–36.
[49] Supportive results can be found in K L Langeland, C M Johnson, and T C Mawhinney, "Improving Staff Performance in a Community Mental Health Setting: Job Analysis, Training, Goal Setting, Feedback, and Years of Data," *Journal of Organizational Behavior Management,* 1998, pp 21–43; and L A Wilk, "The Effects of Feedback and Goal Setting on the Productivity and Satisfaction of University Admissions Staff," *Journal of Organizational Behavior Management,* 1998, pp 45–68.
[50] See Locke and Latham, "Building a Practically Useful Theory of Goal Setting and Task Motivation."
[51] See Ibid.
[52] See J J Donovan and D J Radosevich, "The Moderating Role of Goal Commitment on the Goal Difficulty-Performance Relationship: A Meta-Analytic Review and Critical Reanalysis," *Journal of Applied Psychology,* April 1998, pp 308–15.
[53] See the related discussion in T P Flannery, D A Hofrichter, and P E Platten, *People, Performance, & Pay* (New York: The Free Press, 1996).
[54] See F M Moussa, "Determinants, Process, and Consequences of Personal Goals and Performance," *Journal of Management,* 2000, pp 1259–85; and P M Wright, J M George, S R Farnsworth, and G C McMahan, "Productivity and Extra-Role Behavior: The Effects of Goals and Incentives on Spontaneous Helping," *Journal of Applied Psychology,* June 1993, pp 374–81.
[55] See J A Colquitt and M J Simmering, "Conscientiousness, Goal Orientation, and Motivation to Learn during the Learning Process: A Longitudinal Study," *Journal of Applied Psychology,* August 1998, pp 654–65.
[56] D VandeWalle, S P Brown, W L Cron, and J W Slocum, Jr, "The Influence of Goal Orientation and Self-Regulated Tactics on Sales Performance: A Longitudinal Field Test," *Journal of Applied Psychology,* April 1999, p 250.
[57] See G B Yeo and A Neal, "A Multilevel Analysis of Effort, Practice, and Performance: Effects of Ability, Conscientiousness, and Goal Orientation," *Journal of Applied Psychology,* April 2004, pp 231–47.
[58] Results can be found in D Steele-Johnson, R S Beauregard, P B Hoover, and A M Schmidt, "Goal Orientation and Task Demand Effects on Motivation, Affect, and Performance," *Journal of Applied Psychology,* October 2000, pp 724–38.
[59] E A Locke and G P Latham, *Goal Setting: A Motivational Technique That Works!* (Englewood Cliffs, NJ: Prentice Hall, 1984), p 79.
[60] T R Mitchell, "Motivation: New Directions for Theory, Research, and Practice," *Academy of Management Review,* January 1982, p 81.
[61] Excerpted from C Hymowitz, "Ranking Systems Gain Popularity but Have Many Staffers Riled," *The Wall Street Journal,* May 15, 2001, p B1.
[62] See D J Burrough, "More Firms Rank Employees," *Arizona Republic,* May 20, 2001, p EC1.
[63] "HMO Clerks Who Pare Doctor Visits Rewarded," *Arizona Republic,* May 18, 2002, p A10.
[64] See I Appleby, "HMO to Pay Bonuses for Good Care," *USA Today,* July 11, 2001, p 3B.
[65] See the related discussion in D Cadrain, "Put Success in Sight," *HR Magazine,* May 2003, pp 85–92.
[66] Excerpted from C Bellamy, "Teacher Resigns as School Backs Plagiarizing Kids," *Arizona Republic,* February 10, 2002, p A21.

Chapter 8

[1] From L Buchanan, "For Knowing the Power of Respect," *Inc. Magazine,* April 2004, p 143. Copyright © 2004 Gruner & Jahr USA Publishing. All rights reserved.
[2] Data from S Bates, "Performance Appraisals: Some Improvement Needed," *HR Magazine,* April 2003, p 12.

[3] For example, see "Views Differ on Performance Reviews," *USA Today,* September 10, 2003, p 1B.
[4] As quoted in C Fishman, "Fred Smith," *Fast Company,* June 2001, pp 64, 66.
[5] Data from M Hequet, "Giving Feedback," *Training,* September 1994, pp 72–77.
[6] C Bell and R Zemke, "On-Target Feedback," *Training,* June 1992, p 36.
[7] Both the definition of feedback and the functions of feedback are based on discussion in D R Ilgen, C D Fisher, and M S Taylor, "Consequences of Individual Feedback on Behavior in Organizations," *Journal of Applied Psychology,* August 1979, pp 349–71; and R E Kopelman, *Managing Productivity in Organizations: A Practical People-Oriented Perspective* (New York: McGraw-Hill, 1986), p 175. Also see S E Moss and J I Sanchez, "Are Your Employees Avoiding You? Managerial Strategies for Closing the Feedback Gap," *Academy of Management Executive,* February 2004, pp 32–44; and M Goldsmith, "Leave It at the Stream," *Fast Company,* May 2004, p 103.
[8] See P C Earley, G B Northcraft, C Lee, and T R Lituchy, "Impact of Process and Outcome Feedback on the Relation of Goal Setting to Task Performance," *Academy of Management Journal,* March 1990, pp 87–105. Also see D Rohn, J Austin, and S M Lutrey, "Using Feedback and Performance Accountability to Decrease Cash Register Shortages," *Journal of Organizational Behavior Management,* no 1, 2002, pp 33–46.
[9] For relevant research, see J S Goodman, "The Interactive Effects of Task and External Feedback on Practice Performance and Learning," *Organizational Behavior and Human Decision Processes,* December 1998, pp 223–52.
[10] See J M Jackman and M H Strober, "Fear of Feedback," *Harvard Business Review,* April 2003, pp 101–7.
[11] See B D Bannister, "Performance Outcome Feedback and Attributional Feedback: Interactive Effects on Recipient Responses," *Journal of Applied Psychology,* May 1986, pp 203–10.
[12] For complete details, see P M Podsakoff and J-L Farh, "Effects of Feedback Sign and Credibility on Goal Setting and Task Performance," *Organizational Behavior and Human Decision Processes,* August 1989, pp 45–67. Also see S J Ashford and A S Tsui, "Self-Regulation for Managerial Effectiveness: The Role of Active Feedback Seeking," *Academy of Management Journal,* June 1991, pp 251–80.
[13] See "How to Take the Venom Out of Vitriol," *Training,* June 2000, p 28.
[14] W S Silver, T R Mitchell, and M E Gist, "Responses to Successful and Unsuccessful Performance: The Moderating Effect of Self-Efficacy on the Relationship between Performance and Attributions," *Organizational Behavior and Human Decision Processes,* June 1995, p 297. Also see T A Louie, "Decision Makers' Hindsight Bias after Receiving Favorable and Unfavorable Feedback," *Journal of Applied Psychology,* February 1999, pp 29–41.
[15] See T J DeLong and V Vijayaraghavan, "Let's Hear It for B Players," *Harvard Business Review,* June 2003, pp 96–102.
[16] See D A Waldman, "Does Working with an Executive Coach Enhance the Value of Multisource Performance Feedback?" *Academy of Management Executive,* August 2003, pp 146–48.
[17] See M R Edwards, A J Ewen, and W A Verdini, "Fair Performance Management and Pay Practices for Diverse Work Forces: The Promise of Multisource Assessment," *ACA Journal,* Spring 1995, pp 50–63.
[18] See G D Huet-Cox, T M Nielsen, and E Sundstrom, "Get the Most from 360-Degree Feedback: Put It on the Internet," *HR Magazine,* May 1999, pp 92–103.
[19] This list is based in part on discussion in H J Bernardin, "Subordinate Appraisal: A Valuable Source of Information about Managers," *Human Resource Management,* Fall 1986, pp 421–39.
[20] For a complete list, see "Companies Where Employees Rate Executives," *Fortune,* December 27, 1993, p 128. Also see J A Byrne, "Do You Make the Grade?" *Fast Company,* May 2004, p 101.
[21] Data from D Antonioni, "The Effects of Feedback Accountability on Upward Appraisal Ratings," *Personnel Psychology,* Summer 1994, pp 349–56.
[22] See L Atwater, P Roush, and A Fischthal, "The Influence of Upward Feedback on Self- and Follower Ratings of Leadership," *Personnel Psychology,* Spring 1995, pp 35–59.
[23] Data from J W Smither, M London, N L Vasilopoulos, R R Reilly, R E Millsap, and N Salvemini, "An Examination of the Effects of an Upward Feedback Program over Time," *Personnel Psychology,* Spring 1995, pp 1–34.
[24] C Hymowitz, "Managers See Feedback from Their Staffers as the Most Valuable," *The Wall Street Journal,* November 11, 2003, p. B1. Other recent 360-degree feedback examples may be found in A Jung, "Seek Frank Feedback," *Harvard Business Review,* Special Issue: Inside the Mind of the Leader, January 2004, pp 31–32; the first question-and-answer pairing in "Ask *Inc.:* Do I Deserve a Raise?" *Inc.,* February 2004, p 38; "Best Practices: Executive Coaching; Wachovia," *Training,* March 2004, p 61; and M Goldsmith, "To Help Others Develop, Start with Yourself," *Fast Company,* March 2004, p 100.
[25] Data from J L Seglin, "Reviewing Your Boss," *Fortune,* June 11, 2001, p 248. For a comprehensive overview of 360-degree feedback, see W W Tornow and M London, *Maximizing the Value of 360-Degree Feedback* (San Francisco: Jossey-Bass, 1998). Also see G Toegel and J A Conger, "360-Degree Assessment: Time for Reinvention," *Academy of Management Learning and Education,* September 2003, pp 297–311.
[26] See S Haworth, "The Dark Side of Multi-Rater Assessments," *HR Magazine,* May 1998, pp 106–14; and D A Waldman, L E Atwater, and D Antonioni, "Has 360 Degree Feedback Gone Amok?" *Academy of Management Executive,* May 1998, pp 86–94.
[27] See M M Harris and J Schaubroeck, "A Meta-Analysis of Self-Supervisor, Self-Peer, and Peer-Supervisor Ratings," *Personnel Psychology,* Spring 1988, pp 43–62; and J Lane and P Herriot, "Self-Ratings, Supervisor Ratings, Positions and Performance," *Journal of Occupational Psychology,* March 1990, pp 77–88.
[28] Fisher Hazucha, S A Hezlett, and R J Schneider, "The Impact of 360-Degree Feedback on Managerial Skills Development," *Human Resource Management,* Summer/Fall 1993, p 42. Also see M K Mount, T A Judge, S E Scullen, M R Sytsma, and S A Hezlett, "Trait, Rater and Level Effects in 360-Degree Performance Ratings," *Personnel Psychology,* Autumn 1998, pp 557–76.
[29] F Luthans and S J Peterson, "360-Degree Feedback with Systematic Coaching: Empirical Analysis Suggests a Winning Combination," *Human Resource Management,* Fall 2003, p 243.
[30] See D E Coates, "Don't Tie 360 Feedback to Pay," *Training,* September 1998, pp 68–78.
[31] Adapted from C Bell and R Zemke, "On-Target Feedback," *Training,* June 1992, pp 36–44. A model feedback program at Saint Luke's Hospital of Kansas City is presented in D Jones, "Baldrige Award Honors Record 7 Quality Winners," *USA Today,* November 26, 2003, p 6B. Tips on giving feedback can be found in S Godin, "How to Give Feedback," *Fast Company,* March 2004, p 103.
[32] See R S Allen and R H Kilmann, "Aligning Reward Practices in Support of Total Quality Management," *Business Horizons,* May–June 2001, pp 77–84; and T R Mitchell, B C Holtom, and T W Lee, "How to Keep Your Best Employees: Developing an Effective Retention Policy," *Academy of Management Executive,* November 2001, pp 96–108.
[33] See M Schrage, "Actually, I'd Rather Have That Favor Than a Raise," *Fortune,* April 16, 2001, p 412, and A Etzioni, "The Good Society: Goals Beyond Money," *The Futurist,* July–August 2001, pp 68–66.
[34] For example, see B Nelson, *1001 Ways to Reward Employees* (New York: Workman Publishing, 1994). For more on stock options, see J Pfeffer, "Do Options Really Motivate?" *Business 2.0,* March 2003, p 66; A Sloan, "Running Out of Options," *Newsweek,* July 21, 2003, pp 40–42; and C Taylor, "Out of Options," *HR Magazine,* August 2003, pp 48–52.
[35] W J Wiatrowski, "Family-Related Benefits in the Workplace," *Monthly Labor Review,* March 1990, p 28. Also see J A Byrne, "How to Lead Now: Getting Extraordinary Performance When You Can't Pay for It," *Fast Company,* August 2003, pp 62–70; and S J Wells, "Merging Compensation Strategies," *HR Magazine,* May 2004, pp 66–78.
[36] For complete discussions, see A P Brief and R J Aldag, "The Intrinsic-Extrinsic Dichotomy: Toward Conceptual Clarity," *Academy of Management Review,* July 1977, pp 496–500; E L Deci, *Intrinsic Motivation* (New York: Plenum Press, 1975), ch 2; and E L Deci, R Koestner, and R M Ryan, "A Meta-Analytic Review of Experiments Examining the Effects of Extrinsic Rewards on Intrinsic Motivation," *Psychological Bulletin,* November 1999, pp 627–68.

[37] See K I Kim, H-J Park, and N Suzuki, "Reward Allocations in the United States, Japan, and Korea: A Comparison of Individualistic and Collectivistic Cultures," *Academy of Management Journal,* March 1990, pp 188–98. Also see C C Chen, J R Meindl, and H Hui, "Deciding on Equity or Parity: A Test of Situational, Cultural, and Individual Factors," *Journal of Organizational Behavior,* March 1998, pp 115–29.
[38] For more on this important issue, see L D Tyson, "New Clues to the Pay and Leadership Gap," *Business Week,* October 27, 2003, p 36; S Holmes, "A New Black Eye for Boeing?" *Business Week,* April 26, 2004 pp 90, 92; K Robinson, "For Working Women, Job Equality Elusive," *HR Magazine,* May 2004, p 36; and E Brown, "How to Get Paid What You're Worth," *Business 2.0,* May 2004, pp 102–10.
[39] Based on M Bloom, "The Performance Effects of Pay Dispersion on Individuals and Organizations," *Academy of Management Journal,* February 1999, pp 25–40.
[40] See J Useem, "Have They No Shame?" *Fortune,* April 28, 2003, pp 56–64; E Iwata and B Hansen, "Pay, Performance Don't Always Add Up," *USA Today,* April 30, 2004, pp 1B, 3B; and M Boyle, "When Will They Stop?" *Fortune,* May 3, 2004, pp 123–28.
[41] List adapted from J L Pearce and R H Peters, "A Contradictory Norms View of Employer–Employee Exchange," *Journal of Management,* Spring 1985, pp 19–30.
[42] Ibid., p 25.
[43] M Von Glinow, "Reward Strategies for Attracting, Evaluating, and Retaining Professionals," *Human Resource Management,* Summer 1985, p 193.
[44] A Markels and J S Lublin, "Longevity-Reward Programs Get Short Shrift," *The Wall Street Journal,* April 27, 1995, p B1.
[45] Six reward system objectives are discussed in E E Lawler III, "The New Pay: A Strategic Approach," *Compensation & Benefits Review,* July–August 1995, pp 14–22.
[46] See D Cadrain, "Put Success in Sight," *HR Magazine,* May 2003, pp 84–92; J Kiska, "Customer Satisfaction Pays Off," *HR Magazine,* February 2004, 87–93; and C Taylor, "On-the-Spot Incentives," *HR Magazine,* May 2004, pp 80–84.
[47] For both sides of the "Does money motivate?" debate, see N Gupta and J D Shaw, "Let the Evidence Speak: Financial Incentives *Are* Effective!!" *Compensation & Benefits Review,* March–April 1998, pp 26, 28–32; A Kohn, "Challenging Behaviorist Dogma: Myths about Money and Motivation," *Compensation & Benefits Review;* March–April 1998, pp 27, 33–37; and B Ettorre, "Is Salary a Motivator?" *Management Review,* January 1999, p 8. Also see W J Duncan, "Stock Ownership and Work Motivation," *Organizational Dynamics,* Summer 2001, pp 1–11; and J Pfeffer, "Sins of Commission," *Business 2.0,* May 2004, p 56.
[48] Data from D Kiley, "Crafty Basket Makers Cut Downtime, Waste," *USA Today,* May 10, 2001, p 3B.
[49] Data from N J Perry, "Here Come Richer, Riskier Pay Plans," *Fortune,* December 19, 1998, p 51. Also see W Zellner, "Trickle-Down Is Trickling Down at Work," *Business Week,* March 18, 1996, p 34.
[50] Data from M Bloom and G T Milkovich, "Relationships among Risk, Incentive Pay, and Organizational Performance," *Academy of Management Journal,* June 1998, pp 283–97.
[51] For details, see G D Jenkins, Jr, N Gupta, A Mitra, and J D Shaw, "Are Financial Incentives Related to Performance? A Meta-Analytic Review of Empirical Research," *Journal of Applied Psychology,* October 1998, pp 777–87.
[52] See M J Mandel, "Those Fat Bonuses Don't Seem to Boost Performance," *Business Week.* January 8, 1990, p 26.
[53] Based on discussion in R Ricklefs, "Whither the Payoff on Sales Commissions?" *The Wall Street Journal,* June 6, 1990, p BI.
[54] G Koretz, "Bad Marks for Pay-by-Results," *Business Week,* September 4, 1995, p 28. Also see S Bates, "Now, the Downside of Pay for Performance," *HR Magazine,* March 2002, p 10; and M C Sturman, C O Trevor, J W Boudreau, and B Gerhart, "Is It Worth It to Win the Talent War? Evaluating the Utility of Performance-Based Pay," *Personnel Psychology,* Winter 2003, pp 997–1035.
[55] D R Spitzer, "Power Rewards: Rewards That Really Motivate," *Management Review,* May 1996, p 47. Also see S Kerr, "An Academy Classic: On the Folly of Rewarding A, while Hoping for B," *Academy of Management Executive,* February 1995, pp 7–14.
[56] List adapted from discussion in Spitzer, "Power Rewards: Rewards That Really Motivate," pp 45–50. Also see R Eisenberger and J Cameron, "Detrimental Effects of Reward: Reality or Myth?" *American Psychologist,* November 1996, pp 1153–66; and "What Has Undermined Your Trust in Companies?" *USA Today,* February 10, 2004, p 1B.
[57] See, for example, S Holmes and W Zellner, "The Costco Way," *Business Week,* April 12, 2004, pp 76–77.
[58] For a recent unconventional perspective, see R J DeGrandpre, "A Science of Meaning? Can Behaviorism Bring Meaning to Psychological Science?" *American Psychologist,* July 2000, pp 721–38.
[59] See E L Thorndike, *Educational Psychology: The Psychology of Learning, Vol. II* (New York: Columbia University Teachers College, 1913).
[60] Discussion of an early behaviorist who influenced Skinner's work can be found in P J Kreshel, "John B Watson at J Walter Thompson: The Legitimation of 'Science' in Advertising," *Journal of Advertising,* no. 2, 1990, pp 49–59. Recent discussions involving behaviorism include M R Ruiz, "B F Skinner's Radical Behaviorism: Historical Misconstructions and Grounds for Feminist Reconstructions," *Psychology of Women Quarterly,* June 1995, pp 161–79; J A Nevin, "Behavioral Economics and Behavioral Momentum," *Journal of the Experimental Analysis of Behavior,* November 1995, pp 385–95; and H Rachlin, "Can We Leave Cognition to Cognitive Psychologists? Comments on an Article by George Loewenstein," *Organizational Behavior and Human Decision Processes,* March 1996, pp 296–99.
[61] For more recent discussion, see J W Donahoe, "The Unconventional Wisdom of B F Skinner: The Analysis-Interpretation Distinction," *Journal of the Experimental Analysis of Behavior,* September 1993, pp 453–56.
[62] See B F Skinner, *The Behavior of Organisms* (New York: Appleton-Century-Crofts, 1938).
[63] For modern approaches to respondent behavior, see B Azar, "Classical Conditioning Could Link Disorders and Brain Dysfunction, Researchers Suggest," *APA Monitor,* March 1999, p 17.
[64] For interesting discussions of Skinner and one of his students, see M B Gilbert and T F Gilbert, "What Skinner Gave Us," *Training,* September 1991, pp 42–48; and "HRD Pioneer Gilbert Leaves a Pervasive Legacy," *Training,* January 1996, p 14.
[65] See F Luthans and R Kreitner, *Organizational Behavior Modification and Beyond: An Operant and Social Learning Approach* (Glenview, IL: Scott, Foresman, 1985), pp 49–56.
[66] See K Blanchard and S Johnson, *The One Minute Manager* (New York: Berkley Books, 1981); and K Blanchard and R Lorber, *Putting the One Minute Manager to Work* (New York: Berkley Books, 1984).
[67] Adapted from R Levering and M Moskowitz, "2004 Special Report: The 100 Best Companies to Work For," *Fortune,* January 12, 2004, p 68. Another interesting positive reinforcement example can be found in J McCuan, "The Ultimate Sales Incentive," *Inc.,* May 2004, p 32.
[68] Research on punishment is reported in B P Niehoff, R J Paul, and J F S Bunch, "The Social Effects of Punishment Events: The Influence of Violator Past Performance Record and Severity of the Punishment on Observers' Justice Perceptions and Attitudes," *Journal of Organizational Behavior,* November 1998, pp 589–602.
[69] See C B Ferster and B F Skinner, *Schedules of Reinforcement* (New York: Appleton-Century-Crofts, 1957).
[70] See L M Saari and G P Latham, "Employee Reactions to Continuous and Variable Ratio Reinforcement Schedules Involving a Monetary Incentive," *Journal of Applied Psychology,* August 1982, pp 506–8.
[71] P Brinkley-Rogers and R Collier, "Along the Colorado, the Money's Flowing," *Arizona Republic,* March 4, 1990, p A12.
[72] The topic of managerial credibility is covered in J M Kouzes and B Z Posner, *Credibility* (San Francisco: Jossey-Bass, 1993).
[73] An on-the-job example of behavior shaping can be found in J Case, "Are Your Meetings Like This?" *Inc.,* March 2003, p 79.
[74] Data from K L Alexander, "Continental Airlines Soars to New Heights," *USA Today,* January 23, 1996, p 4B. Also see J Huey, "Outlaw Flyboy CEOs," *Fortune,* November 13, 2000, pp 237–50.
[75] Data from R Levering and M Moskowitz, "100 Best Companies to Work For," *Fortune,* January 20, 2003, p 136.
[76] Excerpted from J A Byrne, "How to Fix Corporate Governance," *Business Week,* May 6, 2002, p 72.

Chapter 9

[1] Excerpted from B Nussbaum, "The Power of Design," *Business Week,* May 17, 2004, pp 88, 90–92, 94. Reprinted with permission.
[2] A thorough discussion of rationality in decision making can be found in N Chater, M Oaksford, R Nakisa, and M Redington, "Fast, Frugal, and Rational: How Rational Norms Explain Behavior," *Organizational Behavior and Human Decision Processes,* January 2003, pp 63–86.
[3] R C Morias, "Mind the Gap," *Forbes,* August 11, 2003, p 58.
[4] M Mangalindan, "The Grown-Up at Google," *The Wall Street Journal,* March 29, 2004, p B1.
[5] H A Simon, "Rational Decision Making in Business Organizations," *American Economic Review,* September 1979, p 510.
[6] For a complete discussion of bounded rationality, see H A Simon, *Administrative Behavior,* 2nd ed (New York: Free Press, 1957).
[7] Biases associated with using shortcuts in decision making are discussed by D Kahneman, "A Perspective on Judgment and Choice," *American Psychologist,* September 2003, pp 697–720.
[8] See T DeAngelis, "Too Many Choices?" *Monitor on Psychology,* June 2004, pp 56–57.
[9] D W De Long and P Seemann, "Confronting Conceptual Confusion and Conflict in Knowledge Management," *Organizational Dynamics,* Summer 2000, p 33.
[10] See S Schwartzman, "Knowledge Management: The Key to CRM Success," *Inc.,* May 2004, p S5; and C Stoll, "Writing the Book on Knowledge Management," *American Society of Association Executives,* April 2004, pp 56–58, 60, 62–63.
[11] These statistics can be found in P Babcock, "Shedding Light on Knowledge Management," *HR Magazine,* May 2004, pp 47–50.
[12] R Lubit, "Tacit Knowledge and Knowledge Management: The Keys to Sustainable Competitive Advantage," *Organizational Dynamics,* 2001, p 166.
[13] A M Hayashi, "When to Trust Your Gut," *Harvard Business Review,* February 2001, p 61.
[14] The role of intuition in decision making is thoroughly discussed by E Bonabeau, "Don't Trust Your Gut," *Harvard Business Review,* May 2003, pp 116–123.
[15] See Lubit, "Tacit Knowledge and Knowledge Management."
[16] R Cross, A Parker, L Prusak, and S P Borgatti, "Knowing What We Know: Supporting Knowledge Creation and Sharing in Social Networks," *Organizational Dynamics,* Fall 2001, p 109.
[17] Ibid.
[18] This definition was derived from A J Rowe and R O Mason, *Managing with Style: A Guide to Understanding, Assessing and Improving Decision Making* (San Francisco: Jossey-Bass, 1987).
[19] The discussion of styles was based on material contained in ibid.
[20] P Shishkin, "Tough Tactics: European Regulators Spark Controversy with 'Dawn Raids,'" *The Wall Street Journal,* March 1, 2002, p A1.
[21] Norms were obtained from Rowe and Mason, *Managing with Style: A Guide to Understanding, Assessing and Improving Decision Making.*
[22] See ibid.; and M J Dollinger and W Danis, "Preferred Decision-Making Styles: A Cross-Cultural Comparison," *Psychological Reports,* 1998, pp 755–61.
[23] A thorough discussion of escalation situations can be found in B M Staw and J Ross, "Behavior in Escalation Situations: Antecedents, Prototypes, and Solutions," in *Research in Organizational Behavior,* vol. 9, eds L L Cummings and B M Staw (Greenwich, CT: JAI Press, 1987), pp 39–78.
[24] The details of this case are discussed in J Ross and B M Staw, "Organizational Escalation and Exit: Lessons from the Shoreham Nuclear Power Plant," *Academy of Management Journal,* August 1993, pp 701–32.
[25] Ibid.
[26] Supportive results can be found in H Moon, "Looking Forward and Looking Back: Integrating Completion and Sunk-Cost Effects within an Escalation-of-Commitment Progress Decision," *Journal of Applied Psychology,* February 2001, pp 104–13.
[27] See D A Hantula and J L D Bragger, "The Effects of Feedback Equivocality on Escalation of Commitment: An Empirical Investigation of Decision Dilemma Theory," *Journal of Applied Social Psychology,* February 1999, pp 424–44.
[28] Results can be found in C R Greer and G K Stephens, "Escalation of Commitment: A Comparison of Differences between Mexican and U.S. Decision Makers," *Journal of Management,* 2001, pp 51–78.
[29] See Ross and Staw, "Organizational Escalation and Exit: Lessons from the Shoreham Nuclear Power Plant."
[30] This definition was based on R J Sternberg, "What Is the Common Thread of Creativity?" *American Psychologist,* April 2001, pp 360–62.
[31] R Langreth and Z Moukheiber, "Medical Merlins," *Forbes,* June 2003, p 115.
[32] See the discussion in O Janssen, E V De Vliert, and M West, "The Bright and Dark Sides of Individual and Group Innovation: A Special Issue Introduction," *Journal of Organizational Behavior,* March 2004, pp 129–45.
[33] Excerpted from T M Burton, "By Learning from Failures, Lilly Keeps Drug Pipeline Full," *The Wall Street Journal,* April 21, 2004, p A1.
[34] Results can be found in E Tahmincioglu, "Gifts that Gall," *Workforce Management,* April 2004, p 45.
[35] Details of this study can be found in M Basadur, "Managing Creativity: A Japanese Model," *Academy of Management Executive,* May 1992, pp 29–42.
[36] Supportive studies can be found in J E Perry-Smith and C E Shalley, "The Social Side of Creativity: A Static and Dynamic Social Network Perspective," *Academy of Management Review,* January 2003, pp 89–106.
[37] Results can be found in C K W De Dreu and M A West, "Minority Dissent and Team Innovation: The Importance of Participation in Decision Making," *Journal of Applied Psychology,* December 2001, pp 1191–201.
[38] These recommendations were derived from R Y Hirokawa, "Group Communication and Decision-Making Performance: A Continued Test of the Functional Perspective," *Human Communication Research,* October 1988, pp 487–515.
[39] See the related discussion in B B Baltes, M W Dickson, M P Sherman, C C Bauer, and J S LaGanke, "Computer-Mediated Communication and Group Decision Making: A Meta-Analysis," *Organizational Behavior and Human Decision Processes,* January 2002, pp 156–79.
[40] These guidelines were derived from G P Huber, *Managerial Decision Making* (Glenview, IL: Scott, Foresman, 1980), p 149.
[41] G W Hill, "Group versus Individual Performance: Are N + 1 Heads Better than One?" *Psychological Bulletin,* May 1982, p 535.
[42] See T Connolly and L Ordóñez, "Judgment and Decision Making," in *Handbook of Psychology,* vol. 12, eds W C Borman, D R Ilgen, and R J Klimoski (Hoboken, NJ: John Wiley & Sons, 2003), pp 493–518.
[43] Results are presented in J T Delaney, "Workplace Cooperation: Current Problems, New Approaches," *Journal of Labor Research,* Winter 1996, pp 45–61.
[44] For an extended discussion of this model, see M Sashkin, "Participative Management Is an Ethical Imperative," *Organizational Dynamics,* Spring 1984, pp 4–22.
[45] S Carey, "The Thrifty Get Thriftier," *The Wall Street Journal,* May 10, 2004, p R7.
[46] For a review of this research, see M J Handel and D I Levine, "Editors' Introduction: The Effects of New Work Practices on Workers," *Industrial Relations,* January 2004, pp 1–43.
[47] Results can be found in B D Cawley, L M Keeping, and P E Levy, "Participation in the Performance Appraisal Process and Employee Reactions: A Meta-Analytic Review of Field Investigations," *Journal of Applied Psychology,* August 1998, pp 615–33.
[48] Results are contained in J A Wagner III, C R Leana, E A Locke, and D M Schweiger, "Cognitive and Motivational Frameworks in US Research on Participation: A Meta-Analysis of Primary Effects," *Journal of Organizational Behavior,* 1997, pp 49–65.
[49] Results are presented in J Barbian, "Decision Making: The Tyranny of Managers," *Training,* January 2002, p 19.
[50] Results can be found in S A Mohrman, E E Lawler III, and G E Ledford, Jr, "Organizational Effectiveness and the Impact of Employee Involvement and TQM Programs: Do Employee Involvement and TQM Programs Work?" *Journal for Quality and Participation,* January–February 1996, pp 6–10.
[51] See R Rodgers, J E Hunter, and D L Rogers, "Influence of Top Management Commitment on Management Program Success," *Journal of Applied Psychology,* February 1993, pp 151–55.

[52] G M Parker, *Team Players and Teamwork: The New Competitive Business Strategy* (San Francisco: Jossey-Bass, 1990).
[53] The effect of group dynamics on brainstorming is discussed by P B Paulus and H-C Yang, "Idea Generation in Groups: A Basis for Creativity in Organizations," *Organizational Behavior and Human Decision Processes,* May 2000, pp 76–87.
[54] These recommendations were obtained from Parker, *Team Players and Teamwork: The New Competitive Business Strategy.*
[55] See A F Osborn, *Applied Imagination: Principles and Procedures of Creative Thinking,* 3rd ed (New York: Scribners, 1979).
[56] See W H Cooper, R Brent Gallupe, S Pollard, and J Cadsby, "Some Liberating Effects of Anonymous Electronic Brainstorming," *Small Group Research,* April 1998, pp 147–78.
[57] These recommendations and descriptions were derived from B Nussbaum, "The Power of Design."
[58] The NGT procedure is discussed by L Thompson, "Improving the Creativity of Organizational Work Groups," *Academy of Management Executive,* February 2003, pp 96–109.
[59] See Ibid.
[60] See N C Dalkey, D L Rourke, R Lewis, and D Snyder, *Studies in the Quality of Life: Delphi and Decision Making* (Lexington, MA: Lexington Books: D C Heath and Co., 1972).
[61] An application of the Delphi technique can be found in K D Joshi, "A Formal Knowledge Management Ontology: Conduct, Activities, Resources, and Influences," *Journal of the American Society for Information Science and Technology,* May 2004, p 593.
[62] A thorough description of computer-aided decision-making systems is provided by M C Er and A C Ng, "The Anonymity and Proximity Factors in Group Decision Support Systems," *Decision Support Systems,* May 1995, pp 75–83.
[63] Excerpted from T E Weber, "How Bringing Doctors Together Online Helps Brothers Build Business," *The Wall Street Journal,* April 2, 2001, p B1.
[64] Supportive results can be found in S S Lam and J Schaubroeck, "Improving Group Decisions by Better Polling Information: A Comparative Advantage of Group Decision Support Systems," *Journal of Applied Psychology,* August 2000, pp 565–73; and I Benbasat and J Lim, "Information Technology Support for Debiasing Group Judgments: An Empirical Evaluation," *Organizational Behavior and Human Decision Processes,* September 2000, pp 167–83.
[65] Results can be found in Baltes, Dickson, Sherman, Bauer, and LaGanke, "Computer-Mediated Communication and Group Decision Making."
[66] Excerpted from E J Pollock, "Limited Partners: Lawyers for Enron Faulted Its Deals, Didn't Force Issue," *The Wall Street Journal,* Eastern Edition, May 22, 2002, pp A1, A18. Copyright 2002 by Dow Jones & Co. Inc. Reproduced with permission of Dow Jones & Co. Inc. via Copyright Clearance Center.

Chapter 10

[1] Reprinted by permission of *Harvard Business Review.* Excerpted from M Bellmann and R H Schaffer, "Freeing Managers to Innovate," *Harvard Business Review,* June 2001, pp 32–33. Copyright © 1999 by the Harvard Business School Publishing Corporation; all rights reserved.
[2] E Van Velsor and J Brittain Leslie, "Why Executives Derail: Perspectives across Time and Cultures," *Academy of Management Executive,* November 1995, p 62.
[3] Ibid., p 63.
[4] According to one survey, "getting along with others who work at the company" was the top-ranked skill believed to be most important for organizational success. See "Gets Along Well with Others," *Training,* August 1996, pp 17–18.
[5] This applies to life in general, as well. See M Elias, "Friends May Make Breast Cancer More Survivable," *USA Today,* March 8, 2001, p 2D.
[6] This definition is based in part on one found in D Horton Smith, "A Parsimonious Definition of 'Group': Toward Conceptual Clarity and Scientific Utility," *Sociological Inquiry,* Spring 1967, pp 141–67. Also see W B Swann, Jr; J T Polzer; D C Seyle; and S J Ko, "Finding Value in Diversity: Verification of Personal and Social Self-Views in Diverse Groups," *Academy of Management Review,* January 2004, pp 9–27.
[7] E H Schein, *Organizational Psychology,* 3rd ed (Englewood Cliffs, NJ: Prentice Hall, 1980), p 145. For more, see L R Weingart, "How Did They Do That? The Ways and Means of Studying Group Process," in *Research in Organizational Behavior,* vol. 19, eds L L Cummings and B M Staw (Greenwich, CT: JAI Press, 1997), pp 189–239.
[8] See R Cross, N Nohria, and A Parker, "Six Myths about Informal Networks—and How to Overcome Them," *MIT Sloan Management Review,* Spring 2002, pp 67–75; C Shirky, "Watching the Patterns Emerge," *Harvard Business Review,* February 2004, pp 34–35; and P Chattopadhyay, M Tluchowska, and E George, "Identifying the Ingroup: A Closer Look at the Influence of Demographic Dissimilarity on Employee Social Identity," *Academy of Management Review,* April 2004, pp 180–202.
[9] Data from "Co-workers Support Each Other," *USA Today,* May 28, 2003, p 1B.
[10] See Schein, *Organizational Psychology,* pp 149–53.
[11] J Castro, "Mazda U," *Time,* October 20, 1986, p 65.
[12] For an instructive overview of five different theories of group development, see J P Wanous, A E Reichers, and S D Malik, "Organizational Socialization and Group Development: Toward an Integrative Perspective," *Academy of Management Review,* October 1984, pp 670–83. Also see L R Offermann and R K Spiros, "The Science and Practice of Team Development: Improving the Link," *Academy of Management Journal,* April 2001, pp 376–92; and A Chang, P Bordia, and J Duck, "Punctuated Equilibrium and Linear Progression: Toward a New Understanding of Group Development," *Academy of Management Journal,* February 2003, pp 106–17.
[13] See B W Tuckman, "Developmental Sequence in Small Groups," *Psychological Bulletin,* June 1965, pp 384–99; and B W Tuckman and M A C Jensen, "Stages of Small-Group Development Revisited," *Group & Organization Studies,* December 1977, pp 419–27. An instructive adaptation of the Tuckman model can be found in L Holpp, "If Empowerment Is So Good, Why Does It Hurt?" *Training,* March 1995, p 56.
[14] A useful resource book is T Ursiny, *The Coward's Guide to Conflict: Empowering Solutions for Those Who Would Rather Run than Fight* (Naperville, IL: Sourcebooks, 2003).
[15] For related research, see M Van Vugt and C M Hart, "Social Identity as Social Glue: The Origins of Group Loyalty," *Journal of Personality and Social Psychology,* April 2004, pp 585–98.
[16] G Graen, "Role-Making Processes within Complex Organizations," in *Handbook of Industrial and Organizational Psychology,* ed M D Dunnette (Chicago: Rand McNally, 1976), p 1201. Also see L Van Dyne and J A LePine, "Helping and Voice Extra-Role Behavior: Evidence of Construct and Predictive Validity," *Academy of Management Journal,* February 1998, pp 108–19; and B E Ashforth, G E Kreiner, and M Fugate, "All in a Day's Work: Boundaries and Micro Role Transitions," *Academy of Management Review,* July 2000, pp 472–91.
[17] See K D Benne and P Sheats, "Functional Roles of Group Members," *Journal of Social Issues,* Spring 1948, pp 41–49.
[18] See H J Klein and P W Mulvey, "Two Investigations of the Relationships among Group Goals, Goal Commitment, Cohesion, and Performance," *Organizational Behavior and Human Decision Processes,* January 1995, pp 44–53; D F Crown and J G Rosse, "Yours, Mine, and Ours: Facilitating Group Productivity through the Integration of Individual and Group Goals," *Organizational Behavior and Human Decision Processes,* November 1995, pp 138–50; and D Knight, C C Durham, and E A Locke, "The Relationship of Team Goals, Incentives, and Efficacy to Strategic Risk, Tactical Implementation, and Performance," *Academy of Management Journal,* April 2001, pp 326–38.
[19] A Zander, "The Value of Belonging to a Group in Japan," *Small Group Behavior,* February 1983, pp 7–8. Also see E Gundling, *Working GlobeSmart: 12 People Skills for Doing Business across Borders* (Palo Alto, CA: Davies-Black Publishing, 2003).
[20] R R Blake and J Srygley Mouton, "Don't Let Group Norms Stifle Creativity," *Personnel,* August 1985, p 28.
[21] See D Kahneman, "Reference Points, Anchors, Norms, and Mixed Feelings," *Organizational Behavior and Human Decision Processes,* March 1992, pp 296–312; and J M Marques, D Abrams, D Paez, and C Martinez-Taboada, "The Role of Categorization and In-Group Norms

in Judgments of Groups and Their Members," *Journal of Personality and Social Psychology,* October 1998, pp 976–88.

[22] A Dunkin, "Pepsi's Marketing Magic: Why Nobody Does It Better," *Business Week,* February 10, 1986, p 52.

[23] See J Pfeffer, "Bring Back Shame," *Business 2.0,* September 2003, p 80.

[24] P Sellers, "Gap's New Guy Upstairs," *Fortune,* April 14, 2003, p 112.

[25] D C Feldman, "The Development and Enforcement of Group Norms," *Academy of Management Review,* January 1984, pp 50–52.

[26] Ibid.

[27] "Top 10 Leadership Tips from Jeff Immelt," *Fast Company,* April 2004, p 96.

[28] J Pfeffer and J F Veiga, "Putting People First for Organizational Success," *Academy of Management Executive,* May 1999, p 41.

[29] See N Enbar, "What Do Women Want? Ask 'Em," *Business Week,* March 29, 1999, p 8; and M Hickins, "Duh! Gen Xers Are Cool with Teamwork," *Management Review,* March 1999, p 7.

[30] J R Katzenbach and D K Smith, *The Wisdom of Teams: Creating the High-Performance Organization* (New York: HarperBusiness, 1999), p 45.

[31] Condensed and adapted from ibid., p 214. Also see B Beersma, J R Hollenbeck, S E Humphrey, H Moon, D Conlon, and D R Ilgen, "Cooperation, Competition, and Team Performance: Toward a Contingency Approach," *Academy of Management Journal,* October 2003, pp 572–90.

[32] See A Levin, "In the Cockpit, Safety Isn't Someone Else's Job," *USA Today,* March 2, 2004, p 4A; and R J Trent, "Becoming an Effective Teaming Organization," *Business Horizons,* March–April 2004, pp 33–40.

[33] J R Katzenbach and D K Smith, "The Discipline of Teams," *Harvard Business Review,* March–April 1993, p 112.

[34] "A Team's-Eye View of Teams," *Training,* November 1995, p 16.

[35] P Burrows, "Cisco's Comeback," *Business Week,* November 24, 2003, p 124.

[36] S Zuboff, "From Subject to Citizen," *Fast Company,* May 2004, p 104. Also see "Minorities Distrust Companies," *USA Today,* January 14, 2004, p 1B; and "Little Faith in Top Executives," *USA Today,* April 5, 2004, p 1B.

[37] L Prusak and D Cohen, "How to Invest in Social Capital," *Harvard Business Review,* June 2001, p 90. Also see V U Druskat and S B Wolff, "Building the Emotional Intelligence of Groups," *Harvard Business Review,* March 2001, pp 80–90.

[38] See D M Rousseau, S B Sitkin, R S Burt, and C Camerer, "Not So Different After All: A Cross-Discipline View of Trust," *Academy of Management Review,* July 1998, pp 393–404; and A C Wicks, S L Berman, and T M Jones, "The Structure of Optimal Trust: Moral and Strategic Implications," *Academy of Management Review,* January 1999, pp 99–116.

[39] J D Lewis and A Weigert, "Trust as a Social Reality," *Social Forces,* June 1985, p 971. Trust is examined as an *indirect* factor in K T Dirks, "The Effects of Interpersonal Trust on Work Group Performance," *Journal of Applied Psychology,* June 1999, pp 445–55. Also see J B Cunningham and J MacGregor, "Trust and the Design of Work: Complementary Constructs in Satisfaction and Performance," *Human Relations,* December 2000, pp 1575–88.

[40] Adapted from C Johnson-George and W C Swap, "Measurement of Specific Interpersonal Trust: Construction and Validation of a Scale to Assess Trust in a Specific Other," *Journal of Personality and Social Psychology,* December 1982, pp 1306–17; and D J McAllister, "Affect- and Cognition-Based Trust as Foundations for Interpersonal Cooperation in Organizations," *Academy of Management Journal,* February 1995, pp 24–59.

[41] See R Zemke, "Little Lies," *Training,* February 2004, p 8.

[42] For support, see G M Spreitzer and A K Mishra, "Giving Up Control without Losing Control: Trust and Its Substitutes' Effects on Managers' Involving Employees in Decision Making," *Group & Organization Management,* June 1999, pp 155–87. Also see G Johnson, "11 Keys to Leadership," *Training,* January 2004, p 18.

[43] Adapted from F Bartolomé, "Nobody Trusts the Boss Completely—Now What?" *Harvard Business Review,* March–April 1989, pp 135–42. For more on building trust, see R Galford and A S Drapeau, "The Enemies of Trust," *Harvard Business Review,* February 2003, pp 88–95; L C Abrams, R Cross, E Lesser, and D Z Levin, "Nurturing Interpersonal Trust in Knowledge-Sharing Networks," *Academy of Management Executive,* November 2003, pp 64–77; C Huxham and S Vangen, "Doing Things Collaboratively: Realizing the Advantage or Succumbing to Inertia?" *Organizational Dynamics,* no 2, 2004, pp 190–201; and S A Joni, "The Geography of Trust," *Harvard Business Review,* March 2004, pp 82–88.

[44] Data from C Joinson, "Teams at Work," *HR Magazine,* May 1999, pp 30–36.

[45] B Dumaine, "Who Needs a Boss?" *Fortune,* May 7, 1990, p 52. Also see D Vredenburgh and I Y He, "Leadership Lessons from a Conductorless Orchestra," *Business Horizons,* September–October 2003, pp 19–24; and C A O'Reilly III and M L Tushman, "The Ambidextrous Organization," *Harvard Business Review,* April 2004, pp 74–81.

[46] Adapted from Table 1 in V U Druskat and J V Wheeler, "Managing from the Boundary: The Effective Leadership of Self-Managing Work Teams," *Academy of Management Journal,* August 2003, pp 435–57.

[47] See A E Randal and K S Jaussi, "Functional Background Identity, Diversity, and Individual Performance in Cross-Functional Teams," *Academy of Management Journal,* December 2003, pp 763–74.

[48] Excerpted from "Fast Talk," *Fast Company,* February 2004, p 50.

[49] See "1996 Industry Report: What Self-Managing Teams Manage," *Training,* October 1996, p 69.

[50] See L L Thompson, *Making the Team: A Guide for Managers* (Upper Saddle River, NJ: Prentice Hall, 2000).

[51] See P S Goodman, R Devadas, and T L Griffith Hughson, "Groups and Productivity: Analyzing the Effectiveness of Self-Managing Teams," in *Productivity in Organizations,* eds J P Campbell, R J Campbell and Associates (San Francisco: Jossey-Bass, 1988), pp 295–327. Also see E F Rogers, W Metlay, I T Kaplan, and T Shapiro, "Self-Managing Work Teams: Do They Really Work?" *Human Resource Planning,* no. 2, 1995, pp 53–57; V U Druskat and S B Wolff, "Effects and Timing of Developmental Peer Appraisals in Self-Managing Work Groups," *Journal of Applied Psychology,* February 1999, pp 58–74; R C Liden, S J Wayne, and M L Kraimer, "Managing Individual Performance in Work Groups," *Human Resource Management,* Spring 2001, pp 63–72; and R Batt, "Who Benefits from Teams? Comparing Workers, Supervisors, and Managers," *Industrial Relations,* January 2004, pp 183–209.

[52] For more, see W F Cascio, "Managing a Virtual Workplace," *Academy of Management Executive,* August 2000, pp 81–90; and the collection of articles on E-leadership and virtual teams in *Organizational Dynamics,* no 4, 2003.

[53] See A M Townsend, S M DeMarie, and A R Hendrickson, "Virtual Teams: Technology and the Workplace of the Future," *Academy of Management Executive,* August 1998, pp 17–29.

[54] See C Saunders, C Van Slyke, and D R Vogel, "My Time or Yours? Managing Time Visions in Global Virtual Teams," *Academy of Management Executive,* February 2004, pp 19–31.

[55] Excerpted from K Naughton, "Styling with Digital Clay," *Newsweek,* April 28, 2003, pp 46–47. For a large-scale example, see S E Ante, "Collaboration: IBM," *Business Week,* November 24, 2003, p 84.

[56] Based on P Bordia, N DiFonzo, and A Chang, "Rumor as Group Problem Solving: Development Patterns in Informal Computer-Mediated Groups," *Small Group Research,* February 1999, pp 8–28.

[57] See K A Graetz, E S Boyle, C E Kimble, P Thompson, and J L Garloch, "Information Sharing in Face-to-Face, Teleconferencing, and Electronic Chat Groups," *Small Group Research,* December 1998, pp 714–43.

[58] Based on F Niederman and R J Volkema, "The Effects of Facilitator Characteristics on Meeting Preparation, Set Up, and Implementation," *Small Group Research,* June 1999, pp 330–60.

[59] Based on J J Sosik, B J Avolio, and S S Kahai, "Inspiring Group Creativity: Comparing Anonymous and Identified Electronic Brainstorming," *Small Group Research,* February 1998, pp 3–31. For practical advice on brainstorming, see C Caggiano, "The Right Way to Brainstorm," *Inc.,* July 1999, p 94.

[60] See B L Kirkman, B Rosen, C B Gibson, P E Tesluk, and S O McPherson, "Five Challenges to Virtual Team Success: Lessons from

Sabre, Inc.," *Academy of Management Executive,* August 2002, pp 67–79; and P J Hinds and D E Bailey, "Out of Sight, Out of Sync: Understanding Conflict in Distributed Teams," *Organization Science,* November–December 2003, pp 615–32.

[61] See E Kelley, "Keys to Effective Virtual Global Teams," *Academy of Management Executive,* May 2001, pp 132–33.

[62] Practical perspectives are offered in "Virtual Teams that Work," *HR Magazine,* July 2003, p 121; D D Davis, "The Tao of Leadership in Virtual Teams," *Organizational Dynamics,* no 1, 2004, pp 47–62; and A Majchrzak, A Malhotra, J Stamps, and J Lipnack, "Can Absence Make a Team Grow Stronger?" *Harvard Business Review,* May 2004, pp 131–37.

[63] For a comprehensive update on groupthink, see the entire February–March 1998 issue of *Organizational Behavior and Human Decision Processes* (12 articles).

[64] I L Janis, *Groupthink,* 2nd ed (Boston: Houghton Mifflin, 1982), p 9. Alternative models are discussed in K Granstrom and D Stiwne, "A Bipolar Model of Groupthink: An Expansion of Janis's Concept," *Small Group Research,* February 1998, pp 32–56; A R Flippen, "Understanding Groupthink from a Self-Regulatory Perspective," *Small Group Research,* April 1999, pp 139–65; and M Harvey, M M Novicevic, M R Buckley, and J R B Halbesleben, "The Abilene Paradox after Thirty Years: A Global Perspective," *Organizational Dynamics,* no 2, 2004, pp 215–26.

[65] Ibid. For an alternative model, see R J Aldag and S Riggs Fuller, "Beyond Fiasco: A Reappraisal of the Groupthink Phenomenon and a New Model of Group Decision Processes," *Psychological Bulletin,* May 1993, pp 533–52. Also see A A Mohamed and F A Wiebe, "Toward a Process Theory of Groupthink," *Small Group Research,* August 1996, pp 416–30.

[66] Adapted from Janis, *Groupthink,* pp 174–75.

[67] L Baum, "The Job Nobody Wants," *Business Week,* September 8, 1986, p 60. Also see L Perlow and S Williams, "Is Silence Killing Your Company?" *Harvard Business Review,* May 2003, pp 52–58; W F Cascio, "Board Governance: A Social Systems Perspective," *Academy of Management Executive,* February 2004, pp 97–100; and L Letendre, "The Dynamics of the Boardroom," *Academy of Management Executive,* February 2004, pp 101–4.

[68] For an ethical perspective, see R R Sims, "Linking Groupthink to Unethical Behavior in Organizations," *Journal of Business Ethics,* September 1992, pp 651–62.

[69] Based on discussion in B Latane, K Williams, and S Harkins, "Many Hands Make Light the Work: The Causes and Consequences of Social Loafing," *Journal of Personality and Social Psychology,* June 1979, pp 822–32; and D A Kravitz and B Martin, "Ringelmann Rediscovered: The Original Article," *Journal of Personality and Social Psychology,* May 1986, pp 936–41.

[70] See S J Karau and K D Williams, "Social Loafing: Meta-Analytic Review and Theoretical Integration," *Journal of Personality and Social Psychology,* October 1993, pp 681–706; and L Thompson, "Improving the Creativity of Organizational Work Groups," *Academy of Management Executive,* February 2003, pp 96–109.

[71] See S J Zaccaro, "Social Loafing: The Role of Task Attractiveness," *Personality and Social Psychology Bulletin,* March 1984, pp 99–106; J M Jackson and K D Williams, "Social Loafing on Difficult Tasks: Working Collectively Can Improve Performance," *Journal of Personality and Social Psychology,* October 1985, pp 937–42; and J M George, "Extrinsic and Intrinsic Origins of Perceived Social Loafing in Organizations," *Academy of Management Journal,* March 1992, pp 191–202.

[72] For complete details, see K Williams, S Harkins, and B Latane, "Identifiability as a Deterrent to Social Loafing: Two Cheering Experiments," *Journal of Personality and Social Psychology,* February 1981, pp 303–11.

[73] See J M Jackson and S G Harkins, "Equity in Effort: An Explanation of the Social Loafing Effect," *Journal of Personality and Social Psychology,* November 1985, pp 1199–1206.

[74] Both studies are reported in S G Harkins and K Szymanski, "Social Loafing and Group Evaluation," *Journal of Personality and Social Psychology,* June 1989, pp 934–41.

[75] Data from J A Wagner III, "Studies of Individualism-Collectivism: Effects on Cooperation in Groups," *Academy of Management Journal,* February 1995, pp 152–72. Also see P W Mulvey and H J Klein, "The Impact of Perceived Loafing and Collective Efficacy on Group Goal Processes and Group Performance," *Organizational Behavior and Human Decision Processes,* April 1998, pp 62–87; P W Mulvey, L Bowes-Sperry, and H J Klein, "The Effects of Perceived Loafing and Defensive Impression Management on Group Effectiveness," *Small Group Research,* June 1998, pp 394–415; and H Goren, R Kurzban, and A Rapoport, "Social Loafing vs. Social Enhancement: Public Goods Provisioning in Real-Time with Irrevocable Commitments," *Organizational Behavior and Human Decision Processes,* March 2003, pp 277–90.

[76] See S G Scott and W O Einstein, "Strategic Performance Appraisal in Team-Based Organizations: One Size Does Not Fit All," *Academy of Management Executive,* May 2001, pp 107–16.

[77] Excerpted from K J Sulkowicz, "The Corporate Shrink," *Fast Company,* May 2004, p 54.

Chapter 11

[1] Excerpted from J S Lublin, "Women Fall Behind When They Don't Hone Negotiation Skills," *The Wall Street Journal,* Eastern Edition, November 4, 2003, p B1. Copyright 2004 by Dow Jones & Co. Inc. Reproduced with permission of Dow Jones & Co. Inc. via Copyright Clearance Center.

[2] D Tjosvold, *Learning to Manage Conflict: Getting People to Work Together Productively* (New York: Lexington Books, 1993), p xi.

[3] Ibid., pp xi–xii.

[4] For recent examples, see R Grover, "Steve Burke: Payback Time for an Ex-Boy Wonder?" *Business Week,* February 23, 2004, p 42; and S Hamm, "A Probe—and a Bitter Feud," *Business Week,* April 12, 2004, pp 78–82.

[5] J A Wall, Jr, and R Robert Callister, "Conflict and Its Management," *Journal of Management,* no. 3, 1995, p 517.

[6] Ibid., p 544.

[7] See O Jones, "Scientific Management, Culture and Control: A First-Hand Account of Taylorism in Practice," *Human Relations,* May 2000, pp 631–53.

[8] See A M O'Leary-Kelly, R W Griffin, and D J Glew, "Organization-Motivated Aggression: A Research Framework," *Academy of Management Review,* January 1996, pp 225–53; D Bencivenga, "Dealing with the Dark Side," *HR Magazine,* January 1999, pp 50–58; L Grensing-Pophal, "Should You Offer Self-Defense Training?" *HR Magazine,* June 2003, pp 80–84; and T Vanden Brook, "Ex-Worker Kills 6 at Chicago Business," *USA Today,* August 28, 2003, p 3A.

[9] See S Alper, D Tjosvold, and K S Law, "Interdependence and Controversy in Group Decision Making: Antecedents to Effective Self-Managing Teams," *Organizational Behavior and Human Decision Processes,* April 1998, pp 33–52.

[10] S P Robbins, "'Conflict Management' and 'Conflict Resolution' Are Not Synonymous Terms," *California Management Review,* Winter 1978, p 70.

[11] Cooperative conflict is discussed in Tjosvold, *Learning to Manage Conflict: Getting People to Work Together Productively.* Also see A C Amason, "Distinguishing the Effects of Functional and Dysfunctional Conflict on Strategic Decision Making: Resolving a Paradox for Top Management Teams," *Academy of Management Journal,* February 1996, pp 123–48; D E Warren, "Constructive and Destructive Deviance in Organizations," *Academy of Management Review,* October 2003, pp 622–32; and H Johnson, "The Next Management Revolution," *Inc.,* July 2004, pp 78–83.

[12] K Brooker, "Can Anyone Replace Herb?" *Fortune,* April 17, 2000, p 190.

[13] K Brooker, "I Built This Company, I Can Save It," *Fortune,* April 30, 2001, p 102. Also see L Stack, "Employees Behaving Badly," *HR Magazine,* October 2003, pp 111–16.

[14] Adapted in part from discussion in A C Filley, *Interpersonal Conflict Resolution* (Glenview, IL: Scott, Foresman, 1975), pp 9–12; and B Fortado, "The Accumulation of Grievance Conflict," *Journal of Management Inquiry,* December 1992, pp 288–303. Also see D Tjosvold and M Poon, "Dealing with Scarce Resources: Open-Minded Interaction for Resolving Budget Conflicts," *Group & Organization Management,* September 1998, pp 237–55.

[15] Excerpted from T Ursiny, *The Coward's Guide to Conflict: Empowering Solutions for Those Who Would Rather Run than Fight* (Naperville, IL: Sourcebooks, 2003), p 27.
[16] Adapted from discussion in Tjosvold, *Learning to Manage Conflict: Getting People to Work Together Productively,* pp 12–13.
[17] L Gardenswartz and A Rowe, *Diverse Teams at Work: Capitalizing on the Power of Diversity* (New York: McGraw-Hill, 1994), p 32.
[18] Data from "Do I Have It?" *Business Week,* July 7, 2003, p 14.
[19] See L M Andersson and C M Pearson, "Tit for Tat? The Spiraling Effect of Incivility in the Workplace," *Academy of Management Review,* July 1999, pp 452–71; C Lee, "The Death of Civility," *Training,* July 1999, pp 24–30; "Good Manners," *USA Today,* December 16, 2003, p 1D; and J Pfeffer, "How to Turn On the Charm," *Business 2.0,* June 2004, p 76.
[20] K Robinson, "Workplace Insults Reduced, but Not Much," *HR Magazine,* April 2004, p 38.
[21] See D L Coutu, "In Praise of Boundaries: A Conversation with Miss Manners," *Harvard Business Review,* December 2003, pp 41–45; and R Kurtz, "Is Etiquette a Core Value?" *Inc.,* May 2004, p 22.
[22] Data from D Stamps, "Yes, Your Boss Is Crazy," *Training,* July 1998, pp 35–39. Also see M F McMillen, "Focusing on ADD in the Workplace," *HR Magazine,* December 2002, pp 56–61; K Tyler, "Mind Matters," *HR Magazine,* August 2003, pp 54–62; J Britt, "Cutting Mental Health Benefits May Not Be Cost-Effective," *HR Magazine,* August 2003, p 10; and C Arnst, "Attention Deficit: Not Just Kid Stuff," *Business Week,* October 27, 2003, pp 84, 86.
[23] See S H Milne and T C Blum, "Organizational Characteristics and Employer Responses to Employee Substance Abuse," *Journal of Management,* no. 6, 1998, pp 693–715; P J Petesch, "Are the Newest ADA Guidelines 'Reasonable?'" *HR Magazine,* June 1999, pp 54–58; T Mauro, "Court Narrows Disability Act, But Expands Rights of the Mentally Ill," *USA Today,* June 23, 1999, p 1A; and K Holland, "Who's Disabled? The Court Rules," *Business Week,* July 5, 1999, p 36.
[24] See N W Janove, "Sexual Harassment and the Three Big Surprises," *HR Magazine,* November 2001, pp 123–30; and M M Clark, "Failure to Cure Harassment Can Be 'Continuing Violation,'" *HR Magazine,* February 2003, p 106.
[25] See D Smith, "Hostility Associated with Immune Function," *Monitor on Psychology,* March 2003, p 47; "The Walking Time Bomb," *Inc.,* December 2003, p 52; and D L Coutu, "Losing It," *Harvard Business Review,* April 2004, pp 37–42.
[26] For practical advice, see N Nicholson, "How to Motivate Your Problem People," *Harvard Business Review,* Special Issue: Motivating People, January 2003, pp 56–65.
[27] Drawn from J C McCune, "The Change Makers," *Management Review,* May 1999, pp 16–22.
[28] Based on discussion in G Labianca, D J Brass, and B Gray, "Social Networks and Perceptions of Intergroup Conflict: The Role of Negative Relationships and Third Parties," *Academy of Management Journal,* February 1998, pp 55–67. Also see C Gómez, B L Kirkman, and D L Shapiro, "The Impact of Collectivism and In-Group/Out-Group Membership on the Evaluation Generosity of Team Members," *Academy of Management Journal,* December 2000, pp 1097–106; and K A Jehn and E A Mannix, "The Dynamic Nature of Conflict: A Longitudinal Study of Intragroup Conflict and Group Performance," *Academy of Management Journal,* April 2001, pp 238–51.
[29] See J Barbian, "Racism Shrugged," *Training,* February 2003, p 68; R J Eidelson and J I Eidelson, "Dangerous Ideas: Five Beliefs That Propel Groups toward Conflict," *American Psychologist,* March 2003, pp 182–92; and T M Glomb and H Liao, "Interpersonal Aggression in Work Groups: Social Influence, Reciprocal, and Individual Effects," *Academy of Management Journal,* August 2003, pp 486–96.
[30] Labianca, Brass, and Gray, "Social Networks and Perceptions of Intergroup Conflict: The Role of Negative Relationships and Third Parties," p 63 (emphasis added).
[31] For example, see S C Wright, A Aron, T McLaughlin-Volpe, and S A Ropp, "The Extended Contact Effect: Knowledge of Cross-Group Friendships and Prejudice," *Journal of Personality and Social Psychology,* July 1997, pp 73–90.
[32] See C D Batson, M P Polycarpou, E Harmon-Jones, H J Imhoff, E C Mitchener, L L Bednar, T R Klein, and L Highberger, "Empathy and Attitudes: Can Feeling for a Member of a Stigmatized Group Improve Feelings toward the Group?" *Journal of Personality and Social Psychology,* January 1997, pp 105–18.
[33] For more, see A K Gupta and V Govindarajan, "Converting Global Presence into Global Competitive Advantage," *Academy of Management Executive,* May 2001, pp 45–56; and N J Adler, *International Dimensions of Organizational Behavior,* 4th ed (Cincinnati: South-Western, 2002).
[34] For an interesting case study, see W Kuemmerle, "Go Global—or No?" *Harvard Business Review,* June 2001, pp 37–49.
[35] "Negotiating South of the Border," *Harvard Management Communication Letter,* August 1999, p 12.
[36] Reprinted from A Rosenbaum, "Testing Cultural Waters," *Management Review,* July–August 1999, p 43. Copyright 1999 American Management Association. Reproduced with permission of American Management Association via Copyright Clearance Center.
[37] See R L Tung, "American Expatriates Abroad: From Neophytes to Cosmopolitans," *Journal of World Business,* Summer 1998, pp 125–44.
[38] R A Cosier and C R Schwenk, "Agreement and Thinking Alike: Ingredients for Poor Decisions," *Academy of Management Executive,* February 1990, p 71. Also see J P Kotter, "Kill Complacency," *Fortune,* August 5, 1996, pp 168–70; and S Caudron, "Keeping Team Conflict Alive," *Training & Development,* September 1998, pp 48–52.
[39] For example, see "Facilitators as Devil's Advocates," *Training,* September 1993, p 10. Also see K L Woodward, "Sainthood for a Pope?" *Newsweek,* June 21, 1999, p 65.
[40] Good background reading on devil's advocacy can be found in C R Schwenk, "Devil's Advocacy in Managerial Decision Making," *Journal of Management Studies,* April 1984, pp 153–68.
[41] See G Katzenstein, "The Debate on Structured Debate: Toward a Unified Theory," *Organizational Behavior and Human Decision Processes,* June 1996, pp 316–32.
[42] W Kiechel III, "How to Escape the Echo Chamber," *Fortune,* June 18, 1990, p 130.
[43] See D M Schweiger, W R Sandberg, and P L Rechner, "Experiential Effects of Dialectical Inquiry, Devil's Advocacy, and Consensus Approaches to Strategic Decision Making," *Academy of Management Journal,* December 1989, pp 745–72.
[44] See J S Valacich and C Schwenk, "Devil's Advocacy and Dialectical Inquiry Effects on Face-to-Face and Computer-Mediated Group Decision Making," *Organizational Behavior and Human Decision Processes,* August 1995, pp 158–73.
[45] Other techniques are presented in Cloke and Goldsmith, *Resolving Conflicts at Work,* pp 229–35.
[46] As quoted in D Jones, "CEOs Need X-Ray Vision in Transition," *USA Today,* April 23, 2001, p 4B.
[47] Based on C K W De Dreu and M A West, "Minority Dissent and Team Innovation: The Importance of Participation in Decision Making," *Journal of Applied Psychology,* December 2001, pp 1191–201.
[48] A statistical validation for this model can be found in M A Rahim and N R Magner, "Confirmatory Factor Analysis of the Styles of Handling Interpersonal Conflict: First-Order Factor Model and Its Invariance across Groups," *Journal of Applied Psychology,* February 1995, pp 122–32.
[49] M A Rahim, "A Strategy for Managing Conflict in Complex Organizations," *Human Relations,* January 1985, p 84.
[50] See R Rubin, "Study: Bullies and Their Victims Tend to Be More Violent," *USA Today,* April 15, 2003, p 9D; and D Salin, "Ways of Explaining Workplace Bullying: A Review of Enabling, Motivating and Precipitating Structures and Processes in the Work Environment," *Human Relations,* October 2003, pp 1213–32.
[51] For more on managing conflict, see K Tyler, "Extending the Olive Branch," *HR Magazine,* November 2002, pp 85–89.
[52] See J Rasley, "The Revolution You Won't See on TV," *Newsweek,* November 25, 2002, p 13; and C Bendersky, "Organizational Dispute Resolution Systems: A Complementarities Model," *Academy of Management Review,* October 2003, pp 643–56.
[53] See M Bordwin, "Do-It-Yourself Justice," *Management Review,* January 1999, pp 56–58.
[54] B Morrow and L M Bernardi, "Resolving Workplace Disputes," *Canadian Manager,* Spring 1999, p 17.

[55] Adapted from discussion in K O Wilburn, "Employment Disputes: Solving Them Out of Court," *Management Review,* March 1998, pp 17–21; and Morrow and Bernardi, "Resolving Workplace Disputes," pp 17–19, 27. Also see L Ioannou, "Can't We Get Along?" *Fortune,* December 7, 1998, p 244[E]; and D Weimer and S A Forest, "Forced into Arbitration? Not Any More," *Business Week,* March 16, 1998, pp 66–68.
[56] For more, see M M Clark, "A Jury of Their Peers," *HR Magazine,* January 2004, pp 54–59.
[57] Wilburn, "Employment Disputes: Solving Them Out of Court," p 19.
[58] For more, see S Armour, "Arbitration's Rise Raises Fairness Issue," *USA Today,* June 12, 2001, pp 1B–2B; and G Weiss and D Serchuk, "Walled Off from Justice?" *Business Week,* March 22, 2004, pp 90–92.
[59] Based on a definition in M A Neale and M H Bazerman, "Negotiating Rationally: The Power and Impact of the Negotiator's Frame," *Academy of Management Executive,* August 1992, pp 42–51.
[60] See, for example, J K Sebenius, "Six Habits of Merely Effective Negotiators," *Harvard Business Review,* April 2001, pp 87–95; and R Walker, "Take It or Leave It: The *Only* Guide to Negotiating You Will *Ever* Need," *Inc.,* August 2003, pp 74–82.
[61] M H Bazerman and M A Neale, *Negotiating Rationally* (New York: The Free Press, 1992), p 16. Also see J F Brett, G B Northcraft, and R L Pinkley, "Stairways to Heaven: An Interlocking Self-Regulation Model of Negotiation," *Academy of Management Review,* July 1999, pp 435–51; G Cullinan, J Le Roux, and R Weddigen, "When to Walk Away from a Deal," *Harvard Business Review,* April 2004, pp 96–104; and G A van Kleef, C K W De Dreu, and A S R Manstead, "The Interpersonal Effects of Anger and Happiness in Negotiations, " *Journal of Personality and Social Psychology,* January 2004, pp 57–76.
[62] Good win-win negotiation strategies can be found in R R Reck and B G Long, *The Win-Win Negotiator: How to Negotiate Favorable Agreements That Last* (New York: Pocket Books, 1987); R Fisher and W Ury, *Getting to YES: Negotiating Agreement without Giving In* (Boston: Houghton Mifflin, 1981); and R Fisher and D Ertel, *Getting Ready to Negotiate: The Getting to YES Workbook* (New York: Penguin Books, 1995).
[63] Adapted from K Albrecht and S Albrecht, "Added Value Negotiating," *Training,* April 1993, pp 26–29. For an interesting look at Donald Trump's negotiating style, see "The Trophy Life," *Fortune,* April 19, 2004, pp 70–83.
[64] L Babcock, S Laschever, M Gelfand, and D Small, "Nice Girls Don't Ask," *Harvard Business Review,* October 2003, p 14. Also see L A Barron, "Ask and You Shall Receive? Gender Differences in Negotiators' Beliefs about Requests for a Higher Salary," *Human Relations,* June 2003, pp 635–62; L D Tyson, "New Clues to the Pay and Leadership Gap," *Business Week,* October 27, 2003, p 36; D Kersten, "Women Need to Learn the Art of the Deal," *USA Today,* November 17, 2003, p 7B; A Fels, "Do Women Lack Ambition?" *Harvard Business Review,* April 2004, pp 50–60; and B Brophy, "Bargaining for Bigger Bucks: A Step-by-Step Guide to Negotiating Your Salary," *Business 2.0,* May 2004, p 107.
[65] Excerpted from S Hamm, "Less Ego, More Success," *Business Week,* July 23, 2001, p 59; for an update, see S Hamm, "A Software Visionary Bows Out," *Business Week,* March 31, 2003, p 61.

Chapter 12

[1] Excerpted from C Hymowitz, "In the Lead: Missing from Work: The Chance to Think, Even to Dream a Little," *The Wall Street Journal,* Eastern Edition, March 23, 2004, p B1. Copyright 2004 by Dow Jones & Co. Inc. Reproduced with permission of Dow Jones & Co. Inc. via Copyright Clearance Center.
[2] C Hymowitz, "In the Lead: What Adecco Can Do to Improve Its Image after Bad News Bungle," *The Wall Street Journal,* January 20, 2004, p B1.
[3] See M A Jaasma and R J Koper, "The Relationship of Student-Faculty Out-of-Class Communication to Instructor Immediacy and Trust and to Student Motivation," *Communication Education,* January 1999, pp 41–47; and P G Clampitt and C W Downs, "Employee Perceptions of the Relationship between Communication and Productivity: A Field Study," *Journal of Business Communication,* 1993, pp 5–28.
[4] J L Bowditch and A F Buono, *A Primer on Organizational Behavior,* 4th ed (New York: John Wiley & Sons, 1997), p 120.
[5] M Orey, "Lawyer's Firing Signals Turmoil in Legal Circles," *The Wall Street Journal,* May 21, 2001, p B1.
[6] For a detailed discussion about selecting an appropriate medium, see B Barry and I Smithey-Fulmer, "The Medium and the Message: The Adaptive Use of Communication Media in Dyadic Influence," *Academy of Management Review,* April 2004, pp 272–92.
[7] Excerpted from J Sandberg, "Cookies, Gossip, Cubes: It's a Wonder Any Work Gets Done at the Office," *The Wall Street Journal,* April 28, 2004, p B1.
[8] For a thorough discussion of communication distortion, see E W Larson and J B King, "The Systematic Distortion of Information: An Ongoing Challenge to Management," *Organizational Dynamics,* Winter 1996, pp 49–61.
[9] J Fulk and S Mani, "Distortion of Communication in Hierarchical Relationships," in *Communication Yearbook 9,* ed M L McLaughlin (Beverly Hills, CA: Sage Publications, 1986), p 483.
[10] For a review of this research, see ibid., pp 483–510.
[11] M Frase-Blunt, "Boss: Understanding and Improve Communications," *HR Magazine,* June 2003, p 96.
[12] Results can be found in J D Johnson, W A Donohue, C K Atkin, and S Johnson, "Communication, Involvement, and Perceived Innovativeness," *Group & Organization Management,* March 2001, pp 24–52; and B Davenport Sypher and T E Zorn, Jr, "Communication-Related Abilities and Upward Mobility: A Longitudinal Investigation," *Human Communication Research,* Spring 1986, pp 420–31.
[13] Communication competence is discussed by J S Hinton and M W Kramer, "The Impact of Self-Directed Videotape Feedback on Students' Self-Reported Levels of Communication Competence and Apprehension," *Communication Education,* April 1998, pp 151–61; and L J Carrell and S C Willmington, "The Relationship between Self-Report Measures of Communication Apprehension and Trained Observers' Ratings of Communication Competence," *Communication Reports,* Winter 1998, pp 87–95.
[14] 1. *False.* Clients always take precedence, and people with the greatest authority or importance should be introduced first.
2. *False.* You should introduce yourself. Say something like "My name is ______. I don't believe we've met."
3. *False.* It's OK to admit you can't remember. Say something like "My mind just went blank, your name is?" Or offer your name and wait for the other person to respond with his or hers.
4. *False.* Business etiquette has become gender neutral.
5. *a. Host.* This enables him or her to lead their guest to the meeting place.
6. *False.* Not only is it rude to invade public areas with your conversation, but you never know who might hear details of your business transaction or personal life.
7. *b. 3 feet.* Closer than this is an invasion of personal space. Farther away forces people to raise their voices. Because communication varies from country to country, you should also inform yourself about cultural differences.
8. *True.* An exception to this would be if your company holds an event at the beach or the pool.
9. *False.* Just wave your hand over it when asked, or say "No thank you."
10. *True.* The person who initiated the call should redial if the connection is broken.
11. *True.* If you must use a speakerphone, you should inform all parties who's present.
12. *True.* You should record a greeting such as "I'm out of the office today, March 12. If you need help, please dial ______ at extension . . ."

[15] See E Raudsepp, "Are You Properly Assertive?" *Supervision,* June 1992, pp 17–18; and D A Infante and W I Gorden, "Superiors' Argumentativeness and Verbal Aggressiveness as Predictors of Subordinates' Satisfaction," *Human Communication Research,* Fall 1985, pp 117–25.
[16] J A Waters, "Managerial Assertiveness," *Business Horizons,* September–October 1982, p 25.
[17] Ibid., p 27.
[18] This statistic was provided by A Fisher, "How Can I Survive a Phone Interview?" *Fortune,* April 19, 2004, p 54.
[19] Problems with body language analysis are discussed by A Pihulyk, "Communicate with Clarity: The Key to Understanding and Influencing Others," *The Canadian Manager,* Summer 2003, pp 12–13.
[20] Related research is summarized by J A Hall, "Male and Female Nonverbal Behavior," in *Multichannel Integrations of Nonverbal*

Behavior, eds A W Siegman and S Feldstein (Hillsdale, NJ: Lawrence Erlbaum, 1985), pp 195–226.
[21] See R E Axtell, *Gestures: The Do's and Taboos of Body Language around the World* (New York: John Wiley & Sons, 1991).
[22] See J A Russell, "Facial Expressions of Emotion: What Lies Beyond Minimal Universality?" *Psychological Bulletin,* November 1995, pp 379–91.
[23] Norms for cross-cultural eye contact are discussed by C Engholm, *When Business East Meets Business West: The Guide to Practice and Protocol in the Pacific Rim* (New York: John Wiley & Sons, 1991).
[24] See D Ray, "Are You Listening?" *Selling Power,* June 1999, pp 28–30; and P Meyer, "So You Want the President's Job," *Business Horizons,* January–February 1998, pp 2–6.
[25] The discussion of listening styles is based on "5 Listening Styles," http://www.crossroadsinstitute.org/listyle.html, June 19, 2004; and "Listening and Thinking: What's Your Style," http://www.pediatricservices.com/prof/prof-10.htm, last modified August 10, 2002.
[26] Additional advice for improving listening skills is provided by S D Boyd, "The Human Side of Business: Effective Listening," *Agency Sales,* February 2004, pp 35–37; and B Brooks, "The Power of Active Listening," *Agency Sales,* December 2003, p 47.
[27] See S R Covey, *The 7 Habits of Highly Effective People* (New York: Simon & Schuster, 1989).
[28] D Tannen, "The Power of Talk: Who Gets Heard and Why," *Harvard Business Review,* September–October 1995, p 139.
[29] For a thorough review of the evolutionary explanation of sex differences in communication, see A H Eagly and W Wood, "The Origins of Sex Differences in Human Behavior," *American Psychologist,* June 1999, pp 408–23.
[30] See D Tannen, "The Power of Talk: Who Gets Heard and Why," in *Negotiation: Readings, Exercises, and Cases,* 3rd ed, eds R J Lewicki and D M Saunders (Boston, MA: Irwin/McGraw-Hill, 1999), pp 160–73; and D Tannen, *You Just Don't Understand: Women and Men in Conversation* (New York: Ballantine Books, 1990).
[31] Research on gender differences in communication can be found in E L MacGeorge, A R Graves, B Feng, S J Gillihan , and B R Burleson, "The Myth of Gender Cultures: Similarities Outweigh Differences in Men's and Women's Provision of and Responses to Supportive Communication," *Sex Roles,* 2004, pp 143–75; and V N Giri and H O Sharma, "Brain-Wiring and Communication Style," *Psychological Studies,* 2003, pp 59–64.
[32] Tannen, "The Power of Talk: Who Gets Heard and Why," pp 147–48.
[33] S N Mehta, "This Is Not a Cellphone," *Fortune,* May 26, 2003, p 142.
[34] This statistic was presented in S Baker, "Where Danger Lurks: Spam, Complexity, and Piracy Could Hinder Tech's Recovery," *Business Week,* August 25, 2003, pp 114–18.
[35] Results can be found in D Smith, "One-Tenth of College Students Are Dependent on the Internet, Research Finds," *Monitor on Psychology,* May 2001, p 10.
[36] Results were reported in A Petersen, "A Fine Line: Companies Face a Delicate Task When It Comes to Deciding What to Put on Their Intranets: How Much Is Too Much?" *The Wall Street Journal,* June 21, 1999, p R8.
[37] See S J Wells, "Communicating Benefits Information Online," *HR Magazine,* February 2001, pp 69–76.
[38] This statistic was reported in H Green, S Rosenbush, R O Crockett, and S Holmes, "Wi-Fi Means Business," *Business Week,* April 28, 2003, pp 86–92.
[39] See D Buss, "Spies Like Us," *Training,* December 2001, pp 44–48.
[40] Results of the survey are presented in "Electronic Monitoring," http://www.nolo.com/lawcenter/ency/article.cfm/ObjectID/C1066E74-A5CA-4EE3-Acd2, June 20, 2004.
[41] Statistics are reported in C Tejada, "Work Week: A Special News Report about Life on the Job—and Trends Taking Shape There," *The Wall Street Journal,* May 8, 2001, p A1; and J Wallace, "The (E-Mail) Postman Rings More Than Twice," *HR Magazine,* March 2001, p 176.
[42] The benefits of using e-mail were derived from discussion in R F Federico and J M Bowley, "The Great E-Mail Debate," *HR Magazine,* January 1996, pp 67–72.
[43] See B Hemphill, "File, Act, or Toss?" *Training & Development,* February 2001, pp 38–41.
[44] Results can be found in J Yaukey, "E-Mail Out of Control for Many: Take Steps to Ease Load," *The Wall Street Journal,* May 8, 2001, p F1.
[45] M Rose and M Peers, "AOL's Latest Internal Woe: 'You've Got Mail'—'Oops, No You Don't,'" *The Wall Street Journal,* March 22, 2002, p B1.
[46] See "US Companies Losing the Spam War," http://www.emarketer.com/Article.aspx?1002870, June 21, 2004.
[47] Results can be found in M S Thompson and M S Feldman, "Electronic Mail and Organizational Communication: Does Saying 'Hi' Really Matter?" *Organization Science,* November–December 1998, pp 685–98.
[48] See the discussion in S Prasso, "Workers, Surf at Your Own Risk," *Business Week,* June 11, 2001, p 14.
[49] E Krell, "Videoconferencing Gets the Call," *Training,* December 2001, p 38.
[50] Challenges associated with virtual operations are discussed by S O'Mahony and S R Barley, "Do Digital Telecommunications Affect Work and Organization? The State of Our Knowledge," in *Research in Organizational Behavior,* vol. 21, eds R I Sutton and B M Staw (Stamford, CT: JAI Press, 1999), pp 125–61.
[51] S Shellenbarger, "Work and Family: 'Telework' Is on the Rise, but It Isn't Just Done from Home Anymore," *The Wall Street Journal,* January 23, 2002, p B1.
[52] Statistics can be found in "Home-Based Telework by U.S. Employees Grows 40% Since 2001," http://www.telecommute.org/news/pr090403.htm, September 4, 2003.
[53] Supporting evidence can be found in B Hemphill, "Telecommuting Productively," *Occupational Health & Safety,* March 2004, pp 16, 18; R Konrad, "Sun's 'iWork' Shuns Desks for Flexibility," *Arizona Republic,* May 28, 2003, p D4; and C Hymowitz, "Remote Managers Find Ways to Narrow the Distance Gap," *The Wall Street Journal,* April 6, 1999, p B1.
[54] See M Tan-Solano and B Kleiner, "Virtual Workers: Are They Worth the Risk?" *Nonprofit World,* November/December 2003, pp 20–22.
[55] The preceding barriers are discussed by J P Scully, "People: The Imperfect Communicators," *Quality Progress,* April 1995, pp 37–39.
[56] For a thorough discussion of these barriers, see C R Rogers and F J Roethlisberger, "Barriers and Gateways to Communication," *Harvard Business Review,* July–August 1952, pp 46–52.
[57] Ibid., p 47.
[58] S Srivastava, "Why India Worries about Outsourcing," *San Francisco Chronicle,* March 21, 2004, p E3.
[59] Excerpted from Yuri Kageyama, "Cellphones with Cameras Creating Trouble: Concerns Include Voyeurism," *Arizona Republic,* July 10, 2003, pp A18.

Chapter 13

[1] Excerpted from Michael Arndt, "3M's Rising Star," *Business Week,* April 12, 2004, pp 62–74. Reprinted with permission.
[2] See D Kipnis, S M Schmidt, and J Wilkinson, "Intraorganizational Influence Tactics: Explorations in Getting One's Way," *Journal of Applied Psychology,* August 1980, pp 440–52. Also see C A Schriesheim and T R Hinkin, "Influence Tactics Used by Subordinates: A Theoretical and Empirical Analysis and Refinement of the Kipnis, Schmidt, and Wilkinson Subscales," *Journal of Applied Psychology,* June 1990, pp 246–57; and G Yukl and C M Falbe, "Influence Tactics and Objectives in Upward, Downward, and Lateral Influence Attempts," *Journal of Applied Psychology,* April 1990, pp 132–40.
[3] Based on Table 1 in G Yukl, C M Falbe, and J Y Youn, "Patterns of Influence Behavior for Managers," *Group & Organization Management,* March 1993, pp 5–28. An additional influence tactic is presented in B P Davis and E S Knowles, "A Disrupt-then-Reframe Technique of Social Influence," *Journal of Personality and Social Psychology,* February 1999, pp 192–99. Also see Table 1 in P P Fu, T K Peng, J C Kennedy, and G Yukl, "Examining the Preferences of Influence Tactics in Chinese Societies: A Comparison of Chinese Managers in Hong Kong, Taiwan and Mainland China," *Organizational Dynamics,* no. 1, 2004, pp 32–46.
[4] For related reading, see L Buchanan, "Who's Managing Whom?" *Inc.,* April 2003, p 44; K D Elsbach, "How to Pitch a Brilliant Idea," *Harvard Business Review,* September 2003, pp 117–23; "Daddy Dearest," *Inc.,*

January 2004, p 46; K Hannon, "Working for the I-Boss," *USA Today,* March 1, 2004, p 5B; J Battelle, "The Net of Influence," *Business 2.0,* March 2004, p 70; B Barry and I S Fulmer, "The Medium and the Message: The Adaptive Use of Communication Media in Dyadic Influence," *Academy of Management Review,* April 2004, pp 272–92; and H Johnson, "The Ins and Outs of Executive Coaching," *Training,* May 2004, pp 36–41.

[5] Based on discussion in G Yukl, H Kim, and C M Falbe, "Antecedents of Influence Outcomes," *Journal of Applied Psychology,* June 1996, pp 309–17.

[6] Excerpted from A Barrett, "Staying on Top," *Business Week,* May 5, 2003, p 60. Reprinted with permission.

[7] Data from Yukl, Kim, and Falbe, "Antecedents of Influence Outcomes."

[8] Data from G Yukl and J B Tracey, "Consequences of Influence Tactics Used with Subordinates, Peers, and the Boss," *Journal of Applied Psychology,* August 1992, pp 525–35. Also see C M Falbe and G Yukl, "Consequences for Managers of Using Single Influence Tactics and Combinations of Tactics," *Academy of Management Journal,* August 1992, pp 638–52.

[9] Data from R A Gordon, "Impact of Ingratiation on Judgments and Evaluations: A Meta-Analytic Investigation," *Journal of Personality and Social Psychology,* July 1996, pp 54–70. Also see S J Wayne, R C Liden, and R T Sparrowe, "Developing Leader-Member Exchanges," *American Behavioral Scientist,* March 1994, pp 697–714; A Oldenburg, "These Days, Hostile Is Fitting for Takeovers Only," *USA Today,* July 22, 1996, pp 8B, 10B; and J H Dulebohn and G R Ferris, "The Role of Influence Tactics in Perceptions of Performance Evaluations' Fairness," *Academy of Management Journal,* June 1999, pp 288–303.

[10] Data from Yukl, Kim, and Falbe, "Antecedents of Influence Outcomes."

[11] Based on C Pornpitakpan, "The Persuasiveness of Source Credibility: A Critical Review of Five Decades' Evidence," *Journal of Applied Social Psychology,* February 2004, pp 243–81.

[12] Data from B J Tepper, R J Eisenbach, S L Kirby, and P W Potter, "Test of a Justice-Based Model of Subordinates' Resistance to Downward Influence Attempts," *Group & Organization Management,* June 1998, pp 144–60. Also see H G Enns and D B McFarlin, "When Executives Influence Peers: Does Function Matter?" *Human Resource Management,* Summer 2003, pp 125–42.

[13] See A R Cohen and D L Bradford, *Influence without Authority* (New York: John Wiley & Sons, 1990), pp 23–24.

[14] Ibid., p 28. Also see R B Cialdini, *Influence* (New York: William Morrow, 1984); R B Cialdini, "Harnessing the Science of Persuasion," *Harvard Business Review,* October 2001, pp 72–79; and G A Williams and R B Miller, "Change the Way You Persuade," *Harvard Business Review,* May 2002, pp 64–73.

[15] See B Salmon, "Fighting Corporate America," *USA Today,* September 8, 2003, p 6B; A Serwer and J Nocera, "Up against the Wall," *Fortune,* November 24, 2003, pp 130–42; and K Hannon, "Author Looks at 'Wild' Private Lives of Business Titans," *USA Today,* June 1, 2004, p 4B.

[16] D Tjosvold, "The Dynamics of Positive Power," *Training and Development Journal,* June 1984, p 72. Also see T A Stewart, "Get with the New Power Game," *Fortune,* January 13, 1997, pp 58–62.

[17] For example, see D Rynecki, "Golf and Power," *Fortune,* April 14, 2003, pp 164–74; P Sellers, "Power: Do Women Really Want It?" *Fortune,* October 13, 2003, pp 80–100; A Harrington and M Shanley, "The Power 50," *Fortune,* October 13, 2003, pp 105–8; B Stone, "At Dell, He's No Second Fiddle," *Newsweek,* February 23, 2004, pp E6–E9; and L Lavelle, "How to Groom the Next Boss," *Business Week,* May 10, 2004, pp 93–94.

[18] M W McCall, Jr, *Power, Influence, and Authority: The Hazards of Carrying a Sword,* Technical Report No. 10 (Greensboro, NC: Center for Creative Leadership, 1978), p 5. For an excellent overview of power, see E P Hollander and L R Offermann, "Power and Leadership in Organizations," *American Psychologist,* February 1990, pp 179–89.

[19] D Weimer, "Daughter Knows Best," *Business Week,* April 19, 1999, pp 132, 134.

[20] See J R P French and B Raven, "The Bases of Social Power," in *Studies in Social Power,* ed D Cartwright (Ann Arbor: University of Michigan Press, 1959), pp 150–67. Also see C M Fiol, E J O'Connor, and H Aguinis, "All for One and One for All? The Development and Transfer of Power across Organizational Levels," *Academy of Management Review,* April 2001, pp 224–42.

[21] Excerpted from C Haddad, "Too Good to Be True," *Business Week,* April 14, 2003, p 71.

[22] Data from J R Larson, Jr, C Christensen, A S Abbott, and T M Franz, "Diagnosing Groups: Charting the Flow of Information in Medical Decision-Making Teams," *Journal of Personality and Social Psychology,* August 1996, pp 315–30.

[23] See H Lancaster, "A Father's Character, Not His Success, Shapes Kids' Careers," *The Wall Street Journal,* February 27, 1996, p B1. Research involving expert and referent power is reported in J S Bunderson, "Team Member Functional Background and Involvement in Management Teams: Direct Effects and the Moderating Role of Power Centralization," *Academy of Management Journal,* August 2003, pp 458–74.

[24] P M Podsakoff and C A Schriesheim, "Field Studies of French and Raven's Bases of Power: Critique, Reanalysis, and Suggestions for Future Research," *Psychological Bulletin,* May 1985, p 388. Also see M A Rahim and G F Buntzman, "Supervisory Power Bases, Styles of Handling Conflict with Subordinates, and Subordinate Compliance and Satisfaction," *Journal of Psychology,* March 1989, pp 195–210; D Tjosvold, "Power and Social Context in Superior-Subordinate Interaction," *Organizational Behavior and Human Decision Processes,* June 1985, pp 281–93; and C A Schriesheim, T R Hinkin, and P M Podsakoff, "Can Ipsative and Single-Item Measures Produce Erroneous Results in Field Studies of French and Raven's (1950) Five Bases of Power? An Empirical Investigation," *Journal of Applied Psychology,* February 1991, pp 106–14.

[25] See T R Hinkin and C A Schriesheim, "Relationships between Subordinate Perceptions and Supervisor Influence Tactics and Attributed Bases of Supervisory Power," *Human Relations,* March 1990, pp 221–37. Also see D J Brass and M E Burkhardt, "Potential Power and Power Use: An Investigation of Structure and Behavior," *Academy of Management Journal,* June 1993, pp 441–70; and K W Mossholder, N Bennett, E R Kemery, and M A Wesolowski, "Relationships between Bases of Power and Work Reactions: The Mediational Role of Procedural Justice," *Journal of Management,* no. 4, 1998, pp 533–52.

[26] See H E Baker III, "'Wax On—Wax Off:' French and Raven at the Movies," *Journal of Management Education,* November 1993, pp 517–19.

[27] See R Forrester, "Empowerment: Rejuvenating a Potent Idea," *Academy of Management Executive,* August 2000, pp 67–80; P Haspeslagh, T Noda, and F Boulos, "It's Not Just about the Numbers," *Harvard Business Review,* July–August 2001, pp 65–73; S Ghoshal and H Bruch, "Going beyond Motivation to the Power of Volition," *MIT Sloan Management Review,* Spring 2003, pp 51–57; P J Sauer, "Open-Door Management," *Inc.,* June 2003, p 44; and L Grensing-Pophal, "Involve Your Employees in Cost Cutting," *HR Magazine,* November 2003, pp 52–56.

[28] J Macdonald, "The Dreaded 'E Word,'" *Training,* September 1998, p 19. Also see R C Liden and S Arad, "A Power Perspective of Empowerment and Work Groups: Implications for Human Resources Management Research," in *Research in Personnel and Human Resources Management,* vol. 14, ed G R Ferris (Greenwich, CT: JAI Press, 1996), pp 205–51.

[29] R M Hodgetts, "A Conversation with Steve Kerr," *Organizational Dynamics,* Spring 1996, p 71. See L Holpp, "If Empowerment Is So Good, Why Does It Hurt?" *Training,* March 1995, pp 52–57; Liden and Arad, "A Power Perspective of Empowerment and Work Groups: Implications for Human Resources Management Research"; and G M Spreitzer, "Social Structural Characteristics of Psychological Empowerment," *Academy of Management Journal,* April 1996, pp 483–504.

[30] L Shaper Walters, "A Leader Redefines Management," *The Christian Science Monitor,* September 22, 1992, p 14.

[31] For related discussion, see M M Broadwell, "Why Command & Control Won't Go Away," *Training,* September 1995, pp 62–68; R E Quinn and G M Spreitzer, "The Road to Empowerment: Seven Questions Every Leader Should Consider," *Organizational Dynamics,* Autumn 1997, pp 37–49; and I Cunningham and L Honold, "Everyone Can Be a Coach," *HR Magazine,* June 1998, pp 63–66.

[32] For recent research, see S H Wagner, C P Parker, and N D Christiansen, "Employees That Think and Act Like Owners: Effects of Ownership Beliefs and Behaviors on Organizational Effectiveness," *Personnel Psychology,* Winter 2003, pp 847–71; D J Leach, T D Wall, and P R Jackson, "The Effect of Empowerment on Job Knowledge: An Empirical Test Involving Operators of Complex Technology," *Journal of Occupational and Organizational Psychology,* March 2003, pp 27–52; P T Coleman, "Implicit Theories of Organizational Power and Priming Effects on Managerial Power-Sharing Decisions: An Experimental Study," *Journal of Applied Social Psychology,* February 2004, pp 297–321; and B L Kirkman, B Rosen, P E Tesluk, and C B Gibson, "The Impact of Team Empowerment on Virtual Team Performance: The Moderating Role of Face-to-Face Interaction," *Academy of Management Journal,* April 2004, pp 175–92.

[33] W A Randolph, "Navigating the Journey to Empowerment," *Organizational Dynamics,* Spring 1995, p 31.

[34] See K Naughton and Marc Peyser, "The World According to Trump," *Newsweek,* March 1, 2004, pp 48–57; "Trump: Paranoia Good for Business," *USA Today,* March 12, 2004, p 3B; D Jones, "It's Nothing Personal? On 'Apprentice,' It's All Personal," *USA Today,* March 26, 2004, p 6B; D Jones and B Keveney, "10 Lessons of 'The Apprentice,'" *USA Today,* April 15, 2004, pp 1A–5A.

[35] C Pasternak, "Corporate Politics May Not Be a Waste of Time," *HR Magazine,* September 1994, p 18. Also see D J Burrough, "Office Politics Mirror Popular TV Program," *Arizona Republic,* February 4, 2001, p EC1.

[36] See G Browning and J James, "Office Politics: The New Game," *Management Today,* May 2003, pp 54–59; P L Perrewé, K L Zellars, G R Ferris, A M Rossi, C J Kacmar, and D A Ralston, "Neutralizing Job Stressors: Political Skills as an Antidote to the Dysfunctional Consequences of Role Conflict," *Academy of Management Journal,* February 2004, pp 141–52; J Sandberg, "From the Front Lines: Bosses Muster Staffs for Border Skirmishes," *The Wall Street Journal,* February 18, 2004, p B1; and K Hannon, "Change the Way You Play: Small Things You Can Do to Get Ahead," *USA Today,* March 15, 2004, p 6B.

[37] R W Allen, D L Madison, L W Porter, P A Renwick, and B T Mayes, "Organizational Politics: Tactics and Characteristics of Its Actors," *California Management Review,* Fall 1979, p 77. Also see K M Kacmar and G R Ferris, "Politics at Work: Sharpening the Focus of Political Behavior in Organizations," *Business Horizons,* July–August 1993, pp 70–74. A comprehensive overview can be found in K M Kacmar and R A Baron, "Organizational Politics: The State of the Field, Links to Related Processes, and an Agenda for Future Research," in *Research in Personnel and Human Resources Management,* vol. 17, ed G R Ferris (Stamford, CT: JAI Press, 1999), pp 1–39.

[38] See P M Fandt and G R Ferris, "The Management of Information and Impressions: When Employees Behave Opportunistically," *Organizational Behavior and Human Decision Processes,* February 1990, pp 140–58; L R Offermann, "When Followers Become Toxic," *Harvard Business Review,* Special Issue: Inside the Mind of the Leader, January 2004, pp 54–60; and K J Sulkowicz, "Worse than Enemies: The CEO's Destructive Confidant," *Harvard Business Review,* February 2004, pp 64–71.

[39] First four based on discussion in D R Beeman and T W Sharkey, "The Use and Abuse of Corporate Politics," *Business Horizons,* March–April 1987, pp 26–30.

[40] A Raia, "Power, Politics, and the Human Resource Professional," *Human Resource Planning,* no. 4, 1985, p 203.

[41] A J DuBrin, "Career Maturity, Organizational Rank, and Political Behavioral Tendencies: A Correlational Analysis of Organizational Politics and Career Experience," *Psychological Reports,* October 1988, p 535.

[42] This three-level distinction comes from A T Cobb, "Political Diagnosis: Applications in Organizational Development," *Academy of Management Review,* July 1986, pp 482–96.

[43] An excellent historical and theoretical perspective of coalitions can be found in W B Stevenson, J L Pearce, and L W Porter, "The Concept of 'Coalition' in Organization Theory and Research," *Academy of Management Review,* April 1985, pp 256–68. Also see A Kleiner, "Are You In with the In Crowd?" *Harvard Business Review,* July 2003, pp 86–92.

[44] See K G Provan and J G Sebastian, "Networks within Networks: Service Link Overlap, Organizational Cliques, and Network Effectiveness," *Academy of Management Journal,* August 1998, pp 453–63.

[45] J Sandberg, "Better Than Great—and Other Tall Tales of Self-Evaluations," *The Wall Street Journal,* March 12, 2003, p B1. Also see J Sandberg, "Sabotage 101: The Sinister Art of Back-Stabbing," *The Wall Street Journal,* February 11, 2004, p B1.

[46] Allen, Madison, Porter, Renwick, and Mayes, "Organizational Politics: Tactics and Characteristics of Its Actors," p 77.

[47] See W L Gardner III, "Lessons in Organizational Dramaturgy: The Art of Impression Management," *Organizational Dynamics,* Summer 1992, pp 33–46.

[48] A Rao, S M Schmidt, and L H Murray, "Upward Impression Management: Goals, Influence Strategies, and Consequences," *Human Relations,* February 1995, p 147. Also see M C Andrews and K M Kacmar, "Impression Management by Association: Construction and Validation of a Scale," *Journal of Vocational Behavior,* February 2001, pp 142–61; and P F Hewlin, "And the Award for Best Actor Goes to . . . : Facades of Conformity in Organizational Settings," *Academy of Management Review,* October 2003, pp 633–42.

[49] For related research, see M G Pratt and A Rafaeli, "Organizational Dress as a Symbol of Multilayered Social Identities," *Academy of Management Journal,* August 1997, pp 862–98. Also see B Leonard, "Casual Dress Policies Can Trip Up Job Applicants," *HR Magazine,* June 2001, pp 33, 35; and W N Davidson III, P Jiraporn, Y S Kim, and C Nemec, "Earnings Management Following Duality-Creating Successions: Ethnostatistics, Impression Management, and Agency Theory," *Academy of Management Journal,* April 2004, pp 267–75.

[50] S Friedman, "What Do You Really Care About? What Are You Most Interested In?" *Fast Company,* March 1999, p 90. Also see B M DePaulo and D A Kashy, "Everyday Lies in Close and Casual Relationships," *Journal of Personality and Social Psychology,* January 1998, pp 63–79.

[51] See S J Wayne and G R Ferris, "Influence Tactics, Affect, and Exchange Quality in Supervisor-Subordinate Interactions: A Laboratory Experiment and Field Study," *Journal of Applied Psychology,* October 1990, pp 487–99. For another version, see Table 1 (p 246) in S J Wayne and R C Liden, "Effects of Impression Management on Performance Ratings: A Longitudinal Study," *Academy of Management Journal,* February 1995, pp 232–60.

[52] See R Vonk, "The Slime Effect: Suspicion and Dislike of Likeable Behavior toward Superiors," *Journal of Personality and Social Psychology,* April 1998, pp 849–64; and M Wells, "How to Schmooze Like the Best of Them," *USA Today,* May 18, 1999, p 14E.

[53] See P Rosenfeld, R A Giacalone, and C A Riordan, "Impression Management Theory and Diversity: Lessons for Organizational Behavior," *American Behavioral Scientist,* March 1994, pp 601–4; R A Giacalone and J W Beard, "Impression Management, Diversity, and International Management," *American Behavioral Scientist,* March 1994, pp 621–36; and A Montagliani and R A Giacalone, "Impression Management and Cross-Cultural Adaptation," *Journal of Social Psychology,* October 1998, pp 598–608.

[54] M E Mendenhall and C Wiley, "Strangers in a Strange Land: The Relationship between Expatriate Adjustment and Impression Management," *American Behavioral Scientist,* March 1994, pp 605–20. Also see J Kurman, "Why Is Self-Enhancement Low in Certain Collectivist Cultures? An Investigation of Two Competing Explanations," *Journal of Cross-Cultural Psychology,* September 2003, pp 496–510.

[55] For a humorous discussion of making a bad impression, see P Hellman, "Looking BAD," *Management Review,* January 2000, p 64.

[56] T E Becker and S L Martin, "Trying to Look Bad at Work: Methods and Motives for Managing Poor Impressions in Organizations," *Academy of Management Journal,* February 1995, p 191.

[57] Ibid., p 181.

[58] Adapted from ibid., pp 180–81.

[59] Based on discussion in ibid., pp 192–93.

[60] A Zaleznik, "Real Work," *Harvard Business Review,* January–February 1989, p 60.

[61] C M Koen, Jr, and S M Crow, "Human Relations and Political Skills," *HR Focus,* December 1995, p 11.

[62] See L A Witt, "Enhancing Organizational Goal Congruence: A Solution to Organizational Politics," *Journal of Applied Psychology,* August 1998, pp 666–74; and F F Reichheld, "Lead for Loyalty," *Harvard Business Review,* July–August 2001, pp 76–84.
[63] Excerpted from K Tse and D Foust, "At Risk from Smoking: Your Job," *Business Week,* April 15, 2002, p 12. Reprinted with permission.

Chapter 14

[1] Excerpted from D Brady, "Act II," *Business Week,* March 29, 2004, pp 73–76, 80. Reprinted with permission.
[2] See S Lieberson and J F O'Connor, "Leadership and Organizational Performance: A Study of Large Corporations," *American Sociological Review,* April 1972, pp 117–30.
[3] Results can be found in K T Dirks, "Trust in Leadership and Team Performance: Evidence from NCAA Basketball," *Journal of Applied Psychology,* December 2000, pp 1004–12; and D Jacobs and L Singell, "Leadership and Organizational Performance: Isolating Links between Managers and Collective Success," *Social Science Research,* June 1993, pp 165–89.
[4] C A Schriesheim, J M Tolliver, and O C Behling, "Leadership Theory: Some Implications for Managers," *MSU Business Topics,* Summer 1978, p 35.
[5] The different levels of leadership are thoroughly discussed by F J Yammarino, F Dansereau, and C J Kennedy, "A Multiple-Level Multidimensional Approach to Leadership: Viewing Leadership through an Elephant's Eye," *Organizational Dynamics,* 2001, pp 149–62.
[6] B Kellerman, "Leadership Warts and All," *Harvard Business Review,* January 2004, p 45.
[7] See the related discussion in M F R Kets de Vries, "Putting Leaders on the Couch," *Harvard Business Review,* January 2004, pp 65–71.
[8] See R Goffee and G Jones, "Followership: It's Personal, Too," *Harvard Business Review,* December 2001, p 148.
[9] See D A Kenny and S J Zaccaro, "An Estimate of Variance Due to Traits in Leadership," *Journal of Applied Psychology,* November 1983, pp 678–85.
[10] See J S Phillips and R G Lord, "Schematic Information Processing and Perceptions of Leadership in Problem-Solving Groups," *Journal of Applied Psychology,* August 1982, pp 486–92.
[11] Results from this study can be found in F C Brodbeck et al., "Cultural Variation of Leadership Prototypes across 22 European Countries," *Journal of Occupational and Organizational Psychology,* March 2000, pp 1–29.
[12] Results can be found in T A Judge, J E Bono, R Ilies, & M W Gerhardt, "Personality and Leadership: A Qualitative and Quantitative Review," *Journal of Applied Psychology,* August 2002, pp 765–80.
[13] See T A Judge, A E Colbert, and R Ilies, "Intelligence and Leadership: A Quantitative Review and Test of Theoretical Propositions," *Journal of Applied Psychology,* June 2004, pp 542–52.
[14] A summary of this research is provided by B J Avolio, J J Soskik, D I Jung, and Y Berson, "Leadership Models, Methods, and Applications," in *Handbook of Psychology,* eds W C Borman, D R Ilgen, R J Klimoski (Hoboken, NJ: John Wiley & Sons, 2003), vol 12, pp 277–307.
[15] Excerpted from C Terhune, B McKay, J S Lublin, "Coke Hunts Outside for Chief as No. 2 Heyer Draws Some Flak," *The Wall Street Journal,* February 23, 2004.
[16] See D Foust, "Coke: Time for a Shakeup," *Business Week,* March 8, 2004, p 40.
[17] Gender and the emergence of leaders was examined by A H Eagly and S J Karau, "Gender and the Emergence of Leaders: A Meta-Analysis," *Journal of Personality and Social Psychology,* May 1991, pp 685–710; and R K Shelly and P T Munroe, "Do Women Engage in Less Task Behavior Than Men?" *Sociological Perspectives,* Spring 1999, pp 49–67.
[18] See A H Eagly, S J Karau, and B T Johnson, "Gender and Leadership Style among School Principals: A Meta-Analysis," *Educational Administration Quarterly,* February 1992, pp 76–102.
[19] Supportive findings are contained in J M Twenge, "Changes in Women's Assertiveness in Response to Status and Roles: A Cross-Temporal Meta-Analysis, 1931–1993," *Journal of Personality and Social Psychology,* July 2001, pp 133–45.
[20] For a summary of this research, see R Sharpe, "As Leaders, Women Rule," *Business Week,* November 20, 2000, pp 74–84.
[21] Results can be found in A H Eagly, M C Johannesen-Schmidt, and M L van Engen, "Transformational, Transactional, and Laissez-Faire Leadership Styles: A Meta-Analysis Comparing Women and Men," *Psychological Bulletin,* June 2003, pp 569–91.
[22] Excerpted from D K Berman and J S Lublin, "Restructuring, Personality Clashes Led to Lucent Executive's Exit," *The Wall Street Journal,* May 16, 2001, p B1.
[23] For corporate examples of leadership development, see H Johnson, "Leveraging Leadership," *Training,* January 2004, pp 20–21; and T Barron, "The Link between Leadership Development and Retention," *Training & Development,* April 2004, pp 59–65.
[24] See B M Bass, *Bass & Stogdill's Handbook of Leadership: Theory, Research, and Managerial Applications,* 3rd ed (New York: The Free Press, 1990), chs 20–25.
[25] The relationships between the frequency and mastery of leader behavior and various outcomes were investigated by F Shipper and C S White, "Mastery, Frequency, and Interaction of Managerial Behaviors Relative to Subunit Effectiveness," *Human Relations,* January 1999, pp 49–66.
[26] F E Fiedler, "Job Engineering for Effective Leadership: A New Approach," *Management Review,* September 1977, p 29.
[27] For more on this theory, see F E Fiedler, "A Contingency Model of Leadership Effectiveness," in *Advances in Experimental Social Psychology,* vol. 1, ed L Berkowitz (New York: Academic Press, 1964); F E Fiedler, *A Theory of Leadership Effectiveness* (New York: McGraw-Hill, 1967).
[28] See L H Peters, D D Hartke, and J T Pohlmann, "Fiedler's Contingency Theory of Leadership: An Application of the Meta-Analyses Procedures of Schmidt and Hunter," *Psychological Bulletin,* March 1985, pp 274–85; and C A Schriesheim, B J Tepper, and L A Tetrault, "Least Preferred Co-Worker Score, Situational Control, and Leadership Effectiveness: A Meta-Analysis of Contingency Model Performance Predictions," *Journal of Applied Psychology,* August 1994, pp 561–73.
[29] Excerpted from D Kirkpatrick, "Inside Sam's $100 Billion Growth Machine," *Fortune,* June 14, 2004, pp 86, 88.
[30] For more detail on this theory, see R J House, "A Path–Goal Theory of Leader Effectiveness," *Administrative Science Quarterly,* September 1971, pp 321–38.
[31] This research is summarized by R J House, "Path–Goal Theory of Leadership: Lessons, Legacy, and a Reformulated Theory," *Leadership Quarterly,* Autumn 1996, pp 323–52.
[32] See ibid.
[33] Supportive results can be found in B Alimo-Metcalfe and R J Alban-Metcalfe, "The Development of a New Transformational Leadership Questionnaire," *Journal of Occupational and Organizational Psychology,* March 2001, pp 1–27.
[34] Excerpted from S Caudron, "Don't Mess with Carly," *Workforce Management,* July 2003, pp 29–30.
[35] Results can be found in P M Podsakoff, S B MacKenzie, M Ahearne, and W H Bommer, "Searching for a Needle in a Haystack: Trying to Identify the Illusive Moderators of Leadership Behaviors," *Journal of Management,* 1995, pp 422–70.
[36] A thorough discussion of this theory is provided by P Hersey and K H Blanchard, *Management of Organizational Behavior: Utilizing Human Resources,* 5th ed (Englewood Cliffs, NJ: Prentice Hall, 1988).
[37] A comparison of the original theory and its latent version is provided by P Hersey and K H Blanchard, "Great Ideas Revisited," *Training & Development,* January 1996, pp 42–47.
[38] See D C Lueder, "Don't Be Misled by LEAD," *Journal of Applied Behavioral Science,* May 1985, pp 143–54; and C L Graeff, "The Situational Leadership Theory: A Critical View," *Academy of Management Review,* April 1983, pp 285–91.
[39] For a complete description of this theory see B J Bass and B J Avolio, *Revised Manual for the Multi-Factor Leadership Questionnaire* (Palo Alto, CA: Mindgarden, 1997).
[40] A definition and description of transactional leadership is provided by J Antonakis and R J House, "The Full-Range Leadership Theory: The Way Forward," in *Transformational and Charismatic Leadership: The Road Ahead,* eds B J Avolio and F J Yammarino (New York: JAI Press, 2002), pp 3–34.

[41] M Arndt, "3M's Rising Star," *Business Week,* April 12, 2004, p 65.
[42] U R Dumdum, K B Lowe, and B J Avolio, "A Meta-Analysis of Transformational and Transactional Leadership Correlates of Effectiveness and Satisfaction: An Update and Extension," in *Transformational and Charismatic Leadership: The Road Ahead,* eds B J Avolio and F J Yammarino (New York: JAI Press, 2002), p 38.
[43] Supportive research is summarized by J Antonakis and R J House, "The Full-Range Leadership Theory: The Way Forward."
[44] M Arndt, "3M's Rising Star," pp 65, 68.
[45] Supportive results can be found in T A Judge and J E Bono, "Five-Factor Model of Personality and Transformational Leadership," *Journal of Applied Psychology,* October 2000, pp 751–65; and A H Eagly, M C Johannesen-Schmidt, and M L van Engen, "Transformational, Transactional, and Laissez-Faire Leadership Styles: A Meta-Analysis Comparing Women and Men."
[46] These definitions are derived from R Kark, B Shamir, and C Chen, "The Two Faces of Transformational Leadership: Empowerment and Dependency," *Journal of Applied Psychology,* April 2003, pp 246–55.
[47] B Nanus, *Visionary Leadership* (San Francisco: Jossey-Bass, 1992), p 8.
[48] A Lashinsky, "Can Moto Find Its Mojo?" *Fortune,* April 5, 2004, p 132.
[49] See R Kark, B Shamir, and G Chen, "The Two Faces of Transformational Leadership," *Journal of Applied Psychology,* April 2003, pp 246–55.
[50] Supportive results can be found in B M Bass, B J Avolio, D I Jung, and Y Berson, "Predicting Unit Performance by Assessing Transformational and Transactional Leadership," *Journal of Applied Psychology,* April 2003, pp 207–18; J E Bono and T A Judge, "Self-Concordance at Work: Toward Understanding the Motivational Effects of Transformational Leaders," *Academy of Management Journal,* October 2003, pp 554–71; and D Charbonneau, J Barling, and E K Kelloway, "Transformational Leadership and Sports Performance: The Mediating Role of Intrinsic Motivation," *Journal of Applied Social Psychology,* July 2001, pp 1521–34.
[51] Results can be found in U R Dumdum, K B Lowe, and B J Avolio, "A Meta-Analysis of Transformational and Transactional Leadership Correlates of Effectiveness and Satisfaction: An Update and Extension."
[52] See K B Lowe, K G Kroeck, and N Sivasubramaniam, "Effectiveness Correlates of Transformational and Transactional Leadership: A Meta-Analytic Review of the MLQ Literature," *Leadership Quarterly,* 1996, pp 385–425.
[53] See A J Towler, "Effects of Charismatic Influence Training on Attitudes, Behavior, and Performance," *Personnel Psychology,* Summer 2003, pp 363–81; and M Frese and S Beimel, "Action Training for Charismatic Leadership: Two Evaluations of Studies of a Commercial Training Module on Inspirational Communication of a Vision," *Personnel Psychology,* Autumn 2003, pp 671–97.
[54] Johnson & Johnson's leadership development program is thoroughly discussed by R M Fulmer, "Johnson & Johnson: Frameworks for Leadership," *Organizational Dynamics,* Winter 2001, pp 211–20.
[55] These recommendations were derived from J M Howell and B J Avolio, "The Ethics of Charismatic Leadership: Submission or Liberation," *The Executive,* May 1992, pp 43–54.
[56] See F Dansereau, Jr, G Graen, and W Haga, "A Vertical Dyad Linkage Approach to Leadership within Formal Organizations," *Organizational Behavior and Human Performance,* February 1975, pp 46–78; and R M Dienesch and R C Liden, "Leader–Member Exchange Model of Leadership: A Critique and Further Development," *Academy of Management Review,* July 1986, pp 618–34.
[57] These descriptions were taken from D Duchon, S G Green, and T D Taber, "Vertical Dyad Linkage: A Longitudinal Assessment of Antecedents, Measures, and Consequences," *Journal of Applied Psychology,* February 1986, pp 56–60.
[58] Supportive results can be found in C Gomez and B Rosen, "The Leader–Member Exchange as a Link between Managerial Trust and Employee Empowerment," *Group & Organization Management,* March 2001, pp 53–69; C A Schriesheim, S L Castro, and F J Yammarino, "Investigating Contingencies: An Examination of the Impact of Span of Supervision and Upward Controllingness on Leader–Member Exchange Using Traditional and Multivariate within—and between—Entities Analysis," *Journal of Applied Psychology,* October 2000, pp 659–77; and C Cogliser and C A Schriesheim, "Exploring Work Unit Context and Leader–Member Exchange: A Multi-Level Perspective," *Journal of Organizational Behavior,* August 2000, pp 487–511.
[59] A turnover study was conducted by G B Graen, R C Liden, and W Hoel, "Role of Leadership in the Employee Withdrawal Process," *Journal of Applied Psychology,* December 1982, pp 868–72. The career progress study was conducted by M Wakabayashi and G B Graen, "The Japanese Career Progress Study: A 7-Year Follow-Up," *Journal of Applied Psychology,* November 1984, pp 603–14.
[60] See D O Adebayo and I B Udegbe, "Gender in the Boss-Subordinate Relationship: A Nigerian Study," *Journal of Organizational Behavior,* June 2004, pp 515–25.
[61] Supportive results can be found in K M Kacmar, L A Witt, S Zivnuska, and S M Gully, "The Interactive-Effect of Leader–Member Exchange and Communication Frequency on Performance Ratings," *Journal of Applied Psychology,* August 2003, pp 764–72; and S J Wayne, L M Shore, and R C Liden, "Perceived Organizational Support and Leader–Member Exchange: A Social Exchange Perspective," *Academy of Management Journal,* February 1997, pp 82–111.
[62] These recommendations were derived from G C Mage, "Leading Despite Your Boss," *HR Magazine,* September 2003, pp 139–44.
[63] R J House and R N Aditya, "The Social Scientific Study of Leadership: Quo Vadis?" *Journal of Management,* 1997, p 457.
[64] A thorough discussion of shared leadership is provided by C L Pearce, "The Future of Leadership: Combining Vertical and Shared Leadership to Transform Knowledge Work," *Academy of Management Executive,* February 2004, pp 47–57.
[65] A Taylor III, "Bill's Brand-New Ford," *Fortune,* June 28, 2004, p 74.
[66] This research is summarized in B J Avolio, J J Soskik, D I Jung, and Y Berson, "Leadership Models, Methods, and Applications," in *Handbook of Psychology.*
[67] An overall summary of servant-leadership is provided by L C Spears, *Reflections on Leadership: How Robert K Greenleaf's Theory of Servant-Leadership Influenced Today's Top Management Thinkers* (New York: John Wiley & Sons, 1995).
[68] J Collins, "What These Extraordinary Leaders Can Teach Today's Troubled Leaders," *Fortune,* July 21, 2003, p 64.
[69] J Stuart, *Fast Company,* September 1999, p 114.
[70] See J Collins, *Good to Great* (New York: Harper Business, 2001).
[71] J Collins, "Level 5 Leadership," *Harvard Business Review,* p 68.
[72] See J Collins, *Good to Great.*

Chapter 15

[1] Excerpted from Jerry Useem, "Should We Admire Wal-Mart?" *Fortune,* March 8, 2004, pp 118, 120. All rights reserved. Also see J Collins, "Bigger, Better, Faster: What I Saw at Wal-Mart . . . and What it Means for the Future of Your Company," *Fast Company,* June 2003, pp 74–78.
[2] See K H Hammonds, "We, Incorporated," *Fast Company,* July 2004, pp 87–89.
[3] C I Barnard, *The Functions of the Executive* (Cambridge, MA: Harvard University Press, 1938), p 73.
[4] Drawn from E H Schein, *Organizational Psychology,* 3rd ed (Englewood Cliffs, NJ: Prentice Hall, 1980), pp 12–15.
[5] For an interesting historical perspective of hierarchy, see P Miller and T O'Leary, "Hierarchies and American Ideals, 1900–1940," *Academy of Management Review,* April 1989, pp 250–65. Also see H J Leavitt, "Why Hierarchies Thrive," *Harvard Business Review,* March 2003, pp 96–102.
[6] For an excellent overview of the span of control concept, see D D Van Fleet and A G Bedeian, "A History of the Span of Management," *Academy of Management Review,* July 1977, pp 356–72. Also see E E Lawler III and J R Galbraith, "New Roles for the Staff: Strategic Support and Service," in *Organizing for the Future: The New Logic for Managing Complex Organizations,* eds J R Galbraith, E E Lawler III, and Associates (San Francisco: Jossey-Bass, 1993), pp 65–83.
[7] M Koslowsky, "Staff/Line Distinctions in Job and Organizational Commitment," *Journal of Occupational Psychology,* June 1990, pp 167–73.
[8] For an illustrative management-related metaphor, see J E Beatty, "Grades as Money and the Role of the Market Metaphor in Management

Education," *Academy of Management Learning and Education,* June 2004, pp 187–96.

[9] K S Cameron, "Effectiveness as Paradox: Consensus and Conflict in Conceptions of Organizational Effectiveness," *Management Science,* May 1986, pp 540–41. Also see S Sackmann, "The Role of Metaphors in Organization Transformation," *Human Relations,* June 1989, pp 463–84; and H Tsoukas, "The Missing Link: A Transformational View of Metaphors in Organizational Science," *Academy of Management Review,* July 1991, pp 566–85.

[10] See W R Scott, "The Mandate Is Still Being Honored: In Defense of Weber's Disciples," *Administrative Science Quarterly,* March 1996, pp 163–71. Also see D Jones, "Military a Model for Execs," *USA Today,* June 9, 2004, p 4B.

[11] Based on M Weber, *The Theory of Social and Economic Organization,* translated by A M Henderson and T Parsons (New York: Oxford University Press, 1947). An instructive analysis of the mistranslation of Weber's work may be found in R M Weiss, "Weber on Bureaucracy: Management Consultant or Political Theorist?" *Academy of Management Review,* April 1983, pp 242–48.

[12] For a critical appraisal of bureaucracy, see R P Hummel, *The Bureaucratic Experience,* 3rd ed (New York: St. Martin's Press, 1987). The positive side of bureaucracy is presented in C T Goodsell, *The Case for Bureaucracy: A Public Administration Polemic* (Chatham, NJ: Chatham House Publishers, 1983).

[13] See G Pinchot and E Pinchot, "Beyond Bureaucracy," *Business Ethics,* March–April 1994, pp 26–29; and O Harari, "Let the Computers Be the Bureaucrats," *Management Review,* September 1996, pp 57–60.

[14] For examples of what managers are doing to counteract bureaucratic tendencies, see B Dumaine, "The Bureaucracy Busters, " *Fortune,* June 17, 1991, pp 36–50; and C J Cantoni, "Eliminating Bureaucracy—Roots and All," *Management Review,* December 1993, pp 30–33.

[15] A management-oriented discussion of general systems theory—an interdisciplinary attempt to integrate the various fragmented sciences—may be found in K E Boulding, "General Systems Theory—The Skeleton of Science," *Management Science,* April 1956, pp 197–208.

[16] J D Thompson, *Organizations in Action* (New York: McGraw-Hill, 1967), pp 6–7. Also see A C Bluedorn, "The Thompson Interdependence Demonstration," *Journal of Management Education,* November 1993, pp 505–9.

[17] For interesting updates on the biological systems metaphor, see A M Webber, "How Business Is a Lot Like Life," *Fast Company,* April 2001, pp 130–36; and E Bonabeau and C Meyer, "Swarm Intelligence: A Whole New Way to Think about Business," *Harvard Business Review,* May 2001, pp 106–14.

[18] R L Daft and K E Weick, "Toward a Model of Organizations as Interpretation Systems," *Academy of Management Review,* April 1984, p 293.

[19] See M Crossan, "Altering Theories of Learning and Action: An Interview with Chris Argyris," *Academy of Management Executive,* May 2003, pp 40–46; D Gray, "Wanted: Chief Ignorance Officer," *Harvard Business Review,* November 2003, pp 22, 24; and G T M Hult, D J Ketchen, Jr, and S F Slater, "Information Processing, Knowledge Development, and Strategic Supply Chain Performance," *Academy of Management Journal,* April 2004, pp 241–253.

[20] For good background reading, see the entire Autumn 1998 issue of *Organizational Dynamics;* D Lei, J W Slocum, and R A Pitts, "Designing Organizations for Competitive Advantage: The Power of Unlearning and Learning," *Organizational Dynamics,* Winter 1999, pp 24–38; L Baird, P Holland, and S Deacon, "Learning from Action: Imbedding More Learning into the Performance Fast Enough to Make a Difference," *Organizational Dynamics,* Spring 1999, pp 19–32; "Leading-Edge Learning: Two Views," *Training & Development,* March 1999, pp 40–42; and A M Webber, "Learning for a Change," *Fast Company,* May 1999, pp 178–88.

[21] Excerpted from M Hopkins, "Zen and the Art of the Self-Managing Company," *Inc.,* November 2000, pp 56, 58.

[22] K Cameron, "Critical Questions in Assessing Organizational Effectiveness," *Organizational Dynamics,* Autumn 1980, p 70. Also see T D Wall, J Michie, M Patterson, S J Wood, M Sheehan, C W Clegg, and M West, "On the Validity of Subjective Measures of Company Performance," *Personnel Psychology,* Spring 2004, pp 95–118.

[23] See G H Seijts, G P Latham, K Tasa, and B W Latham, "Goal Setting and Goal Orientation: An Integration of Two Different yet Related Literatures," *Academy of Management Journal,* April 2004, pp 227–39.

[24] See, for example, R O Brinkerhoff and D E Dressler, *Productivity Measurement: A Guide for Managers and Evaluators* (Newbury Park, CA: Sage Publications, 1990); and D Jones and B Hansen, "Productivity Gains Roll at Their Fastest Clip in 31 Years," *USA Today,* June 14, 2004, pp 1B–2B.

[25] See T J Mullaney, "E-Biz Strikes Again," *Business Week,* May 10, 2004, pp 80, 82; and T C Boyd, A J Rohn, and D T Dunn, "Customer-Focused Online Exchange Strategies: Does One Size Fit All?" *Business Horizons,* May–June 2004, pp 67–74.

[26] Data from M Maynard, "Toyota Promises Custom Order in 5 Days," *USA Today,* August 6, 1999, p 1B.

[27] "Interview: M Scott Peck," *Business Ethics,* March–April 1994, p 17. Also see C B Gibson and J Birkinshaw, "The Antecedents, Consequences, and Mediating Role of Organizational Ambidexterity," *Academy of Management Journal,* April 2004, pp 209–26.

[28] Cameron, "Critical Questions in Assessing Organizational Effectiveness," p 67. Also see W Buxton, "Growth from Top to Bottom," *Management Review,* July–August 1999, p 11.

[29] See R K Mitchell, B R Agle, and D J Wood, "Toward a Theory of Stakeholder Identification and Salience: Defining the Principle of Who and What Really Counts," *Academy of Management Review,* October 1997, pp 853–96; W Beaver, "Is the Stakeholder Model Dead?" *Business Horizons,* March–April 1999, pp 8–12; J Frooman, "Stakeholder Influence Strategies," *Academy of Management Review,* April 1999, pp 191–205; T M Jones and A C Wicks, "Convergent Stakeholder Theory," *Academy of Management Review,* April 1999, pp 206–21; and T J Rowley and M Moldoveanu, "When Will Stakeholder Groups Act? An Interest- and Identity-Based Model of Stakeholder Group Mobilization," *Academy of Management Review,* April 2003, pp 204–19.

[30] S B Shepard, "Steve Ballmer on Microsoft's Future," *Business Week,* December 1, 2003, p 72.

[31] See C Ostroff and N Schmitt, "Configurations of Organizational Effectiveness and Efficiency," *Academy of Management Journal,* December 1993, pp 1345–61.

[32] K S Cameron, "Effectiveness as Paradox: Consensus and Conflict in Conceptions of Organizational Effectiveness," *Management Science,* May 1986, p 542.

[33] Alternative effectiveness criteria are discussed in ibid.; A G Bedeian, "Organization Theory: Current Controversies, Issues, and Directions," in *International Review of Industrial and Organizational Psychology,* eds C L Cooper and I T Robertson (New York: John Wiley & Sons, 1987), pp 1–33; and M Keeley, "Impartiality and Participant-Interest Theories of Organizational Effectiveness," *Administrative Science Quarterly,* March 1984, pp 1–25.

[34] For updates, see J M Pennings, "Structural Contingency Theory: A Reappraisal," *Research in Organizational Behavior* (Greenwich, CT: JAI Press, 1992), vol. 14, pp 267–309; A D Meyer, A S Tsui, and C R Hinings, "Configurational Approaches to Organizational Analysis," *Academy of Management Journal,* December 1993, pp 1175–95; and D H Doty, W H Glick, and G P Huber, "Fit, Equifinality, and Organizational Effectiveness: A Test of Two Configurational Theories," *Academy of Management Journal,* December 1993, pp 1196–250.

[35] B Elgin, "Running the Tightest Ships on the Net," *Business Week,* January 29, 2001, p 126.

[36] See D A Morand, "The Role of Behavioral Formality and Informality in the Enactment of Bureaucratic versus Organic Organizations," *Academy of Management Review,* October 1995, pp 831–72.

[37] See J Huey, "The New Post-Heroic Leadership," *Fortune,* February 21, 1994, pp 42–50; and F Shipper and C C Manz, "Employee Self-Management without Formally Designated Teams: An Alternative Road to Empowerment," *Organizational Dynamics,* Winter 1992, pp 48–61.

[38] See G P Huber, C C Miller, and W H Glick, "Developing More Encompassing Theories about Organizations: The Centralization-Effectiveness Relationship as an Example," *Organization Science,* no. 1, 1990, pp 11–40; and C Handy, "Balancing Corporate Power: A New Federalist Paper," *Harvard Business Review,* November–December 1992, pp 59–72. Also see A Slywotzky and D Nadler, "The Strategy Is the

Structure," *Harvard Business Review,* February 2004, p 16; and N Gull, "Managing on the Front Lines," *Inc.,* May 2004, p 24.
[39] P Kaestle, "A New Rationale for Organizational Structure," *Planning Review,* July–August 1990, p 22.
[40] Details of this study can be found in T Burns and G M Stalker, *The Management of Innovation* (London: Tavistock, 1961).
[41] D J Gillen and S J Carroll, "Relationship of Managerial Ability to Unit Effectiveness in More Organic versus More Mechanistic Departments," *Journal of Management Studies,* November 1985, pp 674–75.
[42] J D Sherman and H L Smith, "The Influence of Organizational Structure on Intrinsic versus Extrinsic Motivation," *Academy of Management Journal,* December 1984, p 883.
[43] See J A Courtright, G T Fairhurst, and L E Rogers, "Interaction Patterns in Organic and Mechanistic Systems," *Academy of Management Journal,* December 1989, pp 773–802.
[44] See J R Galbraith and E E Lawler III, "Effective Organizations: Using the New Logic of Organizing," in J R Galbraith, E E Lawler III, and Associates, eds, *Organizing for the Future: The New Logic for Managing Complex Organizations* (San Francisco: Jossey-Bass, 1993), pp 285–99.
[45] See S Alsop, "I've Seen the Real Future of Tech—And It Is Virtual," *Fortune,* April 14, 2003, p 390.
[46] "David Neeleman, JetBlue," *Business Week,* September 29, 2003, p 124.
[47] J Hopkins, "Other Nations Zip by USA in High-Speed Net Race," *USA Today,* January 19, 2004, p 2B.
[48] See B J Avolio and S S Kahai, "Adding the 'E' to E-Leadership: How It May Impact Your Leadership," *Organizational Dynamics,* no 4, 2003, pp 325–38; and S Parise and A Casher, "Alliance Portfolios: Designing and Managing Your Network of Business-Partner Relationships," *Academy of Management Executive,* November 2003, pp 25–39. A good update on trust is R Zemke, "The Confidence Crisis," *Training,* June 2004, pp 22–30.
[49] C Handy, *The Hungry Spirit: Beyond Capitalism—A Quest for Purpose in the Modern World* (New York: Broadway Books, 1998), p 186. (Emphasis added.)
[50] See B Lessard and S Baldwin, *NetSlaves: True Tales of Working the Web* (New York: McGraw-Hill, 2000).
[51] See M Arndt, "Trade Winds: Made in Wherever," *Business Week,* May 31, 2004, p 14; J E Garten, "Offshoring: You Ain't Seen Nothin' Yet," *Business Week,* June 21, 2004, p 28; and S Hamm, "Services," *Business Week,* June 21, 2004, pp 82–83.
[52] See the series of articles in "Special Report: E-Biz," *Business Week,* May 10, 2004, pp 80–90.
[53] Excerpted from R Richmond, "It's 10 A.M.: Do You Know Where Your Workers Are?" *The Wall Street Journal,* Eastern Edition, January 12, 2004, pp R1, R4. Copyright 2004 by Dow Jones & Co. Inc. Reproduced with permission of Dow Jones & Co. Inc. via Copyright Clearance Center.

Chapter 16

[1] Excerpted from D Brady, "A Thousand and One Noshes," *Business Week,* June 14, 2004, pp 54, 56. Reprinted with permission.
[2] A M Webber, "Learning for a Change," *Fast Company,* May 1999, p 180.
[3] Excerpted from M L Alch, "Get Ready for the Net Generation," *Training & Development,* February 2000, pp 32, 34.
[4] See "Wal-Mart Drives a New Technology," *Fortune,* June 28, 2004, p 202.
[5] This statistic was reported in A Latour, "Defensive Linemen: After 20 Years, Baby Bells Face Some Grown-Up Competition," *The Wall Street Journal,* May 28, 2004, pp A1, A5.
[6] Productivity in the service industry is discussed by S Hamm, S E Ante, A Reinhardt, and M Kripalani, "Services," *Business Week,* June 21, 2004, pp 82–83.
[7] The United example is derived from S Carey, "Friendlier Skies: In Bankruptcy, United Airlines Forges a Path to Better Service," *The Wall Street Journal,* June 15, 2004, pp A1, A12.
[8] For a thorough discussion of the model, see K Lewin, *Field Theory in Social Science* (New York: Harper & Row, 1951).
[9] S Carey, "Friendlier Skies: In Bankruptcy, United Airlines Forges a Path to Better Service," p A12.
[10] C Goldwasser, "Benchmarking: People Make the Process," *Management Review,* June 1995, p 40.
[11] Excerpted from L Lavelle, "KPMG's Brave Leap into the Cold," *Business Week,* May 21, 2001, pp 72, 73.
[12] Systems models of change are discussed by D W Haines, "Letting 'The System' Do the Work," *Journal of Applied Behavioral Science,* September 1999, pp 306–24.
[13] A thorough discussion of the target elements of change can be found in M Beer and B Spector, "Organizational Diagnosis: Its Role in Organizational Learning," *Journal of Counseling & Development,* July/August 1993, pp 642–50.
[14] E Torbenson and S Marta, "Southwest Goes High-Tech to Stay Profitable," *Arizona Republic,* July 7, 2003, p D5.
[15] These errors are discussed by J P Kotter, "Leading Change: The Eight Steps to Transformation," in *The Leader's Change Handbook,* eds J A Conger, G M Spreitzer, and E E Lawler III (San Francisco: Jossey-Bass, 1999), pp 87–99.
[16] The type of leadership needed during organizational change is discussed by R L Englund, R J Graham, and P C Dinsmore, *Creating the Project Office: A Manager's Guide to Leading Organizational Change* (San Francisco: Jossey-Bass, 2003).
[17] M Beer and E Walton, "Developing the Competitive Organization: Interventions and Strategies," *American Psychologist,* February 1990, p 154.
[18] A historical overview of the field of OD can be found in J R Austin and J M Bartunek, "Theories and Practices of Organizational Development," in *Handbook of Psychology,* vol 12, eds W C Borman, D R Ilgen, and R J Klimoski (Hoboken, NJ: John Wiley & Sons, 2003), pp 309–32.
[19] W W Burke, *Organization Development: A Normative View* (Reading, MA: Addison-Wesley, 1987), p 9.
[20] A variety of intervention techniques are summarized in J R Austin and J M Bartunek, "Theories and Practices of Organizational Development."
[21] See R Rodgers, J E Hunter, and D L Rogers, "Influence of Top Management Commitment on Management Program Success," *Journal of Applied Psychology,* February 1993, pp 151–55.
[22] Results can be found in P J Robertson, D R Roberts, and J I Porras, "Dynamics of Planned Organizational Change: Assessing Empirical Support for a Theoretical Model," *Academy of Management Journal,* June 1993, pp 619–34.
[23] Results from the meta-analysis can be found in G A Neuman, J E Edwards, and N S Raju, "Organizational Development Interventions: A Meta-Analysis of Their Effects on Satisfaction and Other Attitudes," *Personnel Psychology,* Autumn 1989, pp 461–90.
[24] Results can be found in C-M Lau and H-Y Ngo, "Organization Development and Firm Performance: A Comparison of Multinational and Local Firms," *Journal of International Business Studies,* First Quarter 2001, pp 95–114.
[25] Adapted in part from B W Armentrout, "Have Your Plans for Change Had a Change of Plan?" *HRFOCUS,* January 1996, p 19; and A S Judson, *Changing Behavior in Organizations: Minimizing Resistance to Change* (Cambridge, MA: Blackwell, 1991).
[26] An individual's predisposition to change was investigated by C R Wanberg and J T Banas, "Predictors and Outcomes of Openness to Changes in a Reorganizing Workplace," *Journal of Applied Psychology,* February 2000, pp 132–42.
[27] See R Moss Kanter, "Managing Traumatic Change: Avoiding the 'Unlucky 13,'" *Management Review,* May 1987, pp 23–24.
[28] Readiness for change is discussed by S R Madsen, "Wellness in the Workplace: Preparing Employees for Change," *Organization Development Journal,* Spring 2003, pp 46–56.
[29] Cognitive hurdles are discussed by W C Kim and R Mauborgne, "Tipping Point Leadership," *Harvard Business Review,* April 2003, pp 60–69.
[30] L Herscovitch and J P Meyer, "Commitment to Organizational Change: Extension of a Three-Component Model," *Journal of Applied Psychology,* June 2003, p 475.
[31] For a discussion of how managers can reduce resistance to change by providing different explanations for an organizational change, see

D M Rousseau and S A Tijoriwala, "What's a Good Reason to Change? Motivated Reasoning and Social Accounts in Promoting Organizational Change," *Journal of Applied Psychology,* August 1999, pp 514–28.

[32] S Reynolds Fisher and M A White, "Downsizing in a Learning Organization: Are There Hidden Costs?" *Academy of Management Review,* January 2000, p 245.

[33] R M Fulmer and J B Keys, "A Conversation with Peter Senger: New Development in Organizational Learning," *Organizational Dynamics,* Autumn 1998, p 35.

[34] A results-oriented approach to learning is discussed by M Crossan, "Alternating Theories of Learning and Action: An Interview with Chris Argyris," *Academy of Management Executive,* May 2003, pp 40–46.

[35] A discussion of learning capabilities and core competencies is provided by R Lubit, "Tacit Knowledge and Knowledge Management," *Organizational Dynamics,* 2001, pp 164–78.

[36] The relationship between organizational learning and various effectiveness criteria is discussed by S F Slater and J C Narver, "Market Orientation and the Learning Organization," *Journal of Marketing,* July 1995, pp 63–74.

[37] A J DiBella, E C Nevis, and J M Gould, "Organizational Learning Style as a Core Capability," in *Organizational Learning and Competitive Advantage,* eds B Moingeon and A Edmondson (Thousand Oaks, CA: Sage, 1996), pp 41–42.

[38] Details of this study can be found in J H Lingle and W A Schiemann, "From Balanced Scorecard to Strategic Gauges: Is Measurement Worth It?" *American Management Association,* March 1996, pp 56–61.

[39] The impact of organizational culture on organizational learning was demonstrated by A Jashapara, "Cognition, Culture and Competition: An Empirical Test of the Learning Organization," *The Learning Organization,* 2003, pp 31–50.

[40] Excerpted from V D Infante, "Men's Wearhouse: Tailored for Any Change That Retail Brings," *Workforce,* March 2001, p 48.

[41] This discussion and definitions are based on D Miller, "A Preliminary Typology of Organizational Learning: Synthesizing the Literature," *Journal of Management,* 1996, pp 485–505.

[42] The role of leadership in organizational learning is thoroughly discussed by D Vera and M Crossan, "Strategic Leadership and Organizational Learning," *Academy of Management Review,* April 2004, pp 222–40.

[43] This discussion is based in part on D Ulrich, T Jick, and M Von Glinow, "High-Impact Learning: Building and Diffusing Learning Capability," *Organizational Dynamics,* Autumn 1993, pp 52–66.

[44] The creation of learning infrastructure is discussed by C R James, "Designing Learning Organizations," *Organizatinal Dynamics,* 2003, pp 46–61.

[45] See N A Wishart, J J Elam, D Robey, "Redrawing the Portrait of a Learning Organization: Inside Knight-Ridder, Inc.," *Academy of Management Executive,* February 1996, pp 7–20; and C Argyris, "Good Communication That Blocks Learning," *Harvard Business Review,* July–August 1994, pp 77–85.

[46] See the related discussion in D Lei, J W Slocum, and R A Pitts, "Designing Organizations for Competitive Advantage: The Power of Unlearning and Learning," *Organizational Dynamics,* Winter 1999, pp 24–38.

PHOTO CREDITS

Page	Photo Credit
p. 1	PhotoDisc Imaging/Getty Images
p. 3	Courtesy, Hewlett-Packard Development Company, L.P.
p. 14	AP/Wide World Photos
p. 16	Joe Raedle/Getty Images
p. 19	© Chuck Nacke/Woodfin Camp & Associates
p. 20	Stewart Cohen/Getty Images
p. 27	AP/Wide World Photos
p. 34	Mark Wilson/Getty Images
p. 41	Tim Boyle/Getty Images
p. 45	Phoenix Newspapers, Inc.
p. 47	Courtesy Southwest Airlines
p. 54	AP/Wide World Photos
p. 58	© Ann States
p. 65	© Namas Bhojani
p. 70	© Reuters
p. 74	Photo Courtesy of InfiniTec Pte Ltd
p. 81	© Esbin-Anderson/The Image Works
p. 89	PhotoDisc/Getty Images
p. 91	Thinkstock/Getty Images
p. 95	PRNewsFoto/Burger King Corporation/AP/Wide World Photos
p. 99	Evan Agostini/Getty Images
p. 106	© Jiang Jin/SuperStock
p. 107	Photo Courtesy of E.piphany
p. 112	© Image Source/SuperStock
p. 125	PhotoDisc/Getty Images
p. 134 left	AP/Wide World Photos
p. 134 right	Tim Mosenfelder/ImageDirect/Getty Images
p. 135	AP/Wide World Photos
p. 140	Spencer Platt/Getty Images

Page	Photo Credit
p. 147	© Rhoda Sidney/Photo Edit
p. 152	© John Van Hasselt/Corbis
p. 155	Keith Brofsky/Getty Images
p. 158	Photo Courtesy of Humanscale
p. 160	Business Wire Photo/AP/Wide World Photos
p. 170	Keith Brofsky/Getty Images
p. 175	RF/Corbis
p. 179	© Michael Newman/PhotoEdit
p. 184 left	© Reuters/Corbis
p. 184 right	AP/Wide World Photos
p. 189	PRNewsFoto/Cutter & Buck Inc./AP/Wide World Photos
p. 195	Nick Wilson/Allsport/Getty Images
p. 201	Photo courtesy of IDG
p. 204	AP/Wide World Photos
p. 214	Courtesy of The Best Present Company
p. 215	Courtesy of the author
p. 217	PhotoLink/Getty Images
p. 223	PhotoDisc/Getty Images
p. 225	Copyright © 2004 by IDEO
p. 230	RF/Corbis
p. 234	AP/Wide World Photos
p. 244	Keith Brofsky/Getty Images
p. 251	Siemens press picture
p. 255	PhotoDisc/Getty Images
p. 261	Courtesy of GMAC Financial Services
p. 262	Marc Pokempner/Getty Images
p. 265	Ryan McVay/Getty Images
p. 271	PhotoDisc/Getty Images
p. 275	Steve Cole/Getty Images
p. 278	Digital Vision/Getty Images

Page	Photo Credit
p. 280	Reprinted with permission of the American Arbitration Association
p. 282	© Reuters/Corbis
p. 291	Nick Koudis/Getty Images
p. 293	Screen shot captured by Christine Scheid/© McGraw-Hill Higher Education, Inc.
p. 297	PhotoDisc/Getty Images
p. 306	John A. Rizzo/Getty Images
p. 312	Photo courtesy of T-Mobile USA
p. 319	© Amy Etra/Photo Edit
p. 324	Mario Tama/Getty Images
p. 326	Walter Hodges/Getty Images
p. 333	Fergus Greer/Icon International
p. 339	Photo Courtesy of Y&R
p. 343	Maxine Hicks/The New York Times
p. 349	"Courtesy of International Business Machines Corporation. Unauthorized use not permitted."
p. 353	AP/Wide World Photos
p. 362	© Louise Gubb/The Image Works
p. 367	RF/Corbis
p. 369	Tim Boyle/Getty Images
p. 377	© Nokia
p. 379	Courtesy of Southwest Airlines
p. 384	© Deborah Davis/PhotoEdit
p. 385	Photo Courtesy of U.S. Army, photo by Staff Sgt. Charles B. Johnson
p. 391	© Susan Van Etten/PhotoEdit
p. 400	© Michael Schmitt
p. 407	Courtesy of WebEx

GLOSSARY

ability Stability characteristic responsible for a person's maximum physical or mental performance.

accountability practices Focus on treating diverse employees fairly.

added-value negotiation Cooperatively developing multiple-deal packages while building a long-term relationship.

affirmative action Focuses on achieving equality of opportunity in an organization.

aggressive style Expressive and self-enhancing, but takes unfair advantage of others.

aided-analytic Using tools to make decisions.

alternative dispute resolution Avoiding costly lawsuits by resolving conflicts informally or through mediation or arbitration.

anticipatory socialization Occurs before an individual joins an organization, and involves the information people learn about different careers, occupations, professions, and organizations.

assertive style Expressive and self-enhancing, but does not take advantage of others.

attention Being consciously aware of something or someone.

attitude Learned predisposition toward a given object.

availability heuristic Tendency to base decisions on information readily available in memory.

benchmarking Process by which a company compares its performance with that of high-performing organizations.

bounded rationality Constraints that restrict decision making.

brainstorming Process to generate a quantity of ideas.

bureaucracy Max Weber's idea of the most rationally efficient form of organization.

care perspective Involves compassion and an ideal of attention and response to need.

case study In-depth study of a single person, group, or organization.

causal attributions Suspected or inferred causes of behavior.

centralized decision making Top managers make all key decisions.

change and acquisition Requires employees to master tasks and roles and to adjust to work group values and norms.

charismatic leadership Transforms employees to pursue organizational goals over self-interests.

closed system A relatively self-sufficient entity.

coalition Temporary groupings of people who actively pursue a single issue.

coercive power Obtaining compliance through threatened or actual punishment.

cognitions A person's knowledge, opinions, or beliefs.

cognitive categories Mental depositories for storing information.

collaborative computing Using computer software and hardware to help people work better together.

collectivist culture Personal goals less important than community goals and interests.

commitment to change A mind-set of doing whatever it takes to effectively implement change.

communication Interpersonal exchange of information and understanding.

communication competence Ability to effectively use communication behaviors in a given context.

communication distortion Purposely modifying the content of a message.

conflict One party perceives its interests are being opposed or set back by another party.

consensus Presenting opinions and gaining agreement to support a decision.

consideration Creating mutual respect and trust with followers.

contingency approach Using management tools and techniques in a situationally appropriate manner; avoiding the one-best-way mentality.

contingency approach to organization design Creating an effective organization–environment fit.

contingency factors Variables that influence the appropriateness of a leadership style.

continuous reinforcement Reinforcing every instance of a behavior.

core job dimensions Job characteristics found to various degrees in all jobs.

creativity Process of developing something new or unique.

cross-cultural training Structured experiences to help people adjust to a new culture/country.

cross-functionalism Team made up of technical specialists from different areas.

culture shock Anxiety and doubt caused by an overload of new expectations and cues.

decentralized decision making Lower-level managers are empowered to make important decisions.

decision making Identifying and choosing solutions that lead to a desired end result.

decision-making style A combination of how individuals perceive and respond to information.

Delphi technique Process to generate ideas from physically dispersed experts.

development practices Focus on preparing diverse employees for greater responsibility and advancement.

developmental relationship strength The quality of relationships among people in a network.

devil's advocacy Assigning someone the role of critic.

dialectic method Fostering a debate of opposing viewpoints to better understand an issue.

distributive justice The perceived fairness of how resources and rewards are distributed.

diversity The host of individual differences that make people different from and similar to each other.

diversity of developmental relationships The variety of people in a network used for developmental assistance.

dysfunctional conflict Threatens organization's interests.

e-business Running the *entire* business via the Internet.

electronic mail Uses the Internet/intranet to send computer-generated text and documents.

emotional intelligence Ability to manage oneself and interact with others in mature and constructive ways.

emotions Complex human reactions to personal achievements and setbacks that may be felt and displayed.

empowerment Sharing varying degrees of power with lower-level employees to better serve the customer.

enacted values The values and norms that are exhibited by employees.

encounter phase Employees learn what the organization is really like and reconcile unmet expectations.

equity sensitivity An individual's tolerance for negative and positive equity.

equity theory Holds that motivation is a function of fairness in social exchanges.

escalation of commitment Sticking to an ineffective course of action too long.

espoused values The stated values and norms that are preferred by an organization.

ethics Study of moral issues and choices.

ethnocentrism Belief that one's native country, culture, language, and behavior are superior.
expatriate Anyone living or working in a foreign country.
expectancy Belief that effort leads to a specific level of performance.
expectancy theory Holds that people are motivated to behave in ways that produce valued outcomes.
expert power Obtaining compliance through one's knowledge or information.
explicit knowledge Information that can be easily put into words and shared with others.
external factors Environmental characteristics that cause behavior.
external forces for change Originate outside the organization.
external locus of control Attributing outcomes to circumstances beyond one's control.
extinction Making behavior occur less often by ignoring or not reinforcing it.
extranet Connects internal employees with selected customers, suppliers, and strategic partners.
extrinsic motivation Motivation caused by the desire to attain specific outcomes.
extrinsic rewards Financial, material, or social rewards from the environment.

feedback Objective information about performance.
field study Examination of variables in real-life settings.
formal group Formed by the organization.
functional conflict Serves organization's interests.
fundamental attribution bias Ignoring environmental factors that affect behavior.

glass ceiling Invisible barrier blocking women and minorities from top management positions.
goal What an individual is trying to accomplish.
goal commitment Amount of commitment to achieving a goal.
goal difficulty The amount of effort required to meet a goal.
goal specificity Quantifiability of a goal.
group Two or more freely interacting people with shared norms and goals and a common identity.
group cohesiveness A "we feeling" binding group members together.
groupthink Janis's term for a cohesive in-group's unwillingness to realistically view alternatives.

high-context cultures Primary meaning derived from nonverbal situational cues.
human capital The productive potential of one's knowledge and actions.
hygiene factors Job characteristics associated with job dissatisfaction.

impression management Getting others to see us in a certain manner.
individualistic culture Primary emphasis on personal freedom and choice.
informal group Formed by friends.
in-group exchange A partnership characterized by mutual trust, respect, and liking.
initiating structure Organizing and defining what group members should be doing.
instrumentality A performance → outcome perception.
intelligence Capacity for constructive thinking, reasoning, problem solving.
interactional justice The perceived fairness of the decision maker's behavior in the process of decision making.
intermittent reinforcement Reinforcing some but not all instances of behavior.
internal factors Personal characteristics that cause behavior.
internal forces for change Originate inside the organization.
internal locus of control Attributing outcomes to one's own actions.
internal motivation Motivation caused by positive internal feelings.
Internet The global system of networked computers.
intranet An organization's private Internet.
intrinsic motivation Motivation caused by positive internal feelings.
intrinsic rewards Self-granted, psychic rewards.

job design Changing the content and/or process of a specific job to increase job satisfaction and performance.
job enlargement Putting more variety into a job.
job enrichment Building achievement, recognition, stimulating work, responsibility, and advancement into a job.
job rotation Moving employees from one specialized job to another.
job satisfaction An affective or emotional response to one's job.
judgmental heuristics Rules of thumb or shortcuts that people use to reduce information-processing demands.
justice perspective Based on the ideal of reciprocal rights and driven by rules and regulations.

knowledge management Implementing systems and practices that increase the sharing of knowledge and information throughout an organization.

laboratory study Manipulation and measurement of variables in contrived situations.
law of effect Behavior with favorable consequences is repeated; behavior with unfavorable consequences disappears.
leadership Influencing employees to voluntarily pursue organizational goals.
leadership prototype Mental representation of the traits and behaviors possessed by leaders.
leader trait Personal characteristics that differentiate leaders from followers.
learned helplessness Debilitating lack of faith in one's ability to control the situation.
learning capabilities The set of core competencies and internal processes that enable an organization to adapt to its environment.
learning modes The various ways in which organizations attempt to create and maximize their learning.
learning organization Proactively creates, acquires, and transfers knowledge throughout the organization.
legitimate power Obtaining compliance through formal authority.
line managers Have authority to make organizational decisions.
linguistic style A person's typical speaking pattern.
listening Actively decoding and interpreting verbal messages.
low-context cultures Primary meaning derived from written and spoken words.

maintenance roles Relationship-building group behavior.
management Process of working with and through others to achieve organizational objectives efficiently and ethically.
management by objectives Management system incorporating participation in decision making, goal setting, and feedback.
managing diversity Creating organizational changes that enable all people to perform up to their maximum potential.
mechanistic organizations Rigid, command-and-control bureaucracies.
mentoring Process of forming and maintaining developmental relationships between a mentor and a junior person.
meta-analysis Pools the results of many studies through statistical procedure.
met expectations The extent to which one receives what he or she expects from a job.
mission statement Summarizes "why" an organization exists.
monochronic time Preference for doing one thing at a time because time is limited, precisely segmented, and schedule driven.
motivation Psychological processes that arouse and direct goal-directed behavior.

motivators Job characteristics associated with job satisfaction.

need for achievement Desire to accomplish something difficult.
need for affiliation Desire to spend time in social relationships and activities.
need for power Desire to influence, coach, teach, or encourage others to achieve.
needs Physiological or psychological deficiencies that arouse behavior.
negative inequity Comparison in which another person receives greater outcomes for similar inputs.
negative reinforcement Making behavior occur more often by contingently withdrawing something negative.
negotiation Give-and-take process between conflicting interdependent parties.
noise Interference with the transmission and understanding of a message.
nominal group technique Process to generate ideas and evaluate solutions.
nonanalytic Using preformulated rules to make decisions.
nonassertive style Timid and self-denying behavior.
nonverbal communication Messages sent outside of the written or spoken word.
norm Shared attitudes, opinions, feelings, or actions that guide social behavior.
normative beliefs Thoughts and beliefs about expected behavior and modes of conduct.

open system Organism that must constantly interact with its environment to survive.
operant behavior Skinner's term for learned, consequence-shaped behavior.
optimizing Choosing the best possible solution.
organic organizations Fluid and flexible network of multitalented people.
organization System of consciously coordinated activities of two or more people.
organizational behavior Interdisciplinary field dedicated to better understanding and managing people at work.
organizational citizenship behaviors (OCBs) Employee behaviors that exceed work-role requirements.
organizational culture Shared values and beliefs that underlie a company's identity.
organizational politics Intentional enhancement of self-interest.
organizational socialization Process by which employees learn an organization's values, norms, and required behaviors.
organization-based self-esteem An organization member's self-perceived value.
organization chart Boxes-and-lines illustration showing chain of formal authority and division of labor.
organization development A set of techniques or tools that are used to implement organizational change.
ostracism Rejection by other group members.
out-group exchange A partnership characterized by a lack of mutual trust, respect, and liking.

participative management Involving employees in various forms of decision making.
pay for performance Monetary incentives tied to one's results or accomplishments.
perception Process of interpreting one's environment.
personality Stable physical and mental characteristics responsible for a person's identity.
personality conflict Interpersonal opposition driven by personal dislike or disagreement.
polychronic time Preference for doing more than one thing at a time because time is flexible and multidimensional.
positive inequity Comparison in which another person receives lesser outcomes for similar inputs.
positive organizational behavior (POB) The study and improvement of employees' positive attributes and capabilities.
positive reinforcement Making behavior occur more often by contingently presenting something positive.
proactive personality Action-oriented person who shows initiative and perseveres to change things.
problem Gap between an actual and desired situation.
procedural justice The perceived fairness of the process and procedures used to make allocation decisions.
process-style listeners Like to discuss issues in detail.
programmed conflict Encourages different opinions without protecting management's personal feelings.
punishment Making behavior occur less often by contingently presenting something negative or withdrawing something positive.

rational model Logical four-step approach to decision making.
readiness Follower's ability and willingness to complete a task.
reasons-style listeners Interested in hearing the rationale behind a message.
reciprocity Widespread belief that people should be paid back for their positive and negative acts.
recruitment practices Attempts to attract qualified, diverse employees at all levels.
referent power Obtaining compliance through charisma or personal attraction.
representativeness heuristic Tendency to assess the likelihood of an event occurring based on impressions about similar occurrences.
resistance to change Emotional/behavioral response to real or imagined work changes.
respondent behavior Skinner's term for unlearned stimulus–response reflexes.
results-style listeners Interested in hearing the bottom line or result of a message.
reward equality norm Everyone should get the same rewards.
reward equity norm Rewards should be tied to contributions.
reward power Obtaining compliance with promised or actual rewards.
roles Expected behaviors for a given position.

sample survey Questionnaire responses from a sample of people.
satisficing Choosing a solution that meets a minimum standard of acceptance.
schema Mental picture of an event or object.
self-concept Person's self-perception as a physical, social, spiritual being.
self-efficacy Belief in one's ability to do a task.
self-esteem One's overall self-evaluation.
self-managed teams Groups of employees granted administrative oversight for their work.
self-monitoring Observing one's own behavior and adapting it to the situation.
self-serving bias Taking more personal responsibility for success than failure.
self-talk Evaluating thoughts about oneself.
sense of choice The ability to use judgment and freedom when completing tasks.
sense of competence Feelings of accomplishment associated with doing high-quality work.
sense of meaningfulness The task purpose is important and meaningful.
sense of progress Feeling that one is accomplishing something important.
servant-leadership Focuses on increased service to others rather than to oneself.
shaping Reinforcing closer and closer approximations to a target behavior.
shared leadership Simultaneous, ongoing, mutual influence process in which people share responsibility for leading.
situational theories Propose that leader styles should match the situation at hand.
social capital The productive potential of strong, trusting, and cooperative relationships.
social loafing Decrease in individual effort as group size increases.

social power Ability to get things done with human, informational, and material resources.

societal culture Socially derived, taken-for-granted assumptions about how to think and act.

span of control The number of people reporting directly to a given manager.

spillover model Describes the reciprocal relationship between job and life satisfaction.

staff personnel Provide research, advice, and recommendations to line managers.

stereotype Beliefs about the characteristics of a group.

strategic constituency Any group of people with a stake in the organization's operation or success.

strategic plan A long-term plan outlining actions needed to achieve planned results.

substitutes for leadership Situational variables that can substitute for, neutralize, or enhance the effects of leadership.

tacit knowledge Information gained through experience that is difficult to express and formalize.

target elements of change Components of an organization that may be changed.

task roles Task-oriented group behavior.

team Small group with complementary skills who hold themselves mutually accountable for common purpose, goals, and approach.

telecommuting Doing work that is generally performed in the office away from the office using different information technologies.

theory Y McGregor's modern and positive assumptions about employees being responsible and creative.

360-degree feedback Comparison of anonymous feedback from one's superior, subordinates, and peers with self-perceptions.

total quality management An organizational culture dedicated to training, continuous improvement, and customer satisfaction.

transactional leadership Focuses on interpersonal interactions between managers and employees.

transformational leadership Transforms employees to pursue organizational goals over self-interests.

trust Reciprocal faith in others' intentions and behavior.

unaided-analytic Analysis is limited to processing information in one's mind.

underemployment The result of taking a job that requires less education, training, or skills than possessed by a worker.

unity of command principle Each employee should report to a single manager.

upward feedback Employees evaluate their boss.

valence The value of a reward or outcome.

value attainment The extent to which a job allows fulfillment of one's work values.

values Enduring belief in a mode of conduct or end-state.

virtual team Information technology allows group members in different locations to conduct business.

NAME INDEX

SUBJECT INDEX